AMERICA VISITED

AMERICA VISITED

The Marquis de Lafayette, Alexis de Tocqueville, Frances Trollope, Harriet Martineau, Charles Dickens, William Makepeace Thackeray, Oscar Wilde, and other famous travelers report on the United States in the 18th and 19th centuries

Arranged by EDITH I. COOMBS

THE BOOK LEAGUE OF AMERICA

New York

PRINTED IN THE UNITED STATES OF AMERICA
AMERICAN BOOK–STRATFORD PRESS, INC., NEW YORK

CONTENTS

Lafayette Liked Us

Marie Jean Paul Roch Yves Gilbert Motier, Marquis de Lafayette (1757–1834), belonged to an ancient family of French aristocrats. Although he was only nineteen when he came to fight in the American Revolution, he was soon chosen to lead a division. He returned to fight for his own country against England early in 1779, but six months later he was again serving under Washington and took part in the battle of Yorktown.

During the French Revolution he commanded the National Guard, struggling unsuccessfully to restrain mob violence. Later he was captured by the Austrians and imprisoned for several years. His escape was assisted by Francis Kinlock Huger, son of his first host in America, but the attempt failed, Lafayette was recaptured and Huger was imprisoned for six months.

On Lafayette's last visit to the United States in 1824–25 he was paid warm universal tribute.

From LAFAYETTE'S AUTOBIOGRAPHY

You ask me at what period I first experienced my ardent love of liberty and glory. I recollect no time of my life anterior to my enthusiasm for anecdotes of glorious deeds, and to my projects of travelling over the world to acquire fame. . . . Republican anecdotes always delighted me; and, when my new connections wished to obtain for me a place at court, I did not hesitate displeasing them to preserve my independence. I was in that frame of mind when I first learnt the troubles in America; they only became thoroughly known in Europe in 1776, and the memorable declaration of the 4th of July reached France at the close of that same year.

After having crowned herself with laurels and enriched herself with conquests; after having become mistress of all seas; and after having insulted all nations,–England had turned her pride against her own colonies. North America had long been displeasing to her; she wished to add new vexations to former injuries, and to destroy the most sacred privileges. The Americans, attached to the mother country, contented themselves at first with merely uttering complaints; they only accused the ministry, and the whole nation rose up against them; they were termed insolent and rebellious, and at length declared the enemies of their country: thus did the obstinacy of the king, the violence of the ministers, and the arrogance of the English nation oblige thirteen of her colonies to render themselves independent. Such a glorious cause had never before attracted the attention of mankind; it was the last struggle of Liberty; and, had she then been vanquished, neither hope nor asylum would have remained for her. The oppressors and oppressed were to receive a powerful lesson; the great work was to be accomplished, or the rights of humanity were to fall beneath its ruin. . . . When I first learnt the subject of this quarrel, my heart espoused warmly the cause of liberty, and I thought of nothing but of adding also the aid of my banner. Some circumstances, which it would be needless to relate, had taught me to expect only obstacles in this case from my own family; I depended, therefore, solely upon myself, and I ventured to adopt for a device on my arms these words—"*Cur non?*" [Why not?] that they might equally serve as an encouragement to myself, and as a reply to others. Silas Deane[1] was then at Paris; but the ministers feared to receive him . . . He despatched privately to America some old arms, which were of little use, and some young officers, who did but little good . . . and when the English ambassador spoke to our court, it denied having sent any cargoes, ordered those that were preparing to be discharged, and dismissed from our ports all American privateers. Whilst wishing to address myself in a direct manner to Mr. Deane, I became the friend of Kalb,[2] a German in our employ, who was applying for service with the *insurgents* (the expression in use at that time), and who became my interpreter. He was the person sent . . . to examine the English colonies; and on his return he received some money, but never succeeded in obtaining an audience, so little did that minister in reality think of the revolution whose retrograde movements some persons have inscribed to him! When I presented to Mr. Deane my boyish face (for I was scarcely nineteen years of age), I spoke more of my ardour in the cause than of my experience; but I dwelt much upon the effect my departure would excite in France, and he signed our mutual agreement. The secrecy with which this negotiation and my preparation were made appears almost a miracle; family, friends, ministers, French spies and English spies, all were kept completely in the dark as to my intentions. Amongst my discreet confidants, I owe much to M. du Boismartin, secretary of the Count de Broglie, and to the Count de Broglie[3] himself, whose affectionate heart, when all his efforts to turn me from this project had proved in vain, entered into my views with even paternal tenderness.

[1]In 1776 Congress sent Silas Deane as a secret agent to induce the French government to give financial aid to America.

[2]Baron Johann de Kalb, a Bavarian then in the French Service, later a general in the American army.

[3]Probably Charles François, Comte de Broglie, who had been the most important member of Louis XV's secret diplomatic service.

Preparations were making to send a vessel to America, when very bad tidings arrived from thence. New York, Long Island, White Plains, Fort Washington, and the Jerseys, had seen the American forces successively destroyed by thirty-three thousand Englishmen or Germans. Three thousand Americans alone remained in arms, and these were closely pursued by General Howe. From that moment all the credit of the insurgents vanished; to obtain a vessel for them was impossible: the envoys themselves thought it right to express to me their own discouragement, and persuade me to abandon my project. I called upon Mr. Deane, and I thanked him for his frankness. "Until now, sir," said I, "you have only seen my ardour in your cause, and that may not prove at present wholly useless, I shall purchase a ship to carry out your officers; we must feel confidence in the future, and it is especially in the hour of danger that I wish to share your fortune." My project was received with approbation; but it was necessary afterwards to find money, and to purchase and arm a vessel secretly: all this was accomplished with the greatest despatch.

Letter to His Wife

"Charleston, 19 June, 1777.

"My last letter to you, my dear love, has informed you, that I arrived safely in this country, after having suffered a little from sea-sickness during the first weeks of the voyage; that I was then, the morning after I landed, at the house of a very kind officer, that I had been nearly two months on the passage, and that I wished to set off immediately. It spoke of every thing most interesting to my heart; of my sorrow at parting from you, and of our dear children; and it said, besides, that I was in excellent health. I give you this abstract of it, because the English may possibly amuse themselves by seizing it on its way. I have such confidence in my lucky star, however, that I hope it will reach you. This same star has befriended me, to the astonishment of every body here. Trust to it yourself, and be assured that it ought to calm all your fears. I landed after having sailed several days along a coast, which swarmed with hostile vessels. When I arrived, every body said that my vessel must inevitably be taken, since two British frigates blockaded the harbour. I even went so far as to send orders to the captain, both by land and sea, to put the men on shore and set fire to the ship, if not yet too late. By a most wonderful good fortune, a gale obliged the frigates to stand out to sea for a short time. My vessel came in at noon-day, without meeting friend or foe.

"At Charleston I have met General [Robert] Howe, an American officer now in the service. The Governor of the State is expected this evening from the country. All with whom I wished to become acquainted here, have shown me the greatest politeness and attention. I feel entirely satisfied with my reception, although I have not thought it best to go into any detail respecting my arrangements and plans. I wish first to see Congress. I hope to set out for Philadelphia in two days. Our route is more than two hundred and fifty leagues by land. We shall divide ourselves into small parties. I have already purchased horses and light carriages for the journey. Some French and American vessels are here, and are to sail together to-morrow morning, taking advantage of a moment when the frigates are out of sight. They are armed, and have promised me to defend themselves stoutly against the small privateers, which they will certainly meet. I shall distribute my letters among the different ships.

"I will now tell you about the country and its inhabitants. They are as agreeable as my enthusiasm had painted them. Simplicity of manners, kindness, love of country and of liberty, and a delightful equality every where prevail. The wealthiest man and the poorest are on a level; and, although there are some large fortunes, I challenge any one to discover the slightest difference between the manners of these two classes respectively towards each other. I first saw the country life at the house of Major Huger. I am now in the city, where every thing is very much after the English fashion, except that there is more simplicity, equality, cordiality, and courtesy here than in England. The city of Charleston is one of the handsomest and best built, and its inhabitants among the most agreeable, that I have ever seen. The American women are very pretty, simple in their manners, and exhibit a neatness, which is every where cultivated even more studiously than in England. What most charms me is, that all the citizens are brethren. In America, there are no poor, nor even what we call peasantry. Each individual has his own honest property, and the same rights as the most wealthy landed proprietor. The inns are very different from those of Europe; the host and hostess sit at table with you, and do the honors of a comfortable meal; and, on going away, you pay your bill without higgling. When one does not wish to go to an inn, there are country-houses where the title of a good American is a sufficient passport to all those civilities paid in Europe to one's friend.

"As to my own reception, it has been most agreeable in every quarter; and to have come with me secures the most flattering welcome. I have just passed five hours at a grand dinner, given in honor of me by an individual of this city. Generals Howe and Moultrie, and several officers of my suite, were present. We drank healths and tried to talk English. I begin to speak it a little. To-morrow I shall go with these gentlemen to call on the Governor of the State, and make arrangements for my departure. The next day the commanding officers here will show me the city and its environs, and then I shall set out for the army.

"Considering the pleasant life I lead in this country, my sympathy with the people, which makes me feel as much at ease in their society as if I had known them for twenty years, the similarity between their mode of thinking and my own, and my love of liberty and of glory, one might suppose that I am very happy. But you are not with me; my friends are not with me; and there is no happiness for me far from you and them. I ask you, if you still love me; but I put the same question much oftener to myself, and my heart always responds, Yes. I am impatient beyond measure to hear from you. I hope to find letters at Philadelphia. My only fear is, that the privateer, which is to bring them, may be captured on her passage. Although I suppose I have drawn upon me the special displeasure of the English, by taking the liberty to depart in spite of them, and by landing in their very face, yet I confess they will not be in arrears with me, should they capture this vessel, my cherished hope, on which I so fondly depend for letters from you. Write frequent and long letters. You do not know the full extent of the joy with which I shall receive them. Embrace Henrietta[4] tenderly. May I say embrace tenderly our *children?* The father of these poor children is a rover, but a good and honest man at heart; a good father, who loves his family dearly, and a good husband, who loves his wife with all his heart.

"Remember me to your friends and my own, to the dear society, once the society of the court, but which by the lapse of time has become the society of the *Wooden Sword.* We republicans think it all the better. I must leave off for want of paper and time; and if I do not repeat to you ten thousand times that I love you, it is not from any want of feeling, but from modesty; since I have the presumption to hope, that I have already convinced you of it. The night is far advanced, and the heat dreadful. I am devoured by insects; so, you see, the best countries have their disadvantages. Adieu.

"Lafayette."

Marquis de Lafayette to George Washington

"*Camp, 30 December, 1777.*—My dear General; I went yesterday morning to head-quarters, with an intention of speaking to your Excellency, but you were too busy, and I shall state in this letter what I wished to say. I need not tell you how sorry I am at what has lately happened;[5] it is a necessary result of my tender and respectful friendship for you, which is as true and candid as the other sentiments of my heart, and much stronger than so new an acquaintance might seem to admit. But another reason for my concern is my ardent and perhaps enthusiastic wish for the happiness and liberty of this country. I see plainly that America can defend herself, if proper measures are taken; but I begin to fear that she may be lost by herself and her own sons.

"When I was in Europe, I thought that here almost every man was a lover of liberty, and would rather die free than live a slave. You can con-

[4]His daughter.

[5]Referring to the Conway Cabal.

ceive my astonishment when I saw, that Toryism was as apparently professed as Whigism itself. There are open dissensions in Congress; parties who hate one another as much as the common enemy; men who, without knowing any thing about war, undertake to judge you. . . . I wish your Excellency could let them know how necessary you are to them, and engage them at the same time to keep peace and reinstate love among themselves, till the moment when these little disputes shall not be attended with such inconveniences. It would be too great a pity, that slavery, dishonor, ruin, and the unhappiness of a whole nation, should issue from trifling differences betwixt a few men.

"You will perhaps find this letter very unimportant; but I was desirous of explaining to you some of my ideas, because it will contribute to my satisfaction to be convinced, that you, my dear General, who have been so indulgent as to permit me to look on you as a friend, should know my sentiments. . . . My desire of deserving your approbation is strong; and, whenever you shall employ me, you can be certain of my trying every exertion in my power to succeed. I am now bound to your fate, and I shall follow it and sustain it, as well by my sword as by all the means in my power. You will pardon my importunity. Youth and friendship perhaps make me too warm, but I feel the greatest concern at recent events. With the most tender and profound respect, I have the honor to be, &c."

Lafayette to General Washington

"St. Jean d'Angely, 12 June, 1779.

"My dear General,

"There is at length a safe occasion of writing to you, and of assuring you what sincere concern I feel at our separation. I had acquired such a habit of being inseparable from you, that I am more and more afflicted at the distance, which keeps me so far from my dearest friend, and especially at this particular time, as I think the campaign is opened, and that you are in the field. I ardently wish I might be near you, know every interesting event, and if possible contribute to your success and glory. . . .

"There is another point upon which you should employ all your influence and popularity. For God's sake prevent the Congress from disputing loudly together. Nothing so much hurts the interests and reputation of America, as these intestine quarrels. On the other hand, there are two parties in France; Mr. Adams and Mr. Lee on one part; Dr. Franklin and his friends on the other. So great is the concern, which these divisions give me, that I cannot wait on these gentlemen as much as I could wish, for fear of mentioning disputes, and bringing them to a greater height. . . .

"I know you wish to hear something about my private affairs. I gave an account of them to Congress, and shall only add, that I am here as happy as possible. My family, my friends, my countrymen, gave me such a reception, and show me every day such an affection, as I could not have hoped. For some days I have been in this place, where are the King's own regiment of dragoons, which I command, and some regiments of infantry, which are for the present under my orders. But what I want, my dear General, and what would make me the happiest of men, is to join again the American colors, or to put under your orders a division of four or five thousand of my countrymen. In case any such co-operation, or any private expedition is wished for, I think, if peace is not settled this winter, that an early demand might be complied with for the next campaign. Our ministers are rather slow in their operations, and have a great desire for peace, provided it is an honorable one; so that I think America must show herself in earnest for war, till such conditions are obtained. American independence is a certain, an undoubted point; but I wish that independence to be acknowledged on advantageous terms. On the whole, between ourselves, as to what concerns the royal and ministerial good will towards America, I, an American citizen, am fully satisfied with it, and I am sure the alliance and friendship between both nations will be established in such a way as will last for ever.

"Be so kind as to present my respects to your lady, and tell her how happy I should feel to present them myself, and at her own house. I have a wife, my dear General, who is in love with you, and affection for you seems to me so well justified, that I cannot oppose that sentiment in her. She begs you will receive her compliments, and make them acceptable to Mrs. Washington. I hope you will come to see us in Europe; and most certainly I give you my word, that, if I am not happy enough to be sent to America before the peace, I shall by all means go there as soon as I can escape. I beg you will present my best compliments to your family, and remind them of my tender regard for them all; and also to the general officers, to all the officers of the army, and to all the friends I have there. I entreat you to let me hear from you. Write to me how you do, and how things are going on. The minutest details will be interesting to me. Do not forget any thing concerning yourself. With the highest respect and the most sincere friendship, I have the honor to be, &c."

To John Jay[6]

Paris, February 11th, 1786.

Dear Sir,

I have not for a long time had the honor to address you, either in public or private letters. This has been owing to a tour I made through several parts of Europe, and to a derangement in the packets which, to my great concern, I found to have taken place during my absence.

In the course of a journey to Prussia, Silesia, the Austrian dominions,

[6]At this time U. S. Secretary of State.

and back again to Berlin, I could not but have many opportunities to improve myself by the inspection of famous fields of battle, the conversation of the greatest Generals, and the sight of excellent troops—those of Prussia particularly exceeding my expectations. I had occasions not less numerous to lament the folly of nations who can bear a despotic Government, and to pay a new tribute of respect and attachment to the constitutional principles we had the happiness to establish. Wherever I went, America was of course a topic in the conversation. Her efforts during the contest are universally admired; and in the transactions which have so gloriously taken place, there is a large field of enthusiasm for the soldier, of wonder and applause for the politician; and to the philosopher and the philanthropist they are a matter of unspeakable delight, and I could say of admiration. Those sentiments I had the pleasure to find generally diffused. But to my great sorrow, (and I will the more candidly tell it in this letter, as it can hurt none more than it hurts myself,) I did not find that every remark equally turned to the advantage of my pride, and of that satisfaction I feel in the admiration of the world for the United States.

In countries so far distant, under constitutions so foreign to republican notions, the affairs of America cannot be thoroughly understood, and such inconveniences as we lament ourselves are greatly exaggerated by her enemies. It would require almost a volume to relate how many mistaken ideas I had the opportunity to set to rights. And it has been painful for me to hear, it is now disagreeable to mention, the bad effect which the want of federal union, and of effective arrangements for the finances and commerce of a general establishment of militia, have had on the minds of European nations. It is foolishly thought by some that democratical constitutions will not, cannot last, that the States will quarrel with each other, that a King, or at least a nobility, are indispensable for the prosperity of a nation. But I would not attend to those absurdities, as they are answered by the smallest particle of unprejudiced common sense, and will, I trust, be forever destroyed by the example of America. But it was impossible for me to feel so much unconcerned when those points were insisted upon for which I could not but acknowledge within myself there was some ground, although it was so unfairly broached upon by the enemies of the United States. It is an object with the European Governments to check and discourage the spirit of emigration, which, I hope, will increase among the Germans with a more perfect knowledge of the situation of America. And while I was enjoying the admiration and respect of those parts of the world for the character of the United States; while I was obliged to hear some remarks which, although they were exaggerated, did not seem to me quite destitute of a foundation, I heartily addressed my prayers to Heaven that, by her known wisdom, patriotism, and liberality of principles, as well as firmness of conduct, America may preserve the consequence she has so well acquired, and continue to command the admiration of the world. . . . LAFAYETTE.

is a most strange place; nothing to be seen in the streets but dogs and negroes, and the few ladies that *pass for white* are to be sure the most unlovely pieces of crockery I ever set my eyes upon. The first object I saw on entering Colonel Hamilton's drawing-room was a harpsichord, which looked like civilisation, and delighted me extremely; and in the evening we had a Miss Mathews, who played and sung very tolerably indeed; but music here is like whistling to a wilderness. She played some of dear Kate's[3] lessons, which brought the tears into my eyes with recollection. I saw some of my own songs among the music-books, and this morning I met with a periodical publication full of extracts from my Anacreon and Little's[4] poems, and speaking of me in the most flattering terms of eulogium. All this is very gratifying; it would be so naturally at any time, and is now particularly so, from the very few hopes I had of being cheered or welcomed by any of those little pleasures or gratifications I have been accustomed to so long. They tell me that the people of Bermuda are very musical, and I find Admiral Mitchell and his squadron winter there, so that I shall not be very much at a loss for society; and as I intend to devote all my leisure hours to the completion of my work, my time may be filled up not unpleasantly. From what I have heard, however, since I came closer to the channels of correct information, I strongly suspect that we shall not, dearest mother, be long separated. I am delighted that we all had the resolution to enable me to make the effort, but as that is the chief point, and almost the only one I ever expected to attain by the step, I believe I shall not find enough, otherwise advantageous, to induce me to absent myself long from my home-opportunities of advancement. My foot is on the ladder pretty firmly, and that is the great point gained.

When I was leaving Portsmouth, just on the instant of my coming away, I folded up a packet in a hurry, which I enclosed to Jasper Erche, but (I believe) forgot to direct it inside. There were some songs in it for Stevenson to arrange. I anxiously hope it arrived safe. At the same time I had a letter written to Captain Atkinson, but not having time to fold it ashore, I was obliged to send it back by the boat which left us to return to Portsmouth. This too I have hopes arrived safe; but my confusion was so great, that I cannot now remember what I wrote or what I did. Explain all this to my dear good friend Atkinson, and tell him he shall hear from me by the next opportunity. If Atkinson could get Lord Moira to write a few words about me to Hamilton, I think it would be of singular service to me while I remain at Bermuda. Show him this letter, and give him with it the warmest remembrances of my heart. . . .

I have this instant received an invitation to dinner from one of the Yankees of this place: if the ambassador and his lady go, of course *I* will. Oh! if you saw the vehicles the people drive about in here, white coaches with black

[3]His sister.

[4]Thomas Little, a pen name of Moore's.

servants, and horses of no colour at all; it is really a most comical place. Poor Mrs. Merry has been as ill-treated by the musquitoes as she is by every one else. They have bit her into a fever. I have escaped their notice entirely, and sleep with a fine net over my bed. The weather now is becoming too cold for them, and indeed a little too much so for me. I shall be glad to escape to the mild climate of Bermuda, which I still hear is the sweetest and most healthy spot in the world; but I am sorry to find that meat is rather a scarcity there, and that it is sometimes no fish, no dinner. He that can't feed well, however, upon good poultry, fish, and fruit of all kinds, ought to be condemned to eat roast mutton all the days of his life; and this, my dear mother, in your mind and mine, would be sufficient punishment for him. Tell my beloved, darling father, that if there is anything in the mercantile way which he can learn, that I may assist him or Mr. Gillespie in here, they shall find me a steadier fellow than I am afraid I have hitherto appeared (at least to Mr. G.), and I shall manage for them like a solid man of business. Seriously, though I know nothing at present about the trade here, it is not impossible but something may occur to Mr. Gillespie in which I may be made useful. . . .

Norfolk, Virginia, Nov. 28. 1803.

My darling Mother,

By a ship which sailed last week for England, I wrote you the first account of my arrival at Norfolk, safely and prosperously, as I could wish. Heaven speed the letter to you, my sweet mother! It is very painful to be uncertain upon a point so interesting, as the little communication we are allowed must be to us all; but it is impossible to answer for the arrival of my letters, and I shall be doomed to still more uncertainty at Bermuda. I must, therefore, take every opportunity that presents itself, and it will be very unfortunate, indeed, if some of my communications do not reach you. I have now been here three weeks, waiting for a ship, to take me to Bermuda. I could scarcely have hoped, dear mother, to bear the voyage and the climate so well, as (thank Heaven!) I hitherto have done. Since I left England, I have had but one day's illness, which was the mere ordinary sea-sickness, upon coming on board. Mr. and Mrs. Merry are gone to Washington, after remaining here more than a fortnight. I am lodged at Col. Hamilton's, the British consul, from whom I have experienced all possible kindness and hospitality; and if any of the squadron off this station touch here in their way from Halifax to Bermuda (where they are to winter), I shall be the luckiest fellow in the world, for I am sure of a passage with them, without expense, and most comfortably. Dear darlings at home! how incessantly I think of you: every night I dream that I am amongst you: sometimes I find you happy and smiling as I could wish: sometimes the picture is not so pleasant, and I awake unhappy, but surely Heaven protects you for me, and we shall meet, and long be united and blessed together. In that hope I bear absence with a lighter heart, and I entreat of you, sweet mother! to look on it with the same cheerful confidence—the same consoling dependence on that God of all pure affection, who sees how we love each other, and has, I trust, much prosperity in store for us. I shall lose no opportunity whatever that occurs of writing to you, and saying how affairs go on. My dear father, I am sure, will often give me the consolation of seeing his hand. Good Kate and Nell[5] too must not be idle, but show me that their thoughts are frequently employed upon me.

I write this merely as a *duplicate* of my last letter, to tell you of my arrival, and let you know how I am at present situated: never was my health or spirits better. . . . I kiss you all. God bless you. Your own,

Tom.

Norfolk, Dec. 2. 1803.

. . . Oh, dear mother! think it is now three months since I had the sweet consolation of seeing any memorial of home. This is a long period, and much may have happened in it; but I hope, I trust, I depend on Heaven that it has preserved you all well and happy for me, and that we shall not long be this dreary distance asunder. My good Father! how often, how dearly, I think of *him*, and *you*, and *all!* I feel how anxious your hearts must be at the long interval you have passed without hearing of me, but the letter I wrote to you in the third week of our passage, and sent by a ship bound for some part of the Continent, if it reached in any reasonable time, must have been a happy relief to your solicitude. I did not regret so much the foul winds we had afterwards, because they were fair for that vessel which bore some tidings of comfort to my dear home. Oh, if the wretches have been neglectful, and not forwarded the letter! But I will hope the best, and think that, long before this, you have seen my handwriting and are comforted, dear mother. The kindness of these good people, the Hamiltons, is fortunate and delightful to me. If I were not so completely thrown upon it though I should be more gratified by, and enjoy it more pleasantly: but is it not a most lucky thing, when I am obliged to remain here, to be received cordially by a family whose hospitality is of that honest kind which sets one at home and at ease, as much as is possible in such a situation. I have been obliged to get a servant, and am fortunate enough to have one who cannot speak a word of English, which will keep me famously alive in my French. It is extraordinary that I cannot, even here, acquire any accurate information with respect to the profits of my registrarship. One thing is *certain*, that a Spanish war *alone* can make it worth a very long sacrifice of my other opportunities, and our government has so long hesitated upon that point, that it seems now more doubtful than ever. However, I am too far from the source of information to guess how politics stand at present. . . . I know that my friends in Dublin will all be very angry that I do not write to them by the same opportunities

[5]Moore's sister.

I have found for writing to you, but I can't help that; till I have satisfied myself pretty well with respect to *your* certainty of hearing from me, I confess I cannot think much about any one else. This is, however, the third letter I have written since my arrival, and the winds and waves must be cruel indeed if they do not suffer at least one of them to reach you. The next opportunity I shall make use of to write to my dear friend Atkinson. Tell him so, and give him my warmest remembrances: they are not the less warm for being Transatlantic. Absence is the best touchstone of affection: it either cools it quite, or makes it ten times warmer than ever it was; and I can never judge how I *love* people till I *leave* them. This is a strange climate; yesterday the glass was at 70°, and to-day it is down to 40°. I consider myself very hardy to bear it so well: my stomach has seldom been in such good order, nor my whole frame more braced and healthy. If Bermuda agrees so perfectly with me, I shall return to you the better for my trip. Return to you! how I like to say that, and think it, and pray for it. Dear mother, kiss Kate and Nell for me. I need not bid Kate read, but I bid little Ellen, and they must both apply closely to their music. I expect such a treat from them when I go home; for, indeed, there is a sad dearth of that luxury in these parts. God bless you again and again. The captain waits for the letters; he goes to Cork. Ever your own.

Norfolk, Virginia, Dec. 10. 1803.

My darling Mother,

You will have received, I hope, long before this arrives, two letters which I wrote since the one I now enclose. I am extremely unhappy at the delay, for I know how you must have suffered in the interval; but the ship Ritson, by which I sent the enclosed letter soon after I landed, returned yesterday so much damaged by the bad weather that she could not get on to England, and had been obliged to put back. Can any thing be more unlucky? I so pleased myself with the idea that you were by this time apprised of my safety, for it is now near five weeks since the Ritson sailed, and to have the letter come back to me thus is quite dreadful. God grant, my dearest and beloved mother, that you have had resolution to combat the solicitude you must have endured so long. I was perfectly happy in the hopes that a quick passage would have attended the ship which bore you the intelligence of my arrival, and every thing else has turned out so fortunate with me, that this is the only subject of regret I have met with. If you however, my dear mother, have got well over it, as I trust in Heaven you have, there is nothing else which at present gives my heart one painful thought: is not this delightful for you to hear? The expectation I expressed in all my letters, that some of the ships of war bound for Bermuda would touch here is gratified most fortunately. Captain Compton of the Driver is arrived, and I go with him. Nothing could be more lucky; beside the safety and comfort of such convoy, it saves me between twenty and thirty guineas, which I should have to pay for passage and provision in a merchantman. He gives me a very favourable account of Bermuda, and I have no doubt of passing my time very pleasantly there. Every thing is succeeding to my utmost wishes, and my spirits are as wild as ever you have witnessed them. Till this cursed Ritson returned with my poor dear letter, I had not one uneasy thought, for even my regrets at the distance that separates us was softened by the hope that you would soon hear of my safety, that you would be happy in the promise of good fortune that awaits us, and that no very distant day would see us in the possession of all our hearts wish for.

I have not time, darling mother, to say more, for the ship that takes this goes away in a few hours. In less than a week, I think, Captain Compton sails for Bermuda, and I shall have an opportunity of writing again before we go. God bless you—Father, Kate, Nell, and all dears. . . .

Bermuda, Jan. 19. 1804.

My darling Mother,

Here have I been more than a week, without any opportunity of sending a letter even to take its chance at sea in some of the cruisers, since none have arrived or left this during that time; and it gives me so much uneasiness to think you should be long without hearing of me, that I am hardly so selfish as to bestow a thought upon my own privation. Yet indeed, dearest mother, it is a very cruel privation to have been now near five months without a whisper of intelligence from home; and if every thing here was as prosperous as I have been flattered into supposing, this dreadful anxiety would embitter it all; and the brightest advantages of the situation would be very dearly purchased. In coming from Norfolk hither we had most tremendous weather: you may guess what it must have been to an inexperienced sailor, when all the officers of the ship declared they seldom, scarcely ever, had encountered such serious and continual gales of wind. The passage, however, was pretty short for this season of the year; we made it in seven days, though for three days of that time we remained without venturing to set a stitch of sail, and of course lost as much as we gained of our way. Yet I bore it all so stoutly, that, would you believe it, dearest mother! on the day of the worst gale we had, I eat the heartiest dinner of beefsteaks and onions that ever I have made in my life; though, as during the whole time of the passage, we were obliged to be tied to the table at dinner; and at night, when the ship was rolling her sides into the water, and when it was in vain to think of sleeping from the noise and the motion, I amused myself in my cot by writing ridiculous verses and laughing at them. Sailors, to be sure, think nothing of all these storms; but I *do* say, for a novice, it requires a little philosophy to be so cool and careless in such new and uncomfortable situations. Indeed, there has never been a severer winter than this upon the coast of America, and often, very often, darling mother, have I dreaded that you would see some accounts of the storms and the accidents that have happened, and that your heart, already too apt to catch at an intimation of danger, would find in these accounts too much food for its solicitude. I felt some regret, indeed not a little, in leaving the Hamiltons at Norfolk. Mrs. Hamilton cried, and said she never parted with any one so reluctantly. The colonel gave me the warmest letters of introduction to every one that could be serviceable or amusing to me here; and as I know dear mother loves to see anything which flatters her boy, and shows he is not neglected in his absence from her, I enclose one of these letters, which by the merest accident has returned into my possession, and which, being to one of the young sea captains, I have reason to think is not half so strong as some others.

These little islands of Bermuda form certainly one of the prettiest and most romantic spots that I could ever have imagined, and the descriptions which represent it as like a place of fairy enchantment are very little beyond the truth. From my window now as I write, I can see five or six different islands, the *most distant* not a mile from the others, and separated by the clearest, sweetest coloured sea you can conceive; for the water here is so singularly transparent, that, in coming in, we could see the rocks under the ship quite plainly. These little islands are thickly covered with cedar groves, through the vistas of which you catch a few pretty white houses, which my poetical short-sightedness always transforms into temples; and I often expect to see Nymphs and Graces come tripping from them, when, to my great disappointment, I find that a few miserable negroes is all "the bloomy flush of life" it has to boast of. Indeed, you must not be surprised, dear mother, if I fall in love with the first pretty face I see on my return home, for certainly the "human face divine" has degenerated wonderfully in these countries; and if I were a painter, and wished to preserve my ideas of beauty immaculate, I would not suffer the brightest belle of Bermuda to be my housemaid. But I shall refer you for a fuller description of this place to a letter I have written to my good friend Atkinson; and to come to the point which is most interesting to us, dear mother, I shall tell you at once that it is *not* worth my while to remain here; that I shall just stop to finish my work for Carpenter,[6] which will occupy me till the spring months come in, when the passages home are always delightfully pleasant, and that then I shall get upon the wing to see my dear friends once more. I perfectly acquit those whose representations have induced me to come out here, because I perceive they were totally ignorant of the nature of the situation. Neither am I sorry for having come; the appointment is respectable, and evidently was considered a matter of great patronage among those who had the disposal of it, which alone is sufficient to make it a valuable step towards preferment. But this is all; so many courts have been established, that this of Bermuda has but few prize causes referred to it, and even a Spanish war would make my income by no means worth staying for. I have entered upon my business, however, and there are two American ships for trial, whose witnesses I have examined, and whose cause will be decided next month: it is well to be

[6]Moore's song-publisher.

acquainted with these things. I have seen too a little more of the world, have got an insight into American character and affairs, have become more used to inconveniences and disappointments, have tried my nerves and resolution a little, and I think very considerably improved my health, for I do not remember ever to have been more perfectly well than I am at present. All these advantages are to be calculated, and as they reconcile me completely to the step I have taken, I have hopes that my darling father and you will consider it in the same favourable light, and not feel much disappointment at the damp our expectations have experienced. Please Heaven! I shall soon embrace you all, and find you in health and happiness once more; and this will amply, dearly repay me for much more exertion than I have yet made towards your welfare. How I shall enjoy dear Kate's playing when I return! The jingle they make here upon things they call pianofortes is, oh! insupportable. . . . Best love to my adored father: I hope Providence favours his exertions for the dear ones about him. Darling Kate and Ellen have my heart with them always. There is a little thing here very like Nell, only much darker, and I go very often to look at her. God bless you, sweet mother, for your own, own affectionate,

T. M.

St. George's, Bermudas, Feb. 17. 1804.

My dearest Mother,

Every ship that comes, I look with impatience to, as bringing me some intelligence from some friends at home; but I am still disappointed, and it is now five months since I saw the last dear paper that brought the *odour of home* on it to me. I begin to fear that it is not unlikely I may be on my return to England before any news of you can reach me; for, unfortunately, I did not know myself, nor therefore could I instruct you in, the most frequent and safe method of forwarding letters to me. . . . My health has never been more perfect or regular than at present; indeed, it is almost impossible to be ill in such a delicious climate as this island enjoys in the winter. Roses are in full blow here now, and my favorite *green peas* smoke every day upon the table. I have been extremely fortunate here (as indeed Providence seems to please I should be everywhere) in conciliating friendship, and interesting those around me in my welfare. The admiral, Sir Andrew Mitchell, has insisted upon my making his table my own during my stay here, and has promised to take me in his ship to America, for the purpose of getting a passage home to England, there being no direct conveyance from this little corner thither. They threaten me here with an impeachment, as being in a fair way to make bankrupts of the whole island. There has been nothing but gaiety since I came, and there never was such a *furor* for dissipation known in the town of St. George's before. The music parties did not long keep up, because they found they were obliged to trust to me for their whole orchestra; but the dances have been innumerable, and still continue with very great spirit indeed. The women dance in general extremely well, though, like Dogberry's "writing and reading," it "comes by nature to them," for they never have any instruction, except when some flying dancing-master, by the kindness of fortune, happens to be wrecked and driven ashore on the island. Poor creatures! I feel real pity for them: many of them have hearts for a more favourable sphere; but they are here thrown together in a secluded nook of the world, where they learn all the corruptions of human nature, without any one of its consolations or ornaments. The ship by which I send this letter goes to Providence, in the Bahamas, an express having arrived from that place to the admiral for a reinforcement, as they dread an attack from the remains of the French army of St. Domingo, who are at this moment actually preparing at Cuba for a descent. If this conduct of the Spaniards does not produce a war, we have peaceable ministers indeed. But I must not talk to you of politics, darling mother, for I have only time to bid you kiss all the dears around you for me. . . . God bless you all, for yours truly and ever,

Tom.

New York, May 7. 1804.

My dearest Mother,

I have but just time to say, *here I am*, after a passage of nine days from Bermuda; never was better; and the novelty of this strange place keeps me in a bustle of spirits and curiosity. The oddest things I have seen yet, however, are young Buonaparte and his bride.[7]

My plans are not settled yet. Captain Douglas, of the Boston frigate, who brought me here, sails in a few days for Norfolk, whither I shall accompany him; and my intention is, if I can manage it, to come up by land through the States, and rejoin him at Halifax, from whence I believe he will be sent to England,—a fine opportunity for me, and I anxiously hope it may occur so. I go to the theatre this evening, and to a concert to-morrow evening. Such a place! such people! barren and secluded as poor Bermuda is, I think it a paradise to any spot in America that I have seen. If there is less barrenness of *soil* here, there is more than enough of barrenness in intellect, taste, and all in which *heart* is concerned. . . .

I have no more time; my heart is full of the prospect of once more seeing and embracing you, dear mother, good father, and my own Kate and Ellen. God bless you. I wrote to Carpenter and Lord Moira by the same ship. Your own Transatlantic Tom.

[7]M. Jerome Buonaparte and Miss Patterson.

Aboard the Boston,
Sandy Hook, thirty miles from New York,
Friday, May 11. 1804.

My darling Mother,

I wrote to you on my arrival at New York, where I have been near a week, and am now returned aboard the frigate, which but waits a fair wind to sail for Norfolk. The Halifax packet is lying along side of us, and I shall take the opportunity of sending this letter by her. At New York I was made happy by my father's letter of the 25th January, and dear Kate's of the 30th, which make four in all that I have received from home. I had so very few opportunities at Bermuda, and they were attended with so much uncertainty, that I fear you may have suffered many an anxious moment, darling mother, from the interruption and delay of the few letters I could dispatch to you. But, please Heaven! we shall soon have those barriers of distance removed; my own tongue shall tell you my "travel's history," and your heart shall go along with me over every billow and step of the way. When I left Bermuda I could not help regretting that the hopes which took me thither could not be even half realised, for I should love to live there, and you would like it too, dear mother; and I think, if the situation would give me but a fourth of what I was so deludingly taught to expect, you should all have come to me; and though set apart from the rest of the world, we should have found in that quiet spot, and under that sweet sky, quite enough to counterbalance what the rest of the world could give us. But I am still to seek, and can only hope that I may find at last.

The environs of New York are pretty, from the number of little fanciful wooden houses that are scattered, to the distance of six to eight miles round the city; but when one reflects upon the cause of this, and that these houses are the retreats of the terrified, desponding inhabitants from the wilderness of death which every autumn produces in the city, there is very little pleasure in the prospect; and, notwithstanding the rich fields, and the various blossoms of their orchards, I prefer the barren, breezy rock of Bermuda to whole continents of such dearly purchased fertility.

While in New York, I employed my time to advantage in witnessing all the novelties possible. I saw young M. Buonaparte, and felt a slight shock of an earthquake, which are two things I could not often meet with upon Usher's Quay. From Norfolk I intend going to Baltimore and Washington; if possible also to Philadelphia and Boston, from thence to Halifax. From Halifax I hope to set sail in the cabin where I now write this letter for the dear old isles of the Old World again; and I think it probable, that twelve months from the time I left England will very nearly see me on its coasts once more. . . .

My first object when I return shall be to discharge my obligations to Carpenter: as I must, for that purpose, seclude myself entirely, the less you say about the time of my return the better. The completion of the work I have in hand will much more than extricate me from all engagements I am under. My dear uncle shall not want his money *one moment* after my arrival: tell him so, with my heart's truest and affectionate remembrances. God bless you, darling mother. Kiss them all round for me, father, Kate, and Nell together. Your own,

T. M.

Baltimore, Wednesday, June 13. 1804.

I am now, dearest mother, more than three hundred miles from Norfolk. I have passed the Potomac, the Rappahannock, the Occoquan, the Potapsio, and many other rivers, with names as barbarous as the inhabitants: every step I take not only *reconciles,* but *endears* to me, not only the excellencies but even the errors of Old England. Such a road as I have come! and in such a conveyance! The mail takes twelve passengers, which generally consist of squalling children, stinking negroes, and republicans smoking cigars! How often it has occurred to me that nothing can be more emblematic of the *government* of this country than its *stages,* filled with a motley mixture, all "hail fellow well met," driving through mud and filth, which *bespatters* them as they *raise* it, and risking an *upset* at every step. God comfort their capacities! as soon as I am away from them, both the stages and the government may have the same fate for what *I* care. I stopped at Washington with Mr. and Mrs. Merry for near a week: they have been treated with the most pointed incivility by the present democratic president, Mr. Jefferson; and it is only the precarious situation of Great Britain which could possibly induce it to overlook such indecent, though, at the same time, petty hostility. I was presented by Mr. Merry to both the secretary of state[8] and the president. . . .

I hope, my darling mother, that all I write to amuse you may meet your eye, and find your heart in a mood to enjoy it. Oh yes, be happy, my own mother! be *you* but well and happy, and no sorrow can come near any of us. I know, in saying this, I speak for *all;* for my dearest, beloved father, and the sweet, good girls; we all hang on you equally. Never did Heaven form a heart more kind than I have found in Mrs. Hamilton of Norfolk, and she has caught the way to my heart by calling herself my *mother.* She sends a pair of ear-rings by me to Kate with the sincerest affection possible: she loves you all through me. I shall leave this place for Philadelphia on to-morrow, or the day after. I shall see there poor Edward Hudson, who, if I am rightly informed, has married the daughter of a very rich bookseller, and is taken into partnership by the father. Surely, surely, *this country* must have cured him of republicanism. Farewell, my sweet mother; Heaven preserve you to me, and to the dear ones about you, who have always my heart and soul with them. Yours and theirs for ever.

I was going to tell you about writing to me, but that is unnecessary, for

[8]James Madison.

in less than six weeks I hope to sail from Halifax for England. I am going to the northward just in right time, before the violent heat sets in, and the Halifax summer is delicious.

Philadelphia, June 16.

I have brought this letter on with me from Baltimore, as there was no opportunity likely to occur from thence. I travelled all night in one of the most rumbling, wretched vehicles. Oh dear! I am almost tired of thus jogging and struggling into experience. I have seen Edward Hudson: the rich bookseller I had heard of is Pat Byrne, whose daughter Hudson has married: they are, I believe, doing well. I dine with them to-day. Oh, if Mrs. Merry were to know that! However, I dined with the Consul-general yesterday, which makes the balance even. I feel awkward with Hudson now; he has perhaps had reason to confirm him in his politics, and God knows I see every reason to change mine. Good by, sweet mother. Your own everywhere.

Passaick Falls, June 26. 1804.

My dearest Mother,

I *must* write to you from this spot, it is so beautiful. Nothing can be more sweetly romantic than the cascade of the Passaick; and yet I could not help wishing, while I looked at it, that some magic could transform it into the waterfall of Wicklow, and then but a few miles should lie between me and those I sigh for. Well, a little lapse of time, and I shall be, please Heaven! in your arms. But there have ships come, darling mother, from Dublin, and I have received no letters; none with a date more recent than January: perhaps they have been sent on to Col. Hamilton, and I shall get them at Halifax. God send I may; but till then I cannot feel at ease. Not a line has reached me from Carpenter since I left England. I sometimes forget the contingencies and accidents which delay and embarrass the forwarding of letters, and almost begin to think myself neglected by those at home; but I ought to recollect how very short a time I have been stationary anywhere, and I shall look with hope to Halifax for the long arrears of comfort which begin to impoverish the treasury of my spirits, rich as it is in stores of consolation and vivacity.

My reception at Philadelphia was extremely flattering: it is the only place in America which can boast any literary society, and my name had prepossessed them more strongly than I deserve. But their affectionate attentions went far beyond this deference to reputation; I was quite caressed while there; and their anxiety to make me known, by introductory letters, to all their friends on my way, and two or three little poems of a very flattering kind, which some of their choicest men addressed to me, all went so warmly to my heart, that I felt quite a regret in leaving them; and the only place I have seen, which I had one wish to pause in, was Philadelphia.

The Boston frigate, in which I expect to return, is now watching the French frigates (off New York), which are come to steal away young Mister Buonaparte:[9] this, perhaps, will a little delay her arrival at Halifax, where I hope to be in less than a fortnight. Never was I in better health; I drink scarcely a drop of wine, which is a plan I am determined to adhere to, as I have always found wine heating and injurious to my stomach. . . .

Saratoga, July 10. 1804.

My darling mother, I hope, has received the letter I wrote from the Passaick Falls. Since that I have passed a week in New York, but was afraid to write from thence, through fear you might be uneasy at my being there in so warm a season. Till the day before I left it, there was no appearance of any infection: on that day, some reports of yellow fever *were* made, and indeed I have no doubt the visitation of this calamity will be as dreadful this year, as any that has preceded. I have now come two hundred miles from New York, and if anything can add to the blessing of the health which I feel, it is the idea of having left such pestilence behind me. Oh that you could see the sweet country I have passed through! The passage up the Hudson river gave me the most bewildering succession of romantic objects that I could ever have conceived. When it was calm, we rowed ashore and visited the little villages that are on the river: one of these places they have called *Athens*, and there, you may imagine, I found myself quite at home. I looked in vain though for my dear *gardens;* there were *hogs* enough, but none of *Epicurus's herd*. If you, or sweet Kate, could read *Latin*, I would quote you here what I allude to; but you have not "been at the great feast of languages, or *stolen the scraps*," so I'll not tease you with it. Two or three days ago I was to see the Coho Falls on the Mohawk river, and was truly gratified. The immense fall of the river over a natural dam of thirty or forty feet high, its roar among the rocks, and the illuminated mist of spray which rises from its foam, were to me objects all new, beautiful, and impressive. I never can forget the scenery of this country, and if it had but any endearing associations of the heart (to diffuse that charm over it, without which the fairest features of nature are but faintly interesting), I should regret very keenly that I cannot renew often the enjoyment of its beauties. But it has none such for me, and I defy the barbarous natives to forge one chain of attachment for any heart that has ever felt the sweets of delicacy or refinement. I believe I must except the *women* from this denunciation; they

[9] Jerome Buonaparte, youngest brother of Napoleon, was cruising among the West Indies when war broke out between England and France in 1803. He took refuge in the United States and met and married Miss Elizabeth Patterson, daughter of a Baltimore merchant. Napoleon declared the marriage null and forced Jerome to marry Catherine, daughter of King Frederick I of Wurttemberg.

are certainly flowers of every climate, and here "waste their sweetness" most deplorably. Dear mother, I know you will be pleased with a little poem I wrote on my way from Philadelphia; it was written very much as a return for the kindnesses I met with there, but chiefly in allusion to a very charming little woman, Mrs. Hopkinson, who was extremely interested by my songs, and flattered me with many attentions. You must observe that the Schuylkill is a river which runs by, or (I believe) through, Philadelphia.

[Here follows, "Alone by the Schuylkill a wanderer rov'd,"]

I am now near the spot where the accomplished but ill-fated Burgoyne incurred the first stain which the arms of England received from the rebel Americans. The country around here seems the very home of savages. Nothing but tall forests of pine, through which the narrow, rocky road with difficulty finds its way; and yet in this neighbourhood is the fashionable resort, the watering-place for ladies and gentlemen from all parts of the United States. At Bell Town Springs, eight miles from this, there are about thirty or forty people at present (and, in the season, triple that number), all stowed together in a miserable boarding house, smoking, drinking the waters, and performing every necessary evolution in concert. They were astonished at our asking for basins and towels in our rooms, and thought we might "condescend, indeed, to come down to the *Public Wash* with the other gentlemen in the morning!" I saw there a poor affectionate mother who had brought her son for the recovery of his health: she sat beside him all day with a large fan, to cool his "feverish brow," and not a moment did she rest from this employment; every time I passed I saw her at it with the sweetest patience imaginable. Oh! there is no love like mother's love; the sight made me think of home, and recalled many circumstances which brought the tears of recollection and gratitude into my eyes.

I enclose you a scrap from a New York paper of last week, which will show you I do not pass unnoticed over this waste. God bless you all. Love to my darling father, and the good girls. From your own devoted son,

Tom.

Geneva, Genessee Country, July 17. 1804.

I just pause a moment on my way to give one word to my dearest mother. I hope the letter I wrote, four or five days since, from Seenectady, will find its way to you. Since then I have been amongst the Oneida Indians, and have been amused very much by the novelty of their appearance. An old chief, Seenando, received me very courteously, and told us as well as he could by broken English and signs, that his nation consisted of 900, divided into three tribes, entitled the Wolf, the Bear, and the Turtle; poor, harmless savages! The government of America are continually deceiving them into a surrender of the lands they occupy, and are driving them back into the woods farther and farther, till at length they will have no retreat but the ocean. This old chief's manners were extremely gentle and intelligent, and almost inclined me to be of the Frenchman's opinion, that the savages are the only well-bred gentlemen in America.

Our journey along the banks of the Mohawk was uncommonly interesting: never did I feel my heart in a better tone of sensibility than that which it derived from the scenery on this river. There is a holy magnificence in the immense bank of woods that overhang it, which does not permit the heart to rest merely in the admiration of *Nature*, but carries it to that something less *vague* than *Nature*, that satisfactory source of all these exquisite wonders, a Divinity! I sometimes on the way forget myself and even you so much, as to wish for ever to remain amidst these romantic scenes; but I *did not* forget you; you were *all inseparable* from the plans of happiness which at that moment might have flattered my fancy. I can form none into which you are not woven, closely and essentially.

To-morrow we shall set out for the *Falls of Niagara!* After seeing these (which I shall consider an era in my life), I shall lose no time in reaching Halifax, so as to be ready for the sailing of the frigate. I told you in a former letter, that it is this lucky opportunity of a passage *gratis* to England which has induced me to devote the expenses of my return to the acquisition of some knowledge respecting this very interesting world, which, with all the defects and disgusting peculiarities of its natives, gives every promise of no very distant competition with the first powers of the Eastern hemisphere.

We travel to Niagara in *a waggon:* you may guess at the cheapness of the inns in this part of the country, when I tell you that, the other night, three of us had supper, beds, and breakfast, besides some drink for two or three Indians who danced for us, and the bill came to something less than seven shillings for all. I must own the accommodations are still lower than their price; nothing was ever so dirty or miserable; but powerful curiosity sweetens all difficulties. I shall not have an opportunity to write again for some time, but I shall send you thoughts enough, and you must imagine them the dearest and most comfortable possible. When I say, "for some time," I mean a fortnight or three weeks. Good by. God bless you, dears. Oh! that I could know how you are at this moment. Your own,

Tom.

Chippewa, Upper Canada, July 22. 1804.

Dearest Mother,

Just arrived within a mile and half of the Falls of Niagara, and their tremendous roar at this moment sounding in my ears. We travelled one whole day through the wilderness, where you would imagine human foot had never ventured to leave its print; and this rough work has given a healthier hue to my cheek than ever it could boast in the Eastern hemisphere of London. If you look at the map of North America, you will be able to trace my situation. I have passed through the Genessee country, and am now between Lake Erie and Lake Ontario. Such scenery as there is around me! it is quite dreadful that any heart, born for sublimities, should be doomed to breathe away its hours amidst the miniature productions of this world, without seeing what shapes Nature *can* assume, what wonders God *can* give birth to.

I have seized this momentary opportunity, dear mother, for writing a line to you, which I will entrust to the waggoner who returns to Geneva, from which place I last wrote to you. Heaven send you may receive all the letters. I feel they would interest even a stranger to me, then what must they be to you! Love to dear father and girls. Your own,

TOM.

I am now on British ground; we arrived yesterday evening to dinner, and drunk the King's health in a bumper. Just going to see the Falls. Good by.

Niagara, July 24. 1804.

MY DEAREST MOTHER,

I have seen the Falls, and am all rapture and amazement. I cannot give you a better idea of what I felt than by transcribing what I wrote off hastily in my journal on returning. "Arrived at Chippewa, within three miles of the Falls, on Saturday, July 21st, to dinner. That evening walked towards the Falls, but got no farther than the Rapids, which gave us a prelibation of the grandeur we had to expect. Next day, Sunday, July 22d, went to visit the Falls. Never shall I forget the impression I felt at the first glimpse of them which we got as the carriage passed over the hill that overlooks them. We were not near enough to be agitated by the terrific effects of the scene; but saw through the trees this mighty flow of waters descending with calm magnificence, and received enough of its grandeur to set imagination on the wing; imagination which, even at Niagara, can outrun reality. I felt as if approaching the very residence of the Deity; the tears started into my eyes; and I remained, for moments after we had lost sight of the scene, in that delicious absorption which pious enthusiasm alone can produce. We arrived at the New Ladder and descended to the bottom. Here all its awful sublimities rushed full upon me. But the former exquisite sensation was gone. I now saw all. The string that had been touched by the first impulse, and which *fancy* would have kept for ever in vibration, now rested at *reality*. Yet, though there was no more to imagine, there was much to feel. My whole heart and soul ascended towards the Divinity in a swell of devout admiration, which I never before experienced. Oh! bring the atheist here, and he cannot return an atheist! I pity the man who can coldly sit down to write a description of these ineffable wonders; much more do I pity him who can submit them to the admeasurement of gallons and yards. It is impossible by pen or pencil to convey even a faint idea of their magnificence. Painting is lifeless; and the most burning words of poetry have all been lavished upon inferior and ordinary subjects. We must have new combinations of language to describe the Falls of Niagara."

* * * * * *

Chippewa, July 25.

On the Sunday morning before I left Chippewa, I wrote you a letter, darling mother, which I entrusted to the waggoner (who was going back) to have it forwarded. Oh! if the stupid scoundrel should have neglected it. Since the day I left New York (July 4) this is the fourth letter I have written to you. How dreadfully provoking if they have miscarried. Never was I in better health than I have been during my journey. This exercise is quite new to me, and I find the invigorating effects of it. My heart, too, feels light with the idea that the moment is approaching when I shall fly on the wings of the wind to the dear embrace of all that is dear to me. God bless you, loves. I pray for you often and fervently; and I feel that Heaven *will* take care of us. A thousand kisses to dear father and the girls, from their own boy on the banks of Lake Ontario. Again God bless you, dearest mother. Ever, ever your

Tom.

Quebec, August 20. 1804.

My darling Mother,

After seventeen hundred miles of rattling and tossing through woods, lakes, rivers, &c., I am at length upon the ground which made Wolfe immortal, and which looks more like the elysium of heroes than their death-place. If any thing can make the beauty of the country more striking, it is the deformity and oddity of the city which it surrounds, and which lies hemmed in by ramparts, amidst this delicious scenery, like a hog in armour upon a bed of roses.

In my passage across Lake Ontario, I met with the same politeness which has been so gratifying, and indeed convenient, to me all along my route. The captain refused to take what I know is always given, and begged me to consider all my friends as included in the same compliment, which a line from me would at any time entitle them to. Even a poor watchmaker at Niagara, who did a very necessary and difficult job for me, insisted I should not think of paying him, but accept it as the only mark of respect he could pay to one he had heard of so much, but never expected to meet with. This is the very nectar of life, and I hope, I *trust*, it is not vanity to which the cordial owes all its sweetness. No; it gives me a feeling towards all mankind, which I am convinced is not unamiable: the impulse which begins with *self*, spreads a circle instantaneously around it, which includes all the sociabilities and benevolences of the heart. Dearest mother! you will feel this with me. I cannot write more now; the fleet which sails for England is on the point of sailing. To-morrow or next day I am off for Halifax, where I shall bid my last adieu to America, and fly home to my darlings once more. Love to all. Your own boy.

The preface and footnotes to Moore's Odes, Epistles and Other Poems *(1806) make further comment on the state of the Union as Moore saw it:*

Though curiosity was certainly not the motive of my voyage to America, yet it happened that the gratification of curiosity was the only advantage which I derived from it. Finding myself in the country of a new people, whose infancy had promised so much, and whose progress to maturity has been an object of such interesting speculation, I determined to employ the short period of time, which my plan of return to Europe afforded me, in travelling through a few of the States, and acquiring some knowledge of the inhabitants.

I went to America, with prepossessions by no means unfavourable, and indeed rather indulged in many of those illusive ideas, with respect to the purity of the government and the primitive happiness of the people, which I had early imbibed in my native country, where, unfortunately, discontent at home enhances every distant temptation, and the western world has long been looked to as a retreat from real or imaginary oppression; as the elysian Atlantis, where persecuted patriots might find their visions realized, and be welcomed by kindred spirits to liberty and repose. I was completely disappointed in every flattering expectation which I had formed, and was inclined to say to America, as Horace says to his mistress, "intentata nites (untried you shine)." Brissot,[10] in the preface to his travels, observes, that "freedom in that country is carried to so high a degree as to border upon a state of nature;" and there certainly is a close approximation to savage life, not only in the liberty which they enjoy, but in the violence of party spirit and of private animosity, which results from it. This illiberal zeal embitters all social intercourse; and, though I scarcely could hesitate in selecting the party whose views appeared the more pure and rational, yet I was sorry to observe that, in asserting their opinions, they both assume an equal share of intolerance; the Democrats, consistently with their principles, exhibiting a vulgarity of rancour, which the Federalists too often are so forgetful of their cause as to imitate.

The rude familiarity of the lower orders, and indeed the unpolished state of society in general, would neither surprise nor disgust, if they seemed to flow from that simplicity of character, that honest ignorance of the gloss of refinement, which may be looked for in a new and inexperienced people. But, when we find them arrived at maturity in most of the vices, and all the pride, of civilization, while they are still so remote from its elegant char-

[10]French revolutionist, originator of the Girondists.

acteristics, it is impossible not to feel that this youthful decay, this crude anticipation of the natural period of corruption, represses every sanguine hope of the future energy and greatness of America.

I am conscious that, in venturing these few remarks, I have said just enough to offend, and by no means sufficient to convince; for the limits of a preface will not allow me to enter into a justification of my opinions, and I am committed on the subject as effectually as if I had written volumes in their defence. . . .

The Marquis de Chastellux,[11] in his wise letter to Mr. Maddison, Professor of Philosophy in the College of William and Mary at Williamsburgh, dwells with much earnestness on the attention which should be paid to dancing. This college, the only one in the state of Virginia, and the first which I saw in America, gave me but a melancholy idea of republican seats of learning. That contempt for the elegances of education, which the American democrats affect, is no where more grossly conspicuous than in Virginia. The young men, who look to advancement, study rather to be demagogues than politicians; and as every thing that distinguishes from the multitude is supposed to be invidious and unpopular, the levelling system is applied to education, and has had all the effect which its partizans could desire, by producing a most extensive equality of ignorance. The Abbé Raynal,[12] in his prophetic admonitions to the Americans, directing their attention very strongly to learned establishments, says, "When the youth of a country are seen depraved, the nation is on the decline." I know not what the Abbé Raynal would pronounce of this nation now, were he alive, to know the morals of the young students at Williamsburgh! But, when he wrote, his countrymen had not yet introduced the "doctrinam deos spernentem (doctrine of spurning the gods)" unto America.

Such romantic works as *The American Farmer's Letters,* and the account of Kentucky, by Imlay, would seduce us into a belief, that innocence, peace, and freedom, had deserted the rest of the world for Martha's Vineyard and the banks of the Ohio. The French travellers too, almost all from revolutionary motives, have contributed their share to the diffusion of this flattering misconception. A visit to the country is, however, quite sufficient to correct even the most enthusiastic prepossession.

In the ferment which the French revolution excited among the democrats of America, and the licentious sympathy with which they shared in the wildest excesses of jacobinism, we may find one source of that vulgarity of vice, that hostility to all the graces of life, which distinguishes the present demagogues of the United States, and has become indeed too generally the

[11]French historian, fought in the American Revolution, wrote several books about the United States.

[12]French political writer and historian, author of Philosophical History of the Two Indies.

characteristic of their countrymen. But there is another cause of the corruption of private morals, which, encouraged as it is by the government, and identified with the interests of the community, seems to threaten the decay of all honest principle in America. I allude to those fraudulent violations of neutrality, to which they are indebted for the most lucrative part of their commerce, and by which they have so long infringed and counteracted the maritime rights and advantages of this country. This unwarrantable trade is necessarily abetted by such a system of collusion, imposture, and perjury, as cannot fail to spread rapid contamination around it.

Norfolk, it must be owned, is an unfavourable specimen of America. The characteristics of Virginia, in general, are not such as can delight either the politician or the moralist, and at Norfolk they are exhibited in their least attractive form. At the time when we arrived, the yellow-fever had not yet disappeared, and every odour that assailed us in the streets very strongly accounted for its visitation. It is in truth a most disagreeable place, and the best the journalist or geographer can say of it is, that it abounds in dogs, in negroes, and in democrats.

Having remained about a week at New-York, where I saw Madame Jerome Bonaparte, and felt a slight shock of an earthquake (the only things that particularly awakened my attention), I sailed again in the Boston for Norfolk, from whence I proceeded on my tour to the northward, through Williamsburgh, Richmond, &c. At Richmond there are a few men of considerable talents. Mr. Wickham, one of their celebrated legal characters, is a gentleman, whose manners and mode of life would do honour to the most cultivated societies. Judge Marshall, the author of Washington's Life, is another very distinguished ornament of Richmond. These gentlemen, I must observe, are of that respectable, but at present unpopular, party, the Federalists.

What Mr. Weld[13] says of the continual necessity of balancing or trimming the stage, in passing over some of the wretched roads in America, is by no means exaggerated. "The driver frequently had to call to the passengers in the stage, to lean out of the carriage first at one side, then at the other, to prevent it from oversetting in the deep ruts with which the road abounds. 'Now, gentlemen, to the right;' upon which the passengers all stretched their bodies half way out of the carriage to balance it on that side: 'Now, gentlemen, to the left;' and so on."

Before the stage can pass one of the bridges, the driver is obliged to stop and arrange the loose planks, of which it is composed, in the manner that best suits his ideas of safety; and, as the planks are again disturbed by the passing of the coach, the next travellers who arrive have, of course,

[13]Isaac Weld (1774–1856), traveled in the United States and Canada, 1795–97; published "Travels" in 1799.

a new arrangement to make. Mahomet (as Sale[14] tells us) was at some pains to imagine a precarious kind of bridge for the entrance of Paradise, in order to enhance the pleasures of arrival; a Virginian bridge, I think, would have answered his purpose completely.

"What will be the old age of this government, if it is thus early decrepit?" Such was the remark of Fauchet, the French minister at Philadelphia, in that famous dispatch to his government which was intercepted by one of our cruisers in the year 1794.

This curious memorial . . . remains a striking monument of republican intrigue on one side, and republican profligacy on the other; and I would recommend the perusal of it to every honest politician, who may labor under a moment's delusion with respect to the purity of American patriotism.

In Virginia the effects of slavery begin to be felt rather seriously. While the master raves of liberty, the slave cannot but catch the contagion, and accordingly there seldom elapses a month without some alarm of insurrection amongst the negroes. The accession of Louisiana, it is feared, will increase this embarrassment; as the numerous emigrations, which are expected to take place, from the southern states to this newly-acquired territory, will considerably diminish the white population, and thus strengthen the proportion of negroes, to a degree which must ultimately be ruinous.

Washington: "On the original location of the ground now allotted for the seat of the Federal City (says Mr. Weld) the identical spot on which the capitol now stands was called Rome. This anecdote is related by many as a certain prognostic of the future magnificence of this city, which is to be, as it were, a second Rome."

A little stream runs through the city, which, with intolerable affectation, they have styled the Tiber. It was originally called Goose-Creek.

"To be under the necessity of going through a deep wood for one or two miles, perhaps, in order to see a next-door neighbour, and in the same city is a curious, and, I believe, a novel, circumstance." Weld.

The Federal City (if it must be called a city) has not been much increased since Mr. Weld visited it. Most of the public buildings, which were then in some degree of forwardness, have been since utterly suspended. The Hotel is already a ruin; a great part of its roof has fallen in, and the rooms are left to be occupied gratuitously by the miserable Scotch and Irish emigrants. The President's House, a very noble structure, is by no means suited to the philosophical humility of its present possessor,[15] who inhabits but a corner of the mansion himself, and abandons the rest to a state of uncleanly desolation, which those who are not philosophers cannot

[14]George Sale (circa 1680–1736), English lawyer, translated the Koran.

[15]Thomas Jefferson.

look at without regret. This grand edifice is encircled by a very rude pale, through which a common rustic stile introduces the visitors of the first man in America.

The private buildings exhibit the same characteristic display of arrogant speculation and premature ruin, and the few ranges of houses which were begun some years ago have remained so long waste and unfinished, that they are now for the most part dilapidated.

In the society of Mr. Dennie[16] and his friends, at Philadelphia, I passed the only agreeable moments which my tour through the States afforded me. Mr. Dennie has succeeded in diffusing through this elegant little circle that love for good literature and sound politics, which he feels so zealously himself, and which is so very rarely the characteristic of his countrymen. They will not, I trust, accuse me of illiberality for the picture which I have given of the ignorance and corruption that surround them. If I did not hate, as I ought, the rabble to which they are opposed, I could not value, as I do, the spirit with which they defy it; and in learning from them what Americans *can be*, I but see with the more indignation what Americans *are*.

[16] Joseph Dennie edited the Portfolio, a weekly newspaper.

Nolte on New Orleans

Vincent Nolte was born in Italy in 1779. At seventeen he was a clerk in his uncle's business in Leghorn when Napoleon entered that city at the head of his army. Young Nolte then joined one of the great financial houses of France and presently took part in a vast transaction which involved famous financiers and European governments. It was this commission that brought him to New Orleans at the beginning of the nineteenth century and made him a factor in the development of business in this country. He was rich and poor by turns, but whatever the state of his fortunes he was destined to cross paths with many famous people. In our own time he appeared by name in the novel ANTHONY ADVERSE.

From FIFTY YEARS IN BOTH HEMISPHERES

SPAIN had, in a treaty of alliance with France, made herself available for a yearly subsidy of 72,000,000 francs, of which 32,000,000 had already [1804] fallen due, without one single franc having been accessible. . . . The treasures which were lying at the command of the Spanish government in Mexico, Peru, and elsewhere, but which could not be reached, on account of the war then going on, were the only resources Spain had to extricate her from the embarrassments that surrounded her; for all other fountains of relief had run completely dry. . . .

Two different methods were devised to lift the immense hoardings of silver on deposit in Mexico, and transport it thence. One of these was to procure from the British government, notwithstanding the war with Spain, permission to transport the silver piastres from Vera Cruz to England. At that time great scarcity of coin prevailed in England, especially of silver change, and in this respect the British East India Company was much inconvenienced, as it required large supplies to pay its hands and keep its various establishments throughout India agoing. The first attempt to obtain such permission failed. Pitt, the British Prime Minister, refused it, because it was evidently contributing to strengthen the enemy's hands, and open sources of aid and comfort which the war had closed against him. But the wisdom and correct feeling of the statesman soon were re-awakened in him, when he perceived and weighed the advantages this supply of silver, once in the hands of the East India Company and the London Exchange, would yield to British trade. . . .

In short, Pitt finally gave his consent to dispatch four frigates, who, in the very midst of the war with Spain, very quietly appeared, one after the other, in the roads of Vera Cruz, and without any interruption took on board about fourteen millions of piastres from the treasury of Mexico, and brought the treasure back to England. Yet, fourteen millions were not more than one quarter of the whole amount which it was desirable to transfer from Mexico to Europe. By far the greater part was not to be transmitted in hard cash, but through the natural channels of trade, by dispatching consignments of goods from America, especially from the United States, to the ports of Europe. The United States, which were at that time wholly in possession of the carrying trade, presented the most extensive field for the purchase of all kinds of colonial produce–not merely their own, such as cotton and tobacco, but also of each and every other kind, such as coffee, sugar, pepper, &c., &c.–since the latter were regularly shipped thither, without the least difficulty, on American account, and under the protection of their neutral flag. But the war between England and the Continent, which obeyed the orders of Napoleon, as well as the watchfulness of the English fleets and cruisers, made the transport of such purchases . . . almost impossible. Measures had therefore to be taken to give them the character of neutral property, not in appearance merely, but in reality; and this could be done only by stimulating the enterprising spirit of the American merchants to send shipments on their own account into Continental Europe, taking out their insurance in England, making advances, and for their amount accepting bills on the drawer. . . . In this manner the home-returning capital accumulated interest and increased, even through the enormously heavy commissions which remained to be raised on these consignments. The whole combination was a most excellent one, but could be easily and naturally carried into execution only in such a country as the United States, where the enterprising spirit knows no bounds, but where the capital of the venturer is limited.

Two great difficulties still lay in the way of an entire realization of the whole plan. The first and most important of these was to effect the realization of the values payable in coin in Mexico, and their transport to the United States. The moneys would have to be exported under the American flag and on American account. But such immense capitals as these could only be made neutral by paying a heavy commission, and respectable houses would in no case have lent themselves to it. People had not yet forgotten that a single house in the North of Europe had, at the beginning of the English and French war, covered such a multitude of ships and cargoes and made them neutral, that the English cruisers, put on their guard by the frequent re-appearance of the same names in the consignment papers and bills of lading, availed themselves of this suspicious circumstance, to call them up and obtain their condemnation as good and lawful prizes. The latter was pronounced because it seemed impossible that any one house could cover the seas with such a huge amount of capital as was here seen afloat at one time. The means of overcoming the first difficulty was to be looked for in the United States themselves. From this arose the second, namely, the selection of a man who should unite sufficient mercantile experience with large intelligence and knowledge of men; and moreover, should possess the capacity for making combinations, so as to devise ways and means of successful exit where they would, otherwise, remain hidden from the eyes of the common observer. . . .

It was not difficult for Mr. Labouchère [representing the Barings and other financiers] to prevail upon [David] Parish to accept the agency of his projected business in America.

Two head agents were still necessary: one for Mexico, to present the bills of exchange and get them cashed, to ship the coin at Vera Cruz, and oversee the sale of the ships' cargoes coming in under license; the other at New Orleans, to receive the coin as it arrived, to dispatch the cargoes of German, English and French manufactured goods coming in from Europe to Vera Cruz under accompanying licenses, and to make over to the merchants in the latter city as many licenses as the opportunity would admit. . . . I consequently embarked [from Amsterdam] during the first days of July, 1805, in the American ship Flora, commanded by Captain Daniel Sterling, for New York. I arrived after a voyage of forty-two days, which was looked upon at that time as a very rapid one. The astonished consignee of the ship, who had not even heard of its arrival in Amsterdam, was standing on the quay to welcome me, its only passenger, and his friend the captain. The world into which I found myself now transported, was entirely new to me. I had, owing to the at that time extreme rarity of authentic works concerning the United States, read so little about them, that I had possessed a very imperfect idea about the country, and had conceived it to be, in consequence of the thoroughly savage condition in which the land had been discovered and gradually peopled, much further behindhand in civilization than I found it.

I distinctly remember a circumstance which will give my readers an excellent conception of the singular ideas I entertained in regard to the state of things in America, as compared with the notions of our captain concerning the perfection of his native country. It simply happened one day that an excellent umbrella was broken on deck during a violent storm, and I asked the captain, if he thought I could replace it with as good a one in New York; when he replied quite sharply: "God bless me! ask me whether the sun shines in New York." It must be remembered that at that time in Germany, America was generally looked upon as a sort of penal colony or rendezvous for all kinds of scamps and worthless fellows. When I first informed my parents that I was going thither, my mother at once exclaimed: "It cannot be possible that you have taken into your head this unfortunate idea of going to America? Who knows what advantage they may take of your inexperience!"

A few days after my arrival in New York, the yellow fever broke out in that city. When I was about starting from Amsterdam, Mr. Labouchère [his employer] had asked me if I was afraid of the yellow fever; "for"—he added—"if you do feel afraid of it, you must not go to America, as you will be certain to die there!" I had said that I felt no apprehension, and as I really did not feel at all timid about it, I was determined to push boldly on for New York. . . . Six weeks after my arrival a rumor was circulated that a ship from Cadiz had entered the bay with the exiled General Moreau[1] on board. It was not long before all the militia drums were heard in every part of the city, and their commander-in-chief, a lawyer by the name of Morton, went galloping about in all directions, on horseback, in the uniform of a general, followed by his adjutants, principally young law-students, as if he imagined that Moreau had also begun his career in the legal profession. At any rate, he dashed about, commanding and countermanding, and urging the greatest haste in the preparations every body was making for a grand display in the long main street of the city, called Broadway, which extends to the public promenade designated as the Battery. It was at the latter point that the distinguished stranger was to land. His debarkation took place about an hour later. The general, clad in citizen's style, with a blue coat and pantaloons, mounted a horse prepared for him, amid music and the acclamations of the crowd, and rode up, surrounded by his staff of parti-colored militia, along the main street to the City Hall. Each separate company of each and every battalion, wore their own peculiar and frequently extremely singular uniform, and it was impossible to look at the *ensemble* of this military assemblage in any other light than as a harlequin parade; but the officers of this remarkable body were in no slight degree proud of it, and when General Moreau had reached the City Hall, he was very gravely asked by General Morton what he really thought of the American troops? The general is said to have replied that he had never seen *such* soldiers in the whole course of his life! which somewhat ambiguous compliment was several times repeated to me, at the same time with the greatest seriousness, as something highly honorable to the American military.

Some American amateurs had got up a great concert on the same evening in the long saloon of the "City Hotel," at that time the largest public house in the place. . . . There was a great crowd present, but the most striking personage in the throng was by no means General Moreau, of whom every body remarked that he did not look at all like a French general, because he simply wore a blue coat; but General Morton in his Washington uniform, with a blue coat and yellow facings, &c. The latter intro-

[1]French general who defeated the Austrians in 1800, later suspected of plotting against Napoleon.

duced to the general every one who wanted to take a good stare at him, and the shaking of hands with ladies and gentlemen went on as if it never would end. At length I managed to force my way close up to these two great leaders, Morton the lawyer and militia hero, and the hero of Hohenlinden. Just as I got there, a quaker had himself introduced to the latter, and shaking him heartily by the hand, uttered the following words: "Glad to see you safe in America!—Pray, General—say, do you remember what was the price of cochineal when you left Cadiz?" The victor of Hohenlinden shrugged his shoulders and was unable to reply.

Some days after this military festival, my friend Lestapis arrived from Amsterdam with a portion of the documents required to carry on our business. We passed our time for several weeks very pleasantly. The well-known hospitality shown to every stranger, possessing the least cultivation, who arrives in the United States, made it easy for us to enjoy ourselves. At length, in the beginning of November, David Parish arrived. The news of some very large commercial enterprise had already preceded him, and, although the nature of the undertaking had not become known, the greatest curiosity followed every step he took. In New York, the whole combination of the enterprise which had been fully discussed at Amsterdam, was unfolded and analyzed, and my friend Lestapis and myself set out, each for his post; he to Vera Cruz and I to New Orleans, where a whole cargo of German linens had arrived, and was awaiting me. The fast-sailing schooner *Aspasia* had brought it to its destination. I went overland to Charleston, and as (contrary to all expectation) there was no suitable craft there on which I could take passage for New Orleans, I purchased the schooner *Regulator*, and went in it to the latter port.

It was on Easter Sunday, 1806, that I first set foot on the soil of Louisiana, where I, five years later, was invested with the rights of citizenship, and I reached the city of New Orleans before nightfall.

Louisiana, originally a French colony, then Spanish, and then again French, had, as every one knows, been sold, shortly before the time of which I speak, to the United States by the French government, for fifteen millions of Spanish dollars, and had been soon afterwards organized as a territory. It possessed an elective legislature, chosen by the people, but the Governor received his appointment from the President of the Confederation, which high post was at that moment occupied by Thomas Jefferson. The political rival of this celebrated man, in the struggle for the Presidency, had been Aaron Burr, and it was said that the vote of a representative from Kentucky, named William Cole Claiborne, had turned the scale at the election, and secured Jefferson's success. Such a service as this had been rewarded by the President elect with no less a mark of favor than Claiborne's appointment to the governorship of Louisiana. To make way for him, the French prefect, Laussat, a man of education and refinement, possessing all the manners of a French courtier, was removed. Claiborne was exactly the reverse; of fine personal appearance, but, in all other respects, a coarse, rude man, and, at the same time, very sharp and *knowing*, as most Americans are. The greater part of the then existing population was of French origin. In the city itself the French number at least three-fifths of the inhabitants; one other fifth was of Spanish race, and another Americans, among whom were some Germans. The city numbered about 16,000 souls, of whom one-third were people of color and slaves. The mercantile class was made up of four or five French establishments, springing from the neighborhood of the Garonne, and founded during the continuance of the French rule; three Scotch counting-houses, one German concern, and eight or ten commission-houses, lately opened by young American merchants from New York, Philadelphia, and Baltimore. The traces of this class, who carried on the early business of New Orleans under the new regime, are now [circa 1853] limited to the sugar-planter Shepherd, who is still living, and now very wealthy, and to the still more opulent Mr. W. M. Montgomery, formerly wholesale grocer, and now the owner of a large portion of the northwestern section of the State, who lives partly at New York and partly at Paris. Shepherd, whom I have just named, who was but two-and-twenty when he came from Baltimore to New Orleans, was accompanied thither by a young American from the same place, who could not have been more than a few years older than himself. The latter brought some six or eight thousand dollars with him, and after, for a considerable time, exploring all sorts of uncultivated lands lying along the Mississippi, made a choice and purchased. This young man was John McDonough, who made such constant parade of the lands he had bought, so well understood the game of making fictitious sales to his friend Shepherd, at very high rates, and through him to others at still higher prices, and pursued this system, observing, at the same time, great frugality at home, so long and so skilfully, that at length real purchasers fell into his net, and made themselves part and parcel of it. McDonough talked very little, and seldom mixed in general conversation, especially with ladies, whose society he avoided as much as possible. When he did open his lips, all that fell from them was praise of certain lands he had just purchased, and this theme was inexhaustible. It was not in Louisiana alone that he carried on this system, but also in neighboring States, and he continued it for more than forty years. He passed his spare time in looking after the education of some children in the neighborhood of his homely residence on an estate, or, as they call it in the South, a *plantation*, belonging to him. He also occupied himself with the amateur study of medicine. McDonough died in October, 1851, and, upon the opening of his will, it was discovered, that at the time of his death he owned four-fifths of all the uncultivated lands in the State of Louisiana, and many tracts of territory in other States, to the very considerable amount of fifteen millions of dollars. . . . McDonough himself died without heirs, either direct or collateral, and has made over his whole property to the government of the United States, that it shall expend the same in the establishment of public schools.

What notions were entertained, in the northern part of the Union, of such a community as made up the population of New Orleans, is clearly conveyed by an anecdote of my friend, Mr. M. Amory, of Boston, whose newly-established house, under the firm of *Amory & Callender*, had received the cargo of Schleswig linens sent from Europe, and then held it in charge for me. Just as he was on the point of starting from Boston for New Orleans he had seen in the newspapers an advertisement of a ship about to sail direct to the latter port, and then looking for passengers and freight. Amory called upon the owner to recommend to him his young house as consignee. The owner told him in confidence that he had not at all intended to send his ship to New Orleans, but that he had published the advertisement only for the purpose of discovering among the passengers who would apply for berths, a rascal who had swindled his brother of a considerable sum of money. "For," added the owner, "I consider it probable that he will try to leave for New Orleans, which, as everybody knows, is a regular rendezvous for all sorts of rogues and rabble."

Among these people, thus generally looked upon as the offscourings of the northern States, I found a man of remarkable intellectual powers and real talent. This man was the celebrated Edward Livingston, originally from the State of New York. He had been a lawyer in the city of New York, and had there, as a member of the Municipal Council, performed the functions of Recorder. In that respect he had played a highly important part, and had once represented the State itself in the Senate at Washington. . . . He then emigrated to New Orleans, and there . . . married the young and fascinating widow of a legitimist and legist by the name of Moreau, from St. Domingo. . . . After the destruction of the colony, she had fled with her mother, sister, and one brother, first to Jamaica, and then to Louisiana. . . .

When I first arrived in New Orleans, there was not a single house there possessed of any capital worth mentioning, and an honorable character seemed to me quite as great a rarity. I believed just as much as I pleased of the representations made by the merchants just established there; and with all their boasting, and great parade of clearness, it was quite remarkable that my experience was not enriched at the beginning, by the knowledge of some unhandsome trick in trade, like those with which every other man seemed to have been proud of having duped his neighbor. The individual who succeeds, with a certain degree of skill, in accomplishing some sharp manœuvre, is too often rewarded in the United States with the epithet of clever fellow.

In Messrs. Amory & Callender I discovered unswerving integrity, combined with a certain distrust of all undertakings which involved the least risk; and it was precisely in consequence of these two qualities, which are rather rare in American business circles, that I made up my mind to employ their house in the execution of my plans. I had not yet passed a fortnight in New Orleans, and had given no one occasion to conjecture what my object was in coming to the place, when the news was all at once buzzed about that a schooner, under the American flag, six days from Vera Cruz, had arrived in the Mississippi, with 150,000 Spanish dollars on board for Vincent Nolte.

"Hullo! who can that be?" every one began to ask; "What, that young man?" They had, however, scarcely ceased to express their wonder, when another schooner from Vera Cruz came in with $200,000 on board, and finally, ten days later, a third one appeared, which, like the first, brought $150,000, and all for the same young man! The French planters had already treated me with some distinction, merely from the fact that I was a stranger. I spoke French, but now, *motif de plus!* their preference knew no bounds. Not a ball or soirée took place at their houses to which I was not invited.

I had already passed more than three months in the city, when, in the beginning of August, I was seized with a terrible attack of yellow fever. A burning headache, as if my brain was on fire, and violent pains in the back, were the first symptoms. The acquaintances by whom I was surrounded, and among them a Spaniard, by the name of Seré, who had become extremely interesting to me through his connection with Vera Cruz, at once called in their favorite physician, a Frenchman by the name of Raoul; and this man, who, in all other respects but intimate knowledge of yellow fever, was a perfect quack, succeeded in saving my life; with the very correct idea that the yellow fever is nothing but a violent inflammation of the gall, he instantly gave me a powerful emetic. Then, on the second day, another one, and on the third a strong purgative. My consciousness gradually returned, and at length I was out of danger, although desperately weakened and unnerved. In the forenoon of the third day the Cashier of the Louisiana Bank, a very honorable man, by the name of Zacharie, came to me, and asked me, with great earnestness, if I had made my will. I replied, "No, why?" "Now," he responded, "I need not tell you that you have the yellow fever, and it is more than probable that you will die to-morrow." I raised my head to listen. "For the fourth day is the critical one, through which the patient seldom survives. You have treasure; large sums lying in the bank to an amount never yet seen here; and were you to die, this capital would fall into extremely unsafe hands. The administrators of the property of foreigners dying here intestate, appointed by the State, are people who not only merit no confidence, but, to tell you the honest truth, are a set of shameless rascals." My reply was that I did not at all feel like dying, and that I would not die. I concluded with the words, "As I am not going to leave the world yet awhile, I don't want to bother my head with making a will." Mr. Zacharie gave me a searching look, and then said, "Well, indeed, my dear Mr. Nolte, with the disposition that you manifest, I do feel quite sure that you are not going to die."

In the autumn of 1806 there circulated, throughout the United States, all kinds of rumors concerning an intended or already organized conspiracy, whose object was to separate the Southern from the Northern States, and to organize a second American Republic. At the head of this conspiracy, and of this projected duplicate republic, stood the American general, Burr; the same who had been the rival candidate of Jefferson for the Presidency, and had killed Washington's celebrated Secretary, Alexander Hamilton, in a duel. This man of evil reputation, of whom, as was generally known, Jefferson was, personally, afraid, had secretly been travelling through the West, and had there won over many partisans. It was even said that General Wilkinson, the commander of the small military force then maintained by the United States, and a militia general, by the name of Adair, from the State of Kentucky, belonged to this conspiracy. In New Orleans, the local militia was organized by the direction of the United States Government, and put in a condition to bear arms. The Frenchmen residing in that city formed two companies, the Irish a third, and the Germans a fourth. The latter, without knowing much about me, appointed me their Captain, probably because they every day heard of my money deposits in the bank. Military capacity I did not possess, and my sub-officers, consisting of store-clerks, grocers and trades-apprentices, learned no more of the service than I had picked up the day before.

Suddenly there appeared in New Orleans, as commander of the garrison, the very general above referred to, who had fallen under suspicion. He at once mustered the local militia, and had them sworn in, so that he might exercise full authority over us all, as though we were regular troops of the line. He then had two young Americans, named Samuel Swartwout and P. V. Ogden, suddenly arrested, put on board a small government vessel, and sent to Washington as accomplices of Burr. A few days later General Adair, of Kentucky, arrived by way of the Mississippi, and he also was arrested and dispatched to the capital. At last I was privately informed that I was looked upon with great suspicion by the commanding general, since he had ascertained that the house of Baring, at London, had placed itself in readiness to furnish the funds necessary to secure the success of Burr's conspiracy, and I was well known to be the agent of that firm. When I learned that Wilkinson had secretly sent for a sergeant and corporal from my company, and questioned them concerning me, it seemed perfectly plain to me that the general was playing with false cards, and I resolved, without further delay, to go right to him, and ask him what was running in his head about me. He received me with a certain degree of solemnity, took me to one side, raised his eyes to heaven, and talked a great deal about his responsibility, and his duties to God and the country, which required that he should exercise the greatest vigilance in all directions. Finally he showed me an intercepted letter, written by one of Burr's accomplices, in which the following words occurred: "B. has undertaken to supply all the funds needed to carry out the whole plan." He then asked me what I thought of that, and what I had to say. My reply was, briefly, to the purport, that he must look to better authority than myself to find out what was meant by those words, and that the letter B. most probably indicated his friend Burr: that I was no agent of the Barings, and that if he would do me the honor to examine them, my books were open for his inspection: above all, I wished to know whether he was satisfied with this voluntary declaration, and would leave me undisturbed. Hereupon he seized my hand with the same solemnity that had characterized his first reception of me, once more rolled up his eyes, and said, "You have above a friend and protector; you are an honorable man, Mr. Nolte; return to your home in peace." And thus the affair terminated. I had carefully watched the man, and had come to the conclusion that he was an impostor, and most likely deeply implicated himself in Burr's plot. The result has proven that my conjectures were correct. From the lawsuits that afterwards arose at Washington, out of the arbitrary arrest of General Adair, and Messrs. Swartwout and Ogden, it was made evident that he had promised his aid to Burr in the scheme, but had withdrawn from it in good season. . . .

I had yet another trial to encounter during the management of the interest intrusted to my care. This was the rencontre between the English man-of-war *Leopard* and the American frigate *Chesapeake*, off the entrance of the bay of the latter name, in the summer of 1807. The English commander had received very accurate and explicit information regarding the enlistment of several deserters from his vessel on board of the American frigate, and when the latter showed herself on the open sea, the *Leopard* bore right down to her, and summoned her captain to surrender the deserting sailors. This the American, very naturally, refused to do. The frigate was poorly manned, and, in all other respects, unfit for action. The first shots from the British vessel were only a few times answered, and then the *Chesapeake* struck her flag. Hereupon the English officers came on board, mustered the crew, selected their five deserters from the throng, and took them back to the *Leopard*. This occurrence aroused the most fearful excitement in the United States; every one spoke with the greatest bitterness in favor of immediate war with England. There was no lack of rash counsellors, who endeavored to persuade me that I ought at once to set out for England or the North with my silver deposits. But I was too well aware that, on the part of England, there could be no good and sufficient cause for war, and that, so far as the United States were concerned, war could only be declared by Congress, which would first have to be called together by the President, and thus several months *must* elapse before the country could be in a position to commence hostilities, even supposing—a case still doubtful—that Congress should deem it necessary and wise to adopt violent measures. . . .

It was in the summer of 1807 when we, Lestapis in Mexico and I in New Orleans, received the first intimation from Parish in Philadelphia, that the existing condition of things in Europe would bring us rapidly nearer the termination of our agencies, which had at first been counted upon for years. So far as I in particular was concerned, there was no necessity for my remaining in New Orleans longer than the settlement of my affairs in that city required. . . . In August, 1807, I . . . returned to the North. . . .

It was exactly at this time that I, then staying at one of the most celebrated boarding-houses in the city of New York, the Widow Gallop's, on Broadway, while engaged in making my preparations for departure, by mere chance, at breakfast, made the acquaintance of a gentleman who was just about to give the world the first example of steam-navigation. The reader will readily guess that I am now referring to Robert Fulton, and his newly-built steamer "Clermont," constructed by him at his own expense. It was then a topic in the mouth of every body, as the attempt he proposed in a short time to make, to carry his plan into execution, was the object of universal curiosity. My new acquaintance wanted me to be present, and witness the departure of his steamboat, which was to take place from the bank of the Hudson river, at twelve o'clock; and, indeed, it did not require much persuasion to induce me to accede to this request. So I saw this curious and wonderful structure—130 feet in length, 16½ feet broad, 7 feet depth of hold, rating 160 tons, as it had been described, and containing about 450 passengers—leave the wharf as the clock struck twelve, make right for the middle of the stream, and describe a circle three times in succession. Then, defying the force of the winds and waves alike, it dashed gallantly along its way to Albany, as though the most favorable breeze were filling its sails. A vociferous cheer arose from the thousands assembled on both banks of the Hudson to witness, with their own eyes, the reality of this truly grand experiment, and its brilliant success. . . . The large steam vessel named *Clermont* for the country-seat of Chancellor Livingston reached Clermont, at a distance of 110 miles, within twenty-four hours, left that point again at nine o'clock, on the next morning, and arrived at Albany, some forty-seven miles farther, in about eight hours. It had thus made nearly five miles per hour against wind and current. . . .

I was anxious to acquire some knowledge of the far western regions, whose rich and manifold productions, of all kinds, were carried down the Ohio and Mississippi rivers, destined to be the sources of the prosperity of New Orleans, although their banks were then but thinly populated, and were almost entirely wild and unreclaimed. In pursuance of this desire, I resolved to cross the Alleghany mountains to Pittsburgh, in the State of Pennsylvania, and there purchase a couple of flat-boats, in which I and my companion would quietly float down the rapid stream to New Orleans, about 2,000 miles.

The only other means usual at that time, for passage or transportation on the two rivers, was by keel-boats, as they are called. These were long narrow barks, which would contain at the farthest about two hundred barrels of flour, and which could complete the journey, by the use of oars, in from thirty to thirty-five days; while the flat-boats, which were only steered, consumed forty or fifty days in making the same distance. The latter, however, were more convenient for the transportation of passengers, since there was space enough on them to put up quite a snug sleeping-room, with beds, &c., and a convenient kitchen and dining-room. I sent my friend Hollander a fortnight in advance of me, to Pittsburgh, to purchase two such flat-boats, one for our own use, and the other to accommodate my horse with a stall. Moreover, we could thus take along with us some four hundred barrels of flour, which could always be disposed of to advantage at New Orleans, and would suffice to pay the expenses of our journey.

I managed to procure an excellent horse in Philadelphia, and, with my saddle-bags strapped to his back, I started in December [1811] alone, on my way to Pittsburgh. It was very cold. I rode, early one morning, entirely alone, over the loftiest summit of the Alleghany ridge, called Laurel Hill, and about ten o'clock arrived at a small inn, close by the Falls of the Juniata river. Here I ordered a substantial breakfast. The landlady showed me into a room, and said, I perhaps would not object to taking my meal at the same table with a strange gentleman, who was already there. As I entered I found the latter personage, who at once struck me as being, what, in common parlance, is called an odd fish. He was sitting at a table, before the fire, with a Madras handkerchief wound around his head, exactly in the style of the French mariners, or laborers, in a seaport town. I stepped up to him, and accosted him politely, with the words, "I hope I don't incommode you, by coming to take my breakfast with you." "Oh no, sir," he replied, with a strong French accent, that made it sound like "No, sare." "Ah," I continued, "you are a Frenchman, sir?" "No, sare," he answered, "hi emm an Heenglishman." "Why," I asked, in return, "how do you make that out? You look like a Frenchman, and you speak like one." "Hi emm an Eenglishman, becas hi got a Heenglish wife," he answered.

Without investigating the matter further, we made up our minds, at breakfast, to remain in company, and to ride together to Pittsburgh. He showed himself to be an original throughout, but at last admitted that he was a Frenchman by birth, and a native of La Rochelle. However, he had come in his early youth to Louisiana, had grown up in the sea-service, and had gradually become a thorough American. "Now," I asked, "how does that accord with your quality of Englishman?" Upon this he found it convenient to reply, in the French language, "When all is said and done, I am somewhat cosmopolitan; I belong to every country." This man, who afterwards won for himself so great a name in natural history, particularly in ornithology, was Audubon, who, however, was by no means thinking, at that time, of occupying himself with the study of natural history.

He wanted to be a merchant, and had married the daughter of an Englishman, named Bakewell, formerly of Philadelphia, but then residing and owning mills at Shippingport, at the Falls of the Ohio, and in the neighborhood of Louisville. It was also his intention to travel down the Ohio into Kentucky. At Pittsburgh, he found no other opportunity of doing so than the one offered by my flat-boats, and, as he was a good companionable man, and, moreover, an accomplished sketcher, I invited him to take a birth in our cabin gratis. He thankfully accepted the invitation, and we left Pittsburgh, in very cold weather, with the Monongahela and Ohio rivers full of drifting ice, in the beginning of January, 1812. I learned nothing further of his travelling plans until we reached Limestone, a little place at the northwestern corner of the State of Ohio. There we had both our horses taken ashore, and I resolved to go with him overland, at first to visit the capital, Lexington, and from there to Louisville, where he expected to find his wife and his parents-in-law. My two boats, which I had left under the charge of Hollander, were to meet me at the same place. We had scarcely finished our breakfast, at Limestone, when Audubon, all at once, sprang to his feet, and exclaimed, in French, "Now I am going to lay the foundation of my establishment." So saying, he took a small packet of address cards and a hammer from his coat pocket, some nails from his vest, and began to nail up one of the cards to the door of the tavern, where we were taking our meal. The address ran as follows: "*Audubon & Bakewell, Commission Merchants* (*Pork, Lard, and Flour*), *New Orleans*." Oh, oh! thought I, there you have competition before you have got to the place yourself. Yet, as this commission house could not refer to the influential name of the Messrs. Hope, or of Messrs. Baring, and as pork and lard, moreover, were not articles which had any very great attraction for me, in the way of trade, I consoled myself with the thought, that competition of this nature could not amount to much.

From Limestone, Audubon and I rode on together as far as Lexington, the capital of Kentucky. It was then a flourishing little town, where I heard a great deal of talk about a highly-gifted lawyer, who, during the elections for members of Congress, had distinguished himself in the taverns and streets, by all sorts of brawls and fisticuff battles. This man was no other than Henry Clay, whose reputation soon after began to rise so rapidly. He was then a member of Congress; but his external appearance was by no means calculated to convey any very high idea of his intellectual capacity, although he had, as early as the period of which I speak, already acquired great celebrity as an orator.

A frightfully cruel practice prevailed at that time among the greater part of the rude inhabitants of the western states. It consisted in allowing the finger-nails to grow so long, that, by cutting them, you could give them the form of a small sickle, and this strange weapon was used, in the broils that constantly occurred, to cut out the eyes of the hostile party. This barbarous action was called *gouging*. Upon this excursion through Kentucky I saw several persons who lacked an eye, and others, both of whose eyes were disfigured. The exasperation then reigning throughout the United States, in relation to the difficulties with England, was much greater in the western provinces than along the sea coast, and the feeling was very intense.

As I passed through Frankfort, on my way from Lexington to Louisville, I was told that the legislature of Kentucky was just then in session. I resolved to go thither, so that I might compare that body with the sessions of the territorial legislature of Louisiana, which I had had the opportunity of observing in New Orleans, and which was made up of the most singular mixture of native born Americans, and men of French and Spanish extraction. I had scarcely entered the legislative hall, when I heard a very enthusiastic orator dealing forth a violent diatribe against England, with the following words: "We must have war with Great Britain—war will ruin her commerce—commerce is the apple in Britain's eye—there we must *gouge* her!" This flower of oratory was received with great applause; and, it must be confessed, that for such a population as most of the inhabitants of Kentucky formed at that period, it was extremely well timed, and betrayed a certain poetic sweep of thought. The North Americans in general possess often an unmistakable keenness of perception, which quickly enables them to catch a certain similarity between two altogether different things. Among them one frequently hears comparisons of the most striking description, from the lips of the most uneducated men. To the happiest of these, which have reached us from the other side of the ocean, perhaps belongs one that was made by the American poet Barlow, the author of the Columbiad. Every one who, during his time, understood and spoke the English language, was full of the splendid phraseology of the English orator Burke, who, in his enthusiasm, so often rose to an almost immeasurable height. Barlow, who had heard him, and who had either been unable to follow him in his logical conclusions, or had, as he thought, found no sound argument in what he said, broke out into the exclamation, "He rises like a rocket, spreads a glaring light, and comes down like a stick!"

I was riding alone through the vast forest which separates Frankfort from Louisville, when, all at once, my horse, as if struck by lightning, suddenly stood still—the trees around us had for some seconds exhibited a strange heaving and waving motion. The animal I bestrode obeyed the spur, when I attempted to force him onward, with a sort of terror, again stood suddenly still for an instant, and then finally advanced in a tremor. It was some time before he fell into his usual pace. Upon my arrival in Louisville I was at once surrounded at the tavern door, and pertinaciously asked if I had noticed anything of the earthquake, and I felt authorized to say that I had. The Ohio had been frozen over for several days, and for more than a week past no boat had descended the stream; hence my boats and my friend Hollander were frozen up on the way between Limestone and Louisville. Three days afterwards, just as we had all sat down to dinner, the whole house was violently shaken; glasses, plates, and bottles jingled, and fell from the board; most of the guests leaped to their feet, exclaiming, "There's the earthquake, by jingo! there is no humbug about it!" as they rushed into the street. But all was still again, and every one gradually returned to his house. Early the next morning I learned that the earthquake had loosened the ice from the Ohio, and had again opened the current of the stream, and that several boats, among others two flats, fastened together, had been carried down over the Falls lying between Louisville and the little town of Shippingport, situated at the distance of a few miles from the former place. I at once rode over to Shippingport, and there found my boats and my companion in safety. So soon as we had replenished and increased our stock of provisions I returned to my boats, and, having recommenced our journey, we in a few days left the clear transparent waters of the Ohio, and passed by its junction with the mighty Mississippi into the thick and turbid flood of the latter stream. We floated on quietly for several days, arresting our course, as was usual, at night, and securing our boats in any way we could to the river bank. In flat-boat journeys like ours it is a rule never to trust your craft in the night to the force of the current, for the surface of the water is so frequently broken by trees (which have been swept away from the shore, and then become fast imbedded in the bottom of the river, where they remain immovable, and are designated by the name of *planters*, as well as by those which are, likewise, fast imbedded, but have a constant up and down motion, whence they are known by the title of *sawyers*), that it is almost an impossibility to avoid them at night, and, in fact, to do so is difficult in broad daylight. In this way we reached the small town of New Madrid, on the 6th of February. Some twenty boats, which had left Shippingport at the same time with us, kept us company. It was a clear moonlight night: my friend Hollander had retired to rest, and I was sitting, about twelve o'clock, at a little table, sketching a caricature of Madison, then President of the United States, and of whom it was said, that he was under petticoat government. Madison had shortly before issued a proclamation, in which he called upon the American people "to put on armor, and assume a warlike attitude." My caricature represented him in a general's uniform, in an attitude as if he were calling out troops; his wife stood beside him, with a military chapeau on her head, a musket on her shoulder, and arrayed in the red breeches which her predecessor Jefferson was known to have brought from France, after the revolutionary period, when he resided at Paris as Ambassador, and was generally asserted to have worn. I had just given the last touches to the somewhat dilapidated red hose, when there came a frightful crash, like a sudden explosion of artillery, and instantly followed by countless flashes of lightning; the Mississippi foamed up like the water in a boiling cauldron, and the stream flowed rushing back, while the forest trees, near which we lay, came cracking and thundering down. This fearful spectacle lasted for several minutes; and the fierce flashes of lightning, the rush of the receding waters, and the crash of the falling trees, seemed as if they would never end. Hollander, starting half-way up from his bed, hurriedly exclaimed, "What is that, Nolte?" What other answer could I give him but that I myself did not know, yet supposed it to be the effect of an earthquake. I clambered up to the roof of our boat. What a spectacle! Our flats were indeed still floating, but far away from the shore where we had moored them at nightfall. The agitated water all around us, full of trees and branches, which the stream, now flowing in its proper current, was rapidly sweeping away, and a light only here and there visible from the town–in short, a real chaos. The feeble crew, which I had brought along with me from Pittsburgh, to man my flat-boats, consisted of three sailors, whom want of employment at the seaports, while the embargo lasted, had driven to that inland city, and a river pilot, acquainted with those streams. They told me that the boats around us had let go the tackle which secured them to the shore, and were now floating down the stream, and asking whether we had not better do the same thing. I at once reflected that if, under the usual circumstances, it was dangerous, and therefore by no means advisable, to trust to the stream in the night, it must now be much more so, when the danger was greatly increased by the trees which the earthquake had loosened and driven away, and that consequently it would be a better plan to remain where we were until daylight had returned, and we could see our way. At sunrise the whole terrible scene was disclosed to our gaze, and the little town of New Madrid, sunken, destroyed, and overflowed to three-fourths of its extent, lay more than five hundred paces from us, with some of its scattered inhabitants here and there visible among the ruins. Our boats were fixed in the middle of an island formed by fallen trees, and several hours passed before the crew could cut a passage for them, and get them out. At length we were again floating on the stream, and continued our course, by day's journeys, until we arrived, on the thirty-second day after our departure from Pittsburgh, in Natchez, in the State of Mississippi. Here, where we heard all kinds of details concerning the earthquake, as it had been noticed in that place, we remained a week, during which time not a single one of the boats arrived that had surrounded us on the evening of the 6th of February. When we reached New Orleans, we learned that the earthquake had not been any farther perceptible there, than that the chandeliers in the ballroom had all at once been observed to rock from side to side, and that a number of ladies had felt quite ill, while others instantly fainted. This remarkable earthquake, which was so disastrous in its consequences, commenced in the northwestern part of the State of Missouri, shook the whole extent of Louisiana more or less, and stretched throughout the whole region lying around the Gulf of Mexico as far as Caraccas, where it finally raged with terrible fury, almost entirely destroying that town itself, and reducing to poverty, or swallowing up, 40,000 inhabitants there, and in several other places in the neighborhood. Of the boats which surrounded us on the evening of February 6th nothing was ever afterwards heard, and we should probably have shared the same fate, had it not been for the plan we adopted of remaining by the shore.

I have always regarded it as a great gift of heaven, that amid the many serious dangers in which I have been frequently exposed during the course of my life, I was ever able to retain a certain tranquillity, and my entire presence of mind.

New Orleans, which I had left more than four and a half years previously, had in that time made no inconsiderable progress—there had been a great deal of new building, and it was much improved. The character of its population, however, had gained nothing. Its old original inhabitants, of French and Spanish origin, had always shown a certain openness, good faith and sincerity, in their mercantile intercourse; but the lawyers who came thither from the northern states, and whose interest it was to stir up litigation to keep themselves from starving, had, by a certain acquaintance with the technicalities of American jurisprudence, and by a spirit of low cunning and adroitness which they introduced, and even managed to communicate to some of the old inhabitants, been the real cause of this moral retrogression. Governor Claiborne it was who brought election intrigue into fashion, and thereby succeeded in undermining the honorable and amiable character of the original Creoles. Social life had rather been impaired than improved in its relations.

I had just procured a dwelling-house, and furnished it, when the news reached us, from Washington, that war had been declared against England on the 18th of June, 1812. This brought all the projects which I had been erecting upon my business relations with Europe to the ground, and all the advantages I was entitled to expect from them vanished out of my hands. Let any one, who can, form an idea of the situation in which I suddenly found myself placed. . . .

Within a few months after the foundation of my establishment, I was suddenly cut off from all resources. The absence of business thence resulting, the difficulty bordering almost upon impossibility, of tracing out under these circumstances, any business combinations at all corresponding to the enterprising mercantile spirit, and yet not calculated to place one's reputation for commercial foresight in jeopardy, made life wearisome among a population such as New Orleans at that time contained. It could, indeed, be borne, but it made the joyless void of existence, when the object of that existence has departed, most keenly felt. It was like a dead calm to the mariner, but with this difference, that the latter continues only for days or weeks, while the termination of my stagnant inactivity could not be calculated, but might extend for years.

The Mississippi was blockaded and narrowly watched by two English vessels of war. After this sad beginning of the war, the whole city and district of country was so additionally unfortunate as to be devastated by a hurricane of the kind which so frequently occurs in tropical climates, at the time of the solstice. Eighteen of the vessels lying in the harbor were thrown on the left bank of the Mississippi, where they remained completely wrecked; many houses, and half-finished buildings were blown down, and most of the roofs in the city were torn away to the last shingle. Such were the reminiscences of the first year of the war! . . .

Party spirit was embittered by the languishing state of things in the city, and day by day increased to such an extent as to cause the greatest division and irreconcilable enmities where social intercourse had just begun. People would gather at the corners of the streets, to hear or circulate all sorts of private scandal. Ready money became scarce. The whole adjacent coast was disquieted and kept in terror by pirates; among the latter, the most conspicuous were the brothers Laffitte, from Bayonne, Sauvelet, Beluche, Dominique, Gamba and others, who were time and again, seen walking about, publicly, in the streets of New Orleans. They had their friends and acquaintances, their depôts of goods, &c., in the city, and sold, almost openly, the wares they had obtained by piracy, particularly English manufactured goods. The slave trade, too, was especially flourishing under their auspices. These pirates captured Spanish and other slave ships on the high seas, and established their main depôt and rendezvous on the little island of Barataria, lying near the coast adjacent to New Orleans. This place was visited by the sugar planters, chiefly of French origin, who bought up the stolen slaves at from 150 to 200 dollars per head, when they could not have procured as good stock in the city for less than 600 or 700 dollars. These were then conveyed to the different plantations, through the innumerable creeks called *bayous*, that communicate by manifold little branches, with each other.

This clandestine traffic was one of the causes to which the scarcity of ready money was to be attributed. The planters, instead of taking bank notes with them, invariably provided themselves with coin to pay for their purchases. This money, however, did not leave the country, but was hoarded away in the private coffers of those who performed the part of secret agents for the pirates, and was thus withdrawn from general circulation. The French and Catalonian population of the city had never been able to persuade themselves that bank-notes are just as good as cash in representing value when based upon the security of a well-managed banking capital, and just when the prejudice against them was passing away, the jealous manœuvring of two cashiers, one *T. L. Harman*, in the Planter's Bank, the other *Joseph Saul*, in the Bank of Orleans, both Englishmen by birth, again revived it. The latter cashier aimed at destroying the credit of the Planter's Bank, and attracting its customers to his own, as they were mostly planters who allowed their deposits to lie longer than the merchants were accustomed to do. The cashier, who could wind the whole Board of Directors belonging to the Bank, around his little finger, had contracted its discounting operations, and thus brought about a much smaller issue of paper than the Planter's Bank had made; he then, carefully, collected the notes of the rival bank as they were coming in, and after getting unfavorable reports into circulation concerning the Planter's Bank, he suddenly presented the accumulated mass of notes, requiring payment of the same in silver, on a day when he knew that his neighbor's supply of that metal was very much reduced. The amount demanded by the notes went far beyond the quantity of silver in the possession of the Planter's Bank, and the clerk of the Bank of Orleans who presented them, instantly returned with word that they would have further consultation on the subject. This was enough. The whole population was thrown into excitement; there was an immediate run upon the Planter's Bank; but there was no distinction drawn by the excited public, between it and the Bank of Orleans, which like its rival and anticipated victim, was likewise brought to a standstill, in the payment of its notes. . . .

Just about this time there was a rumor afloat of a large expedition fitting out, in England, against the southern coasts of the United States, especially the seaboard of Louisiana. A freebooter gang, under an English major named Nicholas, had placed itself in communication with the pirates of Barataria, and English cruisers were from time to time seen in the Gulf of Mexico, and off the mouths of the Mississippi. Navigation on the two lakes, Borgne and Pontchartrain, back of New Orleans, had never been disturbed, and to the entrance of Mobile Bay or Mobile Point, as it is called, to the harbor of Pensacola, which remained opened to the English and their flag, was about six hours sail. At Pensacola, Louisiana cotton could not be procured by the English for less than from twenty-two to twenty-four cents per pound, while in New Orleans it cost only half that rate. Intercourse was then carried on between the country bordering the lakes, and even between New Orleans and Pensacola, by means of small craft, counting from ten to fifteen tons, which conveyed flour, wine, spirituous liquors, etc., etc., to and fro. The whole flotilla amounted to about twenty-five sail. One morning I chartered the larger of these, loaded them with cotton, to the extent of about 250 bales in all, and dispatched them to Mobile Bay, there to await my arrival. A day or two afterwards I reached the place, in a small empty schooner, and lay close to Fort Mobile, before which a small English squadron was cruising, and at length began to make preparations for bombarding the fort. The attack came at last, and continued, right before my eyes, from one o'clock in the afternoon until seven in the evening. The little fort withstood the cannonade of five war vessels most bravely, and responded to it with such effect as evidently to occasion them very great damage. I now brought the whole of my little flotilla from the middle of the bay close to the fort, and waited in my little clipper for the retreat of the British squadron. When this occurred, at sundown, I sailed along close at its heels, yet at a certain distance, and saw that it bore direct for Pensacola, where, thought I, they would be more likely to occupy themselves with repairing their damage than in capturing small craft like mine. So I returned to the bay, hauled out my flotilla, and, favored during the night by a cloudless moon and fair wind, brought it by sunrise safe into the harbor of Pensacola. Here I sold my cotton, on the spot, at twenty-two cents per pound, and in return purchased three packs woollen blankets at five and a half to six dollars. With these I went through Mobile Bay and the small lakes back to New Orleans, where the blankets were worth from ten to eleven dollars. The proper period for the sale of that article is in December, at the beginning of the sugar crop. Everybody thought this little venture of mine a pretty thing, and greeted me on 'Change with, "Ah, you have been to visit your friends the English?" . . .

In Paris in the course of the summer of 1824, I received several visits from General Lafayette, whom I had slightly known some years before. . . . Many invitations had come to him from the United States, once more to visit that land, which had to thank his youthful arms for part of its freedom. Congress had instructed the president to notify him officially, their readiness to receive, as well as their power would admit, and to keep a frigate in readiness for him; he had received from all sides proofs of esteem and affection in such numbers, that he had finally determined, in spite of his advanced age, to undertake the voyage. One difficulty, however, must first be removed. He had no money. "I have here in Paris," said the general to me, "debts to the amount of 100,000 francs, which must be paid before I dare go to another quarter of the world. I could procure the money here if I would give a mortgage upon my estate, Lagrange, but it is the heritage of my children—it belonged to my wife, and now is theirs; and although they are all willing to resign, to help me in my embarrassments, I cannot accept it—I will not disturb it." . . . The general . . . interested me so much, as he did every one who knew him well, that I bade him be of good courage; and promised to visit and inquire among such Americans as were living in independent circumstances in Paris, at the time, and see what could be done with them. And first I went to our ambassador, James Brown, a worthy man, with whom I had become acquainted in Louisiana, and whose esteem and good will I dared flatter myself to possess. Cool and serious as this gentleman was in all his dealings, yet he took hold of this affair right heartily, and with a fire which much encouraged me. He promised to go to work, and pledged himself to furnish one quarter of the sum, and to induce others to follow his example. In what manner the required sum was finally made up I have never learned, but the general himself informed me in a friendly note that the goal of his desires was attained. His note inclosed the request to visit him in the course of the week, that he might introduce me to a couple of English ladies, living in the house with him and under his protection, who expected to visit the United States, and desired to confer with me about some pecuniary difficulties. These two ladies were the authoress, Miss Fanny Wright, afterwards so well known for her eccentricities, and her sister. They desired to make over to me the sum of 120,000 francs, then in the hands of the banker Lafitte, that I might invest this capital in Louisiana, without losing the interest in the meantime; and with power to use the same in the meanwhile, if circumstances should render it necessary. This little negotiation was soon arranged, and when the ladies visited Louisiana, eighteen months later, they received their money back. . . .

Two weeks later the general, accompanied by his son, George Washington Lafayette, and his secretary, M. Levasseur, went to Havre, where he embarked on the 13th of July, in the regular packet Cadmus, for New York. Here he happily arrived after a short voyage, on the 16th of August. The somewhat imperfectly edited memoirs of the general, which appeared after his death, and other contemporaneous writings, describe in detail the extraordinary reception that awaited him there. The enthusiasm which welcomed him, found an echo throughout the entire land. In every State of the Union, (the original thirteen which composed it, after the war of Independence, as well as those which had been afterwards admitted,) gathered young and old together to greet and honor worthily the man who, sprung from the old French noblesse, in the bloom of youth, the darling of the court, had carried over the mighty ocean his strength, his ability, and a great part of his fortune to fight for the young Republic; had been Washington's comrade, friend, and first aid-de-camp. . . . A period of more than forty years had rolled away since the general had left the land for which he fought; the new generation which did not know him, regarded him in the light of a saint, and the old who remained, were so scattered that only here and there came one who could take the stranger by the hand and bid him welcome.

In the beginning of April, 1825, precisely when the wildest spirit of speculation was at work in New Orleans, and was occupying our almost entire attention, came General Lafayette, an arrival which alone could have created a diversion. Although in the whole population of [New Orleans] and its environs not one comrade in the war of independence, nor even one personal acquaintance, except myself, was there to greet him, still the enthusiasm with which he had been received everywhere was intense in Louisiana, from the fact of most of the inhabitants being of French extraction; and men were more anxious to venerate the historic importance of the actor in the French revolution, than of the then young but now gray-haired hero of the American. The general had arrived, before the opening of the Congress of December 8, 1824, in Washington, and had employed the intervening time in visiting the states of New York, Connecticut, Rhode Island, and Massachusetts. He passed through New Jersey, Pennsylvania, Delaware, and Maryland, on his way to Washington, and it was there that the then speaker of the House, the late Henry Clay, introduced him, on the 10th December, into the Hall of Representatives, and presented him to both houses therein assembled.

The roomy and richly-decorated hall held on this occasion 2,000 persons, with all the foreign ministers, except the French ambassador of the Bourbons. The Marquis afterwards told me, that although he had witnessed very many assemblies in his own country, never had he received such an impression as from this one; and that he had never been so thoroughly moved by the eloquence of any man, not even by that of Mirabeau, as by the clear and spirited ring of the voice of Henry Clay. "It was," he said, "the voice of a nation, making itself heard by the mouth of a great man." The whole house, as if stricken by the wand of an enchanter, had risen to their feet as Clay entered, leading Lafayette by the hand. They sat down at the conclusion of the welcoming speech, but arose again at the first signs of a reply. They expected him to take his spectacles and a written answer from his pocket; but after a moment's pause he spoke, extemporaneously, and in English. To Clay's remark, that he was the witness of his own future, he replied, that when he there found, in the sons of his former and now departed friends, the same spirit for the general weal, as well as the same personal friendship for him, no future spread itself before him.

The Congress, as is well known, voted to the general, as a testimonial of the national gratitude, $200,000, and 200,000 acres of land, which the general chose in the newly-received state of Florida, which had just been purchased from Spain, it having been allowed him, as a condition of the present, to choose from any unoccupied public lands in the United States. After this present, the general resolved to visit all the States, if only for a couple of days, which, in the session of Congress, had voted for the present. Therefore he left Washington, and passed through Virginia, North and South Carolina, Georgia and Alabama, to Mobile, where he found a deputation from New Orleans, headed by the governor, who had come to welcome him, and conduct him to their city. As I learned from the governor, his first question about New Orleans was whether I were there, and he seemed pleased at receiving an affirmative answer.

The legislature of the state had arranged his reception with the common council of the city. The residence of the common council, the *Mayory*, was entirely refitted, admirably adorned, and newly and luxuriously furnished. A table, with thirty covers, was set every day during the general's stay, in order that he might become acquainted with the principal inhabitants and planters. I will not speak of other festivities—balls, theatres, &c. Finally, one of the best steamers was procured, and kept ready for a visit to Natchez and the state of Mississippi, with a deputation, consisting of the governor, a member of the legislature, a member of the common council, and a delegate from all the most important classes in the country—planters, lawyers, merchants, &c.—chosen by the general himself. When he looked over the list, and came to the names of the merchants, he designated me as the person who, as an old acquaintance, would be most agreeable to him. By his wish I visited him every morning after breakfast, on which occasions he questioned me freely about men and things in Louisiana. One morning he acknowledged to me that his purse was but meagrely furnished.

"Certainly," he said, "Congress has granted me money enough, but I have not as yet received one cent of the $200,000, because the treasury was not at the moment prepared to pay it; therefore, I am in need of money; can you give it me?"

My answer may be divined. I placed my cash-box at his disposal; but he only wanted $1200, which I brought him the same day. I asked for no receipt.

but begged him merely, when he should return to the North, and visit Boston, at his convenience to give the sum to my friend there, Mr. John Richards. The general insisted on giving a receipt, and put one into my hand the next morning, which I have retained, although the debt has been paid.

The voyage to Natchez gave me better opportunities of seeing the general, and of enjoying his conversation, than would otherwise have been possible. The whole of the great cabin of the steamboat was for the general's convenience. Above this, on the deck, was erected a large convenient saloon, wherein the eating was carried on, and where people passed the time as well as they could. In it were sofas, play-tables, cards, and books. The governor of Louisiana, by name Johnson—a most ordinary kind of man, ill-instructed, and of most unpolished manners, in many respects a true child of nature—sat on the general's right hand. The seat at the left hand was reserved for me; and at breakfast the general was wont to say, "If you have anything to talk about, let us go down to my room and talk." Such invitations were the more welcome because I could not accept them as often as I wished, and I had avoided them, as far as the resting-points of the trip were concerned. As the dwellers on the banks of the Mississippi had expected the arrival and voyage of the general, wherever the steamer that carried the nation's guest was recognized, by the numerous decorative flags, they hastened, so soon as it was seen in the distance, to assemble in some house, and to make the welkin ring with their shouts of welcome. Where the houses were numerous, or in the immediate neighborhood of a village—like Baton Rouge, for instance—the boat would stop, and the general would receive the deputations that came on board to greet him, or the single personages who desired to be presented to him. The deputations usually came with their speaker at the head. Of course, in most instances, the speaker was more occupied in exhibiting his cleverness and oratorical talent, than with the object of his mission, or a desire to give pleasure to the hearer. And the good general had no remedy for this evil, but was compelled to listen attentively to the longest, stupidest, wordiest discourses possible. I never saw a mark of impatience upon his countenance. So soon as the infliction was brought to an end, he always had ready a few suitable and flattering words. The ease with which he performed this task greatly astonished me. I could not refrain one day from asking him how he managed always to reply to the most silly and idealess speeches. "My friend," he answered, "it is not hard. I listen with great attention until the speaker drops something that pleases me, or that gives opportunity for a repartee, and then I think about my reply, and arrange it; but of all the rest I do not hear a syllable—it all blows over me."

But on other less important occasions his readiness and power in answering was really remarkable. At Baton Rouge, two young men were presented to him. The inevitable hand-shaking was the usual prelude to a short dialogue; but the young men stood mute before the general and gazed at him silently. At length he asked one of them, "Are you married?"

"Yes, sir," was the answer. "Happy man," quoth the general. He then put the same question to the other, "and you, sir, are you married?" "No, sir," was the answer; "I am a bachelor." "Lucky dog!" said the general. In these words which fell from the general, both received, married man and bachelor, a witty compliment on his social position.

On my first visit to the general's room, I begged permission to be allowed to address any questions that might come into my head, to him who had a world-full of experience. The occurrences which took place in the first days of the French Revolution, the scenes at Versailles, the leading out of the unfortunate queen, Marie Antoinette, upon the balcony of the palace, where he had kissed her hand, as a proof of peace and good understanding between them, before the thousands who were gathered in the palace court and in the Avenue de Versailles, and many of whom had come there with ill-intent; the joy that followed his assurance to the people that the royal family would go to Paris. To hear all these circumstances described by his own lips, and with the greatest modesty and simpleness, was a genuine treat to me. Great as was his modesty, however, he could not conceal the pleasure caused by these recollections of his earlier popularity and influence. Popularity was the god that ruled him, and to which on no occasion of his life had he ever refused his service. I had already seen this during his stay in New Orleans, and on our trip up the Mississippi, and some years later during the July revolution in Paris, these convictions increased. To be the idol of the people was the deepest desire of his heart, and the fulfillment of this desire he could only attain to in a republic. That he knew—but I would do him injustice were I to ascribe his republicanism to this source alone. He was a republican by conviction, and from the centre of his soul out. The lessons that he had received at the side of Washington, and under the victorious banners of the Union, he faithfully followed throughout his life, and the idea that this form of government and none other could make his country happy was guarded in his breast as a holy thing. In this he found the only panacea for the cure of the many evils under which France was suffering. . . .

The time [1827] for choosing a new president was at hand. The election was to take place in a year, and General Jackson was the favorite candidate. Probably throughout the whole Union there was no man who had more thoroughly disregarded the Constitution than this man; and all who had lived in his immediate neighborhood, who had known and observed him, could not repress the positive conviction, that of all the candidates he was the least fitted for president; since his greatest gifts were only physical courage, intense fieryness, and indomitable will. Respect for law, or the ideas of others, or command over his inborn passionateness of character, had he never felt. He was the first candidate for the presidency who was brought forward and elected by bribery . . . It was an easy matter for the creatures who obeyed his nod to find out the most popular democrats of the various States, who were not always sought for among the most respectable inhabitants; to win them, and to keep them by promises of certain fat and honorable offices; to open their zeal, and, in a word, to make them satellites, prepared to strain every nerve, to silence every suggestion of conscience that stood in their way, and in the way of electing their candidate. . . .

On his candidate voyage Jackson had visited several of the Western States; his own, in which he dwelt as cotton planter, included; and he determined to go to the cradle of his renown, New Orleans, but as simple citizen, sending there also his cotton crop, about eighty bales. The same steamboat that brought the cotton bore also the American hero. A Frenchman would have called that steamboat "the bark that carried Cæsar and his fortunes." He was received with joy; a mob of the more youthful niggers, carefully drilled by Sheriff Morgan, stood at the corners of the streets, and cried "Hurrah for Jackson;" and the general, in simple citizen's guise, surrounded by the electoral committee, stepped on shore. On every occasion, he endeavored to give proof of amiability of character, of esteem for the laws, etc.; hiding carefully from all military display.

To me, who during the defence of the city, had had the general daily and immediately under my eye, and whom no shade of his character could or did escape, all this comedy seemed so mean, and at the same time so absurd, that I, who had little to do, could not withstand the desire to send to my friend Charles King, editor of the New York American, a droll description of the visit, which showed a perfect acquaintance with the city. Mr. King published it. It delighted ordinary readers, but Jackson's partisans in New Orleans, particularly the members of his election committee, were rendered furious. The publisher of the American was written to, and the name of the author demanded—he refused to give it. For the first few weeks no one thought of me, who had so recently returned from Europe; but after a while it was concluded that nobody but I could have written it; and Mr. Slidell, secretary of the committee, was sent to demand a formal explanation. The reader can guess that this had no result, as I only expressed wonder at the presumption, and expressed it mockingly; which I ventured to do, because I lived on the friendliest footing with Mr. Slidell, and at one time, before he sought to still his conscience for this political role, had received him as a most intimate friend at my house. So soon, however, as I observed, that he was allowing himself to be used as the tool of a political faction, all intimacy, and finally all intercourse, ceased. I had seen too many examples of the extremities to which American party spirit will go, not to keep myself clear of any mingling in politics—not to choose my companions with prudence. Also, I felt no interest in the success of this or that party; yet, although I felt no particular esteem for the other candidate, John Quincy Adams, I would very unwillingly have seen him defeated by the filthy intrigues of a most unprincipled man—I mean, of General Jackson. . . . A pure patriot Jackson was not, and could not be, and the results showed that a far better man might have been chosen. The parallel between Jackson and others, who were better fitted for the lofty position at which he was aiming, had taken such possession of me, by reason of my opportunities for observation, and the great attention I had given to it, that I determined, as much for my own pleasure as from any other motive, to write a letter to Adams, wherein the whole position of affairs at the time was set forth, and Jackson's merits and demerits, as well as his own, were contrasted. My friend Custis and others urged me to print this letter, and I did not refuse. It was certainly the best I had ever written in English. But few copies were circulated in New Orleans, but many were sent to the election committees in the north. From the printers the name of the author was discovered, and I need not say that what I had written purely for my own amusement procured for me many enemies, and the deadly hate of most of Jackson's followers. In New Orleans I was a fallen, but not dishonored man. People wondered that I did not follow the American custom of comforting myself in the bar-rooms, and seeking for consolation in brandy, but that I still attended to business, and still held my head high. Most of them could not understand why the loss of my lofty mercantile position did not induce me to descend the social ladder also, and that my self-respect was not in the slightest degree lessened. I was blameless. This steeled me during that last mournful year in New Orleans, while I was bringing about the liquidation there. . . .

Early the next year, 1829, my long-desired return to Europe was rendered possible; I could embark for Havre—but not until one more trial had been passed through. The partisans of Jackson could not let me go without first revenging themselves upon me. One of the most ferocious, F. B. Ogden, to whom Jackson had promised, for his election services, the Liverpool consulate, had determined to attack me in my own house. He had brought a witness with him, in order to lay his misdeed before the public. The twain entered my room lightly, while I was seated at my dinner with my back to the door; but so soon as I caught a glimpse of them, I made one spring behind my writing-desk, on which lay two loaded pistols, which I seized. It was comical to behold how the two good-for-nothings retired, cursing in disappointment. The whole city was informed of the affair by a placard, that same evening, and the larger portion of the citizens, to their honor be it said, were exceedingly incensed.

Day and hour were appointed for my departure. All my former clerks and several friends had assembled to accompany me on board; for the news had gone through the city, that the Jacksonians would make one more attack before my embarkation. I rescinded my resolution to go on board either early in the morning or late at night; and chose to go through the high street, by the clear sunshine of three o'clock P.M. The Levée was thronged with a cheering crowd as I went on board and the vessel moved out to sea. . . .

Thus, then, two-and-twenty years after my first visit, and sixteen since the establishment of my firm, I bade farewell to the city wherein I had hoped to gain the reward of so many struggles, peace and independence for my old age.

Mrs. Trollope was Shocked

Frances Trollope, mother of the novelist, Anthony Trollope, was forty-eight years old when she left England in 1827 to establish a store in Cincinnati. Her husband, Thomas Anthony Trollope, had lost the expectation of a large inheritance and had failed at farming when he decided that a department store in America would restore the family to security. Partly due to his lavish schemes, the undertaking failed before the store-building was finished. After three years her money was gone and life in America was a wretched existence for Mrs. Trollope. With a dim hope of earning a little, she began the book which made a reverberating furore both in America and in England.

From DOMESTIC MANNERS OF THE AMERICANS

New Orleans, Voyage up the Mississippi—Nashoba

On the 4th of November, 1827, I sailed from London, accompanied by my son[1] and two daughters; and after a favourable, though somewhat tedious voyage, arrived on Christmas-day at the mouth of the Mississippi.

I never beheld a scene so utterly desolate as this entrance of the Mississippi. Had Dante seen it, he might have drawn images of another Bolgia from its horrors. One only object rears itself above the eddying waters: this is the mast of a vessel long since wrecked in attempting to cross the bar; and it still stands, a dismal witness of the destruction that has been, and a boding prophet of that which is to come.

On first touching the soil of a new land, of a new continent, of a new world, it is impossible not to feel considerable excitement and deep interest in almost every object that meets us. New Orleans presents very little that can gratify the eye of taste, but nevertheless there is much of novelty and interest for a newly-arrived European. The large proportion of blacks seen in the streets, all labour being performed by them; the grace and beauty of the elegant Quadroons; the occasional groups of wild and savage-looking Indians; the unwonted aspect of the vegetation; the huge and turbid river,

[1]Not the later-famous Anthony, but his brother Henry.

with its low and slimy shore; all help to afford that species of amusement which proceeds from looking at what we never saw before.

The town has much the appearance of a French Ville de Province, and is, in fact, an old Spanish colony taken by the French. The names of the streets are French, and the language about equally French and English. The market is handsome and well supplied, all produce being conveyed by the river. We were much pleased by the chant with which the negro boatmen regulate and beguile their labour on the river; it consists but of very few notes, but they are sweetly harmonious, and the negro voice is almost always rich and powerful. . . .

The first symptom of American equality that I perceived, was my being introduced in form to a milliner. It was not at a boarding-house, under the indistinct outline of 'Miss C—', nor in the street, through the veil of a fashionable toilette; but in the very penetralia of her temple, standing behind her counter, giving laws to ribbon and to wire, and ushering caps and bonnets into existence. She was an English woman, and I was told that she possessed great intellectual endowments and much information; I really believe this was true. Her manner was easy and graceful, with a good deal of French tournure: and the gentleness with which her fine eyes and sweet voice directed the movements of a young female slave, was really touching: the way, too, in which she blended her French talk of modes with her customers, and her English talk of metaphysics with her friends, had a pretty air of indifference in it, that gave her a superiority with both. . . . I heard from many quarters, after I had left New Orleans, that the society of this lady was highly valued by all persons of talent: yet were I, traveller-like, to stop here, and set it down as a national peculiarity, or republican custom, that milliners took the lead in the best society, I should greatly falsify facts. . . . This is one instance, among a thousand, of the impression every circumstance makes on entering a new country, and of the propensity, so irresistible, to class all things, however accidental, as national and peculiar. On the other hand, however, it is certain that if similar anomalies are unfrequent in America, they are nearly impossible elsewhere. . . .

Our stay in New Orleans was not long enough to permit our entering into society; but I was told that it contained two distinct sets of people, both celebrated, in their way, for their social meetings and elegant entertainments. The first of these is composed of Creole families, who are chiefly planters and merchants, with their wives and daughters; these meet together, eat together, and are very grand and aristocratic; each of their balls is a little Almack's,[2] and every portly dame of the set is as exclusive in her principles as a lady patroness. The other set consists of the excluded but amiable Quadroons, and such of the gentlemen of the former class as can by any means escape from the high places, where pure Creole blood swells the veins at the bare mention of any being, tainted in the remotest degree with

[2]At Almack's Assembly Rooms London society gathered for social functions in the eighteenth and nineteenth centuries.

the negro stain. Of all the prejudices I have ever witnessed, this appears to me the most violent, and the most inveterate. Quadroon girls, the acknowledged daughters of wealthy American or Creole fathers, educated with all of style and accomplishments which money can procure at New Orleans, and with all the decorum that care and affection can give—exquisitely beautiful, graceful, gentle, and amiable, are not admitted, nay, are not on any terms admissible, into the society of the Creole families of Louisiana. They cannot marry; that is to say, no ceremony can render a union with them legal or binding; yet such is the powerful effect of their very peculiar grace, beauty, and sweetness of manner, that unfortunately they perpetually become the objects of choice and affection. . . . The unions formed with this unfortunate race are said to be often lasting and happy, as far as any unions can be so to which a certain degree of disgrace is attached.

There is a French and an English theatre in the town; but we were too fresh from Europe to care much for either, or, indeed, for any other of the town delights of the city; and we soon became eager to commence our voyage up the Mississippi.

Miss Wright, then less known . . . than she has since become, was the companion of our voyage from Europe; and it was my purpose to have passed some months with her and her sister at the estate she had purchased in Tennessee. This lady . . . was about, as she said, to seclude herself for life in the deepest forests of the western world, that her fortune, her time, and her talents, might be exclusively devoted to aid the cause of the suffering Africans. Her first object was to show that Nature had made no difference between blacks and whites, excepting in complexion; and this she expected to prove, by giving an education perfectly equal to a class of black and white children. Could this fact be once fully established, she conceived that the negro cause would stand on firmer ground than it had yet done, and the degraded rank which they have ever held amongst civilised nations would be proved to be a gross injustice. This question of the mental equality, or inequality, between us and the negro race, is one of great interest, and has certainly never yet been fairly tried; and I expected for my children and myself both pleasure and information from visiting her establishment, and watching the success of her experiment. . . .

On the first of January, 1828, we embarked on board the Belvidere, a large and handsome boat; though not the largest or handsomest of the many which displayed themselves along the wharfs. We found the room destined for the use of the ladies dismal enough, as its only windows were below the stern gallery; but both this and the gentlemen's cabin were handsomely fitted up, and the latter well carpeted; but oh! that carpet! . . . Let no one who wishes to receive agreeable impressions of American manners, commence his travels in a Mississippi steam-boat; for myself, it is with all sincerity I declare, that I would infinitely prefer sharing the apartment of a party of well-conditioned pigs, to the being confined to its cabin. . . .

We had a full complement of passengers on board. The deck, as is usual, was occupied by the Kentucky flat-boat men, returning from New Orleans, after having disposed of the boat and cargo which they had conveyed thither, with no other labour than that of steering her, the current bringing her down at the rate of four miles an hour. We had about two hundred of these men on board. When we stopped to take in wood they ran, or rather sprung and vaulted over each other's heads to the shore, whence they all assisted in carrying wood to supply the steam-engine; the performance of this duty being a stipulated part of the payment of their passage.

The gentlemen in the cabin (we had no ladies) would certainly, neither from their language, manners, nor appearance, have received that designation in Europe; but we soon found their claim to it rested on more substantial ground; for we heard them nearly all addressed by the titles of general, colonel, and major. . . .

The total want of all the usual courtesies of the table, the voracious rapidity with which the viands were seized and devoured; the strange uncouth phrases and pronunciation; the loathsome spitting, from the contamination of which it was absolutely impossible to protect our dresses; the frightful manner of feeding with their knives, till the whole blade seemed to enter into the mouth; and the still more frightful manner of cleaning the teeth afterwards with a pocket-knife, soon forced us to feel that we were not surrounded by the generals, colonels, and majors of the old world; and that the dinner-hour was to be anything rather than an hour of enjoyment. . . .

As the distance from New Orleans increased, the air of wealth and comfort exhibited in its immediate neighbourhood disappeared, and but for one or two clusters of wooden houses, calling themselves towns, and borrowing some pompous name, generally from Greece or Rome, we might have thought ourselves the first of the human race who had ever penetrated into this territory of bears and alligators. But still, from time to time, appeared the hut of the wood-cutter, who supplies the steam-boats with fuel, at the risk, or rather with the assurance of early death, in exchange for dollars and whiskey. These sad dwellings are nearly all of them inundated during the winter, and the best of them are constructed on piles, which permit the water to reach its highest level without drowning the wretched inhabitants. These unhappy beings are invariably the victims of ague, which they meet recklessly, sustained by the incessant use of ardent spirits. The squalid look of the miserable wives and children of these men was dreadful; and often as the spectacle was renewed, I could never look at it with indifference. . . . A miserable cow and a few pigs, standing knee-deep in water, distinguish the more prosperous of these dwellings; and on the whole I should say, that I never witnessed human nature reduced so low as it appeared in the wood-cutters' huts on the unwholesome banks of the Mississippi. . . .

At length we had the pleasure of being told that we had arrived at Memphis; but this pleasure was considerably abated by the hour of our arrival, which was midnight, and by the rain, which was falling in torrents.

Memphis stands on a high bluff, and at the time of our arrival was nearly inaccessible. The heavy rain which had been falling for many hours would have made any steep ascent difficult; but unfortunately a new road had been recently marked out, which beguiled us into its almost bottomless mud, from the firmer footing of the unbroken cliff. Shoes and gloves were lost in the mire, for we were glad to avail ourselves of all our limbs; and we reached the grand hotel in a most deplorable state.

Miss Wright was well known there; and as soon as her arrival was announced, every one seemed on the alert to receive her, and we soon found ourselves in possession of the best rooms in the hotel. The house was new, and in what appeared to me a very comfortless condition; but I was then new to Western America, and unaccustomed to their mode of "getting along", as they term it. This phrase is eternally in use among them, and seems to mean existing with as few of the comforts of life as possible. . . .

The steam-boat had wearied me of social meals, and I should have been thankful to have eaten my dinner of hard venison and peach-sauce in a private room; but this, Miss Wright said, was impossible; the lady of the house would consider the proposal as a personal affront, and, moreover, it would be assuredly refused. This latter argument carried weight with it; and when the great bell was sounded from an upper window of the house, we proceeded to the dining-room. The table was laid for fifty persons, and was already nearly full. Our party had the honour of sitting near "the lady"; but to check the proud feelings to which such distinction might give birth, my servant, William, sat very nearly opposite to me. The company consisted of all the shopkeepers (storekeepers as they are called throughout the United States) of the little town. . . . They ate in perfect silence, and with such astonishing rapidity that their dinner was over literally before ours was begun; the instant they ceased to eat, they darted from the table in the same moody silence which they had preserved since they entered the room, and a second set took their places, who performed their silent parts in the same manner. The only sounds heard were those produced by the knives and forks, with the unceasing chorus of coughing, etc. No women were present except ourselves and the hostess; the good women of Memphis being well content to let their lords partake of Mrs. Anderson's turkeys and venison, (without their having the trouble of cooking for them,) whilst they regale themselves on mush and milk at home. . . .

Miss Wright was anxious to get home, and we were scarcely less so to see her Nashoba. A clumsy sort of caravan drawn by two horses was prepared for us; and we set off in high spirits for an expedition of fifteen miles through the forest. To avoid passing one of the bridges which was thought insecure, our negro driver took us through a piece of water, which he assured us was not deep "to matter"; however, we soon lost sight of our pole, and as we were evidently descending, we gently remonstrated with him on the danger of proceeding, but he only grinned, and flogged in reply; we soon saw the front wheels disappear, and the horses began to plunge and kick most alarmingly, but still without his looking at all disturbed. At length the splinter-bar gave way, upon which the black philosopher said very composedly, "I expect you'll best be riding out upon the horses, as we've got into an unhandsome fix here." Miss Wright, who sat composedly smiling at the scene, said, "Yes, Jacob, that is what we must do"; and with some difficulty we, in this manner, reached the shore, and soon found ourselves again assembled round Mrs. Anderson's fire. . . .

The next day we started again, and the clear air, the bright sun, the novel wildness of the dark forest, and our keenly awakened curiosity, made the excursion delightful, and enabled us to bear, without shrinking, the bumps and bruises we encountered. We soon lost all trace of a road, at least so it appeared to us; for the stumps of the trees, which had been cut away to open a passage, were left standing three feet high. Over these, the high-hung Deerborn [sic] as our carriage was called, passed safely; but it required some miles of experience to convince us that every stump would not be our last. . . . The forest became thicker and more dreary-looking every mile we advanced; but our ever-grinning negro declared it was a right good road, and that we should be sure to get to Nashoba: and so we did . . . and one glance sufficed to convince me, that every idea I had formed of the place was as far as possible from the truth. Desolation was the only feeling—the only word that presented itself; but it was not spoken. I think, however, that Miss Wright was aware of the painful impression the sight of her forest-home produced on me; and I doubt not that the conviction reached us both at the same moment, that we had erred in thinking that a few months passed together at this spot could be productive of pleasure to either: but to do her justice, I believe her mind was so exclusively occupied by the object she had then in view, that all things else were worthless, or indifferent to her. I never heard or read of any enthusiasm approaching hers, except in some few instances, in ages past, of religious fanaticism. . . . Her whole heart and soul were occupied by the hope of raising the African to the level of European intellect; and even now, that I have seen this favourite fabric of her imagination fall to pieces beneath her feet, I cannot recall the self-devotion with which she gave herself to it without admiration.

The only white persons we found at Nashoba, were my amiable friend, Mrs. W—— (the sister of Miss Wright) and her husband. I think they had between thirty and forty slaves, including children; but when I was there no school had been established. Books and other materials for the great experiment had been collected, and one or two professors engaged; but nothing was yet organised. I found my friend Mrs. W—— in very bad health, which she confessed she attributed to the climate. This naturally so much alarmed me for my children, that I decided upon leaving the place with as little delay as possible, and did so at the end of ten days.

I do not exactly know what was the immediate cause which induced Miss Wright to abandon a scheme which had taken such possession of her imagination, and on which she had expended so much money; but many months had not elapsed before I learnt, with much pleasure, that she and her sister had also left it. I think it probable that she became aware, upon returning to Nashoba, that the climate was too hostile to their health. All I know farther of Nashoba is, that Miss Wright having found (from some cause or other) that it was impossible to pursue her object, herself accompanied her slaves to Hayti, and left them there, free, and under the protection of the President. . . .

Ohio River—Cincinnati

On the 1st of February, 1828, we embarked at Memphis on board the Criterion for Cincinnati, and once more began to float on the "father of waters", as the poor banished Indians were wont to call the Mississippi. The company on board was wonderfully like what we had met in coming from New Orleans; I think they must have all been first cousins; and what was singular, they, too, had all arrived at high rank in the army. For many a wearisome mile above the Wolf River the only scenery was still forest—forest—forest; the only variety was produced by the receding of the river at some points, and its encroaching on the opposite shore. . . . We were now approaching the river which is emphatically called "the beautiful", La Belle Rivière of the New Orleans French; . . . The Ohio is bright and clear; its banks are continually varied as it flows through what is called a rolling country, which seems to mean a district that cannot show a dozen paces of level ground at a time.

So powerful was the effect of this sweet scenery, that we ceased to grumble at our dinners and suppers; nay, we almost learnt to rival our neighbours at table in their voracious rapidity of swallowing, so eager were we to place ourselves again on guard, lest we might lose sight of the beauty that was passing away from us. . . .

We reached Cincinnati on the 10th of February. It is finely situated on the south side of a hill that rises gently from the water's edge: yet it is by no means a city of striking appearance—it wants domes, towers, and steeples; but its landing-place is noble, extending for more than a quarter of a mile. It is well paved, and surrounded by neat, though not handsome, buildings. I have seen fifteen steam-boats lying there at once, and still half the wharf was unoccupied.

On arriving we repaired to the Washington Hotel, and thought ourselves fortunate when we were told that we were just in time for dinner at the table d'hôte; but when the dining-room door was opened, we retreated with a feeling of dismay at seeing between sixty and seventy men already at table. We took our dinner in another room with the females of the family, and then went forth to seek a house for our permanent accommodation. . . .

We had the good fortune to find a dwelling before long, and we returned to our hotel, having determined upon taking possession of it as soon as it could be got ready. Not wishing to take our evening meal either with the threescore and ten gentlemen of the dining-room, nor yet with the half-dozen ladies of the bar-room, I ordered tea in my own chamber. A good-humoured Irish woman came forward with a sort of patronising manner, took my hand, and said: "Och, my honey, ye'll be from the old country. I'll see you will have your tay all to yourselves, honey." With this assurance we retired to my room, which was a handsome one as to its size and bed-furniture; but it had no carpet, and was darkened by blinds of paper such as rooms are hung with, which require to be rolled up, and then fastened with strings very awkwardly attached to the window-frames, whenever light or air was wished for. I afterwards met with these same uncomfortable blinds in every part of America.

Our Irish friend soon reappeared, and brought us tea, together with the never-failing accompaniments of American tea-drinking, hung beef, "chipped up" raw, and sundry sweetmeats of brown-sugar hue and flavour. We took our tea, and were enjoying our family talk, relative to our future arrangements, when a loud sharp knocking was heard at our door. My "come in" was answered by the appearance of a portly personage, who proclaimed himself our landlord.

"Are any of you ill?" he began.

"No, thank you, sir; we are all quite well," was my reply.

"Then, madam, I must tell you, that I cannot accommodate you on these terms; we have no family tea-drinkings here, and you must live either with me and my wife, or not at all in my house."

This was said with an air of authority that almost precluded reply, but I ventured a sort of apologetic hint, that we were strangers, and unaccustomed to the manners of the country.

"Our manners are very good manners, and we don't wish any changes from England," rejoined our sturdy landlord, with an aspect that assuredly did not indicate any very affectionate partiality to the country he named. . . .

We were soon settled in our new dwelling, which looked neat and comfortable enough; but we speedily found that it was devoid of nearly all the accommodation that Europeans conceive necessary to decency and comfort. No pump, no cistern, no drain of any kind, no dustman's cart, or any other visible means of getting rid of the rubbish, which vanishes with such celerity in London, that one has no time to think of its existence; but which accumulated so rapidly at Cincinnati, that I sent for my landlord to know in what manner refuse of all kinds was to be disposed of.

"Your Help will just have to fix them all into the middle of the street; but you must mind, old woman, that it is the middle. I expect you don't know as we have got a law what forbids throwing such things at the sides of the streets; they must just all be cast right into the middle, and the pigs soon takes them off." . . .

I hardly know what I expected to find in this city, fresh risen from the bosom of the wilderness, but certainly it was not a little town, about the size of Salisbury, without even an attempt at beauty in any of its edifices, and with only just enough of the air of a city to make it noisy and bustling. The population is greater than the appearance of the town would lead one to expect. This is partly owing to the number of free negroes who herd together in an obscure part of the city, called little Africa; and partly to the density of the population round the paper-mills and other manufactories. I believe the number of inhabitants exceeds twenty thousand. . . .

Cincinnati is built on the side of a hill that begins to rise at the river's edge; and were it furnished with drains of the simplest arrangement, the heavy showers of the climate would keep them constantly clean: as it is, these showers wash the higher streets, only to deposit their filth on the first level spot; and this happens to be in the street second in importance to Main Street, running at right-angles to it, and containing most of the large warehouses of the town. This deposit is a dreadful nuisance, and must be productive of miasma during the hot weather. . . .

Though I do not quite sympathise with those who consider Cincinnati as one of the wonders of the earth, I certainly think it a city of extraordinary size and importance, when it is remembered that thirty years ago the aboriginal forest occupied the ground where it stands; and every month appears to extend its limits and its wealth.

Some of the native political economists assert, that this rapid conversion of a bear-brake into a prosperous city is the result of free political institutions; not being very deep in such matters, a more obvious cause suggested itself to me, in the unceasing goad which necessity applies to industry in this country, and in the absence of all resource for the idle. During nearly two years that I resided in Cincinnati, or its neighbourhood, I neither saw a beggar, nor a man of sufficient fortune to permit his ceasing his efforts to increase it: thus every bee in the hive is actively employed in search of that honey of Hybla, vulgarly called money; neither art, science, learning, nor pleasure, can seduce them from its pursuit. This unity of purpose, backed by the spirit of enterprise, and joined with an acuteness, and absence of probity where interest is concerned, which might set canny Yorkshire at defiance, may well go far towards obtaining its purpose.

The low rate of taxation, too, unquestionably permits a more rapid accumulation of individual wealth than with us; but, till I had travelled through America, I had no idea how much of the money collected in taxes returns among the people, not only in the purchase of what their industry furnishes, but in the actual enjoyment of what is furnished. Were I an English legislator, instead of sending Sedition to the Tower, I would send her to make a tour of the United States. I had a little leaning towards Sedition myself when I set out; but before I had half completed my tour, I was quite cured.

I have read much of the "few and simple wants of rational man", and I used to give a sort of dreamy acquiescence to the reasoning that went to prove each added want an added woe. Those who reason in a comfortable London drawing-room know little about the matter. . . .

The "simple" manner of living in Western America was more distasteful to me from its levelling effects on the manners of the people, than from the personal privations that it rendered necessary; and yet, till I was without them, I was in no degree aware of the many pleasurable sensations derived from the little elegances and refinements enjoyed by the middle classes in Europe. . . . All animal wants are supplied profusely at Cincinnati, and at a very easy rate; but, alas! these go but a little way in the history of a day's enjoyment. The total and universal want of good, or even pleasing, manners, both in males and females, is so remarkable, that I was constantly endeavouring to account for it. It certainly does not proceed from want of intellect: I have listened to much dull and heavy conversation in America, but rarely to any that I could strictly call silly (if I except the everywhere privileged class of very young ladies). They appear to me to have clear heads and active intellects—to be more ignorant on subjects that are only of conventional value, than on such as are of intrinsic importance; but there is no charm, no grace in their conversation. I very seldom, during my whole stay in the country, heard a sentence elegantly turned, and correctly pronounced from the lips of an American. There is always something either in the expression or the accent that jars the feelings and shocks the taste. . . .

Were Americans, indeed, disposed to assume the plain unpretending deportment of the Switzer, in the days of his picturesque simplicity (when, however, he never chewed tobacco), it would be in bad taste to censure him: but this is not the case; Jonathan will be a fine gentleman, but it must be in his own way—is he not a free-born American? Jonathan, however, must remember, that if he will challenge competition with the old world, the old world will now and then look out to see how he supports his pretensions. . . .

The country is a very fine country, well worth visiting for a thousand reasons; nine hundred and ninety-nine of these are reasons founded on admiration and respect; the thousandth is, that we shall feel the more contented with our own. The more unlike a country through which we travel is to all we have left, the more we are likely to be amused; every thing in Cincinnati had this newness; and I should have thought it a place delightful to visit, but to tarry there was not to feel at home.

My home, however, for a time it was to be. . . . I took a larger house, which, however, I did not obtain without considerable difficulty, as, notwithstanding fourteen hundred new dwellings had been erected the preceding year, the demand for houses greatly exceeded the supply. . . .

We visited the farm which interested us particularly from its wild and lonely situation, and from the entire dependence of the inhabitants upon their own resources. It was a partial clearing in the very heart of the forest. The house was built on the side of a hill, so steep that a high ladder was necessary to enter the front door, while the back one opened against the hill side: at the foot of this sudden eminence ran a clear stream, whose bed had been deepened into a little reservoir, just opposite the house. A noble field of Indian corn stretched away into the forest on one side, and a few half-cleared acres, with a shed or two upon them, occupied the other, giving accommodation to cows, horses, pigs, and chickens innumerable. Immediately before the house was a small potato-garden, with a few peach and apple trees. The house was built of logs, and consisted of two rooms, besides a little shanty or lean-to, that was used as a kitchen. Both rooms were comfortably furnished with good beds, drawers, etc. The farmer's wife, and a young woman who looked like her sister, were spinning, and three little children were playing about. The woman told me that they spun and wove all the cotton and woollen garments of the family, and knit all the stockings; her husband, though not a shoemaker by trade, made all the shoes. She manufactured all the soap and candles they used, and prepared her sugar from the sugar-trees on their farm. All she wanted with money, she said, was to buy coffee, tea, and whiskey; and she could "get enough any day by sending a batch of butter and chicken to market." They used no wheat, nor sold any of their corn, which, though it appeared a very large quantity, was not more than they required to make their bread and cakes of various kinds, and to feed all their live stock during the winter. She did not look in health, and said they had all had ague in "the fall"; but she seemed contented and proud of her independence; though it was in somewhat a mournful accent that she said: " 'Tis strange to us to see company. I expect the sun may rise and set a hundred times, before I shall see another *human* that does not belong to the family."

I have been minute in the description of this forest-farm, as I think it the best specimen I saw of the back-woods independence, of which so much is said in America. These people were indeed independent, Robinson Crusoe was hardly more so, and they eat and drink abundantly; but yet it seemed to me that there was something awful and almost unnatural in their loneliness. No village bell ever summoned them to prayer, where they might meet the friendly greeting of their fellow-men. When they die, no spot sacred by ancient reverence will receive their bones–Religion will not breathe her sweet and solemn farewell upon their graves; the husband or the father will dig the pit that is to hold them, beneath the nearest tree; he will himself deposit them within it, and the wind that whispers through the boughs will be their only requiem: but then they pay neither taxes nor tithes, are never expected to pull off a hat or to make a courtesy, and will live and die without hearing or uttering the dreadful words, "God save the king."

SERVANTS—SOCIETY—EVENING PARTIES—MISS WRIGHT'S MARKET—LECTURE

THE greatest difficulty in organising a family establishment in Ohio, is getting servants, or, as it is there called, "getting help"; for it is more than petty treason to the republic to call a free citizen a *servant*. . . . Hundreds of half-naked girls work in the paper-mills, or in any other manufactory, for less than half the wages they would receive in service; but they think their equality is compromised by the latter, and nothing but the wish to obtain some particular article of finery will ever induce them to submit to it. A kind friend, however, exerted herself so effectually for me, that a tall stately lass soon presented herself, saying "I be come to help you." The intelligence was very agreeable, and I welcomed her in the most gracious manner possible, and asked what I should give her by the year.

"O Gimini!" exclaimed the damsel, with a loud laugh, "you be a downright Englisher, sure enough. I should like to see a young lady engage by the year in America! I hope I shall get a husband before many months, or I expect I shall be an outright old maid, for I be most seventeen already: besides, mayhap I may want to go to school. You must just give me a dollar and a half a week, and mother's slave Phillis must come over once a week, I expect, from t'other side the water, to help me clean."

I agreed to the bargain, of course with all dutiful submission; and seeing she was preparing to set to work in a yellow dress, *parsemé* with red roses, I gently hinted, that I thought it was a pity to spoil so fine a gown, and that she had better change it.

" 'Tis just my best and my worst," she answered; "for I've got no other."

And in truth I found that this young lady had left the paternal mansion with no more clothes of any kind than what she had on. I immediately gave her money to purchase what was necessary for cleanliness and decency, and set to work with my daughters to make her a gown. She grinned applause when our labour was completed; but never uttered the slightest expression of gratitude for that, or for any thing else we could do for her. She was constantly asking us to lend her different articles of dress, and when we declined it, she said: "Well, I never seed such grumpy folks as you be; there is several young ladies of my acquaintance what goes to live out now and then with the old women about the town, and they and their gurls always lends them what they asks for; I guess you English thinks we should poison your things, just as bad as if we was negurs." Here I beg to assure the reader, that whenever I give conversations, they were not made *à loisir*, but were written down immediately after they occurred, with all the verbal fidelity my memory permitted.

This young lady left me at the end of two months; because I refused to lend her money enough to buy a silk dress to go to a ball, saying: "Then 'tis not worth my while to stay any longer."

I cannot imagine it possible that such a state of things can be desirable, or beneficial to any of the parties concerned. I might occupy a hundred pages on the subject, and yet fail to give an adequate idea of the sore, angry, ever-wakeful pride that seemed to torment these poor wretches. In many of them it was so excessive, that all feeling of displeasure, or even of ridicule, was lost in pity. One of these was a pretty girl, whose natural disposition must have been gentle and kind; but her good feelings were soured, and her gentleness turned to morbid sensitiveness, by having heard a thousand and a thousand times that she was as good as any other lady; that all men were equal, and women too; and that it was a sin and a shame for a free-born American to be treated like a servant.

When she found she was to dine in the kitchen, she turned up her pretty lip, and said: "I guess that's cause you don't think I'm good enough to eat with you. You'll find that won't do here." I found afterwards that she rarely ate any dinner at all, and generally passed the time in tears. I did everything in my power to conciliate and make her happy, but I am sure she hated me. I gave her very high wages, and she stayed till she had obtained several expensive articles of dress, and then, *un beau matin*, she came to me full dressed, and said: "I must go."—"When shall you return, Charlotte?"—"I expect you'll see no more of me." And so we parted. Her sister was also living with me; but her wardrobe was not yet completed, and she remained some weeks longer, till it was. . . .

Whatever may be the talents of the persons who meet together in society, the very shape, form, and arrangement of the meeting is sufficient to paralyse conversation. The women invariably herd together at one part of the room, and the men at the other; but, in justice to Cincinnati, I must acknowledge that this arrangement is by no means peculiar to that city, or to the western side of the Alleghanies. Sometimes a small attempt at music produces a partial re-union; a few of the most daring youths, animated by the consciousness of curled hair and smart waistcoats, approach the pianoforte, and begin to mutter a little to the half-grown pretty things, who are comparing with one another "how many quarters' music they have had." Where the mansion is of sufficient dignity to have two drawing-rooms, the piano, the little ladies, and the slender gentlemen, are left to themselves, and on such occasions the sound of laughter is often heard to issue from among them. But the fate of the more dignified personages, who are left in the other room, is extremely dismal. The gentlemen spit, talk of elections and the price of produce, and spit again. The ladies look at each other's dresses till they know every pin by heart; talk of Parson Somebody's last sermon on the day of judgment, on Dr. T'otherbody's new pills for dyspepsia, till the "tea" is announced, when they all console themselves together for whatever they may have suffered in keeping awake, by taking more tea, coffee, hot cake and custard, hoe cake, johnny cake, waffle cake, and dodger cake, pickled peaches and preserved cucumbers, ham, turkey, hung beef, apple-sauce, and pickled oysters, than ever were prepared in any other country of the known world. After this massive meal is over, they return to the drawing-room, and it always appeared to me that they remained together as long as they could bear it, and then they rise *en masse*, cloak, bonnet, shawl, and exit.

Perhaps the most advantageous feature in Cincinnati is its market, which, for excellence, abundance, and cheapness, can hardly, I should think, be surpassed in any part of the world, if I except the luxury of fruits, which are very inferior to any I have seen in Europe. There are no butchers, fish-mongers, or indeed any shops for eatables, except *bakeries*, as they are called, in the town; everything must be purchased at market; and to accomplish this, the busy housewife must be stirring betimes, or, 'spite of the abundant supply, she will find her hopes of breakfast, dinner, and supper for the day defeated, the market being pretty well over by eight o'clock.

The beef is excellent, and the highest price when we were there, four cents (about twopence) the pound. The mutton was inferior, and so was veal to the eye, but it ate well, though not very fat; the price was about the same. The poultry was excellent; fowls or full-sized chickens, ready for table, twelve cents, but much less if bought alive, and not quite fat; turkeys about fifty cents, and geese the same. The Ohio furnishes several sorts of fish, some of them very good, and always to be found cheap and abundant in the market. Eggs, butter, nearly all kinds of vegetables, excellent and at moderate prices. From June till December, tomatoes (the great luxury of the American table in the opinion of most Europeans) may be found in the highest perfection in the market for about sixpence the peck. They have a great variety of beans unknown in England, particularly the Lima bean, the seed of which is dressed like the French haricot; it furnishes a very abundant crop, and is a most delicious vegetable. . . . All the fruit I saw exposed for sale in Cincinnati was most miserable. I passed two summers there, but never tasted a peach worth eating. Of apricots and nectarines I saw none; strawberries very small, raspberries much worse; gooseberries very few, and quite uneatable; currants about half the size of ours, and about double the price; grapes too sour for tarts; apples abundant, but very indifferent, none that would be thought good enough for an English table; pears, cherries, and plums, most miserably bad. The flowers of these regions were at least equally inferior: whether this proceeds from want of cultivation, or from peculiarity of soil, I know not; but after leaving Cincinnati, I was told by a gentleman who appeared to understand the subject, that the state of Ohio had no indigenous flowers or fruits. The water-melons, which in that warm climate furnish a delightful refreshment, were abundant and cheap; but all other melons very inferior to those of France, or even of England when ripened in a common hot-bed.

From the almost total want of pasturage near the city, it is difficult for a stranger to divine how milk is furnished for its supply; but we soon learnt that there are more ways than one of keeping a cow. A large proportion of the families in the town, particularly of the poorer class, have one, though apparently, without any accommodation whatever for it. These animals are fed morning and evening, at the door of the house, with a good mess of Indian corn, boiled with water; while they eat, they are milked, and when the operation is completed, the milk-pail and the meal-tub retreat into the dwelling, leaving the republican cow to walk away, to take her pleasure on the hills, or in the gutters, as may suit her fancy best. They generally return very regularly to give and take the morning and evening meal; though it more than once happened to us, before we were supplied by a regular milk-cart, to have our jug sent home empty, with the sad news that "the cow was not come home, and it was too late to look for her to breakfast now". . . .

Soon a lecturer appeared upon the scene, whose purpose of publicly addressing the people was no sooner made known than the most violent sensation was excited.

That a lady of fortune, family, and education, whose youth had been passed in the most refined circles of private life, should present herself to the people as a public lecturer, would naturally excite surprise any where but in America, where women are guarded by a seven-fold shield of habitual insignificance, it caused an effect that can hardly be described. "Miss Wright, of Nashoba, is going to lecture at the court-house," sounded from street to street, and from house to house. I shared the surprise, but not the wonder; I knew her extraordinary gift of eloquence, her almost unequalled command of words, and the wonderful power of her rich and thrilling voice; . . . I was most anxious to hear her, but was almost deterred from attempting it, by the reports that reached me of the immense crowd that was expected. After many consultations, and hearing that many other ladies intended going, my friend Mrs. P——, and myself, decided upon making the attempt, accompanied by a party of gentlemen, and found the difficulty less than we anticipated, though the building was crowded in every part. We congratulated ourselves that we had had the courage to be among the number, for all my expectations fell far short of the splendour, the brilliance, the overwhelming eloquence of this extraordinary orator.

Her lecture was upon the nature of true knowledge, and it contained little that could be objected to by any sect or party; it was intended as an introduction to the strange and startling theories contained in her subsequent lectures, and could alarm only by the hints it contained that the fabric of human wisdom could rest securely on no other base than that of human knowledge.

There was, however, one passage from which common-sense revolted; it was one wherein she quoted that phrase of mischievous sophistry, "all men are born free and equal."

This false and futile axiom, which has done, is doing, and will do so much harm to this fine country, came from Jefferson; . . . I pretend not to criticise his written works, but common-sense enables me to pronounce this, his favourite maxim, false. . . .

ABSENCE OF PUBLIC AND PRIVATE AMUSEMENT—INFLUENCE OF THE CLERGY—SCHOOLS—CLIMATE—FOURTH OF JULY—MOVING HOUSES—LITERATURE

I NEVER saw any people who appeared to live so much without amusement as the Cincinnatians. Billiards are forbidden by law, so are cards. To sell a pack of cards in Ohio subjects the seller to a penalty of fifty dollars. They have no public balls, excepting, I think, six, during the Christmas holidays. They have no concerts. They have no dinner-parties.

They have a theatre, which is, in fact, the only public amusement of this triste little town; but they seem to care little about it, and either from economy or distaste, it is very poorly attended. Ladies are rarely seen there, and by far the larger proportion of females deem it an offence against religion to witness the representation of a play. It is in the churches and chapels of the town that the ladies are to be seen in full costume: and I am tempted to believe that a stranger from the continent of Europe would be inclined, on first reconnoitring the city, to suppose that the places of worship were the theatres and cafés of the place. No evening in the week but brings throngs of the young and beautiful to the chapels and meeting-houses, all dressed with care, and sometimes with great pretension; it is there that all display is made, and all fashionable distinction sought. The proportion of gentlemen attending these evening meetings is very small, but often, as might be expected, a sprinkling of smart young clerks makes this sedulous display of ribbons and ringlets intelligible and natural. Were it not for the churches, indeed, I think there might be a general bonfire of best bonnets, for I never could discover any other use for them.

The ladies are too actively employed in the interior of their houses to permit much parading in full dress for morning visits. There are no public gardens or lounging shops of fashionable resort, and were it not for public worship, and private tea-drinkings, all the ladies in Cincinnati would be in danger of becoming perfect recluses.

The influence which the ministers of all the innumerable religious sects throughout America have on the females of their respective congregations, approaches very nearly to what we read of in Spain, or in other strictly Roman Catholic countries. There are many causes for this peculiar influence. Where equality of rank is affectedly acknowledged by the rich, and clamorously claimed by the poor, distinction and pre-eminence are allowed to the clergy only. This gives them high importance in the eyes of the ladies. I think, also, that it is from the clergy only that the women of America receive that sort of attention which is so dearly valued by every female heart throughout the world. With the priests of America the women hold that degree of influential importance which, in the countries of Europe, is allowed them throughout all orders and ranks of society, except, perhaps, the very lowest; and in return for this they seem to give their hearts and souls into their keeping. I never saw, or read of, any country where religion had so strong a hold upon the women, or a slighter hold upon the men.

I mean not to assert that I met with no men of sincerely religious feelings, or with no women of no religious feelings at all; but I feel perfectly secure of being correct as to the great majority in the statement I have made.

We had not been many months in Cincinnati when our curiosity was excited by hearing the "revival" talked of by every one we met throughout the town. "The revival will be very full", "We shall be constantly engaged during the revival", were the phrases we constantly heard repeated, and for a long time without in the least comprehending what was meant; but at length I learnt that the un-national church of America required to be roused, at regular intervals, to greater energy and exertion. At these seasons the most enthusiastic of the clergy travel the country, and enter the cities and towns by scores, or by hundreds, as the accommodation of the place may admit, and for a week or fortnight, or, if the population be large, for a month, they preach and pray all day, and often for a considerable portion of the night, in the various churches and chapels of the place. This is called a Revival.

I took considerable pains to obtain information on this subject; but in detailing what I learnt I fear that it is probable I shall be accused of exaggeration; all I can do is cautiously to avoid deserving it. The subject is highly interesting, and it would be a fault of no trifling nature to treat it with levity.

These itinerant clergymen are of all persuasions, I believe, except the Episcopalian, Catholic, Unitarian, and Quaker. I heard of Presbyterians of all varieties; of Baptists of I know not how many divisions; and of Methodists of more denominations than I can remember; whose innumerable shades of varying belief it would require much time to explain and more to comprehend. . . . These Itinerants are, for the most part, lodged in the houses of their respective followers, and every evening that is not spent in the churches and meeting-houses, is devoted to what would be called parties by others, but which they designate as prayer-meetings. Here they eat, drink, pray, sing, hear confessions, and make converts. To these meetings I never got invited, and therefore I have nothing but hearsay evidence to offer, but my information comes from an eye-witness, and one on whom I believe I may depend. If one half of what I heard may be believed, these social prayer-meetings are by no means the least curious, or the least important part of the business.

It is impossible not to smile at the close resemblance to be traced between the feelings of a first-rate Presbyterian or Methodist lady, fortunate enough to have secured a favourite Itinerant for her meeting, and those of a first-rate London Blue, equally blest in the presence of a fashionable poet. There is a strong family likeness among us all the world over.

The best rooms, the best dresses, the choicest refreshments solemnise the meeting. While the party is assembling, the load-star [sic] of the hour is occupied in whispering conversations with the guests as they arrive. They are called brothers and sisters, and the greetings are very affectionate. When the room is full, the company, of whom a vast majority are always women, are invited, entreated, and coaxed to confess before their brothers and sisters, all their thoughts, faults, and follies.

These confessions are strange scenes; the more they confess, the more invariably are they encouraged and caressed. When this is over, they all kneel, and the Itinerant prays extempore. They then eat and drink; and then they sing hymns, pray, exhort, sing, and pray again, till the excitement reaches a very high pitch indeed. These scenes are going on at some house or other every evening during the revival, nay, at many at the same time, for the churches and meeting-houses cannot give occupation to half the Itinerants, though they are all open throughout the day, and till a late hour in the night, and the officiating ministers succeed each other in the occupation of them.

It was at the principal of the Presbyterian churches that I was twice witness to scenes that made me shudder . . . On entering, we found three priests standing side by side, in a sort of tribune, placed where the altar usually is, handsomely fitted up with crimson curtains, and elevated about as high as our pulpits. . . .

The priest who stood in the middle was praying; the prayer was extravagantly vehement, and offensively familiar in expression; when this ended, a hymn was sung, and then another priest took the centre place and preached. The sermon had considerable eloquence, but of a frightful kind. The preacher described, with ghastly minuteness, the last feeble fainting moments of human life, and then the gradual progress of decay after death, which he followed through every process up to the last loathsome stage of decomposition. Suddenly changing his tone, which had been that of sober accurate description, into the shrill voice of horror, he bent forward his head, as if to gaze on some object beneath the pulpit. And as Rebecca made known to Ivanhoe what she saw through the window, so the preacher made known to us what he saw in the pit that seemed to open before him. The device was certainly a happy one for giving effect to his description of hell. No image that fire, flame, brimstone, molten lead, or red hot pincers could supply, with flesh, nerves, and sinews quivering under them, was omitted. . . . The acting was excellent. At length he gave a languishing look to his supporters on each side, as if to express his feeble state, and then sat down, and wiped the drops of agony from his brow.

The other two priests arose, and began to sing a hymn. It was some seconds before the congregation could join as usual; every up-turned face looked pale and horror-struck. When the singing ended, another took the centre place, and began in a sort of coaxing affectionate tone, to ask the congregation if what their dear brother had spoken had reached their hearts? Whether they would avoid the hell he had made them see? "Come, then!" he continued, stretching out his arms towards them; "come to us and tell us so, and we will make you see Jesus, the dear gentle Jesus, who shall save you from it. . . ."

Again a hymn was sung, and while it continued, one of the three was employed in clearing one or two long benches that went across the rail . . . The singing ceased, and again the people were invited, and exhorted not to be ashamed of Jesus, but to put themselves upon "the anxious benches", and lay their heads on his bosom. "Once more we will sing", he concluded, "that we may give you time." . . .

And now in every part of the church a movement was perceptible, slight at first, but by degrees becoming more decided. Young girls arose, and sat down, and rose again; and then the pews opened, and several came tottering out, their hands clasped, their heads hanging on their bosoms, and every limb trembling, and still the hymn went on; but as the poor creatures approached the rail their sobs and groans became audible. They seated themselves on the "anxious benches"; the hymn ceased, and two of the three priests walked down from the tribune, and going, one to the right, and the other to the left, began whispering to the poor tremblers seated there. These whispers were inaudible to us, but the sobs and groans increased to a frightful excess. . . .

Meanwhile the two priests continued to walk among them; they repeatedly mounted on the benches, and trumpet-mouthed proclaimed to the whole congregation "the tidings of salvation", and then from every corner of the building arose in reply, short sharp cries of "Amen!", "Glory!", "Amen!", while the prostrate penitents continued to receive whispered comfortings, and from time to time a mystic caress. More than once I saw a young neck encircled by a reverend arm. Violent hysterics and convulsions seized many of them, and when the tumult was at the highest, the priest who remained above again gave out a hymn as if to drown it.

It was a frightful sight to behold innocent young creatures, in the gay morning of existence, thus seized upon, horror-struck, and rendered feeble and enervated for ever. One young girl, apparently not more than fourteen, was supported in the arms of another some years older; her face was pale as death; her eyes wide open, and perfectly devoid of meaning; her chin and bosom wet with slaver; she had every appearance of idiotism. I saw a priest approach her, he took her delicate hand. "Jesus is with her! Bless the Lord!" he said, and passed on.

Did the men of America value their women as men ought to value their wives and daughters, would such scenes be permitted among them?

It is hardly necessary to say, that all who obeyed the call to place themselves on the "anxious benches" were women, and by far the greater number, very young women. The congregation was, in general, extremely well-dressed, and the smartest and most fashionable ladies of the town were there; during the whole revival, the churches and meeting-houses were every day crowded with well-dressed people.

It is thus the ladies of Cincinnati amuse themselves: to attend the theatre is forbidden; to play cards is unlawful; but they work hard in their families, and must have some relaxation. For myself, I confess that I think the coarsest comedy ever written would be a less detestable exhibition for the eyes of youth and innocence than such a scene.

Cincinnati contains many schools, but of their rank or merit I had very little opportunity of judging; the only one which I visited was kept by Dr. Lock, a gentleman who appears to have liberal and enlarged opinions on the subject of female education. . . . I attended the annual public exhibition at this school, and perceived, with some surprise, that the higher branches of science were among the studies of the pretty creatures I saw assembled there. One lovely girl of sixteen *took her degree* in mathematics, and another was examined in moral philosophy. They blushed so sweetly, and looked so beautifully puzzled and confounded, that it might have been difficult for an abler judge than I was, to decide how far they merited the diplomas they received. . . .

"A quarter's" mathematics, or "two quarters'" political economy, moral philosophy, algebra and quadratic equations, would seldom, I should think, enable the teacher and the scholar, by their joint efforts, to lay in such a stock of these sciences as would stand the wear and tear of half a score of children, and one help.

Towards the end of May we began to feel that we were in a climate warmer than any we had been accustomed to, and my son suffered severely from the effects of it. A bilious complaint, attended by a frightful degree of fever, seized him, and for some days we feared for his life. The treatment he received was, I have no doubt, judicious, but the quantity of calomel prescribed was enormous. I asked one day how many grains I should prepare, and was told to give half a tea-spoonful. The difference of climate must, I imagine, make a difference in the effect of this drug, or the practice of the old and new world could hardly differ so widely as it does in the use of it. . . . Repeated and violent bleeding was also had recourse to, in the case of my son, and in a few days he was able to leave his room, but he was dreadfully emaciated, and it was many weeks before he recovered his strength.

As the heat of the weather increased, we heard of much sickness around us. . . . We were advised to avoid, as much as possible, walking out in the heat of the day; but the mornings and evenings were delightful, particularly the former, if taken sufficiently early. For several weeks I was never in bed after four o'clock, and at this hour I almost daily accompanied my "help" to market, where the busy novelty of the scene afforded me much amusement.

Many waggon-loads of enormous water-melons were brought to market every day, and I was sure to see groups of men, women, and children, seated on the pavement round the spot where they were sold, sucking in prodigious quantities of this watery fruit. Their manner of devouring them is extremely unpleasant; the huge fruit is cut into half-a-dozen sections, of about a foot long, and then, dripping as it is with water, applied to the mouth, from either side of which pour copious streams of the fluid, while, ever and anon, a mouthful of the hard black seeds are shot out in all directions, to the great annoyance of all within reach. When I first tasted this fruit, I thought it very vile stuff indeed; but before the end of the season we all learned to like it. When taken with claret and sugar, it makes delicious wine and water. . . .

And now arrived the 4th of July, that greatest of all American festivals. On the 4th of July, 1776, the declaration of their independence was signed, at the State-house in Philadelphia.

To me the dreary coldness and want of enthusiasm in American manner is one of their greatest defects, and I therefore hailed the demonstrations of general feeling which this day elicits, with real pleasure. On the 4th of July the hearts of the people seem to awaken from a three hundred and sixty-four days' sleep; they appear high-spirited, gay, animated, social, generous, or at least, liberal in expense; and would they but refrain from spitting on that hallowed day, I should say that, on the 4th of July, at least, they appeared to be an amiable people. It is true that the women have but little to do with the pageantry, the splendour, or the gaiety of the day; but, setting this defect aside, it was indeed a glorious sight to behold a jubilee so heartfelt as this; and had they not the bad taste and bad feeling to utter an annual oration, with unvarying abuse of the mother country, to say nothing of the warlike manifesto called the Declaration of Independence, our gracious king himself might look upon the scene and say that it was good; nay, even rejoice, that twelve millions of bustling bodies, at four thousand miles distance from his throne and his altars, should make their own laws, and drink their own tea, after the fashion that pleased them best. . . .

One of the sights to stare at in America is that of houses moving from place to place. . . . The largest dwelling that I saw in motion was one containing two stories of four rooms each; forty oxen were yoked to it. The first few yards brought down the two stacks of chimneys, but it afterwards went on well. . . . This locomotive power was extremely convenient to Cincinnati, as the constant improvements going on there made it often desirable to change a wooden dwelling for one of brick; and whenever this happened, we were sure to see the ex-No. 100 of Main Street, or the ex-No. 55 of Second Street, creeping quietly out of town, to take possession of an humble suburban station on the common above it. . . .

On one occasion . . . I passed an evening in company with a gentleman, said to be a scholar, and a man of reading; he was also what is called a *serious* gentleman, and he appeared to have pleasure in feeling that his claim to distinction was acknowledged in both capacities. There was a very amiable *serious* lady in the company, to whom he seemed to trust for the development of his celestial pretensions, and to me he did the honour of addressing most of his terrestrial superiority. The difference between us was, that when he spoke to her, he spoke as to a being who, if not his equal, was at least deserving high distinction; and he gave her smiles, such as Michael might have vouchsafed to Eve. To me he spoke as Paul to the offending Jews; he did not, indeed, shake his raiment at me, but he used his pocket-handkerchief so as to answer the purpose; and if every sentence did not end with "I am clean", pronounced by his lips, his tone, his look, his action, fully supplied the deficiency.

Our poor Lord Byron, as may be supposed, was the bull's-eye against which every dart in his black little quiver was aimed. I had never heard any serious gentleman talk of Lord Byron at full length before, and I listened attentively. It was evident that the noble passages which are graven on the hearts of the genuine lovers of poetry had altogether escaped the serious gentleman's attention; and it was equally evident that he knew by rote all those that they wish the mighty master had never written. I told him so, and I shall not soon forget the look he gave me.

Of other authors his knowledge was very imperfect, but his criticisms very amusing. Of Pope, he said: "He is so entirely gone by, that in *our* country it is considered quite fustian to speak of him."

But I persevered, and named *The Rape of the Lock* as evincing some little talent, and being in a tone that might still hope for admittance in the drawing-room; but, on the mention of this poem, the serious gentleman became almost as strongly agitated as when he talked of *Don Juan;* and I was unfeignedly at a loss to comprehend the nature of his feelings, till he muttered, with an indignant shake of the handkerchief: "The very title!"

At the name of Dryden he smiled, and the smile spoke as plainly as a smile could speak "How the old woman twaddles!"

"We only know Dryden by quotations, madam, and these, indeed, are found only in books that have long since had their day."

"And Shakspeare, sir?"

"Shakspeare, madam, is obscene, and, thank God, we are sufficiently advanced to have found it out! If we must have the abomination of stage plays, let them at least be marked by the refinement of the age in which we live."

This was certainly being *au courant du jour.*

Of Massinger he knew nothing. Of Ford he had never heard. Gray had had his day. Prior he had never read, but understood he was a very childish writer. Chaucer and Spenser he tied in a couple, and dismissed by saying, that he thought it was neither more nor less than affectation to talk of authors who wrote in a tongue no longer intelligible.

This was the most literary conversation I was ever present at in Cincinnati. . . .

The fact is, that throughout all ranks of society, from the successful merchant, which is the highest, to the domestic serving man, which is the lowest, they are all too actively employed to read, except at such broken moments as may suffice for a peep at a newspaper. It is for this reason, I presume, that every American newspaper is more or less a magazine, wherein the merchant may scan, while he holds out his hand for an invoice, "Stanzas by Mrs. Hemans", or a garbled extract from Moore's *Life of Byron;* the lawyer may study his brief faithfully, and yet contrive to pick up the valuable dictum of some American critic, that "Bulwer's novels are decidedly superior to Sir Walter Scott's"; nay, even the auctioneer may find time, as he bustles to the tub, or his tribune, to support his pretensions to polite learning, by glancing his quick eye over the columns, and reading that "Miss Mitford's descriptions are indescribable". If you buy a yard of ribbon, the shopkeeper lays down his newspaper, perhaps two or three, to measure it. I have seen a brewer's drayman perched on the shaft of his dray and reading one newspaper, while another was tucked under his arm; and I once went into the cottage of a country shoemaker, of the name of Harris, where I saw a newspaper half full of "original" poetry, directed to Madison F. Harris. To be sure of the fact, I asked the man if his name were Madison. "Yes, madam, Madison Franklin Harris is my name." The last and the lyre divided his time, I fear too equally, for he looked pale and poor.

This, I presume, is what is meant by the general diffusion of knowledge, so boasted of in the United States; such as it is, the diffusion of it is general enough, certainly; but I greatly doubt its being advantageous to the population. . . .

Removal to the Country—Equality—Religion

At length, my wish of obtaining a house in the country was gratified. . . . It was situated in a little village about a mile and a half from the town, close to the foot of the hills . . . We found ourselves much more comfortable here than in the city. The house was pretty and commodious, our sitting-rooms were cool and airy; we had got rid of the detestable mosquitoes, and we had an ice-house that never failed. Besides all this, we had the pleasure of gathering our tomatoes from our own garden, and receiving our milk from our own cow. Our manner of life was infinitely more to my taste than before; it gave us all the privileges of rusticity, which are fully as incompatible with the residence in a little town of Western America as with a residence in London. We lived on terms of primeval intimacy with our cow; for if we lay down on our lawn, she did not scruple to take a sniff at the book we were reading, but then she gave us her own sweet breath in return. . . .

We were now in daily expectation of the arrival of Mr. T.; but day after day, and week after week passed by, till we began to fear some untoward circumstance might delay his coming till the spring. At last, when we had almost ceased to look out for him, on the road which led from the town, he arrived, late at night, by that which leads across the country from Pittsburgh. The pleasure we felt at seeing him was greatly increased by his bringing with him our eldest son, which was a happiness we had not hoped for. Our walks and our drives now became doubly interesting. The young men, fresh from a public school, found America so totally unlike all the nations with which their reading had made them acquainted, that it was indeed a new world to them. . . .

The extraordinary familiarity of our poor neighbours startled us at first, and we hardly knew how to receive their uncouth advances, or what was expected of us in return; however, it sometimes produced very laughable scenes. Upon one occasion, two of my children set off upon an exploring walk up the hills; they were absent rather longer than we expected, and the rest of our party determined upon going out to meet them; we knew the direction they had taken, but thought it would be as well to inquire at a little public-house at the bottom of the hill, if such a pair had been seen to pass. A woman, whose appearance more resembled a Covent Garden market-woman than anything else I can remember, came out and answered my question with the most jovial good humour in the affirmative, and prepared to join us in our search. Her look, her voice, her manner, were so exceedingly coarse and vehement, that she almost frightened me; she passed her arm within mine, and to the inexpressible amusement of my young people, she dragged me on, talking and questioning me without ceasing. She lived but a short distance from us, and I am sure intended to be a very good neighbour; but her violent intimacy made me dread to pass her door; my children, including my sons, she always addressed by their Christian names, excepting when she substituted the word "honey": this familiarity of address, however, I afterwards found was universal throughout all ranks in the United States.

My general appellation amongst my neighbours was "the English old woman", but in mentioning each other they constantly employed the term "lady"; and they evidently had a pleasure in using it, for I repeatedly observed, that in speaking of a neighbour, instead of saying Mrs. Such-a-one, they described her as "the lady over the way what takes in washing", or as "that there lady, out by the gully, what is making dip-candles". Mr. Trollope was as constantly called "the old man", while draymen, butchers' boys, and the labourers on the canal, were invariably denominated "them gentlemen"; nay, we once saw one of the most gentleman-like men in Cincinnati introduce a fellow in dirty shirt-sleeves, and all sorts of detestable et cetera, to one of his friends, with this formula, "D——, let me introduce this gentleman to you!"

Our respective titles certainly were not very important; but the eternal shaking hands with these ladies and gentlemen was really an annoyance, and the more so, as the near approach of the gentlemen was always redolent of whiskey and tobacco.

But the point where this republican equality was the most distressing was in the long and frequent visitations that it produced. No one dreams of fastening a door in Western America; I was told that it would be considered as an affront by the whole neighbourhood. I was thus exposed to perpetual, and most vexatious interruptions from people whom I have often never seen, and whose names still oftener were unknown to me.

Those who are native there, and to the manner born, seem to pass over these annoyances with more skill than I could ever acquire. More than once I have seen some of my acquaintance beset in the same way, without appearing at all distressed by it; they continued their employment or conversation with me, much as if no such interruption had taken place; when the visitor entered, they would say "How do you do?" and shake hands.

"Tolerable, I thank ye; how be you?" was the reply.

If it was a female, she took off her hat; if a male, he kept it on, and then taking possession of the first chair in the way, would retain it for an hour together, without uttering another word; at length, rising abruptly, he would again shake hands, with "Well, now I must be going, I guess", and so take himself off, apparently well contented with their reception.

I could never attain this philosophical composure; I could neither write nor read, and I always fancied I must talk to them. I will give the minutes of a conversation which I once set down after one of these visits, as a specimen of their tone and manner of speaking and thinking. My visitor was a milkman.

"Well now, so you be from the old country? Ah—you'll see sights here, I guess."

"I hope I shall see many."

"That's a fact. I expect your little place of an island don't grow such dreadful fine corn as you see here?"

"It grows no corn at all, sir."

"Possible! no wonder, then, that we reads such awful stories of your poor people being starved to death."

"We have wheat, however."

"Ay, for your rich folks, but I calculate the poor seldom gets a belly-full."

"You have certainly much greater abundance here."

"I expect so. Why they do say, that if a poor body contrives to be smart enough to scrape together a few dollars, that your King George always comes down upon 'em, and takes it all away. Don't he?"

"I do not remember hearing of such a transaction."

"I guess they be pretty close about it. Your papers ben't like ourn, I reckon? Now we says and prints just what we likes."

"You spend a good deal of time reading the newspapers."

"And I'd like you to tell me how we can spend it better. How should freemen spend their time, but looking after their government, and watching that them fellers as we gives offices to, doos their duty, and give themselves no airs?"

"But I sometimes think, sir, that your fences might be in more thorough repair, and your roads in better order, if less time was spent in politics."

"The Lord! to see how little you knows of a free country! Why, what's the smoothness of a road, put against the freedom of a free-born American? And what does a broken zigzag signify, comparable to knowing that the men what we have been pleased to send up to Congress, speaks handsome and straight, as we chooses they should?"

"It is from a sense of duty, then, that you all go to the liquor store to read the papers?"

"To be sure it is, and he'd be no true-born American as didn't. I don't say that the father of a family should always be after liquor, but I do say that I'd rather have my son drunk three times in a week, than not look after the affairs of his country." . . .

Our walks were . . . curtailed in several directions by my old Cincinnati enemies, the pigs; immense droves of them were continually arriving from the country by the road that led to most of our favourite walks; they were often fed and lodged in the prettiest valleys, and worse still, were slaughtered beside the prettiest streams. Another evil threatened us from the same quarter, that was yet heavier. Our cottage had an ample piazza (a luxury almost universal in the country houses of America), which, shaded by a group of acacias, made a delightful sitting-room; from this favourite spot we one day perceived symptoms of building in a field close to it; with much anxiety we hastened to the spot, and asked what building was to be erected there.

"'Tis to be a slaughter-house for hogs" was the dreadful reply. As there were several gentlemen's houses in the neighbourhood, I asked if such an erection might not be indicted as a nuisance.

"A what?"

"A nuisance" I repeated, and explained what I meant.

"No, no" was the reply; "that may do very well for your tyrannical country, where a rich man's nose is more thought of than a poor man's mouth; but hogs be profitable produce here, and we be too free for such a law as that, I guess." . . .

All the freedom enjoyed in America, beyond what is enjoyed in England, is enjoyed solely by the disorderly at the expense of the orderly; and were I a stout knight, either of the sword or of the pen, I would fearlessly throw down my gauntlet, and challenge the whole republic to prove the contrary: but being, as I am, a feeble looker-on, with a needle for my spear, and "I talk" for my device, I must be contented with the power of stating the fact, perfectly certain that I shall be contradicted by one loud shout from Maine to Georgia.

I had often heard it observed, before I visited America, that one of the great blessings of its constitution was the absence of a national religion, the country being thus exonerated from all obligation of supporting the clergy; those only contributing to do so whose principles led them to it. My residence in the country has shown me that a religious tyranny may be exerted very effectually without the aid of the government, in a way much more oppressive than the paying of tithe, and without obtaining any of the salutary decorum, which I presume no one will deny is the result of an established mode of worship.

As it was impossible to remain many weeks in the country without being struck with the strange anomalies produced by its religious system, my early notes contain many observations on the subject; but as nearly the same scenes recurred in every part of the country, I state them here, not as belonging to the West alone, but to the whole Union, the same cause producing the same effect everywhere.

The whole people appear to be divided into an almost endless variety of religious factions, and I was told, that to be well received in society, it was necessary to declare yourself as belonging to some one of these. Let your acknowledged belief be what it may, you are said to be *not a Christian,* unless you attach yourself to a particular congregation. Besides the broad and well-known distinctions of Episcopalian, Roman Catholic, Presbyterian, Calvinist, Baptist, Quaker, Swedenborgian, Universalist, Dunker, etc., . . . there are innumerable others springing out of these, each of which assumes a church government of its own; of this, the most intriguing and factious individual is invariably the head; and in order, as it should seem, to show a reason for this separation, each congregation invests itself with some queer variety of external observance that has the melancholy effect of exposing *all* religious ceremonies to contempt. . . .

I believe I am sufficiently tolerant; but this does not prevent my seeing that the object of all religious observances is better obtained, when the government of the church is confided to the wisdom and experience of the most venerated among the people, than when it is placed in the hands of every tinker and tailor who chooses to claim a share in it. Nor is this the only evil attending the want of a national religion, supported by the state. As there is no legal and fixed provision for the clergy, it is hardly surprising that their services are confined to those who can pay them. The vehement expressions of insane or hypocritical zeal, such as were exhibited during "the revival", can but ill atone for the want of village worship, any more than the eternal talk of the admirable and unequalled government can atone for the continual contempt of social order. Church and state hobble along, side by side, notwithstanding their boasted independence. Almost every man you meet will tell you, that he is occupied in labours most abundant for the good of his country; and almost every woman will tell you, that besides those things that are within (her house), she has coming upon her daily the care of all the churches. Yet spite of this universal attention to the government, its laws are half asleep; and spite of the old women and their Dorcas societies, atheism is awake and thriving.

In the smaller cities and towns, prayer-meetings take the place of almost all other amusements; but as the thinly scattered population of most villages can give no parties, and pay no priests, they contrive to marry, christen, and bury, without them. A stranger taking up his residence in any city of America, must think the natives the most religious people upon earth; but if chance lead him among her western villages, he will rarely find either churches or chapels, prayer or preacher; except, indeed, at that most terrific saturnalia, "a camp-meeting." I was much struck with the answer of a poor woman, whom I saw ironing on a Sunday. "Do you make no difference in your occupations on a Sunday?" I said. "I beant a Christian, ma'am; we have got no opportunity" was the reply. It occurred to me, that in a country where "all men are equal", the government would be guilty of no great crime, did it so far interfere as to give them all *an opportunity* of becoming Christians if they wished it. . . .

Peasantry, compared to that of England—Charity—Independence and Equality—Cottage Prayer-Meeting

Mohawk, as our little village was called, gave us an excellent opportunity of comparing the peasants of the United States with those of England, and of judging the average degree of comfort enjoyed by each. I believe Ohio gives as fair a specimen as any part of the Union; if they have the roughness and inconveniences of a new state to contend with, they have higher wages and cheaper provisions; if I err in supposing it a mean state in point of comfort, it certainly is not in taking too low a standard.

Mechanics, if good workmen, are certain of employment and good wages, rather higher than with us; the average wages of a labourer throughout the Union is ten dollars a month, with lodging, boarding, washing, and mending; if he lives at his own expense he has a dollar a day. It appears to me that the necessaries of life, that is to say, meat, bread, butter, tea, and coffee (not to mention whiskey), are within the reach of every sober, industrious, and healthy man who chooses to have them; and yet I think that an English peasant, with the same qualifications, would, in coming to the United States, change for the worse. He would find wages somewhat higher, and provisions in Western America considerably lower; but this statement, true as it is, can lead to nothing but delusion if taken apart from other facts, fully as certain, and not less important but which require more detail in describing, and which perhaps cannot be fully comprehended, except by an eye-witness. The American poor are accustomed to eat meat three times a day; I never inquired into the habits of any cottagers in Western America where this was not the case. I found afterwards in Maryland, Pennsylvania, and other parts of the country, where the price of meat was higher, that it was used with more economy; yet still a much larger portion of the weekly income is thus expended than with us. Ardent spirits, though lamentably cheap, still cost something, and the use of them among the men, with more or less of discretion, according to the character, is universal. Tobacco also grows at their doors, and is not taxed; yet this too costs something, and the air of heaven is not in more general use among the men of America than chewing tobacco. . . . Long, disabling, and expensive fits of sickness are incontestably more frequent in every part of America than in England, and the sufferers have no aid to look to, but what they have saved, or what they may be enabled to sell. I have never seen misery exceed what I witnessed in an American cottage where disease has entered.

But if the condition of the labourer be not superior to that of the English peasant, that of his wife and daughters is incomparably worse. It is they who are indeed the slaves of the soil. One has but to look at the wife of an American cottager, and ask her age, to be convinced that the life she leads is one of hardship, privation, and labour. It is rare to see a woman in this station who has reached the age of thirty, without losing every trace of youth and beauty. You continually see women with infants on the knee, that you feel sure are their grand-children, till some convincing proof of the contrary is displayed. Even the young girls, though often with lovely features, look pale, thin, and haggard. . . . The horror of domestic service, which the reality of slavery, and the fable of equality, have generated, excludes the young women from that sure and most comfortable resource of decent English girls; and the consequence is, that with a most irreverent freedom of manner to the parents, the daughters are, to the full extent of the word, domestic slaves. This condition, which no periodical merry-making, no village *fête*, ever occurs to cheer, is only changed for the still sadder burthens of a teeming wife. They marry very young; . . . The slender childish thing, without vigour of mind or body, is made to stem a sea of troubles that dims her young eye and makes her cheek grow pale, even before nature has given it the last beautiful finish of the full-grown woman.

"We shall get along" is the answer in full for all that can be said in way of advice to a boy and girl, who take it into their heads to go before a magistrate and "get married." They do get along, till sickness overtakes them, by means perhaps of borrowing a kettle from one and a teapot from another; but intemperance, idleness, or sickness, will, in one week, plunge those who are even getting along well, into utter destitution; and where this happens, they are completely without resource.

The absence of poor-laws is, without doubt, a blessing to the country, but they have not that natural and reasonable dependence on the richer classes which, in countries differently constituted, may so well supply their place. I suppose there is less alms-giving in America than in any other Christian country on the face of the globe. It is not in the temper of the people either to give or to receive. . . .

I had not been three days at Mohawk Cottage, before a pair of ragged children came to ask for medicine for a sick mother; and when it was given to them, the eldest produced a handful of cents, and desired to know what he was to pay. The superfluous milk of our cow was sought after eagerly, but every new-comer always proposed to pay for it. When they found out that "the English old woman" did not sell any thing, I am persuaded they by no means liked her the better for it; but they seemed to think, that if she were a fool it was no reason they should be so too, and accordingly the borrowing, as they called it, became very constant, but always in a form that showed their dignity and freedom. One woman sent to borrow a pound of cheese; another half a pound of coffee; and more than once an intimation accompanied the milk-jug, that the milk must be fresh, and unskimmed: on one occasion the messenger refused milk, and said "Mother only wanted a little cream for her coffee."

I could never teach them to believe, during above a year that I lived at this house, that I would not sell the old clothes of the family; and so pertinacious were they in bargain-making, that often, when I had given them the articles which they wanted to purchase, they would say: "Well, I expect I shall have to do a turn of work for this; you may send for me when you want me." But as I never did ask for the turn of work, and as this formula was constantly repeated, I began to suspect that it was spoken solely to avoid uttering that most un-American phrase, "I thank you."

There was one man whose progress in wealth I watched with much interest and pleasure. When I first became his neighbour, himself, his wife, and four children, were living in one room, with plenty of beef-steaks and onions for breakfast, dinner, and supper; but with very few other comforts. He was one of the finest men I ever saw, full of natural intelligence and activity of mind and body, but he could neither read nor write. . . . He made an engagement with the proprietor of the wooded hill before mentioned, by which half the wood he could fell was to be his own. His unwearied industry made this a profitable bargain, and from the proceeds he purchased the materials for building a comfortable frame (or wooden) house; he did the work almost entirely himself. He then got a job for cutting rails; and as he could cut twice as many in a day as any other man in the neighbourhood, he made a good thing of it. He then let half his pretty house, which was admirably constructed, with an ample portico, that kept it always cool. His next step was contracting for the building of a wooden bridge; and when I left Mohawk, he had fitted up his half of the building as a hotel and grocery store; and I have no doubt that every sun that sets sees him a richer man than when it rose. He hopes to make his son a lawyer; and I have little doubt that he will live to see him sit in Congress. When this time arrives, the wood-cutter's son will rank with any other member of Congress, not of courtesy, but of right; and the idea that his origin is a disadvantage, will never occur to the imagination of the most exalted of his fellow-citizens.

This is the only feature in American society that I recognise as indicative of the equality they profess. Any man's son may become the equal of any other man's son; and the consciousness of this is certainly a spur to exertion: on the other hand, it is also a spur to that coarse familiarity, untempered by any shadow of respect, which is assumed by the grossest and the lowest in their intercourse with the highest and most refined. This is a positive evil; and, I think, more than balances its advantages.

And here again it may be observed, that the theory of equality may be very daintily discussed by English gentlemen in a London dining-room, when the servant, having placed a fresh bottle of cool wine on the table, respectfully shuts the door, and leaves them to their walnuts and their wisdom; but it will be found less palatable when it presents itself in the shape of a hard greasy paw, and is claimed in accents that breathe less of freedom than of onions and whiskey. Strong, indeed, must be the love of equality in an English breast, if it can survive a tour through the Union. . . .

Another of our cottage acquaintance was a market-gardener, from whom we frequently bought vegetables; from the wife of this man we one day received a very civil invitation to "please to come and pass the evening with them in prayer." The novelty of the circumstance, and its great dissimilarity to the ways and manners of our own country, induced me to accept the invitation, and also to record the visit here.

We were received with great attention, and a place was assigned us on one of the benches that surrounded the little parlour. Several persons, looking like mechanics and their wives, were present; every one sat in profound silence, and with that quiet subdued air, that serious people assume on entering a church. At length, a long, black, grim-looking man entered; his dress, the cut of his hair, and his whole appearance, strongly recalled the idea of one of Cromwell's fanatics. He stepped solemnly into the middle of the room, and took a chair that stood there, but not to sit upon it; he turned the back towards him, on which he placed his hands, and stoutly uttering a sound between a hem and a cough, he deposited freely on either side of him a considerable portion of masticated tobacco. He then began to preach. His text was "Live in hope", and he continued to expound it for two hours, in a drawling, nasal tone, with no other respite than what he allowed himself for expectoration. If I say that he repeated the words of his text a hundred times, I think I shall not exceed the truth, for that allows more than a minute for each repetition, and in fact the whole discourse was made up of it. The various tones in which he uttered it might have served as a lesson on emphasis; as a question—in accents of triumph—in accents of despair—of pity—of threatening—of authority—of doubt—of hope—of faith. Having exhausted every imaginable variety of tone, he abruptly said: "Let us pray", and twisting his chair round, knelt before it. Every one knelt before the seat they had occupied, and listened for another half-hour to a rant of miserable, low, familiar jargon, that he presumed to *improviser* to his Maker as a prayer. . . . I inquired afterwards of a friend, well acquainted with such matters, how the grim preacher of "Hope" got paid for his labours, and he told me that the trade was an excellent one, for that many a gude wife bestowed more than a tithe of what her gude man trusted to her keeping, in rewarding the zeal of these self-chosen apostles. Those sable ministers walk from house to house, or if the distance be considerable, ride on a comfortable ambling nag. . . . When they see a house that promises comfortable lodging and entertainment, they enter there, and say to the good woman of the house,

"Sister, shall I pray with you?" If the answer be favourable, and it is seldom otherwise, he instals himself and his horse till after breakfast the next morning. The best meat, drink, and lodging are his, while he stays, and he seldom departs without some little contribution in money for the support of the crucified and suffering church. Is it not strange that "the most intelligent people in the world" should prefer such a religion as this, to a form established by the wisdom and piety of the ablest and best among the erring sons of men, solemnly sanctioned by the nation's law, and rendered sacred by the use of their fathers? . . .

Theatre—Fine Arts—Delicacy—Visit of the President

The theatre at Cincinnati is small, and not very brilliant in decoration, but in the absence of every other amusement our young men frequently attended it, and in the bright clear nights of autumn and winter, the mile and a half of distance was not enough to prevent the less enterprising members of the family from sometimes accompanying them. The great inducement to this was the excellent acting of Mr. and Mrs. Alexander Drake, the managers. Nothing could be more distinct than their line of acting, but the great versatility of their powers enabled them often to appear together. . . .

It was painful to see these excellent performers playing to a miserable house, not a third full, and the audience probably not including half a dozen persons who would prefer their playing to that of the vilest strollers. In proof of this, I saw them, as managers, give place to paltry third-rate actors from London, who would immediately draw crowded houses, and be overwhelmed with applause. . . .

The theatre was really not a bad one, though the very poor receipts rendered it impossible to keep it in high order; but an annoyance infinitely greater than decorations indifferently clean, was the style and manner of the audience. Men came into the lower tier of boxes without their coats; and I have seen shirt sleeves tucked up to the shoulder; the spitting was incessant, and the mixed smell of onions and whiskey was enough to make one feel even the Drakes' acting dearly bought by the obligation of enduring its accompaniments. The bearing and attitudes of the men are perfectly indescribable; the heels thrown higher than the head, the entire rear of the person presented to the audience, the whole length supported on the benches, are among the varieties that these exquisite posture-masters exhibit. The noises, too, were perpetual, and of the most unpleasant kind; the applause is expressed by cries and thumping with the feet, instead of clapping; and when a patriotic fit seized them, and *Yankee Doodle* was called for, every man seemed to think his reputation as a citizen depended on the noise he made.

Two very indifferent figurantes, probably from the Ambigue Comique, or la Gaieté, made their appearance at Cincinnati while we were there; and had Mercury stepped down, and danced a *pas seul* upon earth, his godship could not have produced a more violent sensation. But wonder and admiration were by no means the only feelings excited; horror and dismay were produced in at least an equal degree. No one, I believe, doubted their being admirable dancers, but every one agreed that the morals of the Western world would never recover the shock. When I was asked if I had ever seen any thing so dreadful before, I was embarrassed how to answer; for the young women had been exceedingly careful, both in their dress and in their dancing, to meet the taste of the people; but had it been Virginie[3] in her most transparent attire, or Taglioni[4] in her most remarkable pirouette, they could not have been more reprobated. The ladies altogether forsook the theatre; the gentlemen muttered under their breath, and turned their heads aside when the subject was mentioned; the clergy denounced them from the pulpit; and if they were named at the meetings of the saints, it was to show how deep the horror such a theme could produce. I could not but ask myself if virtue were a plant, thriving under one form in one country, and flourishing under a different one in another? If these Western Americans are right, then how dreadfully wrong are we! It is really a very puzzling subject.

But this was not the only point on which I found my notions of right and wrong utterly confounded; hardly a day passed in which I did not discover that something or other that I had been taught to consider lawful as eating, was held in abhorrence by those around me; many words to which I had never heard an objectionable meaning attached, were totally interdicted, and the strangest paraphrastic sentences substituted. I confess it struck me, that notwithstanding a general stiffness of manner, which I think must exceed that of the Scribes and Pharisees, the Americans have imaginations that kindle with alarming facility. I could give many anecdotes to prove this, but will content myself with a few.

A young German gentleman of perfectly good manners, once came to me greatly chagrined at having offended one of the principal families in the neighbourhood, by having pronounced the word *corset* before the ladies of it. An old female friend had kindly overcome her own feelings so far as to mention to him the cause of the coolness he had remarked, and strongly advised his making an apology. He told me that he was perfectly well disposed to do so, but felt himself greatly at a loss how to word it.

An English lady who had long kept a fashionable boarding-school in one of the Atlantic cities, told me that one of her earliest cares with every new-comer, was the endeavour to substitute real delicacy for this affected precision of manner; among many anecdotes she told me one of a young

[3]Probably refers to the heroine of Paul et Virginie, Bernardin de Saint-Pierre's romance.

[4]Maria Taglioni, whose Paris debut in 1827 made a great furore.

lady about fourteen, who on entering the receiving room, where she only expected to see a lady who had inquired for her, and finding a young man with her, put her hands before her eyes, and ran out of the room again, screaming "A man! a man! a man!" . . .

At Cincinnati there is a garden where the people go to eat ices, and to look at roses. For the preservation of the flowers, there is placed at the end of one of the walks a sign-post sort of daub, representing a Swiss peasant girl, holding in her hand a scroll, requesting that the roses might not be gathered. Unhappily for the artist, or for the proprietor, or for both, the petticoat of this figure was so short as to show her ankles. The ladies saw, and shuddered; and it was formally intimated to the proprietor, that if he wished for the patronage of the ladies of Cincinnati, he must have the petticoat of this figure lengthened. The affrighted purveyor of ices sent off an express for the artist and his paint pot. He came, but unluckily not provided with any colour that would match the petticoat; the necessity, however, was too urgent for delay, and a flounce of blue was added to the petticoat of red, giving bright and shining evidence before all men, of the immaculate delicacy of the Cincinnati ladies. . . .

I once mentioned to a young lady that I thought a pic-nic party would be very agreeable, and that I would propose it to some of our friends. She agreed that it would be delightful, but she added: "I fear you will not succeed; we are not used to such sort of things here, and I know it is considered very indelicate for ladies and gentlemen to sit down together on the grass." . . .

And now the time arrived that our domestic circle was again to be broken up. Our eldest son was to be entered at Oxford, and it was necessary that his father should accompany him: and, after considerable indecision, it was at length determined that I and my daughters should remain another year with our second son. It was early in February, and our travellers prepared themselves to encounter some sharp gales upon the mountains, though the great severity of the cold appeared to be past. We got buffalo robes and double shoes prepared for them, and they were on the eve of departure when we heard that General Jackson, the newly-elected President, was expected to arrive immediately at Cincinnati, from his residence in the West, and to proceed by steam-boat to Pittsburgh on his way to Washington. This determined them not to fix the day of their departure till they heard of his arrival, and then, if possible, to start in the same boat with him; the decent dignity of a private conveyance not being deemed necessary for the President of the United States. . . .

The news reached us that the general had arrived at Louisville, and was expected at Cincinnati in a few hours. All was bustle and hurry at Mohawk Cottage; we quickly despatched our packing business, and this being the first opportunity we had had of witnessing such a demonstration of popular feeling, we all determined to be present at the debarkation of the great man. We accordingly walked to Cincinnati, and secured a favourable station at the landing-place, both for the purpose of seeing the first magistrate, and of observing his reception by the people. We had waited but for a few moments when the heavy panting of the steam-engines and then a discharge of cannon told that we were just in time; another moment brought his vessel in sight.

The crowd on the shore awaited her arrival in perfect stillness. When she touched the bank the people on board gave a faint huzza, but it was answered by no note of welcome from the land: this cold silence was certainly not produced by any want of friendly feeling towards the new President; during the whole of the canvassing he had been decidedly the popular candidate at Cincinnati, and for months past we had been accustomed to the cry of "Jackson for ever!" from an overwhelming majority; but enthusiasm is not either the virtue or the vice of America.

More than one private carriage was stationed at the water's edge to await the general's orders, but they were dismissed with the information that he would walk to the hotel. Upon receiving this intimation the silent crowd divided itself in a very orderly manner, leaving a space for him to walk through them. He did so, uncovered, though the distance was considerable, and the weather very cold; but he alone (with the exception of a few European gentlemen who were present) was without a hat. He wore his grey hair carelessly, but not ungracefully arranged, and, spite of his harsh gaunt features, he looks like a gentleman and a soldier. He was in deep mourning, having very recently lost his wife; they were said to have been very happy together, and I was pained by hearing a voice near me exclaim, as he approached the spot where I stood: "There goes Jackson; where is his wife?" Another sharp voice, at a little distance, cried: "Adams for ever!" And these sounds were all I heard to break the silence. . . .

At the hour appointed by the Captain, Mr. T. and his son accompanied the general on board; and by subsequent letters I learnt that they had conversed a good deal with him, and were pleased by his conversation and manners, but deeply disgusted by the brutal familiarity to which they saw him exposed at every place on their progress at which they stopped. . . .

Public Ball—Separation of the Sexes—American Freedom

In noting the various brilliant events which diversified our residence in the western metropolis, I have omitted to mention the Birthday Ball, as it is called, a festivity which, I believe, has place on the 22nd of February, in every town and city throughout the Union. It is the anniversary of the birth of General Washington, and well deserves to be marked by the Americans as a day of jubilee.

I was really astonished at the *coup d'œil* on entering, for I saw a large room filled with extremely well-dressed company, among whom were many very beautiful girls. The gentlemen also were exceedingly smart; but I had not yet been long enough in Western America not to feel startled at recognising in almost every full-dressed *beau* that passed me, the master or shopman that I had been used to see behind the counter, or lolling at the door of every shop in the city. The fairest and finest *belles* smiled and smirked on them with as much zeal and satisfaction as I ever saw bestowed on an eldest son, and I therefore could feel no doubt of their being considered as of the highest rank. Yet it must not be supposed that there is no distinction of classes; at this same ball I was looking among the many very beautiful girls I saw there for one more beautiful still, with whose lovely face I had been particularly struck at the school examination I have mentioned. I could not find her, and asked a gentleman why the beautiful Miss C—— was not there.

"You do not yet understand our aristocracy," he replied; "the family of Miss C—— are mechanics."

"But the young lady has been educated at the same school as these, whom I see here, and I know her brother has a shop in the town, quite as large, and apparently as prosperous, as those belonging to any of these young men. What is the difference?"

"He is a mechanic: he assists in making the articles he sells; the others call themselves merchants." . . .

The arrangements for the supper were very singular, but eminently characteristic of the country. The gentlemen had a splendid entertainment spread for them in another large room of the hotel, while the poor ladies had each a plate put into their hands, as they pensively promenaded the ball-room during their absence; and shortly afterwards servants appeared bearing trays of sweetmeats, cakes, and creams. The fair creatures then sat down on a row of chairs placed round the walls, and each making a table of her knees, began eating her sweet, but sad and sulky, repast. The effect was extremely comic: their gala-dresses and the decorated room forming a contrast the most unaccountable with their uncomfortable and forlorn condition.

This arrangement was owing neither to economy nor want of a room large enough to accommodate the whole party, but purely because the gentlemen liked it better. . . .

I am led to mention this feature of American manners very frequently, not only because it constantly recurs, but because I consider it as being in a great degree the cause of that universal deficiency in good manners and graceful demeanour, both in men and women, which is so remarkable. . . .

The hours of enjoyment are important to human beings every where, and we every where find them preparing to make the most of them. . . . Wherever the highest enjoyment is found by both sexes, in scenes where they meet each other, both will prepare themselves to appear with advantage there. The men will not indulge in the luxury of chewing tobacco, or even of spitting, and the women will contrive to be capable of holding a higher post than that of unwearied tea-makers.

In America, with the exception of dancing, which is almost wholly confined to the unmarried of both sexes, all the enjoyments of the men are found in the absence of the women. They dine, they play cards, they have musical meetings, they have suppers, all in large parties, but all without women. Were it not that such is the custom, it is impossible but that they would have ingenuity enough to find some expedient for sparing the wives and daughters of the opulent the sordid offices of household drudgery, which they almost all perform in their families. Even in the slave-states, though they may not clear-starch and iron, mix puddings and cakes one half of the day, and watch them baking the other half, still the very highest occupy themselves in their household concerns, in a manner that precludes the possibility of their becoming elegant and enlightened companions. In Baltimore, Philadelphia, and New York, I met with some exceptions to this; but speaking of the country generally, it is unquestionably true. . . .

We received, as I have mentioned, much personal kindness; but this by no means interfered with the national feeling of, I believe, unconquerable dislike, which evidently lives at the bottom of every true American heart against the English. This shows itself in a thousand little ways, even in the midst of the most kind and friendly intercourse, but often in a manner more comic than offensive.

Sometimes it was thus: "Well, now, I think your government must just be fit to hang themselves for that last war they cooked up; it has been the ruin of you, I expect, for it has just been the making of us."

Then—"Well, I do begin to understand your broken English better than I did; but no wonder I could not make it out very well at first, as you come from London; for every body knows that London slang is the most dreadful in the world. How queer it is now, that all the people that live in London should put the *h* where it is not, and never will put it where it is."

I was egotistical enough to ask the lady who said this, if she found that I did so.

"No; you do not", was the reply; but she added, with a complacent smile: "It is easy enough to see the pains you take about it; I expect you have heard how we Americans laugh at you all for it, and so you are trying to learn our way of pronouncing."

One lady asked me very gravely, if we had left home in order to get rid of the vermin with which the English of all ranks were afflicted? "I have heard from unquestionable authority", she added, "that it is quite impossible to walk through the streets of London without having the head filled."

I laughed a little, but spoke not a word. She coloured highly, and said: "There is nothing so easy as to laugh, but truth is truth, laughed at or not."

I must preface the following anecdote by observing, that in America nearly the whole of the insect tribe are classed under the general name of bug; the unfortunate cosmopolite known by that name amongst us is almost the only one not included in this term. A lady abruptly addressed me with "Don't you hate chintzes, Mrs. Trollope?"

"No, indeed", I replied; "I think them very pretty."

"There now! if that is not being English! I reckon you call that loving your country. Well, thank God! we Americans have something better to love our country for than that comes to; we are not obliged to say that we like nasty filthy chintzes to show that we are good patriots."

"Chintzes! what are chintzes?"

"Possible! do you pretend you don't know what chintzes are? Why the nasty little stinking blood-suckers that all the beds in London are full of."

I have since been informed that *chinche* is Spanish for bug; but at the time the word suggested only the material of a curtain. . . .

One of my friends startled me one day by saying, in an affectionate, but rather compassionate tone, "How will you bear to go back to England to live, and to bring up your children in a country where you know you are considered as no better than the dirt in the streets?"

I begged she would explain.

"Why, you know I would not affront you for any thing; but the fact is, we Americans know rather more than you think for; and certainly, if I was in England, I should not think of associating with any thing but lords. I have always been among the first here, and if I travelled I should like to do the same. I don't mean, I am sure, that I would not come to see you, but you know you are not lords, and therefore I know very well how you are treated in your own country."

I very rarely contradicted statements of this kind, as I found it less trouble, and infinitely more amusing, to let them pass; indeed, had I done otherwise, it would have been of little avail, as among the many conversations I held in America respecting my own country, I do not recollect a single instance in which it was not clear that I knew much less about it than those I conversed with. . . .

But the favourite, the constant, the universal sneer that met me every where, was on our old-fashioned attachments to things obsolete. Had they a little wit among them, I am certain they would have given us the cognomen of "My Grandmother, the British", for that is the tone they take, and it is thus they reconcile themselves to the crude newness of every thing around them.

"I wonder you are not sick of kings, chancellors, and archbishops, and all your fustian of wigs and gowns" said a very clever gentleman to me once, with an affected yawn. "I protest the very sound almost sets me to sleep."

It is amusing to observe how soothing the idea seems, that they are more modern, more advanced than England. Our classic literature, our princely dignities, our noble institutions, are all gone-by relics of the dark ages.

This, and the vastness of their naked territory, make up the flattering unction which is laid upon the soul, as an antidote to the little misgiving which from time to time arises, lest their large country be not of quite so much importance among the nations as a certain paltry old-fashioned little place which they wot of.

I was once sitting with a party of ladies, among whom were one or two young girls, whose curiosity was greater than their patriotism, and they asked me many questions respecting the splendour and extent of London. I was endeavouring to satisfy them by the best description I could give, when we were interrupted by another lady, who exclaimed, "Do hold your tongues, girls, about London; if you want to know what a beautiful city is, look at Philadelphia; when Mrs. Trollope has been there, I think she will allow that it is better worth talking about than that great overgrown collection of nasty, filthy, dirty streets that they call London." . . .

I do not speak of the police of the Atlantic cities; I believe it is well arranged: in New York it is celebrated for being so; but out of the range of their influence, the contempt of law is greater than I can venture to state, with any hope of being believed. Trespass, assault, robbery, nay even murder, are often committed without the slightest attempt at legal interference.

During the summer that we passed most delightfully in Maryland, our rambles were often restrained in various directions by the advice of our kind friends, who knew the manners and morals of the country. When we asked the cause, we were told "There is a public-house on that road, and it will not be safe to pass it."

The line of the Chesapeake and Ohio canal passed within a few miles of Mrs. S—'s residence. It twice happened during our stay with her, that dead bodies were found partially concealed near it. The circumstance was related as a sort of half-hour's wonder; and when I asked particulars of those who, on one occasion, brought the tale, the reply was "Oh, he was murdered, I expect; or may-be he died of the canal fever; but they say he had marks of being throttled." No inquest was summoned; and certainly no more sensation was produced by the occurrence than if a sheep had been found in the same predicament. . . .

Camp-Meeting

It was in the course of this summer that I found the opportunity I had long wished for, of attending a camp-meeting, and I gladly accepted the invitation of an English lady and gentleman to accompany them in their carriage to the spot where it is held; this was in a wild district on the confines of Indiana.

The prospect of passing a night in the back woods of Indiana was by no means agreeable, but I screwed my courage to the proper pitch, and set forth determined to see with my own eyes, and hear with my own ears, what a camp-meeting really was. I had heard it said that being at a camp-meeting was like standing at the gate of heaven, and seeing it opened before you; I had heard it said, that being at a camp-meeting was like finding yourself within the gates of hell; in either case there must be something to gratify curiosity, and compensate for the fatigues of a long rumbling ride and a sleepless night.

We reached the ground about an hour before midnight, and the approach to it was highly picturesque. The spot chosen was the verge of an unbroken forest, where a space of about twenty acres appeared to have been partially cleared for the purpose. Tents of different sizes were pitched very near together in a circle round the cleared space; behind them were ranged an exterior circle of carriages of every description, and at the back of each were fastened the horses which had drawn them thither. Through this triple circle of defence we distinguished numerous fires burning brightly within it; and still more numerous lights flickering from the trees that were left in the enclosure. The moon was in meridian splendour above our heads.

We left the carriage to the care of a servant, who was to prepare a bed in it for Mrs. B—— and me, and entered the inner circle. The first glance reminded me of Vauxhall, from the effect of the lights among the trees, and the moving crowd below them; but the second showed a scene totally unlike any thing I had ever witnessed. Four high frames, constructed in the form of altars, were placed at the four corners of the enclosure; on these were supported layers of earth and sod, on which burned immense fires of blazing pine-wood. On one side a rude platform was erected to accommodate the preachers, fifteen of whom attended this meeting, and with very short intervals for necessary refreshment and private devotion, preached in rotation, day and night, from Tuesday to Saturday. . . .

Great numbers of persons were walking about the ground, who appeared like ourselves to be present only as spectators; some of these very unceremoniously contrived to raise the drapery of a tent, at one corner, so as to afford us a perfect view of the interior.

The floor was covered with straw, which round the sides was heaped in masses, that might serve as seats, but which at that moment were used to support the heads and the arms of the close-packed circle of men and women who kneeled on the floor.

Out of about thirty persons thus placed, perhaps half a dozen were men. One of these, a handsome-looking youth of eighteen or twenty, kneeled just below the opening through which I looked. His arm was encircling the neck of a young girl who knelt beside him, with her hair hanging dishevelled upon her shoulders, and her features working with the most violent agitation; soon after they both fell forward on the straw, as if unable to endure in any other attitude the burning eloquence of a tall grim figure in black, who, standing erect in the centre, was uttering with incredible vehemence an oration that seemed to hover between praying and preaching; . . . the kneeling circle ceased not to call, in every variety of tone, on the name of Jesus; accompanied with sobs, groans, and a sort of low howling inexpressibly painful to listen to. But my attention was speedily withdrawn from the preacher, and the circle round him, by a figure which knelt alone at some distance; it was a living image of Scott's Macbriar, as young, as wild, and as terrible. His thin arms, tossed above his head, had forced themselves so far out of the sleeves, that they were bare to the elbow; his large eyes glared frightfully, and he continued to scream without an instant's intermission the word "Glory!" with a violence that seemed to swell every vein to bursting. It was too dreadful to look upon long, and we turned away shuddering. . . .

One tent was occupied exclusively by negroes. They were all full-dressed, and looked exactly as if they were performing a scene on the stage. One woman wore a dress of pink gauze trimmed with silver lace; another was dressed in pale yellow silk; one or two had splendid turbans; and all wore a profusion of ornaments. The men were in snow white pantaloons, with gay coloured linen jackets. One of these, a youth of coal-black comeliness, was preaching with the most violent gesticulations, frequently springing high from the ground, and clapping his hands over his head. Could our missionary societies have heard the trash he uttered, by way of an address to the Deity, they might perhaps have doubted whether his conversion had much enlightened his mind.

At midnight a horn sounded through the camp, which, we were told, was to call the people from private to public worship; and we presently saw them flocking from all sides to the front of the preachers' stand. Mrs. B— and I contrived to place ourselves with our backs supported against the lower part of this structure, and we were thus enabled to witness the scene which followed, without personal danger. There were about two thousand persons assembled.

One of the preachers began in a low nasal tone, and, like all other Methodist preachers, assured us of the enormous depravity of man as he comes from the hands of his Maker, and of his perfect sanctification after he had wrestled sufficiently with the Lord to get hold of him, *et cetera*. The admiration of the crowd was evinced by almost constant cries of "Amen! Amen!", "Jesus! Jesus!", "Glory! Glory!" and the like. But this comparative tranquillity did not last long; the preacher told them that "this night was the time fixed upon for anxious sinners to wrestle with the Lord"; that he and his brethren "were at hand to help them"; and that such as needed their help were to come forward into "the pen" . . . the space immediately below the preacher's stand; we were therefore placed on the edge of it, and were enabled to see and hear all that took place in the very centre of this extraordinary exhibition.

The crowd fell back at the mention of the *pen*, and for some minutes there was a vacant space before us. The preachers came down from their stand, and placed themselves in the midst of it, beginning to sing a hymn, calling upon the penitents to come forth. As they sang they kept turning themselves round to every part of the crowd, and, by degrees, the voices of the whole multitude joined in chorus. This was the only moment at which I perceived any thing like the solemn and beautiful effect which I had heard ascribed to this woodland worship . . . but ere I had well enjoyed it, the scene changed, and sublimity gave place to horror and disgust.

The exhortation nearly resembled that which I had heard at "the Revival", but the result was very different; for, instead of the few hysterical women who had distinguished themselves on that occasion, above a hundred persons, nearly all females, came forward, uttering howlings and groans so terrible that I shall never cease to shudder when I recall them. They appeared to drag each other forward, and, on the word being given "Let us pray", they all fell on their knees; but this posture was soon changed for others that permitted greater scope for the convulsive movements of their limbs; and they were soon all lying on the ground in an indescribable confusion of heads and legs. They threw about their limbs with such incessant and violent motion, that I was every instant expecting some serious accident to occur. . . .

Hysterical sobbings, convulsive groans, shrieks and screams the most appalling, burst forth on all sides. I felt sick with horror. As if their hoarse and overstrained voices failed to make noise enough, they soon began to clap their hands violently. . . .

Many of these wretched creatures were beautiful young females. The preachers moved about among them, at once exciting and soothing their agonies. I heard the muttered "Sister! dear sister!" I saw the insidious lips approach the cheeks of the unhappy girls; I heard the murmured confessions of the poor victims, and I watched their tormentors, breathing into their ears consolations that tinged the pale cheek with red. Had I been a man, I am sure I should have been guilty of some rash act of interference; nor do I believe that such a scene could have been acted in the presence of Englishmen without instant punishment being inflicted; not to mention the salutary discipline of the treadmill, which, beyond all question, would, in England, have been applied to check so turbulent and so vicious a scene.

After the first wild burst that followed their prostration, the moanings, in many instances, became loudly articulate; and I then experienced a strange vibration between tragic and comic feeling.

A very pretty girl, who was kneeling in the attitude of Canova's Magdalene immediately before us, amongst an immense quantity of jargon, broke out thus: "Woe! woe to the backsliders! hear it, hear it, Jesus! when I was fifteen my mother died, and I backslided, oh Jesus, I backslided! take me home to my mother, Jesus! take me home to her, for I am weary! Oh John Mitchel! John Mitchel!" and after sobbing piteously behind her raised hands, she lifted her sweet face again, which was as pale as death, and said: "Shall I sit on the sunny bank of salvation with my mother? my own dear mother? oh Jesus, take me home, take me home!"

Who could refuse a tear to this earnest wish for death in one so young and so lovely? But I saw her, ere I left the ground, with her hand fast locked, and her head supported by a man who looked very much as Don Juan might, when sent back to earth as too bad for the regions below. . . .

The stunning noise was sometimes varied by the preachers beginning to sing; but the convulsive movements of the poor maniacs only became more violent. At length the atrocious wickedness of this horrible scene increased to a degree of grossness, that drove us from our station: we returned to the carriage at about three o'clock in the morning, and passed the remainder of the night in listening to the ever increasing tumult at the pen. To sleep was impossible. At day-break the horn again sounded, to send them to private devotion; and in about an hour afterwards I saw the whole camp as joyously and eagerly employed in preparing and devouring their most substantial breakfasts as if the night had been passed in dancing; and I marked many a fair but pale face, that I recognised as a demoniac of the night, simpering beside a swain, to whom she carefully administered hot coffee and eggs. The preaching saint and the howling sinner seemed alike to relish this mode of recruiting their strength.

After enjoying abundance of strong tea, which proved a delightful restorative after a night so strangely spent, I wandered alone into the forest, and I never remember to have found perfect quiet more delightful.

We soon after left the ground; but before our departure we learnt that a very *satisfactory* collection had been made by the preachers, for Bibles, tracts, and *all other religious purposes*. . . .

City of Washington—Congress—Indians

I was delighted with the whole aspect of Washington; light, cheerful, and airy, it reminded me of our fashionable watering-places. It has been laughed at by foreigners, and even by natives, because the original plan of the city was upon an enormous scale, and but a very small part of it has been as yet executed. But I confess I see nothing in the least degree ridiculous about it; the original design, which was as beautiful as it was extensive, has been in no way departed from, and all that has been done has been done well. From the base of the hill on which the capitol stands extends a street of most magnificent width, planted on each side with trees, and ornamented by many splendid shops. This street, which is called Pennsylvania Avenue, is above a mile in length, and at the end of it is the handsome mansion of the President; conveniently near to his residence are the various public offices, all handsome, simple, and commodious; ample areas are left round each, where grass and shrubs refresh the eye. In another of the principal streets is the general post-office, and not far from it a very noble town-hall. Towards the quarter of the President's house are several handsome dwellings, which are chiefly occupied by the foreign ministers.

The houses in the other parts of the city are scattered, but without ever losing sight of the regularity of the original plan; and to a person who has been travelling much through the country, and marked the immense quantity of new manufactories, new canals, new rail-roads, new towns, and new cities, which are springing, as it were, from the earth in every part of it, the appearance of the metropolis rising gradually into life and splendour, is a spectacle of high historic interest. . . .

The residence of the foreign legations and their families gives a tone to the society of this city which distinguishes it greatly from all others. It is also, for a great part of the year, the residence of the senators and representatives, who must be presumed to be the *élite* of the entire body of citizens, both in respect to talent and education. This cannot fail to make Washington a more agreeable abode than any other city in the Union.

The total absence of all sights, sounds, or smells of commerce, adds greatly to the charm. Instead of drays you see handsome carriages; and instead of the busy bustling hustle of men, shuffling on to a sale of "dry goods" or "prime bread stuffs", you see very well-dressed personages lounging leisurely up and down Pennsylvania Avenue.

Mr. Pishey Thompson, the English bookseller, with his pretty collection of all sorts of pretty literature fresh from London, and Mr. Somebody, the jeweller, with his brilliant shop full of trinkets, are the principal points of attraction and business. What a contrast to all other American cities! The members, who pass several months every year in this lounging easy way, with no labour but a little talking, and with the *douceur* of eight dollars a day to pay them for it, must feel the change sadly when their term of public service is over. . . .

But, strange to say, even here a theatre cannot be supported for more than a few weeks at a time. I was told that gambling is the favourite recreation of the gentlemen, and that it is carried to a very considerable extent; but here, as elsewhere within the country, it is kept extremely well out of sight. I do not think I was present with a pack of cards a dozen times during more than three years that I remained in the country. Billiards are much played, though in most places the amusement is illegal. It often appeared to me that the old women of a State made the laws, and the young men broke them.

Notwithstanding the diminutive size of the city, we found much to see and to amuse us. . . .

The purity of the American character, formed and founded on the purity of the American government, was made evident to our senses by the display of all the offerings of esteem and regard which had been presented by various sovereigns to the different American ministers who had been sent to their courts. The object of the law which exacted this deposit from every individual so honoured, was, they told us, to prevent the possibility of bribery being used to corrupt any envoy of the Republic. I should think it would be a better way to select for the office such men as they felt could not be seduced by a sword or a snuff-box. But they, doubtless, know their own business best. . . .

We were at Washington at the time that the measure for chasing the last of several tribes of Indians from their forest homes, was canvassed in Congress, and finally decided upon the *fiat* of the President. If the American character may be judged by their conduct in this matter, they are most lamentably deficient in every feeling of honour and integrity. It is among themselves, and from themselves, that I have heard the statements which represent them as treacherous and false almost beyond belief in their intercourse with the unhappy Indians. Had I, during my residence in the United States, observed any single feature in their national character that could justify their eternal boast of liberality and the love of freedom, I might have respected them, however much my taste might have been offended by what was peculiar in their manners and customs. But it is impossible for any mind of common honesty not to be revolted by the contradictions in their principles and practice. They inveigh against the governments of Europe, because, as they say, they favour the powerful and oppress the weak. You may hear this declaimed upon in Congress, roared out in taverns, discussed in every drawing-room, satirised upon the stage, nay, even anathematised from the pulpit: listen to it, and then look at them at home; you will see them with one hand hoisting the cap of liberty, and with the other flogging their slaves. You will see them one hour lecturing their mob on the indefeasible rights of man, and the next driving from their homes the children of the soil, whom they have bound themselves to protect by the most solemn treaties. . . . The circumstance which renders their expulsion from their own, their native lands, so peculiarly lamentable is, that they were yielding rapidly to the force of example; their lives were no longer those of wandering hunters, but they were becoming agriculturists, and the tyrannical arm of brutal power has not now driven them, as formerly, only from their hunting grounds, their favourite springs, and the sacred bones of their fathers, but it has chased them from the dwellings their advancing knowledge had taught them to make comfortable; from the newly-ploughed fields of their pride; and from the crops their sweat had watered. And for what? To add some thousand acres of territory to the half peopled wilderness which borders them. . . .

Attending the debates in Congress was, of course, one of our great objects; and, as an English woman, I was perhaps the more eager to avail myself of the privilege allowed. It was repeatedly observed to me that, at least in this instance, I must acknowledge the superior gallantry of the Americans, and that they herein give a decided proof of surpassing the English in a wish to honour the ladies, as they have a gallery in the House of Representatives erected expressly for them, while in England they are rigorously excluded from every part of the House of Commons.

But the inference I draw from this is precisely the reverse of that suggested. It is well known that the reason why the House of Commons was closed against ladies was, that their presence was found too attractive, and that so many members were tempted to neglect the business before the House, that they might enjoy the pleasure of conversing with the fair critics in the galleries, that it became a matter of national importance to banish them—and they were banished. It will be long ere the American legislature will find it necessary to pass the same law for the same reason. . . .

The privilege of attending these debates would be more valuable could the speakers be better heard from the gallery; but, with the most earnest attention, I could only follow one or two of the orators, whose voices were peculiarly loud and clear. This made it really a labour to listen; but the extreme beauty of the chamber was of itself a reason for going again and again. It was, however, really mortifying to see this splendid hall, fitted up in so stately and sumptuous a manner, filled with men sitting in the most unseemly attitudes, a large majority with their hats on, and nearly all spitting to an excess that decency forbids me to describe.

Among the crowd, who must be included in this description, a few were distinguished by not wearing their hats, and by sitting on their chairs like other human beings, without throwing their legs above their heads. Whenever I inquired the name of one of these exceptions, I was told that it was Mr. This or Mr. That, of *Virginia*. . . .

If I mistake not, every debate I listened to in the American Congress was upon one and the same subject, namely, the entire independence of each individual state, with regard to the federal government. The jealousy on this point appeared to me to be the very strangest political feeling that ever got possession of the mind of man. I do not pretend to judge the merits of this question. I speak solely of the very singular effect of seeing man after man start eagerly to his feet, to declare that the greatest injury, the basest injustice, the most obnoxious tyranny that could be practised against the state of which he was a member, would be a vote of a few million dollars for the purpose of making their roads or canals; or for drainage; or, in short, for any purposes of improvement whatsoever. . . .

One great boast of the country is, that they have no national debt, or that they shall have none in two years. This seems not very wonderful considering their productive tariff, and that the income paid to their president is 6000*l.* per annum; other government salaries being in proportion, and all internal improvements, at the expense of the government treasury, being voted unconstitutional. . . .

The President has regular evening parties, every other Wednesday, which are called his *levées;* . . . The reception rooms are handsome, particularly the grand saloon, which is elegantly, nay, splendidly furnished; . . . The company are about as select as that of an Easter-day ball at the Mansion-house.

The churches at Washington are not superb; but the Episcopalian and Catholic were filled with elegantly dressed women. I observed a greater proportion of gentlemen at church at Washington than any where else.

The Presbyterian ladies go to church three times in the day, but the general appearance of Washington on a Sunday is much less puritanical than that of most other American towns: the people walk about, and there are no chains in the streets, as at Philadelphia, to prevent their riding or driving, if they like it. . . .

The theatre was not open while we were in Washington, but we afterwards took advantage of our vicinity to the city to visit it. The house is very small, and most astonishingly dirty and void of decoration, considering that it is the only place of public amusement that the city affords. . . .

The spitting was incessant; and not one in ten of the male part of the illustrious legislative audience sat according to the usual custom of human beings; the legs were thrown sometimes over the front of the box, sometimes over the side of it; here and there a senator stretched his entire length along a bench; and in many instances the front rail was preferred as a seat.

I remarked one young man, whose handsome person, and most elaborate toilet, led me to conclude he was a first-rate personage, and so I doubt not he was; nevertheless, I saw him take from the pocket of his silk waistcoat a lump of tobacco, and daintily deposit it within his cheek.

I am inclined to think this most vile and universal habit of chewing tobacco is the cause of a remarkable peculiarity in the male physiognomy of Americans; their lips are almost uniformly thin and compressed. At first I accounted for this upon Lavater's[5] theory, and attributed it to the arid temperament of the people; but it is too universal to be so explained; whereas the habit above mentioned, which pervades all classes (excepting the literary), well accounts for it, as the act of expressing the juices of this loathsome herb enforces exactly that position of the lips, which gives this remarkable peculiarity to the American countenance. . . .

Slavery

It was settled that we should pass the summer in Maryland, and after a month devoted to Washington, we left it for Stonington. . . .

I now, for the first time since I crossed the mountains, found myself sufficiently at leisure to look deliberately round, and mark the different aspects of men and things in a region which, though bearing the same name, and calling itself the same land, was, in many respects, as different from the one I had left, as Amsterdam from St. Petersburg. There every

[5]Swiss theologian, who believed that facial expression indicates disposition and character.

man was straining and struggling, and striving for himself (heaven knows!). Here every white man was waited upon, more or less, by a slave. There, the newly-cleared lands, rich with the vegetable manure accumulated for ages, demanded the slightest labour to return the richest produce; . . . Here the soil had long ago yielded its first fruits; much that had been cleared and cultivated for tobacco (the most exhausting of crops) by the English, required careful and laborious husbandry to produce any return. . . .

The effect produced upon English people by the sight of slavery in every direction is very new, and not very agreeable, and it is not the less painfully felt from hearing upon every breeze the mocking words "All men are born free and equal". . . .

The condition of domestic slaves, however, does not generally appear to be bad; but the ugly feature is, that should it be so, they have no power to change it. I have seen much kind attention bestowed upon the health of slaves; but it is on these occasions impossible to forget, that did this attention fail, a valuable piece of property would be endangered. Unhappily the slaves, too, know this; and the consequence is, that real kindly feeling very rarely can exist between the parties. It is said that slaves born in a family are attached to the children of it, who have grown up with them. This may be the case where the petty acts of infant tyranny have not been sufficient to conquer the kindly feeling naturally produced by long and early association; and this sort of attachment may last as long as the slave can be kept in that state of profound ignorance which precludes reflection. The law of Virginia has taken care of this. The State legislators may truly be said to be "wiser in their generation than the children of light", and they ensure their safety by forbidding light to enter among them. By the law of Virginia it is penal to teach any slave to read, and it is penal to be aiding and abetting in the act of instructing them. This law speaks volumes. Domestic slaves are, generally speaking, tolerably well fed, and decently clothed; and the mode in which they are lodged seems a matter of great indifference to them. They are rarely exposed to the lash, and they are carefully nursed in sickness. These are the favourable features of their situation. The sad one is, that they *may* be sent to *the south*, and sold. This is the dread of all the slaves north of Louisiana. The sugar plantations, and more than all, the rice grounds of Georgia and the Carolinas, are the terror of American negroes; and well they may be, for they open an early grave to thousands; and to *avoid loss*, it is needful to make their previous labour pay their value.

There is something in the system of breeding and rearing negroes in the Northern States, for the express purpose of sending them to be sold in the South, that strikes painfully against every feeling of justice, mercy, or common humanity. During my residence in America I became perfectly persuaded that the state of a domestic slave in a gentleman's family was preferable to that of a hired American "help", both because they are more cared for and valued, and because their condition being born with them, their spirits do not struggle against it with that pining discontent which seems the lot of all free servants in America. But the case is widely different with such as, in their own persons or those of their children "loved in vain", are exposed to the dreadful traffic above-mentioned. In what is their condition better than that of the kidnapped negroes on the coast of Africa? Of the horror in which this enforced migration is held, I had a strong proof during our stay in Virginia. The father of a young slave, who belonged to the lady with whom we boarded, was destined to this fate, and within an hour after it was made known to him, he sharpened the hatchet with which he had been felling timber, and with his right hand severed his left from the wrist.

But this is a subject on which I do not mean to dilate; . . . Its effects on the moral feelings and external manners of the people are all I wish to observe upon, and these are unquestionably most injurious. The same man who beards his wealthier and more educated neighbour with the bullying boast "I'm as good as you," turns to his slave, and knocks him down, if the furrow he has ploughed or the log he has felled, please not this stickler for equality. This is a glaring falsehood on the very surface of such a man's principles that is revolting. It is not among the higher classes that the possession of slaves produces the worst effects. Among the poorer class of landholders, who are often as profoundly ignorant as the negroes they own, the effect of this plenary power over males and females is most demoralising; and the kind of coarse, not to say brutal, authority which is exercised, furnishes the most disgusting moral spectacle I ever witnessed. In all ranks, however, it appeared to me that the greatest and best feelings of the human heart were paralysed by the relative positions of slave and owner. The characters, the hearts of children, are irretrievably injured by it. In Virginia we boarded for some time in a family consisting of a widow and her four daughters, and I there witnessed a scene strongly indicative of the effect I have mentioned. A young female slave, about eight years of age, had found on the shelf of a cupboard a biscuit, temptingly buttered, of which she had eaten a considerable portion before she was observed. The butter had been copiously sprinkled with arsenic for the destruction of rats, and had been thus most incautiously placed by one of the young ladies of the family. As soon as the circumstance was known, the lady of the house came to consult me as to what had best be done for the poor child; I immediately mixed a large cup of mustard and water (the most rapid of all emetics), and got the little girl to swallow it. The desired effect was instantly produced, but the poor child, partly from nausea and partly from the terror of hearing her death proclaimed by half-a-dozen voices round her, trembled so violently that I thought she would fall. I sat down in the court where we were standing, and, as a matter of course, took the little sufferer in my lap. I observed a general titter among the white members of the family, while the black stood aloof ıd looked stupefied. The youngest of the family, a little girl about the age f the young slave, after gazing at me for a few moments in utter astonishment, exclaimed: "My! if Mrs. Trollope has not taken her in her lap, and iped her nasty mouth! Why, I would not have touched her mouth for vo hundred dollars!" . . .

There seems in general a strong feeling throughout America that none f the negro race can be trusted; and as fear, according to their notions, the only principle by which a slave can be actuated, it is not wonderful the imputation be just. But I am persuaded that, were a different mode f moral treatment pursued, most important and beneficial consequences ould result from it. Negroes are very sensible to kindness, and might, I ink, be rendered more profitably obedient by the practice of it towards em, than by any other mode of discipline whatever. . . .

I observed every where throughout the slave states that all articles which an be taken and consumed are constantly locked up, and in large families, here the extent of the establishment multiplies the number of keys, these re deposited in a basket, and consigned to the care of a little negress, who constantly seen following her mistress's steps with this basket on her rm, and this, not only that the keys may be always at hand, but because, hould they be out of sight one moment, that moment would infallibly be mployed for purposes of plunder. It seemed to me in this instance, as in any others, that the close personal attendance of these sable shadows ust be very annoying; but whenever I mentioned it, I was assured that o such feeling existed, and that use rendered them almost unconscious f their presence.

I had, indeed, frequent opportunities of observing this habitual indiference to the presence of their slaves. They talk of them, of their conition, of their faculties, of their conduct, exactly as if they were inapable of hearing. I once saw a young lady who, when seated at table etween a male and a female, was induced by her modesty to intrude n the chair of her female neighbour to avoid the indelicacy of touching he elbow of *a man*. I once saw this very young lady lacing her stays with he most perfect composure before a negro footman. A Virginian gentlenan told me that, ever since he had married, he had been accustomed to ave a negro girl sleep in the same chamber with himself and his wife. I sked for what purpose this nocturnal attendance was necessary? "Good eaven!" was the reply. "If I wanted a glass of water during the night, vhat would become of me?" . . .

City of Philadelphia

ɴ the latter part of August, 1830, we paid a visit to Philadelphia, and, otwithstanding the season, we were so fortunate as to have both bright nd temperate weather for the expedition. . . .

The Americans all seem greatly to admire this city, and to give it th preference in point of beauty to all others in the Union, but I do n agree with them. There are some very handsome buildings, but none o them so placed as to produce a striking effect, as is the case both with th Capitol and the President's house, at Washington. Notwithstanding the fine buildings, one or more of which are to be found in all the princip streets, the *coup d'œil* is every where the same. There is no Place d Louis Quinze or Carrousel, no Regent Street or Green Park, to make on exclaim "How beautiful!" all is even, straight, uniform, and uninteres ing. . . .

Our mornings were spent, as all travellers' mornings must be, in askin questions, and in seeing all that the answers told us it was necessary to se Perhaps this can be done in no city with more facility than in Philadelphi: you have nothing to do but to walk up one straight street, and dow another, till all the parallelograms have been threaded. In doing this yo will see many things worth looking at. The United States and Pennsylvani banks are the most striking buildings, and are both extremely handsome being of white marble, and built after Grecian models. The State Hous has nothing externally to recommend it, but the room shown as that i which the declaration of independence was signed, and in which th estimable Lafayette was received, half a century after he had shed hi noble blood in aiding to obtain it, is an interesting spot. . . .

We visited the nineteenth annual exhibition of the Pennsylvania academ of the fine arts; . . .

One of the rooms of this academy has inscribed over its door

ANTIQUE STATUE GALLERY

The door was open, but just within it was a screen, which prevented any objects in the room being seen from without. Upon my pausing to rea this inscription, an old woman who appeared to officiate as guardian o the gallery, bustled up, and addressing me with an air of much mystery said: "Now, ma'am, now: this is just the time for you—nobody can se you—make haste."

I stared at her with unfeigned surprise, and disengaging my arm, which she had taken apparently to hasten my movements, I very gravely asked he meaning.

"Only, ma'am, that the ladies like to go into that room by themselves when there be no gentlemen watching them."

On entering this mysterious apartment, the first thing I remarked, was a written paper, deprecating the disgusting depravity which had led some of the visitors to mark and deface the casts in a most indecent and shameless manner. This abomination has unquestionably been occasioned by the coarse-minded custom which sends alternate groups of males and females into the room. Were the antique gallery thrown open to mixed parties of ladies and gentlemen, it would soon cease. Till America has reached the

:gree of refinement which permits of this, the antique casts should not : exhibited to ladies at all. I never felt my delicacy shocked at the Louvre, ıt I was strongly tempted to resent as an affront the hint I received, that might steal a glance at what was deemed indecent. Perhaps the arrange-.ents for the exhibition of this room, the feelings which have led to them, ıd the result they have produced, furnish as good a specimen of the nd of delicacy on which the Americans pride themselves, and of the :culiarities arising from it, as can be found. The room contains about fty casts, chiefly from the antique. . . .

I went to the Chesnut Street Theatre to see Mr. Booth, formerly of rury Lane, in the character of Lear, and a Mrs. Duff in Cordelia; but I ave seen too many Lears and Cordelias to be easily pleased; I thought the hole performance very bad. The theatre is of excellently moderate di-ıensions, and prettily decorated. It was not the fashionable season for the ıeatres, which I presume must account for the appearance of the com-any in the boxes, which was any thing but elegant; nor was there more ecorum of demeanour than I had observed elsewhere; I saw one man ı the lower tier of boxes deliberately take off his coat that he might ıjoy the refreshing coolness of shirt sleeves; all the gentlemen wore ıeir hats, and the spitting was unceasing. . . .

The great and most striking contrast between this city and those of urope, is perceived after sun-set; scarcely a sound is heard; hardly a voice r a wheel breaks the stillness. The streets are entirely dark, except where stray lamp marks an hotel or the like; no shops are open, but those of the pothecary, and here and there a cook's shop; scarcely a step is heard, and or a note of music, or the sound of mirth, I listened in vain. . . . This dark-ess, this stillness, is so great, that I almost felt it awful. As we walked home ne fine moonlight evening from the Chesnut Street house, we stopped a ıoment before the United States Bank, to look at its white marble columns y the subdued light, said to be so advantageous to them; the building did, ıdeed, look beautiful; the incongruous objects around were hardly visible, hile the brilliant white of the building, which by daylight is dazzling, was ıellowed into fainter light and softer shadow.

While passing before this modern temple of Theseus, we remarked that e alone seemed alive in this great city; it was ten o'clock, and a most lovely ool evening, after a burning day, yet all was silence. Regent Street, Bond treet, with their blaze of gas-light *bijouterie*, and still more the Italian oulevard of Paris, rose in strong contrast on the memory; the light, which utshines that of day—the gay, graceful, laughing throng—the elegant saloons f Tortoni, with all their varieties of cooling nectar—were all remembered. s it an European prejudice to deem that the solitary dram swallowed by ne gentleman on quitting an American theatre indicates a lower and more icious state of manners, than do the ices so sedulously offered to the ladies n leaving a French one? . . .

The shops, of which there appeared to me to be an unusually large proportion, are very handsome; many of them in a style of European eleganc Lottery offices abound, and that species of gambling is carried to a gre extent. I saw fewer carriages in Philadelphia than either at Baltimore Washington, but in the winter, I was told, they were more numerous.

Many of the best families had left the city for different watering-place and others were daily following. Long Branch is a fashionable bathing pla on the Jersey shore, to which many resort, both from this place and fro New York; the description given of the manner of bathing appeared to m rather extraordinary, but the account was confirmed by so many differe people, that I could not doubt its correctness. The shore, it seems, is too bo to admit of bathing machines, and the ladies have, therefore, recourse another mode for ensuring the enjoyment of a sea-bath with safety. Th accommodation at Long Branch is almost entirely at large boarding-house where all the company live at a *table d'hôte*. It is customary for ladies o arriving to look round among the married gentlemen, the first time the meet at table, and to select the one her fancy leads her to prefer as a pr tector in her purposed visits to the realms of Neptune; she makes h request, which is always graciously received, that he would lead her taste the briny wave; but another fair one must select the same protecto else the arrangement cannot be complete, as custom does not authorise *têt à tête* immersion. . . .

Influence of Females on Society

The religious severity of Philadelphian manners is in nothing more con spicuous than in the number of chains thrown across the streets on a Sunda to prevent horses and carriages from passing. Surely the Jews could nc exceed this country in their external observances. What the gentlemen c Philadelphia do with themselves on a Sunday, I will not pretend to guess, bu the prodigious majority of females in the churches is very remarkable. Al though a large proportion of the population of this city are Quakers, th same extraordinary variety of faith exists here, as every where else in th Union, and the priests have, in some circles, the same unbounded influenc which has been mentioned elsewhere. . . .

There is something in the tone of manners at Philadelphia that I liked; i appeared to me that there was less affectation of ton there than elsewher There is a quietness, a composure in a Philadelphian drawing-room, that i quite characteristic of a city founded by William Penn. The dress of th ladies, even those who are not Quakers, partakes of this; they are mos elegantly neat, and there was a delicacy and good taste in the dress of th young ladies that might serve as a model to the whole Union. There ca hardly be a stronger contrast in the style of dress between any two citie than may be remarked between Baltimore and Philadelphia; both are costly but the former is distinguished by gaudy splendour, the latter by elegan simplicity.

It is said that this city has many gentlemen distinguished by their scientific ursuits; I conversed with several well-informed and intelligent men, but iere is a cold dryness of manner and an apparent want of interest in the ibjects they discuss, that, to my mind, robs conversation of all its harm. . . .

The want of warmth, of interest, of feeling, upon all subjects which do ot immediately touch their own concerns, is universal, and has a most aralysing effect upon conversation. All the enthusiasm of America is con- entrated to the one point of her own emancipation and independence; on iis point nothing can exceed the warmth of her feelings. She may, I think, e compared to a young bride, a sort of Mrs. Major Waddle; her inde- endence is to her as a newly-won bridegroom; for him alone she has eyes, irs, or heart—the honeymoon is not over yet—when it is, America will, erhaps, learn more coquetry, and know better how to *faire l'aimable* to ther nations. . . .

Let me be permitted to describe the day of a Philadelphian lady of the rst class. . . .

It may be said that the most important feature in a woman's history is er maternity. It is so; but the object of the present observation is the social, nd not the domestic influence of woman.

This lady shall be the wife of a senator and a lawyer in the highest repute nd practice. She has a very handsome house, with white marble steps and oor-posts, and a delicate silver knocker and door-handle; she has very andsome drawing-rooms (very handsomely furnished, there is a sideboard 1 one of them, but it is very handsome, and has very handsome decanters nd cut glass water-jugs upon it); she has a very handsome carriage, and a ery handsome free black coachman; she is always very handsomely dressed; nd, moreover, she is very handsome herself.

She rises, and her first hour is spent in the scrupulously nice arrangement f her dress; she descends to her parlour neat, stiff, and silent; her breakfast s brought in by her free black footman; she eats her fried ham and her salt ish, and drinks her coffee in silence, while her husband reads one newspaper, nd puts another under his elbow; and then, perhaps, she washes the cups nd saucers. Her carriage is ordered at eleven; till that hour she is employed n the pastry-room, her snow-white apron protecting her mouse-coloured ilk. Twenty minutes before her carriage should appear, she retires to her hamber, as she calls it, shakes, and folds up her still snow-white apron, mooths her rich dress, and with nice care, sets on her elegant bonnet, and ll her handsome *et cætera;* then walks down stairs, just at the moment that er free black coachman announces to her free black footman that the car- iage waits. She steps into it, and gives the word: "Drive to the Dorcas ociety." Her footman stays at home to clean the knives, but her coachman an trust his horses while he opens the carriage door, and his lady not being ccustomed to a hand or an arm, gets out very safely without, though one f her own is occupied by a work-basket, and the other by a large roll of all those indescribable matters which ladies take as offerings to Dorca societies. She enters the parlour appropriated for the meeting, and find seven other ladies, very like herself, and takes her place among them; sh presents her contribution, which is accepted with a gentle circular smile, an her parings of broad cloth, her ends of ribbon, her gilt paper, and he minikin pins, are added to the parings of broad cloth, the ends of ribbor the gilt paper, and the minikin pins with which the table is already covered she also produces from her basket three ready-made pincushions, four ink wipers, seven paper matches, and a pasteboard watch-case; these are wel comed with acclamations, and the youngest lady present deposits then carefully on shelves, amid a prodigious quantity of similar articles. She the produces her thimble, and asks for work; it is presented to her, and th eight ladies all stitch together for some hours. Their talk is of priests and o missions; of the profits of their last sale, of their hopes from the next; of th doubt whether young Mr. This, or young Mr. That should receive th fruits of it to fit him out for Liberia; of the very ugly bonnet seen at churc on Sabbath morning, of the very handsome preacher who performed o Sabbath afternoon, and of the very large collection made on Sabbath eve ning. This lasts till three, when the carriage again appears, and the lady an her basket return home; she mounts to her chamber, carefully sets aside he bonnet and its appurtenances, puts on her scolloped black silk apron, walk into the kitchen to see that all is right, then into the parlour, where, havin cast a careful glance over the table prepared for dinner, she sits down, wor in hand, to await her spouse. He comes, shakes hands with her, spits, an dines. The conversation is not much, and ten minutes suffice for the dinner fruit and toddy, the newspaper and the work-bag succeed. In the evenin the gentleman, being a savant, goes to the Wister [sic] society,[6] and after wards plays a snug rubber at a neighbour's. The lady receives at tea a youn missionary and three members of the Dorcas society.–And so ends he day.

For some reason or other, which English people are not very likely t understand, a great number of young married persons board by the year instead of "going to houskeeping", as they call having an establishment o their own. Of course this statement does not include persons of large for tune, but it does include very many whose rank in society would make suc a mode of life quite impossible with us. I can hardly imagine a contrivanc more effectual for ensuring the insignificance of a woman, than marryin her at seventeen and placing her in a boarding-house. Nor can I easil imagine a life of more uniform dulness for the lady herself; but this certainl is a matter of taste. I have heard many ladies declare, that it is "just quit the perfection of comfort to have nothing to fix for oneself". Yet despit these assurances, I always experienced a feeling which hovered between pit and contempt, when I contemplated their mode of existence. . . .

[6]Dr. Caspar Wistar held weekly meetings for students, travelers and citizens These discussions were continued long after his death in 1818.

She must rise exactly in time to reach the boarding-table at the hour ppointed for breakfast, or she will get a stiff bow from the lady president, old coffee, and no egg. I have been sometimes greatly amused upon these ccasions by watching a little scene in which the bye-play had much more eaning than the words uttered. The fasting, but tardy lady, looks round he table, and having ascertained that there is no egg left, says distinctly: I will take an egg, if you please." But as this is addressed to no one in articular, no one in particular answers it, unless it happen that her husband s at table before her, and then he says, "There are no eggs, my dear." Whereupon the lady president evidently cannot hear, and the greedy culprit vho has swallowed two eggs (for there are always as many eggs as noses) ooks pretty considerably afraid of being found out. The breakfast proceeds n sombre silence, save that sometimes a parrot, and sometimes a canary bird, entures to utter a timid note. When it is finished, the gentlemen hurry to heir occupations, and the quiet ladies mount the stairs, some to the first, ome to the second, and some to the third stories, in an inverse proportion o the number of dollars paid, and ensconce themselves in their respective hambers. As to what they do there it is not very easy to say; but I believe hey clear-starch a little, and iron a little, and sit in a rocking-chair, and ew a great deal. I always observed that the ladies who boarded wore more laborately worked collars and petticoats than any one else. The plough is ardly a more blessed instrument in America than the needle. How could hey live without it? But time and the needle wear through the longest norning, and happily the American morning is not very long, even though hey breakfast at eight.

It is generally about two o'clock that the boarding gentlemen meet the oarding ladies at dinner. Little is spoken, except a whisper between the narried pairs. Sometimes a sulky bottle of wine flanks the plate of one or wo individuals, but it adds nothing to the mirth of the meeting, and seldom nore than one glass to the good cheer of the owners. It is not then, and it is ot there, that the gentlemen of the Union drink. Soon, very soon, the silent neal is done, and then, if you mount the stairs after them, you will find rom the doors of the more affectionate and indulgent wives, a smell of igars steam forth, which plainly indicates the felicity of the couple within. f the gentleman be a very polite husband, he will, as soon as he has done moking and drinking his toddy, offer his arm to his wife, as far as the orner of the street where his store, or his office is situated, and there he vill leave her to turn which way she likes. As this is the hour for being full lressed, of course she turns the way she can be most seen. Perhaps she pays few visits; perhaps she goes to chapel; or, perhaps, she enters some store vhere her husband deals, and ventures to order a few notions; and then she oes home again—no, not home—I will not give that name to a boarding-ouse, but she re-enters the cold heartless atmosphere in which she dwells, vhere hospitality can never enter, and where interest takes the management nstead of affection. At tea they all meet again, and a little trickery is perceptible to a nice observer in the manner of partaking the pound-cake, etc After this, those who are happy enough to have engagements, hasten to keep them; those who have not, either mount again to the solitude of their chamber, or, what appeared to me much worse, remain in the common sitting room, in a society cemented by no tie, endeared by no connexion, which choice did not bring together, and which the slightest motive would break asunder. I remarked that the gentlemen were generally obliged to go out every evening on business, and, I confess, the arrangement did not surprise me.

It is not thus that the women can obtain that influence in society which is allowed to them in Europe, and to which both sages and men of the world have agreed in ascribing such salutary effects. It is in vain that "collegiate institutes" are formed for young ladies, or that "academic degrees" are conferred upon them. It is after marriage, and when these young attempts upon all the sciences are forgotten, that the lamentable insignificance of the American woman appears; and till this be remedied, I venture to prophesy that the tone of their drawing-rooms will not improve. . . .

American Cooking—Evening Parties—Dress—Sleighing—Money-Getting Habits

In relating all I know of America, I surely must not omit so important a feature as the cooking. . . . The ordinary mode of living is abundant, but not delicate. They consume an extraordinary quantity of bacon. Ham and beef-steaks appear morning, noon, and night. In eating, they mix things together with the strangest incongruity imaginable. I have seen eggs and oysters eaten together; the sempiternal ham with apple-sauce; beef-steak with stewed peaches; and salt fish with onions. The bread is every where excellent, but they rarely enjoy it themselves, as they insist upon eating horrible half-baked hot rolls both morning and evening. The butter is tolerable, but they have seldom such cream as every little dairy produces in England; in fact, the cows are very roughly kept, compared with ours Common vegetables are abundant and very fine. I never saw secale or cauliflowers, and either from the want of summer rain, or the want of care the harvest of green vegetables is much sooner over than with us. They eat the Indian corn in a great variety of forms; sometimes it is dressed green and eaten like peas; sometimes it is broken to pieces when dry, boiled plain and brought to table like rice; this dish is called hominy. The flour of Indian corn is made into at least a dozen different sorts of cakes; but in my opinion all bad. This flour mixed in the proportion of one third with fine wheat makes by far the best bread I ever tasted.

I never saw turbot, salmon, or fresh cod; but the rock and shad are excellent. There is a great want of skill in the composition of sauces; not only with fish, but with every thing. They use very few made dishes, and I never saw any that would be approved by our savants. They have an excellent wild duck, called the Canvas Back, which, if delicately served, would surpass the black cock; but the game is very inferior to ours; they have no hares, and I never saw a pheasant. They seldom indulge in second courses, with all their ingenious temptations to the eating a second dinner; but almost every table has its dessert (invariably pronounced *desart*), which is placed on the table before the cloth is removed, and consists of pastry, preserved fruits, and creams. They are "extravagantly fond", to use their own phrase, of puddings, pies, and all kinds of "sweets", particularly the ladies; but are by no means such connoisseurs in soups and ragoûts as the gastronomes of Europe. Almost every one drinks water at table; and by a strange contradiction, in the country where hard drinking is more prevalent than in any other, there is less wine taken at dinner; ladies rarely exceed one glass, and the great majority of females never take any. In fact, the hard drinking so universally acknowledged, does not take place at jovial dinners, but, to speak plain English, in solitary dram-drinking. Coffee is not served immediately after dinner, but makes part of the serious matter of tea-drinking, which comes some hours later. Mixed dinner parties of ladies and gentlemen are very rare, and unless several foreigners are present, but little conversation passes at table. It certainly does not, in my opinion, add to the well ordering a dinner table, to set the gentlemen at one end of it, and the ladies at the other; but it is very rarely that you find it otherwise.

Their large evening parties are supremely dull; the men sometimes play cards by themselves, but if a lady plays, it must not be for money; no écarté, no chess; very little music, and that little lamentably bad. Among the blacks I heard some good voices, singing in tune; but I scarcely ever heard a white American, male or female, go through an air without being out of tune before the end of it; nor did I ever meet any trace of science in the singing I heard in society. To eat inconceivable quantities of cake, ice, and pickled oysters—and to show half their revenue in silks and satins, seem to be the chief object they have in these parties.

The most agreeable meetings, I was assured by all the young people, were those to which no married women are admitted; of the truth of this statement I have not the least doubt. These exclusive meetings occur frequently, and often last to a late hour; on these occasions, I believe, they generally dance. At regular balls married ladies are admitted, but seldom take much part in the amusement. The refreshments are always profuse and costly, but taken in a most uncomfortable manner. I have known many private balls, where every thing was on the most liberal scale of expense, where the gentlemen sat down to supper in one room, while the ladies took theirs, standing in another.

What we call picnics are very rare, and when attempted, do not often succeed well. The two sexes can hardly mix for the greater part of a day without great restraint and ennui; it is quite contrary to their general habits; the favourite indulgences of the gentlemen (smoking cigars and drinking spirits) can neither be indulged in with decency nor resigned with complacency.

The ladies have strange ways of adding to their charms. They powder themselves immoderately, face, neck, and arms, with pulverised starch; the effect is indescribably disagreeable by day-light, and not very favourable at any time. They are also most unhappily partial to false hair, which they wear in surprising quantities; this is the more to be lamented, as they generally have very fine hair of their own. I suspect this fashion to arise from an indolent mode of making their toilet, and from accomplished ladies' maids not being very abundant; it is less trouble to append a bunch of waving curls here, there, and every where, than to keep their native tresses in perfect order.

Though the expense of the ladies' dress greatly exceeds, in proportion to their general style of living, that of the ladies of Europe, it is very far (excepting in Philadelphia) from being in good taste. They do not consult the seasons in the colours or in the style of their costume; I have often shivered at seeing a young beauty picking her way through the snow with a pale rose-coloured bonnet, set on the very top of her head; I knew one young lady whose pretty little ear was actually frost-bitten from being thus exposed. They never wear muffs or boots, and appear extremely shocked at the sight of comfortable walking shoes and cotton stockings, even when they have to step to their sleighs over ice and snow. They walk in the middle of winter with their poor little toes pinched into a miniature slipper, incapable of excluding as much moisture as might bedew a primrose. I must say in their excuse, however, that they have, almost universally, extremely pretty feet. They do not walk well, nor, in fact, do they ever appear to advantage when in movement. I know not why this should be, for they have abundance of French dancing-masters among them, but somehow or other it is the fact. I fancied I could often trace a mixture of affectation and of shyness in their little mincing unsteady step, and the ever-changing position of the hands. They do not dance well: perhaps I should rather say they do not look well when dancing; lovely as their faces are, they cannot, in a position that exhibits the whole person, atone for the want of *tournure*, and for the universal defect in the formation of the bust, which is rarely full or gracefully formed.

I never saw an American man walk or stand well; notwithstanding their frequent militia drillings, they are nearly all hollow chested and round shouldered: perhaps this is occasioned by no officer daring to say to a brother free-born "Hold up your head"; whatever the cause, the effect is very remarkable to a stranger. In stature, and in physiognomy, a great majority of the population, both male and female, are strikingly handsome, but they know not how to do their own honours; half as much comeliness elsewhere would produce ten times as much effect.

Nothing can exceed their activity and perseverance in all kinds of speculation, handicraft, and enterprise, which promises a profitable pecuniary result. I heard an Englishman, who had been long resident in America, declare that in following, in meeting, or in overtaking, in the street, on the road, or in the field, at the theatre, the coffee-house, or at home, he had never overheard Americans conversing without the word DOLLAR being pronounced between them. Such unity of purpose, such sympathy of feeling, can, I believe, be found nowhere else, except, perhaps, in an ants' nest. The result is exactly what might be anticipated. This sordid object, for ever before their eyes, must inevitably produce a sordid tone of mind, and worse still, it produces a seared and blunted conscience on all questions of probity. I know not a more striking evidence of the low tone of morality which is generated by this universal pursuit of money, than the manner in which the New England States are described by Americans. All agree in saying that they present a spectacle of industry and prosperity delightful to behold, and this is the district and the population most constantly quoted as the finest specimen of their admirable country; yet I never met a single individual in any part of the Union who did not paint these New Englanders as sly, grinding, selfish, and tricking. The Yankees (as the New Englanders are called) will avow these qualities themselves with a complacent smile, and boast that no people on the earth can match them at overreaching in a bargain. I have heard them unblushingly relate stories of their cronies and friends, which, if believed among us, would banish the heroes from the fellowship of honest men for ever; and all this is uttered with a simplicity which sometimes led me to doubt if the speakers knew what honour and honesty meant. Yet the Americans declare that "they are the most moral people upon earth". Again and again I have heard this asserted, not only in conversation, and by their writings, but even from the pulpit. Such broad assumption of superior virtue demands examination, and after four years of attentive and earnest observation and inquiry, my honest conviction is, that the standard of moral character in the United States is very greatly lower than in Europe. Of their religion, as it appears outwardly, I have had occasion to speak frequently; I pretend not to judge the heart, but, without any uncharitable presumption, I must take permission to say, that both Protestant England and Catholic France show an infinitely superior religious and moral aspect to mortal observation, both as to reverend decency of external observance, and as to the inward fruit of honest dealing between man and man.

In other respects I think no one will be disappointed who visits the country expecting to find no more than common sense might teach him to look for, namely, a vast continent, by far the greater part of which is still in the state in which nature left it, and a busy, bustling, industrious population, hacking and hewing their way through it. What greatly increases the interest of this spectacle, is the wonderful facility for internal commerce, furnished by the rivers, lakes, and canals, which thread the country in every direction, producing a rapidity of progress in all commercial and agricultural speculation altogether unequalled. . . .

with Sherlock and Taylor, as much too antiquated to suit the immensely rapid progress of mind which distinguishes America. . . .

They are great novel readers, but the market is chiefly furnished by England. . . . It appeared to me that the style of their imaginative compositions was almost always affected and inflated. Even in treating their great national subject of romance, the Indians, they are seldom either powerful or original. A few well-known general features, moral and physical, are presented over and over again in all their Indian stories, till in reading them you lose all sense of individual character. . . .

It is, I think, Mr. Bryant, who ranks highest as the poet of the Union. This is too lofty an eminence for me to attack; besides, "I am of another parish", and therefore, perhaps, no very fair judge.

From miscellaneous poetry I made a great many extracts; but upon returning to them for transcription, I thought that ill-nature and dulness ("Oh ill-matched pair!") would be more served by their insertion, than wholesome criticism. . . .

They have very few native tragedies: not more than half a dozen, I believe, and those of very recent date. It would be ungenerous to fall heavily upon these; the attempt alone, nearly the most arduous a poet can make, is of itself honourable; and the success at least equal to that in any other department of literature. . . .

I am not, of course, competent to form any opinion of their scientific works; but some papers which I read almost accidentally, appeared to me to be written with great clearness, and neatness of definition.

It appears extraordinary that a people who loudly declare their respect for science, should be entirely without observatories. Neither at their seats of learning, nor in their cities, does any thing of the kind exist; nor did I in any direction hear of individuals given to the study of astronomy. . . .

Jefferson's posthumous works were very generally circulated whilst I was in America. They are a mighty mass of mischief. He wrote with more perspicuity than he thought, and his hot-headed democracy has done a fearful injury to his country. Hollow and unsound as his doctrines are, they are but too palatable to a people, each individual of whom would rather derive his importance from believing that none are above him, than from the consciousness that in his station he makes part of a noble whole. The social system of Mr. Jefferson, if carried into effect, would make of mankind an unamalgamated mass of grating atoms, where the darling "I'm as good as you," would soon take the place of the law and the Gospel. As it is, his principles, though happily not fully put in action, have yet produced most lamentable results. The assumption of equality, however empty, is sufficient to tincture the manners of the poor with brutal insolence, and subjects the rich to the paltry expediency of sanctioning the falsehood, however deep their conviction that it is such. It cannot, I think, be denied that the great men of America attain to power and to fame, by eternally uttering what they know to be untrue. American citizens are not equal. Did Washington feel them to be so, when his word out-weighed (so happily for them) the votes of thousands? Did Franklin think that all were equal when he shouldered his way from the printing press to the cabinet? True, he looked back in high good humour, and with his kindest smile told the poor devils whom he left behind, that they were all his equals; but Franklin did not speak the truth, and he knew it. . . .

In no society in the world can the advantage of travel be so conspicuous as in America. In other countries a tone of unpretending simplicity can more than compensate for the absence of enlarged views or accurate observation; but this tone is not to be found in America, or if it be, it is only among those who, having looked at that insignificant portion of the world not included in the Union, have learnt to know how much is still unknown within the mighty part which is. For the rest, they all declare, and do in truth believe, that they only, among the sons of men, have wit and wisdom, and that one of their exclusive privileges is that of speaking English *elegantly*. There are two reasons for this latter persuasion; the one is, that the great majority have never heard any English but their own, except from the very lowest of the Irish; and the other, that those who have chanced to find themselves in the society of the few educated English who have visited America, have discovered that there is a marked difference between their phrases and accents and those to which they have been accustomed, whereupon they have, of course, decided that no Englishman can speak English.

The reviews of America contain some good clear-headed articles; but I sought in vain for the playful vivacity and the keenly-cutting satire, whose sharp edge, however painful to the patient, is of such high utility in lopping off the excrescences of bad taste, and levelling to its native clay the heavy growth of dulness. Still less could I find any trace of that graceful familiarity of learned allusion and general knowledge which mark the best European reviews, and which make one feel in such perfectly good company while perusing them. But this is a tone not to be found either in the writings or conversation of Americans; as distant from pedantry as from ignorance, it is not learning itself, but the effect of it; and so pervading and subtle is its influence, that it may be traced in the festive halls and gay drawing-rooms of Europe as certainly as in the cloistered library or student's closet; it is, perhaps, the last finish of highly-finished society. . . .

With regard to the fine arts, their paintings, I think, are quite as good, or rather better, than might be expected from the patronage they receive; the wonder is that any man can be found with courage enough to devote himself to a profession in which he has so little chance of finding a maintenance. The trade of a carpenter opens an infinitely better prospect; and this is so well known, that nothing but a genuine passion for the art could beguile any one to pursue it. The entire absence of every means of improvement, and effectual study, is unquestionably the cause why those who manifest this devotion cannot advance farther. I heard of one young artist, whose circumstances did not permit his going to Europe, but who being nevertheless determined that his studies should, as nearly as possible, resemble those of the European academies, was about to commence drawing the human figure, for which purpose he had provided himself with a thin silk dress, in which to clothe his models, as no one of any station, he said, could be found who would submit to sit as a model without clothing. . . .

Much is said about the universal diffusion of education in America, and a vast deal of genuine admiration is felt and expressed at the progress of mind throughout the Union. They believe themselves in all sincerity to have surpassed, to be surpassing, and to be about to surpass, the whole earth in the intellectual race. I am aware that not a single word can be said, hinting a different opinion, which will not bring down a transatlantic anathema on my head; yet the subject is too interesting to be omitted. Before I left England I remember listening with much admiration to an eloquent friend, who deprecated our system of public education, as confining the various and excursive faculties of our children to one beaten path, paying little or no attention to the peculiar powers of the individual.

This objection is extremely plausible, but doubts of its intrinsic value must, I think, occur to every one who has marked the result of a different system throughout the United States.

From every inquiry I could make, and I took much pains to obtain accurate information, it appeared that much is attempted, but very little beyond reading, writing, and book-keeping, is thoroughly acquired. Were we to read a prospectus of the system pursued in any of our public schools, and that of a first-rate seminary in America, we should be struck by the confined scholastic routine of the former, when compared to the varied and expansive scope of the latter; but let the examination go a little farther, and I believe it will be found that the old-fashioned school discipline of England has produced something higher, and deeper too, than that which roars so loud, and thunders in the index.

They will not afford to let their young men study till two or three and twenty, and it is therefore declared, *ex cathedra Americana*, to be unnecessary. At sixteen, often much earlier, education ends, and money-making begins; the idea that more learning is necessary than can be acquired by that time, is generally ridiculed as obsolete monkish bigotry; added to which, if the seniors willed a more prolonged discipline, the juniors would refuse submission. When the money-getting begins, leisure ceases, and all of lore which can be acquired afterwards, is picked up from novels, magazines, and newspapers.

At what time can the taste be formed? How can a correct and polished style, even of speaking, be acquired? or when can the fruit of the two thousand years of past thinking be added to the native growth of American intellect? These are the tools, if I may so express myself, which our elaborate system of school discipline puts into the hands of our scholars; possessed of these, they may use them in whatever direction they please afterwards, they can never be an incumbrance.

No people appear more anxious to excite admiration and receive applause than the Americans, yet none take so little trouble, or make so few sacrifices to obtain it. This may answer among themselves, but it will not with the rest of the world; individual sacrifices must be made and national economy enlarged, before America can compete with the old world in taste, learning, and liberality.

The reception of General Lafayette[7] is the one single instance in which the national pride has overcome the national thrift; and this was clearly referable to the one single feeling of enthusiasm of which they appear capable, namely, the triumph of their successful struggle for national independence. But though this feeling will be universally acknowledged as a worthy and lawful source of triumph and of pride, it will not serve to trade upon for ever, as a fund of glory and high station among the nations. Their fathers were colonists; they fought stoutly, and became an independent people. Success and admiration, even the admiration of those whose yoke they had broken, cheered the successful heroes while living, still sheds a glory round their remote and untitled sepulchres, and will illumine the page of their history for ever.

Their children inherit the independence; they inherit too the honour of being the sons of brave fathers; but this will not give them the reputation at which they aim, of being scholars and gentlemen, nor will it enable them to sit down for evermore to talk of their glory, while they drink mint julap and chew tobacco, swearing by the beard of Jupiter (or some other oath) that they are very graceful, and agreeable, and, moreover, abusing every body who does not cry out Amen!

To doubt that talent and mental power of every kind exist in America would be absurd; why should it not? But in taste and learning they are wofully deficient; and it is this which renders them incapable of graduating a scale by which to measure themselves. Hence arises that overweening complacency and self-esteem, both national and individual, which at once renders them so extremely obnoxious to ridicule, and so peculiarly restive under it.

If they will scorn the process by which other nations have become what they avowedly intend to be, they must rest satisfied with the praise and admiration they receive from each other; and turning a deaf ear to the criticisms of the old world, consent to be their "own prodigious great reward." . . .

New York

I HAVE never seen the bay of Naples, I can therefore make no comparison, but my imagination is incapable of conceiving any thing of the kind more beautiful than the harbour of New York. Various and lovely are the objects

[7] 1824-5.

which meet the eye on every side, but the naming them would only be to give a list of words, without conveying the faintest idea of the scene. I doubt if ever the pencil of Turner could do it justice, bright and glorious as it rose upon us. We seemed to enter the harbour of New York upon waves of liquid gold, and as we darted past the green isles which rise from its bosom, like guardian sentinels of the fair city, the setting sun stretched his horizontal beams farther and farther at each moment, as if to point out to us some new glory in the landscape.

New York, indeed, appeared to us, even when we saw it by a soberer light, a lovely and a noble city. To us who had been so long travelling through half-cleared forests, and sojourning among an "I'm-as-good-as-you" population, it seemed, perhaps, more beautiful, more splendid, and more refined than it might have done, had we arrived there directly from London; but making every allowance for this, I must still declare that I think New York one of the finest cities I ever saw, and as much superior to every other in the Union (Philadelphia not excepted), as London to Liverpool, or Paris to Rouen. Its advantages of position are, perhaps, unequalled any where. Situated on an island, which I think it will one day cover, it rises like Venice, from the sea, and like that fairest of cities in the days of her glory, receives into its lap tribute of all the riches of the earth. . . .

I think it covers nearly as much ground as Paris, but is much less thickly peopled. The extreme point is fortified towards the sea by a battery, and forms an admirable point of defence; but in these piping days of peace, it is converted into a public promenade, and one more beautiful, I should suppose, no city could boast. From hence commences the splendid Broadway, as the fine avenue is called, which runs through the whole city. This noble street may vie with any I ever saw, for its length and breadth, its handsome shops, neat awnings, excellent *trottoir*, and well-dressed pedestrians. It has not the crowded glitter of Bond Street equipages, nor the gorgeous fronted palaces of Regent Street; but it is magnificent in its extent, and ornamented by several handsome buildings, some of them surrounded by grass and trees. The Park, in which stands the noble city-hall, is a very fine area. . . .

The dwelling houses of the higher classes are extremely handsome, and very richly furnished. Silk or satin furniture is as often, or oftener, seen than chintz; the mirrors are as handsome as in London; the cheffoniers, slabs, and marble tables as elegant; and in addition, they have all the pretty tasteful decoration of French porcelain, and ormolu in much greater abundance, because at a much cheaper rate. Every part of their houses is well carpeted, and the exterior finishings, such as steps, railings, and door frames, are very superior. Almost every house has handsome green blinds on the outside; balconies are not very general, nor do the houses display, externally, so many flowers as those of Paris and London; but I saw many rooms decorated within, exactly like those of an European *petite maîtresse*. Little tables, looking and smelling like flower beds, portfolios, nicknacks, bronzes, busts, cameos, and alabaster vases, illustrated copies of lady-like rhymes bound in silk, and, in short, all the coxcomalities of the drawing-room scattered about with the same profuse and studied negligence as with us. . . .

The great defect in the houses is their extreme uniformity—when you have seen one you have seen all. Neither do I quite like the arrangement of the rooms. In nearly all the houses the dining and drawing-rooms are on the same floor, with ample folding doors between them; when thrown together they certainly make a very noble apartment; but no doors can be barrier sufficient between dining and drawing-rooms. Mixed dinner parties of ladies and gentlemen, however, are very rare, which is a great defect in the society, not only as depriving them of the most sociable and hospitable manner of meeting, but as leading to frequent dinner parties of gentlemen without ladies, which certainly does not conduce to refinement.

The evening parties, excepting such as are expressly for young people, are chiefly conversational; we were too late in the season for large parties, but we saw enough to convince us that there is society to be met with in New York, which would be deemed delightful any where. Cards are very seldom used; and music, from their having very little professional aid at their parties, is seldom, I believe, as good as what is heard at private concerts in London.

The Americans have certainly not the same *besoin* of being amused as other people; they may be the wiser for this, perhaps, but it makes them less agreeable to a looker-on.

There are three theatres at New York, all of which we visited. The Park Theatre is the only one licensed by fashion, but the Bowery is infinitely superior in beauty; it is indeed as pretty a theatre as I ever entered, perfect as to size and proportion, elegantly decorated, and the scenery and machinery equal to any in London, but it is not the fashion. The Chatham is so utterly condemned by *bon ton*, that it requires some courage to decide upon going there; nor do I think my curiosity would have penetrated so far, had I had not seen Miss Mitford's *Rienzi* advertised there. It was the first opportunity I had had of seeing it played, and, spite of very indifferent acting, I was delighted. The interest must have been great, for till the curtain fell, I saw not one quarter of the queer things around me: then I observed in the front row of a dress-box a lady performing the most maternal office possible; several gentlemen without their coats, and a general air of contempt for the decencies of life, certainly more than usually revolting. . . .

The Exchange is very handsome, and ranks about midway between the heavy gloom that hangs over our London merchants, and the light and lofty elegance which decorates the Bourse at Paris. The churches are plain, but very neat, and kept in perfect repair within and without; but I saw none which had the least pretension to splendour; the Catholic Cathedral at Baltimore is the only church in America which has.

At New York, as every where else, they show within, during the time of service, like beds of tulips, so gay, so bright, so beautiful, are the long rows of French bonnets and pretty faces; rows but rarely broken by the unribboned heads of the male population; . . . Excepting at New York, I never saw the other side of the picture, but there I did. On the opposite side of the North River, about three miles higher up, is a place called Hoboken. A gentleman who possessed a handsome mansion and grounds there, also possessed the right of ferry, and to render this productive, he has restricted his pleasure grounds to a few beautiful acres, laying out the remainder simply and tastefully as a public walk. It is hardly possible to imagine one of greater attraction; a broad belt of light underwood and flowering shrubs, studded at intervals with lofty forest trees, runs for two miles along a cliff which overhangs the matchless Hudson. . . .

The price of entrance to this little Eden is the six cents you pay at the ferry. We went there on a bright Sunday afternoon, expressly to see the humours of the place. Many thousand persons were scattered through the grounds; of these we ascertained, by repeatedly counting, that nineteen-twentieths were men. The ladies were at church. . . .

How is it that the men of America, who are reckoned good husbands and good fathers, while they themselves enjoy sufficient freedom of spirit to permit their walking forth into the temple of the living God, can leave those they love best on earth bound in the iron chains of a most tyrannical fanaticism? How can they breathe the balmy air, and not think of the tainted atmosphere so heavily weighing upon breasts still dearer than their own? How can they gaze upon the blossoms of the spring, and not remember the fairer cheeks of their young daughters, waxing pale, as they sit for long sultry hours, immured with hundreds of fellow victims, listening to the roaring vanities of a preacher, canonised by a college of old women? They cannot think it needful to salvation, or they would not withdraw themselves. Wherefore is it? Do they fear these self-elected, self-ordained priests, and offer up their wives and daughters to propitiate them? Or do they deem their hebdomadal freedom more complete, because their wives and daughters are shut up four or five times in the day at church or chapel? It is true, that at Hoboken, as everywhere else, there are *reposoirs* [settling tubs for wine], which, as you pass them, blast the sense for a moment, by reeking forth the fumes of whiskey and tobacco, and it may be that these cannot be entered with a wife or daughter. The proprietor of the grounds, however, has contrived with great taste to render these abominations not unpleasing to the eye; there is one in particular, which has quite the air of a Grecian temple, and did they drink wine instead of whiskey, it might be inscribed to Bacchus; but in this particular, as in many others, the ancient and modern republics differ.

It is impossible not to feel, after passing one Sunday in the churches and chapels of New York, and the next in the gardens of Hoboken, that the thousands of well-dressed men you see enjoying themselves at the latter, have made over the thousands of well-dressed women you saw exhibited at the former, into the hands of the priests, at least, for a day. The American people arrogate to themselves a character of superior morality and religion, but this division of their hours of leisure does not give me a favourable idea of either.

I visited all the exhibitions in New York. The Medici of the Republic must exert themselves a little more before these can become even respectable. The worst of the business is, that with the exception of about half a dozen individuals, the good citizens are more than contented, they are delighted.

The newspaper lungs of the Republic breathe forth praise and triumph, nay, almost pant with ecstasy in speaking of their native *chef d'œuvres.* I should be hardly believed were I to relate the instances which fell in my way, of the utter ignorance respecting pictures to be found among persons of the *first standing* in society. Often where a liberal spirit exists, and a wish to patronise the fine arts is expressed, it is joined to a profundity of ignorance on the subject almost inconceivable. A doubt as to the excellence of their artists is very nervously received, and one gentleman, with much civility, told me, that at the present era, all the world were aware that competition was pretty well at an end between our two nations, and that a little envy might naturally be expected to mix with the surprise with which the mother country beheld the distance at which her colonies were leaving her behind them.

I must, however, do the few artists with whom I became acquainted, the justice to say, that their own pretensions are much more modest than those of their patrons for them. I have heard several confess and deplore their ignorance of drawing, and have repeatedly remarked a sensibility to the merit of European artists, though perhaps only known by engravings, and a deference to their authority, which showed a genuine feeling for the art. In fact, I think that there is a very considerable degree of natural talent for painting in America, but it has to make its way through darkness and thick night. When an academy is founded, their first care is to hang the walls of its exhibition room with all the unutterable trash that is offered to them. No living models are sought for; no discipline as to the manner of study is enforced. Boys who know no more of human form, than they do of the eyes, nose, and mouth in the moon, begin painting portraits. If some of them would only throw away their palettes for a year, and learn to draw; if they would attend anatomical lectures, and take notes, not in words, but in forms, of joints and muscles, their exhibitions would soon cease to be so utterly below criticism.

The most interesting exhibition open when I was there was, decidedly, Colonel Trumbull's; and how the patriots of America can permit this truly national collection to remain a profitless burden on the hands of the artist, it is difficult to understand. Many of the sketches are masterly; but, like his illustrious countryman, West, his sketches are his *chef d'œuvres.* . . .

We spent a delightful day in New Jersey, in visiting, with a most agreeable party, the inclined planes, which are used instead of locks on the Morris canal.

This is a very interesting work; it is one among a thousand which prove the people of America to be the most enterprising in the world. . . .

There is no point in the national character of the Americans which commands so much respect as the boldness and energy with which public works are undertaken and carried through. Nothing stops them if a profitable result can be fairly hoped for. It is this which has made cities spring up amidst the forests with such inconceivable rapidity; and could they once be thoroughly persuaded that any point of the ocean had a hoard of dollars beneath it, I have not the slightest doubt that in about eighteen months we should see a snug covered rail-road leading direct to the spot.

I was told at New York, that in many parts of the state it was usual to pay the service of the Presbyterian ministers in the following manner. Once a year a day is fixed, on which some member of every family in a congregation meet at their minister's house in the afternoon. They each bring an offering (according to their means) of articles necessary for housekeeping. The poorer members leave their contributions in a large basket, placed for the purpose close to the door of entrance. Those of more importance, and more calculated to do honour to the piety of the donors, are carried into the room where the company is assembled. Sugar, coffee, tea, cheese, barrels of flour, pieces of Irish linen, sets of china and of glass, were among the articles mentioned to me as usually making parts of these offerings. After the party is assembled, and the business of giving and receiving is dispatched, tea, coffee, and cakes are handed round; but these are not furnished at any expense either of trouble or money to the minister, for selected ladies of the congregation take the whole arrangement upon themselves. These meetings are called spinning visits.

Another New York custom, which does not seem to have so reasonable a cause, is the changing house once a year. On the 1st of May the city of New York has the appearance of sending off a population flying from the plague, or of a town which had surrendered on condition of carrying away all their goods and chattels. Rich furniture and ragged furniture, carts, waggons, and drays, ropes, canvas, and straw, packers, porters, and draymen, white, yellow, and black, occupy the streets from east to west, from north to south, on this day. Every one I spoke to on the subject complained of this custom as most annoying, but all assured me it was unavoidable, if you inhabit a rented house. More than one of my New York friends have built or bought houses solely to avoid this annual inconvenience. . . .

Most of the houses in New York are painted on the outside, but in a manner carefully to avoid disfiguring the material which it preserves: on the contrary, nothing can be neater. They are now using a great deal of a beautiful stone called Jersey freestone; it is of a warm rich brown, and extremely ornamental to the city wherever it has been employed. They have also a grey granite of great beauty. The trottoir paving, in most of the streets, is extremely good, being of large flag stones, very superior to the bricks of Philadelphia.

At night the shops, which are open till very late, are brilliantly illuminated with gas, and all the population seem as much alive as in London or Paris. This makes the solemn stillness of the evening hours in Philadelphia more remarkable. . . .

Ice is in profuse abundance; I do not imagine that there is a house in the city without the luxury of a piece of ice to cool the water, and harden the butter. . . .

The luxury of the New York aristocracy is not confined to the city; hardly an acre of Manhattan Island but shows some pretty villa or stately mansion. The most chosen of these are on the north and east rivers, to whose margins their lawns descend. Among these, perhaps, the loveliest is one situated in the beautiful village of Bloomingdale: here, within the space of sixteen acres, almost every variety of garden scenery may be found. To describe all its diversity of hill and dale, of wood and lawn, of rock and river, would be in vain; nor can I convey an idea of it by comparison, for I never saw any thing like it. How far the elegant hospitality which reigns there may influence my impressions, I know not; but, assuredly, no spot I have ever seen dwells more freshly on my memory, nor did I ever find myself in a circle more calculated to give delight in meeting and regret at parting, than that of Woodlawn.

Conclusion

I SUSPECT that what I have written will make it evident that I do not like America. Now, as it happens that I met with individuals there whom I love and admire, far beyond the love and admiration of ordinary acquaintance; and as I declare the country to be fair to the eye, and most richly teeming with the gifts of plenty, I am led to ask myself why it is that I do not like it. I would willingly know myself, and confess to others, why it is that neither its beauty nor its abundance can suffice to neutralise, or greatly soften, the distaste which the aggregate of my recollections has left upon my mind.

I remember hearing it said . . . that it was the "Who?" and not the "Where?" that made the difference between the pleasant or unpleasant residence. The truth of the observation struck me forcibly when I heard it; and it has been recalled to my mind since, by the constantly recurring evidence of its justness. In applying this to America, I speak not of my friends, nor of my friends' friends. The small patrician band is a race apart; they live with each other, and for each other; mix wondrously little with the high matters of state, which they seem to leave rather supinely to their tailors and tinkers, and are no more to be taken as a sample of the American people, than the head of Lord Byron as a sample of the heads of the British peerage. I speak not of these, but of the population generally, as seen in town and country, among the rich and the poor, in the slave states and the free states. I do not like them. I do not like their principles, I do not like their manners, I do not like their opinions.

Both as a woman, and as a stranger, it might be unseemly for me to say that I do not like their government, and therefore I will not say so. That it is one which pleases themselves is most certain, and this is considerably more important than pleasing all the travelling old ladies in the world. I entered the country at New Orleans, remained for more than two years west of the Alleghanies, and passed another year among the Atlantic cities, and the country around them. I conversed during this time with citizens of all orders and degrees, and I never heard from any one a single disparaging word against their government. It is not, therefore, surprising, that when the people of that country hear strangers questioning the wisdom of their institutions, and expressing disapprobation at some of their effects, they should set it down either to an incapacity of judging, or a malicious feeling of envy and ill-will.

"How can any one in their senses doubt the excellence of a government which we have tried for half a century, and loved the better the longer we have known it?"

Such is the natural inquiry of every American when the excellence of their government is doubted; and I am inclined to answer, that no one in their senses, who has visited their country and known the people, can doubt its fitness for them, such as they now are, or its utter unfitness for any other people.

Whether the government has made the people what they are, or whether the people have made the government what it is, to suit themselves, I know not; but if the latter, they have shown a consummation of wisdom which the assembled world may look upon and admire.

It is matter of historical notoriety, that the original stock of the white population now inhabiting the United States, were persons who had banished themselves, or were banished from the mother country. The land they found was favourable to their increase and prosperity; the colony grew and flourished. Years rolled on, and the children, the grandchildren, and the great-grandchildren of the first settlers, replenished the land, and found it flowing with milk and honey. That they should wish to keep this milk and honey to themselves is not very surprising. What did the mother country do for them? She sent them out gay and gallant officers to guard their frontier; the which they thought they could guard as well themselves; and then she taxed their tea. Now, this was disagreeable; and to atone for it, the distant colony had no great share in her mother's grace and glory. It was not from among them that her high and mighty were chosen; the rays which emanated from that bright sun of honour, the British throne, reached them but feebly. They knew not, they cared not, for her kings nor her heroes; their thriftiest trader was their noblest man; the holy seats of learning were but the cradles of superstition; the splendour of the aristocracy, but a leech that drew their "golden blood". The wealth, the learning, the glory of Britain, was to them nothing; the having their own way every thing.

Can any blame their wish to obtain it? Can any lament that they succeeded?

And now the day was their own, what should they do next? Their elders drew together, and said: "Let us make a government that shall suit us all; let it be rude, and rough, and noisy; let it not affect either dignity, glory, or splendour; let it interfere with no man's will, nor meddle with any man's business: let us have neither tithes, nor taxes, game laws, nor poor laws; let every man have a hand in making the laws, and no man be troubled about keeping them; let not our magistrates wear purple, nor our judges ermine; if a man grow rich, let us take care that his grandson be poor, and then we shall all keep equal; let every man take care of himself, and if England should come to bother us again, why then we will fight all together."

Could any thing be better imagined than such a government for a people so circumstanced? Or is it strange that they are contented with it? Still less is it strange that those who have lived in the repose of order, and felt secure that their country could go on very well and its business proceed without their bawling and squalling, scratching and scrambling to help it, should bless the gods that they are not republicans.

So far all is well. That they should prefer a constitution which suits them so admirably, to one which would not suit them at all, is surely no cause of quarrel on our part; nor should it be such on theirs, if we feel no inclination to exchange the institutions which have made us what we are, for any other on the face of the earth.

But when a native of Europe visits America, a most extraordinary species of tyranny is set in action against him; and as far as my reading and experience have enabled me to judge, it is such as no other country has ever exercised against strangers.

The Frenchman visits England: he is *abîmé d'ennui* [swallowed up by boredom] at our stately dinners; shrugs his shoulders at our *corps de ballet*, and laughs *à gorge déployée* [immoderately] at our passion for driving, and our partial affection for roast beef and plum pudding. The Englishman returns the visit, and the first thing he does on arriving at Paris, is to hasten to *le Théâtre des Variétés*, that he may see "*Les Anglaises pour rire*" [The Englishwomen to laugh at them], and if among the crowd of laughers, you hear a note of more cordial mirth than the rest, seek out the person from whom it proceeds, and you will find the Englishman.

The Italian comes to our green island, and groans at our climate; he vows that the air which destroys a statue cannot be wholesome for man; he sighs for orange trees and macaroni, and smiles at the pretensions of a nation to poetry, while no epics are chaunted through her streets. Yet we welcome the sensitive southern with all kindness, listen to his complaints with interest, cultivate our little orange trees, and teach our children to lisp Tasso, in the hope of becoming more agreeable.

Yet we are not at all superior to the rest of Europe in our endurance of censure, nor is this wish to profit by it at all peculiar to the English; we laugh at, and find fault with, our neighbours quite as freely as they do with us, and they join the laugh, and adopt our fashions and customs. These mutual pleasantries produce no shadow of unkindly feeling; and as long as the governments are at peace with each other, the individuals of every nation in Europe make it a matter of pride, as well as of pleasure, to meet each other frequently, to discuss, compare, and reason upon their national varieties, and to vote it a mark of fashion and good taste to imitate each other in all the external embellishments of life.

The consequence of this is most pleasantly perceptible, at the present time, in every capital of Europe. The long peace has given time for each to catch from each what was best in customs and manners, and the rapid advance of refinement and general information has been the result.

To those who have been accustomed to this state of things, the contrast upon crossing to the new world is inconceivably annoying; and it cannot be doubted that this is one great cause of the general feeling of irksomeness and fatigue of spirits, which hangs upon the memory while recalling the hours passed in American society.

A single word indicative of doubt, that any thing, or every thing, in that country is not the very best in the world, produces an effect which must be seen and felt to be understood. If the citizens of the United States were indeed the devoted patriots they call themselves, they would surely not thus incrust themselves in the hard, dry, stubborn persuasion, that they are the first and best of the human race, that nothing is to be learnt but what they are able to teach, and that nothing is worth having which they do not possess.

The art of man could hardly discover a more effectual antidote to improvement, than this persuasion; and yet I never listened to any public oration, or read any work professedly addressed to the country, in which they did not labour to impress it on the minds of the people.

To hint to the generality of Americans that the silent current of events may change their beloved government, is not the way to please them; but in truth they need be tormented with no such fear. As long as by common consent they can keep down the pre-eminence which nature has assigned to great powers, as long as they can prevent human respect and human honour from resting upon high talent, gracious manners, and exalted station, so long may they be sure of going on as they are.

I have been told, however, that there are some among them who would gladly see a change; some who, with the wisdom of philosophers and the fair candour of gentlemen, shrink from a profession of equality which they feel to be untrue, and believe to be impossible.

I can well believe that such there are, though to me no such opinions were communicated, and most truly should I rejoice to see power pass into such hands.

If this ever happens, if refinement once creeps in among them, if they once learn to cling to the graces, the honours, the chivalry of life, then we shall say farewell to American equality, and welcome to European fellowship one of the finest countries on the earth.

De Tocqueville on Democracy

Although Alexis Charles Henri Clérel de Tocqueville belonged to a family of French aristocrats, several of whom had been executed during the French Revolution, no one has ever written a more impartial or penetrating analysis of democracy.

In 1825, at the age of twenty he was admitted to the French bar, and was appointed to a judicial office the following year. He arrived in America in May, 1831, to remain about nine months, visiting all the principal cities and interviewing Americans of every sort. The next three years were spent writing the first volume of "De la democratie en l'Amerique." The second appeared in 1839. The book was promptly translated into several modern languages.

For nine years de Tocqueville served as a Deputy of the Chamber. He was briefly Minister of Foreign Affairs under Louis Napoleon. After a long period of failing health he died on April 16, 1859, at the age of fifty-three.

From DEMOCRACY IN AMERICA

On the continent of Europe, at the beginning of the seventeenth century, absolute monarchy had everywhere triumphed over the ruins of the oligarchical and feudal liberties of the Middle Ages. Never were the notions of right more completely confounded than in the midst of the splendour and literature of Europe; never was there less political activity among the people; never were the principles of true freedom less widely circulated; and at that very time those principles, which were scorned or unknown by the nations of Europe, were proclaimed in the deserts of the New World, and were accepted as the future creed of a great people. The boldest theories of the human reason were put into practice by a community so humble that not a statesman condescended to attend to it; and a legislation without a precedent was produced offhand by the imagination of the citizens. In the bosom of this obscure democracy, which had as yet brought forth neither generals, nor philosophers, nor authors, a man[1]

[1]John Winthrop, governor of Massachusetts colony.

might stand up in the face of a free people and pronounce the following fine definition of liberty:

"Nor would I have you to mistake in the point of your own liberty. There is a liberty of a corrupt nature which is effected both by men and beasts to do what they list, and this liberty is inconsistent with authority, impatient of all restraint; by this liberty 'sumus omnes deteriores': 'tis the grand enemy of truth and peace, and all the ordinances of God are bent against it. But there is a civil, a moral, a federal liberty which is the proper end and object of authority; it is a liberty for that only which is just and good: for this liberty you are to stand with the hazard of your very lives, and whatsoever crosses it is not authority, but a distemper thereof. This liberty is maintained in a way of subjection to authority; and the authority set over you will, in all administrations for your good, be quietly submitted unto by all but such as have a disposition to shake off the yoke and lose their true liberty, by their murmuring at the honour and power of authority." . . .

The Social Condition of the Anglo-Americans

A social condition is commonly the result of circumstances, sometimes of laws, oftener still of these two causes united; but wherever it exists, it may justly be considered as the source of almost all the laws, the usages, and the ideas which regulate the conduct of nations; whatever it does not produce it modifies. . . . The social condition of the Americans is eminently democratic; this was its character at the foundation of the colonies, and is still more strongly marked at the present day. . . . Great equality existed among the emigrants who settled on the shores of New England. The germ of aristocracy was never planted in that part of the Union. The only influence which obtained there was that of intellect; the people were used to reverence certain names as the emblems of knowledge and virtue. Some of their fellow-citizens acquired a power over the rest which might truly have been called aristocratic, if it had been capable of transmission from father to son.

This was the state of things to the east of the Hudson: to the southwest of that river, and in the direction of the Floridas, the case was different. In most of the States situated to the southwest of the Hudson some great English proprietors had settled, who had imported with them aristocratic principles and the English law of descent. . . . In the South, one man, aided by slaves, could cultivate a great extent of country: it was therefore common to see rich landed proprietors. But their influence was not altogether aristocratic as that term is understood in Europe, since they possessed no privileges; and the cultivation of their estates being carried on by slaves, they had no tenants depending on them, and consequently no patronage. Still, the great proprietors south of the Hudson constituted a superior class, having ideas and tastes of its own, and forming the centre of political action. This kind of aristocracy sympathized with the body of the people, whose passions and interests it easily embraced; but it was too weak and too short-lived to excite either love or hatred for itself. . . .

At the period of which we are now speaking society was shaken to its centre: the people, in whose name the struggle had taken place, conceived the desire of exercising the authority which it had acquired; its democratic tendencies were awakened; and having thrown off the yoke of the mother-country, it aspired to independence of every kind. The influence of individuals gradually ceased to be felt, and custom and law united together to produce the same result.

But the law of descent was the last step to equality. I am surprised that ancient and modern jurists have not attributed to this law a greater influence on human affairs. It is true that these laws belong to civil affairs; but they ought nevertheless to be placed at the head of all political institutions; for, while political laws are only the symbol of a nation's condition, they exercise an incredible influence upon its social state. They have, moreover, a sure and uniform manner of operating upon society, affecting, as it were, generations yet unborn. . . .

When the legislator has regulated the law of inheritance, he may rest from his labour. The machine once put in motion will go on for ages, and advance, as if self-guided, toward a given point. When framed in a particular manner, this law unites, draws together, and vests property and power in a few hands: its tendency is clearly aristocratic. On opposite principles its action is still more rapid; it divides, distributes, and disperses both property and power. Alarmed by the rapidity of its progress, those who despair of arresting its motion endeavour to obstruct it by difficulties and impediments; they vainly seek to counteract its effect by contrary efforts; but it gradually reduces or destroys every obstacle, until by its incessant activity the bulwarks of the influence of wealth are ground down to the fine and shifting sand which is the basis of democracy. . . .

In virtue of the law of partible inheritance, the death of every proprietor brings about a kind of revolution in property; not only do his possessions change hands, but their very nature is altered, since they are parcelled into shares, which become smaller and smaller at each division. . . . It follows, then, that in countries where equality of inheritance is established by law, property, and especially landed property, must have a tendency to perpetual diminution. . . .

When the equal partition of property is established by law, the intimate connection is destroyed between family feeling and the preservation of the paternal estate; the property ceases to represent the family; for as it must inevitably be divided after one or two generations, it has evidently a constant tendency to diminish, and must in the end be completely dispersed. . . .

Now, from the moment that you divest the landowner of that interest in the preservation of his estate which he derives from association, from tradition, and from family pride, you may be certain that sooner or later he will dispose of it; for there is a strong pecuniary interest in favour of selling, as floating capital produces higher interest than real property, and is more readily available to gratify the passions of the moment. . . .

The law of equal distribution proceeds by two methods: by acting upon things, it acts upon persons; by influencing persons, it affects things. By these means the law succeeds in striking at the root of landed property, and dispersing rapidly both families and fortunes. . . .

In the United States it has nearly completed its work of destruction, and there we can best study its results. The English laws concerning the transmission of property were abolished in almost all the States at the time of the Revolution. The law of entail was so modified as not to interrupt the free circulation of property. The first generation having passed away, estates began to be parcelled out, and the change became more and more rapid with the progress of time. At this moment, after a lapse of a little more than sixty years, the aspect of society is totally altered; the families of the great landed proprietors are almost all commingled with the general mass. In the State of New York, which formerly contained many of these, there are but two who still keep their heads above the stream, and they must shortly disappear. The sons of these opulent citizens are become merchants, lawyers, or physicians. Most of them have lapsed into obscurity. The last trace of hereditary ranks and distinctions is destroyed—the law of partition has reduced all to one level. . . .

I do not mean that there is any deficiency of wealthy individuals in the United States; I know of no country, indeed, where the love of money has taken stronger hold upon the affections of men, and where profounder contempt is expressed for the theory of the permanent equality of property. But wealth circulates with inconceivable rapidity, and experience shows that it is rare to find two succeeding generations in the full enjoyment of it. . . .

It is not only the fortunes of men which are equal in America; even their requirements partake in some degree of the same uniformity. I do not believe that there is a country in the world where, in proportion to the population, there are so few uninstructed and at the same time so few learned individuals. Primary instruction is within the reach of everybody; superior instruction is scarcely to be obtained by any. This is not surprising; it is, in fact, the necessary consequence of what we have advanced above. Almost all the Americans are in easy circumstances, and can therefore obtain the first elements of human knowledge.

In America there are comparatively few who are rich enough to live without a profession. Every profession requires an apprenticeship, which limits the time of instruction to the early years of life. At fifteen they enter upon their calling, and thus their education ends at the age when ours begins. Whatever is done afterward is with a view to some special and lucrative object; a science is taken up as a matter of business, and the only branch of it which is attended to is such as admits of an immediate practical application. In America most of the rich men were formerly poor; most of those who now enjoy leisure were absorbed in business during their youth; the consequence of which is, that when they might have had a taste for study they had no time for it, and when time is at their disposal they have no longer the inclination.

There is no class, then, in America in which the taste for intellectual pleasures is transmitted with hereditary fortune and leisure, and by which the labours of the intellect are held in honour. Accordingly, there is an equal want of the desire and the power of application to these objects. . . .

America, then, exhibits in her social state a most extraordinary phenomenon. Men are there seen on a greater equality in point of fortune and intellect, or, in other words, more equal in their strength, than in any other country of the world, or in any age of which history has preserved the remembrance.

The political consequences of such a social condition as this are easily deducible. It is impossible to believe that equality will not eventually find its way into the political world as it does everywhere else. To conceive of men remaining forever unequal upon one single point, yet equal on all others, is impossible; they must come in the end to be equal upon all. Now I know of only two methods of establishing equality in the political world; every citizen must be put in possession of his rights, or rights must be granted to no one. For nations which are arrived at the same stage of social existence as the Anglo-Americans, it is therefore very difficult to discover a medium between the sovereignty of all and the absolute power of one man: and it would be vain to deny that the social condition which I have been describing is equally liable to each of these consequences.

There is, in fact, a manly and lawful passion for equality which excites men to wish all to be powerful and honoured. This passion tends to elevate the humble to the rank of the great; but there exists also in the human heart a depraved taste for equality, which impels the weak to attempt to lower the powerful to their own level, and reduces men to prefer equality in slavery to inequality with freedom. Not that those nations whose social condition is democratic naturally despise liberty; on the contrary, they have an instinctive love of it. But liberty is not the chief and constant object of their desires; equality is their idol: they make rapid and sudden efforts to obtain liberty, and if they miss their aim resign themselves to their disappointment; but nothing can satisfy them except equality, and rather than lose it they resolve to perish.

On the other hand, in a State where the citizens are nearly on an equality, it becomes difficult for them to preserve their independence against the aggressions of power. No one among them being strong enough to engage in the struggle with advantage, nothing but a general combination can protect their liberty. And such a union is not always to be found.

From the same social position, then, nations may derive one or the other of two great political results; these results are extremely different from each other, but they may both proceed from the same cause.

The Anglo-Americans are the first nations who, having been exposed to this formidable alternative, have been happy enough to escape the dominion of absolute power. They have been allowed by their circumstances, their origin, their intelligence, and especially by their moral feeling, to establish and maintain the sovereignty of the people.

Democratic Government in America

In Europe we are at a loss how to judge the true character and the more permanent propensities of democracy, because in Europe two conflicting principles exist, and we do not know what to attribute to the principles themselves, and what to refer to the passions which they bring into collision. Such, however, is not the case in America; there the people reigns without any obstacle, and it has no perils to dread and no injuries to avenge. In America, democracy is swayed by its own free propensities; its course is natural and its activity is unrestrained; the United States consequently afford the most favourable opportunity of studying its real character. And to no people can this inquiry be more vitally interesting than to the French nation, which is blindly driven onward by a daily and irresistible impulse toward a state of things which may prove either despotic or republican, but which will assuredly be democratic.

I have already observed that universal suffrage has been adopted in all the States of the Union; it consequently occurs among different populations which occupy very different positions in the scale of society. I have had opportunities of observing its effects in different localities, and among races of men who are nearly strangers to each other by their language, their religion, and their manner of life; in Louisiana as well as in New England, in Georgia and in Canada. I have remarked that universal suffrage is far from producing in America either all the good or all the evil consequences which are assigned to it in Europe, and that its effects differ very widely from those which are usually attributed to it.

Many people in Europe are apt to believe without saying it, or to say without believing it, that one of the great advantages of universal suffrage is, that it intrusts the direction of public affairs to men who are worthy of the public confidence. They admit that the people is unable to govern for itself, but they aver that it is always sincerely disposed to promote the welfare of the State, and that it instinctively designates those persons who are animated by the same good wishes, and who are the most fit to wield the supreme authority. I confess that the observations I made in America by no means coincide with these opinions. On my arrival in the United States I was surprised to find so much distinguished talent among the subjects, and so little among the heads of the Government. It is a well-authenticated fact, that at the present day the most able men in the United States are very rarely placed at the head of affairs; and it must be acknowledged that such has been the result in proportion as democracy has outstepped all its former limits. The race of American statesmen has evidently dwindled most remarkably in the course of the last fifty years.

Several causes may be assigned to this phenomenon. It is impossible, notwithstanding the most strenuous exertions, to raise the intelligence of the people above a certain level. Whatever may be the facilities of acquiring information, whatever may be the profusion of easy methods and of cheap science, the human mind can never be instructed and educated without devoting a considerable space of time to those objects.

The greater or the lesser possibility of subsisting without labour is therefore the necessary boundary of intellectual improvement. This boundary . . . must exist somewhere as long as the people is constrained to work in order to procure the means of physical subsistence. . . . It is therefore quite as difficult to imagine a State in which all the citizens should be very well informed as a State in which they all should be wealthy. . . . It may very readily be admitted that the mass of the citizens are sincerely disposed to promote the welfare of their country; nay more, it even may be allowed that the lower classes are less apt to be swayed by considerations of personal interest than the higher orders: but it is always more or less impossible for them to discern the best means of attaining the end which they desire with sincerity. Long and patient observation, joined to a multitude of different notions, is required to form a just estimate of the character of a single individual; and can it be supposed that the vulgar have the power of succeeding in an inquiry which misleads the penetration of genius itself? The people has neither the time nor the means which are essential to the prosecution of an investigation of this kind: its conclusions are hastily formed from a superficial inspection of the more prominent features of a question. Hence it often assents to the clamour of a mountebank who knows the secret of stimulating its tastes, while its truest friends frequently fail in their exertions.

Moreover, the democracy is not only deficient in that soundness of judgment which is necessary to select men really deserving of its confidence, but it has neither the desire nor the inclination to find them out. It can not be denied that democratic institutions have a very strong tendency to promote the feeling of envy in the human heart; not so much because they afford to every one the means of rising to the level of any of his fellow-citizens, as because those means perpetually disappoint the persons who employ them. Democratic institutions awaken and foster a passion for equality which they can never entirely satisfy. This complete equality eludes the grasp of the people at the very moment at which it thinks to hold it fast, . . . and the people is excited in the pursuit of an advantage, which is more precious because it is not sufficiently remote to be unknown, or sufficiently near to be enjoyed. The lower orders are agitated by the chance of success, they are irritated by its uncertainty; and they pass from the enthusiasm of pursuit to the exhaustion of ill success, and lastly to the acrimony of disappointment. Whatever transcends their own limits appears to be an obstacle to their desires, and there is no kind of superiority, however legitimate it may be, which is not irksome in their sight. . . .

In the United States the people is not disposed to hate the superior classes of society; but it is not very favourably inclined toward them, and it carefully excludes them from the exercise of authority. It does not entertain any dread of distinguished talents, but it is rarely captivated by them; and it awards its approbation very sparingly to such as have risen without the popular support.

While the natural propensities of democracy induce the people to reject the most distinguished citizens as its rulers, these individuals are no less apt to retire from a political career in which it is almost impossible to retain their independence, or to advance without degrading themselves. This opinion has been very candidly set forth by Chancellor Kent,[2] who says, in speaking with great eulogiums of that part of the Constitution which empowers the Executive to nominate the judges: "It is indeed probable that the men who are best fitted to discharge the duties of this high office would have too much reserve in their manners, and too much austerity in their principles, for them to be returned by the majority at an election where universal suffrage is adopted." Such were the opinions which were printed without contradiction in America in the year 1830.

I hold it to be sufficiently demonstrated that universal suffrage is by no means a guarantee of the wisdom of the popular choice; and that, whatever its advantages may be, this is not one of them.

When a State is threatened by serious dangers, the people frequently succeeds in selecting the citizens who are the most able to save it. It has been observed that man rarely retains his customary level in presence of very critical circumstances; he rises above or he sinks below his usual condition, and the same thing occurs in nations at large. Extreme perils sometimes quench the energy of a people instead of stimulating it; they excite without directing its passions, and instead of clearing they confuse its powers of perception. The Jews deluged the smoking ruins of their temple with the carnage of the remnant of their host. But it is more common, both in the case of nations and in that of individuals, to find extraordinary virtues arising from the very imminence of the danger. Great characters are then thrown into relief, as edifices which are concealed by the gloom of night are illuminated by the glare of a conflagration. At those dangerous times genius no longer abstains from presenting itself in the arena; and

[2]James Kent (1763–1847) chief justice and chancellor of the State of New York, author of *Commentaries on American Law*.

the people, alarmed by the perils of its situation, buries its envious passions in a short oblivion. Great names may then be drawn from the balloting-box.

I have already observed that the American statesmen of the present day are very inferior to those who stood at the head of affairs fifty years ago. This is as much a consequence of the circumstances as of the laws of the country. When America was struggling in the high cause of independence to throw off the yoke of another country, and when it was about to usher a new nation into the world, the spirits of its inhabitants were roused to the height which their great efforts required. In this general excitement the most distinguished men were ready to forestall the wants of the community, and the people clung to them for support, and placed them at its head. But events of this magnitude are rare, and it is from an inspection of the ordinary course of affairs that our judgment must be formed.

If passing occurrences sometimes act as checks upon the passions of democracy, the intelligence and the manners of the community exercise an influence which is not less powerful and far more permanent. This is extremely perceptible in the United States.

In New England the education and the liberties of the communities were engendered by the moral and religious principles of their founders. Where society has acquired a sufficient degree of stability to enable it to hold certain maxims and to retain fixed habits, the lower orders are accustomed to respect intellectual superiority and to submit to it without complaint, although they set at naught all those privileges which wealth and birth have introduced among mankind. The democracy in New England consequently makes a more judicious choice than it does elsewhere.

But as we descend toward the South, to those States in which the constitution of society is more modern and less strong, where instruction is less general, and where the principles of morality, of religion, and of liberty are less happily combined, we perceive that the talents and the virtues of those who are in authority become more and more rare.

Lastly, when we arrive at the new Southwestern States, in which the constitution of society dates but from yesterday, and presents an agglomeration of adventurers and speculators, we are amazed at the persons who are invested with public authority, and we are led to ask by what force, independent of the legislation and of the men who direct it, the State can be protected, and society be made to flourish.

There are certain laws of a democratic nature which contribute, nevertheless, to correct, in some measure, the dangerous tendencies of democracy. On entering the House of Representatives at Washington one is struck by the vulgar demeanour of that great assembly. The eye frequently does not discover a man of celebrity within its walls. Its members are almost all obscure individuals whose names present no associations to the mind: they are mostly village lawyers, men in trade, or even persons belonging to the lower classes of society. In a country in which education is very general, it is said that the representatives of the people do not always know how to write correctly.

At a few yards' distance from this spot is the door of the Senate, which contains within a small space a large proportion of the celebrated men of America. Scarcely an individual is to be perceived in it who does not recall the idea of an active and illustrious career: the Senate is composed of eloquent advocates, distinguished generals, wise magistrates, and statesmen of note, whose language would at all times do honour to the most remarkable parliamentary debates of Europe.

What, then, is the cause of this strange contrast, and why are the most able citizens to be found in one assembly rather than in the other? Why is the former body remarkable for its vulgarity and its poverty of talent, while the latter seems to enjoy a monopoly of intelligence and of sound judgment? Both of these assemblies emanate from the people; both of them are chosen by universal suffrage; and no voice has hitherto been heard to assert in America that the Senate is hostile to the interests of the people. From what cause, then, does so startling a difference arise? The only reason which appears to me adequately to account for it is, that the House of Representatives is elected by the populace directly, and that the Senate is elected by elected bodies. The whole body of the citizens names the legislature of each State, and the Federal Constitution converts these legislatures into so many electoral bodies, which return the members of the Senate. The senators are elected by an indirect application of universal suffrage; for the legislatures which name them are not aristocratic or privileged bodies which exercise the electoral franchise in their own right; but they are chosen by the totality of the citizens; they are generally elected every year, and new members may constantly be chosen who will employ their electoral rights in conformity with the wishes of the public. But this transmission of the popular authority through an assembly of chosen men operates an important change in it, by refining its discretion and improving the forms which it adopts. Men who are chosen in this manner accurately represent the majority of the nation which governs them; but they represent the elevated thoughts which are current in the community, the propensities which prompt its nobler actions, rather than the petty passions which disturb or the vices which disgrace it.

The time already may be anticipated at which the American republics will be obliged to introduce the plan of election by an elected body more frequently into their system of representation, or they will incur no small risk of perishing miserably among the shoals of democracy.

And here I have no scruple in confessing that I look upon this peculiar system of election as the only means of bringing the exercise of political power to the level of all classes of the people. Those thinkers who regard this institution as the exclusive weapon of a party, and those who fear, on the other hand, to make use of it, seem to me to fall into as great an error in the one case as in the other.

When elections recur at long intervals the State is exposed to violent agitation every time they take place. Parties exert themselves to the utmost in order to gain a prize which is so rarely within their reach; and as the evil is almost irremediable for the candidates who fail, the consequences of their disappointed ambition may prove most disastrous: if, on the other hand, the legal struggle can be repeated within a short space of time, the defeated parties take patience. When elections occur frequently, their recurrence keeps society in a perpetual state of feverish excitement, and imparts a continual instability to public affairs.

Thus, on the one hand, the State is exposed to the perils of a revolution, on the other to perpetual mutability; the former system threatens the very existence of the Government, the latter is an obstacle to all steady and consistent policy. The Americans have preferred the second of these evils to the first; but they were led to this conclusion by their instinct much more than by their reason; for a taste for variety is one of the characteristic passions of democracy. An extraordinary mutability has, by this means, been introduced into their legislation. Many of the Americans consider the instability of their laws as a necessary consequence of a system whose general results are beneficial. But no one in the United States affects to deny the fact of this instability, or to contend that it is not a great evil.

Hamilton, after having demonstrated the utility of a power which might prevent, or which might at least impede, the promulgation of bad laws, adds: "It might perhaps be said that the power of preventing bad laws includes that of preventing good ones, and may be used to the one purpose as well as to the other. But this objection will have little weight with those who can properly estimate the mischiefs of that inconstancy and mutability in the laws which form the greatest blemish in the character and genius of our governments" ("Federalist," No. 73). And again in No. 62 of the same work he observes: "The facility and excess of law-making seem to be the diseases to which our governments are most liable. . . . The mischievous effects of the mutability in the public councils arising from a rapid succession of new members would fill a volume: every new election in the States is found to change one half of the representatives. From this change of men must proceed a change of opinions and of measures, which forfeits the respect and confidence of other nations, poisons the blessings of liberty itself, and diminishes the attachment and reverence of the people toward a political system which betrays so many marks of infirmity."

Jefferson himself, the greatest democrat whom the democracy of America has yet produced, pointed out the same evils. "The instability of our laws," said he in a letter to Madison, "is really a very serious inconvenience. I think that we ought to have obviated it by deciding that a whole year should always be allowed to elapse between the bringing in of a bill and the final passing of it. It should afterward be discussed and put to the vote without the possibility of making any alteration in it; and if the circumstances of the case required a more speedy decision, the question should not be decided by a simple majority, but by a majority of at least two thirds of both houses."

Public officers in the United States are commingled with the crowd of citizens; they have neither palaces, nor guards, nor ceremonial costumes. This simple exterior of the persons in authority is connected not only with the peculiarities of the American character, but with the fundamental principles of that society. In the estimation of the democracy a government is not a benefit, but a necessary evil. A certain degree of power must be granted to public officers, for they would be of no use without it. But the ostensible semblance of authority is by no means indispensable to the conduct of affairs, and it is needlessly offensive to the susceptibility of the public. The public officers themselves are well aware that they only enjoy the superiority over their fellow-citizens which they derive from their authority upon condition of putting themselves on a level with the whole community by their manners. A public officer in the United States is uniformly civil, accessible to all the world, attentive to all requests, and obliging in his replies. I was pleased by these characteristics of a democratic government; and I was struck by the manly independence of the citizens, who respect the office more than the officer, and who are less attached to the emblems of authority than to the man who bears them. . . .

A democracy may, however, allow a certain show of magisterial pomp, and clothe its officers in silks and gold, without seriously compromising its principles. Privileges of this kind are transitory; they belong to the place, and are distinct from the individual: but if public officers are not uniformly remunerated by the State, the public charges must be intrusted to men of opulence and independence, who constitute the basis of an aristocracy; and if the people still retains its right of election, that election can only be made from a certain class of citizens. When a democratic republic renders offices which had formerly been remunerated gratuitous, it may safely be believed that the State is advancing to monarchical institutions; and when a monarchy begins to remunerate such officers as had hitherto been unpaid, it is a sure sign that it is approaching toward a despotic or a republican form of government. The substitution of paid for unpaid functionaries is of itself, in my opinion, sufficient to constitute a serious revolution.

I look upon the entire absence of gratuitous functionaries in America as one of the most prominent signs of the absolute dominion which democracy exercises in that country. All public services, of whatsoever nature they may be, are paid; so that every one has not merely the right, but also the means of performing them. Although, in democratic States, all the citizens are qualified to occupy stations in the Government, all are not tempted to try for them. The number and the capacities of the candidates are more apt to restrict the choice of electors than the conditions of the candidateship.

In nations in which the principle of election extends to every place in the State no political career can, properly speaking, be said to exist. Men are promoted as if by chance to the rank which they enjoy, and they are by no means sure of retaining it. The consequence is that in tranquil times public functions offer but few lures to ambition. In the United States the persons who engage in the perplexities of political life are individuals of very moderate pretensions. The pursuit of wealth generally diverts men of great talents and of great passions from the pursuit of power, and it very frequently happens that a man does not undertake to direct the fortune of the State until he has discovered his incompetence to conduct his own affairs. The vast number of very ordinary men who occupy public stations is quite as attributable to these causes as to the bad choice of the democracy. In the United States, I am not sure that the people would return the men of superior abilities who might solicit its support, but it is certain that men of this description do not come forward.

In two different kinds of government the magistrates exercise a considerable degree of arbitrary power; namely, under the absolute government of a single individual, and under that of a democracy. This identical result proceeds from causes which are nearly analogous.

In despotic States the fortune of no citizen is secure; and public officers are not more safe than private individuals. The sovereign, who has under his control the lives, the property, and sometimes the honour of the men whom he employs, does not scruple to allow them a great latitude of action, because he is convinced that they will not use it to his prejudice. In despotic States the sovereign is so attached to the exercise of his power that he dislikes the constraint even of his own regulations; and he is well pleased that his agents should follow a somewhat fortuitous line of conduct, provided he be certain that their actions will never counteract his desires.

In democracies, as the majority has every year the right of depriving the officers whom it has appointed of their power, it has no reason to fear any abuse of their authority. As the people is always able to signify its wishes to those who conduct the Government, it prefers leaving them to make their own exertions to prescribing an invariable rule of conduct which would at once fetter their activity and the popular authority.

It may even be observed, on attentive consideration, that under the rule of a democracy the arbitrary power of the magistrate must be still greater than in despotic States. In the latter the sovereign has the power of punishing all the faults with which he becomes acquainted, but it would be vain for him to hope to become acquainted with all those which are committed. In the former the sovereign power is not only supreme, but it is universally present. The American functionaries are, in point of fact, much more independent in the sphere of action which the law traces out for them than any public officer in Europe. Very frequently the object which they are to accomplish is simply pointed out to them, and the choice of the means is left to their own discretion.

In New England, for instance, the selectmen of each township are bound to draw up the list of persons who are to serve on the jury; the only rule which is laid down to guide them in their choice is that they are to select citizens possessing the elective franchise and enjoying a fair reputation. In France the lives and liberties of the subject would be thought to be in danger if a public officer of any kind was intrusted with so formidable a right. In New England the same magistrates are empowered to post the names of habitual drunkards in public-houses, and to prohibit the inhabitants of a town from supplying them with liquor. A censorial power of this excessive kind would be revolting to the population of the most absolute monarchies; here, however, it is submitted to without difficulty. . . .

The authority which public men possess in America is so brief, and they are so soon commingled with the ever-changing population of the country, that the acts of a community frequently leave fewer traces than the occurrences of a private family. The public administration is, so to speak, oral and traditionary. But little is committed to writing, and that little is wafted away forever, like the leaves of the Sibyl, by the smallest breeze.

The only historical remains in the United States are the newspapers; but if a number be wanting, the chain of time is broken, and the present is severed from the past, I am convinced that in fifty years it will be more difficult to collect authentic documents concerning the social condition of the Americans at the present day than it is to find remains of the administration of France during the Middle Ages; and if the United States were ever invaded by barbarians, it would be necessary to have recourse to the history of other nations in order to learn anything of the people which now inhabits them.

The instability of the administration has penetrated into the habits of the people: it even appears to suit the general taste, and no one cares for what occurred before his time. No methodical system is pursued; no archives are formed; and no documents are brought together when it would be very easy to do so. Where they exist, little store is set upon them; and I have among my papers several original public documents which were given to me in answer to some of my inquiries. In America society seems to live from hand to mouth, like an army in the field. Nevertheless, the art of administration may undoubtedly be ranked as a science, and no sciences can be improved if the discoveries and observations of successive generations are not connected together in the order in which they occur. One man, in the short space of his life remarks a fact; another conceives an idea; the former invents a means of execution, the latter reduces a truth to a fixed proposition; and mankind gathers the fruits of individual experience upon its way and gradually forms the sciences. But the persons who conduct the administration in America can seldom afford any instruction to each other; and when they assume the direction of society, they simply possess those attainments which are most widely disseminated in the community, and no experience peculiar to themselves. Democracy, carried to its furthest limits, is therefore prejudicial to the art of government; and for this reason it is better adapted to a people already versed in the conduct of an administration than to a nation which is uninitiated in public affairs.

This remark, indeed, is not exclusively applicable to the science of administration. Although a democratic government is founded upon a very simple and natural principle, it always presupposes the existence of a high degree of culture and enlightenment in society. At the first glance it may be imagined to belong to the earliest ages of the world; but maturer observation will convince us that it could only come last in the succession of human history.

Before we can affirm whether a democratic form of government is economical or not, we must establish a suitable standard of comparison. The question would be one of easy solution if we were to attempt to draw a parallel between a democratic republic and an absolute monarchy. The public expenditure would be found to be more considerable under the former than under the latter; such is the case with all free States compared to those which are not so. It is certain that despotism ruins individuals by preventing them from producing wealth, much more than by depriving them of the wealth they have produced; it dries up the source of riches, while it usually respects acquired property. Freedom, on the contrary, engenders far more benefits than it destroys; and the nations which are favoured by free institutions invariably find that their resources increase even more rapidly than their taxes.

My present object is to compare free nations to each other, and to point out the influence of democracy upon the finances of a State.

Communities, as well as organic bodies, are subject to certain fixed rules in their formation which they can not evade. They are composed of certain elements which are common to them at all times and under all circumstances. The people may always be mentally divided into three distinct classes. The first of these classes consists of the wealthy; the second, of those who are in easy circumstances; and the third is composed of those who have little or no property, and who subsist more especially by the work which they perform for the two superior orders. The proportion of the individuals who are included in these three divisions may vary according to the condition of society, but the divisions themselves can never be obliterated.

It is evident that each of these classes will exercise an influence peculiar to its own propensities upon the administration of the finances of the State. If the first of the three exclusively possesses the legislative power, it is probable that it will not be sparing of the public funds, because the taxes which are levied on a large fortune only tend to diminish the sum of superfluous enjoyment, and are, in point of fact, but little felt. If the second class has the power of making the laws, it will certainly not be lavish of taxes, because nothing is so onerous as a large impost which is levied upon a small income. The government of the middle classes appears to me to be the most economical, though perhaps not the most enlightened, and certainly not the most generous, of free governments.

But let us now suppose that the legislative authority is vested in the lowest orders: there are two striking reasons which show that the tendency of the expenditure will be to increase, not to diminish. As the great majority of those who create the laws are possessed of no property upon which taxes can be imposed, all the money which is spent for the community appears to be spent for their advantage, at no cost of their own; and those who are possessed of some little property readily find means of regulating the taxes so that they are burdensome to the wealthy and profitable to the poor, although the rich are unable to take the same advantage when they are in possession of the Government.

In countries in which the poor should be exclusively invested with the power of making the laws no great economy of public expenditure ought to be expected: that expenditure will always be considerable; either because the taxes do not weigh upon those who levy them, or because they are levied in such a manner as not to weigh upon those classes. In other words, the government of the democracy is the only one under which the power which lays on taxes escapes the payment of them.

It may be objected (but the argument has no real weight) that the true interest of the people is indissolubly connected with that of the wealthier portion of the community, since it can not but suffer by the severe measures to which it resorts. But is it not the true interest of kings to render their subjects happy, and the true interest of nobles to admit recruits into their order on suitable grounds? If remote advantages had power to prevail over the passions and the exigencies of the moment, no such thing as a tyrannical sovereign or an exclusive aristocracy could ever exist.

Again, it may be objected that the poor are never invested with the sole power of making the laws; but I reply, that wherever universal suffrage has been established the majority of the community unquestionably exercises the legislative authority; and if it be proved that the poor always constitute the majority, it may be added, with perfect truth, that in the countries in which they possess the elective franchise they possess the sole power of making laws. But it is certain that in all the nations of the world the greater number has always consisted of those persons who hold no property, or of those whose property is insufficient to exempt them from the necessity of working in order to procure an easy subsistence. Universal suffrage does therefore, in point of fact, invest the poor with the government of society. . . .

The extravagance of democracy is, however, less to be dreaded in proportion as the people acquires a share of property, because on the one hand the contributions of the rich are then less needed, and, on the other, it is more difficult to lay on taxes which do not affect the interests of the lower classes. On this account universal suffrage would be less dangerous in France than in England, because in the latter country the property on which taxes may be levied is vested in fewer hands. America, where the great majority of the citizens possess some fortune, is in a still more favourable position than France.

There are still further causes which may increase the sum of public expenditure in democratic countries. When the aristocracy governs, the individuals who conduct the affairs of State are exempted by their own station in society from every kind of privation; they are contented with their position; power and renown are the objects for which they strive; and, as they are placed far above the obscurer throng of citizens, they do not always distinctly perceive how the well-being of the mass of the people ought to redound to their own honour. They are not indeed callous to the sufferings of the poor, but they can not feel those miseries as acutely as if they were themselves partakers of them. Provided that the people appear to submit to its lot, the rulers are satisfied, and they demand nothing further from the Government. An aristocracy is more intent upon the means of maintaining its influence than upon the means of improving its condition.

When, on the contrary, the people is invested with the supreme authority, the perpetual sense of their own miseries impels the rulers of society to seek for perpetual ameliorations. A thousand different objects are subjected to improvement; the most trivial details are sought out as susceptible of amendment; and those changes which are accompanied with considerable expense are more especially advocated, since the object is to render the condition of the poor more tolerable, who can not pay for themselves. . . .

In monarchies and aristocracies the natural taste which the rulers have for power and for renown is stimulated by the promptings of ambition, and they are frequently incited by these temptations to very costly undertakings. In democracies, where the rulers labour under privations, they can only be courted by such means as improve their well-being, and these improvements can not take place without a sacrifice of money. When a people begins to reflect upon its situation, it discovers a multitude of wants to which it had not before been subject, and to satisfy these exigencies recourse must be had to the coffers of the State. Hence it arises that the public charges increase in proportion as civilization spreads, and that imposts are augmented as knowledge pervades the community.

The last cause which frequently renders a democratic government dearer than any other is, that a democracy does not always succeed in moderating its expenditure, because it does not understand the art of being economical.

As the designs which it entertains are frequently changed, and the agents of those designs are still more frequently removed, its undertakings are often ill conducted or left unfinished: in the former case the State spends sums out of all proportion to the end which it proposes to accomplish; in the second, the expense itself is unprofitable.

There is a powerful reason which usually induces democracies to economize upon the salaries of public officers. As the number of citizens who dispense the remuneration is extremely large in democratic countries, so the number of persons who can hope to be benefited by the receipt of it is comparatively small. . . .

It must be allowed, however, that a democratic State is most parsimonious toward its principal agents. In America the secondary officers are much better paid, and the dignitaries of the administration much worse, than they are elsewhere.

These opposite effects result from the same cause; the people fixes the salaries of the public officers in both cases; and the scale of remuneration is determined by the consideration of its own wants. It is held to be fair that the servants of the public should be placed in the same easy circumstances as the public itself; but when the question turns upon the salaries of the great officers of State, this rule fails, and chance alone can guide the popular decision. The poor have no adequate conception of the wants which the higher classes of society may feel. The sum which is scanty to the rich appears enormous to the poor man whose wants do not extend beyond the necessaries of life; and in his estimation the Governor of a State, with his two or three hundred a year, is a very fortunate and enviable being. If you undertake to convince him that the representative of a great people ought to be able to maintain some show of splendour in the eyes of foreign nations, he will perhaps assent to your meaning; but when he reflects on his own humble dwelling, and on the hard-earned produce of his wearisome toil, he remembers all that he could do with a salary which you say is insufficient, and he is startled or almost frightened at the sight of such uncommon wealth. Besides, the secondary public officer is almost on a level with the people, while the others are raised above it. The former may therefore excite his interest, but the latter begins to arouse his envy. This is very clearly seen in the United States, where the salaries seem to decrease as the authority of those who receive them augments. . . .

On casting my eyes over the different republics which form the confederation, I perceive that their Governments lack perseverance in their undertakings, and that they exercise no steady control over the men whom they employ. Whence I naturally infer that they must often spend the money of the people to no purpose, or consume more of it than is really necessary to their undertakings. Great efforts are made, in accordance with the democratic origin of society, to satisfy the exigencies of the lower orders, to open the career of power to their endeavours, and to diffuse knowledge and comfort among them. The poor are maintained, immense sums are annually devoted to public instruction, all services whatsoever are remunerated, and the most subordinate agents are liberally paid. If this kind of government appears to me to be useful and rational, I am nevertheless constrained to admit that it is expensive.

Wherever the poor direct public affairs and dispose of the national resources, it appears certain that, as they profit by the expenditure of the State, they are apt to augment that expenditure.

I conclude, therefore, without having recourse to inaccurate computations, and without hazarding a comparison which might prove incorrect, that the democratic government of the Americans is not a cheap government, as is sometimes asserted; and I have no hesitation in predicting that, if the people of the United States is ever involved in serious difficulties, its taxation will speedily be increased to the rate of that which prevails in the greater part of the aristocracies and the monarchies of Europe.

A distinction must be made, when the aristocratic and the democratic principles mutually inveigh against each other, as tending to facilitate corruption. In aristocratic governments the individuals who are placed at the head of affairs are rich men, who are solely desirous of power. In democracies statesmen are poor, and they have their fortunes to make. The consequence is that in aristocratic States the rulers are rarely accessible to corruption, and have very little craving for money; while the reverse is the case in democratic nations.

But in aristocracies, as those who are desirous of arriving at the head of affairs are possessed of considerable wealth, and as the number of persons by whose assistance they may rise is comparatively small, the government is, if I may use the expression, put up to a sort of auction. In democracies, on the contrary, those who are covetous of power are very seldom wealthy, and the number of citizens who confer that power is extremely great. Perhaps in democracies the number of men who might be bought is by no means smaller, but buyers are rarely to be met with; and, besides, it would be necessary to buy so many persons at once that the attempt is rendered nugatory. . . .

In France the practice of bribing electors is almost unknown, while it is notoriously and publicly carried on in England. In the United States I never heard a man accused of spending his wealth in corrupting the populace; but I have often heard the probity of public officers questioned; still more frequently have I heard their success attributed to low intrigues and immoral practices. . . .

It is difficult to say what degree of exertion a democratic government may be capable of making at a crisis in the history of the nation. But no great democratic republic has hitherto existed in the world. To style the oligarchy which ruled over France in 1793 by that name would be to offer an insult to the republican form of government. The United States afford the first example of the kind.

The American Union has now subsisted for half a century, in the course of which time its existence has only once been attacked, namely, during the War of Independence. At the commencement of that long war, various occurrences took place which betokened an extraordinary zeal for the service of the country. But as the contest was prolonged, symptoms of private egotism began to show themselves. No money was poured into the public treasury; few recruits could be raised to join the army; the people wished to acquire independence, but was very ill disposed to undergo the privations by which alone it could be obtained. . . .

The United States have not had any serious war to carry on since that period. In order, therefore, to appreciate the sacrifices which democratic nations may impose upon themselves, we must wait until the American people is obliged to put half its entire income at the disposal of the Government, as was done by the English; or until it sends forth a twentieth part of its population to the field of battle, as was done by France. . . .

It is incontestable that in times of danger a free people displays far more energy than one which is not so. But I incline to believe that this is more especially the case in those free nations in which the democratic element preponderates. Democracy appears to me to be much better adapted for the peaceful conduct of society, or for an occasional effort of remarkable vigour, than for the hardy and prolonged endurance of the storms which beset the political existence of nations. The reason is very evident; it is enthusiasm which prompts men to expose themselves to dangers and privations, but they will not support them long without reflection. There is more calculation, even in the impulses of bravery, than is generally attributed to them; and although the first efforts are suggested by passion, perseverance is maintained by a distinct regard of the purpose in view. A portion of what we value is exposed, in order to save the remainder.

But it is this distinct perception of the future, founded upon a sound judgment and an enlightened experience, which is most frequently wanting in democracies. The populace is more apt to feel than to reason; and if its present sufferings are great, it is to be feared that the still greater sufferings attendant upon defeat will be forgotten. Another cause tends to render the efforts of a democratic government less persevering than those of an aristocracy. Not only are the lower classes less awakened than the higher orders to the good or evil chances of the future, but they are liable to suffer far more acutely from present privations. The noble exposes his life, indeed, but the chance of glory is equal to the chance of harm. If he sacrifices a large portion of his income to the State, he deprives himself for a time of the pleasures of affluence; but to the poor man death is embellished by no pomp or renown, and the imposts which are irksome to the rich are fatal to him. . . .

I am of opinion that a democratic government tends in the end to increase the real strength of society; but it can never combine, upon a single point and at a given time, so much power as an aristocracy or a monarchy.

If a democratic country remained during a whole century subject to a republican government, it would probably at the end of that period be more populous and more prosperous than the neighbouring despotic States. But it would have incurred the risk of being conquered much oftener than they would in that lapse of years.

The difficulty which a democracy has in conquering the passions and in subduing the exigencies of the moment, with a view to the future, is conspicuous in the most trivial occurrences of the United States. The people, which is surrounded by flatterers, has great difficulty in surmounting its inclinations, and whenever it is solicited to undergo a privation or any kind of inconvenience, even to attain an end which is sanctioned by its own rational conviction, it almost always refuses to comply at first. The deference of the Americans to the laws has been very justly applauded; but it must be added that in America the legislation is made by the people and for the people. Consequently, in the United States, the law favours those classes which are most interested in evading it elsewhere. It may therefore be supposed that an offensive law, which should not be acknowledged to be one of immediate utility, would either not be enacted or would not be obeyed. . . .

The great privilege of the Americans does not simply consist in their being more enlightened than other nations, but in their being able to repair the faults they may commit.

The Real Advantages That American Society Derives From Democratic Government

The political institutions of the United States appear to me to be one of the forms of government which a democracy may adopt; but I do not regard the American Constitution as the best, or as the only one, which a democratic people may establish. In showing the advantages which the Americans derive from the government of democracy, I am therefore very far from meaning, or from believing, that similar advantages can only be obtained from the same laws.

The defects and the weaknesses of a democratic government may be discovered very readily; they are demonstrated by the most flagrant instances, while its beneficial influence is less perceptibly exercised. A single glance suffices to detect its evil consequences, but its good qualities can only be discerned by long observation. The laws of the American democracy are frequently defective or incomplete; they sometimes attack vested rights, or give a sanction to others which are dangerous to the community; but even if they were good, the frequent changes which they undergo would be an evil. How comes it, then, that the American republics prosper and maintain their position?

In the consideration of laws a distinction must be carefully observed between the end at which they aim and the means by which they are directed to that end, between their absolute and their relative excellence. If it be the intention of the legislator to favour the interests of the minority at the expense of the majority, and if the measures he takes are so combined as to accomplish the object he has in view with the least possible expense of time and exertion, the law may be well drawn up, although its purpose be bad; and the more efficacious it is, the greater is the mischief which it causes.

Democratic laws generally tend to promote the welfare of the greatest possible number; for they emanate from the majority of the citizens, who are subject to error, but who can not have an interest opposed to their own advantage. The laws of an aristocracy tend, on the contrary, to concentrate wealth and power in the hands of the minority, because an aristocracy, by its very nature, constitutes a minority. It therefore may be asserted, as a general proposition, that the purpose of a democracy in the conduct of its legislation is useful to a greater number of citizens than that of an aristocracy. This is, however, the sum total of its advantages.

Aristocracies are infinitely more expert in the science of legislation than democracies ever can be. They are possessed of a self-control which protects them from the errors of temporary excitement, and they form lasting designs which they mature with the assistance of favourable opportunities. Aristocratic government proceeds with the dexterity of art; it understands how to make the collective force of all its laws converge at the same time to a given point. Such is not the case with democracies, whose laws are almost always ineffective or inopportune. The means of democracy are therefore more imperfect than those of aristocracy, and the measures which it unwittingly adopts are frequently opposed to its own cause; but the object it has in view is more useful.

Let us now imagine a community so organized by nature, or by its constitution, that it can support the transitory action of bad laws, and that it can await, without destruction, the general tendency of the legislation: we shall then be able to conceive that a democratic government, notwithstanding its defects, will be most fitted to conduce to the prosperity of this community. This is precisely what has occurred in the United States; and I repeat, what I have before remarked, that the great advantage of the Americans consists in their being able to commit faults which they may afterward repair.

An analogous observation may be made respecting public officers. It is easy to perceive that the American democracy frequently errs in the choice of the individuals to whom it intrusts the power of the administration; but it is more difficult to say why the State prospers under their rule. In the first place, it is to be remarked that if in a democratic State the governors have less honesty and less capacity than elsewhere, the governed, on the other hand, are more enlightened and more attentive to their interests. As the people in democracies is more incessantly vigilant in its affairs and more jealous of its rights, it prevents its representatives from abandoning that general line of conduct which its own interest prescribes. In the second place, it must be remembered that if the democratic magistrate is more apt to misuse his power, he possesses it for a shorter period of time. But there is yet another reason which is still more general and conclusive. It is no doubt of importance to the welfare of nations that they should be governed by men of talents and virtue: but it is perhaps still more important that the interests of those men should not differ from the interests of the community at large; for, if such were the case, virtues of a high order might become useless, and talents might be turned to a bad account. I say that it is important that the interests of the persons in authority should not conflict with or oppose the interests of the community at large; but I do not insist upon their having the same interests as the whole population, because I am not aware that such a state of things ever existed in any country.

No political form has been discovered hitherto which is equally favourable to the prosperity and the development of all the classes into which society is divided. These classes continue to form, as it were, a certain number of distinct nations in the same nation; and experience has shown that it is no less dangerous to place the fate of these classes exclusively in the hands of any one of them than it is to make one people the arbiter of the destiny of another. When the rich alone govern, the interest of the poor is always endangered; and when the poor make the laws, that of the rich incurs very serious risks. The advantage of democracy does not consist, therefore, as has sometimes been asserted, in favouring the prosperity of all, but simply in contributing to the well-being of the greatest possible number.

The men who are intrusted with the direction of public affairs in the United States are frequently inferior, both in point of capacity and of morality, to those whom aristocratic institutions would raise to power. But their interest is identified and confounded with that of the majority of their fellow-citizens. They may frequently be faithless and frequently mistaken, but they will never systematically adopt a line of conduct opposed to the will of the majority; and it is impossible that they should give a dangerous or an exclusive tendency to the government.

The maladministration of a democratic magistrate is a mere isolated fact, which only occurs during the short period for which he is elected. Corruption and incapacity do not act as common interests, which may connect men permanently with one another. A corrupt or an incapable magistrate will not concert his measures with another magistrate, simply because that individual is as corrupt and as incapable as himself; and these two men will never unite their endeavours to promote the corruption and inaptitude of their remote posterity. The ambition and the manœuvres of the one will serve, on the contrary, to unmask the other. The vices of a magistrate, in democratic states, are usually peculiar to his own person.

But under aristocratic governments public men are swayed by the interest of their order, which, if it is sometimes confounded with the interests of the majority, is very frequently distinct from them. This interest is the common and lasting bond which unites them together; it induces them to coalesce, and to combine their efforts in order to attain an end which does not always insure the greatest happiness of the greatest number; and it serves not only to connect the persons in authority, but to unite them to a considerable portion of the community, since a numerous body of citizens belongs to the aristocracy, without being invested with official functions. The aristocratic magistrate is therefore constantly supported by a portion of the community, as well as by the Government of which he is a member.

The common purpose which connects the interest of the magistrates in aristocracies with that of a portion of their contemporaries identifies it with that of future generations; their influence belongs to the future as much as to the present. The aristocratic magistrate is urged at the same time toward the same point by the passions of the community, by his own, and I may almost add by those of his posterity. Is it, then, wonderful that he does not resist such repeated impulses? And, indeed, aristocracies are often carried away by the spirit of their order without being corrupted by it; and they unconsciously fashion society to their own ends, and prepare it for their own descendants.

The English aristocracy is perhaps the most liberal which ever existed, and no body of men has ever uninterruptedly furnished so many honourable and enlightened individuals to the government of a country. It can not, however, escape observation that in the legislation of England the good of the poor has been sacrificed to the advantage of the rich, and the rights of the majority to the privileges of the few. The consequence is, that England, at the present day, combines the extremes of fortune in the bosom of her society, and her perils and calamities are almost equal to her power and her renown.

In the United States, where the public officers have no interests to promote connected with their caste, the general and constant influence of the Government is beneficial, although the individuals who conduct it are frequently unskilful and sometimes contemptible. There is, indeed, a secret tendency in democratic institutions to render the exertions of the citizens subservient to the prosperity of the community, notwithstanding their private vices and mistakes; while in aristocratic institutions there is a secret propensity which, notwithstanding the talents and the virtues of those who conduct the government, leads them to contribute to the evils which oppress their fellow-creatures. In aristocratic governments public men may frequently do injuries which they do not intend, and in democratic states they produce advantages which they never thought of.

There is one sort of patriotic attachment which principally arises from that instinctive, disinterested, and undefinable feeling which connects the affections of man with his birthplace. This natural fondness is united to a taste for ancient customs, and to a reverence for ancestral traditions of the past; those who cherish it love their country as they love the mansion of their fathers. They enjoy the tranquility which it affords them; they cling to the peaceful habits which they have contracted within its bosom; they are attached to the reminiscences which it awakens, and they are even pleased by the state of obedience in which they are placed. This patriotism is sometimes stimulated by religious enthusiasm, and then it is capable of making the most prodigious efforts. It is in itself a kind of religion; it does not reason, but it acts from the impulse of faith and of sentiment. By some nations the monarch has been regarded as a personification of the country; and the fervour of patriotism being converted into the fervour of loyalty, they took a sympathetic pride in his conquests, and gloried in his power. At one time, under the ancient monarchy, the French felt a sort of satisfaction in the sense of their dependence upon the arbitrary pleasure of their king, and they were wont to say with pride, "We are the subjects of the most powerful king in the world."

But, like all instinctive passions, this kind of patriotism is more apt to prompt transient exertion than to supply the motives of continuous endeavour. It may save the State in critical circumstances, but it will not infrequently allow the nation to decline in the midst of peace. While the manners of a people are simple and its faith unshaken, while society is steadily based upon traditional institutions whose legitimacy has never been contested, this instinctive patriotism is wont to endure.

But there is another species of attachment to a country which is more rational than the one we have been describing. It is perhaps less generous and less ardent, but it is more fruitful and more lasting; it is coeval with the spread of knowledge, it is nurtured by the laws, it grows by the exercise of civil rights, and, in the end, it is confounded with the personal interest of the citizen. A man comprehends the influence which the prosperity of his country has upon his own welfare; he is aware that the laws authorize him to contribute his assistance to that prosperity, and he labours to promote it as a portion of his interest in the first place, and as a portion of his right in the second.

But epochs sometimes occur, in the course of the existence of a nation, at which the ancient customs of a people are changed, public morality destroyed, religious belief disturbed, and the spell of tradition broken, while the diffusion of knowledge is yet imperfect, and the civil rights of the community are ill secured, or confined within very narrow limits. The country then assumes a dim and dubious shape in the eyes of the citizens; they no longer behold it in the soil which they inhabit, for that soil is to them a dull inanimate clod; nor in the usages of their forefathers, which they have been taught to look upon as a debasing yoke; nor in religion, for of that they doubt; nor in the laws, which do not originate in their own authority; nor in the legislator, whom they fear and despise. The country is lost to their senses, they can neither discover it under its own nor under borrowed features, and they intrench themselves within the dull precincts of a narrow egotism. They are emancipated from prejudice without having acknowledged the empire of reason; they are neither animated by the instinctive patriotism of monarchical subjects nor by the thinking patriotism of republican citizens; but they have stopped half-way between the two, in the midst of confusion and of distress.

In this predicament, to retreat is impossible; for a people can not restore the vivacity of its earlier times, any more than a man can return to the innocence and the bloom of childhood; such things may be regretted, but they can not be renewed. The only thing, then, which remains to be done is to proceed, and to accelerate the union of private with public interests, since the period of disinterested patriotism is gone by forever.

I am certainly very far from averring that, in order to obtain this result, the exercise of political rights should be immediately granted to all the members of the community. But I maintain that the most powerful, and perhaps the only, means of interesting men in the welfare of their country which we still possess is to make them partakers in the Government. At the present time civic zeal seems to me to be inseparable from the exercise of political rights; and I hold that the number of citizens will be found to augment or to decrease in Europe in proportion as those rights are extended.

In the United States the inhabitants were thrown but as yesterday upon the soil which they now occupy, and they brought neither customs nor traditions with them there; they meet each other for the first time with no previous acquaintance; in short, the instinctive love of their country can scarcely exist in their minds; but every one takes as zealous an interest in the affairs of his township, his county, and of the whole State, as if they were his own, because every one, in his sphere, takes an active part in the government of society.

The lower orders in the United States are alive to the perception of the influence exercised by the general prosperity upon their own welfare; and simple as this observation is, it is one which is but too rarely made by the people. But in America the people regards this prosperity as the result of its own exertions; the citizen looks upon the fortune of the public as his private interest, and he co-operates in its success, not so much from a sense of pride or of duty, as from what I shall venture to term cupidity.

It is unnecessary to study the institutions and the history of the Americans in order to discover the truth of this remark, for their manners render it sufficiently evident. As the American participates in all that is done in his country, he thinks himself obliged to defend whatever may be censured; for it is not only his country which is attacked upon these occasions, but it is himself. The consequence is, that his national pride resorts to a thousand artifices, and to all the petty tricks of individual vanity.

Nothing is more embarrassing in the ordinary intercourse of life than this irritable patriotism of the Americans. A stranger may be very well inclined to praise many of the institutions of their country, but he begs permission to blame some of the peculiarities which he observes—a permission which is, however, inexorably refused. America is therefore a free country, in which, lest anybody should be hurt by your remarks, you are not allowed to speak freely of private individuals or of the State, of the citizens or of the authorities, of public or of private undertakings, or, in short, of anything at all, except it be of the climate and the soil; and even then Americans will be found ready to defend either the one or the other, as if they had been contrived by the inhabitants of the country.

In our times option must be made between the patriotism of all and the government of a few; for the force and activity which the first confers are irreconcilable with the guarantees of tranquility which the second furnishes.

After the idea of virtue, I know no higher principle than that of right; or, to speak more accurately, these two ideas are commingled in one. The idea of right is simply that of virtue introduced into the political world. It is the idea of right which enabled men to define anarchy and tyranny; and which taught them to remain independent without arrogance, as well as to obey without servility. The man who submits to violence is debased by his compliance; but when he obeys the mandate of one who possesses that right of authority which he acknowledges in a fellow-creature, he rises in some measure above the person who delivers the command. There are no great men without virtue, and there are no great nations—it may almost be added that there would be no society—without the notion of rights; for what is the condition of a mass of rational and intelligent beings who are only united together by the bond of force?

I am persuaded that the only means which we possess at the present time of inculcating the notion of rights, and of rendering it, as it were, palpable to the senses, is to invest all the members of the community with the peaceful exercise of certain rights: this is very clearly seen in children, who are men without the strength and the experience of manhood. When a child begins to move in the midst of the objects which surround him, he is instinctively led to turn everything which he can lay his hands upon to his own purposes; he has no notion of the property of others; but as he gradually learns the value of things, and begins to perceive that he may in his turn be deprived of his possessions, he becomes more circumspect, and he observes those rights in others which he wishes to have respected in himself. The principle which the child derives from the possession of his toys is taught to the man by the objects which he may call his own. In America those complaints against property in general which are so frequent in Europe are never heard, because in America there are no paupers; and as every one has property of his own to defend, every one recognises the principle upon which he holds it.

The same thing occurs in the political world. In America the lowest classes have conceived a very high notion of political rights, because they exercise those rights; and they refrain from attacking those of other people, in order to insure their own from attack. While in Europe the same classes sometimes recalcitrate even against the supreme power, the American submits without a murmur to the authority of the pettiest magistrate.

This truth is exemplified by the most trivial details of national peculiarities. In France very few pleasures are exclusively reserved for the higher classes; the poor are admitted wherever the rich are received, and they consequently behave with propriety, and respect whatever contributes to the enjoyments in which they themselves participate. In England, where wealth has a monopoly of amusement as well as of power, complaints are made that whenever the poor happen to steal into the inclosures which are reserved for the pleasures of the rich, they commit acts of wanton mischief: can this be wondered at, since care has been taken that they should have nothing to lose?

The government of democracy brings the notion of political rights to the level of the humblest citizens, just as the dissemination of wealth brings the notion of property within the reach of all the members of the community; and I confess that, to my mind, this is one of its greatest advantages. I do not assert that it is easy to teach men to exercise political rights; but I maintain that, when it is possible, the effects which result from it are highly important; and I add that, if there ever was a time at which such an attempt ought to be made, that time is our own. It is clear that the influence of religious belief is shaken, and that the notion of divine rights is declining; it is evident that public morality is vitiated, and the notion of moral rights is also disappearing: these are general symptoms of the substitution of argument for faith, and of calculation for the impulses of sentiment. If, in the midst of this general disruption, you do not succeed in connecting the notion of rights with that of personal interest, which is the only immutable point in the human heart, what means will you have of governing the world except by fear? When I am told that, since the laws are weak and the populace is wild, since passions are excited and the authority of virtue is paralyzed, no measures must be taken to increase the rights of the democracy, I reply, that it is for these very reasons that some measures of the kind must be taken; and I am persuaded that governments are still more interested in taking them than society at large, because governments are liable to be destroyed and society can not perish.

I am not, however, inclined to exaggerate the example which America furnishes. In those States the people were invested with political rights at a time when they could scarcely be abused, for the citizens were few in number and simple in their manners. As they have increased, the Americans have not augmented the power of the democracy, but they have, if I may use the expression, extended its dominions.

It can not be doubted that the moment at which political rights are granted to a people that before has been without them is a very critical, though it be a necessary, one. A child may kill before he is aware of the value of life; and he may deprive another person of his property before he is aware that his own may be taken away from him. The lower orders, when first they are invested with political rights, stand, in relation to those rights, in the same position as the child does to the whole of Nature. . . . This truth may even be perceived in America. The States in which the citizens have enjoyed their rights longest are those in which they make the best use of them.

It can not be repeated too often that nothing is more fertile in prodigies than the art of being free; but there is nothing more arduous than the apprenticeship of liberty. Such is not the case with despotic institutions: despotism often promises to make amends for a thousand previous ills; it supports the right, it protects the oppressed, and it maintains public order. The nation is lulled by the temporary prosperity which accrues to it, until it is roused to a sense of its own misery. Liberty, on the contrary, is generally established in the midst of agitation, it is perfected by civil discord, and its benefits can not be appreciated until it is already old.

It is not always feasible to consult the whole people, either directly or indirectly, in the formation of the law; but it can not be denied that, when such a measure is possible, the authority of the law is very much augmented. This popular origin, which impairs the excellence and the wisdom of legislation, contributes prodigiously to increase its power. There is an amazing strength in the expression of the determination of a whole people, and when it declares itself the imagination of those who are most inclined to contest it is overawed by its authority. The truth of this fact is very well known by parties, and they consequently strive to make out a majority whenever they can. If they have not the greater number of voters on their side, they assert that the true majority abstained from voting; and if they are foiled even there, they have recourse to the body of those persons who had no votes to give.

In the United States, except slaves, servants, and paupers in the receipt of relief from the townships, there is no class of persons who do not exercise the elective franchise, and who do not indirectly contribute to make the laws. Those who design to attack the laws must consequently either modify the opinion of the nation or trample upon its decision.

A second reason, which is still more weighty, may be further adduced: in the United States every one is personally interested in enforcing the obedience of the whole community to the law; for as the minority may shortly rally the majority to its principles, it is interested in professing that respect for the decrees of the legislator which it may soon have occasion to claim for its own. However irksome an enactment may be, the citizen of the United States complies with it, not only because it is the work of the majority, but because it originates in his own authority, and he regards it as a contract to which he is himself a party.

In the United States, then, that numerous and turbulent multitude does not exist which always looks upon the law as its natural enemy, and accordingly surveys it with fear and with distrust. It is impossible, on the other hand, not to perceive that all classes display the utmost reliance upon the legislation of their country, and that they are attached to it by a kind of parental affection.

I am wrong, however, in saying all classes; for as in America the European scale of authority is inverted, the wealthy are there placed in a position analogous to that of the poor in the Old World, and it is the opulent classes which frequently look upon the law with suspicion. I have already observed that the advantage of democracy is not, as has been sometimes asserted, that it protects the interests of the whole community, but simply that it protects those of the majority. In the United States, where the poor rule, the rich have always some reason to dread the abuses of their power. This natural anxiety of the rich may produce a sullen dissatisfaction, but society is not disturbed by it; for the same reason which induces the rich to withhold their confidence in the legislative authority makes them obey its mandates; their wealth, which prevents them from making the law, prevents them from withstanding it. Among civilized nations revolts are rarely excited, except by such persons as have nothing to lose by them; and if the laws of a democracy are not always worthy of respect, at least they always obtain it; for those who usually infringe the laws have no excuse for not complying with the enactments they have themselves made, and by which they are themselves benefited, while the citizens whose interests might be promoted by the infraction of them are induced, by their character and their stations, to submit to the decisions of the legislature, whatever they may be. Besides which, the people in America obeys the law not only because it emanates from the popular authority, but because that authority may modify it in any points which may prove vexatious; a law is observed because it is a self-imposed evil in the first place, and an evil of transient duration in the second.

On passing from a country in which free institutions are established to one where they do not exist, the traveller is struck by the change; in the former all is bustle and activity, in the latter everything is calm and motionless. In the one, amelioration and progress are the general topics of inquiry; in the other, it seems as if the community only aspired to repose in the enjoyment of the advantages which it has acquired. Nevertheless, the country which exerts itself so strenuously to promote its welfare is generally more wealthy and more prosperous than that which appears to be so contented with its lot; and when we compare them together, we can scarcely conceive how so many new wants are daily felt in the former, while so few seem to occur in the latter.

If this remark is applicable to those free countries in which monarchical and aristocratic institutions subsist, it is still more striking with regard to democratic republics. In these States it is not only a portion of the people which is busied with the amelioration of its social condition, but the whole community is engaged in the task; and it is not the exigencies and the convenience of a single class for which a provision is to be made, but the exigencies and the convenience of all ranks of life.

It is not impossible to conceive the surpassing liberty which the Americans enjoy; some idea may likewise be formed of the extreme equality which subsists among them, but the political activity which pervades the United States must be seen in order to be understood. No sooner do you set foot upon American soil than you are stunned by a kind of tumult; a confused clamour is heard on every side; and a thousand simultaneous voices demand the immediate satisfaction of their social wants. Everything is in motion around you; here, the people of one quarter of a town are met to decide upon the building of a church; there, the election of a representative is going on; a little farther the delegates of a district are posting to the town in order to consult upon some local improvements; or in another place the labourers of a village quit their ploughs to deliberate upon the project of a road or a public school. Meetings are called for the sole purpose of declaring their disapprobation of the line of conduct pursued by the Government; while in other assemblies the citizens salute the authorities of the day as the fathers of their country. Societies are formed which regard drunkenness as the principal cause of the evils under which the State labours, and which solemnly bind themselves to give a constant example of temperance.

The great political agitation of the American legislative bodies, which is the only kind of excitement that attracts the attention of foreign countries, is a mere episode or a sort of continuation of that universal movement which originates in the lowest classes of the people and extends successively to all the ranks of society. It is impossible to spend more efforts in the pursuit of enjoyment.

The cares of political life take a most prominent place in the occupation of a citizen in the United States, and almost the only pleasure of which an American has any idea is to take a part in the Government, and to discuss the part he has taken. This feeling pervades the most trifling habits of life; even the women frequently attend public meetings and listen to political harangues as a recreation after their household labours. Debating clubs are to a certain extent a substitute for theatrical entertainments: an American can not converse, but he can discuss; and when he attempts to talk he falls into a dissertation. He speaks to you as if he was addressing a meeting; and if he should chance to warm in the course of the discussion, he will infallibly say, "Gentlemen," to the person with whom he is conversing.

In some countries the inhabitants display a certain repugnance to avail themselves of the political privileges with which the law invests them; it would seem that they set too high a value upon their time to spend it on the interests of the community; and they prefer to withdraw within the exact limits of a wholesome egotism, marked out by four sunk fences and a quickset hedge. But if an American were condemned to confine his activity to his own affairs, he would be robbed of one half of his existence; he would feel an immense void in the life which he is accustomed to lead, and his wretchedness would be unbearable. I am persuaded that, if ever a despotic government is established in America, it will find it more difficult to surmount the habits which free institutions have engendered than to conquer the attachment of the citizens to freedom.

This ceaseless agitation which democratic government has introduced into the political world influences all social intercourse. I am not sure that upon the whole this is not the greatest advantage of democracy. And I am much less inclined to applaud it for what it does than for what it causes to be done.

It is incontestable that the people frequently conducts public business very badly; but it is impossible that the lower orders should take a part in public business without extending the circle of their ideas, and without quitting the ordinary routine of their mental acquirements. The humblest individual who is called upon to co-operate in the government of society acquires a certain degree of self-respect; and as he possesses authority, he can command the services of minds much more enlightened than his own. He is canvassed by a multitude of applicants, who seek to deceive him in a thousand different ways, but who instruct him by their deceit. He takes a part in political undertakings which did not originate in his own conception, but which give him a taste for undertakings of the kind. New ameliorations are daily pointed out in the property which he holds in common with others, and this gives him the desire of improving that property which is more peculiarly his own. He is perhaps neither happier nor better than those who came before him, but he is better informed and more active. I have no doubt that the democratic institutions of the United States, joined to the physical constitution of the country, are the cause (not the direct, as is so often asserted, but the indirect cause) of the prodigious commercial activity of the inhabitants. It is not engendered by the laws, but the people learns how to promote it by the experience derived from legislation.

When the opponents of democracy assert that a single individual performs the duties which he undertakes much better than the government of the community, it appears to me that they are perfectly right. The government of an individual, supposing an equality of instruction on either side, is more consistent, more persevering, and more accurate than that of a multitude, and it is much better qualified judiciously to discriminate the characters of the men it employs. If any deny what I advance, they have certainly never seen a democratic government, or have formed their opinion upon very partial evidence. It is true that even when local circumstances and the disposition of the people allow democratic institutions to subsist, they never display a regular and methodical system of government. Democratic liberty is far from accomplishing all the projects it undertakes, with the skill of an adroit despotism. It frequently abandons them before they have borne their fruits, or risks them when the consequences may prove dangerous; but in the end it produces more than any absolute government, and if it do fewer things well, it does a greater number of things. Under its sway the transactions of the public administration are not nearly so important as what is done by private exertion. Democracy does not confer the most skilful kind of government upon the people, but it produces that which the most skilful governments are frequently unable to awaken, namely, an all-pervading and restless activity, a superabundant force, and an energy which is inseparable from it, and which may, under favourable circumstances, beget the most amazing benefits. These are the true advantages of democracy.

In the present age, when the destinies of Christendom seem to be in suspense, some hasten to assail democracy as its foe while it is yet in its early growth; and others are ready with their vows of adoration for this new deity which is springing forth from chaos: but both parties are very imperfectly acquainted with the object of their hatred or of their desires; they strike in the dark, and distribute their blows by mere chance.

We must first understand what the purport of society and the aims of government are held to be. If it be your intention to confer a certain elevation upon the human mind, and to teach it to regard the things of this world with generous feelings, to inspire men with a scorn of mere temporal advantage, to give birth to living convictions, and to keep alive the spirit of honourable devotedness; if you hold it to be a good thing to refine the habits, to embellish the manners, to cultivate the arts of a nation, and to promote the love of poetry, of beauty, and of renown; if you would constitute a people not unfitted to act with power upon all other nations, nor unprepared for those high enterprises which, whatever be the result of its efforts, will leave a name forever famous in time—if you believe such to be the principal object of society, you must avoid the government of democracy, which would be a very uncertain guide to the end you have in view.

But if you hold it to be expedient to divert the moral and intellectual activity of man to the production of comfort, and to the acquirement of the necessaries of life; if a clear understanding be more profitable to man than genius; if your object be not to stimulate the virtues of heroism, but to create habits of peace; if you had rather witness vices than crimes and are content to meet with fewer noble deeds, provided offences be diminished in the same proportion; if, instead of living in the midst of a brilliant state of society, you are contented to have prosperity around you: if, in short, you are of opinion that the principal object of a Government is not to confer the greatest possible share of power and of glory upon the body of the nation, but to insure the greatest degree of enjoyment and the least degree of misery to each of the individuals who compose it—if such be your desires, you can have no surer means of satisfying them than by equalizing the conditions of men, and establishing democratic institutions. . . .

Unlimited Power of the Majority in the United States, and Its Consequences

The very essence of democratic government consists in the absolute sovereignty of the majority; for there is nothing in democratic States which is capable of resisting it. Most of the American Constitutions have sought to increase this natural strength of the majority by artificial means.

The legislature is, of all political institutions, the one which is most easily swayed by the wishes of the majority. The Americans determined that the members of the legislature should be elected by the people immediately, and for a very brief term, in order to subject them, not only to the general convictions, but even to the daily passions, of their constituents. The members of both Houses are taken from the same class in society, and are nominated in the same manner; so that the modifications of the legislative bodies are almost as rapid and quite as irresistible as those of a single assembly. It is to a legislature thus constituted that almost all the authority of the government has been intrusted.

But while the law increased the strength of those authorities which of themselves were strong, it enfeebled more and more those which were naturally weak. It deprived the representatives of the executive of all stability and independence, and by subjecting them completely to the caprices of the legislature, it robbed them of the slender influence which the nature of a democratic government might have allowed them to retain. In several States the judicial power was also submitted to the elective discretion of the majority, and in all of them its existence was made to depend on the pleasure of the legislative authority, since the representatives were empowered annually to regulate the stipend of the judges.

Custom, however, has done even more than law. A proceeding which will in the end set all the guarantees of representative government at naught is becoming more and more general in the United States: it frequently happens that the electors, who choose a delegate, point out a certain line of conduct to him, and impose upon him a certain number of positive obligations which he is pledged to fulfil. With the exception of the tumult, this comes to the same thing as if the majority of the populace held its deliberations in the market-place.

Several other circumstances concur in rendering the power of the majority in America not only preponderant, but irresistible. The moral authority of the majority is partly based upon the notion that there is more intelligence and more wisdom in a great number of men collected together than in a single individual, and that the number of legislators is more important than their quality. The theory of equality is, in fact, applied to the intellect of man: and human pride is thus assailed in its last retreat by a doctrine which the minority hesitate to admit, and in which they very slowly concur. Like all other powers, and perhaps more than all other powers, the authority of the many requires the sanction of time; at first it enforces obedience by constraint, but its laws are not respected until they have long been maintained.

The right of governing society, which the majority supposes itself to derive from its superior intelligence, was introduced into the United States by the first settlers, and this idea, which would be sufficient of itself to create a free nation, has now been amalgamated with the manners of the people and the minor incidents of social intercourse.

The French, under the old monarchy, held it for a maxim (which is still a fundamental principle of the English Constitution) that the King could do no wrong; and if he did do wrong, the blame was imputed to his advisers. This notion was highly favourable to habits of obedience, and it enabled the subject to complain of the law without ceasing to love and honour the lawgiver. The Americans entertain the same opinion with respect to the majority.

The moral power of the majority is founded upon yet another principle, which is, that the interests of the many are to be preferred to those of the few. It readily will be perceived that the respect here professed for the rights of the majority must naturally increase or diminish according to the state of parties. When a nation is divided into several irreconcilable factions, the privilege of the majority is often overlooked, because it is intolerable to comply with its demands.

If there existed in America a class of citizens whom the legislating majority sought to deprive of exclusive privileges which they had possessed for ages, and to bring down from an elevated station to the level of the ranks of the multitude, it is probable that the minority would be less ready to comply with its laws. But as the United States were colonized by men holding equal rank among themselves, there is as yet no natural or permanent source of dissension between the interests of its different inhabitants.

There are certain communities in which the persons who constitute the minority can never hope to draw over the majority to their side, because they must then give up the very point which is at issue between them. Thus, an aristocracy can never become a majority while it retains its exclusive privileges, and it can not cede its privileges without ceasing to be an aristocracy.

In the United States political questions can not be taken up in so general and absolute a manner, and all parties are willing to recognise the rights of the majority, because they all hope to turn those rights to their own advantage at some future time. The majority therefore in that country exercises a prodigious actual authority, and a moral influence which is scarcely less preponderant; no obstacles exist which can impede or so much as retard its progress, or which can induce it to heed the complaints of those whom it crushes upon its path. This state of things is fatal in itself and dangerous for the future.

I have already spoken of the natural defects of democratic institutions, and they all of them increase in the exact ratio of the power of the majority. To begin with the most evident: the mutability of the laws is an evil inherent in democratic government, because it is natural to democracies to raise men to power in very rapid succession. But this evil is more or less sensible in proportion to the authority and the means of action which the legislature possesses.

In America the authority exercised by the legislative bodies is supreme; nothing prevents them from accomplishing their wishes with celerity, and with irresistible power, while they are supplied by new representatives every year. That is to say, the circumstances which contribute most powerfully to democratic instability, and which admit of the free application of caprice to every object in the State, are here in full operation. In conformity with this principle, America is, at the present day, the country in the world where laws last the shortest time. Almost all the American constitutions have been amended within the course of thirty years: there is therefore not a single American State which has not modified the principles of its legislation in that lapse of time. As for the laws themselves, a single glance upon the archives of the different States of the Union suffices to convince one that in America the activity of the legislator never slackens. Not that the American democracy is naturally less stable than any other, but that it is allowed to follow its capricious propensities in the formation of the laws.

The omnipotence of the majority, and the rapid as well as absolute manner in which its decisions are executed in the United States, has not only the effect of rendering the law unstable, but it exercises the same influence upon the execution of the law and the conduct of the public administration. As the majority is the only power which it is important to court, all its projects are taken up with the greatest ardour, but no sooner is its attention distracted than all this ardour ceases; while in the free States of Europe the administration is at once independent and secure, so that the projects of the legislature are put into execution, although its immediate attention may be directed to other objects.

In America certain ameliorations are undertaken with much more zeal and activity than elsewhere; in Europe the same ends are promoted by much less social effort, more continuously applied.

Some years ago several pious individuals undertook to ameliorate the condition of the prisons. The public was excited by the statements which they put forward, and the regeneration of criminals became a very popular undertaking. New prisons were built, and for the first time the idea of reforming as well as of punishing the delinquent formed a part of prison discipline. But this happy alteration, in which the public had taken so hearty an interest, and which the exertions of the citizens had irresistibly accelerated, could not be completed in a moment. While the new penitentiaries were being erected (and it was the pleasure of the majority that they should be terminated with all possible celerity), the old prisons existed, which still contained a great number of offenders. These jails became more unwholesome and more corrupt in proportion as the new establishments were beautified and improved, forming a contrast which may readily be understood. The majority was so eagerly employed in founding the new prisons that those which already existed were forgotten; and as the general attention was diverted to a novel object, the care which hitherto had been bestowed upon the others ceased. The salutary regulations of discipline were first relaxed, and afterward broken; so that in the immediate neighbourhood of a prison which bore witness to the mild and enlightened spirit of our time, dungeons might be met with which reminded the visitor of the barbarity of the Middle Ages.

I hold it to be an impious and an execrable maxim that, politically speaking, a people has a right to do whatsoever it pleases, and yet I have asserted that all authority originates in the will of the majority. Am I, then, in contradiction with myself?

A general law—which bears the name of Justice—has been made and sanctioned, not only by a majority of this or that people, but by a majority of mankind. The rights of every people are consequently confined within the limits of what is just. A nation may be considered in the light of a jury which is empowered to represent society at large, and to apply the great and general law of justice. Ought such a jury, which represents society, to have more power than the society in which the laws it applies originate?

When I refuse to obey an unjust law, I do not contest the right which the majority has of commanding, but I simply appeal from the sovereignty of the people to the sovereignty of mankind. It has been asserted that a people can never entirely outstep the boundaries of justice and of reason in those affairs which are more peculiarly its own, and that consequently full power may fearlessly be given to the majority by which it is represented. But this language is that of a slave.

A majority taken collectively may be regarded as a being whose opinions, and most frequently whose interests, are opposed to those of another being, which is styled a minority. If it be admitted that a man, possessing absolute power, may misuse that power by wronging his adversaries, why should a majority not be liable to the same reproach? Men are not apt to change their characters by agglomeration; nor does their patience in the presence of obstacles increase with the consciousness of their strength. And for these reasons I can never willingly invest any number of my fellow-creatures with that unlimited authority which I should refuse to any one of them.

I do not think that it is possible to combine several principles in the same government, so as at the same time to maintain freedom, and really to oppose them to one another. The form of government which is usually termed mixed has always appeared to me to be a mere chimera. Accurately speaking, there is no such thing as a mixed government (with the meaning usually given to that word), because in all communities some one principle of action may be discovered which preponderates over the others. England in the last century, which has been more especially cited as an example of this form of Government, was in point of fact an essentially aristocratic State, although it comprised very powerful elements of democracy; for the laws and customs of the country were such that the aristocracy could not but preponderate in the end, and subject the direction of public affairs to its own will. The error arose from too much attention being paid to the actual struggle which was going on between the nobles and the people, without considering the probable issue of the contest, which was in reality the important point. When a community really has a mixed government—that is to say, when it is equally divided between two adverse principles—it must either pass through a revolution or fall into complete dissolution.

I am therefore of opinion that some one social power must always be made to predominate over the others; but I think that liberty is endangered when this power is checked by no obstacles which may retard its course, and force it to moderate its own vehemence. . . .

It is in the examination of the display of public opinion in the United States that we clearly perceive how far the power of the majority surpasses all the powers with which we are acquainted in Europe. Intellectual principles exercise an influence which is so invisible, and often so inappreciable, that they baffle the toils of oppression. At the present time the most absolute monarchs in Europe are unable to prevent certain notions, which are opposed to their authority, from circulating in secret throughout their dominions, and even in their courts. Such is not the case in America; as long as the majority is still undecided, discussion is carried on; but as soon as its decision is irrevocably pronounced, a submissive silence is observed, and the friends, as well as the opponents, of the measure unite in assenting to its propriety. The reason of this is perfectly clear: no monarch is so absolute as to combine all the powers of society in his own hands, and to conquer all opposition with the energy of a majority which is invested with the right of making and of executing the laws.

The authority of a king is purely physical, and it controls the actions of the subject without subduing his private will; but the majority possesses a power which is physical and moral at the same time; it acts upon the will as well as upon the actions of men, and it represses not only all contest, but all controversy.

I know no country in which there is so little true independence of mind and freedom of discussion as in America. In any constitutional state in Europe every sort of religious and political theory may be advocated and propagated abroad; for there is no country in Europe so subdued by any single authority as not to contain citizens who are ready to protect the man who raises his voice in the cause of truth from the consequences of his hardihood. If he is unfortunate enough to live under an absolute government, the people is upon his side; if he inhabits a free country, he may find a shelter behind the authority of the throne, if he require one. The aristocratic part of society supports him in some countries, and the democracy in others. But in a nation where democratic institutions exist, organized like those of the United States, there is but one sole authority, one single element of strength and of success, with nothing beyond it.

In America, the majority raises very formidable barriers to the liberty of opinion: within these barriers an author may write whatever he pleases, but he will repent it if he ever step beyond them. Not that he is exposed to the terrors of an auto-da-fé, but he is tormented by the slights and persecutions of daily obloquy. His political career is closed forever, since he has offended the only authority which is able to promote his success. Every sort of compensation, even that of celebrity, is refused to him. Before he published his opinions he imagined that he held them in common with many others; but no sooner has he declared them openly than he is loudly censured by his overbearing opponents, while those who think like him, without having the courage to speak, abandon him in silence. He yields at length, oppressed by the daily efforts he has been making, and he subsides into silence, as if he was tormented by remorse for having spoken the truth.

Fetters and headsmen were the coarse instruments which tyranny formerly employed; but the civilization of our age has refined the arts of despotism, which seemed, however, to have been sufficiently perfected before. The excesses of monarchical power had devised a variety of physical means of oppression: the democratic republics of the present day have rendered it as entirely an affair of the mind as that will which it is intended to coerce. Under the absolute sway of an individual despot the body was attacked in order to subdue the soul, and the soul escaped the blows which were directed against it and rose superior to the attempt; but such is not the course adopted by tyranny in democratic republics; there the body is left free, and the soul is enslaved. The sovereign can no longer say, "You shall think as I do on pain of death"; but he says: "You are free to think differently from me, and to retain your life, your property, and all that you possess; but if such be your determination, you are henceforth an alien among your people. You may retain your civil rights, but they will be useless to you, for you will never be chosen by your fellow-citizens if you solicit their suffrages, and they will affect to scorn you if you solicit their esteem. You will remain among men, but you will be deprived of the rights of mankind. Your fellow-creatures will shun you like an impure being, and those who are most persuaded of your innocence will abandon you too, lest they should be shunned in their turn. Go in peace! I have given you your life, but it is an existence incomparably worse than death." . . .

Causes Which Mitigate the Tyranny of the Majority in the United States

In visiting the Americans and in studying their laws we perceive that the authority they have intrusted to members of the legal profession, and the influence which these individuals exercise in the Government, is the most powerful existing security against the excesses of democracy. . . .

The members of the legal profession have taken an important part in all the vicissitudes of political society in Europe during the last five hundred years. At one time they have been the instruments of those who were invested with political authority, and at another they have succeeded in converting political authorities into their instrument. In the Middle Ages they afforded a powerful support to the Crown, and since that period they have exerted themselves to the utmost to limit the royal prerogative. In England they have contracted a close alliance with the aristocracy; in France they have proved to be the most dangerous enemies of that class. It is my object to inquire whether, under all these circumstances, the members of the legal profession have been swayed by sudden and momentary impulses; or whether they have been impelled by principles which are inherent in their pursuits, and which will always recur in history. I am incited to this investigation by reflecting that this particular class of men will play most likely a prominent part in that order of things to which the events of our time are giving birth.

Men who have more especially devoted themselves to legal pursuits derive from those occupations certain habits of order, a taste for formalities, and a kind of instinctive regard for the regular connection of ideas, which naturally render them very hostile to the revolutionary spirit and the unreflecting passions of the multitude.

The special information which lawyers derive from their studies insures them a separate station in society, and they constitute a sort of privileged body in the scale of intelligence. This notion of their superiority perpetually recurs to them in the practice of their profession: they are the masters of a science which is necessary, but which is not very generally known; they serve as arbiters between the citizens; and the habit of directing the blind passions of parties in litigation to their purpose inspires them with a certain contempt for the judgment of the multitude. To this it may be added that they naturally constitute a body, not by any previous understanding, or by an agreement which directs them to a common end; but the analogy of their studies and the uniformity of their proceedings connect their minds together, as much as a common interest could combine their endeavours. . . .

I do not . . . assert that all the members of the legal profession are at all times the friends of order and the opponents of innovation, but merely that most of them usually are so. In a community in which lawyers are allowed to occupy, without opposition, that high station which naturally belongs to them, their general spirit will be eminently conservative and anti-democratic. When an aristocracy excludes the leaders of that profession from its ranks, it excites enemies which are the more formidable to its security as they are independent of the nobility by their industrious pursuits; and they feel themselves to be its equal in point of intelligence, although they enjoy less opulence and less power. But whenever an aristocracy consents to impart some of its privileges to these same individuals, the two classes coalesce very readily, and assume, as it were, the consistency of a single order of family interests. . . .

Lawyers are attached to public order beyond every other consideration, and the best security of public order is authority. It must not be forgotten that, if they prize the free institutions of their country much, they nevertheless value the legality of those institutions far more: they are less afrai of tyranny than of arbitrary power; and provided that the legislature tak upon itself to deprive men of their independence, they are not dissatis fied. . . .

The government of democracy is favourable to the political power o lawyers; for when the wealthy, the noble, and the prince are excluded fron the government, they are sure to occupy the highest stations, in their ow right, as it were, since they are the only men of information and sagacity beyond the sphere of the people, who can be the objects of the popula choice. If, then, they are led by their tastes to combine with the aristocrac and to support the Crown, they are naturally brought into contact wit the people by their interests. They like the government of democracy without participating in its propensities and without imitating its weaknesses whence they derive a twofold authority, from it and over it. The people i democratic States does not mistrust the members of the legal professio because it is well known that they are interested in serving the popula cause; and it listens to them without irritation, because it does not attribut to them any sinister designs. The object of lawyers is not, indeed, to over throw the institutions of democracy, but they constantly endeavour to giv it an impulse which diverts it from its real tendency, by means which ar foreign to its nature. Lawyers belong to the people by birth and interest to the aristocracy by habit and by taste, and they may be looked upon a the natural bond and connecting link of the two great classes of society

The profession of the law is the only aristocratic element which can b amalgamated without violence with the natural elements of democracy, an which can be advantageously and permanently combined with them. I an not unacquainted with the defects which are inherent in the character o that body of men; but without this admixture of lawyer-like sobriety wit the democratic principle, I question whether democratic institutions coul long be maintained, and I can not believe that a republic could subsist a the present time if the influence of lawyers in public business did not increase in proportion to the power of the people.

This aristocratic character, which I hold to be common to the legal profession, is much more distinctly marked in the United States and in England than in any other country. This proceeds not only from the legal studies o the English and American lawyers, but from the nature of the legislation and the position which those persons occupy in the two countries. The English and the Americans have retained the law of precedents; that is to say, they continue to found their legal opinions and the decisions of their courts upon the opinions and the decisions of their forefathers. In the mind of an English or American lawyer a taste and a reverence for what is old is almost always united to a love of regular and lawful proceedings. . . .

In America there are no nobles or men of letters, and the people is apt to mistrust the wealthy; lawyers consequently form the highest political class, and the most cultivated circle of society. They have, therefore, nothing to gain by innovation, which adds a conservative interest to their natural taste for public order. If I were asked where I place the American aristocracy, I should reply without hesitation that it is not composed of the rich, who are united together by no common tie, but that it occupies the judicial bench and the bar.

The more we reflect upon all that occurs in the United States the more shall we be persuaded that the lawyers as a body form the most powerful, if not the only, counterpoise to the democratic element. In that country we perceive how eminently the legal profession is qualified by its powers, and even by its defects, to neutralize the vices which are inherent in popular government. When the American people is intoxicated by passion, or carried away by the impetuosity of its ideas, it is checked and stopped by the almost invisible influence of its legal counsellors, who secretly oppose their aristocratic propensities to its democratic instincts, their superstitious attachment to what is antique to its love of novelty, their narrow views to its immense designs, and their habitual procrastination to its ardent impatience. . . .

Armed with the power of declaring the laws to be unconstitutional, the American magistrate perpetually interferes in political affairs. He can not force the people to make laws, but at least he can oblige it not to disobey its own enactments, or to act inconsistently with its own principles. I am aware that a secret tendency to diminish the judicial power exists in the United States, and by most of the constitutions of the several States the Government can, upon the demand of the two houses of the legislature, remove the judges from their station. By some other constitutions the members of the tribunals are elected, and they are even subjected to frequent re-elections. I venture to predict that these innovations will sooner or later be attended with fatal consequences, and that it will be found out at some future period that the attack which is made upon the judicial power has affected the democratic republic itself.

It must not, however, be supposed that the legal spirit of which I have been speaking has been confined, in the United States, to the courts of justice; it extends far beyond them. As the lawyers constitute the only enlightened class which the people does not mistrust, they are naturally called upon to occupy most of the public stations. They fill the legislative assemblies, and they conduct the administration; they consequently exercise a powerful influence upon the formation of the law, and upon its execution. The lawyers are, however, obliged to yield to the current of public opinion, which is too strong for them to resist it, but it is easy to find indications of what their conduct would be if they were free to act as they chose. The Americans, who have made such copious innovations in their political legislation, have introduced very sparing alterations in their civil laws, and that with great difficulty, although those laws are frequently repugnant to their social condition. The reason of this is, that in matters of civil law the majority is obliged to defer to the authority of the legal profession, and that the American lawyers are disinclined to innovate when they are left to their own choice. . . .

The influence of the legal habits which are common in America extends beyond the limits I have just pointed out. Scarcely any question arises in the United States which does not become, sooner or later, a subject of judicial debate; hence all parties are obliged to borrow the ideas, and even the language, usual in judicial proceedings in their daily controversies. As most public men are, or have been, legal practitioners, they introduce the customs and technicalities of their profession into the affairs of the country. The jury extends this habitude to all classes. The language of the law thus becomes, in some measure, a vulgar tongue; the spirit of the law, which is produced in the schools and courts of justice, gradually penetrates beyond their walls into the bosom of society, where it descends to the lowest classes, so that the whole people contracts the habits and the tastes of the magistrate. The lawyers of the United States form a party which is but little feared and scarcely perceived, which has no badge peculiar to itself, which adapts itself with great flexibility to the exigencies of the time, and accommodates itself to all the movements of the social body; but this party extends over the whole community, and it penetrates into all classes of society; it acts upon the country imperceptibly, but it finally fashions it to suit its purposes.

Since I have been led by my subject to recur to the administration of justice in the United States, I will not pass over this point without adverting to the institution of the jury. . . .

By the jury I mean a certain number of citizens chosen indiscriminately, and invested with a temporary right of judging. Trial by jury, as applied to the repression of crime, appears to me to introduce an eminently republican element into the Government upon the following grounds:

The institution of the jury may be aristocratic or democratic, according to the class of society from which the jurors are selected; but it always preserves its republican character, inasmuch as it places the real direction of society in the hands of the governed, or of a portion of the governed, instead of leaving it under the authority of the Government. Force is never more than a transient element of success; and after force comes the notion of right. A government which should only be able to crush its enemies upon a field of battle would very soon be destroyed. The true sanction of political laws is to be found in penal legislation, and if that sanction be wanting the law will sooner or later lose its cogency. He who punishes infractions of the law is therefore the real master of society. Now the institution of the jury raises the people itself, or at least a class of citizens, to the bench of judicial authority. The institution of the jury consequently invests the people, or that class of citizens, with the direction of society.

In England the jury is returned from the aristocratic portion of the nation; the aristocracy makes the laws, applies the laws, and punishes all infractions of the laws; everything is established upon a consistent footing, and England may with truth be said to constitute an aristocratic republic. In the United States the same system is applied to the whole people. Every American citizen is qualified to be an elector, a juror, and is eligible to office. The system of the jury, as it is understood in America, appears to me to be as direct and as extreme a consequence of the sovereignty of the people as universal suffrage. These institutions are two instruments of equal power, which contribute to the supremacy of the majority. All the sovereigns who have chosen to govern by their own authority, and to direct society instead of obeying its directions, have destroyed or enfeebled the institution of the jury. The monarchs of the House of Tudor sent to prison jurors who refused to convict, and Napoleon caused them to be returned by his agents. . . .

In whatever manner the jury be applied, it can not fail to exercise a powerful influence upon the national character; but this influence is prodigiously increased when it is introduced into civil causes. The jury, and more especially the jury in civil cases, serves to communicate the spirit of the judges to the minds of all the citizens; and this spirit, with the habits which attend it, is the soundest preparation for free institutions. It imbues all classes with a respect for the thing judged, and with the notion of right. If these two elements be removed, the love of independence is reduced to a mere destructive passion. It teaches men to practise equity, every man learns to judge his neighbour as he would himself be judged; and this is especially true of the jury in civil causes, for, while the number of persons who have reason to apprehend a criminal prosecution is small, every one is liable to have a civil action brought against him. The jury teaches every man not to recoil before the responsibility of his own actions, and impresses him with that manly confidence without which political virtue can not exist. It invests each citizen with a kind of magistracy, it makes them all feel the duties which they are bound to discharge toward society, and the part which they take in the Government. By obliging men to turn their attention to affairs which are not exclusively their own, it rubs off that individual egotism which is the rust of society.

The jury contributes most powerfully to form the judgment and to increase the natural intelligence of a people, and this is, in my opinion, its greatest advantage. It may be regarded as a gratuitous public school ever open, in which every juror learns to exercise his rights, enters into daily communication with the most learned and enlightened members of the upper classes, and becomes practically acquainted with the laws of his country, which are brought within the reach of his capacity by the efforts of the bar, the advice of the judge, and even by the passions of the parties. I think that the practical intelligence and political good sense of the Americans are mainly attributable to the long use which they have made of the jury in civil causes. I do not know whether the jury is useful to those who are in litigation; but I am certain it is highly beneficial to those who decide the litigation; and I look upon it as one of the most efficacious means for the education of the people which society can employ.

What I have hitherto said applies to all nations, but the remark I am now about to make is peculiar to the Americans and to democratic peoples. I have already observed that in democracies the members of the legal profession and the magistrates constitute the only aristocratic body which can check the irregularities of the people. This aristocracy is invested with no physical power, but it exercises its conservative influence upon the minds of men, and the most abundant source of its authority is the institution of the civil jury. In criminal causes, when society is armed against a single individual, the jury is apt to look upon the judge as the passive instrument of social power, and to mistrust his advice. Moreover, criminal causes are entirely founded upon the evidence of facts which common sense can readily appreciate; upon this ground the judge and the jury are equal. Such, however, is not the case in civil causes; then the judge appears as a disinterested arbiter between the conflicting passions of the parties. The jurors look up to him with confidence and listen to him with respect, for in this instance their intelligence is completely under the control of his learning. It is the judge who sums up the various arguments with which their memory has been wearied out, and who guides them through the devious course of the proceedings; he points their attention to the exact question of fact which they are called upon to solve, and he puts the answer to the question of law into their mouths. His influence upon their verdict is almost unlimited.

If I am called upon to explain why I am but little moved by the arguments derived from the ignorance of jurors in civil causes, I reply, that in these proceedings, whenever the question to be solved is not a mere question of fact, the jury has only the semblance of a judicial body. The jury sanctions the decision of the judge, they by the authority of society which they represent, and he by that of reason and of law.

In England and in America the judges exercise an influence upon criminal trials which the French judges have never possessed. The reason of this difference easily may be discovered: the English and American magistrates establish their authority in civil causes, and only transfer it afterward to tribunals of another kind, where that authority was not acquired. In some cases (and they are frequently the most important ones) the American judges have the right of deciding causes alone. Upon these occasions they are accidentally placed in the position which the French judges habitually occupy, but they are invested with far more power than the latter; they are still surrounded by the reminiscence of the jury, and their judgment has almost as much authority as the voice of the community at large, represented by that institution. Their influence extends beyond the limits of the courts; in the recreations of private life as well as in the turmoil of public business, abroad and in the legislative assemblies, the American judge is constantly surrounded by men who are accustomed to regard his intelligence as superior to their own, and after having exercised his power in the decision of causes, he continues to influence the habits of thought and the characters of the individuals who took a part in his judgment.

The jury, then, which seems to restrict the rights of magistracy, does in reality consolidate its power, and in no country are the judges so powerful as there, where the people partakes their privileges. It is more especially by means of the jury in civil causes that the American magistrates imbue all classes of society with the spirit of their profession. Thus the jury, which is the most energetic means of making the people rule, is also the most efficacious means of teaching it to rule well.

Principal Causes Which Tend to Maintain the Democratic Republic in the United States

The chief circumstance which has favoured the establishment and the maintenance of a democratic republic in the United States is the nature of the territory which the Americans inhabit. Their ancestors gave them the love of equality and of freedom, but God himself gave them the means of remaining equal and free, by placing them upon a boundless continent, which is open to their exertions. General prosperity is favourable to the stability of all governments, but more particularly of a democratic constitution, which depends upon the dispositions of the majority, and more particularly of that portion of the community which is most exposed to feel the pressure of want. When the people rules, it must be rendered happy, or it will overturn the State, and misery is apt to stimulate it to those excesses to which ambition rouses kings. The physical causes, independent of the laws, which contribute to promote general prosperity, are more numerous in America than they have ever been in any other country in the world, at any other period of history. In the United States not only is legislation democratic, but Nature herself favours the cause of the people.

In what part of human tradition can be found anything at all similar to that which is occurring under our eyes in North America? The celebrated communities of antiquity were all founded in the midst of hostile nations, which they were obliged to subjugate before they could flourish in their place. Even the moderns have found, in some parts of South America, vast regions inhabited by a people of inferior civilization, but which occupied and cultivated the soil. To found their new States it was necessary to extirpate or to subdue a numerous population, until civilization has been made to blush for their success. But North America was only inhabited by wandering tribes, who took no thought of the natural riches of the soil, and that vast country was still, properly speaking, an empty continent, a desert land awaiting its inhabitants.

Everything is extraordinary in America, the social condition of the inhabitants, as well as the laws; but the soil upon which these institutions are founded is more extraordinary than all the rest. When man was first placed upon the earth by the Creator, the earth was inexhaustible in its youth, but man was weak and ignorant; and when he had learned to explore the treasures which it contained, hosts of his fellow-creatures covered its surface, and he was obliged to earn an asylum for repose and for freedom by the sword. At that same period North America was discovered, as if it had been kept in reserve by the Deity, and had just risen from beneath the waters of the deluge.

That continent still presents, as it did in the primeval time, rivers which rise from never-failing sources, green and moist solitudes, and fields which the ploughshare of the husbandman has never turned. In this state it is offered to man, not in the barbarous and isolated condition of the early ages, but to a being who is already in possession of the most potent secrets of the natural world, who is united to his fellow-men, and instructed by the experience of fifty centuries. At this very time thirteen millions of civilized Europeans are peaceably spreading over those fertile plains, with whose resources and whose extent they are not yet themselves accurately acquainted. Three or four thousand soldiers drive the wandering races of the aborigines before them; these are followed by the pioneers, who pierce the woods, scare off the beasts of prey, explore the courses of the inland streams, and make ready the triumphal procession of civilization across the waste.

The favourable influence of the temporal prosperity of America upon the institutions of that country has been so often described by others, and adverted to by myself, that I shall not enlarge upon it beyond the addition of a few facts. An erroneous notion is generally entertained that the deserts of America are peopled by European emigrants, who annually disembark upon the coasts of the New World, while the American population increases and multiplies upon the soil which its forefathers tilled. The European settler, however, usually arrives in the United States without friends, and sometimes without resources; in order to subsist he is obliged to work for hire, and he rarely proceeds beyond that belt of industrious population which adjoins the ocean. The desert can not be explored without capital or credit; and the body must be accustomed to the rigours of a new climate before it can be exposed to the chances of forest life. It is the Americans themselves who daily quit the spots which gave them birth to acquire extensive domains in a remote country. Thus the European leaves his cottage for the transatlantic shores; and the American, who is born on that very coast, plunges in his turn into the wilds of central America. This double emigration is incessant; it begins in the remotest parts of Europe, it crosses the Atlantic Ocean, and it advances over the solitudes of the New World. Millions of men are marching at once toward the same horizon; their language, their religion, their manners differ, their object is the same. The gifts of fortune are promised in the West, and to the West they bend their course. . . .

The future still conceals from us the ulterior consequences of this emigration of the Americans toward the West; but we can readily apprehend its more immediate results. As a portion of the inhabitants annually leave the States in which they were born, the population of these States increases very slowly, although they have long been established: thus in Connecticut, which contains only fifty-nine inhabitants to the square mile, the population has not been increased by more than one quarter in forty years, while that of England has been augmented by one third in the lapse of the same period. The European emigrant always lands, therefore, in a country which is but half full, and where hands are in request: he becomes a workman in easy circumstances; his son goes to seek his fortune in unpeopled regions, and he becomes a rich land-owner. The former amasses the capital which the latter invests, and the stranger as well as the native is unacquainted with want. . . .

It is difficult to describe the rapacity with which the American rushes forward to secure the immense booty which fortune proffers to him. In the pursuit he fearlessly braves the arrow of the Indian and the distempers of the forest; he is unimpressed by the silence of the woods; the approach of beasts of prey does not disturb him; for he is goaded onward by a passion more intense than the love of life. Before him lies a boundless continent, and he urges onward as if time pressed, and he was afraid of finding no room for his exertions. I have spoken of the emigration from the older States, but how shall I describe that which takes place from the more recent ones? Fifty years have scarcely elapsed since that of Ohio was founded; the greater part of its inhabitants were not born within its confines; its capital has only been built thirty years, and its territory is still covered by an immense extent of uncultivated fields; nevertheless, the population of Ohio is already proceeding westward, and most of the settlers who descend to the fertile savannas of Illinois are citizens of Ohio. These men left their first country to improve their condition; they quit their resting-place to ameliorate it still more; fortune awaits them everywhere, but happiness they can not attain. The desire of prosperity is become an ardent and restless passion in their minds which grows by what it gains. They early broke the ties which bound them to their natal earth, and they have contracted no fresh ones on their way. Emigration was at first necessary to them as a means of subsistence; and it soon becomes a sort of game of chance, which they pursue for the emotions it excites as much as for the gain it procures. . . .

In Europe we are wont to look upon a restless disposition, an unbounded desire of riches, and an excessive love of independence, as propensities very formidable to society. Yet these are the very elements which insure a long and peaceful duration to the republics of America. Without these unquiet passions the population would collect in certain spots, and would soon be subject to wants like those of the Old World, which it is difficult to satisfy; for such is the present good fortune of the New World, that the vices of its inhabitants are scarcely less favourable to society than their virtues. These circumstances exercise a great influence on the estimation in which human actions are held in the two hemispheres. The Americans frequently term what we should call cupidity a laudable industry; and they blame as faint-heartedness what we consider to be the virtue of moderate desires. . . .

At the present time America presents a field for human effort far more extensive than any sum of labour which can be applied to work it. In America too much knowledge can not be diffused; for all knowledge, while it may serve him who possesses it, turns also to the advantage of those who are without it. New wants are not to be feared, since they can be satisfied without difficulty; the growth of human passions need not be dreaded, since all passions may find an easy and a legitimate object; nor can men be put in possession of too much freedom, since they are scarcely ever tempted to misuse their liberties. . . .

Three circumstances seem to me to contribute most powerfully to the maintenance of the democratic republic in the United States:

The first is that Federal form of Government which the Americans have adopted, and which enables the Union to combine the power of a great empire with the security of a small State.

The second consists in those municipal institutions which limit the despotism of the majority, and at the same time impart a taste for freedom and a knowledge of the art of being free to the people.

The third is to be met with in the constitution of the judicial power. I have shown in what manner the courts of justice serve to repress the excesses of democracy, and how they check and direct the impulses of the majority without stopping its activity.

I have previously remarked that the manners of the people may be considered as one of the general causes to which the maintenance of a democratic republic in the United States is attributable. I here used the word manners with the meaning which the ancients attached to the word mores; for I apply it not only to manners in their proper sense of what constitutes the character of social intercourse, but I extend it to the various notions and opinions current among men, and to the mass of those ideas which constitute their character of mind. I comprise, therefore, under this term the whole moral and intellectual condition of a people. My intention is not to draw a picture of American manners, but simply to point out such features of them as are favourable to the maintenance of political institutions. . . .

The imagination of the Americans, even in its greatest flights, is circumspect and undecided; its impulses are checked, and its works unfinished. These habits of restraint recur in political society, and are singularly favourable both to the tranquility of the people and to the durability of the institutions it has established. Nature and circumstances concurred to make the inhabitants of the United States bold men, as is sufficiently attested by the enterprising spirit with which they seek for fortune. If the mind of the Americans were free from all trammels, they would very shortly become the most daring innovators and the most implacable disputants in the world. But the revolutionists of America are obliged to profess an ostensible respect for Christian morality and equity, which does not easily permit them to violate the laws that oppose their designs; nor would they find it easy to surmount the scruples of their partisans, even if they were able to get over their own. Hitherto no one in the United States has dared to advance the maxim that everything is permissible with a view to the interests of society; an impious adage which seems to have been invented in an age of freedom to shelter all the tyrants of future ages. Thus while the law permits the Americans to do what they please, religion prevents them from conceiving, and forbids them to commit, what is rash or unjust.

Religion in America takes no direct part in the government of society, but nevertheless it must be regarded as the foremost of the political institutions of that country; for if it does not impart a taste for freedom, it facilitates the use of free institutions. Indeed, it is in this same point of view that the inhabitants of the United States themselves look upon religious belief. I do not know whether all the Americans have a sincere faith in their religion, for who can search the human heart? but I am certain that they hold it to be indispensable to the maintenance of republican institutions. This opinion is not peculiar to a class of citizens or to a party, but it belongs to the whole nation, and to every rank of society. . . .

The Americans never use the word "peasant," because they have no idea of the peculiar class which that term denotes; the ignorance of more remote ages, the simplicity of rural life, and the rusticity of the villager have not been preserved among them; and they are alike unacquainted with the virtues, the vices, the coarse habits, and the simple graces of an early stage of civilization. At the extreme borders of the confederate States, upon the confines of society and of the wilderness, a population of bold adventurers have taken up their abode, who pierce the solitudes of the American woods, and seek a country there, in order to escape that poverty which awaited them in their native provinces. As soon as the pioneer arrives upon the spot which is to serve him for a retreat, he fells a few trees and builds a log-house. Nothing can offer a more miserable aspect than these isolated dwellings. The traveller who approaches one of them toward nightfall, sees the flicker of the hearth-flame through the chinks in the walls; and at night, if the wind rises, he hears the roof of boughs shake to and fro in the midst of the great forest trees. Who would not suppose that this poor hut is the asylum of rudeness and ignorance? Yet no sort of comparison can be drawn between the pioneer and the dwelling which shelters him. Everything about him is primitive and unformed, but he is himself the result of the labour and the experience of eighteen centuries. He wears the dress and he speaks the language of cities; he is acquainted with the past, curious of the future, and ready for argument upon the present; he is, in short, a highly civilized being, who consents, for a time, to inhabit the backwoods, and who penetrates into the wilds of the New World with the Bible, an axe, and a file of newspapers.

It is difficult to imagine the incredible rapidity with which public opinion circulates in the midst of these deserts. I do not think that so much intellectual intercourse takes place in the most enlightened and populous districts of France. It can not be doubted that, in the United States, the instruction of the people powerfully contributes to the support of a democratic republic; and such must always be the case, I believe, where instruction which awakens the understanding is not separated from moral education which amends the heart. But I by no means exaggerate this benefit, and I am still further from thinking, as so many people do think in Europe, that men can be made citizens instantaneously by teaching them to read and write. True information is mainly derived from experience; and if the Americans had not been gradually accustomed to govern themselves, their book-learning would not assist them much at the present day.

I have lived a great deal with the people in the United States, and I can not express how much I admire their experience and their good sense. An American should never be allowed to speak of Europe; for he will then probably display a vast deal of presumption and very foolish pride. He will take up with those crude and vague notions which are so useful to the ignorant all over the world. But if you question him respecting his own country, the cloud which dimmed his intelligence will immediately disperse; his language will become as clear and as precise as his thoughts. He will inform you what his rights are, and by what means he exercises them; he will be able to point out the customs which obtain in the political world. You will find that he is well acquainted with the rules of the administration, and that he is familiar with the mechanism of the laws. The citizen of the United States does not acquire his practical science and his positive notions from books; the instruction he has acquired may have prepared him for receiving those ideas, but it did not furnish them. The American learns to know the laws by participating in the act of legislation; and he takes a lesson in the forms of government from governing. The great work of society is ever going on beneath his eyes, and, as it were, under his hands. . . .

I am far from supposing that the American laws are pre-eminently good in themselves; I do not hold them to be applicable to all democratic peoples; and several of them seem to me to be dangerous, even in the United States. Nevertheless, it can not be denied that the American legislation, taken collectively, is extremely well adapted to the genius of the people and the nature of the country which it is intended to govern. The American laws are therefore good, and to them must be attributed a large portion of the success which attends the government of democracy in America: but I do not believe them to be the principal cause of that success; and if they seem to me to have more influence upon the social happiness of the Americans than the nature of the country, on the other hand there is reason to believe that their effect is still inferior to that produced by the manners of the people.

The Federal laws undoubtedly constitute the most important part of the legislation of the United States. Mexico, which is not less fortunately situated than the Anglo-American Union, has adopted the same laws, but is unable to accustom itself to the government of democracy. Some other cause is therefore at work, independently of those physical circumstances and peculiar laws which enable the democracy to rule in the United States.

Another still more striking proof may be adduced. Almost all the inhabitants of the territory of the Union are the descendants of a common stock; they speak the same language, they worship God in the same manner, they are affected by the same physical causes, and they obey the same laws. Whence, then, do their characteristic differences arise? Why, in the Eastern States of the Union, does the republican Government display vigour and regularity, and proceed with mature deliberation? Whence does it derive the wisdom and the durability which mark its acts, while in the Western States, on the contrary, society seems to be ruled by the powers of chance? There, public business is conducted with an irregularity and a passionate and feverish excitement, which does not announce a long or sure duration. . . .

It is in the Eastern States that the Anglo-Americans have been longest accustomed to the government of democracy, and that they have adopted the habits and conceived the notions most favourable to its maintenance. Democracy has gradually penetrated into their customs, their opinions, and the forms of social intercourse; it is to be found in all the details of daily life as equally as in the laws. In the Eastern States the instruction and practical education of the people have been most perfected, and religion has been most thoroughly amalgamated with liberty. Now these habits, opinions, customs, and convictions are precisely the constituent elements of that which I have denominated manners.

In the Western States, on the contrary, a portion of the same advantages is still wanting. Many of the Americans of the West were born in the woods, and they mix the ideas and the customs of savage life with the civilization of their parents. Their passions are more intense; their religious morality less authoritative; and their convictions less secure. The inhabitants exercise no sort of control over their fellow-citizens, for they are scarcely acquainted with each other. The nations of the West display, to a certain extent, the inexperience and the rude habits of a people in its infancy; for although they are composed of old elements, their assemblage is of recent date.

The manners of the Americans of the United States are, then, the real cause which renders that people the only one of the American nations that is able to support a democratic Government; and it is the influence of manners which produces the different degrees of order and of prosperity that may be distinguished in the several Anglo-American democracies. Thus the effect which the geographical position of a country may have upon the duration of democratic institutions is exaggerated in Europe. Too much importance is attributed to legislation, too little to manners. These three great causes serve, no doubt, to regulate and direct the American democracy; but if they were to be classed in their proper order, I should say that the physical circumstances are less efficient than the laws, and the laws very subordinate to the manners of the people. I am convinced that the most advantageous situation and the best possible laws can not maintain a constitution in spite of the manners of a country; while the latter may turn the most unfavourable positions and the worst laws to some advantage. The importance of manners is a common truth to which study and experience incessantly direct our attention. It may be regarded as a central point in the range of human observation, and the common termination of all inquiry. . . .

I have asserted that the success of democratic institutions in the United States is more intimately connected with the laws themselves, and the manners of the people, than with the nature of the country. But does it follow that the same causes would of themselves produce the same results if they were put into operation elsewhere; and if the country is no adequate substitute for laws and manners, can laws and manners in their turn prove a substitute for the country? It will readily be understood that the necessary elements of a reply to this question are wanting: other peoples are to found in the New World besides the Anglo-Americans, and as these people are affected by the same physical circumstances as the latter, they may fairly be compared together. But there are no nations out of America which have adopted the same laws and manners, being destitute of the physical advantages peculiar to the Anglo-Americans. No standard of comparison therefore exists, and we can only hazard an opinion upon this subject.

It appears to me, in the first place, that a careful distinction must be made between the institutions of the United States and democratic institutions in general. When I reflect upon the state of Europe, its mighty nations, its populous cities, its formidable armies, and the complex nature of its politics, I can not suppose that even the Anglo-Americans, if they were transported to our hemisphere, with their ideas, their religion, and their manners, could exist without considerably altering their laws. But a democratic nation may be imagined, organized differently from the American people. It is not impossible to conceive a government really established upon the will of the majority; but in which the majority, repressing its natural propensity to equality, should consent, with a view to the order and the stability of the State, to invest a family or an individual with all the prerogatives of the executive. A democratic society might exist, in which the forces of the nation would be more centralized than they are in the United States; the people would exercise a less direct and less irresistible influence upon public affairs, and yet every citizen invested with certain rights would participate, within his sphere, in the conduct of the government. The observations I made among the Anglo-Americans induce me to believe that democratic institutions of this kind, prudently introduced into society, so as gradually to mix with the habits and to be interfused with the opinions of the people, might subsist in other countries besides America. If the laws of the United States were the only imaginable democratic laws, or the most perfect which it is possible to conceive, I should admit that the success of those institutions affords no proof of the success of democratic institutions in general, in a country less favoured by natural circumstances. But as the laws of America appear to me to be defective in several respects, and as I can readily imagine others of the same general nature, the peculiar advantages of that country do not prove that democratic institutions can not succeed in a nation less favoured by circumstances, if ruled by better laws.

If human nature were different in America from what it is elsewhere; or if the social condition of the Americans engendered habits and opinions among them different from those which originate in the same social condition in the Old World, the American democracies would afford no means of predicting what may occur in other democracies. If the Americans displayed the same propensities as all other democratic nations, and if their legislators had relied upon the nature of the country and the favour of circumstances to restrain those propensities within due limits, the prosperity of the United States would be exclusively attributable to physical causes, and it would afford no encouragement to a people inclined to imitate their example, without sharing their natural advantages. But neither of these suppositions is borne out by facts.

In America the same passions are to be met with as in Europe; some originating in human nature, others in the democratic condition of society. Thus in the United States I found that restlessness of heart which is natural to men, when all ranks are nearly equal and the chances of elevation are the same to all. I found the democratic feeling of envy expressed under a thousand different forms. I remarked that the people frequently displayed, in the conduct of affairs, a consummate mixture of ignorance and presumption; and I inferred that in America men are liable to the same failings and the same absurdities as among ourselves. But upon examining the state of society more attentively, I speedily discovered that the Americans had made great and successful efforts to counteract these imperfections of human nature, and to correct the natural defects of democracy. Their divers municipal laws appeared to me to be a means of restraining the ambition of the citizens within a narrow sphere, and of turning those same passions which might have worked havoc in the State, to the good of the township or the parish. The American legislators have succeeded to a certain extent in opposing the notion of rights to the feelings of envy; the permanence of the religious world to the continual shifting of politics; the experience of the people to its theoretical ignorance; and its practical knowledge of business to the impatience of its desires.

The Americans, then, have not relied upon the nature of their country to counterpoise those dangers which originate in their Constitution and in their political laws. To evils which are common to all democratic peoples they have applied remedies which none but themselves had ever thought of before; and although they were the first to make the experiment, they have succeeded in it.

The manners and laws of the Americans are not the only ones which may suit a democratic people; but the Americans have shown that it would be wrong to despair of regulating democracy by the aid of manners and of laws. If other nations should borrow this general and pregnant idea from the Americans, without, however, intending to imitate them in the peculiar application which they have made of it; if they should attempt to fit themselves for that social condition, which it seems to be the will of Providence to impose upon the generations of this age, and so to escape from the despotism or the anarchy which threatens them; what reason is there to suppose that their efforts would not be crowned with success? The organization and the establishment of democracy in Christendom is the great political problem of the time. The Americans, unquestionably, have not resolved this problem, but they furnish useful data to those who undertake the task.

It may readily be discovered with what intention I undertook the foregoing inquiries. The question here discussed is interesting not only to the United States, but to the whole world; it concerns, not a nation, but all mankind. If those nations whose social condition is democratic could only remain free as long as they are inhabitants of the wilds, we could not but despair of the future destiny of the human race; for democracy is rapidly acquiring a more extended sway, and the wilds are gradually peopled with men. If it were true that laws and manners are insufficient to maintain democratic institutions, what refuge would remain open to the nations, except the despotism of a single individual? I am aware that there are many worthy persons at the present time who are not alarmed at this latter alternative, and who are so tired of liberty as to be glad of repose, far from those storms by which it is attended. But these individuals are ill acquainted with the haven toward which they are bound. They are so deluded by their recollections as to judge the tendency of absolute power by what it was formerly, and not by what it might become at the present time.

If absolute power were re-established among the democratic nations of Europe, I am persuaded that it would assume a new form, and appear under features unknown to our forefathers. There was a time in Europe when the laws and the consent of the people had invested princes with almost unlimited authority; but they scarcely ever availed themselves of it. I do not speak of the prerogatives of the nobility, of the authority of supreme courts of justice, of corporations and their chartered rights, or of provincial privileges, which served to break the blows of the sovereign authority, and to maintain a spirit of resistance in the nation. Independently of these political institutions—which, however opposed they might be to personal liberty, served to keep alive the love of freedom in the mind of the public, and which may be esteemed to have been useful in this respect—the manners and opinions of the nation confined the royal authority within barriers which were not less powerful, although they were less conspicuous. Religion, the affections of the people, the benevolence of the prince, the sense of honour, family pride, provincial prejudices, custom, and public opinion limited the power of kings, and restrained their authority within an invisible circle. The constitution of nations was despotic at that time, but their manners were free. Princes had the right, but they had neither the means nor the desire, of doing whatever they pleased.

But what now remains of those barriers which formerly arrested the aggressions of tyranny? Since religion has lost its empire over the souls of men, the most prominent boundary which divided good from evil is overthrown; the very elements of the moral world are indeterminate; the princes and the peoples of the earth are guided by chance, and none can define the natural limits of despotism and the bounds of license. Long revolutions have forever destroyed the respect which surrounded the rulers of the State; and since they have been relieved from the burden of public esteem, princes may henceforward surrender themselves without fear to the seductions of arbitrary power.

When kings find that the hearts of their subjects are turned toward them, they are clement, because they are conscious of their strength, and they are chary of the affection of their people, because the affection of their people is the bulwark of the throne. A mutual interchange of good-will then takes place between the prince and the people, which resembles the gracious intercourse of domestic society. The subjects may murmur at the sovereign's decree, but they are grieved to displease him; and the sovereign chastises his subjects with the light hand of parental affection.

But when once the spell of royalty is broken in the tumult of revolution; when successive monarchs have crossed the throne, so as alternately to display to the people the weakness of their right and the harshness of their power, the sovereign is no longer regarded by any as the Father of the State, and he is feared by all as its master. If he be weak, he is despised; if he be strong, he is detested. He is himself full of animosity and alarm; he finds that he is as a stranger in his own country, and he treats his subjects like conquered enemies.

When the provinces and the towns formed so many different nations in the midst of their common country, each of them had a will of its own, which was opposed to the general spirit of subjection; but now that all the parts of the same empire, after having lost their immunities, their customs, their prejudices, their traditions, and their names, are subjected and accustomed to the same laws, it is not more difficult to oppress them collectively than it was formerly to oppress them singly.

While the nobles enjoyed their power, and indeed long after that power was lost, the honour of aristocracy conferred an extraordinary degree of force upon their personal opposition. They afforded instances of men who, notwithstanding their weakness, still entertained a high opinion of their personal value, and dared to cope singlehanded with the efforts of the public authority. But at the present day, when all ranks are more and more confounded, when the individual disappears in the throng, and is easily lost in the midst of a common obscurity, when the honour of monarchy has almost lost its empire without being succeeded by public virtue, and when nothing can enable man to rise above himself, who shall say at what point the exigencies of power and the servility of weakness will stop?

As long as family feeling was kept alive, the antagonist of oppression was never alone; he looked about him, and found his clients, his hereditary friends, and his kinsfolk. If this support was wanting, he was sustained by his ancestors and animated by his posterity. But when patrimonial estates are divided, and when a few years suffice to confound the distinctions of a race, where can family feeling be found? What force can there be in the customs of a country which has changed and is still perpetually changing its aspect; in which every act of tyranny has a precedent, and every crime an example; in which there is nothing so old that its antiquity can save it from destruction, and nothing so unparalleled that its novelty can prevent it from being done? What resistance can be offered by manners of so pliant a make that they have already often yielded? What strength can even public opinion have retained, when no twenty persons are connected by a common tie; when not a man, nor a family, nor chartered corporation, nor class, nor free institution, has the power of representing or exerting that opinion; and when every citizen—being equally weak, equally poor, and equally dependent—has only his personal impotence to oppose to the organized force of the Government? . . .

Those who hope to revive the monarchy of Henry IV or of Louis XIV appear to me to be afflicted with mental blindness; and when I consider the present condition of several European nations—a condition to which all the others tend—I am led to believe that they will soon be left with no other alternative than democratic liberty, or the tyranny of the Cæsars.

And, indeed, it is deserving of consideration, whether men are to be entirely emancipated or entirely enslaved; whether their rights are to be made equal, or wholly taken away from them. If the rulers of society were reduced either gradually to raise the crowd to their own level, or to sink the citizens below that of humanity, would not the doubts of many be resolved, the consciences of many be healed, and the community prepared to make great sacrifices with little difficulty? In that case, the gradual growth of democratic manners and institutions should be regarded, not as the best, but as the only means of preserving freedom; and without liking the government of democracy, it might be adopted as the most applicable and the fairest remedy for the present ills of society.

It is difficult to associate a people in the work of government; but it is still more difficult to supply it with experience, and to inspire it with the feelings which it requires in order to govern well. I grant that the caprices of democracy are perpetual; its instruments are rude; its laws imperfect. But if it were true that soon no just medium would exist between the empire of democracy and the dominion of a single arm, should we not rather incline toward the former than submit voluntarily to the latter? And if complete equality be our fate, is it not better to be levelled by free institutions than by despotic power?

Those who, after having read this book, should imagine that my intention in writing it has been to propose the laws and manners of the Anglo-Americans for the imitation of all democratic peoples, would commit a very great mistake; they must have paid more attention to the form than to the substance of my ideas. My aim has been to show, by the example of America, that laws, and especially manners, may exist which will allow a democratic people to remain free. But I am very far from thinking that we ought to follow the example of the American democracy, and copy the means which it has employed to attain its ends; for I am well aware of the influence which the nature of a country and its political precedents exercise upon a constitution; and I should regard it as a great misfortune for mankind if liberty were to exist over all the world under the same forms.

But I am of opinion that if we do not succeed in gradually introducing democratic institutions into France, and if we despair of imparting to the citizens those ideas and sentiments which first prepare them for freedom, and afterward allow them to enjoy it, there will be no independence at all, either for the middle classes or the nobility, for the poor or for the rich, but an equal tyranny over all; and I foresee that if the peaceable empire of the majority be not founded among us in time, we shall sooner or later arrive at the unlimited authority of a single despot.

Indian Tribes

When the Indians were the sole inhabitants of the wilds from whence they have since been expelled, their wants were few. Their arms were of their own manufacture, their only drink was the water of the brook, and their clothes consisted of the skins of animals, whose flesh furnished them with food.

The Europeans introduced among the savages of North America fire-arms, ardent spirits, and iron: they taught them to exchange for manufactured stuffs the rough garments which had previously satisfied their untutored simplicity. Having acquired new tastes, without the arts by which they could be gratified, the Indians were obliged to have recourse to the workmanship of the Whites; but in return for their productions the savage had nothing to offer except the rich furs which still abounded in his woods. Hence the chase became necessary, not merely to provide for his subsistence, but in order to procure the only objects of barter which he could furnish to Europe. While the wants of the natives were thus increasing, their resources continued to diminish.

From the moment when a European settlement is formed in the neighbourhood of the territory occupied by the Indians, the beasts of chase take the alarm. Thousands of savages, wandering in the forests and destitute of any fixed dwelling, did not disturb them; but as soon as the continuous sounds of European labour are heard in their neighbourhood, they begin to flee away, and retire to the West, where their instinct teaches them that they will find deserts of immeasurable extent. . . .

To drive away their game is to deprive the Indians of the means of existence as effectually as if the fields of our agriculturists were stricken with barrenness; and they are reduced, like famished wolves, to prowl through the forsaken woods in quest of prey. Their instinctive love of their country attaches them to the soil which gave them birth, even after it has ceased to yield anything but misery and death. At length they are compelled to acquiesce, and to depart: they follow the traces of the elk, the buffalo, and the beaver, and are guided by these wild animals in the choice of their future country. Properly speaking, therefore, it is not the Europeans who drive away the native inhabitants of America; it is famine which compels them to recede; a happy distinction which had escaped the casuists of former times, and for which we are indebted to modern discovery!

It is impossible to conceive the extent of the sufferings which attend these forced emigrations. They are undertaken by a people already exhausted and reduced; and the countries to which the new-comers betake themselves are inhabited by other tribes which receive them with jealous hostility. Hunger is in the rear; war awaits them, and misery besets them on all sides. In the hope of escaping from such a host of enemies, they separate, and each individual endeavours to procure the means of supporting his existence in solitude and secrecy, living in the immensity of the desert like an outcast in civilized society. The social tie, which distress had long since weakened, is then dissolved; they have lost their country, and their people soon desert them: their very families are obliterated; the names they bore in common are forgotten; their language perishes, and all traces of their origin disappear. Their nation has ceased to exist, except in the recollection of the antiquaries of America and a few of the learned of Europe. . . .

If the Indian tribes which now inhabit the heart of the continent could summon up energy enough to attempt to civilize themselves, they might possibly succeed. Superior already to the barbarous nations which surround them, they would gradually gain strength and experience, and when the Europeans should appear upon their borders, they would be in a state, if not to maintain their independence, at least to assert their right to the soil, and to incorporate themselves with the conquerors. But it is the misfortune of Indians to be brought into contact with a civilized people, which is also (it must be owned) the most avaricious nation on the globe, while they are still semi-barbarian: to find despots in their instructors, and to receive knowledge from the hand of oppression. Living in the freedom of the woods, the North American Indian was destitute, but he had no feeling of inferiority toward any one; as soon, however, as the desires to penetrate into the social scale of the Whites, he takes the lowest rank in society, for he enters, ignorant and poor, within the pale of science and wealth. After having led a life of agitation, beset with evils and dangers, but at the same time filled with proud emotions, he is obliged to submit to a wearisome, obscure, and degraded state; and to gain the bread which nourishes him by hard and ignoble labour; such are in his eyes the only results of which civilization can boast: and even this much he is not sure to obtain.

When the Indians undertake to imitate their European neighbours, and to till the earth like the settlers, they are immediately exposed to a very formidable competition. The white man is skilled in the craft of agriculture; the Indian is a rough beginner in an art with which he is unacquainted. The former reaps abundant crops without difficulty, the latter meets with a thousand obstacles in raising the fruits of the earth.

The European is placed among a population whose wants he knows and partakes. The savage is isolated in the midst of a hostile people, with whose manners, language, and laws he is imperfectly acquainted, but without whose assistance he can not live. He can only procure the materials of comfort by bartering his commodities against the goods of the European, for the assistance of his countrymen is wholly insufficient to supply his wants. When the Indian wishes to sell the produce of his labour, he can not always meet with a purchaser, while the European readily finds a market; and the former can only produce at a considerable cost that which the latter vends at a very low rate. Thus the Indian has no sooner escaped those evils to which barbarous nations are exposed, than he is subjected to the still greater miseries of civilized communities; and he finds it scarcely less difficult to live in the midst of our abundance than in the depth of his own wilderness. . . .

Washington said in one of his messages to Congress, "We are more enlightened and more powerful than the Indian nations, we are therefore bound in honour to treat them with kindness and even with generosity." But this virtuous and high-minded policy has not been followed. The rapacity of the settlers is usually backed by the tyranny of the Government. Although the Cherokees and the Creeks are established upon the territory which they inhabited before the settlement of the Europeans, and although the Americans have frequently treated with them as with foreign nations, the surrounding States have not consented to acknowledge them as independent peoples, and attempts have been made to subject these children of the woods to Anglo-American magistrates, laws, and customs. Destitution had driven these unfortunate Indians to civilization, and oppression now drives them back to their former condition: many of them abandon the soil which they had begun to clear, and return to their savage course of life.

If we consider the tyrannical measures which have been adopted by the Legislatures of the Southern States, the conduct of their Governors, and the decrees of their courts of justice, we shall be convinced that the entire expulsion of the Indians is the final result to which the efforts of their policy are directed. The Americans of that part of the Union look with jealousy upon the Aborigines, they are aware that these tribes have not yet lost the traditions of savage life, and before civilization has permanently fixed them to the soil, it is intended to force them to recede by reducing them to despair. The Creeks and Cherokees, oppressed by the several States, have appealed to the central Government, which is by no means insensible to their misfortunes, and is sincerely desirous of saving the remnant of the natives, and of maintaining them in the free possession of that territory, which the Union is pledged to respect. But the several States oppose so formidable a resistance to the execution of this design, that the Government is obliged to consent to the extirpation of a few barbarous tribes in order not to endanger the safety of the American Union.

But the Federal Government, which is not able to protect the Indians, would fain mitigate the hardships of their lot; and, with this intention, proposals have been made to transport them into more remote regions at the public cost.

Between the thirty-third and thirty-seventh degrees of north latitude lies a vast tract of country, which has taken the name of Arkansas, from the principal river that waters its extent. It is bounded on the one side by the confines of Mexico, on the other by the Mississippi. Numberless streams cross it in every direction; the climate is mild, and the soil productive, but it is only inhabited by a few wandering hordes of savages. The Government of the Union wishes to transport the broken remnants of the indigenous population of the South to the portion of this country which is nearest to Mexico, and at a great distance from the American settlements.

We were assured, toward the end of the year 1831, that ten thousand Indians had already gone down to the shores of the Arkansas; and fresh detachments were constantly following them; but Congress has been unable to excite a unanimous determination in those whom it is disposed to protect.

Some, indeed, are willing to quit the seat of oppression, but the most enlightened members of the community refuse to abandon their recent dwellings and their springing crops; they are of opinion that the work of civilization, once interrupted, will never be resumed; they fear that those domestic habits which have been so recently contracted may be irrevocably lost in the midst of a country which is still barbarous, and where nothing is prepared for the subsistence of an agricultural people; they know that their entrance into those wilds will be opposed by inimical hordes, and that they have lost the energy of barbarians, without acquiring the resources of civilization to resist their attacks. Moreover, the Indians readily discover that the settlement which is proposed to them is merely a temporary expedient. Who can assure them that they will at length be allowed to dwell in peace in their new retreat? The United States pledge themselves to the observance of the obligation; but the territory which they at present occupy was formerly secured to them by the most solemn oaths of Anglo-American faith. The American Government does not indeed rob them of their lands, but it allows perpetual incursions to be made on them. In a few years the same white population which now flocks around them will track them to the solitudes of the Arkansas; they will then be exposed to the same evils without the same remedies, and as the limits of the earth will at last fail them, their only refuge is the grave.

The Union treats the Indians with less cupidity and rigour than the policy of the several States, but the two Governments are alike destitute of good faith. The States extend what they are pleased to term the benefits of their laws to the Indians, with a belief that the tribes will recede rather than submit; and the central Government, which promises a permanent refuge to these unhappy beings, is well aware of its inability to secure it to them.

Thus the tyranny of the States obliges the savages to retire; the Union, by its promises and resources, facilitates their retreat; and these measures tend to precisely the same end. "By the will of our Father in Heaven, the Governor of the whole world," said the Cherokees in their petition to Congress,[3] "the red man of America has become small, and the white man great and renowned. When the ancestors of the people of these United States first came to the shores of America they found the red man strong: though he was ignorant and savage, yet he received them kindly, and gave them dry land to rest their weary feet. They met in peace, and shook hands in token of friendship. Whatever the white man wanted and asked of the Indian, the latter willingly gave. At that time the Indian was the lord, and the white man the suppliant. But now the scene has changed. The strength of the red man has become weakness. As his neighbours increased in numbers his power became less and less, and now, of the many and powerful tribes who once covered these United States, only a few are to be seen—a few whom a sweeping pestilence has left. The northern tribes, who

[3]December 18, 1829.

were once so numerous and powerful, are now nearly extinct. Thus it has happened to the red man of America. Shall we, who are remnants, share the same fate?

"The land on which we stand we have received as an inheritance from our fathers, who possessed it from time immemorial as a gift from our common Father in Heaven. They bequeathed it to us as their children, and we have sacredly kept it, as containing the remains of our beloved men. This right of inheritance we have never ceded nor ever forfeited. Permit us to ask what better right the people can have to a country than the right of inheritance and immemorial peaceable possession? We know it is said of late by the State of Georgia and by the Executive of the United States that we have forfeited this right; but we think this is said gratuitously. At what time have we made the forfeit? What great crime have we committed whereby we must forever be divested of our country and rights? Was it when we were hostile to the United States, and took part with the King of Great Britain, during the struggle for independence? If so, why was not this forfeiture declared in the first treaty of peace between the United States and our beloved men? Why was not such an article as the following inserted in the treaty: 'The United States give peace to the Cherokees, but, for the part they took in the late war, declare them to be but tenants at will, to be removed when the convenience of the States, within whose chartered limits they live, shall require it'? That was the proper time to assume such a possession. But it was not thought of, nor would our forefathers have agreed to any treaty whose tendency was to deprive them of their rights and their country."

Such is the language of the Indians: their assertions are true, their forebodings inevitable. From whatever side we consider the destinies of the aborigines of North America, their calamities appear to be irremediable: if they continue barbarous, they are forced to retire; if they attempt to civilize their manners, the contact of a more civilized community subjects them to oppression and destitution. They perish if they continue to wander from waste to waste, and if they attempt to settle they still must perish; the assistance of Europeans is necessary to instruct them, but the approach of Europeans corrupts and repels them into savage life; they refuse to change their habits as long as their solitudes are their own, and it is too late to change them when they are constrained to submit.

The Spaniards pursued the Indians with blood-hounds, like wild beasts; they sacked the New World with no more temper or compassion than a city taken by storm; but destruction must cease, and frenzy be stayed; the remnant of the Indian population which had escaped the massacre mixed with its conquerors, and adopted in the end their religion and their manners. The conduct of the Americans of the United States toward the aborigines is characterized, on the other hand, by a singular attachment to the formalities of law. Provided that the Indians retain their barbarous condition, the Americans take no part in their affairs; they treat them as independent nations, and do not possess themselves of their hunting grounds without a treaty of purchase; and if an Indian nation happens to be so encroached upon as to be unable to subsist upon its territory, they afford it brotherly assistance in transporting it to a grave sufficiently remote from the land of its fathers.

The Spaniards were unable to exterminate the Indian race by those unparalleled atrocities which brand them with indelible shame, nor did they even succeed in wholly depriving it of its rights; but the Americans of the United States have accomplished this twofold purpose with singular felicity; tranquilly, legally, philanthropically, without shedding blood, and without violating a single great principle of morality in the eyes of the world. It is impossible to destroy men with more respect for the laws of humanity. . . .

Individualism in Democratic Countries

The first and most intense passion that is engendered by the equality of conditions is, I need hardly say, the love of that same equality. My readers will therefore not be surprised that I speak of it before all others. Everybody has remarked that in our time, and especially in France, this passion for equality is every day gaining ground in the human heart. It has been said a hundred times that our contemporaries are far more ardently and tenaciously attached to equality than to freedom; but as I do not find that the causes of the fact have been sufficiently analyzed, I shall endeavour to point them out.

It is possible to imagine an extreme point at which freedom and equality would meet and be confounded together. Let us suppose that all the members of the community take a part in the government, and that each one of them has an equal right to take a part in it. As none is different from his fellows, none can exercise a tyrannical power: men will be perfectly free, because they will all be entirely equal; and they will all be perfectly equal, because they will be entirely free. To this ideal state democratic nations tend. Such is the completest form that equality can assume upon earth; but there are a thousand others which, without being equally perfect, are not less cherished by those nations.

The principle of equality may be established in civil society without prevailing in the political world. Equal rights may exist of indulging in the same pleasures, of entering the same professions, of frequenting the same places—in a word, of living in the same manner and seeking wealth by the same means, although all men do not take an equal share in the government. A kind of equality may even be established in the political world, though there should be no political freedom there. A man may be the equal of all his countrymen save one, who is the master of all without distinction, and who selects equally from among them all the agents of his power. Several other combinations might be easily imagined, by which very great equality would be united to institutions more or less free, or even to institutions wholly without freedom. Although men can not become absolutely equal unless they be entirely free, and consequently equality, pushed to its farthest extent, may be confounded with freedom, yet there is good reason for distinguishing the one from the other. The taste which men have for liberty, and that which they feel for equality, are, in fact, two different things; and I am not afraid to add that, among democratic nations, they are two unequal things.

Upon close inspection, it will be seen that there is in every age some peculiar and preponderating fact with which all others are connected; this fact almost always gives birth to some pregnant idea or some ruling passion, that attracts to itself, and bears away in its course, all the feelings and opinions of the time: it is like a great stream, toward which each of the surrounding rivulets seems to flow.

Freedom has appeared in the world at different times and under various forms; it has not been exclusively bound to any social condition, and it is not confined to democracies. Freedom can not, therefore, form the distinguishing characteristic of democratic ages. The peculiar and preponderating fact which marks those ages as its own is the equality of conditions; the ruling passion of men in those periods is the love of this equality. Ask not what singular charm the men of democratic ages find in being equal, or what special reasons they may have for clinging so tenaciously to equality rather than to the other advantages which society holds out to them: equality is the distinguishing characteristic of the age they live in; that, of itself, is enough to explain that they prefer it to all the rest.

But independently of this reason there are several others, that will at all times habitually lead men to prefer equality to freedom. If a people could ever succeed in destroying, or even in diminishing, the equality which prevails in its own body, this could only be accomplished by long and laborious efforts. Its social condition must be modified, its laws abolished, its opinions superseded, its habits changed, its manners corrupted. But political liberty is more easily lost; to neglect to hold it fast is to allow it to escape. Men therefore not only cling to equality because it is dear to them; they also adhere to it because they think it will last forever.

That political freedom may compromise in its excesses the tranquility, the property, the lives of individuals, is obvious to the narrowest and most unthinking minds. But, on the contrary, none but attentive and clear-sighted men perceive the perils with which equality threatens us, and they commonly avoid pointing them out. They know that the calamities they apprehend are remote, and flatter themselves that they will only fall upon future generations, for which the present generation takes but little thought. The evils which freedom sometimes brings with it are immediate; they are apparent to all, and all are more or less affected by them. The evils which extreme equality may produce are slowly disclosed; they creep gradually into the social frame; they are only seen at intervals, and at the moment at which they become most violent habit already causes them to be no longer felt. The advantages which freedom brings are only shown by length of time; and it is always easy to mistake the cause in which they originate. The advantages of equality are instantaneous, and they may be traced constantly from their source. Political liberty bestows exalted pleasures, from time to time, upon a certain number of citizens. Equality every day confers a number of small enjoyments on every man. The charms of equality are felt every instant, and are within the reach of all; the noblest hearts are not insensible to them, and the most vulgar souls exult in them. The passion which equality engenders must therefore be at once strong and general. Men can not enjoy political liberty unpurchased by some sacrifices, and they never obtain it without great exertions. But the pleasures of equality are self-proffered: each of the petty incidents of life seems to occasion them, and in order to taste them nothing is required but to live.

Democratic nations are at all times fond of equality, but there are certain epochs at which the passion they entertain for it swells to the height of fury. This occurs at the moment when the old social system, long menaced, completes its own destruction after a last intestine struggle, and when the barriers of rank are at length thrown down. At such times men pounce upon equality as their booty, and they cling to it as to some precious treasure which they fear to lose. The passion for equality penetrates on every side into men's hearts, expands there, and fills them entirely. Tell them not that by this blind surrender of themselves to an exclusive passion they risk their dearest interests: they are deaf. Show them not freedom escaping from their grasp, while they are looking another way: they are blind—or rather, they can discern but one sole object to be desired in the universe. . . .

I think that democratic communities have a natural taste for freedom: left to themselves, they will seek it, cherish it, and view any privation of it with regret. But for equality, their passion is ardent, insatiable, incessant, invincible: they call for equality in freedom; and if they can not obtain that, they still call for equality in slavery. They will endure poverty, servitude, barbarism—but they will not endure aristocracy. This is true at all times, and especially true in our own. All men and all powers seeking to cope with this irresistible passion will be overthrown and destroyed by it. In our age, freedom can not be established without it, and despotism itself can not reign without its support.

I have shown how it is that in ages of equality every man seeks for his opinions within himself: I am now about to show how it is that, in the same ages, all his feelings are turned toward himself alone. Individualism is a novel expression, to which a novel idea has given birth. Our fathers were only acquainted with egotism. Egotism is a passionate and exaggerated love of self, which leads a man to connect everything with his own person, and to prefer himself to everything in the world. Individualism is a mature and calm feeling, which disposes each member of the community to sever himself from the mass of his fellow-creatures; and to draw apart with his family and his friends; so that, after he has thus formed a little circle of his own, he willingly leaves society at large to itself. Egotism originates in blind instinct: individualism proceeds from erroneous judgment more than from depraved feelings; it originates as much in the deficiencies of the mind as in the perversity of the heart. Egotism blights the germ of all virtue; individualism, at first, only saps the virtues of public life; but, in the long run, it attacks and destroys all others, and is at length absorbed in downright egotism. Egotism is a vice as old as the world, which does not belong to one form of society more than to another: individualism is of democratic origin, and it threatens to spread in the same ratio as the equality of conditions.

Among aristocratic nations, as families remain for centuries in the same condition, often on the same spot, all generations become, as it were, contemporaneous. A man almost always knows his forefathers, and respects them: he thinks he already sees his remote descendants, and he loves them. He willingly imposes duties on himself toward the former and the latter; and he will frequently sacrifice his personal gratifications to those who went before and to those who will come after him. Aristocratic institutions have, moreover, the effect of closely binding every man to several of his fellow-citizens. As the classes of an aristocratic people are strongly marked and permanent, each of them is regarded by its own members as a sort of lesser country, more tangible and more cherished than the country at large. As in aristocratic communities all the citizens occupy fixed positions, one above the other, the result is that each of them always sees a man above himself whose patronage is necessary to him, and below himself another man whose co-operation he may claim. Men living in aristocratic ages are therefore almost always closely attached to something placed out of their own sphere, and they are often disposed to forget themselves. It is true that in those ages the notion of human fellowship is faint, and that men seldom think of sacrificing themselves for mankind; but they often sacrifice themselves for other men. In democratic ages, on the contrary, when the duties of each individual to the race are much more clear, devoted service to any one man becomes more rare; the bond of human affection is extended, but it is relaxed.

Among democratic nations new families are constantly springing up, others are constantly falling away, and all that remain change their condition; the woof of time is every instant broken, and the track of generations effaced. Those who went before are soon forgotten; of those who will come after no one has any idea: the interest of man is confined to those in close propinquity to himself. As each class approximates to other classes, and intermingles with them, its members become indifferent and as strangers to one another. Aristocracy had made a chain of all the members of the community, from the peasant to the king: democracy breaks that chain, and severs every link of it. As social conditions become more equal, the number of persons increases who, although they are neither rich enough nor powerful enough to exercise any great influence over their fellow-creatures, have nevertheless acquired or retained sufficient education and fortune to satisfy their own wants. They owe nothing to any man, they expect nothing from any man; they acquire the habit of always considering themselves as standing alone, and they are apt to imagine that their whole destiny is in their own hands. Thus not only does democracy make every man forget his ancestors, but it hides his descendants, and separates his contemporaries from him; it throws him back forever upon himself alone, and threatens in the end to confine him entirely within the solitude of his own heart.

The period when the construction of democratic society upon the ruins of an aristocracy has just been completed, is especially that at which this separation of men from one another, and the egotism resulting from it, most forcibly strike the observation. Democratic communities not only contain a large number of independent citizens, but they are filled constantly with men who, having entered but yesterday upon their independent condition, are intoxicated with their new power. They entertain a presumptuous confidence in their strength, and as they do not suppose that they can henceforward ever have occasion to claim the assistance of their fellow-creatures, they do not scruple to show that they care for nobody but themselves. . . .

Democracy leads men not to draw near to their fellow-creatures; but democratic revolutions lead them to shun each other, and perpetuate in a state of equality the animosities which the state of inequality engendered. The great advantage of the Americans is that they have arrived at a state of democracy without having to endure a democratic revolution; and that they are born equal, instead of becoming so.

Despotism, which is of a very timorous nature, is never more secure of continuance than when it can keep men asunder; and all its influence is commonly exerted for that purpose. No vice of the human heart is so acceptable to it as egotism: a despot easily forgives his subjects for not loving him, provided they do not love each other. He does not ask them to assist him in governing the state; it is enough that they do not aspire to govern it themselves. He stigmatizes as turbulent and unruly spirits those who would combine their exertions to promote the prosperity of the community, and, perverting the natural meaning of words, he applauds as good citizens those who have no sympathy for any but themselves. Thus the vices that despotism engenders are precisely those that equality fosters. These two things mutually and perniciously complete and assist each other. Equality places men side by side, unconnected by any common tie; despotism raises barriers to keep them asunder; the former predisposes them not to consider their fellow-creatures, the latter makes general indifference a sort of public virtue.

Despotism, then, which is at all times dangerous, is more particularly to be feared in democratic ages. It is easy to see that in those same ages men stand most in need of freedom. When the members of a community are forced to attend to public affairs, they are necessarily drawn from the circle of their own interests, and snatched at times from self-observation. As soon as a man begins to treat of public affairs in public, he begins to perceive that he is not so independent of his fellow-men as he had at first imagined, and that, in order to obtain their support, he must often lend them his co-operation.

When the public is supreme, there is no man who does not feel the value of public good-will, or who does not endeavour to court it by drawing to himself the esteem and affection of those among whom he is to live. Many of the passions which congeal and keep asunder human hearts are then obliged to retire and hide below the surface. Pride must be dissembled; disdain dares not break out; egotism fears its own self. Under a free government, as most public offices are elective, the men whose elevated minds or aspiring hopes are too closely circumscribed in private life, constantly feel that they can not do without the population which surrounds them. Men learn at such times to think of their fellow-men from ambitious motives; and they frequently find it, in a manner, their interest to forget themselves. . . .

The Americans have combated by free institutions the tendency of equality to keep men asunder, and they have subdued it. The legislators of America did not suppose that a general representation of the whole nation would suffice to ward off a disorder at once so natural to the frame of democratic society, and so fatal: they also thought that it would be well to infuse political life into each portion of the territory, in order to multiply to an infinite extent opportunities of acting in concert for all the members of the community, and to make them constantly feel their mutual dependence on each other. The plan was a wise one. The general affairs of a country only engage the attention of leading politicians, who assemble from time to time in the same places; and as they often lose sight of each other afterward, no lasting ties are established between them. But if the object be to have the local affairs of a district conducted by the men who reside there, the same persons are always in contact, and they are, in a manner, forced to be acquainted, and to adapt themselves to one another.

It is difficult to draw a man out of his own circle to interest him in the destiny of the state, because he does not clearly understand what influence the destiny of the state can have upon his own lot. But if it be proposed to make a road across the end of his estate, he will see at a glance that there is a connection between this small public affair and his greatest private affairs; and he will discover, without its being shown to him, the close tie which unites private to general interest. Thus, far more may be done by intrusting to the citizens the administration of minor affairs than by surrendering to them the control of important ones, toward interesting them in the public welfare, and convincing them that they constantly stand in need one of the other in order to provide for it. A brilliant achievement may win for you the favour of a people at one stroke; but to earn the love and respect of the population which surrounds you, a long succession of little services rendered and of obscure good deeds—a constant habit of kindness, and an established reputation for disinterestedness—will be required. Local freedom, then, which leads a great number of citizens to value the affection of their neighbours and of their kindred, perpetually brings men together, and forces them to help one another, in spite of the propensities which sever them.

In the United States the more opulent citizens take great care not to stand aloof from the people; on the contrary, they constantly keep on easy terms with the lower classes: they listen to them, they speak to them every day. They know that the rich in democracies always stand in need of the poor; and that in democratic ages you attach a poor man to you more by your manner than by benefits conferred. The magnitude of such benefits, which sets off the difference of conditions, causes a secret irritation to those who reap advantage from them; but the charm of simplicity of manners is almost irresistible: their affability carries men away, and even their want of polish is not always displeasing. This truth does not take root at once in the minds of the rich. They generally resist it as long as the democratic revolution lasts, and they do not acknowledge it immediately after that revolution is accomplished. They are very ready to do good to the people, but they still choose to keep them at arm's length; they think that is sufficient, but they are mistaken. They might spend fortunes thus without warming the hearts of the population around them—that population does not ask them for the sacrifice of their money, but of their pride.

It would seem as if every imagination in the United States were upon the stretch to invent means of increasing the wealth and satisfying the wants of the public. The best-informed inhabitants of each district constantly use their information to discover new truths which may augment the general prosperity; and if they have made any such discoveries, they eagerly surrender them to the mass of the people.

When the vices and weaknesses, frequently exhibited by those who govern in America, are closely examined, the prosperity of the people occasions—but improperly occasions—surprise. Elected magistrates do not make the American democracy flourish; it flourishes because the magistrates are elective.

It would be unjust to suppose that the patriotism and the zeal that every American displays for the welfare of his fellow-citizens are wholly insincere. Although private interest directs the greater part of human actions in the United States as well as elsewhere, it does not regulate them all. I must say that I have often seen Americans make great and real sacrifices to the public welfare; and I have remarked a hundred instances in which they hardly ever failed to lend faithful support to each other. The free institutions which the inhabitants of the United States possess, and the political rights of which they make so much use, remind every citizen, and in a thousand ways, that he lives in society. They every instant impress upon his mind the notion that it is the duty, as well as the interest of men, to make themselves useful to their fellow-creatures; and as he sees no particular ground of animosity to them, since he is never either their master or their slave, his heart readily leans to the side of kindness. Men attend to the interests of the public, first by necessity, afterward by choice: what was intentional becomes an instinct; and by dint of working for the good of one's fellow-citizens, the habit and the taste for serving them is at length acquired.

Many people in France consider equality of conditions as one evil, and political freedom as a second. When they are obliged to yield to the former, they strive at least to escape from the latter. But I contend that in order to combat the evils which equality may produce, there is only one effectual remedy—namely, political freedom.

The New State of the World

Before I close forever the theme that has detained me so long, I would fain take a parting survey of all the various characteristics of modern society, and appreciate at last the general influence to be exercised by the principle of equality upon the fate of mankind; but I am stopped by the difficulty of the task, and in presence of so great an object my sight is troubled and my reason fails. The society of the modern world which I have sought to delineate, and which I seek to judge, has but just come into existence. Time has not yet shaped it into perfect form: the great revolution by which it has been created is not yet over: and amid the occurrences of our time, it is almost impossible to discern what will pass away with the revolution itself, and what will survive its close. The world which is rising into existence is still half encumbered by the remains of the world which is waning into decay; and amid the vast perplexity of human affairs, none can say how much of ancient institutions and former manners will remain, or how much will completely disappear. Although the revolution that is taking place in the social condition, the laws, the opinions, and the feelings of men, is still very far from being terminated, yet its results already admit of no comparison with anything that the world has ever before witnessed. I go back from age to age up to the remotest antiquity; but I find no parallel to what is occurring before my eyes: as the past has ceased to throw its light upon the future, the mind of man wanders in obscurity.

Nevertheless, in the midst of a prospect so wide, so novel, and so confused, some of the more prominent characteristics may already be discerned and pointed out. The good things and the evils of life are more equally distributed in the world: great wealth tends to disappear, the number of small fortunes to increase; desires and gratifications are multiplied, but extraordinary prosperity and irremediable penury are alike unknown. The sentiment of ambition is universal, but the scope of ambition is seldom vast. Each individual stands apart in solitary weakness; but society at large is active, provident, and powerful: the performances of private persons are insignificant, those of the state immense. There is little energy of character; but manners are mild, and laws humane. If there be few instances of exalted heroism or of virtues of the highest, brightest, and purest temper, men's habits are regular, violence is rare, and cruelty almost unknown. Human existence becomes longer, and property more secure: life is not adorned with brilliant trophies, but it is extremely easy and tranquil. Few pleasures are either very refined or very coarse; and highly polished manners are as uncommon as great brutality of tastes. Neither men of great learning, nor extremely ignorant communities, are to be met with; genius becomes more rare, information more diffused. The human mind is impelled by the small efforts of all mankind combined together, not by the strenuous activity of certain men. There is less perfection, but more abundance, in all the productions of the arts. The ties of race, of rank, and of country are relaxed; the great bond of humanity is strengthened. If I endeavour to find out the most general and the most prominent of all these different characteristics, I shall have occasion to perceive that what is taking place in men's fortunes manifests itself under a thousand other forms. Almost all extremes are softened or blunted: all that was most prominent is superseded by some mean term, at once less lofty and less low, less brilliant and less obscure, than what before existed in the world.

When I survey this countless multitude of beings, shaped in each other's likeness, amid whom nothing rises and nothing falls, the sight of such universal uniformity saddens and chills me, and I am tempted to regret that state of society which has ceased to be. When the world was full of men of great importance and extreme insignificance, of great wealth and extreme poverty, of great learning and extreme ignorance, I turned aside from the latter to fix my observation on the former alone, who gratified my sympathies. But I admit that this gratification arose from my own weakness: it is because I am unable to see at once all that is around me that I am allowed thus to select and separate the objects of my predilection from among so many others. Such is not the case with that Almighty and Eternal Being, whose gaze necessarily includes the whole of created things, and who surveys distinctly, though at once, mankind and man. We may naturally believe that it is not the singular prosperity of the few, but the greater well-being of all, which is most pleasing in the sight of the Creator and Preserver of men. What appears to me to be man's decline is to his eye advancement; what afflicts me is acceptable to him. A state of equality is perhaps less elevated, but it is more just; and its justice constitutes its greatness and its beauty. I would strive, then, to raise myself to this point of the divine contemplation, and thence to view and to judge the concerns of men.

No man, upon the earth, can as yet affirm absolutely and generally that the new state of the world is better than its former one; but it is already easy to perceive that this state is different. Some vices and some virtues were so inherent in the constitution of an aristocratic nation, and are so opposite to the character of a modern people, that they can never be infused into it; some good tendencies and some bad propensities which were unknown to the former are natural to the latter; some ideas suggest themselves spontaneously to the imagination of the one which are utterly repugnant to the mind of the other. They are like two distinct orders of human beings, each of which has its own merits and defects, its own advantages and its own evils. Care must therefore be taken not to judge the state of society, which is now coming into existence, by notions derived from a state of society which no longer exists; for as these states of society are exceedingly different in their structure, they can not be submitted to a just or fair comparison. It would be scarcely more reasonable to require of our own contemporaries the peculiar virtues which originated in the social condition of their forefathers, since that social condition is itself fallen, and has drawn into one promiscuous ruin the good and evil which belonged to it.

But as yet these things are imperfectly understood. I find that a great number of my contemporaries undertake to make a certain selection from among the institutions, the opinions, and the ideas which originated in the aristocratic constitution of society as it was: a portion of these elements they would willingly relinquish, but they would keep the remainder and transplant them into their new world. I apprehend that such men are wasting their time and their strength in virtuous but unprofitable efforts. The object is not to retain the peculiar advantages which the inequality of conditions bestows upon mankind, but to secure the new benefits which equality may supply. We have not to seek to make ourselves like our progenitors, but to strive to work out that species of greatness and happiness which is our own. For myself, who now look back from this extreme limit of my task, and discover from afar, but at once, the various objects which have attracted my more attentive investigation upon my way, I am full of apprehensions and of hopes. I perceive mighty dangers which it is possible to ward off—mighty evils which may be avoided or alleviated; and I cling with a firmer hold to the belief, that for democratic nations to be virtuous and prosperous they require but to will it. I am aware that many of my contemporaries maintain that nations are never their own masters here below, and that they necessarily obey some insurmountable and unintelligent power, arising from anterior events, from their race, or from the soil and climate of their country. Such principles are false and cowardly; such principles can never produce aught but feeble men and pusillanimous nations. Providence has not created mankind entirely independent or entirely free. It is true that around every man a fatal circle is traced, beyond which he can not pass;

but within the wide verge of that circle he is powerful and free: as it is with man, so with communities. The nations of our time can not prevent the conditions of men from becoming equal; but it depends upon themselves whether the principle of equality is to lead them to servitude or freedom, to knowledge or barbarism, to prosperity or to wretchedness.

Miss Martineau on Slavery

At nineteen Harriet Martineau began to write anonymously for the Monthly Repository; *eight years later, when she had been left penniless, she undertook to earn her living by writing. In 1831 some stories called "Illustrations of Political Economy" were successful in spite of their title. When she visited America in 1834 her support of the Abolitionists, then a small minority, was resented and her two books on America intensified her unpopularity.*

In London her friends included Wordsworth, Sidney Smith, Henry Hallam, and Carlyle. Twice she declined an English civil pension to avoid any compromise of her political independence. She contracted a heart ailment in 1855 and began to write her autobiography, but she lived for twenty-one years longer.

From RETROSPECT OF WESTERN TRAVEL

[September 19, 1834]

First Impressions

The moment of first landing in a foreign city is commonly spoken of as a perfect realization of forlornness. My entrance upon American life was anything but this. The spirits of my companions and myself were in a holyday dance while we were receiving our first impressions; and New York always afterward bore an air of gayety to me from the association of the early pleasures of foreign travel.

Apartments had been secured for us at a boarding-house in Broadway, and a hackney-coach was in waiting at the wharf. The moonlight was flickering through the trees of the Battery, the insects were buzzing all about us, the catydids were grinding, and all the sounds, except human voices, were quite unlike all we had heard for six weeks. . . . As we rattled over the stones, I was surprised to find that the street we were in was Broadway; the lower and narrower end, however; but nothing that I saw, after all I had heard, and the panorama of New York that I had visited in London, disappointed me so much as Broadway. Its length is remarkable, but neither its width nor the style of its houses. The trees with which it is lined gave it, this first evening, a foreign air. . . .

In our rooms we found beds with four posts, looking as if meant to hang gowns and bonnets upon; for there was no tester. The washstand was without tumbler, glass, soap, or brush-tray. The candlestick had no snuffers. There was, however, the luxury, sufficient for the occasion, that every article of furniture stood still in its place, and that the apartment itself did not rock up and down. The first few days after a voyage go far towards making one believe that some things have a quality of stability, however one may be metaphysically convinced that the sea affords a far truer hint of the incessant flux and change which are the law of the universe. If I had rejoiced in the emblem at sea, I now enjoyed the deception on land.

At five in the morning I threw up my sash to see what I could see. I cannot conceive what travellers mean by saying that there is little that is foreign in the aspect of New York. I beheld nothing at this moment that I could have seen at home, except the sky and the grass of the courtyard. The houses were all neatly and brightly painted, had green outside blinds to every window, and an apparatus for drying linen on the roof. A young lady in black silk, with her hair neatly dressed, was mopping the steps of one house, and a similar young lady was dusting the parlour of another. A large locust-tree grew in the middle of the courtyard of the house I was in, and under it was a truly American wood-pile. Two negroes were at the pump, and a third was carrying muskmelons.

When the breakfast-bell rang the long and cross tables in the eating-room were filled in five minutes. The cross table, at which our hostess presided, was occupied by General Mason's family, a party of Spaniards, and ourselves. The long one was filled up with families returning southward from the springs; married persons without children, who preferred boarding to housekeeping; and single gentlemen, chiefly merchants. I found this mode of living rather formidable the first day; and not all the good manners that I saw at public tables ever reconciled me to it. . . .

In the streets I was in danger of being run down by the fire-engines, so busy were my eyes with the novelties about me. These fire-engines run along the side-pavement, stopping for nobody; and I scarcely ever walked out in New York without seeing one or more out on business, or for an airing. The novelties which amused me were the spruce appearance of all the people; the pervading neatness and brightness, and the business-like air of the children. The carmen were all well dressed, and even two poor boys who were selling matches had clean shirt-collars and whole coats, though they were barefooted. The stocks of goods seemed large and handsome, and we were less struck with the indifference of manner commonly ascribed to American storekeepers than frequently afterward. The most unpleasant circumstance was the appearance and manner of the ladies whom we saw in the streets and stores. It was now the end of a very hot summer, and every lady we met looked as if she were emerging from the yellow fever; and the languid and unsteady step betokened the reverse of health. . . .

I feel some doubt about giving any account of the public men of the United States; I do not mean scruples of conscience; for when a man comes forward in political or other kind of public life, he makes a present of himself to society at large, and his person, mind, and manners become a legitimate subject of observation and remark. My doubts arise from the want of interest in the English about the great men of America; a want of interest which arises from no fault in either party, I believe, but from the baseness of the newspapers, whose revilings of all persons in turn who fill a public station are so disgusting as to discourage curiosity, and set all friendly interest at defiance. The names of the English political leaders of the day are almost as familiar in the mouths of Americans as of natives, while people in London are asking who Mr. Clay is, and what part of the Union Mr. Calhoun comes from. The deeds of Mr. Clay and the aspirations of Mr. Calhoun would be at least as interesting in London as the proceedings of French and German statesmen, if they could be fairly placed under observation; but every man of feeling and taste recoils from wading through such a slough of rancour, folly, and falsehood as the American newspapers present as the only medium through which the object is to be attained. . . .

I was assured at the outset that the late abolition riots in New York were the work of the Irish emigrants, who feared the increase of a free black population as likely to interfere with their monopoly of certain kinds of labour. This I afterward found to be untrue. Some Irish may have joined in "the row," but the mischief originated with natives. It is remarkable that I heard no more of abolition for many weeks; I think not till I was about leaving Philadelphia. . . .

I was shown . . . the spot where Hamilton received his death-wound from Colonel Burr. It was once made a qualification for office that the candidate should never have fought a duel. Duelling is an institution not to be reached by such a provision as this. No man under provocation to fight would refrain from fear of disqualifying himself for office hereafter; and the operation of the restriction was accordingly found to be this; that duels were as frequent as ever, and that desirable candidates were excluded. The provision was got rid of on the plea that promissory oaths are bad in principle. The cure of duelling, as of every other encroachment of passion and selfishness on such higher principles as, being passive, cannot be imbodied in acts, must be the natural result of the improved moral condition of the individual or of society. No one believes that the legal penalties of duelling have had much effect in stopping the practice; and it is an injury to society to choose out of the ample range of penalties disqualification for social duty as one. . . .

One of the first impressions of a foreigner in New York is of the extreme insolence and vulgarity of certain young Englishmen, who thus make themselves very conspicuous. Well-mannered Englishmen are scarcely distinguishable from the natives, and thus escape observation; while every commercial traveller who sneers at republicanism all day long, and every impertinent boy, leaving home for the first time, with no understanding or sympathy for anything but what he has been accustomed to see at home, obtrudes himself upon the notice, and challenges the congeniality of such countrymen and countrywomen as he can contrive to put himself in the way of. . . .

Weddings

I was present at three weddings in the United States, and at an offer of marriage.

The offer of marriage ought hardly to be so called, however. It was a petition from a slave to be allowed to wed (as slaves wed) the nursemaid of a lady in whose house I was staying. The young man could either write a little, or had employed some one who could to prepare his epistle for him. It ran from corner to corner of the paper, which was daubed with diluted wafer, like certain love-letters nearer home than Georgia. Here are the contents:

"Miss Cunningham it is My wishes to companion in your Present and I hope you will Be peeze at it and I hope that you will not think Hard of Me I have Ben to the Doctor and he was very well satafide with Me and I hope you is and Miss Mahuw all so

"that's all I has to say now wiheshen you will grant Me that honour I will Be very glad.

"S. B. Smith."

The nursemaid was granted; and as it was a love-match, and as the girl's mistress is one of the tender, the sore-hearted about having slaves, I hope the poor creatures are as happy as love in debasement can make them.

The first wedding I saw in Boston was very like the common run of weddings in England. It happened to be convenient that the parties should be married in church; and in the Unitarian church in which they usually worshipped we accordingly awaited them. I had no acquaintance with the family, but went on the invitation of the pastor who married them. The family connexion was large, and the church, therefore, about half full. The form of celebration is at the pleasure of the pastor; but, by consent, the administration by pastors of the same sect is very nearly alike. The promises of the married parties are made reciprocal, I observed. The service in this instance struck me as being very beautiful from its simplicity, tenderness, and brevity. There was one variation from the usual method, in the offering of one of the prayers by a second pastor, who, being the uncle of the bridegroom, was invited to take a share in the service.

The young people were to set out for Europe in the afternoon, the bride being out of health, the dreary drawback upon almost every extensive plan of action and fair promise of happiness in America. The lady has, I rejoice to hear, been quite restored by travel; but her sickness threw a gloom over the celebration, even in the minds of strangers. She and her husband walked up the middle aisle to the desk where the pastors sat. They were attended by only one bridesmaid and one groomsman, and were all in plain travelling dresses. They said steadily and quietly what they had to say, and walked down the aisle again as they came. Nothing could be simpler and better, for this was not a marriage where festivity could have place. If there is any natural scope for joy, let weddings by all means be joyous; but here there was sickness, with the prospect of a long family separation, and there was most truth in quietness.

The other wedding I saw in Boston was as gay a one as is often seen. The parties were opulent, and in the first rank in society. They were married in the drawing-room of the bride's house, at half past eight in the evening, by Dr. Channing. The moment the ceremony was over, crowds of company began to arrive; and the bride, young and delicate, and her maidens, were niched in a corner of one of the drawing-rooms to courtesy to all comers. They were so formally placed, so richly and (as it then seemed) formally dressed, for the present revived antique style of dress was then quite new, that, in the interval of their courtesies, they looked like an old picture brought from Windsor Castle. The bride's mother presided in the other drawing-room, and the bridegroom flitted about, universally attentive, and on the watch to introduce all visitors to his lady. The transition from the solemnity of Dr. Channing's service to the noisy gayeties of a rout was not at all to my taste. I imagined that it was not to Dr. Channing's either, for his talk with me was on matters very little resembling anything that we had before our eyes; and he soon went away. The noise became such as to silence all who were not inured to the gabble of an American party, the noisiest kind of assemblage, I imagine (not excepting a Jew's synagogue), on the face of the globe. I doubt whether any pagans in their worship can raise any hubbub to equal it. I constantly found in a large party, after trying in vain every kind of scream that I was capable of, that I must give up, and satisfy myself with nodding and shaking my head. If I was rightly understood, well and good; if not, I must let it pass. As the noise thickened and the heat grew more oppressive, I glanced towards the poor bride in her corner, still standing, still courtesying; her pale face growing paler; her nonchalant manner (perhaps the best she could assume) more indifferent. I was afraid that if all this went on much longer, she would faint or die upon the spot. It did not last much longer. By eleven some of the company began to go away, and by a quarter before twelve all were gone but the comparatively small party (including ourselves) who were invited to stay to supper.

The chandelier and mantelpieces, I then saw, were dressed with flowers. There was a splendid supper; and, before we departed, we were carried up to a well-lighted apartment, where bride cake and the wedding presents were set out in bright array.

Five days afterward we went, in common with all her acquaintance, to pay our respects to the bride. The courtyard of her mother's house was thronged with carriages, though no one seemed to stay five minutes. The bridegroom received us at the head of the stairs, and led us to his lady, who courtesied as before. Cake, wine, and liqueurs were handed round, the visiters all standing. A few words on common subjects were exchanged, and we were gone to make way for others.

A Quaker marriage which I saw at Philadelphia was scarcely less showy in its way. It took place at the Cherry-street church, belonging to the Hicksites. The reformed Quaker Church, consisting of the followers of Elias Hicks, bears about the same relation to the old Quakerism as the Church of England to that of Rome; and, it seems to me, the mutual dislike is as intense. I question whether religious enmity ever attained a greater extreme than among the orthodox Friends of Philadelphia. The Hicksites are more moderate, but are sometimes naturally worried out of their patience by the meddling, the denunciations, and the calumnies of the old Quaker societies. The new church is thinking of reforming and relaxing a good deal farther, and in the celebration of marriage among other things. It is under consideration (or was when I was there) whether the process of betrothment should not be simplified, and marriage in the father's house permitted to such as prefer it to the church. The wedding at which I was present was, however, performed with all the formalities. . . .

The spacious church was crowded; and for three or four hours the poor bride had to sit facing the assemblage, aware, doubtless, that during the time of silence the occupation of the strangers present, if not of the friends themselves, would be watching her and her party. She was pretty, and most beautifully dressed. I have seldom pitied anybody more than I did her, while she sat palpitating for three hours under the gaze of some hundreds of people. . . .

Of the five speakers, one was an old gentleman whose discourse was an entire perplexity to me. For nearly an hour he discoursed on Jacob's ladder; but in a style so rambling, and in a chant so singularly unmusical as to set attention and remembrance at defiance. . . . What a contrast was the brief discourse of my Quaker friend which followed! Her noble countenance was radiant as the morning; her soft voice, though low, so firm that she was heard to the farthest corner, and her little sermon as philosophical as it was devout. "Send forth thy light and thy truth," was her text. She spoke gratefully of intellectual light as a guide to spiritual truth, and anticipated and prayed for an ultimate universal diffusion of both. The certificate of the marriage was read by Dr. Parrish, an elderly physician of Philadelphia, the very realization of all my imaginings of the personal appearance of William Penn; with all the dignity and bonhommie that one fancies Penn invested with in his dealings with the Indians. Dr. Parrish speaks with affection of the Indians, from the experience some ancestors of his had of the hospitality of these poor people when they were in a condition to show hospitality. His grandfather's family were shipwrecked, and the Indians took the poor lady and her children home to an inhabited cave, and fed them for many weeks or months. The tree stump round which they used to sit at meals is still standing; and Dr. Parrish says that, let it stand as long as it will, the love of his family to the Indians shall outlast it.

The matrimonial promise was distinctly and well spoken by both the parties. At the request of the bride and bridegroom, Dr. Parrish asked me to put the first signature, after their own, to the certificate of the marriage; and we adjourned for the purpose to an apartment connected with the church. Most ample sheets of parchment were provided for the signatures; and there was a prodigious array of names before we left, when a crowd was still waiting to testify. This multitudinous witnessing is the pleasantest part of being married by acclamation. If weddings are not to be private, there seems no question of the superiority of this Quaker method to that of the Boston marriage I beheld, where there was all the publicity, without the co-operation and sanction. . . .

First Sight of Slavery

From the day of my entering the States till that of my leaving Philadelphia I had seen society basking in one bright sunshine of good-will. The sweet temper and kindly manners of the Americans are so striking to foreigners, that it is some time before the dazzled stranger perceives that, genuine as is all this good, evils as black as night exist along with it. I had been received with such hearty hospitality everywhere, and had lived among friends so conscientious in their regard for human rights, that, though I had heard of abolition riots, and had observed somewhat of the degradation of the blacks, my mind had not yet been really troubled about the enmity of the races. The time of awakening must come. It began just before I left Philadelphia.

I was calling on a lady whom I had heard speak with strong horror of the abolitionists (with whom I had then no acquaintance), and she turned round upon me with the question whether I would not prevent, if I could, the marriage of a white person with a person of colour. I saw at once the beginning of endless troubles in this inquiry, and was very sorry it had been made; but my determination had been adopted long before, never to evade the great question of colour; never to provoke it; but always to meet it plainly in whatever form it should be presented. I replied that I would never, under any circumstances, try to separate persons who really loved, believing such to be truly those whom God had joined; but I observed that the case she put was one not likely to happen, as I believed the blacks were no more disposed to marry the whites than the whites to marry the blacks. "You are an amalgamationist!" cried she. I told her that the party term was new to me; but that she must give what name she pleased to the principle I had declared in answer to her question. This lady is an eminent religionist, and denunciations spread rapidly from her. The day before I left Philadelphia my old shipmate, the Prussian physician, arrived there, and lost no time in calling to tell me, with much agitation, that I must not go a step farther south; that he had heard on all hands, within two hours of his arrival, that I was an amalgamationist, and that my having published a story against slavery would be fatal to me in the slave states. I did not give much credit to the latter part of this news, and saw plainly that all I had to do was to go straight on. I really desired to see the working of the slave system, and was glad that my having published against its principles divested me altogether of the character of a spy, and gave me an unquestioned liberty to publish the results of what I might observe. In order to see things as they were, it was necessary that people's minds should not be prepossessed by my friends as to my opinions and conduct; and I therefore forbade my Philadelphia friends to publish in the newspapers, as they wished, an antidote to the charges already current against me.

The next day I first set foot in a slave state, arriving in the evening at Baltimore. I dreaded inexpressibly the first sight of a slave, and could not help speculating on the lot of every person of colour I saw from the windows the first few days. The servants in the house where I was were free blacks.

Before a week was over I perceived that all that is said in England of the hatred of the whites to the blacks in America is short of the truth. The slanders that I heard of the free blacks were too gross to injure my estimation of any but those who spoke them. In Baltimore the bodies of coloured people exclusively are taken for dissection, "because the whites do not like it, and the coloured people cannot resist." It is wonderful that the bodily structure can be (with the exception of the colouring of the skin) thus assumed to be the pattern of that of the whites; that the exquisite nervous system, the instrument of moral as well as physical pleasures and pains, can be nicely investigated, on the ground of its being analogous with that of the whites; that not only the mechanism, but the sensibilities of the degraded race should be argued from to those of the exalted order, and that men come from such a study with contempt for these brethren in their countenances, hatred in their hearts, and insult on their tongues. These students are the men who cannot say that the coloured people have not nerves that quiver under moral injury, nor a brain that is on fire with insult, nor pulses that throb under oppression. These are the men who should stay the hand of the rash and ignorant possessors of power, who crush the being of creatures, like themselves, "fearfully and wonderfully made." But to speak the right word, to hold out the helping hand, these searchers into man have not light nor strength.

It was in Baltimore that I heard Miss Edgeworth denounced as a woman of no intelligence or delicacy, whose works could never be cared for again, because, in Belinda, poor Juba was married, at length, to an English farmer's daughter! The incident is so subordinate that I had entirely forgotten it; but a clergyman's lady threw the volume to the opposite corner of the floor when she came to the page. As I have said elsewhere, Miss Edgeworth is worshipped throughout the United States; but it is in spite of this terrible passage, this clause of a sentence in Belinda, which nobody in America can tolerate, while no one elsewhere ever, I should think, dreamed of finding fault with it.

A lady from New England, staying in Baltimore, was one day talking over slavery with me, her detestation of it being great, when I told her I dreaded seeing a slave. "You have seen one," said she. "You were waited on by a slave yesterday evening." She told me of a gentleman who let out and lent out his slaves to wait at gentlemen's houses, and that the tall handsome mulatto who handed the tea at a party the evening before was one of these. I was glad it was over for once; but I never lost the painful feeling caused to a stranger by intercourse with slaves. No familiarity with them, no mirth and contentment on their part, ever soothed the miserable restlessness caused by the presence of a deeply-injured fellow-being. No wonder or ridicule on the spot avails anything to the stranger. He suffers, and must suffer from this, deeply and long, as surely as he is human and hates oppression.

The next slave that I saw, knowing that it was a slave, was at Washington, where a little negro child took hold of my gown in the passage of our boarding-house, and entered our drawing-room with me. She shut the door softly, as asking leave to stay. I took up a newspaper. She sat at my feet, and began amusing herself with my shoestrings. Finding herself not discouraged, she presently begged play by peeping at me above and on each side the newspaper. She was a brighteyed, merry-hearted child; confiding, like other children, and dreading no evil, but doomed, hopelessly doomed, to ignorance, privation, and moral degradation. When I looked at her, and thought of the fearful disobedience to the first of moral laws, the cowardly treachery, the cruel abuse of power involved in thus dooming to blight a being so helpless, so confiding, and so full of promise, a horror came over me which sickened my very soul. To see slaves is not to be reconciled to slavery.

At Baltimore and Washington again I was warned, in various stealthy ways, of perils awaiting me in the South. I had no means of ascertaining the justness of these warnings but by going on, and turning back for such vague reasons was not to be thought of. So I determined to say no word to my companions (who were in no danger), but to see the truth for myself. The threats proved idle, as I suspected they would. Throughout the South I met with very candid and kind treatment. I mention these warnings partly because they are a fact connected with the state of the country, and partly because it will afterward appear that the stranger's real danger lies in the North and West, over which the South had, in my case, greatly the advantage in liberality.

Life at Washington

Washington is no place for persons of domestic tastes. Persons who love dissipation, persons who love to watch the game of politics, and those who make a study of strong minds under strong excitements, like a season at Washington; but it is dreary to those whose pursuits and affections are domestic. I spent five weeks there, and was heartily glad when they were over. I felt the satisfaction all the time of doing something that was highly useful; of getting knowledge that was necessary to me, and could not be otherwise obtained; but the quiet delights of my Philadelphia home (though there half our time was spent in visiting) had spoiled me for such a life as every one leads at the metropolis. I have always looked back upon the five weeks at Washington as one of the most profitable, but by far the least agreeable, of my residences in the United States.

Yet we were remarkably fortunate in our domestic arrangements there. We joined a party of highly esteemed and kind friends: a member of the House of Representatives from Massachusetts, his wife and sister-in-law, and a senator from Maine. We (the above party) had a drawing-room to ourselves and a separate table at Mrs. Peyton's boarding-house; so that we formed a quiet family group enough, if only we had had any quiet in which to enjoy the privilege.

We arrived at Washington on the 13th of January, 1835, the year of the short session of Congress which closes on the 4th of March, so that we continued to see the proceedings of Congress at its busiest and most interesting time. . . .

In Philadelphia I had found perpetual difficulty in remembering that I was in a foreign country. The pronunciation of a few words by our host and hostess, the dinner-table, and the inquiries of visiters were almost all that occurred to remind me that I was not in a brother's house. At Washington it was very different. The city itself is unlike any other that ever was seen, straggling out hither and thither, with a small house or two a quarter of a mile from any other; so that, in making calls "in the city," we had to cross ditches and stiles, and walk alternately on grass and pavements, and strike across a field to reach a street. . . . Then we were waited upon by a slave appointed for the exclusive service of our party during our stay. Then there were canvass-back ducks, and all manner of other ducks on the table, in greater profusion than any single article of food, except turkeys, that I ever saw. Then there was the society, singularly compounded from the largest variety of elements: foreign ambassadors, the American government, members of Congress, from Clay and Webster down to Davy Crockett, Benton from Missouri, and Cuthbert, with the freshest Irish brogue, from Georgia; flippant young belles, "pious" wives dutifully attending their husbands, and groaning over the frivolities of the place; grave judges, saucy travellers, pert newspaper reporters, melancholy Indian chiefs, and timid New England ladies, trembling on the verge of the vortex; all this was wholly unlike anything that is to be seen in any other city in the world; for all these are mixed up together in daily intercourse, like the higher circle of a little village, and there is nothing else. You have this or nothing; you pass your days among these people, or you spend them alone. . . .

Our pleasantest evenings were some spent at home in a society of the highest order. Ladies, literary, fashionable, or domestic, would spend an hour with us on their way from a dinner or to a ball. Members of Congress would repose themselves by our fireside. Mr. Clay, sitting upright on the sofa, with his snuffbox ever in his hand, would discourse for many an hour in his even, soft, deliberate tone, on any one of the great subjects of American policy which we might happen to start, always amazing us with the moderation of estimate and speech which so impetuous a nature has been able to attain. Mr. Webster, leaning back at his ease, telling stories, cracking jokes, shaking the sofa with burst after burst of laughter, or smoothly discoursing to the perfect felicity of the logical part of one's constitution, would illuminate an evening now and then. Mr. Calhoun, the cast-iron man, who looks as if he had never been born and never could be extinguished, would come in sometimes to keep our understandings upon a painful stretch for a short while, and leave us to take to pieces his close, rapid, theoretical, illustrated talk, and see what we could make of it. We found it usually more worth retaining as a curiosity than as either very just or useful. His speech abounds in figures, truly illustrative, if that which they illustrate were but true also. But his theories of government (almost the only subject on which his thoughts are employed), the squarest and compactest that ever were made, are composed out of limited elements, and are not, therefore, likely to stand service very well. It is at first extremely interesting to hear Mr. Calhoun talk; and there is a never-failing evidence of power in all he says and does which commands intellectual reverence; but the admiration is too soon turned into regret, into absolute melancholy. It is impossible to resist the conviction that all this force can be at best but useless, and is but too likely to be very mischievous. His mind has long lost all power of communicating with any other. I know of no man who lives in such utter intellectual solitude. He meets men, and harangues them by the fireside as in the Senate; he is wrought like a piece of machinery, set a going vehemently by a weight, and stops while you answer; he either passes by what you say, or twists it into a suitability with what is in his head, and begins to lecture again. Of course, a mind like this can have little influence in the Senate, except by virtue, perpetually wearing out, of what it did in its less eccentric days; but its influence at home is to be dreaded. There is no hope that an intellect so cast in narrow theories will accommodate itself to varying circumstances; and there is every danger that it will break up all that it can, in order to remould the materials in its own way. Mr. Calhoun is as full as ever of his nullification doctrines; and those who know the force that is in him, and his utter incapacity of modific: tion by other minds (after having gone through as remarkable a revolution of political opinion as perhaps any man ever experienced), will no more expect repose and self-retention from him than from a volcano in full force. Relaxation is no longer in the power of his will. I never saw any one who so completely gave me the idea of possession. Half an hour's conversation with him is enough to make a necessarian of anybody. Accordingly, he is more complained of than blamed by his enemies. His moments of softness in his family, and when recurring to old college days, are hailed by all as a relief to the vehement working of the intellectual machine; a relief equally to himself and others. Those moments are as touching to the observer as tears on the face of a soldier. . . .

Our active-minded, genial friend, Judge Story, found time to visit us frequently, though he is one of the busiest men in the world; writing half a dozen great law-books every year; having his full share of the business of the Supreme Court upon his hands; his professorship to attend to; the District Courts at home in Massachusetts, and a correspondence which spreads half over the world. . . .

With Judge Story sometimes came the man to whom he looked up with feelings little short of adoration—the aged Chief-justice Marshall. There was almost too much mutual respect in our first meeting; we knew something of his individual merits and services; and he maintained through life, and carried to his grave, a reverence for woman as rare in its kind as in its degree. It had all the theoretical fervour and magnificence of Uncle Toby's, with the advantage of being grounded upon an extensive knowledge of the sex. He was the father and the grandfather of women; and out of this experience he brought, not only the love and pity which their offices and position command, and the awe of purity which they excite in the minds of the pure, but a steady conviction of their intellectual equality with men; and, with this, a deep sense of their social injuries. Throughout life he so invariably sustained their cause, that no indulgent libertine dared to flatter and humour; no skeptic, secure in the possession of power, dared to scoff at the claims of woman in the presence of Marshall, who, made clearsighted by his purity, knew the sex far better than either.

How delighted we were to see Judge Story bring in the tall, majestic, brighteyed old man! old by chronology, by the lines on his composed face, and by his services to the republic; but so dignified, so fresh, so present to the time, that no feeling of compassionate consideration for age dared to mix with the contemplation of him. The first evening he asked me much about English politics, and especially whether the people were not fast ripening for the abolition of our religious establishment; an institution which, after a long study of it, he considered so monstrous in principle, and so injurious to true religion in practice, that he could not imagine that it could be upheld for anything but political purposes. There was no prejudice here on account of American modes being different; for he observed that the clergy were there, as elsewhere, far from being in the van of society, and lamented the existence of much fanaticism in the United States; but he saw the evils of an establishment the more clearly, not the less, from being aware of the faults in the administration of religion at home. The most animated moment of our conversation was when I told him I was going to visit Mr. Madison on leaving Washington. He instantly sat upright in his chair, and with beaming eyes began to praise Mr. Madison. Madison received the mention of Marshall's name in just the same manner; yet these men were strongly opposed in politics, and their magnanimous appreciation of each other underwent no slight or brief trial. . . .

We highly enjoyed our dinings at the British legation, where we felt ourselves at home among our countrymen. Once, indeed, we were invited to help to do the honours as English ladies to the seven Judges of the Supreme Court, and seven great lawyers besides, when we had the merriest day that could well be. Mr. Webster fell chiefly to my share, and there is no merrier man than he; and Judge Story would enliven a dinner-table at Pekin. One laughable peculiarity at the British legation was the confusion of tongues among the servants, who ask you to take fish, flesh, and fowl in Spanish, Italian, German, Dutch, Irish, or French. The foreign ambassadors are terribly plagued about servants. No American will wear livery, and there is no reason why any American should. But the British ambassador must have livery servants. He makes what compromise he can, allowing his people to appear without livery out of doors except on state occasions; but yet he is obliged to pick up his domestics from among foreigners who are in want of a subsistence for a short time, and are sure to go away as soon as they can find any employment in which the wearing a livery is not requisite. . . .

At the president's[1] I met a very large party, among whom there was more stiffness than I saw in any other society in America. It was not the fault of the president or his family, but of the way in which the company was unavoidably brought together. With the exception of my party, the name of everybody present began with J, K, or L; that is to say, it consisted of members of Congress, who are invited alphabetically, to ensure none being left out. . . . At dinner the president was quite disposed for conversation. Indeed, he did nothing but talk. His health is poor, and his diet of the sparest. We both talked freely of the governments of England and France; I, novice in American politics as I was, entirely forgetting that the great French question was pending, and that the president and the King of the French were then bandying very hard words. I was most struck and surprised with the president's complaints of the American Senate, in which there was at that time a small majority against the administration. He told me that I must not judge of the body by what I saw it then, and that after the 4th of March I should behold a Senate more worthy of the country. After the 4th of March there was, if I remember rightly, a majority of two in favour of the government. The ground of his complaint was, that the

[1]President Andrew Jackson.

senators had sacrificed their dignity by disregarding the wishes of their constituents. The other side of the question is, that the dignity of the Senate is best consulted by its members following their own convictions, declining instructions for the term for which they are elected. It is a serious difficulty, originating in the very construction of the body, and not to be settled by dispute.

The president offered me bonbons for a child belonging to our party at home, and told me how many children (of his nephew's and his adopted son's) he had about him, with a mildness and kindliness which contrasted well with his tone upon some public occasions. He did the honours of his house with gentleness and politeness to myself, and, as far as I saw, to every one else. About an hour after dinner he rose, and we led the way into the drawing-room, where the whole company, gentlemen as well as ladies, followed to take coffee; after which every one departed, some homeward, some to make evening calls, and others, among whom were ourselves, to a splendid ball at the other extremity of the city.

General Jackson is extremely tall and thin, with a slight stoop, betokening more weakness than naturally belongs to his years. He has a profusion of stiff gray hair, which gives to his appearance whatever there is of formidable in it. His countenance bears commonly an expression of melancholy gravity; though, when roused, the fire of passion flashes from his eyes, and his whole person looks then formidable enough. His mode of speech is slow and quiet, and his phraseology sufficiently betokens that his time has not been passed among books. When I was at Washington albums were the fashion and the plague of the day. I scarcely ever came home but I found an album on my table or requests for autographs; but some ladies went much further than petitioning a foreigner who might be supposed to have leisure. I have actually seen them stand at the door of the Senate Chamber, and send the doorkeeper with an album, and a request to write in it, to Mr. Webster and other eminent members. I have seen them do worse; stand at the door of the Supreme Court, and send in their albums to Chief-justice Marshall while he was on the bench hearing pleadings. The poor president was terribly persecuted; and to him it was a real nuisance, as he had no poetical resource but Watts's hymns. I have seen verses and stanzas of a most ominous purport from Watts, in the president's very conspicuous handwriting, standing in the midst of the crowquill compliments and translucent charades which are the staple of albums. Nothing was done to repress this atrocious impertinence of the ladies. I always declined writing more than name and date; but senators, judges, and statesmen submitted to write gallant nonsense at the request of any woman who would stoop to desire it. . . .

There is nothing remarkable in the appearance of Mr. Van Buren, whom I . . . saw frequently at Washington. He is small in person, with light hair and blue eyes. I was often asked whether I did not think his manners gentlemanly. There is much friendliness in his manners, for he is a kind-hearted man; he is also rich in information, and lets it come out on subjects in which he cannot contrive to see any danger in speaking. But his manners want the frankness and confidence which are essential to good breeding. He questions closely, without giving anything in return. Moreover, he flatters to a degree which so cautious a man should long ago have found out to be disagreeable; and his flattery is not merely praise of the person he is speaking to, but a worse kind still; a skepticism and ridicule of objects and persons supposed to be distasteful to the one he is conversing with. I fully believe that he is an amiable and indulgent domestic man, and a reasonable political master, a good scholar, and a shrewd man of business; but he has the skepticism which marks the lower order of politicians. His public career exhibits no one exercise of that faith in men and preference of principle to petty expediency by which a statesman shows himself to be great.

The consequence is, that, with all his opportunities, no great deed has ever been put to his account, and his shrewdness has been at fault in some of the most trying crises of his career. The man who so little trusts others, and so intensely regards self as to make it the study of his life not to commit himself, is liable to a more than ordinary danger of judging wrong when compelled, by the pressure of circumstances, to act a decided part. It has already been so with Mr. Van Buren more than once; and now[2] that he is placed in a position where he must sometimes visibly lead, and cannot always appear to follow, it will be seen whether a due reverence of men and a forgetfulness of self would not have furnished him with more practical wisdom than all his "sounding on his dim and perilous way." Mr. Calhoun is, I believe, Mr. Van Buren's evil genius. Mr. Calhoun was understood to be in expectation of succeeding to the presidential chair when Mr. Van Buren was appointed minister to Great Britain. This appointment of President Jackson's did not receive the necessary sanction from the Senate, and the new minister was recalled on the first possible day, Mr. Calhoun being very active in bringing him back. Mr. Calhoun was not aware that he was recalling one who was to prove a successful rival. Mr. Calhoun has not been president; Mr. Van Buren is so; but the successful rival has a mortal dread of the great nullifier; a dread so obvious, and causing such a prostration of all principle and all dignity, as to oblige observers to conclude that there is more in the matter than they see; that it will come out some day why the disappointed aspirant is still to be propitiated, when he seems to be deprived of power to do mischief. . . .

Perhaps Mr. Van Buren may entertain the opinion which many hold, that that business is not over yet, and that the slavery question is made a pretext by the nullifiers of the South for a line of action to which they are impelled by the disappointed personal ambition of one or two, and the wounded pride of the many, who cannot endure the contrast between the increase of the free states of the North and the deterioration of the slave states of the South. However this may be, to propitiate Mr. Calhoun seems to have been Mr. Van Buren's great object for a long time past; an object probably

[2]Martin Van Buren was President of the United States from 1837 to 1841.

hopeless in itself, and in the pursuit of which he is likely to lose the confidence of the North far faster than he could, at best, disarm the enmity of the South.

In the spring of 1836, when Mr. Van Buren was still vice-president, and the presidential election was drawing near, Mr. Calhoun brought forward in the Senate his bill (commonly called the Gag Bill) to violate the post-office function, by authorizing postmasters to investigate the contents of the mails, and to keep back all papers whatsoever relating to the subject of slavery. The bill was, by consent, read the first and second times without debate; and the Senate was to be divided on the question whether it should go to a third reading. The votes were equal, 18 to 18. "Where's the vice-president?" shouted Mr. Calhoun's mighty voice. The vice-president was behind a pillar, talking. He was compelled to give the casting vote, to commit himself for once; a cruel necessity to a man of his caution. He voted for the third reading, and there was a bitter cry on the instant, "The Northern States are sold." The bill was thrown out on the division on the third reading, and the vice-president lost by his vote the good-will of the whole body of abolitionists, who had till then supported him as the democratic and supposed anti-slavery candidate. As it was, most of the abolitionists did not vote at all, for want of a good candidate, and Mr. Van Buren's majority was so reduced as to justify a belief, that if the people had had another year to consider his conduct in, or if another democratic candidate could have been put forward, he would have been emphatically rejected. Having once committed himself, he has gone further still in propitiation of Mr. Calhoun. On the day of his presidential installation he declared that under no circumstances would he give his assent to any bill for the abolition of slavery in the District of Columbia. This declaration does not arise out of a belief that Congress has not power to abolish slavery in the District; for he did, not long before, when hard pressed, declare that he believed Congress to possess that power. He has therefore hazarded the extraordinary declaration that he will not, under any circumstances, assent to what may become the will of the people constitutionally imbodied. This is a bold intimation for a "non-committal man" to make. It remains to be seen whether Mr. Calhoun, if really dangerous, can be kept quiet by such fawning as this; and whether the will of the people may not be rather stimulated than restrained by this sacrifice of them to the South, so as either to compel the president to retract his declaration before his four years are out, or to prevent his re-election.

How strange it is to recall one's first impressions of public men in the midst of one's matured opinions of them! How freshly I remember the chat about West Point and Stockbridge acquaintances that I had that afternoon at Albany, with the conspicuous man about whom I was then ignorant and indifferent, and whom I have since seen committed to the lowest political principles and practices, while elected as professing some of the highest! It only remains to be said, that if Mr. Van Buren feels himself aggrieved by the interpretation which is commonly put upon the facts of his political life, he has no one to blame but himself; for such misinterpretation (if it exists) is owing to his singular reserve; a reserve which all men agree in considering incompatible with the simple honesty and cheerful admission of responsibility which democratic republicans have a right to require of their rulers. . . .

I was fortunate enough once to catch a glimpse of the invisible Amos Kendall, one of the most remarkable men in America. He is supposed to be the moving spring of the whole administration; the thinker, planner, and doer; but it is all in the dark. Documents are issued of an excellence which prevents their being attributed to persons who take the responsibility of them; a correspondence is kept up all over the country for which no one seems to be answerable; work is done, of goblin extent and with goblin speed, which makes men look about them with a superstitious wonder; and the invisible Amos Kendall has the credit of it all. President Jackson's Letters to his Cabinet are said to be Kendall's; the Report on Sunday Mails is attributed to Kendall; the letters sent from Washington to appear in remote country newspapers, whence they are collected and published in the Globe as demonstrations of public opinion, are pronounced to be written by Kendall. Every mysterious paragraph in opposition newspapers relates to Kendall; and it is some relief to the timid that his having now the office of postmaster-general affords opportunity for open attacks upon this twilight personage; who is proved, by the faults in the postoffice administration, not to be able to do quite everything well. But he is undoubtedly a great genius. He unites with his "great talent for silence" a splendid audacity. . . .

His countenance does not help the superstitious to throw off their dread of him. He probably does not desire this superstition to melt away; for there is no calculating how much influence was given to Jackson's administration by the universal belief that there was a concealed eye and hand behind the machinery of government, by which everything could be foreseen, and the hardest deeds done. . . .

I was more vividly impressed with the past and present state of Ireland while I was in America than ever I was at home. Besides being frequently questioned as to what was likely to be done for the relief of her suffering millions—suffering to a degree that it is inconceivable to Americans that freeborn whites should ever be—I met from time to time with refugee Irish gentry, still burning with the injuries they or their fathers sustained in the time of the rebellion. . . . The descendants of "the rebels" cannot be comforted with tidings of anything to be done for their country. Naturally believing that nothing good can come out of England—nothing good for Ireland—they passionately ask that their country shall be left to govern herself. With tears and scornful laughter they beg that nothing may be "done for her" by hands that have ravaged her with gibbet, fire, and sword, but that she may be left to whatever hopefulness may yet be smouldering under the ashes of her despair. Such is the representation of Ireland to American minds. It may be imagined what a monument of idiotcy the forcible maintenance of the Church of England in Ireland must appear to American statesmen. "I do not understand this Lord John Russell of yours," said one of the most sagacious of them. "Is he serious in supposing that he can allow a penny of the revenues, a plait of the lawn-sleeves of that Irish Church to be touched, and keep the whole from coming down, in Ireland first, and in England afterward?" We fully agree in the difficulty of supposing Lord John Russell serious. The comparison of various, but, I believe, pretty extensive American opinions about the Church of England yields rather a curious result. No one dreams of the establishment being necessary or being designed for the maintenance of religion; it is seen by Chief-justice Marshall and a host of others to be an institution turned to political purposes. Mr. Van Buren, among many, considers that the church has supported the state for many years. Mr Clay, and a multitude with him, anticipates the speedy fall of the establishment. The result yielded by all this is a persuasion not very favourable (to use the American phrase) "to the permanence of our institutions." . . .

We took advantage of a mild day to ascend to the skylight of the dome of the Capitol, in order to obtain a view of the surrounding country. . . .

There was a funeral of a member of Congress on the 30th of January. . . . Some of the fiercest political foes in the country; some who never meet on any other occasion—the president and the South Carolina senators, for instance—now sat knee to knee, necessarily looking into each others' faces. With a coffin beside them, and such an event awaiting their exit, how out of place was hatred here!

After prayers there was a sermon, in which warning of death was brought home to all, and particularly to the aged; and the vanity of all disturbances of human passion when in view of the grave was dwelt upon. There sat the gray-headed old president, at that time feeble, and looking scarcely able to go through this ceremonial. I saw him apparently listening to the discourse; I saw him rise when it was over, and follow the coffin in his turn, somewhat feebly; I saw him disappear in the doorway, and immediately descended with my party to the Rotundo [sic], in order to behold the departure of the procession for the grave. At the bottom of the stairs a member of Congress met us, pale and trembling, with the news that the president had been twice fired at with a pistol by an assassin who had waylaid him in the portico, but that both pistols had missed fire. At this moment the assassin rushed into the Rotundo where we were standing, pursued and instantly surrounded by a crowd. I saw his hands and half-bare arms struggling above the heads of the crowd in resistance to being handcuffed. He was presently overpowered, conveyed to a carriage, and taken before a magistrate. The attack threw the old soldier into a tremendous passion. He fears nothing, but his temper is not equal to his courage. Instead of his putting the event calmly aside, and proceeding with the business of the hour, it was found necessary to put him into his carriage and take him home.

We feared what the consequences would be. We had little doubt that the assassin Lawrence was mad; and as little that, before the day was out, we should hear the crime imputed to more than one political party or individual. And so it was. Before two hours were over, the name of almost every eminent politician was mixed up with that of the poor maniac who caused the uproar. The president's misconduct on the occasion was the most virulent and protracted. A deadly enmity had long subsisted between General Jackson and Mr. Poindexter, a senator[3] of the United States, which had been much aggravated since General Jackson's accession by some unwarrantable language which he had publicly used in relation to Mr. Poindexter's private affairs. There was a prevalent expectation of a duel as soon as the expiration of the president's term of office should enable his foe to send him a challenge. Under these circumstances the president thought proper to charge Mr. Poindexter with being the instigator of Lawrence's attempt. He did this in conversation so frequently and openly, that Mr. Poindexter wrote a letter, brief and manly, stating that he understood this charge was made against him, but that he would not believe it till it was confirmed by the president himself; his not replying to this letter being understood to be such a confirmation. The president showed this letter to visiters at the White House, and did not answer it. He went further; obtaining affidavits (tending to implicate Poindexter) from weak and vile persons whose evidence utterly failed; having personal interviews with these creatures, and openly showing a disposition to hunt his foe to destruction at all hazards. The issue was, that Lawrence was proved to have acted from sheer insanity; Poindexter made a sort of triumphal progress through the states, and an irretrievable stain was left upon President Jackson's name.

Every one was anxiously anticipating the fierce meeting of these foes on the president's retirement from office, when Mr. Poindexter last year, in a fit either of somnambulism or of delirium from illness, walked out of a chamber window in the middle of the night, and was so much injured that he soon died.

It so happened that we were engaged to a party at Mr. Poindexter's the very evening of this attack upon the president. There was so tremendous a thunder-storm that our host and hostess were disappointed of almost all their guests except ourselves, and we had difficulty in merely crossing the street, being obliged to have planks laid across the flood which gushed between the carriage and the steps of the door. The conversation naturally turned on the event of the morning. I knew little of the quarrel which was now to be so dreadfully aggravated; but the more I afterward heard, the more I admired the moderation with which Mr. Poindexter spoke of his foe that night, and as often as I subsequently met him. . . .

It would be amusing, if it were possible to furnish a complete set of the rumours, injurious (if they had not been too absurd) to all parties in turn, upon this single and very common act of a madman. One would have thought that no maniac had ever before attacked a chief magistrate. The

[3]From Missouri.

act might so easily have remained fruitless! but it was made to bear a full and poisonous crop of folly, wickedness, and wo. I feared on the instant how it would be, and felt that, though the president was safe, it was very bad news. When will it come to be thought possible for politicians to have faith in one another, though they may differ, and to be jealous for their rivals rather than for themselves?

The Capitol

. . . Judge Story was kind enough to send us notice when any cause was to be argued in the Supreme Court which it was probable we might be able to understand, and we passed a few mornings there. . . .

At some moments this court presents a singular spectacle. I have watched the assemblage while the chief-justice[4] was delivering a judgment; the three judges on either hand gazing at him more like learners than associates; Webster standing firm as a rock, his large, deep-set eyes wide awake, his lips compressed, and his whole countenance in that intent stillness which easily fixes the eye of the stranger; Clay leaning against the desk in an attitude whose grace contrasts strangely with the slovenly make of his dress, his snuffbox for the moment unopened in his hand, his small gray eye and placid half-smile conveying an expression of pleasure which redeems his face from its usual unaccountable commonness; the attorney-general, his fingers playing among his papers, his quick black eye, and thin tremulous lips for once fixed, his small face, pale with thought, contrasting remarkably with the other two; these men, absorbed in what they are listening to, thinking neither of themselves nor of each other, while they are watched by the groups of idlers and listeners around them; the newspaper corps, the dark Cherokee chiefs, the stragglers from the Far West, the gay ladies in their waving plumes, and the members of either house that have stepped in to listen; all these I have seen at one moment constitute one silent assemblage, while the mild voice of the aged chief-justice sounded through the court. . . .

It was amusing to see how the court would fill after the entrance of Webster, and empty when he had gone back to the Senate Chamber. The chief interest to me in Webster's pleading, and also in his speaking in the Senate, was from seeing one so dreamy and *nonchalant* roused into strong excitement. . . . Webster is a lover of ease and pleasure, and has an air of the most unaffected indolence and careless self-sufficiency. It is something to see him moved with anxiety and the toil of intellectual conflict; to see his lips tremble, his nostrils expand, the perspiration start upon his brow; to hear his voice vary with emotion, and to watch the expression of laborious thought while he pauses, for minutes together, to consider his notes, and decide upon the arrangement of his argument. These are the moments when

[4]John Marshall.

it becomes clear that this pleasure-loving man works for his honours and his gains. He seems to have the desire which other remarkable men have shown, to conceal the extent of his toils, and his wish has been favoured by some accidents; some sudden, unexpected call upon him for a display of knowledge and power which has electrified the beholders. But on such occasions he has been able to bring into use acquisitions and exercises intended for other occasions, on which they may or may not have been wanted. No one will suppose that this is said in disparagement of Mr. Webster. It is only saying that he owes to his own industry what he must otherwise owe to miracle. . . .

Mr. Webster has for some years been considered the head of the federal party, and he is therefore now on the losing side in politics. His last great triumph was his exposure of the nullification doctrine in 1833. Since that time he has maintained his influence in Congress by virtue of his great talents and former services; but, his politics being in opposition to those of the great body of the people, he is unable to do more than head the opposition in the Senate. . . .

Mr. Webster owes his rise to the institutions under which he lives; institutions which open the race to the swift and the battle to the strong; but there is little in him that is congenial with them. He is aristocratic in his tastes and habits, and but little republican simplicity is to be recognised in him. Neither his private conversation nor his public transactions usually convey an impression that he is in earnest. When he is so, his power is majestic, irresistible; but his ambition for office, and for the good opinion of those who surround him, is seen too often in alternation with his love of ease and luxury to allow of his being confided in as he is admired. If it had been otherwise, if his moral had equalled his intellectual supremacy, if his aims had been as single as his reason is unclouded, he would long ago have carried all before him, and been the virtual monarch of the United States. But to have expected this would have been unreasonable. The very best men of any society are rarely or never to be found among its eminent statesmen; and it is not fair to look for them in offices which, in the present condition of human affairs, would yield to such no other choice than of speedy failure or protracted martyrdom. Taking great politicians as they are, Mr. Webster's general consistency may be found not to have fallen below the average, though it has not been so remarkable as to ensure on his behalf a confidence at all to be compared with the universal admiration of his talents.

Mr. Webster speaks seldom in the Senate. When he does, it is generally on some constitutional question, where his reasoning powers and knowledge are brought into play, and where his authority is considered so high, that he has the glorious satisfaction of knowing that he is listened to as an oracle by an assemblage of the first men in the country. Previous to such an exercise he may be seen leaning back in his chair, not, as usual, biting the top of his pen, or twirling his thumbs, or bursting into sudden and transient laughter at Colonel Benton's oratorical absurdities, but absent and thoughtful, making notes, and seeing nothing that is before his eyes. When he rises, his voice is moderate and his manner quiet, with the slightest possible mixture of embarrassment; his right hand rests upon his desk, and the left hangs by his side. Before his first head is finished, however, his voice has risen so as to fill the chamber and ring again, and he has fallen into his favourite attitude, with his left hand under his coat-tail, and the right in full action. At this moment the eye rests upon him as upon one under the true inspiration of seeing the invisible and grasping the impalpable. When the vision has passed away, the change is astonishing. He sits at his desk, writing letters or dreaming, so that he does not always discover when the Senate is going to a division. Some one of his party has not seldom to jog his elbow, and tell him that his vote is wanted.

There can scarcely be a stronger contrast than between the eloquence of Webster and that of Clay. . . . Clay's appearance is plain in the extreme, being that of a mere west-country farmer. He is tall and thin, with a weather-beaten complexion, small gray eyes, which convey an idea of something more than his well-known sagacity, even of slyness. . . . Mr. Clay is a man of an irritable and impetuous nature, over which he has obtained a truly noble mastery. His moderation is now his most striking characteristic; obtained, no doubt, at the cost of prodigious self-denial on his own part, and on that of his friends of some of the ease, naturalness, and self-forgetfulness of his manners and discourse. . . .

Mr. Clay is sometimes spoken of as a "disappointed statesman." . . . He once held the balance of the Union in his hand, and now belongs to the losing party; he more than once expected to be president, and has now no chance of ever being so. Thus far he is a disappointed statesman; but, at the same time, he is in possession of more than an equivalent for what he has lost, not only in the disciplined moderation of his temper, but in the imperishable reality of great deeds done. No possession of office could now add to his dignity any more than the total neglect of the present generation of the people could detract from it. The fact that Mr. Clay's political opinions are not in accordance with those now held by the great body of the people is no disgrace to him or them, while the dignity of his former services, supported by his present patience and quietness, places him far above compassion, and every feeling but respect and admiration. This admiration is exalted to enthusiasm in those who know how difficult it is to a man of Mr. Clay's nature, who has lived in public all his life, to fall back into obscurity; an obscurity not relieved, alas! by the solace of a cheerful home. Few spectacles can be more noble than he is in that obscurity, discoursing of public men and affairs with a justice which no rivalship can impair, and a hopefulness which no personal disappointment can relax. . . .

The one act of Mr. Clay's public life for which he must be held to require pardon from posterity, is that by which he secured the continuance of slavery in Missouri, and, in consequence, its establishment in Arkansas and Florida; the one an admitted state, the other a territory destined to be so. Mr. Clay is not an advocate of slavery, though, instead of being a friend to abolition, he is a dupe of colonization. When he held the destinies of American slavery in his hand, he had, unhappily, more regard for precedent in human arrangements than for the spirit of the divine laws in the light of which such arrangements should be ever regarded. He acted to avert the conflict which cannot be averted. It was still to take place; it is now taking place, under less favourable circumstances; and his measure of expediency is already meeting with the retribution which ever follows upon the subordination of a higher principle to a lower. For many of his public acts Mr. Clay will be permanently honoured; with regard to others, the honour will be mingled with allowance for error in philosophy; for this one he will have to be forgiven. . . .

The finest speech I heard from Mr. Clay in the Senate was on the sad subject of the injuries of the Indians. He exposed the facts of the treatment of the Cherokees by Georgia. He told how the lands in Georgia, guaranteed by solemn treaties to the Cherokees, had been surveyed and partitioned off to white citizens of the state; that, though there is a nominal right of appeal awarded to the complainants, this is a mere mockery, as an acknowledgment of the right of Georgia to divide the lands is made a necessary preliminary to the exercise of the right; in other words, the Indians must lay down their claims on the threshold of the courts which they enter for the purpose of enforcing these claims! The object of Mr. Clay's plea was to have the Supreme Court open to the Cherokees, their case being, he contended, contemplated by the Constitution. A minor proposition was that Congress should assist, with territory and appliances, a body of Cherokees who desired to emigrate beyond the Mississippi.

It was known that Mr. Clay would probably bring forward his great topic that day. Some of the foreign ambassadors might be seen leaning against the pillars behind the chair, and many members of the other house appeared behind and in the passages; and one sat on the steps of the platform, his hands clasped, and his eyes fixed on Mr. Clay, as if life hung upon his words. As many as could crowd into the gallery leaned over the balustrade; and the lower circle was thronged with ladies and gentlemen, in the centre of whom stood a group of Cherokee chiefs, listening immoveably. I never saw so deep a moral impression produced by a speech. The best testimony to this was the disgust excited by the empty and abusive reply of the senator from Georgia. . . .

The American Senate is a most imposing assemblage. When I first entered it I thought I never saw a finer set of heads than the forty-six before my eyes: two only being absent, and the Union then consisting of twenty-four states. . . . No English person who has not travelled over half the world can form an idea of such differences among men forming one assembly for the same purposes, and speaking the same language. Some were descended from Dutch farmers, some from French Huguenots, some from Scotch Puritans, some from English cavaliers, some from Irish chieftains. They were brought together out of law-courts, sugar-fields, merchants' stores, mountain farms, forests, and prairies. The stamp of originality was impressed upon every one, and inspired a deep, involuntary respect. I have seen no assembly of chosen men, and no company of the highborn, invested with the antique dignities of an antique realm, half so imposing to the imagination as this collection of stout-souled, full-grown, original men, brought together on the ground of their supposed sufficiency, to work out the will of their diverse constituencies. . . .

I wished every day that the ladies would conduct themselves in a more dignified manner than they did in the Senate. They came in with waving plumes, and glittering in all the colours of the rainbow, causing no little bustle in the place, no little annoyance to the gentlemen spectators, and rarely sat still for any length of time. I know that these ladies are no fair specimen of the women who would attend parliamentary proceedings in any other metropolis. I know that they were the wives, daughters, and sisters of legislators, women thronging to Washington for purposes of convenience or pleasure, leaving their usual employments behind them, and seeking to pass away the time. I knew this, and made allowance accordingly; but I still wished that they could understand the gravity of such an assembly, and show so much respect to it as to repay the privilege of admission by striving to excite as little attention as possible, and by having the patience to sit still when they happened not to be amused, till some interruption gave them opportunity to depart quietly. If they had done this, Judge Porter[5] would not have moved that they should be appointed seats in the gallery instead of below; and they would have been guiltless of furnishing a plea for the exclusion of women, who would probably make a better use of the privilege, from the galleries of other houses of parliament. . . .

The gallery of the splendid Hall of Representatives is not well contrived for hearing, and I rarely went into it for more than a passing view of what was going on. . . . My chief interest was watching Mr. Adams.[6] He is one of the most remarkable men in America. He is an imbodiment of the pure, simple morals which are assumed to prevail in the thriving young republic. His term of office was marked by nothing so much as by the subordination of glory to goodness, of showy objects to moral ones. The eccentricity of thought and action in Mr. Adams, of which his admirers bitterly or sorrowfully complain, and which renders him an impracticable member of a party, arises from the same honest simplicity which crowns his virtues, mingled with a faulty taste and an imperfect temper. . . . His occasional starts out of the ranks of his party, without notice

[5]Senator from Louisiana.

[6]John Quincy Adams.

and without apparent cause, have been in vain attempted to be explained on suppositions of interest or vanity; they may be more easily accounted for in other ways. Between one day and another, some new idea of justice and impartiality may strike his brain, and send him to the house warm with invective against his party and sympathy with their foes. He rises, and speaks out all his new mind, to the perplexity of the whole assembly . . . perplexity which gives way to dismay on the one hand and triumph on the other. The triumphant party begins to coax and honour him; but, before the process is well begun, he is off again, finding that he had gone too far; and the probability is, that he finishes by placing himself between two fires. . . . He was well described to me before I saw him. "Study Mr. Adams," was the exhortation. "You will find him well worth it. He runs in veins; if you light upon one, you will find him marvellously rich; if not, you may chance to meet rubbish. In action he is very peculiar. He will do ninety-nine things nobly, excellently; but the hundredth will be so bad in taste and temper, that it will drive all the rest out of your head, if you don't take care." His countrymen will "take care." Whatever the heats of party may be, however the tone of disappointment against Mr. Adams may sometimes rise to something too like hatred, there is undoubtedly a deep reverence and affection for the man in the nation's heart. . . . He fought a stout and noble battle in Congress last session in favour of discussion of the slavery question, and in defence of the right of petition upon it; on behalf of women as well as of men. While hunted, held at bay, almost torn to pieces by an outrageous majority . . . he preserved a boldness and coolness as amusing as they were admirable. Though he now and then vents his spleen with violence when disappointed in a favourite object, he seems able to bear perfectly well that which it is the great fault of Americans to shrink from, singularity and blame. He seems, at times, reckless of opinion; and this is the point of his character which his countrymen seem, naturally, least to comprehend.

Madison

While I was at Washington I received a kind invitation from Mr. and Mrs. Madison to visit them at their seat, Montpelier, Virginia. I was happy to avail myself of it, and paid the visit on my way down to Richmond. . . .

We were warmly welcomed by Mrs. Madison and a niece, a young lady who was on a visit to her; and when I left my room I was conducted to the apartment of Mr. Madison. He had, the preceding season, suffered so severely from rheumatism, that, during this winter, he confined himself to one room, rising after breakfast, before nine o'clock, and sitting in his easy-chair till ten at night. He appeared perfectly well during my visit, and was a wonderful man of eighty-three. He complained of one ear being deaf, and that his sight, which had never been perfect, prevented his reading much, so that his studies "lay in a nutshell;" but he could hear Mrs. Madison read, and I did not perceive that he lost any part of the conversation. He was in his chair, with a pillow behind him, when I first saw him; his little person wrapped in a black silk gown; a warm gray and white cap upon his head, which his lady took care should always sit becomingly; and gray worsted gloves, his hands having been rheumatic. His voice was clear and strong, and his manner of speaking particularly lively, often playful. . . .

There is no need to add another to the many eulogies of Madison; I will only mention that the finest of his characteristics appeared to me to be his inexhaustible faith; faith that a well-founded commonwealth may, as our motto declares, be immortal; not only because the people, its constituency, never die, but because the principles of justice in which such a commonwealth originates never die out of the people's heart and mind. This faith shone brightly through the whole of Mr. Madison's conversation except on one subject. With regard to slavery he owned himself almost to be in despair. He had been quite so till the institution of the Colonization Society. How such a mind as his could derive any alleviation to its anxiety from that source is surprising. I think it must have been from his overflowing faith; for the facts were before him that in eighteen years the Colonization Society had removed only between two and three thousand persons, while the annual increase of the slave population in the United States was upward of sixty thousand.

He talked more on the subject of slavery than on any other, acknowledging, without limitation or hesitation, all the evils with which it has ever been charged. He told me that the black population in Virginia increases far faster than the white; and that the licentiousness only stops short of the destruction of the race; every slave girl being expected to be a mother by the time she is fifteen. He assumed from this, I could not make out why, that the negroes must go somewhere, and pointed out how the free states discourage the settlement of blacks; how Canada disagrees with them; how Hayti shuts them out; so that Africa is their only refuge. He did not assign any reason why they should not remain where they are when freed. He found, by the last returns from his estates, that one third of his own slaves were under five years of age. He had parted with some of his best land to feed the increasing numbers, and had yet been obliged to sell a dozen of his slaves the preceding week. He observed that the whole Bible is against negro slavery; but that the clergy do not preach this, and the people do not see it. He became animated in describing . . . the eagerness of the clergy of the four denominations to catch converts among the slaves, and the effect of religious teaching of this kind upon those who, having no rights, can have no duties. He thought the condition of slaves much improved in his time, and, of course, their intellects. This remark was, I think, intended to apply to Virginia alone, for it is certainly not applicable to the southwestern states. He accounted for his selling his slaves by mentioning their horror of going to Liberia, a horror which he admitted to be prevalent among the blacks, and which appears to me decisive as to the unnaturalness of the scheme. The willing mind is the first requisite to the emigrant's success. Mr. Madison complained of the difficulty and risk of throwing an additional population into the colony, at the rate of two or three cargoes a year; complained of it because he believed it was the fault of the residents, who were bent upon trading with the interior for luxuries, instead of raising food for the new comers. This again seems fatal to the scheme, since the compulsory direction of industry, if it could be enforced, would be almost as bad as slavery at home; and there are no means of preventing the emigrants being wholly idle, if they are not allowed to work in their own way for their own objects. Mr. Madison admitted the great and various difficulties attending the scheme, and recurred to the expression that he was only "less in despair than formerly about slavery." He spoke with deep feeling of the sufferings of ladies under the system, declaring that he pitied them even more than their negroes, and that the saddest slavery of all was that of conscientious Southern women. They cannot trust their slaves in the smallest particulars, and have to superintend the execution of all their own orders; and they know that their estates are surrounded by vicious free blacks, who induce thievery among the negroes, and keep the minds of the owners in a state of perpetual suspicion, fear, and anger.

Mr. Madison spoke strongly of the helplessness of all countries cursed with a servile population in a conflict with a people wholly free; ridiculed the idea of the Southern States being able to maintain a rising against the North; and wondered that all thinkers were not agreed in a thing so plain. He believed that Congress has power to prohibit the internal slave-trade. . . .

Country Life in the South

THERE was no end to the kind cautions given me against travelling through the Southern States, not only on account of my opinions on slavery, but because of the badness of the roads and the poverty of the wayside accommodations. . . . The evil prognostications went on multiplying as we advanced. . . . At Richmond we were cautioned about the journey into South Carolina; at Charleston we were met with dreadful reports of travelling in Georgia; in Georgia people spoke of the horrors of Alabama, and so on; and, after all, nothing could well be easier than the whole undertaking. I do not remember a single difficulty that occurred all the way.

There was much fatigue, of course. In going down from Richmond to Charleston with a party of friends, we were nine days on the road, and had only three nights' rest. Throughout the journey we were obliged to accommodate ourselves to the stage hours, setting off sometimes in the evening, sometimes at midnight; or, of all uncomfortable seasons, at two or three in the morning. On a journey of many days, we had to inform ourselves of the longest time that the stage would stop at a supping or breakfasting place, so that we might manage to snatch an hour's sleep. While the meal was preparing, it was my wont to lie down and doze, in spite of hunger; if I could find a bed or sofa, it was well; if not, I could wrap myself in my cloak, and make a pillow on the floor of my carpet-bag. I found that a sleep somewhat longer than this, when I could go to bed for two hours, was more fatiguing than refreshing. The being waked up at two, when I had lain down at midnight, was the greatest discomfort I experienced. But little sleep can be obtained in the stage from the badness of the roads. It was only when quite wearied out that I could forget myself for an hour or two amid the joltings and rollings of the vehicle. In Alabama, some of the passengers in the stage were Southern gentlemen coming from New York, in comparison with whose fatigues ours were nothing. I think they had then travelled eleven days and nights with very short intervals of rest, and the badness of the roads at the end of a severe winter had obliged them to walk a good deal. They looked dreadfully haggard and nervous. . . . It is not necessary, of course, to proceed without stopping in such a way as this; but it is necessary to be patient of fatigue to travel in the South at all.

Yet I was very fond of these long journeys. The traveller (if he be not an abolitionist) is perfectly secure of good treatment, and fatigue and indifferent fare are the only evils which need be anticipated. The toils of society in the cities were so great to me that I generally felt my spirits rise when our packing began; and, the sorrow of parting with kind hosts once over, the prospect of a journey of many days was a very cheerful one. The novelty and the beauty of the scenery seemed inexhaustible; and the delightful American stages, open or closed all round at the will of the traveller, allow of everything being seen. . . .

When the sun has gone down all is still within the stage; the passengers grow drowsy unless hunger keeps them awake. Each one nods upon his neighbour's shoulder, till a red light, gradually illuminating all the faces, and every moment growing brighter, rouses the dullest. Each tells somebody else that we are coming to a fire in the woods. First there are lines of little yellow flames on each side the path; the blazing up of twigs too dry to have been made incombustible by the morning's rain. Then there is a pond of red fire on either hand, and pillars of light rising from it; tall burning stems, throwing out jets of flame on all sides, or emitting a flood of sparks when touched by the night breeze. The succeeding darkness is intense. The horses seem to feel it, for they slacken to a footpace, and the grazing of a wheel against a pinestem, or the zigzag motion of the vehicle, intimates that the driver's eyes have been dazzled. Presently the horses set off again, and the passengers sink once more into silence. They are next roused by the discordant horn of the driver, sending out as many distinct blasts as there are passengers, each blast more of a screech than the last, and the final flourish causing a shout of laughter in the coach; laughter animated a little, perhaps, by the prospect of supper. Right or left soon appears the loghouse, its open shutters and door giving token that a large fire is blazing within. The gentlemen hand out the ladies at the door, and then stand yawning and stretching, or draw to the fire while they can, before the ladies take possession of the best places. The hostess, who is busy cooking, points to a lamp, with which the ladies light themselves to her chamber, to put up their hair under their bonnets for the night. Little impish blacks peep and grin from behind the stove or shine in the heat of the chimney-corner. . . . An observer may see some fun going on behind the mistress's back; a whisk of a carving-knife across a companion's throat, or a flourish of two plates like cymbals over the head.

At last supper is ready; the broiled venison, the ham collops and eggs, and apple-sauce; the infusion which is called tea or coffee; and the reeking corn-bread. Before the clatter of knives has ceased, the stage, with its fresh horses, is at the door; the ladies snatch a final warming while the driver finishes his protracted meal, their eyes being now at liberty to study the apartment, looking round for some other object than the old story, the six presidents who smile from the walls of almost every loghouse in America, and the great map of the United States, with a thumbmark, amounting to an erasure, on the spot of the very territory where this particular loghouse happens to be. If we wanted to consult a map in a hurry in such places as these, we never had to hunt out our present situation. There was always the worn spot to serve as the centre to our investigations. The passengers, however wearily they might have descended from the stage, are pretty sure to enter it again with a spring; warm and satisfied, with a joke on their tongues, and a good supper to sleep or muse upon. . . .

If the teambolt or other fastening of equal consequence should happen to break, there is a chance of two hours' rest or so. Something snaps; the vehicle stops; the gentlemen get out; the ladies gaze from the windows, while somebody half-dressed comes out with a lantern from any dwelling that may be in sight, and goes back again for hammer and nail, or, at worst, a piece of cord, and you proceed at a slow foot-pace to the nearest hotel. There the slaves, roused from the floor, where they are lying like dogs, go winking about, putting fresh logs on the smouldering fire, and lighting a lamp or two. After repeated inquiries on the part of the ladies, who feel the first minutes of their two hours slipping away without any promise of rest, a female slave at last appears, staring as if she had never seen anybody before. The ladies have already taken out nightcap, soap, and towel from their carpet-bags. They motion the woman up stairs, and follow her. They find the water-jug, if there be one, empty, of course. With infinite coaxing they get the attendant to fill it. Long after they are undressed it comes, clear or "sort o' muddy," as may be. If there are no sheets or yellow ones, the ladies spread their dressing-gowns over the bed, and use their cloaks for a covering. As soon as they have lain down, a draught begins to blow in the strangest way on the top of their heads. They examine, and find a broken window behind the bed. They wrap up their heads and lie down again. As soon as they are fairly dreaming that they are at home, and need not get up till they please, the horn startles them; they raise their heads, see a light under the door, and the black woman looks in to drawl out that they must please to make haste. It seems like a week since they lay down; but they are not rested, and turn away sick and dizzy from the flickering light.

In the morning you wonder where your fatigue is gone. As the day steals through the forest, kindling up beauty as it goes, the traveller's whole being is refreshed. The young aloes under the fallen trunks glitter with dew; the gray moss, dangling from the trees, waves in the breath of the morning. The busy little chameleons run along the fences, and the squirrel erects his brush as you pass. While the crescent moon and the morning star glittered low down in the sky, you had longed to stay the sun beneath the horizon; but, now that he is come, fresh vigour and enjoyment seem to be shed down with his rays. . . .

Our stationary rural life in the South was various and pleasant enough; all shaded with the presence of slavery, but without any other drawback. There is something in the make-shift, irregular mode of life which exists where there are slaves, that is amusing when the cause is forgotten.

The waking in the morning is accomplished by two or three black women staring at you from the bedposts. Then it is five minutes' work to get them out of the room. Perhaps, before you are half dressed, you are summoned to breakfast. You look at your watch, and listen whether it has stopped, for it seems not to be seven o'clock yet. You hasten, however, and find your hostess making the coffee. The young people drop in when the meal is half done, and then it is discovered that breakfast has been served an hour too early, because the clock has stopped, and the cook has ordered affairs according to her own conjectures. Everybody laughs, and nothing ensues. After breakfast a farmer in homespun—blue trousers and an orange-brown coat, or all over gray—comes to speak with your host. A drunken white has shot one of his negroes, and he fears no punishment can be obtained, because there were no witnesses of the deed but blacks. A consultation is held whether the affair shall go into court; and, before the farmer departs, he is offered cake and liqueur.

Your hostess, meantime, has given her orders, and is now engaged in a back room, or out in the piazza behind the house, cutting out clothes for her slaves; very laborious work in warm weather. There may be a pretence of lessons among the young people, and something more than pretence if they happen to have a tutor or governess; but the probability is that their occupations are as various as their tempers. Rosa cannot be found; she is lying on the bed in her own room reading a novel; Clara is weeping for her canary, which has flown away while she was playing with it; Alfred is trying to ascertain how soon we may all go out to ride; and the little ones are lounging about the court, with their arms round the necks of blacks of their own size. You sit down to the piano or to read, and one slave or another enters every half hour to ask what is o'clock. Your hostess comes in at length, and you sit down to work with her; she gratifies your curiosity about her "people," telling you how soon they burn out their shoes at the toes, and wear out their winter woollens, and tear up their summer cottons; and how impossible it is to get black women to learn to cut out clothes without waste; and how she never inquires when and where the whipping is done, as it is the overseer's business, and not hers. She has not been seated many minutes when she is called away, and returns saying how babyish these people are, that they will not take medicine unless she gives it to them; and how careless of each other, so that she has been obliged to stand by and see Diana put clean linen upon her infant, and to compel Bet to get her sick husband some breakfast.

Morning visiters next arrive. It may be the clergyman, with some new book that you want to look at; and inquiries whether your host sees any prospect of getting the requisite number of professors for the new college or whether the present head of the institution is to continue to fill all the chairs. It may be a lank judge from some raw district, with a quid in his cheek, a swordcane in his hand, and a legal doubt in his mind which he wants your host to resolve. It may be a sensible woman, with courtesy in her countenance and decision in her air, who is accustomed really to rule her household, and to make the most of such human material and such a human lot as are pressing around and upon her. . . .

Meantime Clara has dried her tears, for some one has recovered her canary, and the door of the cage is shut. The carriage and saddle-horses are scrambling on the gravel before the door. . . .

You admire the horsemanship of your host on his white horse, and the boys on their black ponies. The carriage goes at good speed, and yet the fast *pace* of the saddle-horses enables the party to keep together. . .

Your host paces up to the carriage window to tell you that you are now on A.'s plantation. You are overtaking a long train of negroes going to their work from dinner. They look all over the colour of the soil they are walking on: dusky in clothing, dusky in complexion. An old man, blacker than the rest, is indicated to you as a native African; and you point out a child so light as to make you doubt whether he be a slave. A glance at the long heel settles the matter. You feel that it would be a relief to be assured that this was a troop of monkeys dressed up for sport, rather than that these dull, shuffling animals should be human.

There is something inexpressibly disgusting in the sight of a slave woman in the field. I do not share in the horror of the Americans at the idea of women being employed in outdoor labour. It did not particularly gratify me to see the cows always milked by men (where there were no slaves); and the hay and harvest fields would have looked brighter in my eyes if women had been there to share the wholesome and cheerful toil. But a negro woman behind the plough presents a very different object from the English mother with her children in the turnip-field, or the Scotch lassie among the reapers. In her pre-eminently ugly costume, the long, scanty, dirty woollen garment, with the shabby large bonnet at the back of her head, the perspiration streaming down her dull face, the heavy tread of the splay foot, the slovenly air with which she guides her plough, a more hideous object cannot well be conceived, unless it be the same woman at home, in the negro quarter, as the cluster of slave dwellings is called.

You are now taken to the cotton-gin, the building to your left, where you are shown how the cotton, as picked from the pods, is drawn between cylinders so as to leave the seeds behind; and how it is afterward packed, by hard pressure, into bales. The neighbouring creek is dammed up to supply the water-wheel by which this gin is worked. You afterward see the cotton-seed laid in handfuls round the stalks of the young springing corn, and used in the cotton field as manure.

Meantime you attempt to talk with the slaves. You ask how old that very aged man is, or that boy; they will give you no intelligible answer. Slaves never know, or never will tell their ages, and this is the reason why the census presents such extraordinary reports on this point, declaring a great number to be above a hundred years old. If they have a kind master, they will boast to you of how much he gave for each of them, and what sums he has refused for them. If they have a hard master, they will tell you that they would have more to eat and be less flogged, but that massa is busy, and has no time to come down and see that they have enough to eat. . . .

You are then invited to see the house, learning by the way the extent and value of the estate you are visiting, and of the "force" upon it. You admire the lofty, cool rooms, with their green blinds, and the width of the piazzas on both sides the house, built to compensate for the want of shade from trees, which cannot be allowed near the dwelling for fear of moschetoes. . . .

You are glad to find, on arriving at home, that you have half an hour to lie down before you dress, and are surprised, on rising, to feel how you are refreshed. You have not very far to go to dinner; only to Mr. E.'s cottage on the Sand Hills. . . .

The dinner is plentiful, including, of course, turkey, ham, and sweet potatoes; excellent claret, and large blocks of icecream. A slave makes gentle war against the flies with the enormous bunch of peacocks' feathers; and the agitation of the air is pleasant while the ladies are engaged in eating, so that they cannot use their own fans, which are hung by loops on the backs of their chairs. The afternoon is spent in the piazza, where coffee is served. There the ladies sit, whisking their feather fans, jesting with the children, and talking over the last English poem or American novel, or complaining bitterly of the dreadful incendiary publications which Mr. E. heard from Mr. H., who had heard it from Mr. M., that Judge R. had said that somebody had seen circulated among the negroes by some vile agent of the horrid abolitionists of the North.

You go in to tea, and find the table strewed with prints, and the piano open, and Mrs. F. plays and sings. The gentlemen have done discussing the French war and the currency, and are praising the conduct of the Committee of Vigilance; frankly informing you, as a stranger, of the reasons of its formation, and the modes of its operation in deterring abolitionists from coming into the neighbourhood, in arresting them on any suspicion of tampering with the negroes, and in punishing them summarily if any facts are established against them. . . .

Charleston

Charleston is the place in which to see those contrasting scenes of human life brought under the eye which moralists gather together for the purpose of impressing the imagination. The stranger has but to pass from street to street, to live from hour to hour in this city, to see in conjunction the extremes between which there is everywhere else a wide interval. The sights of one morning I should remember if every other particular of my travels were forgotten. I was driven round the city by a friend whose conversation was delightful all the way. Though I did not agree in all his views of society, the thoughtfulness of his mind and the benevolence of his exertions betokened a healthy state of feeling, and gave value to all he said. . . .

I went into the slave market, a place which the traveller ought not to avoid to spare his feelings. There was a table on which stood two auctioneers, one with a hammer, the other to exhibit "the article" and count the bids. The slaves for sale were some of them in groups below, and some in a long row behind the auctioneers. The sale of a man was just concluding when we entered the market. A woman, with two children, one at the breast, and another holding by her apron, composed the next lot. The restless, jocose zeal of the auctioneer who counted the bids was the most infernal sight I ever beheld. The woman was a mulatto; she was neatly dressed, with a clean apron and a yellow head-handkerchief. The elder child clung to her. She hung her head low, lower, and still lower on her breast, yet turning her eyes incessantly from side to side, with an intensity of expectation which showed that she had not reached the last stage of despair. I should have thought that her agony of shame and dread would have silenced the tongue of every spectator; but it was not so. A lady chose this moment to turn to me and say, with a cheerful air of complacency, "You know my theory, that one race must be subservient to the other. I do not care which; and if the blacks should ever have the upper hand, I should not mind standing on that table, and being sold with two of my children." Who could help saying within himself, "Would you were! so that that mother were released!" Who could help seeing in vision the blacks driving the whites into the field, and preaching from the pulpits of Christian churches the doctrines now given out there, that God has respect of persons; that men are to hold each other as property, instead of regarding each other as brethren; and that the right interpretation of the golden rule by the slaveholder is, "Do unto your slaves as you would wish your master to do unto you if you were a slave!" A little boy of eight or nine years old, apparently, was next put up alone. There was no bearing the child's look of helplessness and shame. It seemed like an outrage to be among the starers from whom he shrunk, and we went away before he was disposed of.

We next entered a number of fine houses, where we were presented with flowers, and entertained with lively talk about the small affairs of gay society, which to little minds are great. To me every laugh had lost its gayety, every courtesy had lost its grace, all intercourse had lost its innocence. . . . If there be a scene which might stagger the faith of the spirit of Christianity itself; if there be an experience which might overthrow its serenity, it is the transition from the slavemarket to the abodes of the slavemasters, bright with sunshine, and gay with flowers, with courtesies, and mirth.

If the moral gloom which oppresses the spirit of the stranger were felt by the residents, of course this condition of society would not endure another day. . . . Every day shows how many mansions there are in this hell; how variously the universally allowed evil visits minds of different strength and discernment. All suffer, from the frivolous and sophisticated child to the far-seeing and disciplined saint. The difficulty is to have patience with the diversity, and to wait, as God waits, till the moral gloom strikes upon every heart, and causes every eye to turn for light where some already see it. At the same hour when the customary sins of the slavemarket were being perpetrated, hundreds of the little people of Charleston were preparing for their childish pleasures—their merry dancing-schools, their juvenile fancy balls—ordering their little slaves about, and allowing themselves to be fanned by black attendants while reposing in preparation for the fatigues of the evening; ministers of the Gospel were agreeing to deprive persons of colour of all religious education; a distant Lynch mob was outraging the person of a free and innocent citizen; elegant ladies were administering hospitality, and exchanging gossip and sentiment; and Angelina Grimké[7] was penning the letter which contains the following pas-

[7]She spoke publicly against slavery, whereupon the General Association of Congregational Ministers of Massachusetts called upon the clergy to close their churches against women speakers. Whittier attacked their action in *The Pastoral Letter.*

sages, a private letter to a friend[8] who was shortly to undergo the strengthening process of being mobbed:—

"I can hardly express to thee the deep and solemn interest with which I have viewed the violent proceedings of the last few weeks. Although I expected opposition, yet I was not prepared for it so soon; it took me by surprise, and I greatly feared abolitionists would be driven back in the first onset, and thrown into confusion. So fearful was I, that, though I clung with unflinching firmness to our principles, yet I was afraid of even opening one of thy papers, lest I should see some indications of compromise, some surrender, some palliation. Under these feelings I was urged to read thy appeal to the citizens of Boston. Judge, then, what were my feelings on finding that my fears were utterly groundless, and that thou stoodst firm in the midst of the storm, determined to suffer and to die rather than yield one inch.

"Religious persecution always begins with mobs. It is always unprecedented in the age or country in which it commences, and, therefore, there are no laws by which reformers can be punished; consequently, a lawless band of unprincipled men determine to take the matter into their own hands, and act out in mobs what they know are the principles of a large majority of those who are too high in church and state to condescend to mingle with them, though they secretly approve and rejoice over their violent measures. The first Christian martyr was stoned by a lawless mob; and if we look at the rise of various sects, Methodists, Friends, &c., we shall find that mobs began the persecution against them, and that it was not until after the people had spoken out their wishes that laws were framed to fine, imprison, or destroy them. Let us, then, be prepared for the enactment of laws, even in our free states, against abolitionists. And how ardently has the prayer been breathed, that God would prepare us for all that he is preparing for us!

"My mind has been especially turned towards those who are standing in the forefront of the battle, and the prayer has gone up for their preservation; not the preservation of their lives, but the preservation of their minds in humility and patience, faith, hope, and *charity*. If persecution is the means which God has ordained for the accomplishment of this great end, emancipation, then, in dependance upon him for strength to bear it, I feel as if I could say, 'Let it come;' for it is my deep, solemn, deliberate conviction, that this is a cause worth dying for.

"At one time I thought this system would be overthrown in blood, with the confused noise of the warrior; but a hope gleams across my mind that our blood will be spilt instead of the slaveholders'; our lives will be taken, and theirs spared. I say 'a hope,' for, of all things, I desire to be spared the anguish of seeing our beloved country desolated with the horrors of a servile war."

The writer of this letter was born into the system, under the same

[8]Probably William Lloyd Garrison.

circumstances with the ladies who repeatedly asked me if I did not find that the slaves were very happy. So widely different are the influences of the same circumstances upon different minds!

Our evening engagements were as strangely contrasted as those of the morning. We were at parties where we heard loud talk of justice and oppression; appeals to the eternal principles of the one, when the tariff was the subject, and expressions of the most passionate detestation of the other, which might, but for the presence of black faces in the rooms, lead a stranger to suppose that he was in the very sanctuary of human rights. We were at a young heiress's first ball, where every guest was presented with a bouquet on entering; where the young ladies waltzed, and the young gentlemen gave a loose to their spirits, and all who were present had kindly greetings for the stranger. Nothing could be gayer than the external aspect of these entertainments; but it is impossible for the stranger to avoid being struck with the anxiety which shows itself through it all. I think I never was in society in any of the Southern cities without being asked what I would do if I had a legacy of slaves, or told, in vindictiveness or sorrow, that the prosperity of the North was obtained at the expense of the South. I was never in Southern society without perceiving that its characteristic is a want of repose. It is restlessly gay or restlessly sorrowful. It is angry or exulting; it is hopeful or apprehensive. It is never content; never in such a state of calm satisfaction as to forget itself. This peculiarity poisons the satisfaction of the stranger in the midst of the free and joyous hospitality to which he would otherwise surrender himself with inconsiderate delight. While everything is done that can be conceived of to make you happy, there is a weight pulling at your heartstrings, because you see that other hearts are heavy, and the nobler the heavier. While the host's little child comes to you at first sight, and holds up her mouth for a kiss, and offers to tell you a story, and pours out all her mirth and all her generosity upon you, the child's father tells you that there is a dark prospect before these young creatures, and Heaven knows what lot is in store for them. Your vigilance is kept active by continual suggestions that society is composed of two classes, which entertain a mortal dread of each other. If ever you forget this for an hour, it is recalled by the sight of a soldier at the corner of a street, of a decaying mansion or deserted estate, or of some anti-republican arrangement for social or domestic defence. You reproach yourself because you are anxious and cannot be deceived; and feel as if it were ingratitude to your entertainers not to think them the secure and happy people which, in alternation with their complaints of all the external world, they assure you they are. . . .

I was strongly urged not to omit the Saturday night's market held by the slaves. I should have been sorry to miss this spectacle. The slaves enjoy the amusement and profit yielded by this market. They sit in rows, by lamplight, some with heaps of fruit and vegetables before them, or surrounded by articles of their own manufacture: boxes, bedsteads, baskets, and other handiworks, very cheap, and of good workmanship. The bananas, pines, imported apples, and oranges, which are seen in great abundance, are usually the property of the master; while the manufactured articles, made at spare hours, are nominally the slave's own. Some are allowed to make use of their leisure in preparing for the market, on condition of bringing their masters six dollars each per week, retaining whatever surplus they may gain. I could not learn the consequence of failing to bring in the six dollars per week. They enjoy the fun and bustle of the market, and look with complacency on any white customers who will attend it. Their activity and merriment at market were pointed out to me as an assurance of their satisfaction with their condition, their conviction that their present position is the one they were made for, and in which their true happiness is to be found.

At the very same moment I was shown the ruins of the church of St. Philip, destroyed by fire, as they frowned in the rear of the lamplight; and I was informed that the church had once before been on fire, but had been saved by the exertions of a slave, who "had his liberty given him for a reward."

"A reward!" said I. "What! when the slaves are convinced that their true happiness lies in slavery?"

The conversation had come to an awkward pass. A lady advanced to the rescue, saying that some few, too many, were haunted by a pernicious fancy, put into their heads by others, about liberty; a mere fancy, which, however, made them like the idea of freedom.

"So the benefactor of the city was rewarded by being indulged, to his own hurt, in a pernicious fancy?"

"Why . . . yes." . . .

The prospects of the citizens are "dark every way," as some declared; for the rising generation must either ascend, through a severe discipline and prodigious sacrifices, to a conformity with republican principles, or descend into a condition of solitary feudalism, neither sanctioned by the example nor cheered by the sympathy of the world; but, on the contrary, regarded with that compassion which is precisely the last species of regard which the feudal spirit is able to endure.

We left Charleston in company with Mr. Calhoun and his family. . . . I feared how it would be; what part he would take in the present struggle between the two principles of greatness, physical force with territorial conquest, and moral power shown in self-conquest. I feared that Mr. Calhoun would organize and head the feudal party, as he has done; but I never had any fears that that party would prevail. When we parted at Branchville he little knew—he might have been offended if he had known—with what affectionate solicitude those whom he left behind looked on into his perilous political path. I am glad we could not foresee how soon our fears would be justified. Mr. Calhoun is at present insisting that the pirate colony of Texas shall be admitted into the honourable American

Union; that a new impulse shall thereby be given to the slave-trade, and a new extension to slavery; and that his country shall thereby surrender her moral supremacy among the nations for a gross and antiquated feudal ambition. He vows, taking the whole Union to witness, that these things shall be. The words have publicly passed his pen and his lips, "Texas shall be annexed to the United States." His best friends must hope that the whole world will say, "It shall not."

Restless Slaves

The traveller in America hears on every hand of the fondness of slaves for slavery. If he points to the little picture of a runaway prefixed to advertisements of fugitives, and repeated down whole columns of the first newspaper that comes to hand, he is met with anecdotes of slaves who have been offered their freedom, and prefer remaining in bondage. Both aspects of the question are true, and yet more may be said on both sides. The traveller finds, as he proceeds, that suicides are very frequent among slaves; and that there is a race of Africans who will not endure bondage at all, and who, when smuggled from Africa into Louisiana, are avoided in the market by purchasers, though they have great bodily strength and comeliness. When one of this race is accidentally purchased and taken home, he is generally missed before twenty-four hours are over, and found hanging behind a door or drowned in the nearest pond. . . . On the other hand, the traveller may meet with a few negroes who have returned into slaveland from a state of freedom, and besought their masters to take them back.

These seeming contradictions admit of an easy explanation. Slaves are more or less degraded by slavery in proportion to their original strength of character or educational discipline of mind. The most degraded are satisfied, the least degraded are dissatisfied with slavery. The lowest order prefer release from duties and cares to the enjoyment of rights and the possession of themselves; and the highest order have a directly opposite taste. The mistake lies in not perceiving that slavery is emphatically condemned by the conduct of both.

The stories on the one side of the question are all alike. The master offers freedom—of course, to the worst of his slaves—to those who are more plague than profit. Perhaps he sends the fellow he wants to get rid of on some errand into a free state, hoping that he will not return. The man comes back; and, if questioned as to why he did not stay where he might have been free, he replies that he knows better than to work hard for a precarious living when he can be fed by his master without anxiety of his own as long as he lives. As for those who return after having been free, they are usually the weak-minded, who have been persuaded into remaining in a free state, where they have been carried in attendance on their masters' families, and who want courage to sustain their unprotected freedom. I do not remember ever hearing of the return of a slave who, having long nourished the idea and purpose of liberty, had absconded with danger and difficulty. The prosecution of such a purpose argues a strength of mind worthy of freedom. . . .

Slavery is nowhere more hopeless and helpless than in Alabama. The richness of the soil and the paucity of inhabitants make the labourer a most valuable possession; while his distance from any free state—the extent of country overspread with enemies which the fugitive has to traverse—makes the attempt to escape desperate. All coloured persons travelling in the slave states without a pass—a certificate of freedom or of leave—are liable to be arrested and advertised, and, if unclaimed at the end of a certain time, sold in the market. Yet slaves do continue to escape from the farthest corners of Alabama or Mississippi. Two slaves in Alabama, who had from their early manhood cherished the idea of freedom, planned their escape in concert, and laboured for many years at their scheme. They were allowed the profits of their labour at over-hours; and, by strenuous toil and self-denial, saved and hid a large sum of money. Last year they found they had enough, and that the time was come for the execution of their purpose. They engaged the services of "a mean white;" one of the extremely degraded class who are driven by loss of character to labour in the slave states, where, labour by whites being disgraceful, they are looked down upon by the slaves no less than the slaves are by the superior whites. These two slaves hired a "mean white man" to personate a gentleman; bought him a suit of good clothes, a portmanteau, a carriage and horses, and proper costume for themselves. One night the three set off in style, as master, coachman, and footman, and travelled rapidly through the whole country, without the slightest hinderance, to Buffalo. There the slaves sold their carriage, horses, and finery, paid off their white man, and escaped into Canada, where they now are in safety.

They found in Canada a society of their own colour prepared to welcome and aid them. In Upper Canada there are upward of ten thousand people of colour, chiefly fugitive slaves, who prosper in the country which they have chosen for a refuge. Scarcely an instance is known of any of them having received alms, and they are as respectable for their intelligence as for their morals. One peculiarity in them is the extravagance of their loyalty. They exert themselves vehemently in defence of all the acts of the executive, whatever they may be. The reason for this is obvious: they exceedingly dread the barest mention of the annexation of Canada to the United States.

It is astonishing that, in the face of facts of daily occurrence like that of the escape of these men, it can be pleaded in behalf of slavery that negroes cannot take care of themselves, and that they prefer being held as property. A lady of New York favoured me with some of her recollections of slavery in that state. She told me of a favourite servant who had been her father's property for five-and-twenty years. I believe the woman was the family nurse. She was treated with all possible indulgence, and was the object of the attachment of the whole household. The woman was never happy. During all these dreary years she was haunted with the longing for freedom, and at last fell ill, apparently from anxiety of mind. From her sick-bed she implored her master so movingly to make her free, and her medical attendant was so convinced that her life depended on her request being granted, that her master made the desired promise, but very unwillingly, as he thought freedom would be more of a care than a blessing to her. She immediately recovered, and in spite of all entreaty, pecuniary inducement, and appeals to her gratitude, left the family. She shed many tears, mourned over parting with the children, and thanked the family for all the favour with which she had been treated, but declared that she could not remain. Everything savoured too strongly of the bondage she had been unable to endure. She took a service not far off, deposited her earnings with her old master, and frequently visited the family, but, to the last, shrank from all mention of returning to them.

While I was in the United States, a New York friend of mine was counsel for a native African who sued his mistress for his earnings of many years. This man had been landed in the South after the year 1808, the date fixed by the Constitution for the cessation of the importation of negroes. He was purchased by a lady to whom he proved very profitable, his services being of a superior kind. She let him out, and he paid over to her all the money he earned. After many years she visited New York, bringing this man with her, not anticipating that, in that free city, he would gain new lights as to his relation to her. He refused to return, and brought his mistress into court to answer his demand for the repayment of all the money he had earned abroad, with interest, and compensation for his services at home during his illegal bondage. As a knowledge of the law was necessarily supposed on both sides, the counsel for the slave made compulsion his plea. This was not allowed. The slave's maintenance was decided to be a sufficient compensation for his services at home, and he was decreed to receive only the earnings of his hired labour, without interest. His counsel had, however, the pleasure of seeing him, in the strength of his manhood, free, and in possession of a large sum of money to begin life with on his own account. . . .

The energies of slaves sometimes take a direction which their masters contrive to render profitable, when they take to religion as a pursuit. The universal, unquenchable reverence for religion in the human mind is taken advantage of when the imagination of the slave has been turned into the channel of superstition. It is a fact, that in the newspapers of New Orleans may be seen an advertisement now and then of a lot of "pious negroes." Such "pious negroes" are convenient on a plantation where the treatment is not particularly mild; as they consider nonresistance a Christian duty, and are able to inspire a wonderful degree of patience into their fellow-sufferers.

The vigour which negroes show when their destiny is fairly placed in their own hands, is an answer to all arguments about their helplessness drawn from their dulness in a state of bondage. A highly satisfactory experiment upon the will, judgment, and talents of a large body of slaves was made a few years ago by a relative of Chief-justice Marshall. This gentleman and his family had attached their negroes to them by a long course of judicious kindness. At length an estate at some distance was left to the gentleman, and he saw, with much regret, that it was his duty to leave the plantation on which he was living. He could not bear the idea of turning over his people to the tender mercies or unproved judgment of a stranger overseer. He called his negroes together, told them the case, and asked whether they thought they could manage the estate themselves. If they were willing to undertake the task, they must choose an overseer from among themselves, provide comfortably for their own wants, and remit him the surplus of the profits. The negroes were full of grief at losing the family, but willing to try what they could do. They had an election for overseer, and chose the man their master would have pointed out; decidedly the strongest head on the estate. All being arranged, the master left them, with a parting charge to keep their festivals, and take their appointed holydays as if he were present. After some time he rode over to see how all went on, choosing a festival day, that he might meet them in their holyday gayety. He was surprised, on approaching, to hear no merriment; and, on entering his fields, he found his "force" all hard at work. As they flocked round him, he inquired why they were not making holyday. They told him that the crop would suffer in its present state by the loss of a day, and that they had therefore put off their holyday, which, however, they meant to take by-and-by. Not many days after an express arrived to inform the proprietor that there was an insurrection on his estate. He would not believe it; declared it impossible, as there was nobody to rise against; but the messenger, who had been sent by the neighbouring gentlemen, was so confident of the facts, that the master galloped, with the utmost speed, to his plantation, arriving as night was coming on. As he rode in a cry of joy arose from his negroes, who pressed round to shake hands with him. They were in their holyday clothes, and had been singing and dancing. They were only enjoying the deferred festival. The neighbours, hearing the noise on a quiet working day, had jumped to the conclusion that it was an insurrection.

There is no catastrophe yet to this story. When the proprietor related it, he said that no trouble had arisen; and that for some seasons, ever since this estate had been wholly in the hands of his negroes, it had been more productive than it ever was while he managed it himself.

The finest harvest-field of romance perhaps in the world is the frontier between the United States and Canada. The vowed student of human nature could not do better than take up his abode there, and hear what fugitives and their friends have to tell. There have been no exhibitions of the forces of human character in any political revolution or religious reformation more wonderful and more interesting than may almost daily be seen there. The impression on even careless minds on the spot is very strong. I remember observing to a friend in the ferry-boat, when we were crossing the Niagara from Lewistown to Queenstown, that it seemed very absurd, on looking at the opposite banks of the river, to think that, while the one belonged to the people who lived on it, the other was called the property of a nation three thousand miles off, the shores looking so much alike as they do. My friend replied with a smile, "Runaway slaves see a great difference." "That they do!" cried the ferryman, in a tone of the deepest earnestness. He said that the leap ashore of an escaped slave is a sight unlike any other that can be seen. . . .

New Orleans

When we arrived at the extreme southwest point of our journey, it was amusing to refer to the warnings of our kind friends about its inconveniences and dangers. We had brought away tokens of the hospitality of Charleston in the shape of a large basket of provision which had been prepared, on the supposition that we should find little that we could eat on the road. There was wine, tea, and cocoa; cases of French preserved meat, crackers (biscuits), and gingerbread. All these good things, except the wine and crackers, we found it expedient to leave behind, from place to place. There was no use in determining beforehand to eat them at any particular meal; when it came to the point, we always found hunger or disgust so much more bearable than the shame of being ungracious to entertainers who were doing their best for us, that we could never bring ourselves to produce our stores. We took what was set before us, and found ourselves, at length, alive and well at New Orleans. . . .

All was very new, very foreign in its aspect. Many of the ladies in the streets wore caps or veils instead of bonnets; the negroes who passed shouted their very peculiar kind of French; and everything seemed to tell us that we had plunged into the dogdays. I never knew before how impressions of heat can be conveyed through the eye. The intensity of glare and shadow in the streets, and the many evidences that the fear of heat is the prevailing idea of the place, affect the imagination even more than the scorching power of the sun does the bodily frame. . . .

The ladies of New Orleans walk more than their country-women of other cities, from the streets being in such bad order as to make walking the safest means of locomotion. The streets are not very numerous; they are well distinguished, and lie at right angles, and their names are clearly printed up; so that strangers find no difficulty in going about, except when a fall of rain has made the crossings impassable. The heat is far less oppressive in the streets than in the open country, as there is generally a shady side. We were never kept within doors by the heat, though summer weather had fairly set in before our arrival. We made calls, and went shopping and sight-seeing, much as we do in London; and, moreover, walked to dinner visits, to the theatre, and to church, while the sun was blazing as if he had drawn that part of the world some millions of miles nearer to himself than that in which we had been accustomed to live. It is in vain to attempt describing what the moonlight is like. We walked under the long rows of Pride-of-India trees on the Ramparts, amid the picturesque low dwellings of the Quadroons, and almost felt the glow of the moonlight, so warm, so golden, so soft as I never saw it elsewhere. We were never tired of watching the lightning from our balcony, flashing through the first shades of twilight, and keeping the whole heaven in night-long conflagration. The moschetoes were a great and perpetual plague, except while we were asleep. We found our moscheto-curtains a sufficient protection at night; but we had to be on the watch against these malicious insects all day, and to wage war against them during the whole evening. Many ladies are accustomed, during the summer months, to get after breakfast into a large sack of muslin tied round the throat, with smaller sacks for the arms, and to sit thus at work or book, fanning themselves to protect their faces. Others sit all the morning on the bed, within their moscheto-curtains. I wore gloves and prunella boots all day long, but hands and feet were stung through all the defences I could devise. . . .

Sunday is the busiest day of the week to the stranger in New Orleans. There is first the negro market to be seen at five o'clock. We missed this sight, as the mornings were foggy, and it was accounted unsafe to go out in the early damp. Then there is the Cathedral to be attended, a place which the European gladly visits, as the only one in the United States where all men meet together as brethren. As he goes, the streets are noisy with traffic. Some of those who keep the Sunday sit at their doors or windows reading the newspapers or chatting with their acquaintance. Merchants are seen hastening to the counting-house or the wharf, or busy in the stores. Others are streaming into the church doors. There are groups about the Cathedral gates, the blacks and the whites parting company as if they had not been worshipping side by side. Within the edifice there is no separation. Some few persons may be in pews; but kneeling on the pavement may be seen a multitude, of every shade of complexion, from the fair Scotchwoman or German to the jet-black pure African. The Spanish eye flashes from beneath the veil; the French creole countenance, painted high, is surmounted by the neat cap or the showy bonnet; while between them may be thrust a gray-headed mulatto, following with his stupid eyes the evolutions of the priest; or the devout negro woman telling her beads —a string of berries—as if her life depended on her task. During the preaching, the multitude of anxious faces, thus various in tint and expression, turned up towards the pulpit, afforded one of those few spectacles which are apt to haunt the whole future life of the observer like a dream. . . .

I was persuaded that, if a ritual religion be ever a good, it is so in the case of the most, not the least, enlightened; if those who accept the ritual as symbolical, and not of those who pay it literal worship. I could not but think that, if the undisguised story of Jesus were presented to these last as it was to the fishermen of Galilee and the peasants on the reedy banks of Jordan, they would embrace a Christianity, in comparison with which their present religion is an unintelligible and effectual mythology. But such a primitive Christianity they, as slaves, never will and never can have, as its whole spirit is destructive of slavery. . . .

Whatever may be thought of the duty or expediency of a strict observance of the Sunday, no one can contend that in this city the observance is strict. In the market there is traffic in meat and vegetables, and the groups of foreigners make a Babel of the place with their loud talk in many tongues. The men are smoking outside their houses; the girls, with broad coloured ribands streaming from the ends of their long braids of hair, are walking or flirting; while veiled ladies are stealing through the streets, or the graceful Quadroon women are taking their evening airing on the Levée. The river is crowded with shipping, to the hulls of which the walkers look up from a distance, the river being above the level of the neighbouring streets. It rushes along through the busy region, seeming to be touched with mercy, or to disdain its power of mischief. It might overwhelm in an instant the swarming inhabitants of the boundless level; it looks as if it could scarcely avoid doing so; yet it rolls on within its banks so steadily, that the citizens forget their insecurity. . . .

The road to the lake winds for five miles through the swamp, and is bordered by cypress, flowering reeds, fleurs-de-lis of every colour, palmetto, and a hundred aquatic shrubs new to the eye of the stranger. The gray moss common in damp situations floats in streamers from the branches. . . . It was along this road that Madame Lalaurie escaped from the hands of her exasperated countrymen about five years ago. . . . I was requested on the spot not to publish it as exhibiting a fair specimen of slaveholding in New Orleans, and no one could suppose it to be so; but it is a revelation of what may happen in a slaveholding country, and can happen nowhere else. Even on the mildest supposition that the case admits of, that Madame Lalaurie was insane, there remains the fact that the insanity could have taken such a direction, and perpetrated such deeds nowhere but in a slave country. . . .

Madame Lalaurie . . . was a French creole, and her third husband, M. Lalaurie, was, I believe, a Frenchman. He was many years younger than his lady, and had nothing to do with the management of her property, so that he has been in no degree mixed up with her affairs and disgraces. It had been long observed that Madame Lalaurie's slaves looked singularly haggard and wretched, except the coachman, whose appearance was sleek and comfortable enough. Two daughters by a former marriage, who lived with her, were also thought to be spiritless and unhappy-looking. But the lady was so graceful and accomplished, so charming in her manners and so hospitable, that no one ventured openly to question her perfect goodness. If a murmur of doubt began among the Americans, the French resented it. If the French had occasional suspicions, they concealed them for the credit of their faction. "She was very pleasant to whites," I was told, and sometimes to blacks, but so broadly so as to excite suspicions of hypocrisy. When she had a dinner-party at home, she would hand the remains of her glass of wine to the emaciated negro behind her chair, with a smooth audible whisper, "Here, my friend, take this; it will do you good." At length rumours spread which induced a friend of mine, an eminent lawyer, to send her a hint about the law which ordains that slaves who can be proved to have been cruelly treated shall be taken from the owner, and sold in the market for the benefit of the State. My friend, being of the American party, did not appear in the matter himself, but sent a young French creole, who was studying law with him. The young man returned full of indignation against all who could suspect this amiable woman of doing anything wrong. He was confident that she could not harm a fly, or give pain to any human being.

Soon after this a lady, living in a house which joined the premises of Madame Lalaurie, was going up stairs, when she heard a piercing shriek from the next courtyard. She looked out, and saw a little negro girl, apparently about eight years old, flying across the yard towards the house, and Madame Lalaurie pursuing her, cowhide in hand. The lady saw the poor child run from story to story, her mistress following, till both came out upon the top of the house. Seeing the child about to spring over, the witness put her hands before her eyes; but she heard the fall, and saw the child taken up, her body bending and limbs hanging as if every bone was broken. The lady watched for many hours, and at night she saw the body brought out, a shallow hole dug by torchlight in the corner of the yard, and the corpse covered over. No secret was made of what had been seen. Inquiry was instituted, and illegal cruelty proved in the case of nine slaves, who were forfeited according to law. It afterward came out that this woman induced some family connexions of her own to purchase these slaves, and sell them again to her, conveying them back to her premises in the night. She must have desired to have them for purposes of torture, for she could not let them be seen in a neighbourhood where they were known.

During all this time she does not appear to have lost caste, though it appears that she beat her daughters as often as they attempted in her absence to convey food to her miserable victims. She always knew of such attempts by means of the sleek coachman, who was her spy. It was necessary to have a spy, to preserve her life from the vengeance of her household; so she pampered this obsequious negro, and at length owed her escape to him.

She kept her cook chained within eight yards of the fireplace, where sumptuous dinners were cooked in the most sultry season. It is a pity that some of the admiring guests whom she assembled round her hospitable table could not see through the floor, and be made aware at what a cost they were entertained. One morning the cook declared that they had better all be burned together than lead such a life, and she set the house on fire. The alarm spread over the city; the gallant French creoles all ran to the aid of their accomplished friend, and the fire was presently extinguished. Many, whose curiosity had been roused about the domestic proceedings of the lady, seized the opportunity of entering those parts of the premises from which the whole world had been hitherto carefully excluded. They perceived that, as often as they approached a particular outhouse, the lady became excessively uneasy lest some property in an opposite direction should be burned. When the fire was extinguished, they made bold to break open this outhouse. A horrible sight met their eyes. Of the nine slaves, the skeletons of two were afterward found poked into the ground; the other seven could scarcely be recognised as human. Their faces had the wildness of famine, and their bones were coming through the skin. They were chained and tied in constrained postures, some on their knees, some with their hands above their heads. They had iron collars with spikes which kept their heads in one position. The cowhide, stiff with blood, hung against the wall; and there was a stepladder on which this fiend stood while flogging her victims, in order to lay on the lashes with more effect. Every morning, it was her first employment after breakfast to lock herself in with her captives, and flog them till her strength failed.

Amid shouts and groans, the sufferers were brought out into the air and light. Food was given them with too much haste, for two of them died in the course of the day. The rest, maimed and helpless, are pensioners of the city.

The rage of the crowd, especially of the French creoles, was excessive. The lady shut herself up in the house with her trembling daughters, while the street was filled from end to end with a yelling crowd of gentlemen. She consulted her coachman as to what she had best do. He advised that she should have her coach to the door after dinner, and appear to go forth for her afternoon drive, as usual; escaping or returning, according to the aspect of affairs. It is not told whether she ate her dinner that day, or prevailed on her remaining slaves to wait upon her. The carriage appeared at the door; she was ready, and stepped into it. Her assurance seems to have paralyzed the crowd. The moment the door was shut they appeared to repent having allowed her to enter, and they tried to upset the carriage, to hold the horses, to make a snatch at the lady. But the coachman laid about him with his whip, made the horses plunge, and drove off. He took the road to the lake, where he could not be intercepted, as it winds through the swamp. He outstripped the crowd, galloped to the lake, bribed the master of a schooner which was lying there to put off instantly with the lady to Mobile. She escaped to France, and took up her abode in Paris under a feigned name, but not for long. Late one evening a party of gentlemen called on her, and told her she was Madame Lalaurie, and that she had better be off. She fled that night, and is supposed to be now skulking about in some French province under a false name.

The New Orleans mob met the carriage returning from the lake. What became of the coachman I do not know. The carriage was broken to pieces and thrown into the swamp, and the horses stabbed and left dead upon the road. The house was gutted, the two poor girls having just time to escape from a window. They are now living, in great poverty, in one of the faubourgs. The piano, tables, and chairs were burned before the house. The feather-beds were ripped up, and the feathers emptied into the street, where they afforded a delicate footing for some days. The house stands, and is meant to stand, in its ruined state. It was the strange sight of its gaping windows and empty walls, in the midst of a busy street, which excited my wonder, and was the cause of my being told the story the first time. I gathered other particulars afterward from eyewitnesses.

The crowd at first intended to proceed to the examination of other premises, whose proprietors were under suspicion of cruelty to their slaves; but the shouts of triumph which went up from the whole negro population of the city showed that this would not be safe. Fearing a general rising, the gentlemen organized themselves into a patrol, to watch the city night and day till the commotion should have subsided. They sent circulars to all proprietors suspected of cruelty, warning them that the eyes of the city were upon them. This is the only benefit the negroes have derived from the exposure. In reply to inquiries, I was told that it was very possible that cruelties like those of Madame Lalaurie might be incessantly in course of perpetration. It may be doubted whether any more such people exist; but if they do, there is nothing to prevent their following her example with impunity as long as they can manage to preserve that secrecy which was put an end to by accident in her case.

I could never get out of the way of the horrors of slavery in this region. Under one form or another, they met me in every house, in every street; everywhere but in the intelligence pages of newspapers, where I might read on in perfect security of exemption from the subject. In the advertising columns there were offers of reward for runaways, restored dead or alive; and notices of the capture of a fugitive with so many brands on his limbs and shoulders, and so many scars on his back. But from the other half of the newspaper, the existence of slavery could be discovered only by inference. . . .

The stranger has great difficulty in satisfying himself as to the bounds of the unconsciousness of oppression which he finds urged as the exculpatory plea of the slaveholder, while he mourns over it as the great hinderance in the way of social reformation. It has been seen that an audience at the theatre will quietly receive a hit which would subject the author to punishment if he were an abolitionist. When I listened to the stories told by ladies to each other in their morning calls, showing the cleverness of their slaves, I often saw that they could not but be as fully convinced as I was that their slaves were as altogether human as themselves. . . .

I was sought by some, and met accidentally with other persons who were on the eve of departure for Texas. Attempts were made to induce me to go myself, and also to convince me of the eligibility of the country as a place of settlement for British emigrants, in the hope that the arrival of a cargo of settlers from England might afford to the Texans a plea of countenance from the British government. The subject of Texas is now so well understood, that there is no occasion to enlarge upon the state of the question as it was two years and a half ago; and besides, if I were to give a precise account of the conversations between myself and the friends of the Texan aggression, my story would not be believed. The folly and romance of some of the agents employed, and the villainy which peeped out of every admission extorted from the advocates of the scheme, would make my readers as astonished as I was myself, that any attempts should be made in the neighbourhood of the scene to gain the sympathy of strangers who were at all above the rank of knaves and fools. Suffice it that one class of advocates told me that I should be perfectly safe there, as the inhabitants were chiefly persons who could fight bravely against the Mexicans, from having nothing to lose, and from their having been compelled to leave the United States by their too free use of arms: while the opposite species of agent enlarged, not only on the beauty of the sunsets and the greenness of the savannahs, but on the delightful security of living under the same laws as the people of the United States, and amid a condition of morals kept perfectly pure by Colonel Austin's[9] practice of having every person whom he conceived to have offended whipped at the cart's tail; the fact being carefully concealed that Colonel Austin was at that time, and had been for two years, in jail in the Mexican capital. . . .

After eleven days of housekeeping in New Orleans we were obliged to depart, having been fortunate enough to secure berths in a capital boat which started northward on the 6th of May. The slaves in our temporary abode had served us intelligently and well. Wishing to see what they could do, we did not give any orders about our table. We were rarely at home at dinner, but our breakfasts and occasional dinners were more luxurious than if we had provided for ourselves. Excellent coffee, French bread, radishes, and strawberries at breakfast; and at dinner, broth, fowls, beefsteak, with peas, young asparagus, salad, new potatoes, and spinach, all well cooked; claret at dinner, and coffee worthy of Paris after it; this was the kind of provision with which we were favoured. Everything was done to make us cool. The beds were literally as hard as the floor. We had a bath of the coldest water prepared morning and night; all the doors and windows were kept open, and the curtains drawn, to establish draughts and keep out

[9]Colonel Stephen Fuller Austin, who established an American colony in Mexican territory on the site of the present city of Austin.

the sun. There was ice in the water-jug, ice on the lump of butter, ice in the wineglass, and icecream for dessert.

Abroad, all was, as in every other American city, hospitality and gayety. I had rather dreaded the visit to New Orleans, and went more from a sense of duty than from inclination. A friendship that I formed there, though already eclipsed by death, left me no feeling but rejoicing that I had gone; and I also learned much that was useful in helping me to interpret some things which met my observation both previously and subsequently. But my strongest impression of New Orleans is, that while it affords an instructive study, and yields some enjoyment to a stranger, it is the last place in which men are gathered together where one who prizes his humanity would wish to live.

Compromise

The greatest advantage of long life, at least to those who know how and wherefore to live, is the opportunity which it gives of seeing moral experiments worked out, of being present at the fructification of social causes, and of thus gaining a kind of wisdom which in ordinary cases seems reserved for a future life. An equivalent for this advantage is possessed by such as live in those critical periods of society when retribution is hastened, or displayed in clear connexion with the origin of its events. The present seems to be such an age. It is an age in which the societies of the whole world are daily learning the consequences of what their fathers did, the connexion of cause and effect being too palpable to be disputed; it is an age when the active men of the New World are beholding the results of their own early counsels and deeds. It seems, indeed, as if the march of events were everywhere accelerated for a time, so as to furnish some who are not aged with a few complete pieces of experience. Some dispensation—like the political condition of France, for instance—will still be centuries in the working out; but in other cases—the influence of eminent men, for example—results seem to follow more closely than in the slower and quieter past ages of the world. It is known to all how in England, and also in America, the men of the greatest intellectual force have sunk from a higher to a far lower degree of influence from the want of high morals. It seems as if no degree of talent and vigour can long avail to keep a man eminent in either politics or literature, unless his morals are also above the average. Selfish vanity, double-dealing, supreme regard to expediency, are as fatal to the most gifted men in these days, and almost as speedily fatal, as intellectual capacity to a pretender. Men of far inferior knowledge and power rise over their heads in the strength of honesty; and by dint of honesty (positive or comparative) retain the supremacy, even through a display of intellectual weakness and error of which the fallen make their sport. This is a cheering sign of the times, indicating that the days are past when men were possessed by their leaders, and that the time is coming when power will be less unfairly distributed, and held on a better tenure than it has been. It indicates that traitors and oppressors will not, in future, be permitted to work their will and compass their purposes at the expense of others, till guilty will and purpose are prostrated on the threshold of eternity. It indicates that that glorious and beautiful spectacle of judgment may be beheld in this world which religious men have referred to another, when the lowly shall be exalted; when, unconscious of their dignity, they shall, with amazement, hear themselves greeted as the blessed of the Father. . . .

However long it may be before the last shred of tinsel may be cast into the fire, and the last chaff of false pretence winnowed away, the revolution is good and secure as far as it goes. Moral power has begun its long series of conquests over physical force and selfish cunning, and the diviner part of man is a guarantee that not one inch of the ground gained shall ever be lost. For our encouragement, we are presented with a more condensed evidence of retribution than has hitherto been afforded to the world. Moral causes seem to be quickened as well as strengthened in their operation by the new and more earnest heed which is given to them.

In the New World, however long some moral causes may be in exhibiting their results, there have been certain deeds done which have produced their consequences with extraordinary rapidity and an indisputable clearness. May all men open their eyes to see them, and their hearts to understand them!

The people of the United States were never under a greater temptation to follow temporary expediency in preference to everlasting principle than in the case of the admission of Missouri, with slave institutions, into the Union. To this temptation they yielded, by a small majority of their representatives. The final decision rested, as it happened, in the hands of one man, Mr. Clay; but it is to the shame of the North (which had abolished slavery) that it did so happen. The decision was made to prefer custom and expediency to principle; it was hoped that, if the wind were once got under confinement, something would prevent its bursting forth as the whirlwind.

The plea of slaveholders, and a plausible one up to the year 1820, was that slavery was not an institution of their choice or for which they were answerable: it was an inherited institution. Since the year 1820 this plea has become hypocrisy; for in that year a deliberate vote was passed by Congress to perpetuate slavery in the Union by admitting a new state whose institutions had this basis. The new states northwest of the Ohio were prohibited from introducing slavery by the very act of cession of the land; and nothing could have been easier than to procure the exclusion of slavery from Missouri by simply refusing to admit any new state whose distinguishing institution was one incompatible in principle with the principles on which the American Constitution was founded. Missouri would undoubtedly have surrendered slavery, been admitted, and virtuously flourished, like her neighbour Illinois. But there was division of opinion; and, because the political device of the Union seemed in danger, the eternal principles of justice were set aside, and protection was deliberately pledged to slavery, not only in Missouri, but, as a consequence, in Arkansas and Florida. The Constitution and Declaration of Rights of Missouri, therefore, exhibit the following singular mixture of declarations and provisions. It will be seen afterward how they are observed.

"The general assembly shall not have power to pass laws,

"1. For the emancipation of slaves without the consent of the owners; or without paying them, before such emancipation, a full equivalent for such slaves so emancipated; and,

"2. To prevent *bonâ fide* emigrants to this state, or actual settlers therein, from bringing from any of the United States, or from any of their territories, such persons as may there be deemed to be slaves, so long as any persons of the same description are allowed to be held as slaves by the laws of this state.

"It shall be their duty, as soon as may be, to pass such laws as may be necessary,

"1. To prevent free negroes and mulattoes from coming to and settling in this state, under any pretext whatsoever.

"Schools and the means of education shall for ever be encouraged in this state.

"That the right of trial by jury shall remain inviolate.

"That the accused cannot be deprived of life, liberty, or property, but by the judgment of his peers or the law of the land.

"That cruel and unusual punishments shall not be inflicted.

"That the free communication of thoughts and opinions is one of the invaluable rights of man, and that every person may freely speak, write, and print on any subject, being responsible for the abuse of that liberty."

The consequences of the compromise began to show themselves first in the difference between the character of the population in Missouri and Illinois, the latter of which is two years older than the former. They lie opposite each other on the Mississippi, and both are rich in advantages of soil, climate, and natural productions. They showed, however, social differences from the very beginning of their independent career, which are becoming more striking every day. Rapacious adventurers, who know that the utmost profit of slaves is made by working them hard on a virgin soil, began flocking to Missouri, while settlers who preferred smaller gains to holding slaves sat down in Illinois. When it was found, as it soon was, that slavery does not answer so well in the farming parts of Missouri as on the new plantations of the South, a farther difference took place. New settlers perceived that, in point of immediate interest merely, the fine lands of Missouri were less worth having, with the curse of slavery upon them, than those of Illinois without it. In vain has the price of land been lowered in Missouri as that in Illinois rose. Settlers go first and look at the cheaper land; some remain upon it; but many recross the river and settle in the rival state. This enrages the people of Missouri. Their soreness and jealousy, combined with other influences of slavery, so exasperate their prejudices against the people of colour as to give a perfectly diabolical character to their hatred of negroes and the friends of negroes. That such is the temper of those who conduct popular action in the state is shown by some events which happened in the year 1836. In the very bottom of the souls of the American statesmen who admitted Missouri on unrighteous terms, these events must kindle a burning comparison between what the social condition of the frontier states of their honourable Union is and what it might have been.

A man of colour in St. Louis was arrested for some offence, and rescued by a free man of his own colour, a citizen of Pennsylvania, named Mackintosh, who was steward on board a steamboat then at St. Louis. Mackintosh was conveyed to jail for rescuing his comrade, whose side of the question we have no means of knowing. Mackintosh appears to have been a violent man, or, at least, to have been in a state of desperation at the time that he was on his way to jail, guarded by two peace-officers. He drew a knife from his side (almost every man on the western frontier being accustomed to carry arms), killed one of the officers, and wounded the other. He was immediately lodged in the prison. The wife and children of the murdered officer bewailed him in the street, and excited the rage of the people against Mackintosh. Some of the citizens acknowledged to me that his colour was the provocation which aggravated their rage so far beyond what it had ever been in somewhat similar cases of personal violence, and that no one would have dreamed of treating any white man as this mulatto was treated. The citizens assembled round the jail in the afternoon, demanding the prisoner, and the jailer delivered him up. He was led into the woods on the outskirts of the city; and, when there, they did not know what to do with him. While deliberating they tied him to a tree. This seemed to suggest the act which followed. A voice cried out, "Burn him!" Many tongues echoed the cry. Brushwood was rooted up, and a heap of green wood piled about the man. Who furnished the fire does not seem to be known. Between two and three thousand of the citizens of St. Louis were present. Two gentlemen of the place assured me that the deed was done by the hands of not more than six; but they could give no account of the reasons why the two or three thousand stood by in silence to behold the act of the six, further than that they were afraid to interfere! . . .

I saw the first notice which was given of this in the St. Louis newspapers. The paragraph briefly related that a ruffian of colour had murdered a citizen, had been demanded by the indignant fellow-citizens of the murdered man, and burned in the neighbourhood of the city; that this unjustifiable act was to be regretted, but that it was hoped that the veil of oblivion would be drawn over the deed. Some of the most respectable of the citizens were in despair when they found that the newspapers of the Union generally were disposed to grant the last request; and it is plain that, on the spot, no one dared to speak out about the act. The charge of Judge Lawless (his real name) to the grand jury is a sufficient commentary upon the state of St. Louis society. He told the jury that a bad and lamentable deed had been committed in burning a man alive without trial, but that it was quite another question whether they were to take any notice of it. If it should be proved to be the act of the few, every one of those few ought undoubtedly to be indicted and punished; but if it should be proved to be the act of the many, incited by that electric and metaphysical influence which occasionally carries on a multitude to do deeds above and beyond the law, it was no affair for a jury to interfere in. He spoke of Mackintosh as connected with the body of abolitionists. Of course, the affair was found to be electric and metaphysical, and all proceedings were dropped.

All proceedings in favour of law and order; others of an opposite character were vigorously instituted by magistrates, in defiance of some of those clauses of the constitution which I have quoted above. The magistrates of St. Louis prosecuted a domiciliary inquisition into the periodical publications of the city, visiting the newspaper offices, prying and threatening, and offering rewards for the discovery of any probability that the institution of slavery would be spoken against in print. In the face of the law, the press was rigidly controlled.

Information was given, while the city was in this excited state, of every indication of favour to the coloured people, and of disapprobation of slavery; and the savages of St. Louis were on the alert to inflict vengeance. In Marion College, Palmyra (Missouri), two students were undoubtedly guilty of teaching two coloured boys to read. These boys were carried by them to the college for service, the one being employed on the farm, and the other in the college, to clean shoes and wait on the young men. One afternoon a large number of citizens from St. Louis, well mounted, appeared on the Palmyra road, and they made no secret of their intention to Lynch the two students who taught their servants to read. The venerable Dr. Nelson, who was, I believe, at the head of the institution, came out of his house to implore the mob with tears not to proceed, and the ladies of his family threw themselves down in the road in the way of the horses. The way was forcibly cleared, and the persecutors proceeded. The young men came forth as soon as summoned. They were conducted to the edge of the forest where it opens upon a prairie. There a circle was formed, and they were told that they stood in a Lynch court.

The younger one was first set in the midst. He acknowledged the act with which he was charged. He was offered the alternative of receiving twenty lashes with the horrid cowhide (which was shown him), or of immediately leaving the state for ever. He engaged to leave the state for ever, and was set across the river into Illinois.

The elder student made his trial a longer one. He acknowledged the act of teaching his servant to read, and made himself heard while he defended it. He pleaded that he was a citizen of Missouri, being of age, and having exercised the suffrage at the last election. He demanded a fair trial in a court of law, and pledged himself to meet any accusation there. At last it came to their binding him to a tree, and offering him the choice of two hundred lashes with the cowhide, or of promising to leave the state, and never to return to it. He knew that a sentence of two hundred lashes meant death by torture (it is so understood in Lynch courts), and he knew that a promise thus extorted was not binding; so he promised. He was also set across the river, where he immediately published a narrative of the whole transaction, and declared his intention of returning to his state, to resume the duties and privileges of citizenship, as soon as he could be personally safe.

The St. Louis Lynchers next ordered the heads of Marion College to hold a public meeting, and declare their convictions and feelings on the subject of slavery. They were obeyed, and they put pretty close questions to the professors, especially to Dr. Ely, who was a suspected man.

Dr. Ely came from one of the Eastern states, and was considered by the abolitionists of his own religious persuasion to be one of their body. Some time after he went into Missouri, it appeared incidentally in some newspaper communciations that he had bought a slave. His friends at the East resented the imputation, and were earnest in his vindication; but were presently stopped and thrown into amazement by his coming out with an acknowledgment and defence of the act. He thought that the way in which he could do most good was by purchasing negroes for purposes of enlightenment. So he bought his man Abraham, designing to enlighten him for nine years, and then set him free, employing the proceeds of his nine years' labour in purchasing two other slaves, to be enlightened and robbed in the same manner, for the purpose of purchasing four more at the expiration of another series of years, and so on. It seems astonishing that a clergyman should thus deliberately propose to confer his charities through the medium of the grossest injustice: but so it was. When, at the enforced meeting, he was questioned by the Lynchers as to his principles, he declared himself opposed to the unchristian fanaticism of abolitionism; spurned the imputation of being one of the body, and, in proof of his sincerity, declared himself to be the master of one slave, and to be already contracting for more.

The Lynchers returned to St. Louis without having committed murder. They had triumphantly broken the laws, and trodden under foot their constitution of sixteen years old. If it could be made known at what expense they were saved from bloodshed; if it could be revealed what violence they offered to conscience, what feelings they lacerated, what convictions they stifled, what passions they kindled, what an undying worm they fixed at the core of many a heart, at the root of many a life, it might have been clear to all eyes that the halter and the cowhide would have been mercy in comparison with the tortures with which they strewed their way.

I have told enough to show what comes of compromise. There is no need to lengthen out my story of persecutions. I will just mention that the last news from Missouri that I saw was in the form of an account of the proceedings of its legislature, but which yet seems to me incredible. It is stated to have been enacted that any person of any complexion, coming into or found in the State of Missouri, who shall be proved to have spoken, written, or printed a word in disapprobation of slavery or in favour of abolition, shall be sold into slavery for the benefit of the state. If, in the fury of the moment, such a law should really have been passed, it must speedily be repealed. The general expectation is that slavery itself will soon be abolished in Missouri, as it is found to be unprofitable and perilous, and a serious drawback to the prosperity of the region.

What a lesson is meantime afforded as to the results of compromise! Missouri might now have been a peaceful and orderly region, inhabited by settlers as creditable to their country as those of the neighbouring free states, instead of being a nest of vagabond slavedealers, rapacious slave-drivers, and ferocious rioters. If the inhabitants think it hard that all should be included in a censure which only some have deserved, they must bestir themselves to show in their legislature, and by their improved social order, that the majority are more respectable than they have yet shown themselves to be. At present it seems as if one who might have been a prophet preaching in the wilderness had preferred the profession of a bandit of the desert. But it should never be forgotten whence came the power to inflict injury, by a permission being given where there should have been a prohibition. Whatever danger there ever was to the Union from difference of opinion on the subject of the compromise is now increased. The battle has still to be fought at a greater disadvantage than when a bad deed was done to avert it.

Cincinnati

We reached Cincinnati by descending the Ohio from Maysville, Kentucky, whence we took passage in the first boat going down to the great City of the West. It happened to be an inferior boat; but, as we were not to spend a night on board, this was of little consequence. . . .

Some time after dark we came in sight of long rows of yellow lights, with a flaring and smoking furnace here and there, which seemed to occupy a space of nearly two miles from the wharf where we at length stopped. . . .

After waiting some time in the boat for the arrival of a hack, we proceeded up the steep pavement above the wharf to the Broadway Hotel and Boarding-house. There we were requested to register our names, and were then presented with the cards of some of the inhabitants who had called to inquire for us. We were well and willingly served, and I went to rest intensely thankful to be once more out of sight of slavery.

The next morning was bright, and I scarcely remember a pleasanter day during all my travels than this 16th of June. We found ourselves in a large boarding-house, managed by a singularly zealous and kindly master. . . . The ladies at the breakfast-table looked somewhat vulgar; and it is undeniable that the mustard was spilled, and that the relics of the meal were left in some disorder by the gentlemen who were most in a hurry to be off to business. But every one was obliging; and I saw at that table a better thing than I saw at any other table in the United States, a lady of colour breakfasting in the midst of us! . . .

The first of our visiters was an English gentleman, who was settled in business in Cincinnati. He immediately undertook a commission of inquiry, with which I had been charged from England, about a family of settlers, and sent me a pile of new books, and tickets for a concert which was to be held in Mrs. Trollope's bazar the next evening but one. He was followed by . . . Dr. Drake, the first physician in the place; and Miss Beecher,[10] daughter of the Rev. Dr. Beecher, head of Lane Seminary, near Cincinnati, then on his trial for heresy, and justly confident of acquittal. Miss Beecher is a lady eminent for learning and talents, and for her zeal in the cause of education. These were followed by several merchants, with their ladies, sisters, and daughters. The impression their visits left on our minds was of high respect for the society of Cincinnati, if these were, in manners, dress, and conversation, fair specimens. Dr. Drake and his daughter proposed to call for us for an afternoon's drive, and take us home to tea with them; a plan to which we gladly agreed. . . .

Dr. Drake took us for a delightful drive, the pleasure of which was much enhanced by his very interesting conversation. He is a complete and favourable specimen of a Westerner. He entered Ohio just forty-seven years before this time, when there were not above a hundred white persons in the state, and they all French, and when the shores were one expanse of canebrake, infested by buffalo. He had seen the foundations of the great city laid; he had watched its growth till he was now able to point out to the stranger, not only the apparatus for the exportation of 6,000,000 dollars' worth a year of produce and manufactures, but things which he values far more: the ten or twelve edifices erected for the use of the common schools, the new church of St. Paul, the two fine banking-houses, and the hundred and fifty handsome private dwellings, all the creations of the year 1835. He points to the periodicals, the respectable monthlies, and the four daily and six weekly papers of the city. He looks with a sort of paternal complacency on the 35,000 inhabitants, scarcely one of whom is without the comforts of life, the means of education, and a bright prospect for the future. Though a true Westerner, and devoutly believing the *buckeyes* (natives of Ohio) to be superior to all others of God's creatures, he hails every accession of intelligent members to his darling society. He observed to me, with his calm enthusiasm (the concomitant of a conviction which has grown out of experience rather than books), on the good effects of emigration on the posterity of emigrants; and told how, with the same apparent means of education, they surpass the descendants of natives. They combine the influences of two countries. Thus believing, he carries a cheerful face into the homes of his Welsh, Irish, English, German, and Yankee patients; he bids them welcome,

[10]Catherine, elder sister of Harriet Beecher Stowe.

and says, from the bottom of his heart, that he is glad to see them. His knowledge of the case of the emigrant enables him to alleviate, more or less, with the power which an honest and friendly physician carries about with him, an evil which he considers the worst that attends emigration. He told me that, unless the head of the emigrant family be timely and judiciously warned, the peace of the household is broken up by the pining of the wife. The husband soon finds interests in his new abode; he becomes a citizen, a man of business, a man of consequence, with brightening prospects; while the poor wife, surrounded by difficulties or vexed with hardships at home, provided with no compensation for what she has left behind, pines away, and wonders that her husband can be so happy when she is so miserable. When there is an end of congeniality, all is over; and a couple who would in their own land have gone through life cheerily, hand in hand, become uneasy yoke-fellows in the midst of a much-improved outward condition or prospect. . . .

The doctor had at present a patient in Dr. Beecher's house, so we returned by the Theological Seminary. Dr. Beecher and his daughters were not at home. We met them on the road in their cart, the ladies returning from their school in the city, and we spent an evening there the next week. The seminary (Presbyterian) was then in a depressed condition, in consequence of the expulsion of most of the pupils for their refusal to avoid discussion of the slavery question. These expelled youths have since been founders and supporters of abolition societies; and the good cause has gained even more than the seminary has lost by the absurd tyranny practised against the students. . . .

The teatable was set out in the garden at Dr. Drake's. We were waited upon, for the first time for many months, by a free servant. The long grass grew thick under our feet; fireflies were flitting about us, and I doubted whether I had ever heard more sense and eloquence at any Old World tea-table than we were entertained with as the twilight drew on.

As we walked home through the busy streets, where there was neither the apathy of the South nor the disorder consequent on the presence of a pauper class, I felt strongly tempted to jump to some hasty conclusions about the happiness of citizenship in Cincinnati. I made a virtuous determination to suspend every kind of judgment: but I found each day as exhilarating as the first, and, when I left the city, my impressions were much like what they were after an observation of twenty-four hours. . . .

The most threatening evil to Cincinnati is from that faithlessness which manifests itself in illiberality. . . . One direction in which this illiberality shows itself is towards the Catholics. The Catholic religion spreads rapidly in many or most of the recently-settled parts of the United States, and its increase produces an almost insane dread among some Protestants, who fail to see that no evils that the Catholic religion can produce in the present state of society can be so afflictive and dangerous as the bigotry by which it is proposed to put it down. The removal to Cincinnati of Dr. Beecher, the ostentatious and virulent foe of the Catholics, has much quickened the spirit of alarm in that region. It is to be hoped that Dr. Beecher and the people of Cincinnati will remember what has been the invariable consequence in America of public denunciations of assumed offences which the law does not reach; namely, mobbing. It is to be hoped that all parties will remember that Dr. Beecher preached in Boston three sermons vituperative of the Catholics the Sunday before the burning of the Charlestown convent by a Boston mob. Circumstances may also have shown them by this time how any kind of faith grows under persecution; and, above all, it may be hoped that the richer classes of citizens will become more aware than they have yet proved themselves to be of their republican (to say nothing of their human) obligation to refrain from encroaching, in the smallest particulars, on their brethren's rights of opinion and liberty of conscience. . . .

Cambridge Commencement

The Pilgrim Fathers early testified to the value of education. "When New England was poor, and they were but few in number, there was a spirit to encourage learning." One of their primary requisitions, first by custom and then by law, was, "That none of the brethren shall suffer so much barbarism in their families as not to teach their children and apprentices so much learning as may enable them perfectly to read the English tongue." They next ordered, "To the end that learning may not be buried in the graves of our forefathers, every township, after the Lord hath increased them to the number of fifty householders, shall appoint one to teach all children to write and read; and where any town shall increase to the number of one hundred families, they shall set up a grammar-school, the masters thereof being able to instruct youth so far as they may be fitted for the University."

This university was Harvard. In 1636 the General Court had voted a sum equal to a year's rate of the whole colony towards the erection of a college. Two years afterward, John Harvard, who arrived at the settlements only to die, left to the infant institution one half of his estate and all his library. The state set apart for the college the rent of a ferry. The wealthiest men of the community gave presents which were thought profuse at the time, and beside their names in the record stand entries of humbler gifts; from each family in the colonies twelvepence, or a peck of corn, or an equivalent in wampum-peag; and from individuals the sums of five shillings, nine shillings, one pound, and two pounds. There were legacies also; from one colonist a flock of sheep; from another cotton cloth worth nine shillings; from others a pewter flagon worth ten shillings, a fruit-dish, a sugar-spoon, a silver-tipped jug, one great salt, one small trencher salt. Afterward the celebrated Theophilus Gale bequeathed his library to the college; and in 1731 Bishop Berkeley, after visiting the institution, presented it with some of the Greek and Latin classics.

The year following John Harvard's bequest the Cambridge printing-press was set up, the only press in America north of Mexico. The General Court appointed licensers of this press, and did not scruple to interfere with the licensers themselves when any suspicion of heresy occurred to torment the minds of the worthy fathers. . . .

When I was at Boston the state of the University was a subject of great mourning among its friends. Attempts had been made to obtain the services of three gentlemen of some eminence as professors, but in vain. The salaries offered were insufficient to maintain the families of these gentlemen in comfort, in such a place as Cambridge; though, at that very time, the managers of the affairs of the institution were purchasing lands in Maine. . . .

The number of undergraduates in the years 1833, 4 was two hundred and sixteen. They cannot live at Harvard for less than 200 dollars a year, independently of personal expenses. Seventy-five dollars must be contributed by each to the current expenses; fuel is dear; fifteen dollars are charged for lodging within the college walls, and eighty are paid for board by those who use their option of living in the college commons. The fact is, I believe, generally acknowledged, that the comparative expensiveness of living is a cause of the depression of Harvard in comparison with its former standing among other colleges; but this leads to a supposition which does not to all appear a just one, that if the expenses of poor students could be defrayed by a public fund, to be raised for the purpose, the sons of the yeomanry would repair once more to Harvard. . . .

We had so arranged our movements as to arrive at Cambridge just in time for commencement, which always takes place on the last Wednesday in August. . . .

A great variety of exercises were gone through by the young men: orations were delivered, and poems, and dialogues, and addresses. Some of these appeared to me to have a good deal of merit; two or three were delivered by students who relied on their reputation at college, with a manner mixed up of pomposity and effrontery, which contrasted amusingly with the modesty of some of their companions, who did things much more worthy of honour. I discovered that many, if not most of the compositions, contained allusions to mob-law; of course, reprobating it. This was very satisfactory, particularly if the reprobation was accompanied with a knowledge of the causes and a recognition of the real perpetrators of the recent illegal violences; a knowledge that they have invariably sprung out of a conflict of selfish interests with eternal principles; and a recognition that their perpetrators have universally been, at first or second hand, aristocratic members of American society. . . .

The president then got into the antique chair from which the honours of the University are dispensed, and delivered their diplomas to the students. During this process we departed, at half past four o'clock, the business being concluded except the final blessing, given by the oldest clerical professor.

At home we assembled, a party of ladies, without any gentlemen. The gentlemen were all to dine in the College-hall. Our hostess had happened to collect round her table a company of ladies more or less distinguished in literature, and all, on the present occasion at least, as merry as children; or, which is saying as much, as merry as Americans usually are. . . .

After dinner several of the gentlemen came in to tell us what had been done and said at the hall. Their departure was a signal that it was time to be dressing for the president's levee. It was the most tremendous squeeze I encountered in America, for it is an indispensable civility to the president and the University to be seen at the levee. The band which had refreshed us in the morning was playing in the hall, and in the drawing-rooms there was a splendid choice of good company. I believe almost every eminent person in the state, for official rank or scientific and literary accomplishment, was there. I was presented with flowers as usual, and was favoured with some delightful introductions, so that I much enjoyed the brief hour of our stay. We were home by eight o'clock, and felt ourselves quite at rest again in our hostess's cool drawing-room, where the family party sat refreshing themselves with Champagne and conversation till the fatigues of commencement were forgotten. . . .

Mr. Sparks[11] breakfasted with us on the morning of the 27th. He brought with him the pass given by Arnold to André, and the papers found in André's boots. He possesses also the Reports of the West Point fortifications in Arnold's undisguised handwriting. The effect is singular of going from André's monument in Westminster Abbey to the shores of the Hudson, where the treachery was transacted, and to Mr. Sparks's study, where the evidence lies clear and complete.

After breakfast we proceeded once more to the church, in which were to be performed the rites of the Phi Beta Kappa Society. . . .

Prayers were said by the chaplain of the society, and then a member delivered an address. This address was and is to me a matter of great surprise. I do not know what was thought of it by the members generally; but if its doctrine and sentiments are at all sanctioned by them, I must regard this as another evidence, in addition to many, that the minority in America are, with regard to social principles, eminently in the wrong. The traveller is met everywhere among the aristocracy of the country with what seems to him the error of concluding that letters are wisdom, and that scholarship is education. Among a people whose profession is social equality, and whose rule of association is universal self-government, he is surprised to behold the assumptions of a class, and the contempt which the few express for the many, with as much assurance as if they lived in Russia or England. Much of this is doubtless owing to the minds of the lettered class having been nourished upon the literature of the Old World, so that their ideas have grown into a conformity with those of the subjects of feudal institutions, and the least strong-minded and original indiscriminately adopt, not merely

[11]Jared Sparks edited the writings of Washington and of Franklin; was editor of *North American Review*, later president of Harvard College.

the language, but the hopes and apprehensions, the notions of good and evil which have been generated amid the antiquated arrangements of European society; but, making allowance for this, as quite to be expected of all but very strong and original minds, it is still surprising that, within the bounds of the republic, the insolence should be so very complacent, the contempt of the majority so ludicrously decisive as it is. Self-satisfied, oracular ignorance and error are always as absurd as they are mournful; but when they are seen in full display among a body whose very ground of association is superiority of knowledge and of the love of it, the inconsistency affords a most striking lesson to the observer. Of course I am not passing a general censure on the association now under notice; for I know no more of it than what I could learn from the public exercises of this day, and a few printed addresses and poems. I am speaking of the tone and doctrine of the orator of the day, who might be no faithful organ of the society, but whose ways of thinking and expressing himself were but too like those of many literary and professional men whom I met in New England society.

The subject of the address was the "Duties of Educated men in a Republic;" a noble subject, of which the orator seemed to be aware at the beginning of his exercise. He well explained that whereas, in all the nominal republics of the Old World, men had still been under subjection to arbitrary human will, the new republic was established on the principle that men might live in allegiance to truth under the form of law. He told that the primary social duty of educated men was to enlighten public sentiment as to what truth is, and what law ought, therefore, to be. But here he diverged into a set of monstrous suppositions, expressed or assumed: that men of letters are the educated men of society in regard not only to literature and speculative truth, but to morals, politics, and the conduct of all social affairs; that power and property were made to go eternally together; that the "masses" are ignorant; that the ignorant masses naturally form a party against the enlightened few; that the masses desire to wrest power from the wealthy few; that, therefore, the masses wage war against property; that industry is to be the possession of the many, and property of the few; that the masses naturally desire to make the right instead of to find it; that they are, consequently, opposed to law; and that a struggle was impending in which the whole power of mind must be arrayed against brute force. This extraordinary collection of fallacies was not given in the form of an array of propositions, but they were all taken for granted when not announced. The orator made large reference to recent outrages in the country; but, happily for the truth and for the reputation of "the masses," the facts of the year supplied as complete a contradiction as could be desired to the orator of the hour. The violences were not perpetrated by industry against property, but by property against principle. The violators of law were, almost without an exception, members of the wealthy and "educated" class, while the victorious upholders of the law were the "industrious" masses. The rapid series of victories since gained by principle over the opposition of property, and without injury to property—holy and harmless victories—the failure of the law-breakers in all their objects, and their virtual surrender to the sense and principle of the majority, are sufficient, one would hope, to enlighten the "enlightened;" to indicate to the lettered class of American society, that while it is truly their duty to extend all the benefits of education which it is in their power to dispense to "the masses," it is highly necessary that the benefit should be reciprocated, and that the few should be also receiving an education from the many. There are a thousand mechanics' shops, a thousand loghouses where certain members of the Phi Beta Kappa Society, the orator of the day for one, might learn new and useful lessons on morals and politics, on the first principles of human relations. . . .

Signs of the Times in Massachusetts

Some few years hence it will be difficult to believe what the state of the times was in some parts of the United States, and even in the maritime cities, in 1835. The system of terrorism seems now to be over. It did not answer its purpose, and is dropped; but in 1835 it was new and dreadful. One of the most hideous features of the times was the ignorance and unconcern of a large portion of society about what was being done and suffered by other divisions of its members. I suppose, while Luther was toiling and thundering, German ladies and gentlemen were supping and dancing as usual; and while the Lollards were burning, perhaps little was known or cared about it in warehouses and upon farms. So it was in America. The gentry with whom I chiefly associated in New York knew little of the troubles of the abolitionists in that city, and nothing about the state of the anti-slavery question in their own region. In Boston I heard very striking facts which had taken place in broad daylight vehemently and honestly denied by many who happened to be ignorant of what had been done in their very streets. Not a few persons applied to me, a stranger, for information about the grand revolution of the time which was being transacted, not only on their own soil, but in the very city of their residence. A brief sketch of what I saw and experienced in Boston during the autumn of 1835 will afford some little information as to what the state of society actually was.

At the end of August a grand meeting was held at Faneuil Hall in Boston. The hall was completely filled with the gentry of the city, and some of the leading citizens took the responsibility and conducted the proceedings of the day. The object of the meeting was to sooth the South, by directing public indignation upon the abolitionists. The pretext of the assembly was, that the Union was in danger; and though the preamble to the resolutions declared disapprobation of the institution of slavery, the resolutions themselves were all inspired by fear of or sympathy with slaveholders. They reprobated all agitation of the question, and held out assurances to the South that every consideration should be made subordinate to the grand one of preserving the Union. The speeches were a disgrace to the constituents of a democratic republic, pointed as they were against those rights of free discussion and association at the time acted upon by fellow-citizens, and imbued with deference for the South. In the crowded assembly no voice was raised in disapprobation except when a speaker pointed to the portrait of Washington as "that slaveholder;" and even then the murmur soon died into silence. The gentlemen went home, trusting that they had put down the abolitionists and conciliated the South. In how short a time did the new legislature of the State pass, in that very city, a series of thorough-going abolition resolutions, sixteen constituting the minority! while the South had already been long despising the half-and-half doctrine of the Faneuil Hall meeting!

Meantime, the immediate result of the proceeding was the mob of which I have elsewhere given an account. After that mob the regular meetings of the abolitionists were suspended for want of a place to meet in. Incessant attempts were made to hire any kind of public building, but no one would take the risk of having his property destroyed by letting it to so obnoxious a set of people. For six weeks exertions were made in vain. At last a Boston merchant, who had built a pleasant house for himself and his family, said, that while he had a roof over his head, his neighbours should not want a place in which to hold a legal meeting for honest objects; and he sent an offer of his house to the ladies of the Anti-slavery Society. They appointed their meeting for three o'clock in the afternoon of Wednesday, November 18. They were obliged to make known their intentions as they best could, for no newspaper would admit their advertisements, and the clergy rarely ventured to give out their notices, among others, from the pulpit.

I was at this time slightly acquainted with three or four abolitionists, and I was distrusted by most or all of the body who took any interest in me at all. My feelings were very different from theirs about the slaveholders of the South; naturally enough, as these Southern slaveholders were nothing else in the eyes of abolitionists, while to me they were, in some cases, personal friends, and, in more, hospitable entertainers. It was known, however, that I had declared my intention of attending an abolition meeting. This was no new resolution. From the outset of my inquiry into the question, I had declared that, having attended colonization meetings, and heard all that the slaveholders had to say for themselves and against abolitionists, I felt myself bound to listen to the other side of the question. I always professed my intention of seeking acquaintance with the abolitionists, though I then fully and involuntarily believed two or three charges against them which I found to be wholly groundless. The time was now come for discharging this duty.

On the Monday, two friends, then only new acquaintances, called on me at the house of a clergyman where I was staying, three miles from Boston. A late riot at Salem was talked over, a riot in which the family of Mr. Thompson had been driven from one house to another three times in one night, the children being snatched from their beds, carried abroad in the cold, and injuriously terrified. It was mentioned that the ladies of the Anti-slavery Society were going to attempt a meeting on the next Wednesday, and I was asked whether I was in earnest in saying that I would attend one of their meetings. Would I go to this one if I should be invited? I replied that it depended entirely on the nature of the meeting. If it was merely a meeting for the settlement of accounts and the despatch of business, where I should not learn what I wanted, I should wait for a less perilous time; if it was a *bonâ fide* public meeting, a true reflection of the spirit and circumstances of the time and the cause, I would go. The matter was presently decided by the arrival of a regular official invitation to me to attend the meeting, and to carry with me the friend who was my travelling companion, and any one else who might be disposed to accompany me.

Trifling as these circumstances may now appear, they were no trifles at the time; and many considerations were involved in the smallest movement a stranger made on the question. The two first things I had to take care of were to avoid involving my host in any trouble I might get into, and to afford opportunity to my companion to judge for herself what she would do. My host had been reviled in the newspapers already for having read a notice (among several others) of an anti-slavery meeting from Dr. Channing's pulpit, where he was accidentally preaching. My object was to prevent his giving an opinion on anything that I should do, that he might not be made more or less responsible for my proceedings. I handed the invitation to my companion, with a hint not to speak of it. We separately made up our minds to go, and announced our determination to our host and hostess. Between joke and earnest, they told us we should be mobbed; and the same thing was repeated by many who were not in joke at all.

At two o'clock on the Wednesday we arrived at the house of a gentleman where we were to meet a few of the leading abolitionists, and dine, previous to the meeting. . . . During dinner, the conversation was all about the Southern gentry, in whose favour I said all I could, and much more than the party could readily receive; which was natural enough, considering that they and I looked at the people of the South from different points of view. Before we issued forth on our expedition I was warned once more that exertions had been made to get up a mob, and that it was possible we might be dispersed by violence. When we turned into the street where the house of meeting stood, there were about a dozen boys hooting before the door, as they saw ladies of colour entering. We were admitted without having to wait an instant on the steps, and the door was secured behind us.

The ladies assembled in two drawing-rooms, thrown into one by the folding-doors being opened. The total number was a hundred and thirty. . . . There were only three gentlemen in the house, its inhabitant, the gentleman who escorted us, and a clergyman who had dined with us. They remained in the hall, keeping the front door fastened, and the back way clear for our retreat, if retreat should be necessary. But the number of hooters in the streets at no time exceeded thirty, and they treated us to nothing worse than a few yells.

A lady who sat next me amused me by inquiring, with kindness, whether it revolted my feelings to meet thus in assembly with people of colour. She was as much surprised as pleased with my English deficiency of all feeling on the subject. My next neighbour on the other hand was Mrs. Thompson, the wife of the anti-slavery lecturer, who had just effected his escape, and was then on the sea. The proceedings began with the reading of a few texts of Scripture by the president. My first impression was that the selection of these texts gave out a little vainglory about the endurance of persecution; but when I remembered that this was the reunion of persons who had been dispersed by a mob, and when I afterward became aware how cruelly many of the members had been wounded in their moral sense, their domestic affections, and their prospects in life, I was quite ready to yield my too nice criticism. A prayer then followed, the spirit of which appeared to me perfect in hopefulness, meekness, and gentleness. While the secretary was afterward reading her report, a note was handed to me, the contents of which sunk my spirits fathom deep for the hour. It was a short pencil note from one of the gentlemen in the hall; and it asked me whether I had any objection to give a word of sympathy to the meeting, fellow-labourers as we had long been in behalf of the principles in whose defence they were met. The case was clear as daylight to my conscience. If I had been a mere stranger, attending with a mere stranger's interest to the proceedings of a party of natives, I might and ought to have declined mixing myself up with their proceedings. But I had long before published against slavery, and always declared my conviction that this was a question of humanity, not of country or race; a moral, not a merely political question; a general affair, and not one of city, state, party, or nation. Having thus declared on the safe side of the Atlantic, I was bound to act up to my declaration on the unsafe side, if called upon. I thought it a pity that the call had been made, though I am now very glad that it was, as it was the means of teaching me more of the temper and affairs of the times than I could have known by any other means, . . . but, at the moment, I foresaw none of these good consequences, but a formidable array of very unpleasant ones. I foresaw that almost every house in Boston, except those of the abolitionists, would be shut against me; that my relation to the country would be completely changed, as I should be suddenly transformed from being a guest and an observer to being considered a missionary or a spy; and results even more serious than this might reasonably be anticipated. During the few minutes I had for consideration, the wife of the writer of the note came to me, and asked what I thought of it, begging me to feel quite at liberty to attend to it or not, as I liked. I felt that I had no such liberty. I was presently introduced to the meeting, when I offered the note as my reason for breaking the silence of a stranger, and made the same declarations of my abhorrence of slavery and my agreement in the principles of the abolitionists which I had expressed throughout the whole of my travels through the South.

Of the consequences of this simple affair it is not my intention to give any account, chiefly because it would be impossible to convey to my English readers my conviction of the smallness of the portion of American society which was concerned in the treatment inflicted upon me. The hubbub was so great, and the modes of insult were so various, as to justify distant observers in concluding that the whole nation had risen against me. I soon found how few can make a great noise, while the many are careless or ignorant of what is going on about a person or a party with whom they have nothing to do; and while not a few are rendered more hearty in their regard and more generous in their hospitality by the disgraces of the individual who is under the oppression of public censure. All that I anticipated at the moment of reading the note came to pass, but only for a time. Eventually, nothing remained which in the slightest degree modified my opinions or impaired my hopes of the society I was investigating.

The secretary's report was drawn up with remarkable ability, and some animating and beautiful letters were read from distant members of the association. The business which had been interrupted by violence was put in train again; and, when the meeting broke up, a strong feeling of satisfaction visibly pervaded it. The right of meeting was vindicated; righteous pertinacity had conquered violence, and no immediate check to the efforts of the society was to be apprehended.

The trials of the abolitionists of Boston were, however, not yet over. Two months before, the attorney-general of the state had advocated in council the expected demand of the South, that abolitionists should be delivered up to the Slave States for trial and punishment under Southern laws. This fact is credible to those, and, perhaps, to those only, who have seen the pamphlet in reply to Dr. Channing's work on Slavery attributed to this gentleman. The South was not long in making the demand. Letters arrived from the governors of Southern States to the new governor of Massachusetts, demanding the passing of laws against abolitionism in all its forms. The governor, as was his business, laid these letters before the legislature of his state. This was the only thing he could do on this occasion. Just before, at his entrance upon his office, he had aimed his blow at the abolitionists in the following passages of his address. The same delusion (if it be mere delusion) is visible here that is shared by all persons in power, who cannot deny that an evil exists, but have not courage to remove it; a vague hope that "fate, or Providence, or something," will do the work which men are created to perform; men of principle and men of peace, like the abolitionists; victims, not perpetrators of violence. "As the genius of our institutions and the character of our people are entirely repugnant to laws impairing the liberty of speech and of the press, even for the sake of repressing its abuses, the patriotism of all classes of citizens must be invoked to abstain from a discussion which, by exasperating the master, can have no other effect than to render more oppressive the condition of the slave; and which, if not abandoned, there is great reason to fear will prove the rock on which the Union will split." . . . "A conciliatory forbearance," he proceeds to say, "would leave this whole painful subject where the Constitution leaves it, with the states where it exists, and in the hands of an all-wise Providence, who in his own good time is able to cause it to disappear, like the slavery of the ancient world, under the gradual operation of the gentle spirit of Christianity." The time is at hand. The "gradual operation of the gentle spirit of Christianity" had already educated the minds and hearts of the abolitionists for the work they are doing, but which the governor would fain have put off. It thus appears that they had the governor and attorney-general of the state against them, and the wealth, learning, and power of their city. It will be seen how their legislature was affected towards them.

As soon as they were aware of the demands of the Southern governors, they petitioned their legislature for a hearing, according to the invariable practice of persons who believe that they may be injured by the passing of any proposed law. The hearing was granted, as a matter of course; and a committee of five members of the legislature was appointed to hear what the abolitionists had to say. The place and time appointed were the Senate Chamber, on the afternoon of Friday, the 4th of March.

The expectation had been that few or none but the parties immediately concerned would be present at the discussion of such "a low subject;" but the event proved that more curiosity was abroad than had been supposed. I went just before the appointed hour, and took my seat with my party, in the empty gallery of the Senate Chamber. The abolitionists dropped in one by one; Garrison, May, Goodell, Follen, E. G. Loring, and others. The committee treated them with ostentatious neglect, dawdling away the time, and keeping them waiting a full hour beyond the appointed time. The gallery filled rapidly, and more and more citizens entered the room below. To our great delight, Dr. Channing made his appearance there. At length it was manifest that the Senate Chamber was not large enough; and we adjourned to the Hall of Representatives, which was soon about two thirds filled.

I could not have conceived that such conduct could have been ventured upon as that of the chairman of the committee. It was so insulting as to disgust the citizens present, whatever might be their way of thinking on the question which brought them together. The chairman and another of the five were evidently predetermined. They spared no pains in showing it, twisting the meaning of expressions employed by the pleaders, noting down any disjointed phrase which could be made to tell against those who used it, conveying sarcasms in their questions and insult in their remarks. Two others evidenced a desire to fulfil their function, to hear what the abolitionists had to say. Dr. Channing took his seat behind the pleaders; and I saw with pleasure that he was handing them notes, acting on their side as decisively, and almost as publicly as if he had spoken. After several unanswerable defences against charges had been made, and Mr. Loring had extorted the respect of the committee by a speech in which he showed that a legislative censure is more injurious than penal laws, it was Dr. Follen's turn to speak. He was presently stopped by the chairman, with a command that he should be respectful to the committee; with an intimation that the gentlemen were heard only as a matter of favour. They protested against this, their hearing having been demanded as a matter of right; they refused to proceed, and broke up the conference.

Much good was done by this afternoon's proceedings. The feeling of the bystanders was, on the whole, decidedly in favour of the pleaders, and the issue of the affair was watched with much interest. The next day the abolitionists demanded a hearing as a matter of right; and it was granted likewise as an affair of course. The second hearing was appointed for Tuesday the 8th, at the same place and hour.

Some well-meaning friends of the abolitionists had in the interval advised that the most accomplished, popular, and gentlemanly of the abolitionists should conduct the business of the second day; that the speeches should be made by Dr. Follen, Messrs. Loring and Sewall, and one or two more; and that Garrison and Goodell, the homely, primitive, and eminently suffering men of the apostleship, should be induced to remain in the background. The advice was righteously rejected; and, as it happened, theirs were the speeches that went farthest in winning over the feeling of the audience to their side. I shall never forget the swimming eye and tremulous voice with which a noble lady of the persecuted party answered such a suggestion as I have mentioned. "Oh," said she, "above all things, we must be just and faithful to Garrison. You do not know what we know; that, unless we put him, on every occasion, into the midst of the *gentlemen* of the party, he will be torn to pieces. Nothing can save him but his being made one with those whom his enemies will not dare to touch." As for Mr. Goodell, he had been frequently stoned. "He was used to it." They appeared in the midst of the professional gentlemen of the association, and did the most eminent service of the day.

The hall was crowded, and shouts of applause broke forth as the pleaders demolished an accusation or successfully rebutted the insolence of the chairman. Dr. Follen was again stopped, as he was showing that mobs had been the invariable consequence of censures of abolitionism passed by public meetings in the absence of gag-laws. He was desired to hold his tongue, or to be respectful to the committee; to which he replied, in his gentlest and most musical voice, "Am I, then, to understand that, in speaking ill of mobs, I am disrespectful to the committee?" The chairman looked foolish enough during the applauses which followed this question. Dr. Follen fought his ground inch by inch, and got out all he had to say. The conduct of the chairman became at last so insufferable, that several spectators attempted a remonstrance. A merchant was silenced; a physician was listened to, his speech being seasoned with wit so irresistible as to put all parties into good-humour.

The loudly-expressed opinion of the spectators as they dispersed was, that the chairman had ruined his political career, and, probably, filled the chair of a committee of the legislature for the last time. The result of the affair was that the report of the committee "spoke disrespectfully" of the exertions of the abolitionists, but rejected the suggestion of penal laws being passed to control their operations. The letters from the South therefore remained unanswered.

The abolitionists held a consultation whether they should complain to the legislature of the treatment their statements had received, and of the impediments thrown in the way of their self-justification. They decided to let the matter rest, trusting that there were witnesses enough of their case to enlighten the public mind on their position. A member of the legislature declared in his place what he had seen of the treatment of the appellants by the chairman, and proposed that the committee should be censured. As the aggrieved persons made no formal complaint, however, the matter was dropped. But the faith of the abolitionists was justified. The people were enlightened as to their position; and in the next election they returned a set of representatives, one of whose earliest acts was to pass a series of anti-slavery resolutions by a majority of 378 to 16.

These were a few of the signs of the times in Massachusetts when I was there. They proved that, while the aristocracy of the great cities were not to be trusted to maintain the great principles on which their society was based, the body of the people were sound.

Hot and Cold Weather

I believe no one attempts to praise the climate of New England. The very low average of health there, the prevalence of consumption and of decay of the teeth, are evidences of an unwholesome climate which I believe are universally received as such. The mortality among children throughout the whole country is a dark feature of life in the United States. . . . . One acquaintance of mine had lost four out of six children; another five out of seven; another six out of seven; another thirteen out of sixteen; and one mourner tells me that a fatality seems to attend the females of his family, for, out of eighteen, only one little granddaughter survives; and most of this family died very young, and of different kinds of disease. Never did I see so many wo-worn mothers as in America. Wherever we went in the North, we heard of "the lung fever" as of a common complaint, and children seemed to be as liable to it as grown persons. The climate is doubtless chiefly to blame for all this, and I do not see how any degree of care could obviate much of the evil. The children must be kept warm within doors; and the only way of affording them the range of the house is by warming the whole, from the cellar to the garret, by means of a furnace in the hall. This makes all comfortable within; but, then, the risk of going out is very great. There is far less fog and damp than in England, and the perfectly calm, sunny days of midwinter are endurable; but the least breath of wind seems to chill one's very life. I had no idea what the suffering from extreme cold amounted to till one day, in Boston, I walked the length of the city and back again in a wind, with the thermometer seven degrees and a half below zero. I had been warned of the cold, but was anxious to keep an appointment to attend a meeting. We put on all the merinoes and furs we could muster; but we were insensible of them from the moment the wind reached us. My muff seemed to be made of ice; I almost fancied I should have been warmer without it. We managed getting to the meeting pretty well, the stock of warmth we had brought out with us lasting till then. But we set out cold on our return; and, by the time I got home, I did not very well know where I was and what I was about. The stupefaction from cold is particularly disagreeable, the sense of pain remaining through it; and I determined not to expose myself to it again. All this must be dangerous to children; and if, to avoid it, they are shut up during the winter, there remains the danger of encountering the ungenial spring. . . .

Every season, however, has its peculiar pleasures; and in the retrospect these shine out brightly, while the evils disappear.

On a December morning you are awakened by the domestic scraping at your hearth. Your anthracite fire has been in all night; and now the ashes are carried away, more coal is put on, and the blower hides the kindly red from you for a time. In half an hour the fire is intense, though, at the other end of the room, everything you touch seems to blister your fingers with cold. If you happen to turn up a corner of the carpet with your foot, it gives out a flash; and your hair crackles as you brush it. Breakfast is always hot, be the weather what it may. The coffee is scalding, and the buckwheat cakes steam when the cover is taken off. . . . You may see boys coasting on Boston Common all the winter day through; and too many in the streets, where it is not so safe. To coast is to ride on a board down a frozen slope; and many children do this in the steep streets which lead down to the Common, as well as on the snowy slopes within the enclosure where no carriages go. Some sit on their heels on the board, some on their crossed legs. Some strike their legs out, put their arms a-kimbo, and so assume an air of defiance amid their velocity. Others prefer lying on their stomachs, and so going headforemost; an attitude whose comfort I never could enter into. Coasting is a wholesome exercise for hardy boys. Of course they have to walk up the ascent, carrying their boards between every feat of coasting; and this affords them more exercise than they are at all aware of taking.

As for the sleighing, I heard much more than I experienced of its charms. . . . On a perfectly level and crisp surface I can fancy the smooth rapid motion to be exceedingly pleasant; but such surfaces are rare in the neighbourhood of populous cities. . . . I do not know the author of a description of sleighing which was quoted to me, but I admire it for its fidelity. "Do you want to know what sleighing is like? You can soon try. Set your chair on a springboard out in the porch on Christmas day; put your feet in a pailful of powdered ice; have somebody to jingle a bell in one ear, and somebody else to blow into the other with the bellows, and you will have an exact idea of sleighing."

I was surprised to find that young people whose health is too delicate to allow them to do many simple things, are not too delicate to go out sleighing in an open sleigh. They put hot bricks under their feet, and wrap up in furs; but the face remains exposed, and the breathing the frosty air of a winter's night, after dancing, may be easily conceived to be the cause of much of the "lung fever" of which the stranger hears. The gayest sleighing that I saw was on the day when all the schools in Boston have a holyday, and the pupils go abroad in a long procession of sleighs. The multitude of happy young faces, though pinched with cold, was a pretty sight.

If the morning be fine, you have calls to make, or shopping to do, or some meeting to attend. If the streets be coated with ice, you put on your India-rubber shoes–unsoled–to guard you from slipping. If not, you are pretty sure to measure your length on the pavement before your own door. . . . Nothing is seen in England like the streets of Boston and New York at the end of the season while the thaw is proceeding. The area of the street had been so raised that passengers could look over the blinds of your ground-floor rooms; when the sidewalks become full of holes and puddles, they are cleared, and the passengers are reduced to their proper level; but the middle of the street remains exalted, and the carriages drive along a ridge. Of course, this soon becomes too dangerous, and for a season ladies and gentlemen walk; carts tumble, slip, and slide, and get on as they can; while the mass, now dirty, not only with thaw, but with quantities of refuse vegetables, sweepings of the poor people's houses, and other rubbish which it was difficult to know what to do with while every place was frozen up, daily sinks and dissolves into a composite mud. It was in New York and some of the inferior streets of Boston that I saw this process in its completeness.

If the morning drives are extended beyond the city, there is much to delight the eye. The trees are cased in ice; and when the sun shines out suddenly, the whole scene looks like one diffused rainbow, dressed in a brilliancy which can hardly be conceived of in England. On days less bright, the blue harbour spreads in strong contrast with the sheeted snow which extends to its very brink.

The winter evenings begin joyously with the festival of Thanksgiving Day, which is, if I remember rightly, held on the first Thursday of December. The festival is ordered by proclamation of the governor of the state, which proclamation is read in all the churches. . . . Boston friends invited us to join their family gathering on that great annual festival. We went to church in the morning, and listened to the thanksgiving for the mercies of the year, and to an exemplification of the truth that national prosperity is of value only as it is sanctified to individual progression; an important doctrine, well enforced. This is the occasion chosen by the boldest of the clergy to say what they think of the faults of the nation, and particularly to reprobate apathy on the slavery question. There are few who dare do this, though it seems to be understood that this is an occasion on which "particular preaching" may go a greater length than on common Sundays. . . .

At three o'clock a family party of about thirty were assembled round two wellspread tables. There was only one drawback, that five of the children were absent, being ill of the measles. There was much merriment among us grown people at the long-table; but the bursts of laughter from the children's side-table, where a kind aunt presided, were incessant. After dinner we played hunt-the-slipper with the children, while the gentlemen were at their wine; and then went to spend an hour with a poor boy in the measles, who was within hearing of the mirth, but unable to leave his easy-chair. When we had made him laugh as much as was good for him with some of our most ludicrous English Christmas games, we went down to communicate more of this curious kind of learning in the drawing-rooms. There we introduced a set of games quite new to the company; and it was delightful to see with what spirit and wit they were entered into and carried on. Dumb Crambo was made to yield its ultimate rhymes, and the storytelling in Old Coach was of the richest. When we were all quite tired with laughing, the children began to go away; some fresh visiters dropped in from other houses, and music and supper followed. We got home by eleven o'clock, very favourably impressed with the institution of Thanksgiving Day. . . .

Christmas evening was very differently passed, but in a way to me even more interesting. We were in a country village, Hingham, near the shores of Massachusetts Bay, and were staying in the house of the pastor, our clerical shipmate. . . . The church was dressed up with evergreens in great quantity, and arranged with much taste. The organist had composed a new anthem, which was well sung by the young men and women of the congregation. At home the rooms were prettily dressed with green, and an ample supply of lights was provided against the evening. Soon after dinner some little girls arrived to play with the children of the house, and we resumed the teaching of English Christmas games. The little things were tired, and went away early enough to leave us a quiet hour before the doors were thrown open to "the parish," whose custom it is to flock to the pastor's house, to exchange greetings with him on Christmas night. What I saw makes me think this a delightful custom. There is no expensive or laborious preparation for their reception. The rooms are well lighted, and cake and lemonade are provided, and this is all. . . .

An excellent woman, the general benefactress of the village, is always ready to nurse the sick and help the afflicted, and to be of eminent service in another way to her young neighbours. She assembles them in the evenings once or twice a week, and reads with them and to them; and thus the young women of the village are obtaining a knowledge of Italian and French, as well as English literature, which would have been unattainable without her help. The daughters of the fishermen, bucket and net-makers, and farmers of Hingham, are far more accomplished than many a highbred young lady in England and New York. Such a village population is one of the true glories of America. Many such girls were at their pastor's this evening, dressed in silk gowns of the latest make, with rich French pelerines, and their well-arranged hair bound with coloured riband; as pretty a set of girls as could be collected anywhere.

When it appeared that the rooms were beginning to thin, the organist called the young people round him, and they sang the new Christmas anthem extremely well. Finally, a Christmas hymn was sung by all to the tune of Old Hundred; the pastor and his people exchanged the blessing of the season, and in a few minutes the house was cleared. . . .

I was present at the introduction into the new country of the spectacle of the German Christmas-tree. My little friend Charley and three companions had been long preparing for this pretty show. The cook had broken her eggs carefully in the middle for some weeks past, that Charley might have the shells for cups; and these cups were gilded and coloured very prettily. I rather think it was, generally speaking, a secret out of the house; but I knew what to expect. It was a Newyear's tree, however; for I could not go on Christmas-eve, and it was kindly settled that Newyear's-eve would do as well. We were sent for before dinner, and we took up two round-faced boys by the way. Early as it was, we were all so busy that we could scarcely spare a respectful attention to our plum-pudding. It was desirable that our preparations should be completed before the little folks should begin to arrive; and we were all engaged in sticking on the last of the seven dozen of wax-tapers, and in filling the gilded egg-cups and gay paper cornucopiæ with comfits, lozenges, and barley-sugar. The tree was the top of a young fir, planted in a tub, which was ornamented with moss. Smart dolls and other whimsies glittered in the evergreen, and there was not a twig which had not something sparkling upon it. When the sound of wheels was heard, we had just finished; and we shut up the tree by itself in the front drawing-room, while we went into the other, trying to look as if nothing was going to happen. Charley looked a good deal like himself, only now and then twisting himself about in an unaccountable fit of giggling. It was a very large party; for, besides the tribes of children, there were papas and mammas, uncles, aunts, and elder sisters. When all were come we shut out the cold; the great fire burned clearly; the tea and coffee were as hot as possible, and the cheeks of the little ones grew rosier and their eyes brighter every moment. It had been settled that, in order to cover our designs, I was to resume my vocation of teaching Christmas games after tea, while Charley's mother and her maids went to light up the front room. So all found seats, many of the children on the floor, for Old Coach. . . . When they were fairly practised in the game, I turned over my story to a neighbour, and got away to help to light up the tree. . . .

I mounted the steps behind the tree to see the effect of opening the doors. It was delightful. The children poured in, but in a moment every voice was hushed. Their faces were upturned to the blaze, all eyes wide open, all lips parted, all steps arrested. Nobody spoke, only Charley leaped for joy. The first symptom of recovery was the children's wandering round the tree. At last a quick pair of eyes discovered that it bore something eatable, and from that moment the babble began again. They were told that they might get what they could without burning themselves; and we tall people kept watch, and helped them with good things from the higher branches. When all had had enough, we returned to the larger room, and finished the evening with dancing. By ten o'clock all were well warmed for the ride home with steaming mulled wine, and the prosperous evening closed with shouts of mirth. By a little after eleven Charley's father and mother and I were left by ourselves to sit in the Newyear. I have little doubt the Christmas-tree will become one of the most flourishing exotics of New England. . . .

William Lloyd Garrison

William lloyd garrison was, not many years ago, a printer's boy. . . . By some accident his attention was turned to the condition of the coloured race, and to colonization as a means of rescue. . . .

Garrison . . . engaged to deliver a lecture on colonization; and, in order to prepare himself, he went down to Baltimore to master the details of the scheme on the spot where it was in actual operation. His studies soon convinced him of the fallacies and iniquities involved in the plan, and he saw that nothing short of the abolition of the slave system would redeem the coloured race from their social depression. A visitation of persecution came at this time in aid of his convictions. A merchant of Newburyport, Massachusetts, gave permission to the master of a vessel of which he was the owner to freight the ship with slaves at Baltimore, and carry them down to the New Orleans market. Garrison commented upon this transaction in a newspaper in the terms which it deserved, but which were libellous, and he was, in consequence, brought to a civil and criminal trial, thrown into prison, and fined 1000 dollars, which he had not the remotest prospect of being able to pay. When he had been imprisoned three months, he was released by the fine being paid by Arthur Tappan, of New York; a gentleman who was an entire stranger to Garrison, and who did this act (the first of a long series of munificent deeds) for the sake of the principle in volved in the case.

Of this gentleman a few words before we proceed. He is one of the few wealthy original abolitionists, and his money has been poured out freely in the cause. He has been one of the most persecuted, and his nerves have never appeared to be shaken. He has been a mark for insult from the whole body of his countrymen (except a handful of abolitionists) for a series of years; and he has never, on this account, altered his countenance towards man or woman. His house was attacked in New York, and his family driven from the city; he quietly took up his abode on Long Island. . . . His partners early remonstrated with him on the injury he was doing to his trade by publicly opposing slavery, and supported one another in declaring to him that he must give up his connexion with the abolitionists. He heard them to an end; said, "I will be hanged first," and walked off. When I was in America, immense rewards for the head, and even for the ears of Mr. Tappan, were offered from the South, through advertisements in the newspapers and handbills. . . . Mr. Tappan's house on Long Island is in an exposed situation; but he hired no guard, and lost not an hour's sleep. . . . A cause involving a broad principle, and supported to the point of martyrdom by men of this make, is victorious from the beginning. Its complete triumph is merely a question of time.

Garrison lectured in New York in favour of the abolition of slavery, and in exposure of the colonization scheme, and was warmly encouraged by a few choice spirits. He went to Boston for the same purpose; but in the enlightened and religious city of Boston, every place in which he could lecture was shut against him. He declared his intention of lecturing on the Common if he could get no door opened to him, and this threat procured for him what he wanted. At his first lecture he fired the souls of some of his hearers; among others, of Mr. May, the first Unitarian clergyman who embraced the cause. On the next Sunday Mr. May, in pursuance of the custom of praying for all distressed persons, prayed for the slaves; and was asked, on descending from the pulpit, whether he was mad.

Garrison and his fellow-workman, both in the printing-office and the cause—his friend Isaac Knapp—set up the Liberator, in its first days a little sheet of shabby paper, printed with old types, and now a handsome and flourishing newspaper. These two heroes, in order to publish their paper, lived for a series of years in one room on bread and water, "with sometimes," when the paper sold unusually well, "the luxury of a bowl of milk." In course of time twelve men formed themselves into an abolition society at Boston, and the cause was fairly afoot.

It was undergoing its worst persecutions just before I entered Boston for the winter. I had resolved some time before, that, having heard every species of abuse of Garrison, I ought in fairness to see him. The relation of the above particulars quickened my purpose, and I mentioned my wish to the relator, who engaged that we should meet, mentioning that he supposed I was aware what I should encounter by acknowledging a wish to see Garrison. I was staying at the house of a clergyman in Boston, when a note was brought in which told me that Mr. Garrison was in town, and would meet me at any hour, at any friend's house, the next day. My host . . . kindly insisted that Mr. Garrison should call on me at home. At ten o'clock he came, accompanied by his introducer. His aspect put to flight in an instant what prejudices his slanderers had raised in me. I was wholly taken by surprise. It was a countenance glowing with health, and wholly expressive of purity, animation, and gentleness. . . . Garrison has a good deal of a Quaker air; and his speech is deliberate like a Quaker's, but gentle as a woman's. The only thing that I did not like was his excessive agitation when he came in, and his thanks to me for desiring to meet one "so odious" as himself. I was, however, as I told him, nearly as odious as himself at that time; so it was fit that we should be acquainted. On mentioning afterward to his introducer my impression of something like a want of manliness in Garrison's agitation, he replied that I could not know what it was to be an object of insult and hatred to the whole of society for a series of years; that Garrison could bear what he met with from street to street, and from town to town; but that a kind look and shake of the hand from a stranger unmanned him for the moment. How little did the great man know our feelings towards him on our meeting; how we, who had done next to nothing, were looking up to him who is achieving the work of an age, and, as a stimulus, that of a nation!

His conversation was more about peace principles than the great subject. It was of the most practical cast. Every conversation I had with him confirmed my opinion that sagacity is the most striking attribute of his conversation. It has none of the severity, the harshness, the bad taste of his writing; it is as gladsome as his countenance, and as gentle as his voice. Through the whole of his deportment breathes the evidence of a heart at ease; and this it is, I think, more than all his distinct claims, which attaches his personal friends to him with an almost idolatrous affection.

I do not pretend to like or to approve the tone of Garrison's printed censures. I could not use such language myself towards any class of offenders, nor can I sympathize in its use by others. But it is only fair to mention that Garrison adopts it warily; and that I am persuaded that he is elevated above passion, and has no unrighteous anger to vent in harsh expressions. He considers his task to be the exposure of fallacy, the denunciation of hypocrisy, and the rebuke of selfish timidity. He is looked upon by those who defend him in this particular as holding the branding-iron; and it seems true enough that no one branded by Garrison ever recovers it. He gives his reasons for his severity with a calmness, meekness, and softness which contrast strongly with the subject of the discourse, and which convince the objector that there is principle at the bottom of the practice. . . .

Garrison gayly promised me that he would come over whenever his work is done in the United States, that we may keep jubilee in London. I believe it would be safe to promise him a hundred thousand welcomes as warm as mine.

Traveller's Retrospect

What is gained by living and travelling?

One of the most striking and even amusing results is the perception of the transient nature of troubles. The thoughtful traveller feels something like wonder and amusement at himself for being so depressed by evils as he finds himself in the midst of long-idealized objects. He is surprised at his own sufferings from hunger, cold, heat, and weariness; and at his being only prevented by shame from passing some great object unseen, if he has to rouse himself from sleep to look at it, or to forego a meal for its sake. The next time he is refreshed, he wonders how his troubles could ever so affect him; and, when at home, he looks through the picture-gallery of his memory, the afflictions of past hours would have vanished, their very occurrence would be denied but for the record in the journal. The contemptible entries about cold, hunger, and sleepiness stand, ludicrously enough, among notices of cataracts and mountains, and of moral conflicts in the senates of nations. And so with life. We look back upon our pangs about objects of desire, as if it were the object and not the temper of pursuit which was of importance. We look back on our sufferings from disease, from disappointment, from suspense, in times when the great moral events of our lives, or even of the age, were impending, and we disregarded them. We were mourning over some petty loss or injury while a new region of the moral universe was about to be disclosed to us; or fretting about our "roast chicken and our little game at cards," while the liberties of an empire were being lost or won. . . .

Nothing is more conspicuous in the traveller's retrospect than the fact how little external possession has to do with happiness. As he wanders back over city and village, plantation and prairie, he sees again care on the brow of the merchant and mirth in the eyes of the labourer; the soulless faces of the rich Shakers rise up before him, side by side with the gladsome countenance of the ruined abolitionist. Each class kindly pities the one below it in power and wealth; the traveller pities none but those who are wasting their energies in the exclusive pursuit of either. Generally speaking, they have all an equal endowment of the things from which happiness is really derived. They have, in pretty equal distribution, health, senses, and their pleasures, homes, children, pursuits, and successes. With all these things in common, the one point of difference in their respective amounts of possession of more than they can at present eat, use, and enjoy, seems to him quite unworthy of all the compassion excited by it; though the compassion, having something amiable in it, is of a kindly use as far as it goes. . . . In the retrospect of the recent traveller in America, the happiest class is clearly that small one of the original abolitionists; men and women wholly devoted to a lofty pursuit, and surrendering for it much that others most prize: and, in the retrospect of the traveller through life, the most eminently blessed come forth from among all ranks and orders of men, some being rich and others poor; some illustrious and others obscure; but all having one point of resemblance, that they have not staked their peace on anything so unreal as money or fame.

Dickens Sympathized

The publication of SKETCHES BY BOZ, OLIVER TWIST, NICHOLAS NICKLEBY *and the* PICKWICK PAPERS *had made their author well known in America when he arrived in 1842. Charles Dickens (1812–70) knew the miseries of the poor, for he had shared them. His father had been held in a debtors' prison and he himself had been a child drudge in a blacking warehouse. He looked at the United States with the social reformer's eye and wrote frankly of all that stirred him; but his observations of the more casual aspects of American civilization were seasoned with the vast warm humor that helped make him probably the most widely read of all English novelists.*

From AMERICAN NOTES

Going Away

I SHALL never forget the one-fourth serious and three-fourths comical astonishment, with which, on the morning of the third of January eighteen-hundred-and-forty-two, I opened the door of, and put my head into, a 'state-room' on board the Britannia steam-packet, twelve hundred tons burthen per register, bound for Halifax and Boston, and carrying Her Majesty's mails.

That this state-room had been specially engaged for 'Charles Dickens, Esquire, and Lady,' was rendered sufficiently clear even to my scared intellect by a very small manuscript, announcing the fact, which was pinned on a very flat quilt, covering a very thin mattress, spread like a surgical plaster on a most inaccessible shelf. . . .

By very nearly closing the door, and twining in and out like serpents, and by counting the little washing slab as standing-room,—we could manage to insinuate four people into it, all at one time. . . . I do not verily believe that, deducting the two berths, one above the other, than which nothing smaller for sleeping in was ever made except coffins, it was no bigger than one of those hackney cabriolets which have the door behind, and shoot their fares out, like sacks of coals, upon the pavement. . . .

We all dined together that day. . . . I could not but observe that very few remained long over their wine; and that everybody had an unusual love of the open air; and that the favourite and most coveted seats were invariably those nearest to the door. The tea-table, too, was by no means as well attended as the dinner-table; and there was less whist-playing than might have been expected. Still . . . there were no invalids as yet; and walking, and smoking, and drinking of brandy-and-water (but always in the open air), went on with unabated spirit, until eleven o'clock or thereabouts, when 'turning in' . . . became the order of the night. The perpetual tramp of boot-heels on the decks gave place to a heavy silence, and the whole human freight was stowed away below, excepting a very few stragglers, like myself, who were probably, like me, afraid to go there. . . .

I crept below at midnight. It was not exactly comfortable below. It was decidedly close; and it was impossible to be unconscious of the presence of that extraordinary compound of strange smells, which is to be found nowhere but on board ship, and which is such a subtle perfume that it seems to enter at every pore of the skin, and whisper of the hold. Two passengers' wives (one of them my own) lay already in silent agonies on the sofa; and one lady's maid (*my* lady's) was a mere bundle on the floor, execrating her destiny, and pounding her curl-papers among the stray boxes. Everything sloped the wrong way: which in itself was an aggravation scarcely to be borne. I had left the door open, a moment before, in the bosom of a gentle declivity, and, when I turned to shut it, it was on the summit of a lofty eminence. Now every plank and timber creaked, as if the ship were made of wicker-work; and now crackled, like an enormous fire of the driest possible twigs. There was nothing for it but bed; so I went to bed.

It was pretty much the same for the next two days, with a tolerably fair wind and dry weather. I read in bed (but to this hour I don't know what) a good deal; and reeled on deck a little; drank cold brandy-and-water with an unspeakable disgust, and ate hard biscuit perseveringly: not ill, but going to be.

It is the third morning. I am awakened out of my sleep by a dismal shriek from my wife, who demands to know whether there's any danger. I rouse myself, and look out of bed. The water-jug is plunging and leaping like a lively dolphin; all the smaller articles are afloat, except my shoes, which are stranded on a carpet-bag, high and dry, like a couple of coal-barges. Suddenly I see them spring into the air, and behold the looking-glass, which is nailed to the wall, sticking fast upon the ceiling. At the same time the door entirely disappears, and a new one is opened in the floor. Then I begin to comprehend that the state-room is standing on its head. . . .

I say nothing of what may be called the domestic noises of the ship: such as the breaking of glass and crockery, the tumbling down of stewards, the gambols, overhead, of loose casks and truant dozens of bottled porter, and the very remarkable and far from exhilarating sounds raised in their various state-rooms by the seventy passengers who were too ill to get up to breakfast. I say nothing of them: for although I lay listening to this concert for three or four days, I don't think I heard it for more than a quarter of a minute, at the expiration of which term, I lay down again, excessively sea-sick.

Not sea-sick, be it understood, in the ordinary acceptation of the term: I wish I had been: but in a form which I have never seen or heard described, though I have no doubt it is very common. I lay there, all the day long, quite coolly and contentedly; with no sense of weariness, with no desire to get up, or get better, or take the air; with no curiosity, or care, or regret, of any sort or degree, saving that I think I can remember, in this universal indifference, having a kind of lazy joy–of fiendish delight, if anything so lethargic can be dignified with the title–in the fact of my wife being too ill to talk to me. If . . . a goblin postman, with a scarlet coat and bell, had come into that little kennel before me, broad awake in broad day, and, apologising for being damp through walking in the sea, had handed me a letter directed to myself, in familiar characters, I am certain I should not have felt one atom of astonishment: I should have been perfectly satisfied. If Neptune himself had walked in, with a toasted shark on his trident, I should have looked upon the event as one of the very commonest everyday occurrences.

Once–once–I found myself on deck. I don't know how I got there, or what possessed me to go there, but there I was; and completely dressed too, with a huge pea-coat on, and a pair of boots such as no weak man in his senses could ever have got into. I found myself standing, when a gleam of consciousness came upon me, holding on to something. I don't know what. I think it was the boatswain: or it may have been the pump: or possibly the cow. I can't say how long I had been there; whether a day or a minute. I recollect trying to think about something (about anything in the whole wide world, I was not particular) without the smallest effect. I could not even make out which was the sea, and which the sky, for the horizon seemed drunk, and was flying wildly about in all directions. Even in that incapable state, however, I recognised the lazy gentleman standing before me: nautically clad in a suit of shaggy blue, with an oilskin hat. But I was too imbecile, although I knew it to be he, to separate him from his dress; and tried to call him, I remember, *Pilot*. After another interval of total unconsciousness, I found he had gone, and recognised another figure in its place. It seemed to wave and fluctuate before me as though I saw it reflected in an unsteady looking-glass; but I knew it for the captain; and such was the cheerful influence of his face, that I tried to smile: yes, even then I tried to smile. I saw by his gestures that he addressed me; but it was a long time before I could make out that he remonstrated against my standing up to my knees in water–as I was; of course I don't know why. I tried to thank him, but couldn't. I could only point to my boots–or wherever I supposed my boots to be–and say in a plaintive voice, 'Cork soles:' at the same time endeavouring, I am told, to sit down in the pool. Finding that I was quite insensible, and for the time a maniac, he humanely conducted me below.

There I remained until I got better: suffering, whenever I was recommended to eat anything, an amount of anguish only second to that which is said to be endured by the apparently drowned, in the process of restoration to life. One gentleman on board had a letter of introduction to me from a mutual friend in London. He sent it below with his card, on the morning of the head-wind; and I was long troubled with the idea that he might be up, and well, and a hundred times a day expecting me to call upon him in the saloon. I imagined him one of those cast-iron images—I will not call them men—who ask, with red faces, and lusty voices, what sea-sickness means, and whether it really is as bad as it is represented to be. This was very torturing indeed; and I don't think I ever felt such perfect gratification and gratitude of heart, as I did when I heard from the ship's doctor that he had been obliged to put a large mustard poultice on this very gentleman's stomach. I date my recovery from the receipt of that intelligence. . . .

Boston

In all the public establishments of America, the utmost courtesy prevails. Most of our Departments are susceptible of considerable improvement in this respect, but the Custom-house above all others would do well to take example from the United States and render itself somewhat less odious and offensive to foreigners. The servile rapacity of the French officials is sufficiently contemptible; but there is a surly boorish incivility about our men, alike disgusting to all persons who fall into their hands, and discreditable to the nation that keeps such ill-conditioned curs snarling about its gates.

When I landed in America, I could not help being strongly impressed with the contrast their Custom-house presented, and the attention, politeness and good humour with which its officers discharged their duty.

As we did not land at Boston, in consequence of some detention at the wharf, until after dark, I received my first impressions of the city in walking down to the Custom-house on the morning after our arrival, which was Sunday. . . . When I got into the streets upon this Sunday morning, the air was so clear, the houses were so bright and gay; the signboards were painted in such gaudy colours; the gilded letters were so very golden; the bricks were so very red, the stone was so very white, the blinds and area railings were so very green, the knobs and plates upon the street doors so marvellously bright and twinkling; and all so slight and unsubstantial in appearance—that every thoroughfare in the city looked exactly like a scene in a pantomime. It rarely happens in the business streets that a tradesman, if

I may venture to call anybody a tradesman, where everybody is a merchant, resides above his store; so that many occupations are often carried on in one house, and the whole front is covered with boards and inscriptions. As I walked along, I kept glancing up at these boards, confidently expecting to see a few of them change into something; and I never turned a corner suddenly without looking out for the clown and pantaloon, who, I had no doubt, were hiding in a doorway or behind some pillar close at hand. As to Harlequin and Columbine, I discovered immediately that they lodged (they are always looking after lodgings in a pantomime) at a very small clockmaker's one story high, near the hotel; which, in addition to various symbols and devices, almost covering the whole front, had a great dial hanging out–to be jumped through, of course. . . .

The city is a beautiful one, and cannot fail, I should imagine, to impress all strangers very favourably. The private dwelling-houses are, for the most part, large and elegant; the shops extremely good; and the public buildings handsome. The State House is built upon the summit of a hill, which rises gradually at first, and afterwards by a steep ascent, almost from the water's edge. In front is a green enclosure, called the Common. The site is beautiful: and from the top there is a charming panoramic view of the whole town and neighbourhood. In addition to a variety of commodious offices, it contains two handsome chambers; in one the House of Representatives of the State hold their meetings: in the other, the Senate. Such proceedings as I saw here, were conducted with perfect gravity and decorum; and were certainly calculated to inspire attention and respect.

There is no doubt that much of the intellectual refinement and superiority of Boston is referable to the quiet influence of the University of Cambridge, which is within three or four miles of the city. The resident professors at that university are gentlemen of learning and varied attainments; and are, without one exception that I can call to mind, men who would shed a grace upon, and do honour to, any society in the civilised world. . . . Whatever the defects of American universities may be, they disseminate no prejudices; rear no bigots; dig up the buried ashes of no old superstitions; never interpose between the people and their improvement; exclude no man because of his religious opinions; above all, in their whole course of study and instruction, recognise a world, and a broad one too, lying beyond the college walls.

It was a source of inexpressible pleasure to me to observe the almost imperceptible, but not less certain effect, wrought by this institution among the small community of Boston; and to note at every turn the humanising tastes and desires it has engendered; the affectionate friendships to which it has given rise; the amount of vanity and prejudice it has dispelled. The golden calf they worship at Boston is a pigmy compared with the giant effigies set up in other parts of that vast counting-house which lies beyond the Atlantic; and the almighty dollar sinks into something comparatively insignificant, amidst a whole Pantheon of better gods.

Above all, I sincerely believe that the public institutions and charities of this capital of Massachusetts are as nearly perfect, as the most considerate wisdom, benevolence, and humanity, can make them. I never in my life was more affected by the contemplation of happiness, under circumstances of privation and bereavement, than in my visits to these establishments.

It is a great and pleasant feature of all such institutions in America, that they are either supported by the State or assisted by the State; or (in the event of their not needing its helping hand) that they act in concert with it, and are emphatically the people's. I cannot but think, with a view to the principle and its tendency to elevate or depress the character of the industrious classes, that a Public Charity is immeasurably better than a Private Foundation, no matter how munificently the latter may be endowed. In our own country, where it has not, until within these later days, been a very popular fashion with governments to display any extraordinary regard for the great mass of the people or to recognise their existence as improvable creatures, private charities, unexampled in the history of the earth, have arisen, to do an incalculable amount of good among the destitute and afflicted. But the government of the country, having neither act nor part in them, is not in the receipt of any portion of the gratitude they inspire; and, offering very little shelter or relief beyond that which is to be found in the workhouse and the jail, has come, not unnaturally, to be looked upon by the poor rather as a stern master, quick to correct and punish, than a kind protector, merciful and vigilant in their hour of need. . . .

At South Boston, as it is called, in a situation excellently adapted for the purpose, several charitable institutions are clustered together. One of these is the State Hospital for the insane; admirably conducted on those enlightened principles of conciliation and kindness, which twenty years ago would have been worse than heretical, and which have been acted upon with so much success in our own pauper Asylum at Hanwell. 'Evince a desire to show some confidence, and repose some trust, even in mad people,' said the resident physican, as we walked along the galleries, his patients flocking round us unrestrained. Of those who deny or doubt the wisdom of this maxim after witnessing its effects, if there be such people still alive, I can only say that I hope I may never be summoned as a Juryman on a Commission of Lunacy whereof they are the subjects; for I should certainly find them out of their senses, on such evidence alone.

Each ward in this institution is shaped like a long gallery or hall, with the dormitories of the patients opening from it on either hand. Here they work, read, play at skittles, and other games; and when the weather does not admit of their taking exercise out of doors, pass the day together. In one of these rooms, seated, calmly, and quite as a matter of course, among a throng of mad-women, black and white, were the physician's wife and another lady, with a couple of children. These ladies were graceful and handsome; and it was not difficult to perceive at a glance that even their presence there, had a highly beneficial influence on the patients who were grouped about them. . . .

Every patient in this asylum sits down to dinner every day with a knife and fork; and in the midst of them sits the resident physician. . . . At every meal, moral influence alone restrains the more violent among them from cutting the throats of the rest; but the effect of that influence is reduced to an absolute certainty, and is found, even as a means of restraint, to say nothing of it as a means of cure, a hundred times more efficacious than all the strait-waistcoats, fetters, and handcuffs, that ignorance, prejudice, and cruelty have manufactured since the creation of the world.

In the labour department, every patient is as freely trusted with the tools of his trade as if he were a sane man. In the garden, and on the farm, they work with spades, rakes, and hoes. For amusement, they walk, run, fish, paint, read, and ride out to take the air in carriages provided for the purpose. They have among themselves a sewing society to make clothes for the poor, which holds meetings, passes resolutions, never comes to fisty-cuffs or bowie-knives as sane assemblies have been known to do elsewhere; and conducts all its proceedings with the greatest decorum. The irritability, which would otherwise be expended on their own flesh, clothes, and furniture, is dissipated in these pursuits. They are cheerful, tranquil, and healthy.

Once a week they have a ball, in which the Doctor and his family, with all the nurses and attendants, take an active part. Dances and marches are performed alternately, to the enlivening strains of a piano; and now and then some gentleman or lady (whose proficiency has been previously ascertained) obliges the company with a song. . . .

It is obvious that one great feature of this system, is the inculcation and encouragement, even among such unhappy persons, of a decent self-respect. Something of the same spirit pervades all the Institutions at South Boston.

There is the House of Industry. In that branch of it, which is devoted to the reception of old or otherwise helpless paupers, these words are painted on the walls: 'WORTHY OF NOTICE. SELF-GOVERNMENT, QUIETUDE, AND PEACE, ARE BLESSINGS.' It is not assumed and taken for granted that being there they must be evil-disposed and wicked people, before whose vicious eyes it is necessary to flourish threats and harsh restraints. They are met at the very threshold with this mild appeal. All within-doors is very plain and simple, as it ought to be, but arranged with a view to peace and comfort. It costs no more than any other plan of arrangement, but it speaks an amount of consideration for those who are reduced to seek a shelter there, which puts them at once upon their gratitude and good behaviour. Instead of being parcelled out in great, long, rambling wards, where a certain amount of weazen life may mope, and pine, and shiver, all day long, the building is divided into separate rooms, each with its share of light and air. In these, the better kind of paupers live. They have a motive for exertion and becoming pride, in the desire to make these little chambers comfortable and decent.

I do not remember one but it was clean and neat, and had its plant or two upon the window-sill, or row of crockery upon the shelf, or small display of coloured prints upon the whitewashed wall, or, perhaps, its wooden clock behind the door.

The orphans and young children are in an adjoining building; separate from this, but a part of the same Institution. Some are such little creatures, that the stairs are of Lilliputian measurement, fitted to their tiny strides. The same consideration for their years and weakness is expressed in their very seats, which are perfect curiosities, and look like articles of furniture for a pauper doll's-house. I can imagine the glee of our Poor Law Commissioners at the notion of these seats having arms and backs; but small spines being of older date than their occupation of the Board-room at Somerset House, I thought even this provision very merciful. . . .

One other establishment closes the catalogue. It is the House of Correction for the State, in which silence is strictly maintained, but where the prisoners have the comfort and mental relief of seeing each other, and of working together. This is the improved system of Prison Discipline which we have imported into England, and which has been in successful operation among us for some years past.

America, as a new and not over-populated country, has in all her prisons, the one great advantage, of being enabled to find useful and profitable work for the inmates; whereas, with us, the prejudice against prison labour is naturally very strong, and almost insurmountable, when honest men who have not offended against the laws are frequently doomed to seek employment in vain. Even in the United States, the principle of bringing convict labour and free labour into a competition which must obviously be to the disadvantage of the latter, has already found many opponents, whose number is not likely to diminish with access of years.

For this very reason though, our best prisons would seem at the first glance to be better conducted than those of America. The treadmill is conducted with little or no noise; five hundred men may pick oakum in the same room, without a sound; and both kinds of labour admit of such keen and vigilant superintendence, as will render even a word of personal communication amongst the prisoners almost impossible. On the other hand, the noise of the loom, the forge, the carpenter's hammer, or the stonemason's saw, greatly favour those opportunities of intercourse—hurried and brief no doubt, but opportunities still—which these several kinds of work, by rendering it necessary for men to be employed very near to each other, and often side by side, without any barrier or partition between them, in their very nature present. . . . In an American state prison or house of correction, I found it difficult at first to persuade myself that I was really in a jail: a place of ignominious punishment and endurance. And to this hour I very much question whether the humane boast that it is not like one has its root in the true wisdom or philosophy of the matter.

I hope I may not be misunderstood on this subject, for it is one in which I take a strong and deep interest. I incline as little to the sickly feeling which makes every canting lie or maudlin speech of a notorious criminal a subject of newspaper report and general sympathy, as I do to those good old customs of the good old times which made England, even so recently as in the reign of the Third King George, in respect of her criminal code and her prison regulations, one of the most bloody-minded and barbarous countries on the earth. . . . At the same time I know, as all men do or should, that the subject of Prison Discipline is one of the highest importance to any community; and that in her sweeping reform and bright example to other countries on this head, America has shown great wisdom, great benevolence, and exalted policy. In contrasting her system with that which we have modelled upon it, I merely seek to show that with all its drawbacks, ours has some advantages of its own.

The House of Correction which has led to these remarks, is not walled, like other prisons, but is palisaded round about with tall rough stakes, something after the manner of an enclosure for keeping elephants in, as we see it represented in Eastern prints and pictures. The prisoners wear a parti-coloured dress; and those who are sentenced to hard labour, work at nail-making, or stone-cutting. When I was there, the latter class of labourers were employed upon the stone for a new custom-house in course of erection at Boston. They appeared to shape it skilfully and with expedition, though there were very few among them (if any) who had not acquired the art within the prison gates. . . .

Such are the Institutions at South Boston! In all of them, the unfortunate or degenerate citizens of the State are carefully instructed in their duties both to God and man; are surrounded by all reasonable means of comfort and happiness that their condition will admit of; are appealed to, as members of the great human family, however afflicted, indigent, or fallen; are ruled by the strong Heart, and not by the strong (though immeasurably weaker) Hand. . . . I mean to take them for a model, and to content myself with saying of others we may come to, whose design and purpose are the same, that in this or that respect they practically fail, or differ.

I wish by this account of them, imperfect in its execution, but in its just intention, honest, I could hope to convey to my readers one-hundredth part of the gratification, the sights I have described, afforded me.

To an Englishman, accustomed to the paraphernalia of Westminster Hall, an American Court of Law is as odd a sight as, I suppose, an English Court of Law would be to an American. Except in the Supreme Court at Washington (where the judges wear a plain black robe), there is no such thing as a wig or gown connected with the administration of justice. The gentlemen of the bar being barristers and attorneys too (for there is no division of those functions as in England) are no more removed from their clients than attorneys in our Court for the Relief of Insolvent Debtors are, from theirs. The jury are quite at home, and make themselves as comfortable as circumstances will permit. The witness is so little elevated above, or put aloof from, the crowd in the court, that a stranger entering during a pause in the proceedings would find it difficult to pick him out from the rest. And if it chanced to be a criminal trial, his eyes, in nine cases out of ten, would wander to the dock in search of the prisoner, in vain; for that gentleman would most likely be lounging among the most distinguished ornaments of the legal profession, whispering suggestions in his counsel's ear, or making a toothpick out of an old quill with his penknife.

I could not but notice these differences, when I visited the courts at Boston. I was much surprised at first, too, to observe that the counsel who interrogated the witness under examination at the time, did so *sitting*. But seeing that he was also occupied in writing down the answers, and remembering that he was alone and had no 'junior,' I quickly consoled myself with the reflection that law was not quite so expensive an article here, as at home; and that the absence of sundry formalities which we regard as indispensable, had doubtless a very favourable influence upon the bill of costs.

In every Court, ample and commodious provision is made for the accommodation of the citizens. This is the case all through America. In every Public Institution, the right of the people to attend, and to have an interest in the proceedings, is most fully and distinctly recognised. There are no grim door-keepers to dole out their tardy civility by the sixpenny-worth; nor is there, I sincerely believe, any insolence of office of any kind. Nothing national is exhibited for money; and no public officer is a showman. We have begun of late years to imitate this good example. I hope we shall continue to do so; and that in the fulness of time, even deans and chapters may be converted. . . .

I am by no means a wholesale admirer of our legal solemnities, many of which impress me as being exceedingly ludicrous. Strange as it may seem too, there is undoubtedly a degree of protection in the wig and gown —a dismissal of individual responsibility in dressing for the part—which encourages that insolent bearing and language, and that gross perversion of the office of a pleader for The Truth, so frequent in our courts of law. Still, I cannot help doubting whether America, in her desire to shake off the absurdities and abuses of the old system, may not have gone too far into the opposite extreme; and whether it is not desirable, especially in the small community of a city like this, where each man knows the other, to surround the administration of justice with some artificial barriers against the 'Hail fellow, well met' deportment of everyday life. All the aid it can have in the very high character and ability of the Bench, not only here but elsewhere, it has, and well deserves to have; but it may need something more: not to impress the thoughtful and the well-informed, but the ignorant and heedless; a class which includes some prisoners and many witnesses. These institutions were established, no doubt, upon the principle that those who had so large a share in making the laws, would certainly respect them. But experience has proved this hope to be fallacious; for no men know better than the Judges of America, that on the occasion of any great popular excitement the law is powerless, and cannot, for the time, assert its own supremacy.

The tone of society in Boston is one of perfect politeness, courtesy, and good breeding. The ladies are unquestionably very beautiful–in face: but there I am compelled to stop. Their education is much as with us; neither better nor worse. I had heard some very marvellous stories in this respect; but not believing them, was not disappointed. Blue ladies there are, in Boston; but like philosophers of that colour and sex in most other latitudes, they rather desire to be thought superior than to be so. Evangelical ladies there are, likewise, whose attachment to the forms of religion, and horror of theatrical entertainments, are most exemplary. Ladies who have a passion for attending lectures are to be found among all classes and all conditions. In the kind of provincial life which prevails in cities such as this, the Pulpit has great influence. The peculiar province of the Pulpit in New England (always excepting the Unitarian Ministry) would appear to be the denouncement of all innocent and rational amusements. The church, the chapel, and the lecture-room, are the only means of excitement excepted; and to the church, the chapel, and the lecture-room, the ladies resort in crowds.

Wherever religion is resorted to, as a strong drink, and as an escape from the dull monotonous round of home, those of its ministers who pepper the highest will be the surest to please. They who strew the Eternal Path with the greatest amount of brimstone, and who most ruthlessly tread down the flowers and leaves that grow by the wayside, will be voted the most righteous; and they who enlarge with the greatest pertinacity on the difficulty of getting into heaven, will be considered by all true believers certain of going there: though it would be hard to say by what process of reasoning this conclusion is arrived at. It is so at home, and it is so abroad. With regard to the other means of excitement, the Lecture, it has at least the merit of being always new. One lecture treads so quickly on the heels of another, that none are remembered; and the course of this month may be safely repeated next, with its charm of novelty unbroken, and its interest unabated. . . . Such of its [Boston's] social customs as I have not mentioned . . . may be told in a very few words.

The usual dinner-hour is two o'clock. A dinner party takes place at five; and at an evening party, they seldom sup later than eleven; so that it goes hard but one gets home, even from a rout, by midnight. I never could find out any difference between a party at Boston and a party in London, saving that at the former place all assemblies are held at more rational hours; that the conversation may possibly be a little louder and more cheerful; and a guest is usually expected to ascend to the very top of the house to take his cloak off; that he is certain to see, at every dinner, an unusual amount of poultry on the table; and at every supper, at least two mighty bowls of hot stewed oysters, in any one of which a half-grown Duke of Clarence might be smothered easily.

There are two theatres in Boston, of good size and construction, but sadly in want of patronage. The few ladies who resort to them, sit, as of right, in the front rows of the boxes.

The bar is a large room with a stone floor, and there people stand and smoke, and lounge about, all the evening: dropping in and out as the humour takes them. There too the stranger is initiated into the mysteries of Gin-sling, Cock-tail, Sangaree, Mint Julep, Sherrycobbler, Timber Doodle, and other rare drinks. The house is full of boarders, both married and single, many of whom sleep upon the premises, and contract by the week for their board and lodging: the charge for which diminishes as they go nearer the sky to roost. A public table is laid in a very handsome hall for breakfast, and for dinner, and for supper. The party sitting down together to these meals will vary in number from one to two hundred: sometimes more. The advent of each of these epochs in the day is proclaimed by an awful gong, which shakes the very window-frames as it reverberates through the house, and horribly disturbs nervous foreigners. There is an ordinary for ladies, and an ordinary for gentlemen.

In our private room the cloth could not, for any earthly consideration, have been laid for dinner without a huge glass dish of cranberries in the middle of the table; and breakfast would have been no breakfast unless the principal dish were a deformed beef-steak with a great flat bone in the centre, swimming in hot butter, and sprinkled with the very blackest of all possible pepper. Our bedroom was spacious and airy, but (like every bedroom on this side of the Atlantic) very bare of furniture, having no curtains to the French bedstead or to the window. It had one unusual luxury, however, in the shape of a wardrobe of painted wood, something smaller than an English watch-box; or if this comparison should be insufficient to convey a just idea of its dimensions, they may be estimated from the fact of my having lived for fourteen days and nights in the firm belief that it was a shower-bath.

An American Railroad. Lowell and Its Factory System

Before leaving Boston, I devoted one day to an excursion to Lowell. . . . I made acquaintance with an American railroad, on this occasion, for the first time. As these works are pretty much alike all through the States, their general characteristics are easily described.

There are no first and second class carriages as with us; but there is a gentleman's car and a ladies' car: the main distinction between which is that in the first, everybody smokes; and in the second, nobody does. As a black man never travels with a white one, there is also a negro car; which is a great, blundering, clumsy chest, such as Gulliver put to sea in, from the kingdom of Brobdingnag. There is a great deal of jolting, a great deal of noise, a great deal of wall, not much window, a locomotive engine, a shriek, and a bell.

The cars are like shabby omnibuses, but larger: holding thirty, forty, fifty, people. The seats, instead of stretching from end to end, are placed crosswise. Each seat holds two persons. There is a long row of them on each side of the caravan, a narrow passage up the middle, and a door at both ends. In the centre of the carriage there is usually a stove, fed with charcoal or anthracite coal; which is for the most part red-hot. It is insufferably close; and you see the hot air fluttering between yourself and any other object you may happen to look at, like the ghost of smoke.

In the ladies' car, there are a great many gentlemen who have ladies with them. There are also a great many ladies who have nobody with them: for any lady may travel alone, from one end of the United States to the other, and be certain of the most courteous and considerate treatment everywhere. . . . A great many newspapers are pulled out, and a few of them are read. Everybody talks to you, or to anybody else who hits his fancy. If you are an Englishman, he expects that that railroad is pretty much like an English railroad. If you say 'No,' he says 'Yes?' (interrogatively), and asks in what respect they differ. You enumerate the heads of difference, one by one, and he says 'Yes?' (still interrogatively) to each. Then he guesses that you don't travel faster in England; and on your replying that you do, says 'Yes?' again (still interrogatively), and it is quite evident, don't believe it. After a long pause he remarks, partly to you, and partly to the knob on the top of his stick, that 'Yankees are reckoned to be considerable of a go-ahead people too;' upon which *you* say 'Yes,' and then *he* says 'Yes' again (affirmatively this time). . . .

If a lady take a fancy to any male passenger's seat, the gentleman who accompanies her gives him notice of the fact, and he immediately vacates it with great politeness. Politics are much discussed, so are banks, so is cotton. Quiet people avoid the question of the Presidency, for there will be a new election in three years and a half, and party feeling runs very high: the great constitutional feature of this institution being, that directly the acrimony of the last election is over, the acrimony of the next one begins; which is an unspeakable comfort to all strong politicians and true lovers of their country: that is to say, to ninety-nine men and boys out of every ninety-nine and a quarter. . . .

Although only just of age—for if my recollection serve me, it has been a manufacturing town barely one-and-twenty years—Lowell is a large, populous, thriving place. Those indications of its youth which first attract the eye, give it a quaintness and oddity of character which, to a visitor from the old country, is amusing enough. It was a very dirty winter's day, and nothing in the whole town looked old to me, except the mud, which in some parts was almost knee-deep, and might have been deposited there, on the subsiding of the waters after the Deluge. In one place, there was a new wooden church, which, having no steeple, and being yet unpainted, looked like an enormous packing-case without any direction upon it. In another there was a large hotel, whose walls and colonnades were so crisp, and thin, and slight, that it had exactly the appearance of being built with cards. I was careful not to draw my breath as we passed, and trembled when I saw a workman come out upon the roof, lest with one thoughtless stamp of his foot he should crush the structure beneath him, and bring it rattling down. . . . One would swear that every 'Bakery,' 'Grocery,' and 'Bookbindery,' and other kind of store, took its shutters down for the first time, and started in business yesterday. The golden pestles and mortars fixed as signs upon the sun-blind frames outside the Druggists', appear to have been just turned out of the United States' Mint. . . .

There are several factories in Lowell. . . . I went over several of these; such as a woollen factory, a carpet factory, and a cotton factory: examined them in every part; and saw them in their ordinary working aspect, with no preparation of any kind, or departure from their ordinary everyday proceedings. I may add that I am well acquainted with our manufacturing towns in England, and have visited many mills in Manchester and elsewhere in the same manner.

I happened to arrive at the first factory just as the dinner hour was over, and the girls were returning to their work. . . . They were all well dressed, but not to my thinking above their condition; for I like to see the humbler classes of society careful of their dress and appearance, and even, if they please, decorated with such little trinkets as come within the compass of their means. Supposing it confined within reasonable limits, I would always encourage this kind of pride, as a worthy element of self-respect, in any person I employed. . . .

These girls, as I have said, were all well dressed: and that phrase necessarily includes extreme cleanliness. They had serviceable bonnets, good warm cloaks, and shawls; and were not above clogs and pattens. Moreover, there were places in the mill in which they could deposit these things without injury; and there were conveniences for washing. They were healthy in appearance, many of them remarkably so, and had the manners and deportment of young women: not of degraded brutes of burden. If I had seen in one of those mills (but I did not, though I looked for something of this kind with a sharp eye), the most lisping, mincing, affected, and ridiculous young creature that my imagination could suggest, I should have thought of the careless, moping, slatternly, degraded, dull reverse (I *have* seen that), and should have been still well pleased to look upon her.

The rooms in which they worked, were as well ordered as themselves. In the windows of some, there were green plants, which were trained to shade the glass; in all, there was as much fresh air, cleanliness, and comfort, as the nature of the occupation would possibly admit of. . . . I solemnly declare, that from all the crowd I saw in the different factories that day, I cannot recall or separate one young face that gave me a painful impression; not one young girl whom, assuming it to be a matter of necessity that she should gain her daily bread by the labour of her hands, I would have removed from those works if I had had the power.

They reside in various boarding-houses near at hand. The owners of the mills are particularly careful to allow no persons to enter upon the possession of these houses, whose characters have not undergone the most searching and thorough inquiry. Any complaint that is made against them, by the boarders, or by any one else, is fully investigated; and if good ground of complaint be shown to exist against them, they are removed, and their occupation is handed over to some more deserving person. There are a few children employed in these factories, but not many. The laws of the State forbid their working more than nine months in the year, and require that they be educated during the other three. . . .

At some distance from the factories, and on the highest and pleasantest ground in the neighbourhood, stands their hospital, or boarding-house for the sick: it is the best house in those parts, and was built by an eminent merchant for his own residence. . . . It is divided into convenient chambers, each of which has all the comforts of a very comfortable home. The principal medical attendant resides under the same roof; and were the patients members of his own family, they could not be better cared for, or attended with greater gentleness and consideration. The weekly charge in this establishment for each female patient is three dollars, or twelve shillings English; but no girl employed by any of the corporations is ever excluded for want of the means of payment. That they do not very often want the means, may be gathered from the fact, that in July, 1841, no fewer than nine hundred and seventy-eight of these girls were depositors in the Lowell Savings Bank: the amount of whose joint savings was estimated at one hundred thousand dollars, or twenty thousand English pounds.

I am now going to state three facts, which will startle a large class of readers on this side of the Atlantic, very much.

Firstly, there is a joint-stock piano in a great many of the boarding-houses. Secondly, nearly all these young ladies subscribe to circulating libraries. Thirdly, they have got up among themselves a periodical called THE LOWELL OFFERING, 'A repository of original articles, written exclusively by females actively employed in the mills,'—which is duly printed, published, and sold; and whereof I brought away from Lowell four hundred good solid pages, which I have read from beginning to end.

The large class of readers, startled by these facts, will exclaim, with one voice, 'How very preposterous!' On my deferentially inquiring why, they will answer, 'These things are above their station.' In reply to that objection, I would beg to ask what their station is.

It is their station to work. And they *do* work. They labour in these mills, upon an average, twelve hours a day, which is unquestionably work, and pretty tight work too. Perhaps it is above their station to indulge in such amusements, on any terms. Are we quite sure that we in England have not formed our ideas of the 'station' of working people, from accustoming ourselves to the contemplation of that class as they are, and not as they might be? I think that if we examine our own feelings, we shall find that the pianos, and the circulating libraries, and even the Lowell Offering, startle us by their novelty, and not by their bearing upon any abstract question of right or wrong.

For myself, I know no station in which, the occupation of to-day cheerfully done and the occupation of to-morrow cheerfully looked to, any one of these pursuits is not most humanising and laudable. I know no station which is rendered more endurable to the person in it, or more safe to the person out of it, by having ignorance for its associate. I know no station which has a right to monopolise the means of mutual instruction, improvement, and rational entertainment; or which has ever continued to be a station very long, after seeking to do so.

Of the merits of the Lowell Offering as a literary production, I will only observe . . . that it will compare advantageously with a great many English Annuals. . . . Some persons might object to the papers being signed occasionally with rather fine names, but this is an American fashion. One of the provinces of the state legislature of Massachusetts is to alter ugly names into pretty ones, as the children improve upon the tastes of their parents. These changes costing little or nothing, scores of Mary Annes are solemnly converted into Bevelinas every session. . . .

In this brief account of Lowell, and inadequate expression of the gratification it yielded me, and cannot fail to afford to any foreigner to whom the condition of such people at home is a subject of interest and anxious speculation, I have carefully abstained from drawing a comparison between these factories and those of our own land. Many of the circumstances whose strong influence has been at work for years in our manufacturing towns have not arisen here; and there is no manufacturing population in Lowell, so to speak: for these girls (often the daughters of small farmers) come from other States, remain a few years in the mills, and then go home for good.

The contrast would be a strong one, for it would be between the Good and Evil, the living light and deepest shadow. I abstain from it, because I deem it just to do so. But I only the more earnestly adjure all those whose eyes may rest on these pages, to pause and reflect upon the difference between this town and those great haunts of desperate misery: to call to mind, if they can in the midst of party strife and squabble, the efforts that must be made to purge them of their suffering and danger: and last, and foremost, to remember how the precious Time is rushing by. . . .

New York

The beautiful metropolis of America is by no means so clean a city as Boston, but many of its streets have the same characteristics; except that the houses are not quite so fresh-coloured, the sign-boards are not quite so gaudy, the gilded letters not quite so golden, the bricks not quite so red, the stone not quite so white, the blinds and area railings not quite so green, the knobs and plates upon the street doors not quite so bright and twinkling. There are many by-streets, almost as neutral in clean colours, and positive in dirty ones, as by-streets in London; and there is one quarter, commonly called the Five Points, which, in respect of filth and wretchedness, may be safely backed against Seven Dials, or any other part of famed St. Giles's.

The great promenade and thoroughfare, as most people know, is Broadway; a wide and bustling street, which, from the Battery Gardens to its opposite termination in a country road, may be four miles long. Shall we sit down in an upper floor of the Carlton House Hotel (situated in the best part of this main artery of New York), and when we are tired of looking down upon the life below, sally forth arm-in-arm, and mingle with the stream? . . .

Was there ever such a sunny street as this Broadway! The pavement stones are polished with the tread of feet until they shine again; the red bricks of the houses might be yet in the dry, hot kilns; and the roofs of those omnibuses look as though, if water were poured on them, they would hiss and smoke, and smell like half-quenched fires. No stint of omnibuses here! Half-a-dozen have gone by within as many minutes. Plenty of hackney cabs and coaches too; gigs, phaetons, large-wheeled tilburies, and private carriages—rather of a clumsy make, and not very different from the public vehicles, but built for the heavy roads beyond the city pavement. Negro coachmen and white; in straw hats, black hats, white hats, glazed caps, fur caps; in coats of drab, black, brown, green, blue, nankeen, striped jean and linen; and there, in that one instance (look while it passes, or it will be too late), in suits of livery. Some southern republican that, who puts his blacks in uniform, and swells with Sultan pomp and power. . . . Heaven save the ladies, how they dress! We have seen more colours in these ten minutes, than we should have seen elsewhere, in as many days. What various parasols! what rainbow silks and satins! what pinking of thin stockings, and pinching of thin shoes, and fluttering of ribbons and silk tassels, and display of rich cloaks with gaudy hoods and linings! The young gentlemen are fond, you see, of turning down their shirt-collars and cultivating their whiskers, especially under the chin; but they cannot approach the ladies in their dress or bearing, being, to say the truth, humanity of quite another sort. Byrons of the desk and counter, pass on, and let us see what kind of men those are behind ye: those two labourers in holiday clothes, of whom one carries in his hand a crumpled scrap of paper from which he tries to spell out a hard name, while the other looks about for it on all the doors and windows.

Irishmen both! You might know them, if they were masked, by their long-tailed blue coats and bright buttons, and their drab trousers, which they wear like men well used to working dresses, who are easy in no others. It would be hard to keep your model republics going, without the countrymen and countrywomen of those two labourers. For who else would dig, and delve, and drudge, and do domestic work, and make canals and roads, and execute great lines of Internal Improvement! . . .

This narrow thoroughfare, baking and blistering in the sun, is Wall Street: the Stock Exchange and Lombard Street of New York. Many a rapid fortune has been made in this street, and many a no less rapid ruin. Some of these very merchants whom you see hanging about here now, have locked up money in their strong-boxes, like the man in the Arabian Nights, and opening them again, have found but withered leaves. Below, here by the water-side, where the bowsprits of ships stretch across the footway, and almost thrust themselves into the windows, lie the noble American vessels which have made their Packet Service the finest in the world. They have brought hither the foreigners who abound in all the streets: not, perhaps, that there are more here, than in other commercial cities; but elsewhere, they have particular haunts, and you must find them out; here, they pervade the town. . . .

What is this dismal-fronted pile of bastard Egyptian, like an enchanter's palace in a melodrama!—a famous prison, called The Tombs. Shall we go in?

So. A long, narrow, lofty building, stove-heated as usual, with four galleries, one above the other, going round it, and communicating by stairs. Between the two sides of each gallery, and in its centre, a bridge, for the greater convenience of crossing. On each of these bridges sits a man: dozing or reading, or talking to an idle companion. On each tier, are two opposite rows of small iron doors. They look like furnace-doors, but are cold and black, as though the fires within had all gone out. Some two or three are open, and women, with drooping heads bent down, are talking to the inmates. The whole is lighted by a skylight, but it is fast closed; and from the roof there dangle, limp and drooping, two useless windsails.

A man with keys appears, to show us round. A good-looking fellow, and, in his way, civil and obliging.

'Are those black doors the cells?'

'Yes.'

'Are they all full?'

'Well, they're pretty nigh full, and that's a fact, and no two ways about it.'

'Those at the bottom are unwholesome, surely?'

'Why, we *do* only put coloured people in 'em. That's the truth.'

'When do the prisoners take exercise?'

'Well, they do without it pretty much.' . . .

'But suppose a man were here for a twelvemonth. I know this is only a prison for criminals who are charged with grave offences, while they are awaiting their trial, or under remand, but the law here affords criminals many means of delay. What with motions for new trials, and in arrest of judgment, and what not, a prisoner might be here for twelve months, I take it, might he not?'

'Well, I guess he might.'

'Do you mean to say that in all that time he would never come out at that little iron door, for exercise?'

'He might walk some, perhaps–not much.'

'Will you open one of the doors?'

'All, if you like.'

The fastenings jar and rattle, and one of the doors turns slowly on its hinges. Let us look in. A small bare cell, into which the light enters through a high chink in the wall. There is a rude means of washing, a table, and a bedstead. Upon the latter, sits a man of sixty; reading. He looks up for a moment; gives an impatient dogged shake; and fixes his eyes upon his book again. As we withdraw our heads, the door closes on him, and is fastened as before. This man has murdered his wife, and will probably be hanged.

'How long has he been here?'

'A month.'

'When will he be tried?'

'Next term.'

'When is that?'

'Next month.'

'In England, if a man be under sentence of death, even he has air and exercise at certain periods of the day.'

'Possible?'

With what stupendous and untranslatable coolness he says this, and how loungingly he leads on to the women's side: making, as he goes, a kind of iron castanet of the key and the stair-rail!

Each cell door on this side has a square aperture in it. Some of the women peep anxiously through it at the sound of footsteps; others shrink away in shame.–For what offence can that lonely child, of ten or twelve years old, be shut up here? Oh! that boy? He is the son of the prisoner we saw just now; is a witness against his father; and is detained here for safe keeping, until the trial; that's all.

But it is a dreadful place for the child to pass the long days and nights in. This is rather hard treatment for a young witness, is it not?–What says our conductor?

'Well, it ain't a very rowdy life, and *that's* a fact!' . . .

The prison-yard in which he pauses now, has been the scene of terrible performances. Into this narrow, grave-like place, men are brought out to die. The wretched creature stands beneath the gibbet on the ground; the rope about his neck; and when the sign is given, a weight at its other end comes running down, and swings him up into the air—a corpse.

The law requires that there be present at this dismal spectacle, the judge, the jury, and citizens to the amount of twenty-five. From the community it is hidden. To the dissolute and bad, the thing remains a frightful mystery. Between the criminal and them, the prison-wall is interposed as a thick gloomy veil. It is the curtain to his bed of death, his winding-sheet, and grave. From him it shuts out life, and all the motives to unrepenting hardihood in that last hour, which its mere sight and presence is often all-sufficient to sustain. There are no bold eyes to make him bold; no ruffians to uphold a ruffian's name before. All beyond the pitiless stone wall, is unknown space.

Let us go forth again into the cheerful streets.

Once more in Broadway! . . . We are going to cross here. Take care of the pigs. Two portly sows are trotting up behind this carriage, and a select party of half-a-dozen gentlemen hogs have just now turned the corner.

Here is a solitary swine lounging homeward by himself. He . . . leads a roving, gentlemanly, vagabond kind of life, somewhat answering to that of our club-men at home. He leaves his lodgings every morning at a certain hour, throws himself upon the town, gets through his day in some manner quite satisfactory to himself, and regularly appears at the door of his own house again at night, like the mysterious master of Gil Blas. He is a free-and-easy, careless, indifferent kind of pig, having a very large acquaintance among other pigs of the same character, whom he rather knows by sight than conversation, as he seldom troubles himself to stop and exchange civilities, but goes grunting down the kennel, turning up the news and small-talk of the city in the shape of cabbage-stalks and offal, and bearing no tails but his own: which is a very short one, for his old enemies, the dogs, have been at that too, and have left him hardly enough to swear by. He is in every respect a republican pig, going wherever he pleases, and mingling with the best society, on an equal, if not superior footing, for every one makes way when he appears, and the haughtiest give him the wall, if he prefer it. He is a great philosopher, and seldom moved, unless by the dogs before mentioned. Sometimes, indeed, you may see his small eye twinkling on a slaughtered friend, whose carcase garnishes a butcher's door-post, but he grunts out 'Such is life: all flesh is pork!' . . .

But how quiet the streets are! Are there no itinerant bands; no wind or stringed instruments? No, not one. By day, are there no Punches, Fantoccini [puppets], Dancing-dogs, Jugglers, Conjurers, Orchestrinas, or even Barrel-organs? No, not one. Yes, I remember one. One barrel-organ and a dancing-monkey—sportive by nature, but fast fading into a dull, lumpish monkey, of the Utilitarian school. . . .

Are there no amusements? Yes. There is a lecture-room across the way, from which that glare of light proceeds, and there may be evening service for the ladies thrice a week, or oftener. For the young gentlemen, there is the counting-house, the store, the bar-room: the latter, as you may see through these windows, pretty full. Hark! to the clinking sound of hammers breaking lumps of ice, and to the cool gurgling of the pounded bits, as, in the process of mixing, they are poured from glass to glass! No amusements? What are these suckers of cigars and swallowers of strong drinks, whose hats and legs we see in every possible variety of twist, doing, but amusing themselves? What are the fifty newspapers, which those precocious urchins are bawling down the street, and which are kept filed within, what are they but amusements? Not vapid, waterish amusements, but good strong stuff; dealing in round abuse and blackguard names; pulling off the roofs of private houses, as the Halting Devil did in Spain; pimping and pandering for all degrees of vicious taste, and gorging with coined lies the most voracious maw; imputing to every man in public life the coarsest and the vilest motives; scaring away from the stabbed and prostrate body-politic, every Samaritan of clear conscience and good deeds; and setting on, with yell and whistle and the clapping of foul hands, the vilest vermin and worst birds of prey.—No amusements!

Let us go on again; and . . . plunge into the Five Points. But it is needful, first, that we take as our escort these two heads of the police, whom you would know for sharp and well-trained officers if you met them in the Great Desert. So true it is, that certain pursuits, wherever carried on, will stamp men with the same character. These two might have been begotten, born, and bred, in Bow Street.[1]

We have seen no beggars in the streets by night or day; but of other kinds of strollers, plenty. Poverty, wretchedness, and vice, are rife enough where we are going now.

This is the place: these narrow ways, diverging to the right and left, and reeking everywhere with dirt and filth. Such lives as are led here, bear the same fruits here as elsewhere. The coarse and bloated faces at the doors, have counterparts at home, and all the wide world over. Debauchery has made the very houses prematurely old. See how the rotten beams are tumbling down, and how the patched and broken windows seem to scowl dimly, like eyes that have been hurt in drunken frays. Many of those pigs live here. Do they ever wonder why their masters walk upright in lieu of going on all-fours? and why they talk instead of grunting? . . .

Ascend these pitch-dark stairs, heedful of a false footing on the trembling boards, and grope your way with me into this wolfish den, where neither ray of light nor breath of air, appears to come. A negro lad, startled from his sleep by the officer's voice—he knows it well—but comforted by his assurance that he has not come on business, officiously bestirs himself to light a candle. The match flickers for a moment, and shows great mounds of dusty rags upon the ground; then dies away and leaves a denser darkness than before, if there can be degrees in such extremes. He stumbles down the stairs and presently comes back, shading a flaring taper with his hand.

[1]In Bow Street is located London's principal police court.

Then the mounds of rags are seen to be astir, and rise slowly up, and the floor is covered with heaps of negro women, waking from their sleep: their white teeth chattering, and their bright eyes glistening and winking on all sides with surprise and fear, like the countless repetition of one astonished African face in some strange mirror.

Mount up these other stairs with no less caution (there are traps and pitfalls here, for those who are not so well escorted as ourselves) into the housetop; where the bare beams and rafters meet overhead, and calm night looks down through the crevices in the roof. Open the door of one of these cramped hutches full of sleeping negroes. Pah! They have a charcoal fire within; there is a smell of singeing clothes, or flesh, so close they gather round the brazier; and vapours issue forth that blind and suffocate. From every corner, as you glance about you in these dark retreats, some figure crawls half-awakened, as if the judgment-hour were near at hand, and every obscene grave were giving up its dead. Where dogs would howl to lie, women, and men, and boys slink off to sleep, forcing the dislodged rats to move away in quest of better lodgings. . . .

Our leader has his hand upon the latch of 'Almack's,' and calls to us from the bottom of the steps; for the assembly-room of the Five Point fashionables is approached by a descent. Shall we go in? It is but a moment.

Heyday! the landlady of Almack's thrives! A buxom fat mulatto woman, with sparkling eyes, whose head is daintily ornamented with a handkerchief of many colours. Nor is the landlord much behind her in his finery, being attired in a smart blue jacket, like a ship's steward, with a thick gold ring upon his little finger, and round his neck a gleaming golden watch-guard. How glad he is to see us! What will we please to call for? A dance? It shall be done directly, sir: 'a regular break-down.' . . .

. . . The dance commences. Every gentleman sets as long as he likes to the opposite lady, and the opposite lady to him, and all are so long about it that the sport begins to languish, when suddenly the lively hero dashes in to the rescue. Instantly the fiddler grins, and goes at it tooth and nail; there is new energy in the tambourine; new laughter in the dancers; new smiles in the landlady; new confidence in the landlord; new brightness in the very candles. Single shuffle, double shuffle, cut and cross-cut; snapping his fingers, rolling his eyes, turning in his knees, presenting the backs of his legs in front, spinning about on his toes and heels like nothing but the man's fingers on the tambourine; dancing with two left legs, two right legs, two wooden legs, two wire legs, two spring legs—all sorts of legs and no legs—what is this to him? And in what walk of life, or dance of life, does man ever get such stimulating applause as thunders about him, when, having danced his partner off her feet, and himself too, he finishes by leaping gloriously on the bar-counter, and calling for something to drink, with the chuckle of a million of counterfeit Jim Crows, in one inimitable sound!

The air, even in these distempered parts, is fresh after the stifling atmosphere of the houses; and now, as we emerge into a broader street, it blows upon us with a purer breath, and the stars look bright again. Here are The Tombs once more. The city watch-house is a part of the building. It follows naturally on the sights we have just left. Let us see that, and then to bed.

What! do you thrust your common offenders against the police discipline of the town, into such holes as these? Do men and women, against whom no crime is proved, lie here all night in perfect darkness, surrounded by the noisome vapours which encircle that flagging lamp you light us with, and breathing this filthy and offensive stench! Why, such indecent and disgusting dungeons as these cells, would bring disgrace upon the most despotic empire in the world! Look at them, man—you, who see them every night, and keep the keys. Do you see what they are? Do you know how drains are made below the streets, and wherein these human sewers differ, except in being always stagnant?

Well, he don't know. He has had five-and-twenty young women locked up in this very cell at one time, and you'd hardly realise what handsome faces there were among 'em.

In God's name! shut the door upon the wretched creature who is in it now, and put its screen before a place, quite unsurpassed in all the vice, neglect, and devilry, of the worst old town in Europe.

Are people really left all night, untried, in those black sties?—Every night. The watch is set at seven in the evening. The magistrate opens his court at five in the morning. That is the earliest hour at which the first prisoner can be released; and if an officer appear against him, he is not taken out till nine o'clock or ten.—But if any one among them die in the interval, as one man did, not long ago? Then he is half-eaten by the rats in an hour's time; as that man was; and there an end. . . .

One day, during my stay in New York, I paid a visit to the different public institutions on Long Island, or Rhode Island: I forget which. One of them is a Lunatic Asylum. The building is handsome; and is remarkable for a spacious and elegant staircase. The whole structure is not yet finished, but it is already one of considerable size and extent, and is capable of accommodating a very large number of patients.

The terrible crowd with which these halls and galleries were filled, so shocked me, that I abridged my stay within the shortest limits. . . . I have no doubt that the gentleman who presided over this establishment at the time I write of, was competent to manage it, and had done all in his power to promote its usefulness: but will it be believed that the miserable strife of Party feeling is carried even into this sad refuge of afflicted and degraded humanity? Will it be believed that the eyes which are to watch over and control the wanderings of minds on which the most dreadful visitation to which our nature is exposed has fallen, must wear the glasses of some wretched side in Politics? Will it be believed that the governor of such a house as this, is appointed, and deposed, and changed perpetually, as Parties fluctuate and vary, and as their despicable weathercocks are blown this way or that? A hundred times in every week, some new most paltry exhibition of that narrow-minded and injurious Party Spirit, which is the Simoom of America, sickening and blighting everything of wholesome life within its reach, was forced upon my notice; but I never turned my back upon it with feelings of such deep disgust and measureless contempt, as when I crossed the threshold of this madhouse.

At a short distance from this building is another called the Alms House, that is to say, the workhouse of New York. This is a large Institution also: lodging, I believe, when I was there, nearly a thousand poor. It was badly ventilated, and badly lighted; was not too clean; and impressed me, on the whole, very uncomfortably. But it must be remembered that New York, as a great emporium of commerce, and as a place of general resort, not only from all parts of the States, but from most parts of the world, has always a large pauper population to provide for; and labours, therefore, under peculiar difficulties in this respect. Nor must it be forgotten that New York is a large town, and that in all large towns a vast amount of good and evil is intermixed and jumbled up together. . . .

I was taken to these Institutions by water, in a boat belonging to the Island Jail, and rowed by a crew of prisoners, who were dressed in a striped uniform of black and buff, in which they looked like faded tigers. They took me, by the same conveyance, to the Jail itself.

It is an old prison, and quite a pioneer establishment, on the plan I have already described. I was glad to hear this, for it is unquestionably a very indifferent one. The most is made, however, of the means it possesses, and it is as well regulated as such a place can be.

The women work in covered sheds, erected for that purpose. If I remember right, there are no shops for the men, but be that as it may, the greater part of them labour in certain stone-quarries near at hand. The day being very wet indeed, this labour was suspended, and the prisoners were in their cells. Imagine these cells, some two or three hundred in number, and in every one a man locked up; this one at his door for air, with his hands thrust through the grate; this one in bed (in the middle of the day, remember); and this one flung down in a heap upon the ground, with his head against the bars, like a wild beast. Make the rain pour down, outside, in torrents. Put the everlasting stove in the midst; hot, and suffocating, and vaporous, as a witch's cauldron. Add a collection of gentle odours, such as would arise from a thousand mildewed umbrellas, wet through, and a thousand buck-baskets, full of half-washed linen—and there is the prison, as it was that day.

The prison for the State at Sing Sing is, on the other hand, a model jail. That, and Auburn, are, I believe, the largest and best examples of the silent system.

In another part of the city, is the Refuge for the Destitute: an Institution whose object is to reclaim youthful offenders, male and female, black and white, without distinction; to teach them useful trades, apprentice them to respectable masters, and make them worthy members of society. Its design,

Every cell has double doors: the outer one of sturdy oak, the other of grated iron, wherein there is a trap through which his food is handed. He has a Bible, and a slate and pencil, and, under certain restrictions, has sometimes other books, provided for the purpose, and pen and ink and paper. His razor, plate, and can, and basin, hang upon the wall, or shine upon the little shelf. Fresh water is laid on in every cell, and he can draw it at his pleasure. During the day, his bedstead turns up against the wall, and leaves more space for him to work in. His loom, or bench, or wheel, is there; and there he labours, sleeps and wakes, and counts the seasons as they change, and grows old.

The first man I saw, was seated at his loom, at work. He had been there six years, and was to remain, I think, three more. He had been convicted as a receiver of stolen goods, but even after his long imprisonment, denied his guilt, and said he had been hardly dealt by. It was his second offence.

He stopped his work when we went in, took off his spectacles, and answered freely to everything that was said to him, but always with a strange kind of pause first, and in a low, thoughtful voice. He wore a paper hat of his own making, and was pleased to have it noticed and commended. He had very ingeniously manufactured a sort of Dutch clock from some disregarded odds and ends; and his vinegar-bottle served for the pendulum. Seeing me interested in this contrivance, he looked up at it with a great deal of pride, and said that he had been thinking of improving it, and that he hoped the hammer and a little piece of broken glass beside it 'would play music before long.' He had extracted some colours from the yarn with which he worked, and painted a few poor figures on the wall. One, of a female, over the door, he called 'The Lady of the Lake.'

He smiled as I looked at these contrivances to while away the time; but when I looked from them to him, I saw that his lip trembled, and could have counted the beating of his heart. I forget how it came about, but some allusion was made to his having a wife. He shook his head at the word, turned aside, and covered his face with his hands.

'But you are resigned now!' said one of the gentlemen after a short pause, during which he had resumed his former manner. He answered with a sigh that seemed quite reckless in its hopelessness, 'Oh yes, oh yes! I am resigned to it.' 'And are a better man, you think?' 'Well, I hope so: I'm sure I hope I may be.' 'And time goes pretty quickly?' 'Time is very long, gentlemen, within these four walls!'

He gazed about him—Heaven only knows how wearily!—as he said these words; and in the act of doing so, fell into a strange stare as if he had forgotten something. A moment afterwards he sighed heavily, put on his spectacles, and went about his work again. . . .

Sitting upon the stairs, engaged in some slight work, was a pretty coloured boy. 'Is there no refuge for young criminals in Philadelphia, then?' said I. 'Yes, but only for white children.' Noble aristocracy in crime!

There was a sailor who had been there upwards of eleven years, and who in a few months' time would be free. Eleven years of solitary confinement!

'I am very glad to hear your time is nearly out.' What does he say? Nothing. Why does he stare at his hands, and pick the flesh upon his fingers, and raise his eyes for an instant, every now and then, to those bare walls which have seen his head turn grey? It is a way he has sometimes.

Does he never look men in the face, and does he always pluck at those hands of his, as though he were bent on parting skin and bone? It is his humour: nothing more.

It is his humour too, to say that he does not look forward to going out; that he is not glad the time is drawing near; that he did look forward to it once, but that was very long ago; that he has lost all care for everything. It is his humour to be a helpless, crushed, and broken man. And, Heaven be his witness that he has his humour thoroughly gratified! . . .

I went from cell to cell that day; and every face I saw, or word I heard, or incident I noted, is present to my mind in all its painfulness. But let me pass them by, for one, more pleasant, glance of a prison on the same plan which I afterwards saw at Pittsburgh.

When I had gone over that, in the same manner, I asked the governor if he had any person in his charge who was shortly going out. He had one, he said, whose time was up next day; but he had only been a prisoner two years.

Two years! I looked back through two years of my own life—out of jail, prosperous, happy, surrounded by blessings, comforts, good fortune—and thought how wide a gap it was, and how long those two years passed in solitary captivity would have been. I have the face of this man, who was going to be released next day, before me now. It is almost more memorable in its happiness than the other faces in their misery. How easy and how natural it was for him to say that the system was a good one; and that the time went 'pretty quick—considering;' and that when a man once felt that he had offended the law, and must satisfy it, 'he got along, somehow:' and so forth!

'What did he call you back to say to you, in that strange flutter?' I asked of my conductor, when he had locked the door and joined me in the passage.

'Oh! That he was afraid the soles of his boots were not fit for walking, as they were a good deal worn when he came in; and that he would thank me very much to have them mended, ready.'

Those boots had been taken off his feet, and put away with the rest of his clothes, two years before!

I took that opportunity of inquiring how they conducted themselves immediately before going out; adding that I presumed they trembled very much.

'Well, it's not so much a trembling,' was the answer—'though they do quiver—as a complete derangement of the nervous system. They can't sign their names to the book; sometimes can't even hold the pen; look about 'em without appearing to know why, or where they are; and sometimes get up and sit down again, twenty times in a minute. This is when they're in the office, where they are taken with the hood on, as they were brought in. When they get outside the gate; they stop, and look first one way and then the other; not knowing which to take. Sometimes they stagger as if they were drunk, and sometimes are forced to lean against the fence, they're so bad:—but they clear off in course of time.' . . .

On the haggard face of every man among these prisoners, the same expression sat. I know not what to liken it to. It had something of that strained attention which we see upon the faces of the blind and deaf, mingled with a kind of horror, as though they had all been secretly terrified. In every little chamber that I entered, and at every grate through which I looked, I seemed to see the same appalling countenance. It lives in my memory, with the fascination of a remarkable picture. Parade before my eyes a hundred men, with one among them newly released from this solitary suffering, and I would point him out. . . .

My firm conviction is that, independent of the mental anguish it occasions—an anguish so acute and so tremendous, that all imagination of it must fall far short of the reality—it wears the mind into a morbid state, which renders it unfit for the rough contact and busy action of the world. It is my fixed opinion that those who have undergone this punishment, MUST pass into society again morally unhealthy and diseased. There are many instances on record, of men who have chosen, or have been condemned, to lives of perfect solitude, but I scarcely remember one, even among sages of strong and vigorous intellect, where its effect has not become apparent, in some disordered train of thought, or some gloomy hallucination. What monstrous phantoms, bred of despondency and doubt, and born and reared in solitude, have stalked upon the earth, making creation ugly, and darkening the face of Heaven!

Suicides are rare among these prisoners: are almost, indeed, unknown. But no argument in favour of the system, can reasonably be deduced from this circumstance, although it is very often urged. All men who have made diseases of the mind their study, know perfectly well that such extreme depression and despair as will change the whole character, and beat down all its powers of elasticity and self-resistance, may be at work within a man, and yet stop short of self-destruction. This is a common case.

That it makes the senses dull, and by degrees impairs the bodily faculties, I am quite sure. I remarked to those who were with me in this very establishment at Philadelphia, that the criminals who had been there long, were deaf. They, who were in the habit of seeing these men constantly, were perfectly amazed at the idea, which they regarded as groundless and fanciful. And yet the very first prisoner to whom they appealed—one of their own selection—confirmed my impression (which was unknown to him) instantly, and said, with a genuine air it was impossible to doubt, that he couldn't think how it happened, but he *was* growing very dull of hearing.

That it is a singularly unequal punishment, and affects the worst man least, there is no doubt. In its superior efficiency as a means of reformation, compared with that other code of regulations which allows the prisoners to work in company without communicating together, I have not the smallest faith. All the instances of reformation that were mentioned to me, were of a kind that might have been. . . .

Washington. The Legislature. The President's House

We left Philadelphia by steamboat, at six o'clock one very cold morning, and turned our faces towards Washington.

In the course of this day's journey, as on subsequent occasions, we encountered some Englishmen (small farmers, perhaps, or country publicans at home) who were settled in America, and were travelling on their own affairs. Of all grades and kinds of men that jostle one in the public conveyances of the States, these are often the most intolerable and the most insufferable companions. United to every disagreeable characteristic that the worst kind of American travellers possess, these countrymen of ours display an amount of insolent conceit and cool assumption of superiority, quite monstrous to behold. In the coarse familiarity of their approach, and the effrontery of their inquisitiveness (which they are in great haste to assert, as if they panted to revenge themselves upon the decent old restraints of home), they surpass any native specimens that came within my range of observation: and I often grew so patriotic when I saw and heard them, that I would cheerfully have submitted to a reasonable fine, if I could have given any other country in the whole world, the honour of claiming them for its children.

As Washington may be called the head-quarters of tobacco-tinctured saliva, the time is come when I must confess, without any disguise, that the prevalence of those two odious practices of chewing and expectorating began about this time to be anything but agreeable, and soon became most offensive and sickening. In all the public places of America, this filthy custom is recognised. In the courts of law, the judge has his spittoon, the crier his, the witness his, and the prisoner his; while the jurymen and spectators are provided for, as so many men who in the course of nature must desire to spit incessantly. In the hospitals, the students of medicine are requested, by notices upon the wall, to eject their tobacco juice into the boxes provided for that purpose, and not to discolour the stairs. In public buildings, visitors are implored, through the same agency, to squirt the essence of their quids, or 'plugs,' as I have heard them called by gentlemen learned in this kind of sweetmeat, into the national spittoons, and not about the bases of the marble columns. But in some parts, this custom is inseparably mixed up with every meal and morning call, and with all the transactions of social life. The stranger, who follows in the track I took myself, will find it in its full bloom and glory, luxuriant in all its alarming recklessness, at Washington. And let him not persuade himself (as I once did, to my shame) that previous tourists have exaggerated its extent. The thing itself is an exaggeration of nastiness, which cannot be outdone. . . .

We stopped to dine at Baltimore, and being now in Maryland, were waited on, for the first time, by slaves. The sensation of exacting any service from human creatures who are bought and sold, and being, for the time, a party as it were to their condition, is not an enviable one. The institution exists, perhaps, in its least repulsive and most mitigated form in such a town as this; but it *is* slavery; and though I was, with respect to it, an innocent man, its presence filled me with a sense of shame and self-reproach.

After dinner, we went down to the railroad again, and took our seats in the cars for Washington. Being rather early, those men and boys who happened to have nothing particular to do, and were curious in foreigners, came (according to custom) round the carriage in which I sat; let down all the windows; thrust in their heads and shoulders; hooked themselves on conveniently, by their elbows; and fell to comparing notes on the subject of my personal appearance, with as much indifference as if I were a stuffed figure. I never gained so much uncompromising information with reference to my own nose and eyes, and various impressions wrought by my mouth and chin on different minds, and how my head looks when it is viewed from behind, as on these occasions. Some gentlemen were only satisfied by exercising their sense of touch; and the boys (who are surprisingly precocious in America) were seldom satisfied, even by that, but would return to the charge over and over again. Many a budding president has walked into my room with his cap on his head and his hands in his pockets, and stared at me for two whole hours: occasionally refreshing himself with a tweak of his nose, or a draught from the water-jug; or by walking to the windows and inviting other boys in the street below, to come up and do likewise: crying, 'Here he is!' 'Come on!' 'Bring all your brothers!' with other hospitable entreaties of that nature.

We reached Washington at about half-past six that evening, and had upon the way a beautiful view of the Capitol, which is a fine building of the Corinthian order, placed upon a noble and commanding eminence. Arrived at the hotel; I saw no more of the place that night; being very tired, and glad to get to bed.

Breakfast over next morning, I walk about the streets for an hour or two. . . . Here is Washington, fresh in my mind and under my eye. . . .

It is sometimes called the City of Magnificent Distances, but it might with greater propriety be termed the City of Magnificent Intentions; for it is only on taking a bird's-eye view of it from the top of the Capitol, that one can at all comprehend the vast designs of its projector, an aspiring Frenchman.[2] Spacious avenues, that begin in nothing, and lead nowhere; streets, mile-long, that only want houses, roads and inhabitants; public buildings

[2]Pierre L'Enfant.

that need but a public to be complete; and ornaments of great thoroughfares, which only lack great thoroughfares to ornament—are its leading features. One might fancy the season over, and most of the houses gone out of town for ever with their masters. To the admirers of cities it is a Barmecide Feast: a pleasant field for the imagination to rove in; a monument raised to a deceased project, with not even a legible inscription to record its departed greatness.

Such as it is, it is likely to remain. It was originally chosen for the seat of Government, as a means of averting the conflicting jealousies and interests of the different States; and very probably, too, as being remote from mobs: a consideration not to be slighted, even in America. It has no trade or commerce of its own: having little or no population beyond the President and his establishment; the members of the legislature who reside there during the session; the Government clerks and officers employed in the various departments; the keepers of the hotels and boarding-houses; and the tradesmen who supply their tables. It is very unhealthy. Few people would live in Washington, I take it, who were not obliged to reside there; and the tides of emigration and speculation, those rapid and regardless currents, are little likely to flow at any time towards such dull and sluggish water. . . .

I do not remember having ever fainted away, or having even been moved to tears of joyful pride, at sight of any legislative body. I have borne the House of Commons like a man, and have yielded to no weakness, but slumber, in the House of Lords. I have seen elections for borough and county, and have never been impelled (no matter which party won) to damage my hat by throwing it up into the air in triumph, or to crack my voice by shouting forth any reference to our Glorious Constitution, to the noble purity of our independent voters, or the unimpeachable integrity of our independent members. Having withstood such strong attacks upon my fortitude, it is possible that I may be of a cold and insensible temperament, amounting to iciness, in such matters; and therefore my impressions of the live pillars of the Capitol at Washington must be received with such grains of allowance as this free confession may seem to demand.

Did I see in this public body an assemblage of men, bound together in the sacred names of Liberty and Freedom, and so asserting the chaste dignity of those twin goddesses, in all their discussions, as to exalt at once the Eternal Principles to which their names are given, and their own character and the character of their countrymen, in the admiring eyes of the whole world?

It was but a week, since an aged, grey-haired man, a lasting honour to the land that gave him birth, who has done good service to his country, as his forefathers did, and who will be remembered scores upon scores of years after the worms bred in its corruption are but so many grains of dust—it was but a week, since this old man had stood for days upon his trial before this very body, charged with having dared to assert the infamy of that traffic, which has for its accursed merchandise men and women, and their unborn children. Yes. And publicly exhibited in the same city all the while;

gilded, framed and glazed; hung up for general admiration; shown to strangers not with shame, but pride; its face not turned towards the wall, itself not taken down and burned; is the Unanimous Declaration of the Thirteen United States of America, which solemnly declares that All Men are created Equal; and are endowed by their Creator with the Inalienable Rights of Life, Liberty, and the Pursuit of Happiness!

It was not a month, since this same body had sat calmly by, and heard a man, one of themselves, with oaths which beggars in their drink reject, threaten to cut another's throat from ear to ear. There he sat, among them; not crushed by the general feeling of the assembly, but as good a man as any.

There was but a week to come, and another of that body, for doing his duty to those who sent him there; for claiming in a Republic the Liberty and Freedom of expressing their sentiments, and making known their prayer; would be tried, found guilty, and have strong censure passed upon him by the rest. His was a grave offence indeed; for years before, he had risen up and said, 'A gang of male and female slaves for sale, warranted to breed like cattle, linked to each other by iron fetters, are passing now along the open street beneath the windows of your Temple of Equality! Look!' But there are many kinds of hunters engaged in the Pursuit of Happiness, and they go variously armed. It is the Inalienable Right of some among them, to take the field after *their* Happiness equipped with cat and cartwhip, stocks, and iron collar, and to shout their view halloa! (always in praise of Liberty) to the music of clanking chains and bloody stripes.

Where sat the many legislators of coarse threats; of words and blows such as coalheavers deal upon each other, when they forget their breeding? On every side. Every session had its anecdotes of that kind, and the actors were all there.

Did I recognise in this assembly, a body of men, who, applying themselves in a new world to correct some of the falsehoods and vices of the old, purified the avenues to Public Life, paved the dirty ways to Place and Power, debated and made laws for the Common Good, and had no party but their Country?

I saw in them, the wheels that move the meanest perversion of virtuous Political Machinery that the worst tools ever wrought. Despicable trickery at elections; under-handed tamperings with public officers; cowardly attacks upon opponents, with scurrilous newspapers for shields, and hired pens for daggers; shameful trucklings to mercenary knaves, whose claim to be considered, is, that every day and week they sow new crops of ruin with their venal types, which are the dragon's teeth of yore, in everything but sharpness; aidings and abettings of every bad inclination in the popular mind, and artful suppressions of all its good influences: such things as these, and in a word, Dishonest Faction in its most depraved and most unblushing form, stared out from every corner of the crowded hall.

Did I see among them, the intelligence and refinement: the true, honest, patriotic heart of America? Here and there, were drops of its blood and life, but they scarcely coloured the stream of desperate adventures which sets that way for profit and for pay. It is the game of these men, and of their profligate organs, to make the strife of politics so fierce and brutal, and so destructive of all self-respect in worthy men, that sensitive and delicate-minded persons shall be kept aloof, and they, and such as they, be left to battle out their selfish views unchecked. And thus this lowest of all scrambling fights goes on, and they who in other countries would, from their intelligence and station, most aspire to make the laws, do here recoil the farthest from that degradation.

That there are, among the representatives of the people in both Houses, and among all parties, some men of high character and great abilities, I need not say. The foremost among those politicians who are known in Europe, have been already described, and I see no reason to depart from the rule I have laid down for my guidance, of abstaining from all mention of individuals. It will be sufficient to add, that to the most favourable accounts that have been written of them, I more than fully and most heartily subscribe; and that personal intercourse and free communication have bred within me, not the result predicted in the very doubtful proverb, but increased admiration and respect. They are striking men to look at, hard to deceive, prompt to act, lions in energy, Crichtons in varied accomplishments, Indians in fire of eye and gesture, Americans in strong and generous impulse; and they as well represent the honour and wisdom of their country at home, as the distinguished gentleman who is now its Minister at the British Court sustains its highest character abroad. . . .

The Senate is a dignified and decorous body, and its proceedings are conducted with much gravity and order. Both houses are handsomely carpeted; but the state to which these carpets are reduced by the universal disregard of the spittoon with which every honourable member is accommodated, and the extraordinary improvements on the pattern which are squirted and dabbled upon it in every direction, do not admit of being described. I will merely observe, that I strongly recommend all strangers not to look at the floor; and if they happen to drop anything, though it be their purse, not to pick it up with an ungloved hand on any account. . . .

The President's mansion is more like an English club-house, both within and without, than any other kind of establishment with which I can compare it. The ornamental ground about it has been laid out in garden walks; they are pretty, and agreeable to the eye; though they have that uncomfortable air of having been made yesterday, which is far from favourable to the display of such beauties.

My first visit to this house was on the morning after my arrival, when I was carried thither by an official gentleman, who was so kind as to charge himself with my presentation to the President.[3]

We entered a large hall, and having twice or thrice rung a bell which

[3]John Tyler.

nobody answered, walked without further ceremony through the rooms on the ground floor, as divers other gentlemen (mostly with their hats on, and their hands in their pockets) were doing very leisurely. Some of these had ladies with them, to whom they were showing the premises; others were lounging on the chairs and sofas; others, in a perfect state of exhaustion from listlessness, were yawning drearily. The greater portion of this assemblage were rather asserting their supremacy than doing anything else, as they had no particular business there, that anybody knew of. A few were closely eyeing the movables, as if to make quite sure that the President (who was far from popular) had not made away with any of the furniture, or sold the fixtures for his private benefit.

After glancing at these loungers; who were scattered over a pretty drawing-room, opening upon a terrace which commanded a beautiful prospect of the river and the adjacent country; and who were sauntering, too, about a larger state-room called the Eastern Drawing-room; we went upstairs into another chamber, where were certain visitors, waiting for audiences. At sight of my conductor, a black in plain clothes and yellow slippers who was gliding noiselessly about, and whispering messages in the ears of the more impatient, made a sign of recognition, and glided off to announce him. . . .

We had not waited in this room many minutes, before the black messenger returned, and conducted us into another of smaller dimensions, where, at a business-like table covered with papers, sat the President himself. He looked somewhat worn and anxious, and well he might; being at war with everybody—but the expression of his face was mild and pleasant, and his manner was remarkably unaffected, gentlemanly, and agreeable. I thought that in his whole carriage and demeanour, he became his station singularly well.

Being advised that the sensible etiquette of the republican court admitted of a traveller, like myself, declining, without any impropriety, an invitation to dinner, which did not reach me until I had concluded my arrangements for leaving Washington some days before that to which it referred, I only returned to this house once. It was on the occasion of one of those general assemblies which are held on certain nights, between the hours of nine and twelve o'clock, and are called, rather oddly, Levees.

I went, with my wife, at about ten. There was a pretty dense crowd of carriages and people in the court-yard, and so far as I could make out, there were no very clear regulations for the taking up or setting down of company. There were certainly no policemen to soothe startled horses, either by sawing at their bridles or flourishing truncheons in their eyes; and I am ready to make oath that no inoffensive persons were knocked violently on the head, or poked acutely in their backs or stomachs; or brought to a standstill by any such gentle means, and then taken into custody for not moving on. But there was no confusion or disorder. Our carriage reached the porch in its turn, without any blustering, swearing, shouting, backing, or other disturbance: and we dismounted with as much ease and comfort as though we had been escorted by the whole Metropolitan Force from A to Z inclusive.

The suite of rooms on the ground-floor were lighted up, and a military band was playing in the hall. In the smaller drawing-room, the centre of a circle of company, were the President and his daughter-in-law, who acted as the lady of the mansion; and a very interesting, graceful, and accomplished lady too. One gentleman who stood among this group, appeared to take upon himself the functions of a master of the ceremonies. I saw no other officers or attendants, and none were needed.

The great drawing-room, which I have already mentioned, and the other chambers on the ground-floor, were crowded to excess. The company was not, in our sense of the term, select, for it comprehended persons of very many grades and classes; nor was there any great display of costly attire: indeed, some of the costumes may have been, for aught I know, grotesque enough. But the decorum and propriety of behaviour which prevailed, were unbroken by any rude or disagreeable incident; and every man, even among the miscellaneous crowd in the hall who were admitted without any orders or tickets to look on, appeared to feel that he was a part of the Institution, and was responsible for its preserving a becoming character, and appearing to the best advantage.

That these visitors, too, whatever their station, were not without some refinement of taste and appreciation of intellectual gifts, and gratitude to those men who, by the peaceful exercise of great abilities, shed new charms and associations upon the homes of their countrymen, and elevate their character in other lands, was most earnestly testified by their reception of Washington Irving, my dear friend, who had recently been appointed Minister at the court of Spain, and who was among them that night, in his new character, for the first and last time before going abroad. I sincerely believe that in all the madness of American politics, few public men would have been so earnestly, devotedly, and affectionately caressed, as this most charming writer: and I have seldom respected a public assembly more, than I did this eager throng, when I saw them turning with one mind from noisy orators and officers of state, and flocking with a generous and honest impulse round the man of quiet pursuits: proud in his promotion as reflecting back upon their country: and grateful to him with their whole hearts for the store of graceful fancies he had poured out among them. Long may he dispense such treasures with unsparing hand; and long may they remember him as worthily! . . .

Richmond. Harrisburg

We were to proceed in the first instance by steamboat; and as it is usual to sleep on board, in consequence of the starting-hour being four o'clock in the morning, we went down to where she lay, at that very uncomfortable time for such expeditions when slippers are most valuable, and a familiar bed, in the perspective of an hour or two, looks uncommonly pleasant.

It is ten o'clock at night: say half-past ten: moonlight, warm, and dull enough. The steamer (not unlike a child's Noah's ark in form, with the machinery on the top of the roof) is riding lazily up and down, and bumping clumsily against the wooden pier, as the ripple of the river trifles with its unwieldy carcase. . . . As soon as our footsteps are heard upon the planks, a fat negress, particularly favoured by nature in respect of bustle, emerges from some dark stairs, and marshals my wife towards the ladies' cabin, to which retreat she goes, followed by a mighty bale of cloaks and great-coats. . . .

I . . . open the door of the gentlemen's cabin; and walk in. Somehow or other—from its being so quiet, I suppose—I have taken it into my head that there is nobody there. To my horror and amazement it is full of sleepers in every stage, shape, attitude, and variety of slumber: in the berths, on the chairs, on the floors, on the tables, and particularly round the stove, my detested enemy. I take another step forward, and slip on the shining face of a black steward, who lies rolled in a blanket on the floor. He jumps up, grins, half in pain and half in hospitality; whispers my own name in my ear; and groping among the sleepers, leads me to my berth. . . . Having but partially undressed, I clamber on my shelf, . . . turn round: and go to sleep.

I wake, of course, when we get under weigh, for there is a good deal of noise. . . . I huddle on my clothes, go down into the fore-cabin, get shaved by the barber, and wash myself. The washing and dressing apparatus for the passengers generally, consists of two jack-towels, three small wooden basins, a keg of water and a ladle to serve it out with, six square inches of looking-glass, two ditto ditto of yellow soap, a comb and brush for the head, and nothing for the teeth. Everybody uses the comb and brush, except myself. Everybody stares to see me using my own; and two or three gentlemen are strongly disposed to banter me on my prejudices, but don't. . . .

Soon after nine o'clock we come to Potomac Creek, where we are to land; and then comes the oddest part of the journey. Seven stage-coaches are preparing to carry us on. . . . The coaches are something like the French coaches, but not nearly so good. In lieu of springs, they are hung on bands of the strongest leather. There is very little choice or difference between them; and they may be likened to the car portion of the swings at an English fair, roofed, put upon axle-trees and wheels, and curtained with painted canvas. They are covered with mud from the roof to the wheel-tire, and have never been cleaned since they were first built. . . .

I throw my coat on the box, and hoist my wife and her maid into the inside. It has only one step, and that being about a yard from the ground, is usually approached by a chair: when there is no chair, ladies trust in

Providence. The coach holds nine inside, having a seat across from door to door, where we in England put our legs: so that there is only one feat more difficult in the performance than getting in, and that is, getting out again. There is only one outside passenger, and he sits upon the box. As I am that one, I climb up; . . . somebody in authority cries 'Go ahead!' . . . The mail takes the lead in a four-horse waggon, and all the coaches follow in procession. . . .

By the way, whenever an Englishman would cry 'All right!' an American cries 'Go ahead!' which is somewhat expressive of the national character of the two countries.

The first half-mile of the road is over bridges made of loose planks laid across two parallel poles, which tilt up as the wheels roll over them; and IN the river. The river has a clayey bottom and is full of holes, so that half a horse is constantly disappearing unexpectedly, and can't be found again for some time.

But we get past even this, and come to the road itself, which is a series of alternate swamps and gravel pits. A tremendous place is close before us, the black driver rolls his eyes, screws his mouth up very round. . . . He takes a rein in each hand; jerks and pulls at both; and dances on the splashboard with both feet (keeping his seat, of course). . . . We come to the spot, sink down in the mire nearly to the coach windows, tilt on one side at an angle of forty-five degrees, and stick there. The insides scream dismally; the coach stops; the horses flounder; all the other six coaches stop; and their four-and-twenty horses flounder likewise: but merely for company, and in sympathy with ours. . . .

They run up the bank, and go down again on the other side at a fearful pace. It is impossible to stop them, and at the botton there is a deep hollow, full of water. The coach rolls frightfully. The insides scream. The mud and water fly about us. The black driver dances like a madman. Suddenly we are all right by some extraordinary means, and stop to breathe. . . .

And so we do the ten miles or thereabouts in two hours and a half; breaking no bones, though bruising a great many. . . .

This singular kind of coaching terminates at Fredericksburgh, whence there is a railway to Richmond. The tract of country through which it takes its course was once productive; but the soil has been exhausted by the system of employing a great amount of slave labour in forcing crops, without strengthening the land: and it is now little better than a sandy desert overgrown with trees. Dreary and uninteresting as its aspect is, I was glad to the heart to find anything on which one of the curses of this horrible institution has fallen; and had greater pleasure in contemplating the withered ground, than the richest and most thriving cultivation in the same place could possibly have afforded me.

In this district as in all others where slavery sits brooding (I have frequently heard this admitted, even by those who are its warmest advocates:) there is an air of ruin and decay abroad, which is inseparable from the system. The barns and outhouses are mouldering away; the sheds are patched and half roofless; the log cabins (built in Virginia with external chimneys made of clay or wood) are squalid in the last degree. There is no look of decent comfort anywhere. The miserable stations by the railway side; the great wild wood-yards, whence the engine is supplied with fuel; the negro children rolling on the ground before the cabin doors, with dogs and pigs; the biped beasts of burden slinking past: gloom and dejection are upon them all.

In the negro car belonging to the train in which we made this journey, were a mother and her children who had just been purchased; the husband and father being left behind with their old owner. The children cried the whole way, and the mother was misery's picture. The champion of Life, Liberty, and the Pursuit of Happiness, who had bought them, rode in the same train; and, every time we stopped, got down to see that they were safe. The black in Sinbad's Travels with one eye in the middle of his forehead which shone like a burning coal, was nature's aristocrat compared with this white gentleman. . . .

On the following day, I visited a plantation or farm, of about twelve hundred acres, on the opposite bank of the river from Richmond. Here . . . although I went down with the owner of the estate, to 'the quarter,' as that part of it in which the slaves live is called, I was not invited to enter into any of their huts. All I saw of them, was, that they were very crazy, wretched cabins, near to which groups of half-naked children basked in the sun, or wallowed on the dusty ground. But I believe that this gentleman is a considerate and excellent master, who inherited his fifty slaves, and is neither a buyer nor a seller of human stock; and I am sure, from my own observation and conviction, that he is a kind-hearted, worthy man.

The planter's house was an airy, rustic dwelling, that brought Defoe's description of such places strongly to my recollection. The day was very warm, but the blinds being all closed, and the windows and doors set wide open, a shady coolness rustled through the rooms, which was exquisitely refreshing after the glare and heat without. Before the windows was an open piazza, where, in what they call the hot weather—whatever that may be—they sling hammocks, and drink and doze luxuriously. I do not know how their cool refections may taste within the hammocks, but, having experience, I can report that, out of them, the mounds of ices and the bowls of mint-julep and sherry-cobbler they make in these latitudes, are refreshments never to be thought of afterwards, in summer, by those who would preserve contented minds. . . .

The same decay and gloom that overhang the way by which it is approached, hover above the town of Richmond. There are pretty villas and cheerful houses in its streets, and Nature smiles upon the country round; but jostling its handsome residences, like slavery itself going hand in hand with many lofty virtues, are deplorable tenements, fences unrepaired, walls crumbling into ruinous heaps. Hinting gloomily at things below the surface, these, and many other tokens of the same description, force themselves upon the notice, and are remembered with depressing influence, when livelier features are forgotten.

To those who are happily unaccustomed to them, the countenances in the streets and labouring-places, too, are shocking. All men who know that there are laws against instructing slaves, of which the pains and penalties greatly exceed in their amount the fines imposed on those who maim and torture them, must be prepared to find their faces very low in the scale of intellectual expression. But the darkness—not of skin, but mind—which meets the stranger's eye at every turn; the brutalizing and blotting out of all fairer characters traced by Nature's hand; immeasurably outdo his worst belief. That travelled creation of the great satirist's brain, who fresh from living among horses, peered from a high casement down upon his own kind with trembling horror, was scarcely more repelled and daunted by the sight, than those who look upon some of these faces for the first time must surely be.

I left the last of them behind me in the person of a wretched drudge, who, after running to and fro all day till midnight, and moping in his stealthy winks of sleep upon the stairs betweenwhiles, was washing the dark passages at four o'clock in the morning; and went upon my way with a grateful heart that I was not doomed to live where slavery was, and had never had my senses blunted to its wrongs and horrors in a slave-rocked cradle. . . .

I . . . resolved to set forward on our western journey without any more delay. . . . We left Baltimore at half-past eight in the morning, and reached the town of York, some sixty miles off, by the early dinner-time of the Hotel which was the starting-place of the four-horse coach, wherein we were to proceed to Harrisburg. . . .

'If here ain't the Harrisburg mail at last, and dreadful bright and smart to look at too,' cried an elderly gentleman in some excitement, 'darn my mother!'

I don't know what the sensation of being darned may be, or whether a man's mother has a keener relish or disrelish of the process than anybody else; but if the endurance of this mysterious ceremony by the old lady in question had depended on the accuracy of her son's vision in respect to the abstract brightness and smartness of the Harrisburg mail, she would certainly have undergone its infliction. However, they booked twelve people inside; and the luggage (including such trifles as a large rocking-chair, and a good-sized dining-table) being at length made fast upon the roof, we started off in great state. . . .

The coachmen always change with the horses, and are usually as dirty as the coach. The first was dressed like a very shabby English baker; the second like a Russian peasant: for he wore a loose purple camlet robe, with a fur collar, tied round his waist with a parti-coloured worsted sash; grey trousers; light blue gloves: and a cap of bearskin. It had by this time come on to rain very heavily, and there was a cold damp mist besides, which penetrated to the skin. I was glad to take advantage of a stoppage and get down to stretch my legs, shake the water off my great-coat, and swallow the usual anti-temperance recipe for keeping out the cold.

When I mounted to my seat again, I observed a new parcel lying on the coach roof, which I took to be a rather large fiddle in a brown bag. In the course of a few miles, however, I discovered that it had a glazed cap at one end and a pair of muddy shoes at the other; and further observation demonstrated it to be a small boy in a snuff-coloured coat, with his arms quite pinioned to his sides, by deep forcing into his pockets. He was, I presume, a relative or friend of the coachman's, as he lay a-top of the luggage with his face towards the rain; and except when a change of position brought his shoes in contact with my hat, he appeared to be asleep. At last, on some occasion of our stopping, this thing slowly upreared itself to the height of three feet six, and fixing its eyes on me, observed in piping accents, with a complaisant yawn, half quenched in an obliging air of friendly patronage, 'Well now, stranger, I guess you find this a'most like an English arternoon, hey?' . . .

At length . . . we emerged upon the streets of Harrisburg, whose feeble lights, reflected dismally from the wet ground, did not shine out upon a very cheerful city. We were soon established in a snug hotel, which though smaller and far less splendid than many we put up at, it raised above them all in my remembrance, by having for its landlord the most obliging, considerate, and gentlemanly person I ever had to deal with.

As we were not to proceed upon our journey until the afternoon, I walked out, after breakfast the next morning, to look about me; and was duly shown a model prison on the solitary system, just erected, and as yet without an inmate; the trunk of an old tree to which Harris, the first settler here (afterwards buried under it), was tied by hostile Indians, with his funeral pile about him, when he was saved by the timely appearance of a friendly party on the opposite shore of the river; the local legislature (for there was another of those bodies here again, in full debate); and the other curiosities of the town.

I was very much interested in looking over a number of treaties made from time to time with the poor Indians, signed by the different chiefs at the period of their ratification, and preserved in the office of the Secretary to the Commonwealth. These signatures, traced of course by their own hands, are rough drawings of the creatures or weapons they were called after. Thus, the Great Turtle makes a crooked pen-and-ink outline of a great turtle; the Buffalo sketches a buffalo; the War Hatchet sets a rough image of that weapon for his mark. So with the Arrow, the Fish, the Scalp, the Big Canoe, and all of them.

I could not but think—as I looked at these feeble and tremulous productions of hands which could draw the longest arrow to the head in a stout elk-horn bow, or split a bead or feather with a rifle-ball—of Crabbe's musings over the Parish Register, and the irregular scratches made with a pen, by men who would plough a lengthy furrow straight from end to end. Nor could I help bestowing many sorrowful thoughts upon the simple warriors whose hands and hearts were set there, in all truth and honesty; and who only learned in course of time from white men how to break their faith, and quibble out of forms and bonds. I wonder, too, how many times the credulous Big Turtle, or trusting Little Hatchet, had put his mark to treaties which were falsely read to him; and had signed away, he knew not what, until it went and cast him loose upon the new possessors of the land, a savage indeed. . . .

Canal Boat. Pittsburgh

It still continued to rain heavily, and when we went down to the canal boat (for that was the mode of conveyance by which we were to proceed) after dinner, the weather was as unpromising and obstinately wet as one would desire to see. Nor was the sight of this canal boat, in which we were to spend three or four days, by any means a cheerful one; as it involved some uneasy speculations concerning the disposal of the passengers at night, and opened a wide field of inquiry touching the other domestic arrangements of the establishment, which was sufficiently disconcerting.

However, there it was—a barge with a little house in it, viewed from the outside; and a caravan at a fair, viewed from within: the gentlemen being accommodated, as the spectators usually are, in one of those locomotive museums of penny wonders; and the ladies being partitioned off by a red curtain, after the manner of the dwarfs and giants in the same establishments, whose private lives are passed in rather close exclusiveness. . . .

No doubt it would have been a thought more comfortable if the driving rain, which now poured down more soakingly than ever, had admitted of a window being opened, or if our number had been something less than thirty; but there was scarcely time to think as much, when a train of three horses was attached to the tow-rope, the boy upon the leader smacked his whip, the rudder creaked and groaned complainingly, and we had begun our journey.

As it continued to rain most perseveringly, we all remained below: the damp gentlemen round the stove, gradually becoming mildewed by the action of the fire; and the dry gentlemen lying at full length upon the seats, or slumbering uneasily with their faces on the tables, or walking up and down the cabin, which it was barely possible for a man of the middle height to do, without making bald places on his head by scraping it against the roof. At about six o'clock, all the small tables were put together to form one long table, and everybody sat down to tea, coffee, bread, butter, salmon, shad, liver, steaks, potatoes, pickles, ham, chops, black-puddings, and sausages.

'Will you try,' said my opposite neighbour, handing me a dish of potatoes, broken up in milk and butter, 'will you try some of these fixings?'

There are few words which perform such various duties as this word 'fix.' It is the Caleb Quotem of the American vocabulary. You call upon a gentleman in a country town, and his help informs you that he is 'fixing himself' just now, but will be down directly: by which you are to understand that he is dressing. You inquire, on board a steamboat, of a fellow-passenger, whether breakfast will be ready soon, and he tells you he should think so, for when he was last below, they were 'fixing the tables:' in other words, laying the cloth. You beg a porter to collect your luggage, and he entreats you not to be uneasy, for he'll 'fix it presently:' and if you complain of indisposition, you are advised to have recourse to Doctor So-and-so, who will 'fix you' in no time.

One night, I ordered a bottle of mulled wine at an hotel where I was staying, and waited a long time for it; at length it was put upon the table with an apology from the landlord that he feared it wasn't 'fixed properly.' And I recollect once, at a stage-coach dinner, overhearing a very stern gentleman demand of a waiter who presented him with a plate of under-done roast-beef, 'whether he called *that*, fixing God A'mighty's vittles?'

There is no doubt that the meal, at which the invitation was tendered to me which has occasioned this digression, was disposed of somewhat ravenously; and that the gentlemen thrust the broad-bladed knives and the two-pronged forks further down their throats than I ever saw the same weapons go before, except in the hands of a skilful juggler: but no man sat down until the ladies were seated; or omitted any little act of politeness which could contribute to their comfort. Nor did I ever once, on any occasion, anywhere, during my rambles in America, see a woman exposed to the slightest act of rudeness, incivility, or even inattention.

By the time the meal was over, the rain, which seemed to have worn itself out by coming down so fast, was nearly over too; and it became feasible to go on deck: which was a great relief, notwithstanding its being a very small deck, and being rendered still smaller by the luggage, which was heaped together in the middle under a tarpaulin covering; leaving, on either side, a path so narrow, that it became a science to walk to and fro without tumbling overboard into the canal. It was somewhat embarrassing at first, too, to have to duck nimbly every five minutes whenever the man at the helm cried 'Bridge!' and sometimes, when the cry was 'Low Bridge,' to lie down nearly flat. But custom familiarises one to anything, and there were so many bridges that it took a very short time to get used to this.

As night came on, and we drew in sight of the first range of hills, which are the outposts of the Alleghany Mountains, the scenery, which had been uninteresting hitherto, became more bold and striking. The wet ground reeked and smoked, after the heavy fall of rain; and the croaking of the frogs (whose noise in these parts is almost incredible) sounded as though a million of fairy teams with bells were travelling through the air, and keeping pace with us. The night was cloudy yet, but moonlight too: and when we crossed the Susquehanna river—over which there is an extraordinary wooden bridge with two galleries, one above the other, so that even there, two boat teams meeting, may pass without confusion—it was wild and grand.

I have mentioned my having been in some uncertainty and doubt, at first, relative to the sleeping arrangements on board this boat. I remained in the same vague state of mind until ten o'clock or thereabouts, when going below, I found suspended on either side of the cabin, three long tiers of hanging book-shelves, designed apparently for volumes of the small octavo size. Looking with greater attention at these contrivances (wondering to find such literary preparations in such a place), I descried on each shelf a sort of microscopic sheet and blanket; then I began dimly to comprehend that the passengers were the library, and that they were to be arranged, edge-wise, on these shelves, till morning.

I was assisted to this conclusion by seeing some of them gathered round the master of the boat, at one of the tables, drawing lots with all the anxieties and passions of gamesters depicted in their countenances; while others, with small pieces of cardboard in their hands, were groping among the shelves in search of numbers corresponding with those they had drawn. As soon as any gentleman found his number, he took possession of it by immediately undressing himself and crawling into bed. The rapidity with which an agitated gambler subsided into a snoring slumberer, was one of the most singular effects I have ever witnessed. As to the ladies, they were already abed, behind the red curtain, which was carefully drawn and pinned up the centre; though as every cough, or sneeze, or whisper, behind this curtain, was perfectly audible before it, was had still a lively consciousness of their society.

The politeness of the person in authority had secured to me a shelf in a nook near this red curtain, in some degree removed from the great body of sleepers: to which place I retired, with many acknowledgments to him for his attention. I found it, on after-measurement, just the width of an ordinary sheet of Bath post letter-paper; and I was at first in some uncertainty as to the best means of getting into it. But the shelf being a bottom one, I finally determined on lying upon the floor, rolling gently in, stopping immediately I touched the mattress, and remaining for the night with that side uppermost, whatever it might be. Luckily, I came upon my back at exactly the right moment. I was much alarmed on looking upward, to see, by the shape of his half-yard of sacking (which his weight had bent into an exceedingly tight bag), that there was a very heavy gentleman above me, whom the slender cords seemed quite incapable of holding; and I could not help reflecting upon the grief of my wife and family in the event of his coming down in the night. But as I could not have got up again without a severe bodily struggle, which might have alarmed the ladies; and as I had nowhere to go to, even if I had; I shut my eyes upon the danger, and remained there. . . .

Between five and six o'clock in the morning we got up, and some of us went on deck, to give them an opportunity of taking the shelves down; while others, the morning being very cold, crowded round the rusty stove, cherishing the newly kindled fire, and filling the grate with those voluntary contributions of which they had been so liberal all night. The washing accommodations were primitive. There was a tin ladle chained to the deck, with which every gentleman who thought it necessary to cleanse himself (many were superior to this weakness), fished the dirty water out of the canal, and poured it into a tin basin, secured in like manner. There was also a jack-towel. And, hanging up before a little looking-glass in the bar, in the immediate vicinity of the bread and cheese and biscuits, were a public comb and hair-brush.

At eight o'clock, the shelves being taken down and put away and the tables joined together, everybody sat down to the tea, coffee, bread, butter, salmon, shad, liver, steak, potatoes, pickles, ham, chops, black-puddings, and sausages, all over again. Some were fond of compounding this variety, and having it all on their plates at once. As each gentleman got through his own personal amount of tea, coffee, bread, butter, salmon, shad, liver, steak, potatoes, pickles, ham, chops, black-puddings, and sausages, he rose up and walked off. When everybody had done with everything, the fragments were cleared away: and one of the waiters appearing anew in the character of a barber, shaved such of the company as desired to be shaved; while the remainder looked on, or yawned over their newspapers. Dinner was breakfast again, without the tea and coffee; and supper and breakfast were identical.

There was a man on board this boat, with a light fresh-coloured face, and a pepper-and-salt suit of clothes, who was the most inquisitive fellow that can possibly be imagined. He never spoke otherwise than interrogatively. He was an embodied inquiry. . . . Every button in his clothes said, 'Eh? What's that? Did you speak? Say that again, will you?' He was always wide awake, like the enchanted bride who drove her husband frantic; always restless; always thirsting for answers; perpetually seeking and never finding. There never was such a curious man.

I wore a fur great-coat at that time, and before we were well clear of the wharf, he questioned me concerning it, and its price, and where I bought it, and when, and what fur it was, and what it weighed, and what it cost. Then he took notice of my watch, and asked me what *that* cost, and whether it was a French watch, and where I got it, and how I got it, and whether I bought it or had it given me, and how it went, and where the key-hole was, and when I wound it, every night or every morning, and whether I ever forgot to wind it at all, and if I did, what then? Where had I been to last, and where was I going next, and where was I going after that, and had I seen the President, and what did he say, and what did I say, and what did he say when I had said that? Eh? Lor now! do tell!

Finding that nothing would satisfy him, I evaded his questions after the first score or two, and in particular pleaded ignorance respecting the name of the fur whereof the coat was made. I am unable to say whether this was the reason, but that coat fascinated him afterwards; he usually kept close behind me as I walked, and moved as I moved, that he might look at it the better; and he frequently dived into narrow places after me at the risk of his life, that he might have the satisfaction of passing his hand up the back, and rubbing it the wrong way.

We had another odd specimen on board, of a different kind. This was a thin-faced, spare-figured man of middle age and stature, dressed in a dusty drabbish-coloured suit, such as I never saw before. He was perfectly quiet during the first part of the journey: indeed I don't remember having so much as seen him until he was brought out by circumstances, as great men often are. The conjunction of events which made him famous, happened, briefly, thus.

The canal extends to the foot of the mountain, and there, of course, it stops; the passengers being conveyed across it by land carriage, and taken on afterwards by another canal boat, the counterpart of the first, which awaits them on the other side. There are two canal lines of passage-boats; one is called The Express, and one (a cheaper one) The Pioneer. The Pioneer gets first to the mountain, and waits for the Express people to come up; both sets of passengers being conveyed across it at the same time. We were the Express company; but when we had crossed the mountain, and had come to the second boat, the proprietors took it into their heads to draft all the Pioneers into it likewise, so that we were five-and-forty at least, and the accession of passengers was not at all of that kind which improved the prospect of sleeping at night. Our people grumbled at this, as people do in such cases; but suffered the boat to be towed off with the whole freight aboard nevertheless; and away we went down the canal. At home, I should have protested lustily, but being a foreigner here, I held my peace. Not so this passenger. He cleft a path among the people on deck (we were nearly all on deck), and without addressing anybody whomsoever, soliloquised as follows:

'This may suit *you*, this may, but it don't suit *me*. This may be all very well with Down Easters, and men of Boston raising, but it won't suit my figure nohow; and no two ways about *that;* and so I tell you. Now! I'm from the brown forests of Mississippi, *I* am, and when the sun shines on me, it does shine—a little. It don't glimmer where *I* live, the sun don't. No. I'm a brown forester, I am. I an't a Johnny Cake. There are no smooth skins where I live. We're rough men there. Rather. If Down Easters and men of Boston raising like this, I'm glad of it, but I'm none of that raising nor of that breed. No. This company wants a little fixing, *it* does. I'm the wrong sort of man for 'em, *I* am. They won't like me, *they* won't. This is piling of it up, a little too mountainous, this is.' At the end of every one of these short sentences he turned upon his heel, and walked the other way; checking himself abruptly when he had finished another short sentence, and turning back again.

It is impossible for me to say what terrific meaning was hidden in the words of this brown forester, but I know that the other passengers looked on in a sort of admiring horror, and that presently the boat was put back to the wharf, and as many of the Pioneers as could be coaxed or bullied into going away, were got rid of.

When we started again, some of the boldest spirits on board, made bold to say to the obvious occasion of this improvement in our prospects, 'Much obliged to you, sir;' whereunto the brown forester (waving his hand, and still walking up and down as before), replied, 'No you an't. You're none o' my raising. You may act for yourselves, *you* may. I have pinted out the way. Down Easters and Johnny Cakes can follow if they please. I an't a Johnny Cake, *I* an't. I am from the brown forests of the Mississippi, *I* am.' . . .

As we have not reached Pittsburgh yet, however, in the order of our narrative, I may go on to remark that breakfast was perhaps the least desirable meal of the day, as in addition to the many savoury odours arising from the eatables already mentioned, there were whiffs of gin, whiskey, brandy, and rum, from the little bar hard by, and a decided seasoning of stale tobacco. Many of the gentlemen passengers were far from particular in respect of their linen, which was in some cases as yellow as the little rivulets that had trickled from the corners of their mouths in chewing, and dried there. Nor was the atmosphere quite free from zephyr whisperings of the thirty beds which had just been cleared away, and of which we were further and more pressingly reminded by the occasional appearance on the table-cloth of a kind of Game, not mentioned in the Bill of Fare.

And yet despite these oddities—and even they had, for me at least, a humour of their own—there was much in this mode of travelling which I heartily enjoyed at the time, and look back upon with great pleasure. Even the running up, bare-necked, at five o'clock in the morning, from the tainted cabin to the dirty deck; scooping up the icy water, plunging one's head into it, and drawing it out, all fresh and glowing with the cold; was a good thing. The fast, brisk walk upon the towing-path, between that time and breakfast, when every vein and artery seemed to tingle with health; the exquisite beauty of the opening day, when light came gleaming off from everything; the lazy motion of the boat, when one lay idly on the deck, looking through, rather than at, the deep blue sky; the gliding on at night, so noiselessly, past frowning hills, sullen with dark trees, and sometimes angry in one red, burning spot high up, where unseen men lay crouching round a fire; the shining out of the bright stars undisturbed by noise of wheels or steam, or any other sound than the limpid rippling of the water as the boat went on: all these were pure delights.

Then there were new settlements and detached log-cabins and frame-houses, full of interest for strangers from an old country: cabins with simple ovens, outside, made of clay; and lodgings for the pigs nearly as good as many of the human quarters; broken windows, patched with worn-out hats, old clothes, old boards, fragments of blankets and paper; and home-made dressers standing in the open air without the door, whereon was ranged the household store, not hard to count, of earthen jars and pots. The eye was pained to see the stumps of great trees thickly strewn in every field of wheat, and seldom to lose the eternal swamp and dull morass, with hundreds of rotten trunks and twisted branches steeped in its unwholesome water. It was quite sad and oppressive, to come upon great tracts where settlers had been burning down the trees, and where their wounded bodies lay about, like those of murdered creatures, while here and there some charred and blackened giant reared aloft two withered arms, and seemed to call down curses on his foes. Sometimes, at night, the way wound through some lonely gorge, like a mountain pass in Scotland, shining and coldly glittering in the light of the moon, and so closed in by high steep hills all round, that there seemed to be no egress save through the narrower path by which we had come, until one rugged hill-side seemed to open, and shutting out the moonlight as we passed into its gloomy throat, wrapped our new course in shade and darkness.

We had left Harrisburg on Friday. On Sunday morning we arrived at the foot of the mountain, which is crossed by railroad. There are ten inclined planes; five *a*scending, and five *de*scending; the carriages are dragged up the former, and let slowly down the latter, by means of stationary engines; the comparatively level spaces between, being traversed, sometimes by horse, and sometimes by engine power, as the case demands. Occasionally the rails are laid upon the extreme verge of a giddy precipice; and looking from the carriage window, the traveller gazes sheer down, without a stone or scrap of fence between, into the mountain depths below. The journey is very carefully made, however; only two carriages travelling together; and while proper precautions are taken, is not to be dreaded for it dangers. . . .

On the Monday evening, furnace fires and clanking hammers on the banks of the canal, warned us that we approached the termination of this part of our journey. After going through another dreamy place—a long aqueduct across the Alleghany River, . . . we emerged upon that ugly confusion of backs of buildings and crazy galleries and stairs, which always abuts on water, whether it be river, sea, canal, or ditch: and were at Pittsburgh.

Pittsburgh is like Birmingham in England; at least its townspeople say so. Setting aside the streets, the shops, the houses, waggons, factories, public buildings, and population, perhaps it may be. It certainly has a great quantity of smoke hanging about it, and is famous for its iron-works. Besides the prison to which I have already referred, this town contains a pretty arsenal and other institutions. It is very beautifully situated on the Alleghany River, over which there are two bridges; and the villas of the wealthier citizens sprinkled about the high grounds in the neighbourhood, are pretty enough. We lodged at a most excellent hotel, and were admirably served. As usual it was full of boarders, was very large, and had a broad colonnade to every story of the house.

We tarried here three days. Our next point was Cincinnati: and as this was a steamboat journey, and western steamboats usually blow up one or two a week in the season, it was advisable to collect opinions in reference to the comparative safety of the vessels bound that way, then lying in the river. One called the Messenger was the best recommended. She had been advertised to start positively, every day for a fortnight or so, and had not gone yet, nor did her captain seem to have any very fixed intention on the subject. But this is the custom: for if the law were to bind down a free and independent citizen to keep his word with the public, what would become of the liberty of the subject? Besides, it is in the way of trade. And if passengers be decoyed in the way of trade, and people be inconvenienced in the way of trade, what man, who is a sharp tradesman himself, shall say, 'We must put a stop to this?'

Impressed by the deep solemnity of the public announcement, I (being then ignorant of these usages) was for hurrying on board in a breathless state, immediately; but receiving private and confidential information that the boat would certainly not start until Friday, April the First, we made ourselves very comfortable in the mean while, and went on board at noon that day.

Cincinnati

The Messenger was one among a crowd of high-pressure steamboats, clustered together by a wharf-side, which, looked down upon from the rising ground that forms the landing-place, and backed by the lofty bank on the opposite side of the river, appeared no larger than so many floating models. She had some forty passengers on board, exclusive of the poorer persons on the lower deck; and in half an hour, or less, proceeded on her way.

We had, for ourselves, a tiny state-room with two berths in it, opening out of the ladies' cabin. There was, undoubtedly, something satisfactory in this 'location,' inasmuch as it was in the stern, and we had been a great many times very gravely recommended to keep as far aft as possible, 'because the steamboats generally blew up forward.' Nor was this an unnecessary caution, as the occurrence and circumstances of more than one such fatality during our stay sufficiently testified. Apart from this source of self-congratulation, it was an unspeakable relief to have any place, no matter how confined, where one could be alone: and as the row of little chambers of which this was one, had each a second glass-door besides that in the ladies' cabin, which opened on a narrow gallery outside the vessel, where the other passengers seldom came, and where one could sit in peace and gaze upon the shifting prospect, we took possession of our new quarters with much pleasure.

If the native packets I have already described be unlike anything we are in the habit of seeing on water, these western vessels are still more foreign to all the ideas we are accustomed to entertain of boats. I hardly know what to liken them to, or how to describe them.

In the first place, they have no mast, cordage, tackle, rigging, or other such boat-like gear; nor have they anything in their shape at all calculated to remind one of a boat's head, stern, sides, or keel. Except that they are in the water, and display a couple of paddle-boxes, they might be intended, for anything that appears to the contrary, to perform some unknown service, high and dry, upon a mountain top. There is no visible deck, even: nothing but a long, black, ugly roof, covered with burnt-out feathery sparks; above which tower two iron chimneys, and a hoarse escape valve, and a glass steerage-house. Then, in order as the eye descends towards the water, are the sides, and doors, and windows of the state-rooms, jumbled as oddly together as though they formed a small street, built by the varying tastes of a dozen men: the whole is supported on beams and pillars resting on a dirty barge, but a few inches above the water's edge: and in the narrow space between this upper structure and this barge's deck, are the furnace fires and machinery, open at the sides to every wind that blows, and every storm of rain it drives along its path.

Passing one of these boats at night, and seeing the great body of fire, exposed as I have just described, that rages and roars beneath the frail pile of painted wood: the machinery, not warded off or guarded in any way, but doing its work in the midst of the crowd of idlers and emigrants and children, who throng the lower deck: under the management, too, of reckless men whose acquaintance with its mysteries may have been of six months' standing: one feels directly that the wonder is, not that there should be so many fatal accidents, but that any journey should be safely made.

Within, there is one long narrow cabin, the whole length of the boat; from which the state-rooms open, on both sides. A small portion of it at the stern is partitioned off for the ladies; and the bar is at the opposite extreme. There is a long table down the centre, and at either end a stove. The washing apparatus is forward, on the deck. It is a little better than on board the canal boat, but not much. In all modes of travelling, the American customs, with reference to the means of personal cleanliness and wholesome ablution, are extremely negligent and filthy; and I strongly incline to the belief that a considerable amount of illness is referable to this cause.

We are to be on board the Messenger three days: arriving at Cincinnati (barring accidents) on Monday morning. There are three meals a day. Breakfast at seven, dinner at half-past twelve, supper about six. At each, there are a great many small dishes and plates upon the table, with very little in them; so that although there is every appearance of a mighty 'spread,' there is seldom really more than a joint: except for those who fancy slices of beet-root, shreds of dried beef, complicated entanglements of yellow pickle; maize, Indian corn, apple-sauce, and pumpkin.

Some people fancy all these little dainties together (and sweet preserves beside), by way of relish to their roast pig. They are generally those dyspeptic ladies and gentlemen who eat unheard-of quantities of hot corn bread (almost as good for the digestion as a kneaded pin-cushion), for breakfast, and for supper. Those who do not observe this custom, and who help themselves several times instead, usually suck their knives and forks meditatively, until they have decided what to take next: then pull them out of their mouths: put them in the dish; help themselves; and fall to work again. At dinner, there is nothing to drink upon the table, but great jugs full of cold water. Nobody says anything, at any meal, to anybody. All the passengers are very dismal, and seem to have tremendous secrets weighing on their minds. There is no conversation, no laughter, no cheerfulness, no sociality, except in spitting; and that is done in silent fellowship round the stove, when the meal is over. Every man sits down, dull and languid; swallows his fare as if breakfasts, dinners, and suppers, were necessities of nature never to be coupled with recreation or enjoyment; and having bolted his food in a gloomy silence, bolts himself, in the same state. But for these animal observances, you might suppose the whole male portion of the company to be the melancholy ghosts of departed bookkeepers, who had fallen dead at the desk: such is their weary air of business and calculation. Undertakers on duty would be sprightly beside them; and a collation of funeral-baked meats, in comparison with these meals, would be a sparkling festivity. . . .

Evening slowly steals upon the landscape and changes it before me, when we stop to set some emigrants ashore.

Five men, as many women, and a little girl. All their worldly goods are a bag, a large chest and an old chair: one, old, high-backed, rush-bottomed chair: a solitary settler in itself. They are rowed ashore in the boat, while the vessel stands a little off awaiting its return, the water being shallow. They are landed at the foot of a high bank, on the summit of which are a few log cabins, attainable only by a long winding path. It is growing dusk; but the sun is very red, and shines in the water and on some of the tree-tops, like fire.

The men get out of the boat first; help out the women; take out the bag, the chest, the chair; bid the rowers 'good-bye;' and shove the boat off for them. At the first plash of the oars in the water, the oldest woman of the party sits down in the old chair, close to the water's edge, without speaking a word. None of the others sit down, though the chest is large enough for many seats. They all stand where they landed, as if stricken into stone;

and look after the boat. So they remain, quite still and silent: the old woman and her old chair, in the centre; the bag and chest upon the shore, without anybody heeding them: all eyes fixed upon the boat. It comes alongside, is made fast, the men jump on board, the engine is put in motion, and we go hoarsely on again. There they stand yet, without the motion of a hand. I can see them through my glass, when, in the distance and increasing darkness, they are mere specks to the eye: lingering there still: the old woman in the old chair, and all the rest about her: not stirring in the least degree. And thus I slowly lose them.

The night is dark, and we proceed within the shadow of the wooded bank, which makes it darker. After gliding past the sombre maze of boughs for a long time, we come upon an open space where the tall trees are burning. The shape of every branch and twig is expressed in a deep red glow, and as the light wind stirs and ruffles it, they seem to vegetate in fire. It is such a sight as we read of in legends of enchanted forests: saving that it is sad to see these noble works wasting away so awfully, alone; and to think how many years must come and go before the magic that created them will rear their like upon this ground again. But the time will come; and when, in their changed ashes, the growth of centuries unborn has struck its roots, the restless men of distant ages will repair to these again unpeopled solitudes; and their fellows, in cities far away, that slumber now, perhaps, beneath the rolling sea, will read in language strange to any ears in being now, but very old to them, of primeval forests where the axe was never heard, and where the jungled ground was never trodden by a human foot. . . .

When the morning shines again, it gilds the house-tops of a lively city, before whose broad paved wharf the boat is moored; with other boats, and flags, and moving wheels, and hum of men around it; as though there were not a solitary or silent rood of ground within the compass of a thousand miles.

Cincinnati is a beautiful city; cheerful, thriving, and animated. I have not often seen a place that commends itself so favourably and pleasantly to a stranger at the first glance as this does: with its clean houses of red and white, its well-paved roads, and foot-ways of bright tile. Nor does it become less prepossessing on a closer acquaintance. The streets are broad and airy, the shops extremely good, the private residences remarkable for their elegance and neatness. There is something of invention and fancy in the varying styles of these latter erections, which, after the dull company of the steamboat, is perfectly delightful, as conveying an assurance that there are such qualities still in existence. The disposition to ornament these pretty villas and render them attractive, leads to the culture of trees and flowers, and the laying out of well-kept gardens, the sight of which, to those who walk along the streets, is inexpressibly refreshing and agreeable. I was quite charmed with the appearance of the town, and its adjoining suburb of Mount Auburn: from which the city, lying in an amphitheatre of hills, forms a picture of remarkable beauty, and is seen to great advantage.

There happened to be a great Temperance Convention held here on the day after our arrival; and as the order of march brought the procession under the windows of the hotel in which we lodged, when they started in the morning, I had a good opportunity of seeing it. It comprised several thousand men; the members of various 'Washington Auxiliary Temperance Societies;' and was marshalled by officers on horseback, who cantered briskly up and down the line, with scarves and ribbons of bright colours fluttering out behind them gaily. There were bands of music too, and banners out of number: and it was a fresh, holiday-looking concourse altogether.

I was particularly pleased to see the Irishmen, who formed a distinct society among themselves, and mustered very strong with their green scarves; carrying their national Harp and their Portrait of Father Mathew, high above the people's heads. They looked as jolly and good-humoured as ever; and, working (here) the hardest for their living and doing any kind of sturdy labour that came in their way, were the most independent fellows there, I thought. . . .

After going round the town, the procession repaired to a certain appointed place, where, as the printed programme set forth, it would be received by the children of the different free schools, 'singing Temperance Songs.' I was prevented from getting there, in time to hear these Little Warblers, or to report upon this novel kind of vocal entertainment: novel, at least, to me: but I found in a large open space, each society gathered round its own banners, and listening in silent attention to its own orator. The speeches, judging from the little I could hear of them, were certainly adapted to the occasion, as having that degree of relationship to cold water which wet blankets may claim: but the main thing was the conduct and appearance of the audience throughout the day; and that was admirable and full of promise.

Cincinnati is honourably famous for its free schools, of which it has so many that no person's child among its population can, by possibility, want the means of education, which are extended, upon an average, to four thousand pupils, annually. I was only present in one of these establishments during the hours of instruction. In the boys' department, which was full of little urchins (varying in their ages, I should say, from six years old to ten or twelve), the master offered to institute an extemporary examination of the pupils in algebra; a proposal, which, as I was by no means confident of my ability to detect mistakes in that science, I declined with some alarm. In the girls' school, reading was proposed; and as I felt tolerably equal to that art, I expressed my willingness to hear a class. Books were distributed accordingly, and some half-dozen girls relieved each other in reading paragraphs from English History. But it seemed to be a dry compilation, infinitely above their powers; and when they had blundered through three or four dreary passages concerning the Treaty of Amiens, and other thrilling topics of the same nature (obviously without comprehending ten words), I expressed myself quite satisfied. . . .

As in every other place I visited, the Judges here were gentlemen of high character and attainments. I was in one of the courts for a few minutes, and found it like those to which I have already referred. A nuisance cause was trying; there were not many spectators; and the witnesses, counsel, and jury, formed a sort of family circle, sufficiently jocose and snug.

The society with which I mingled, was intelligent, courteous, and agreeable. The inhabitants of Cincinnati are proud of their city as one of the most interesting in America: and with good reason: for beautiful and thriving as it is now, and containing, as it does, a population of fifty thousand souls, but two-and-fifty years have passed away since the ground on which it stands (bought at that time for a few dollars) was a wild wood, and its citizens were but a handful of dwellers in scattered log huts upon the river's shore.

Louisville and St. Louis

Leaving Cincinnati at eleven o'clock in the forenoon, we embarked for Louisville in the Pike steamboat, which, carrying the mails, was a packet of a much better class than that in which we had come from Pittsburgh. As this passage does not occupy more than twelve or thirteen hours, we arranged to go ashore that night: not coveting the distinction of sleeping in a state-room, when it was possible to sleep anywhere else.

There chanced to be on board this boat, in addition to the usual dreary crowd of passengers, one Pitchlynn, a chief of the Choctaw tribe of Indians, who *sent in his card* to me, and with whom I had the pleasure of a long conversation.

He spoke English perfectly well, though he had not begun to learn the language, he told me, until he was a young man grown. He had read many books; and Scott's poetry appeared to have left a strong impression on his mind: especially the opening of The Lady of the Lake, and the great battle scene in Marmion, in which, no doubt from the congeniality of the subjects to his own pursuits and tastes, he had great interest and delight. He appeared to understand correctly all he had read; and whatever fiction had enlisted his sympathy in its belief, had done so keenly and earnestly. I might almost say fiercely. He was dressed in our ordinary every-day costume, which hung about his fine figure loosely, and with indifferent grace. On my telling him that I regretted not to see him in his own attire, he threw up his right arm, for a moment, as though he were brandishing some heavy weapon, and answered, as he let it fall again, that his race were losing many things besides their dress, and would soon be seen upon the earth no more: but he wore it at home, he added proudly.

He told me that he had been away from his home, west of the Mississippi, seventeen months: and was now returning. He had been chiefly at Washington on some negotiations pending between his Tribe and the Government: which were not settled yet (he said in a melancholy way), and he feared never would be: for what could a few poor Indians do, against such well-skilled men of business as the whites? He had no love for Washington; tired of towns and cities very soon; and longed for the Forest and the Prairie.

I asked him what he thought of Congress? He answered, with a smile, that it wanted dignity, in an Indian's eyes. . . .

There were but twenty thousand of the Choctaws left, he said, and their number was decreasing every day. A few of his brother chiefs had been obliged to become civilised, and to make themselves acquainted with what the whites knew, for it was their only chance of existence. But they were not many; and the rest were as they always had been. He dwelt on this: and said several times that unless they tried to assimilate themselves to their conquerors, they must be swept away before the strides of civilised society. . . .

There was nothing very interesting in the scenery of this day's journey, which brought us at midnight to Louisville. We slept at the Galt House; a splendid hotel; and were as handsomely lodged as though we had been in Paris, rather than hundreds of miles beyond the Alleghanies.

The city presenting no objects of sufficient interest to detain us on our way, we resolved to proceed next day by another steamboat, the Fulton, and to join it, about noon, at a suburb called Portland, where it would be delayed some time in passing through a canal.

The interval, after breakfast, we devoted to riding through the town, which is regular and cheerful: the streets being laid out at right angles, and planted with young trees. The buildings are smoky and blackened, from the use of bituminous coal, but an Englishman is well used to that appearance, and indisposed to quarrel with it. There did not appear to be much business stirring; and some unfinished buildings and improvements seemed to intimate that the city had been overbuilt in the ardour of 'going-a-head,' and was suffering under the re-action consequent upon such feverish forcing of its powers.

On our way to Portland, we passed a 'Magistrate's office,' which amused me, as looking far more like a dame school than any police establishment: for this awful Institution was nothing but a little lazy, good-for-nothing front parlour, open to the street; wherein two or three figures (I presume the magistrate and his myrmidons) were basking in the sunshine, the very effigies of languor and repose. It was a perfect picture of Justice retired from business for want of customers; her sword and scales sold off; napping comfortably with her legs upon the table. . . .

We found the steamboat in the canal, waiting for the slow process of getting through the lock, and went on board, where we shortly afterwards had a new kind of visitor in the person of a certain Kentucky Giant whose name is Porter, and who is of the moderate height of seven feet eight inches, in his stockings.

There never was a race of people who so completely gave the lie to history as these giants, or whom all the chroniclers have so cruelly libelled. Instead of roaring and ravaging about the world, constantly catering for their cannibal larders, and perpetually going to market in an unlawful manner, they are the meekest people in any man's acquaintance: rather inclining to milk and vegetable diet, and bearing anything for a quiet life. So decidedly are amiability and mildness their characteristics, that I confess I look upon that youth who distinguished himself by the slaughter of these inoffensive persons, as a false-hearted brigand, who, pretending to philanthropic motives, was secretly influenced only by the wealth stored up within their castles, and the hope of plunder. And I lean the more to this opinion from finding that even the historian of those exploits, with all his partiality for his hero, is fain to admit that the slaughtered monsters in question were of a very innocent and simple turn; extremely guileless and ready of belief; lending a credulous ear to the most improbable tales; suffering themselves to be easily entrapped into pits; and even (as in the case of the Welsh Giant) with an excess of the hospitable politeness of a landlord, ripping themselves open, rather than hint at the possibility of their guests being versed in the vagabond arts of sleight-of-hand and hocus-pocus.

The Kentucky Giant was but another illustration of the truth of this position. He had a weakness in the region of the knees, and a trustfulness in his long face, which appealed even to five-feet nine for encouragement and support. He was only twenty-five years old, he said, and had grown recently, for it had been found necessary to make an addition to the legs of his inexpressibles. At fifteen he was a short boy, and in those days his English father and his Irish mother had rather snubbed him, as being too small of stature to sustain the credit of the family. He added that his health had not been good, though it was better now; but short people are not wanting who whisper that he drinks too hard.

I understand he drives a hackney-coach, though how he does it, unless he stands on the footboard behind, and lies along the roof upon his chest, with his chin in the box, it would be difficult to comprehend. He brought his gun with him, as a curiosity. Christened 'The Little Rifle,' and displayed outside a shop-window, it would make the fortune of any retail business in Holborn. When he had shown himself and talked a little while, he withdrew with his pocket-instrument, and went bobbing down the cabin, among men of six feet high and upwards, like a light-house walking among lamp-posts.

Within a few minutes afterwards, we were out of the canal, and in the Ohio river again.

The arrangements of the boat were like those of the Messenger, and the passengers were of the same order of people. . . . I never in my life did see such listless, heavy dulness as brooded over these meals: the very recollection of it weighs me down, and makes me, for the moment, wretched. Reading and writing on my knee, in our little cabin, I really dreaded the coming of the hour that summoned us to table; and was as glad to escape from it again, as if it had been a penance or a punishment. Healthy cheerfulness and good spirits forming a part of the banquet, I could soak my crusts in the fountain with Le Sage's strolling player, and revel in their glad enjoyment: but sitting down with so many fellow-animals to ward off thirst and hunger as a business; to empty, each creature, his Yahoo's[4] trough as quickly as he can, and then slink sullenly away; to have these social sacraments stripped of everything but the mere greedy satisfaction of the natural cravings; goes so against the grain with me, that I seriously believe the recollection of these funeral feasts will be a waking nightmare to me all my life. . . .

Nor was the scenery, as we approached the junction of the Ohio and Mississippi rivers, at all inspiriting in its influence. The trees were stunted in their growth; the banks were low and flat; the settlements and log cabins fewer in number: their inhabitants more wan and wretched than any we had encountered yet. No songs of birds were in the air, no pleasant scents, no moving lights and shadows from swift passing clouds. Hour after hour, the changeless glare of the hot, unwinking sky, shone upon the same monotonous objects. Hour after hour, the river rolled along, as wearily and slowly as the time itself.

At length, upon the morning of the third day, we arrived at a spot so much more desolate than any we had yet beheld, that the forlornest places we had passed, were, in comparison with it, full of interest. At the junction of the two rivers, on ground so flat and low and marshy, that at certain seasons of the year it is inundated to the house-tops, lies a breeding-place of fever, ague, and death; vaunted in England as a mine of Golden Hope, and speculated in, on the faith of monstrous representations, to many people's ruin.[5] A dismal swamp, on which the half-built houses rot away: cleared here and there for the space of a few yards; and teeming, then, with rank unwholesome vegetation, in whose baleful shade the wretched wanderers who are tempted hither, droop, and die, and lay their bones; the hateful Mississippi circling and eddying before it, and turning off upon its southern course a slimy monster hideous to behold; a hotbed of disease, an ugly sepulchre, a grave uncheered by any gleam of promise: a place without one single quality, in earth or air or water, to commend it: such is this dismal Cairo.

But what words shall describe the Mississippi, great father of rivers, who

[4]In Swift's *Gulliver's Travels*, Yahoos are beasts in the shape of men.

[5]John Law's disastrous speculation called "The Mississippi Bubble."

(praise be to Heaven) has no young children like him! An enormous ditch, sometimes two or three miles wide, running liquid mud, six miles an hour: its strong and frothy current choked and obstructed everywhere by huge logs and whole forest trees: now twining themselves together in great rafts, from the interstices of which a sedgy, lazy foam works up, to float upon the water's top; now rolling past like monstrous bodies, their tangled roots showing like matted hair; now glancing singly by like giant leeches; and now writhing round and round in the vortex of some small whirlpool, like wounded snakes. The banks low, the trees dwarfish, the marshes swarming with frogs, the wretched cabins few and far apart, their inmates hollow-cheeked and pale, the weather very hot, mosquitoes penetrating into every crack and crevice of the boat, mud and slime on everything; nothing pleasant in its aspect, but the harmless lightning which flickers every night upon the dark horizon.

For two days we toiled up this foul stream, striking constantly against the floating timber, or stopping to avoid those more dangerous obstacles, the snags, or sawyers, which are the hidden trunks of trees that have their roots below the tide. When the nights are very dark, the look-out stationed in the head of the boat, knows by the ripple of the water if any great impediment be near at hand, and rings a bell beside him, which is the signal for the engine to be stopped: but always in the night this bell has work to do, and after every ring, there comes a blow which renders it no easy matter to remain in bed. . . .

We drank the muddy water of this river while we were upon it. It is considered wholesome by the natives, and is something more opaque than gruel. I have seen water like it at the Filter-shops, but nowhere else. We went to a large hotel, called the Planter's House: built like an English hospital, with long passages and bare walls, and sky-lights above the room-doors for the free circulation of air. There were a great many boarders in it; and as many lights sparkled and glistened from the windows down into the street below, when we drove up, as if it had been illuminated on some occasion of rejoicing. It is an excellent house, and the proprietors have most bountiful notions of providing the creature comforts. Dining alone with my wife in our own room, one day, I counted fourteen dishes on the table at once.

In the old French portion of the town, the thoroughfares are narrow and crooked, and some of the houses are very quaint and picturesque: being built of wood, with tumble-down galleries before the windows, approachable by stairs or rather ladders from the street. There are queer little barbers' shops and drinking-houses too, in this quarter; and abundance of crazy old tenements with blinking casements, such as may be seen in Flanders. Some of these ancient habitations, with high garret gable-windows perking into the roofs, have a kind of French shrug about them; and being lop-sided with age, appear to hold their heads askew, besides, as if they were grimacing in astonishment at the American Improvements.

It is hardly necessary to say, that these consist of wharfs and warehouses, and new buildings in all directions; and of a great many vast plans which are still 'progressing.' Already, however, some very good houses, broad streets, and marble-fronted shops, have gone so far a-head as to be in a state of completion; and the town bids fair in a few years to improve considerably: though it is not likely ever to vie, in point of elegance or beauty, with Cincinnati. . . .

No man ever admits the unhealthiness of the place he dwells in (unless he is going away from it), and I shall therefore, I have no doubt, be at issue with the inhabitants of St. Louis, in questioning the perfect salubrity of its climate, and in hinting that I think it must rather dispose to fever, in the summer and autumnal seasons. Just adding, that it is very hot, lies among great rivers, and has vast tracts of undrained swampy land around it, I leave the reader to form his own opinion. . . .

Slavery

The upholders of slavery in America—of the atrocities of which system, I shall not write one word for which I have not had ample proof and warrant—may be divided into three great classes.

The first, are those more moderate and rational owners of human cattle, who have come into the possession of them as so many coins in their trading capital, but who admit the frightful nature of the Institution in the abstract, and perceive the dangers to society with which it is fraught: dangers which however distant they may be, or howsoever tardy in their coming on, are as certain to fall upon its guilty head, as is the Day of Judgment.

The second, consists of all those owners, breeders, users, buyers and sellers of slaves, who will, until the bloody chapter has a bloody end, own, breed, use, buy, and sell them at all hazards; who doggedly deny the horrors of the system in the teeth of such a mass of evidence as never was brought to bear on any other subject, and to which the experience of every day contributes its immense amount; who would at this or any other moment, gladly involve America in a war, civil or foreign, provided that it had for its sole end and object the assertion of their right to perpetuate slavery, and to whip and work and torture slaves, unquestioned by any human authority, and unassailed by any human power; who, when they speak of Freedom, mean the Freedom to oppress their kind, and to be savage, merciless, and cruel; and of whom every man on his own ground, in republican America, is a more exacting, and a sterner, and a less responsible despot than the Caliph Haroun Alraschid in his angry robe of scarlet.

The third, and not the least numerous or influential, is composed of all that delicate gentility which cannot bear a superior, and cannot brook an equal; of that class whose Republicanism means, 'I will not tolerate a man above me: and of those below, none must approach too near;' whose pride, in a land where voluntary servitude is shunned as a disgrace, must be ministered to by slaves; and whose inalienable rights can only have their growth in negro wrongs.

It has been sometimes urged that, in the unavailing efforts which have been made to advance the cause of Human Freedom in the republic of America (strange cause for history to treat of!), sufficient regard has not been had to the existence of the first class of persons; and it has been contended that they are hardly used, in being confounded with the second. This is, no doubt, the case; noble instances of pecuniary and personal sacrifice have already had their growth among them; and it is much to be regretted that the gulf between them and the advocates of emancipation should have been widened and deepened by any means: the rather, as there are, beyond dispute, among these slave-owners, many kind masters who are tender in the exercise of their unnatural power. Still, it is to be feared that this injustice is inseparable from the state of things with which humanity and truth are called upon to deal. Slavery is not a whit the more endurable because some hearts are to be found which can partially resist its hardening influences; nor can the indignant tide of honest wrath stand still, because in its onward course it overwhelms a few who are comparatively innocent, among a host of guilty.

The ground most commonly taken by these better men among the advocates of slavery, is this: 'It is a bad system; and for myself I would willingly get rid of it, if I could; most willingly. But it is not so bad, as you in England take it to be. You are deceived by the representations of the emancipationists. The greater part of my slaves are much attached to me. You will say that I do not allow them to be severely treated; but I will put it to you whether you believe that it can be a general practice to treat them inhumanly, when it would impair their value, and would be obviously against the interests of their masters.'

Is it the interest of any man to steal, to game, to waste his health and mental faculties by drunkenness, to lie, forswear himself, indulge hatred, seek desperate revenge, or do murder? No. All these are roads to ruin. And why, then, do men tread them? Because such inclinations are among the vicious qualities of mankind. Blot out, ye friends of slavery, from the catalogue of human passions, brutal lust, cruelty, and the abuse of irresponsible power (of all earthly temptations the most difficult to be resisted), and when ye have done so, and not before, we will inquire whether it be the interest of a master to lash and maim the slaves, over whose lives and limbs he has an absolute control!

But again: this class, together with that last one I have named, the miserable aristocracy spawned of a false republic, lift up their voices and exclaim 'Public opinion is all-sufficient to prevent such cruelty as you denounce.' Public opinion! Why, public opinion in the slave States *is* slavery, is it not? Public opinion, in the slave States, has delivered the slaves over, to the gentle mercies of their masters. Public opinion has made the laws, and denied the slaves legislative protection. Public opinion has knotted the lash, heated the branding-iron, loaded the rifle, and shielded the murderer. Public opinion threatens the abolitionist with death, if he venture to the South; and drags him with a rope about his middle, in broad unblushing noon, through the first city in the East.[6] Public opinion has, within a few years, burned a slave alive at a slow fire in the city of St. Louis; and public opinion has to this day maintained upon the bench that estimable Judge who charged the Jury, impanelled there to try his murderers, that their most horrid deed was an act of public opinion, and being so, must not be punished by the laws the public sentiment had made. Public opinion hailed this doctrine with a howl of wild applause, and set the prisoners free, to walk the city, men of mark, and influence, and station, as they had been before.

Public opinion! what class of men have an immense preponderance over the rest of the community, in their power of representing public opinion in the legislature? the slave-owners. They send from their twelve States one hundred members, while the fourteen free States, with a free population nearly double, return but a hundred and forty-two. Before whom do the presidential candidates bow down the most humbly, on whom do they fawn the most fondly, and for whose tastes do they cater the most assiduously in their servile protestations? The slave-owners always.

Public opinion! hear the public opinion of the free South, as expressed by its own members in the House of Representatives at Washington. 'I have a great respect for the chair,' quoth North Carolina, 'I have a great respect for the chair as an officer of the house, and a great respect for him personally; nothing but that respect prevents me from rushing to the table and tearing that petition which has just been presented for the abolition of slavery in the district of Columbia, to pieces.'–'I warn the abolitionists,' says South Carolina, 'ignorant, infuriated barbarians as they are, that if chance shall throw any of them into our hands, he may expect a felon's death.'–'Let an abolitionist come within the borders of South Carolina,' cries a third; mild Carolina's colleague; 'and if we can catch him, we will try him, and notwithstanding the interference of all the governments on earth, including the Federal government, we will HANG him.'

Public opinion has made this law.–It has declared that in Washington, in that city which takes its name from the father of American liberty, any justice of the peace may bind with fetters any negro passing down the street and thrust him into jail: no offence on the black man's part is necessary. The justice says, 'I choose to think this man a runaway:' and locks him up. Public opinion impowers the man of law when this is done, to advertise the negro in the newspapers, warning his owner to come and claim him, or he will be sold to pay the jail fees. But supposing he is a free black, and has no owner, it may naturally be presumed that he is set at liberty. No: HE IS SOLD TO RECOMPENSE HIS JAILER. This has been done again, and

[6]This probably refers to the mobbing of William Lloyd Garrison in Boston.

again, and again. He has no means of proving his freedom; has no adviser, messenger, or assistance of any sort or kind; no investigation into his case is made, or inquiry instituted. He, a free man, who may have served for years, and bought his liberty, is thrown into jail on no process, for no crime, and on no pretence of crime: and is sold to pay the jail fees. This seems incredible, even of America, but it is the law.

Public opinion is deferred to, in such cases as the following which is reported in the newspapers:

'An interesting case is now on trial in the Supreme Court, arising out of the following facts. A gentleman residing in Maryland had allowed an aged pair of his slaves, substantial though not legal freedom for several years. While thus living, a daughter was born to them, who grew up in the same liberty, until she married a free negro, and went with him to reside in Pennsylvania. They had several children, and lived unmolested until the original owner died, when his heir attempted to regain them; but the magistrate before whom they were brought, decided that he had no jurisdiction in the case. *The owner seized the woman and her children in the night, and carried them to Maryland.*'

'Cash for negroes,' 'cash for negroes,' 'cash for negroes,' is the heading of advertisements in great capitals down the long columns of the crowded journals. Woodcuts of a runaway negro with manacled hands, crouching beneath a bluff pursuer in top boots, who, having caught him, grasps him by the throat, agreeably diversify the pleasant text. The leading article protests against 'that abominable and hellish doctrine of abolition, which is repugnant alike to every law of God and nature.' . . .

Let us try this public opinion by another test, which is important in three points of view: first, as showing how desperately timid of the public opinion slave-owners are, in their delicate descriptions of fugitive slaves in widely circulated newspapers; secondly, as showing how perfectly contented the slaves are, and how very seldom they run away; thirdly, as exhibiting their entire freedom from scar, or blemish, or any mark of cruel infliction, as their pictures are drawn, not by lying abolitionists, but by their own truthful masters.

The following are a few specimens of the advertisements in the public papers. It is only four years since the oldest among them appeared; and others of the same nature continue to be published every day, in shoals.

'Ran away, Negress Caroline. Had on a collar with one prong turned down.'

'Ran away, a black woman, Betsy. Had an iron bar on her right leg.'

'Ran away, the negro Manuel. Much marked with irons.'

'Ran away, the negress Fanny. Had on an iron band about her neck.'

'Ran away, a negro boy about twelve years old. Had round his neck a chain dog-collar with "De Lampert" engraved on it.'

'Ran away, the negro Hown. Has a ring of iron on his left foot. Also, Grise, *his wife*, having a ring and chain on the left leg.'

'Ran away, a negro boy named James. Said boy was ironed when he left me.'

'Committed to jail, a man who calls his name John. He has a clog of iron on his right foot which will weigh four or five pounds.'

'Detained at the police jail, the negro wench, Myra. Has several marks of LASHING, and has irons on her feet.'

'Ran away, a negro woman and two children. A few days before she went off, I burnt her with a hot iron, on the left side of her face. I tried to make the letter M.'

'Ran away, a negro man named Henry; his left eye out, some scars from a dirk on and under his left arm, and much scarred with the whip.' . . .

'Ran away, a negro named Arthur. Has a considerable scar across his breast and each arm, made by a knife; loves to talk much of the goodness of God.'

'Twenty-five dollars reward for my man Isaac. He has a scar on his forehead, caused by a blow; and one on his back, made by a shot from a pistol.'

'Ran away, a negro girl called Mary. Has a small scar over her eye, a good many teeth missing, the letter A is branded on her cheek and forehead.'

'Ran away, negro Ben. Has a scar on his right hand; his thumb and forefinger being injured by being shot last fall. A part of the bone came out. He has also one or two large scars on his back and hips.'

'Detained at the jail, a mulatto, named Tom. Has a scar on the right cheek, and appears to have been burned with powder on the face.' . . .

'Was committed to jail, a negro man. Says his name is Josiah. His back very much scarred by the whip; and branded on the thigh and hips in three or four places, thus (J M). The rim of his right ear has been bit or cut off.'

'Fifty dollars reward, for my fellow Edward. He has a scar on the corner of his mouth, two cuts on and under his arm, and the letter E on his arm.' . . .

'Ran away, Anthony. One of his ears cut off, and his left hand cut with an axe.'

'Fifty dollars reward for the negro Jim Blake. Has a piece cut out of each ear, and the middle finger of the left hand cut off to the second joint.' . . .

'Ran away, the Mulatto wench Mary. Has a cut on the left arm, a scar on the left shoulder, and two upper teeth missing.'

I should say, perhaps, in explanation of this latter piece of description, that among the other blessings which public opinion secures to the negroes, is the common practice of violently punching out their teeth. To make them wear iron collars by day and night, and to worry them with dogs, are practices almost too ordinary to deserve mention.

'Ran away, my man Fountain. Has holes in his ears, a scar on the right side of his forehead, has been shot in the hind part of his legs, and is marked on the back with the whip.'

'Two hundred and fifty dollars reward for my negro man Jim. He is much marked with shot in his right thigh. The shot entered on the outside, halfway between the hip and knee joints.' . . .

'Taken up, a negro man. Is very much scarred about the face and body, and has the left ear bit off.' . . .

'Ran away, a negro man, NAMED WASHINGTON. Has lost a part of his middle finger, and the end of his little finger.'

'Twenty-five dollars reward for my man John. The tip of his nose is bit off.'

'Twenty-five dollars reward for the negro slave, Sally. Walks *as though* crippled in the back.' . . .

'Ran away, a negro man, named Ivory. Has a small piece cut out of the top of each ear.'

While upon the subject of ears, I may observe that a distinguished abolitionist in New York once received a negro's ear, which had been cut off close to the head, in a general post letter. It was forwarded by the free and independent gentleman who had caused it to be amputated, with a polite request that he would place the specimen in his 'collection.'

I could enlarge this catalogue with broken arms, and broken legs, and gashed flesh, and missing teeth, and lacerated backs, and bites of dogs, and brands of red-hot irons innumerable: but as my readers will be sufficiently sickened and repelled already, I will turn to another branch of the subject.

These advertisements, of which a similar collection might be made for every year, and month, and week, and day; and which are coolly read in families as things of course, and as a part of the current news and small-talk; will serve to show how very much the slaves profit by public opinion, and how tender it is in their behalf. . . .

Now, I appeal to every human mind, imbued with the commonest of common sense, and the commonest of common humanity; to all dispassionate, reasoning creatures, of any shade of opinion; and ask, . . . can they have a doubt of the real condition of the slave, or can they for a moment make a compromise between the institution or any of its flagrant, fearful features, and their own just consciences? . . . Do we not know that the man who has been born and bred among slavery's wrongs; who has seen in his childhood husbands obliged at the word of command to flog their wives; women, indecently compelled to hold up their own garments that men might lay the heavier stripes upon their legs, driven and harried by brutal overseers in their time of travail, and becoming mothers on the field of toil, under the very lash itself; who has read in youth, and seen his virgin sisters read, descriptions of runaway men and women, and their disfigured persons, which could not be published elsewhere, of so much stock upon a farm, or at a show of beasts:—do we not know that that man, whenever his wrath is kindled up, will be a brutal savage? . . .

What! shall we declaim against the ignorant peasantry of Ireland, and mince the matter when these American taskmasters are in question? Shall we cry shame on the brutality of those who hamstring cattle: and spare the lights of Freedom upon earth who notch the ears of men and women, cut pleasant posies in the shrinking flesh, learn to write with pens of red-hot iron on the human face, rack their poetic fancies for liveries of mutilation which their slaves shall wear for life and carry to the grave, breaking living limbs as did the soldiery who mocked and slew the Saviour of the world, and set defenceless creatures up for targets! Shall we whimper over legends of the tortures practised on each other by the Pagan Indians, and smile upon the cruelties of Christian men! Shall we, so long as these things last, exult above the scattered remnants of that race, and triumph in the white enjoyment of their possessions? Rather, for me, restore the forest and the Indian village; in lieu of stars and stripes, let some poor feather flutter in the breeze; replace the streets and squares by wigwams; and though the death-song of a hundred haughty warriors fill the air, it will be music to the shriek of one unhappy slave.

On one theme, which is commonly before our eyes, and in respect of which our national character is changing fast, let the plain Truth be spoken, and let us not, like dastards, beat about the bush by hinting at the Spaniard and the fierce Italian. When knives are drawn by Englishmen in conflict let it be said and known: 'We owe this change to Republican Slavery. These are the weapons of Freedom. With sharp points and edges such as these, Liberty in America hews and hacks her slaves. . . .'

Concluding Remarks

I may be pardoned, if on such a theme as the general character of the American people, and the general character of their social system, as presented to a stranger's eyes, I desire to express my own opinions in a few words, before I bring these volumes to a close.

They are, by nature, frank, brave, cordial, hospitable, and affectionate. Cultivation and refinement seem but to enhance their warmth of heart and ardent enthusiasm; and it is the possession of these latter qualities in a most remarkable degree, which renders an educated American one of the most endearing and most generous of friends. I never was so won upon, as by this class; never yielded up my full confidence and esteem so readily and pleasurably, as to them; never can make again, in half a year, so many friends for whom I seem to entertain the regard of half a life.

These qualities are natural, I implicitly believe, to the whole people. That they are, however, sadly sapped and blighted in their growth among the mass; and that there are influences at work which endanger them still more, and give but little present promise of their healthy restoration; is a truth that ought to be told.

It is an essential part of every national character to pique itself mightily upon its faults, and to deduce tokens of its virtue or its wisdom from their very exaggeration. One great blemish in the popular mind of America, and the prolific parent of an innumerable brood of evils, is Universal Distrust. Yet the American citizen plumes himself upon this spirit, even when he is sufficiently dispassionate to perceive the ruin it works; and will often adduce it, in spite of his own reason, as an instance of the great sagacity and acuteness of the people, and their superior shrewdness and independence.

'You carry,' says the stranger, 'this jealousy and distrust into every transaction of public life. By repelling worthy men from your legislative assemblies, it has bred up a class of candidates for the suffrage, who, in their very act, disgrace your Institutions and your people's choice. It has rendered you so fickle, and so given to change, that your inconstancy has passed into a proverb; for you no sooner set up an idol firmly, than you are sure to pull it down and dash it into fragments: and this, because directly you reward a benefactor, or a public servant, you distrust him, merely because he *is* rewarded; and immediately apply yourselves to find out, either that you have been too bountiful in your acknowledgments, or he remiss in his deserts. Any man who attains a high place among you, from the President downwards, may date his downfall from that moment; for any printed lie that any notorious villain pens, although it militate directly against the character and conduct of a life, appeals at once to your distrust, and is believed. You will strain at a gnat in the way of trustfulness and confidence, however fairly won and well deserved; but you will swallow a whole caravan of camels, if they be laden with unworthy doubts and mean suspicions. Is this well, think you, or likely to elevate the character of the governors or the governed, among you?'

The answer is invariably the same: 'There's freedom of opinion here, you know. Every man thinks for himself, and we are not to be easily overreached. That's how our people come to be suspicious.'

Another prominent feature is the love of 'smart' dealing: which gilds over many a swindle and gross breach of trust; many a defalcation, public and private; and enables many a knave to hold his head up with the best, who well deserves a halter; though it has not been without its retributive operation, for this smartness has done more in a few years to impair the public credit, and to cripple the public resources, than dull honesty, however rash, could have effected in a century. The merits of a broken speculation, or a bankruptcy, or of a successful scoundrel, are not gauged by its or his observance of the golden rule, 'Do as you would be done by,' but are considered with reference to their smartness. I recollect, on both occasions of our passing that ill-fated Cairo on the Mississippi, remarking on the bad effects such gross deceits must have when they exploded, in generating a want of confidence abroad, and discouraging foreign investment: but I was given to understand that this was a very smart scheme by which a deal of money had been made: and that its smartest feature was, that they forgot these things abroad, in a very short time, and speculated again, as freely as ever. The following dialogue I have held a hundred times: "Is it not a very disgraceful circumstance that such a man as So-and-so should be acquiring a large property by the most infamous and odious means, and notwithstanding all the crimes of which he has been guilty, should be tolerated and abetted by your Citizens? He is a public nuisance, is he not?" "Yes, sir." "A convicted liar?" "Yes, sir." "He has been kicked, and cuffed, and caned?" "Yes, sir." "And he is utterly dishonourable, debased, and profligate?" "Yes, sir." "In the name of wonder, then, what is his merit?" "Well, sir, he is a smart man."

In like manner, all kinds of deficient and impolitic usages are referred to the national love of trade; though, oddly enough, it would be a weighty charge against a foreigner that he regarded the Americans as a trading people. The love of trade is assigned as a reason for that comfortless custom, so very prevalent in country towns, of married persons living in hotels, having no fireside of their own, and seldom meeting from early morning until late at night, but at the hasty public meals. The love of trade is a reason why the literature of America is to remain for ever unprotected: 'For we are a trading people, and don't care for poetry:' though we *do*, by the way, profess to be very proud of our poets: while healthful amusements, cheerful means of recreation, and wholesome fancies, must fade before the stern utilitarian joys of trade.

These three characteristics are strongly presented at every turn, full in the stranger's view. But, the foul growth of America has a more tangled root than this; and it strikes its fibres, deep in its licentious Press.

Schools may be erected, East, West, North, and South; pupils be taught, and masters reared, by scores upon scores of thousands; colleges may thrive, churches may be crammed, temperance may be diffused, and advancing knowledge in all other forms walk through the land with giant strides: but while the newspaper press of America is in, or near, its present abject state, high moral improvement in that country is hopeless. Year by year, it must and will go back; year by year, the tone of public feeling must sink lower down; year by year, the Congress and the Senate must become of less account before all decent men; and year by year, the memory of the Great Fathers of the Revolution must be outraged more and more, in the bad life of their degenerate child.

Among the herd of journals which are published in the States, there are some, the reader scarcely need be told, of character and credit. From personal intercourse with accomplished gentlemen connected with publications of this class, I have derived both pleasure and profit. But the name of these is Few, and of the others Legion; and the influence of the good, is powerless to counteract the moral poison of the bad.

Among the gentry of America; among the well-informed and moderate: in the learned professions; at the bar and on the bench: there is, as there can be, but one opinion, in reference to the vicious character of these infamous journals. It is sometimes contended—I will not say strangely, for it is natural to seek excuses for such a disgrace—that their influence is not so great as a visitor would suppose. I must be pardoned for saying that there is no warrant for this plea, and that every fact and circumstance tends directly to the opposite conclusion.

When any man, of any grade of desert in intellect or character, can climb to any public distinction, no matter what, in America, without first grovelling down upon the earth, and bending the knee before this monster of depravity; when any private excellence is safe from its attacks; when any social confidence is left unbroken by it, or any tie of social decency and honour is held in the least regard; when any man in that free country has freedom of opinion, and presumes to think for himself, and speak for himself, without humble reference to a censorship which, for its rampant ignorance and base dishonesty, he utterly loathes and despises in his heart; when those who most acutely feel its infamy and the reproach it casts upon the nation, and who most denounce it to each other, dare to set their heels upon, and crush it openly, in the sight of all men: then, I will believe that its influence is lessening, and men are returning to their manly senses. But while that Press has its evil eye in every house, and its black hand in every appointment in the state, from a president to a postman; while, with ribald slander for its only stock in trade, it is the standard literature of an enormous class, who must find their reading in a newspaper, or they will not read at all; so long must its odium be upon the country's head, and so long must the evil it works, be plainly visible in the Republic.

To those who are accustomed to the leading English journals, or to the respectable journals of the Continent of Europe; to those who are accustomed to anything else in print and paper; it would be impossible, without an amount of extract for which I have neither space nor inclination, to convey an adequate idea of this frightful engine in America. But if any man desire confirmation of my statement on this head, let him repair to any place in this city of London, where scattered numbers of these publications are to be found; and there, let him form his own opinion.

It would be well, there can be no doubt, for the American people as a whole, if they loved the Real less, and the Ideal somewhat more. It would be well, if there were greater encouragement to lightness of heart and gaiety, and a wider cultivation of what is beautiful, without being eminently and directly useful. But here, I think the general remonstrance, 'we are a new country,' which is so often advanced as an excuse for defects which are quite unjustifiable, as being, of right, only the slow growth of an old one, may be very reasonably urged: and I yet hope to hear of there being some other national amusement in the United States, besides newspaper politics.

They certainly are not a humorous people, and their temperament always impressed me as being of a dull and gloomy character. In shrewdness of remark, and a certain cast-iron quaintness, the Yankees, or people of New England, unquestionably take the lead; as they do in most other evidences of intelligence. But in travelling about, out of the large cities—as I have remarked in former parts of these volumes—I was quite oppressed by the prevailing seriousness and melancholy air of business: which was so general and unvarying, that at every new town I came to, I seemed to meet the very same people whom I had left behind me, at the last. Such defects as are perceptible in the national manners, seem, to me, to be referable, in a great degree, to this cause: which has generated a dull, sullen persistence in coarse usages, and rejected the graces of life as undeserving of attention. There is no doubt that Washington, who was always most scrupulous and exact on points of ceremony, perceived the tendency towards this mistake, even in his time, and did his utmost to correct it.

I cannot hold with other writers on these subjects that the prevalence of various forms of dissent in America, is in any way attributable to the non-existence there of an established church: indeed, I think the temper of the people, if it admitted of such an Institution being founded amongst them, would lead them to desert it, as a matter of course, merely because it *was* established. But, supposing it to exist, I doubt its probable efficacy in summoning the wandering sheep to one great fold, simply because of the immense amount of dissent which prevails at home; and because I do not find in America any one form of religion with which we in Europe, or even in England, are unacquainted. Dissenters resort thither in great numbers, as other people do, simply because it is a land of resort; and great settlements of them are founded, because ground can be purchased, and towns and villages reared, where there were none of the human creation before. But even the Shakers emigrated from England; our country is not unknown to Mr. Joseph Smith, the apostle of Mormonism, or to his benighted disciples; I have beheld religious scenes myself in some of our populous towns which can hardly be surpassed by an American camp-meeting; and I am not aware that any instance of superstitious imposture on the one hand, and superstitious credulity on the other, has had its origin in the United States, which we cannot more than parallel. . . .

The Republican Institutions of America undoubtedly lead the people to assert their self-respect and their equality; but a traveller is bound to bear those Institutions in his mind, and not hastily to resent the near approach of a class of strangers, who, at home, would keep aloof. This characteristic, when it was tinctured with no foolish pride, and stopped short of no honest service, never offended me; and I very seldom, if ever, experienced its rude or unbecoming display. . . .

There is but one other head on which I wish to offer a remark; and that has reference to the public health. In so vast a country, where there are thousands of millions of acres of land yet unsettled and uncleared, and on every rood of which vegetable decomposition is annually taking place; where there are so many great rivers, and such opposite varieties of climate; there cannot fail to be a great amount of sickness at certain seasons. But I may venture to say, after conversing with many members of the medical profession in America, that I am not singular in the opinion that much of the disease which does prevail, might be avoided, if a few common precautions were observed. Greater means of personal cleanliness, are indispensable to this end; the custom of hastily swallowing large quantities of animal food, three times a-day, and rushing back to sedentary pursuits after each meal, must be changed; the gentler sex must go more wisely clad, and take more healthful exercise; and in the latter clause, the males must be included also. Above all, in public institutions, and throughout the whole of every town and city, the system of ventilation, and drainage, and removal of impurities requires to be thoroughly revised. There is no local Legislature in America which may not study Mr. Chadwick's excellent Report upon the Sanitary Condition of our Labouring Classes, with immense advantage.

I have now arrived at the close of this book. I have little reason to believe, from certain warnings I have had since I returned to England, that it will be tenderly or favourably received by the American people; and as I have written the Truth in relation to the mass of those who form their judgments and express their opinions, it will be seen that I have no desire to court, by any adventitious means, the popular applause.

It is enough for me, to know, that what I have set down in these pages, cannot cost me a single friend on the other side of the Atlantic, who is, in anything, deserving of the name. For the rest, I put my trust, implicitly, in the spirit in which they have been conceived and penned; and I can bide my time.

I have made no reference to my reception, nor have I suffered it to influence me in what I have written; for, in either case, I should have offered but a sorry acknowledgment, compared with that I bear within my breast, towards those partial readers of my former books, across the Water, who met me with an open hand, and not with one that closed upon an iron muzzle.

Thackeray Took Notes

William Makepeace Thackeray (1811–1863) was born in Calcutta and sent to England when he was about six. Although he began the study of law in 1831, he soon turned to writing and sketching. Thackeray was married in 1836 but after four years he was parted from his wife because of her insanity. He never remarried.

The Snob Papers, *published in* Punch *in 1847, first made Thackeray famous and his reputation as a novelist was firmly established with the appearance of* VANITY FAIR *(1847–48). While he was lecturing in America on "English Humourists of the Eighteenth Century" he wrote these letters, chiefly to his friends the Reverend William Henry Brookfield and his wife. "A Mississippi Bubble" was first published as one of the* ROUNDABOUT PAPERS *in the* CORNHILL MAGAZINE, *of which Thackeray was editor.*

From His LETTERS

CLARENDON HOTEL, NEW YORK
Tuesday, 23 Dec. [1852]

MY DEAR LADY:

I send you a little line and shake your hand across the water. God bless you and yours. . . .

The passage is nothing, now it is over; I am rather ashamed of gloom and disquietude about such a trifling journey. I have made scores of new acquaintances and lighted on my legs as usual. I didn't expect to like people as I do, but am agreeably disappointed and find many most pleasant companions, natural and good; natural and well read and well bred too; and I suppose am none the worse pleased because everybody has read all my books and praises my lectures; (I preach in a Unitarian Church, and the parson comes to hear me. His name is Mr. Bellows, it isn't a pretty name), and there are 2,000 people nearly who come, and the lectures are so well liked that it is probable I shall do them over again. So really there is a chance of making a pretty little sum of money for old age, imbecility, and those young ladies[1] afterwards.

[1]His children.

Had Lady Ashburton told you of the moving tables? Try, six or seven of you, a wooden table without brass castors; sit round it, lay your hands flat on it, not touching each other, and in half an hour or so perhaps it will begin to turn round and round. It is the most wonderful thing, but I have tried twice in vain since I saw it and did it at Mr. Bancroft's.[2] I have not been into fashionable society yet, what they call the upper ten thousand here, but have met very likeable of the lower sort. On Sunday I went into the country, and there was a great rosy jolly family of sixteen or eighteen people, round a great tea-table; and the lady of the house told me to make myself at home—remarking my bashfulness, you know—and said, with a jolly face, and twinkling of her little eyes, "Lord bless you, we know you *all to pieces!*" and there was sitting by me O! such a pretty girl, the very picture of Rubens's second wife, and face and figure. Most of the ladies, all except this family, are as lean as greyhounds; they dress prodigiously fine, taking for their models the French actresses, I think, of the *Boulevard* theatres.

Broadway is miles upon miles long, a rush of life such as I never have seen; not so full as the Strand, but so rapid. The houses are always being torn down and built up again, the railroad cars drive slap into the midst of the city. There are barricades and scaffoldings banging everywhere. I have not been into a house except the fat country one, but something new is being done to it, and the hammerings are clattering in the passage, or a wall, or steps are down, or the family is going to move. Nobody is quiet here, no more am I. The rush and restlessness pleases me, and I like, for a little, the dash of the stream. I am not received as a god, which I like too. There is one paper which goes on every morning saying I am a snob, and I don't say no. Six people were reading it at breakfast this morning, and the man opposite me popped it under the table cloth. But the other papers roar with approbation. . . .

Here comes in a man with a paper I hadn't seen; I must cut out a bit just as the actors do, but then I think you will like it, and that is why I do it. There was a very rich biography about me in one of the papers the other day, with an account of a servant, maintained in the splendour of his menial decorations—Poor old John whose picture is in *Pendennis*. And I have filled my paper, and I shake my dear lady's hand across the roaring sea, and I know that you will be glad to know that I prosper and that I am well, and that I am yours

W. M. T.

Cutting from the New York Evening Post Enclosed in the Foregoing

The building was crowded to its utmost capacity with the celebrities of literature and fashion in this metropolis, all of whom, we believe, left, perfectly united in the opinion that they never remembered to have spent

[2]Probably George Bancroft, the historian.

an hour more delightfully in their lives, and that the room in which they had been receiving so much enjoyment, was very badly lighted. We fear, also, that it was the impression of the many who were disappointed in getting tickets, that the room was not spacious enough for the purpose in which it has been appropriated.

Every one who saw Mr. Thackeray last evening for the first, seemed to have had their impressions of his appearance and manner of speech, corrected. Few expected to see so large a man; he is gigantic, six feet four at least; few expected to see so old a person; his hair appears to have kept silvery record over fifty years; and then there was a notion in the minds of many that there must be something dashing and "fast" in his appearance, whereas his costume was perfectly plain; the expression of his face grave and earnest; his address perfectly unaffected, and such as we might expect to meet with, in a well bred man somewhat advanced in years. His elocution, also, surprised those who had derived their impressions from the English journals. His voice is a superb tenor, and possesses that pathetic tremble which is so effective in what is called emotive eloquence, while his delivery was as well suited to the communication he had to make as could well have been imagined.

His enunciation is perfect. Every word he uttered might have been heard in the remotest quarters of the room, yet he scarcely lifted his voice above a colloquial tone. The most striking feature in his whole manner was the utter absence of affectation of any kind. He did not permit himself to appear conscious that he was an object of peculiar interest in the audience, neither was he guilty of the greater error of not appearing to care whether they were interested in him or not. In other words, he inspired his audience with a respect for him, as a man proportioned to the admiration, which his books have inspired for him as an author.

Of the lecture itself, as a work of art, it would be difficult to speak too strongly. Though written with the utmost simplicity and apparent inattention to effects, it overflowed with every characteristic of the author's happiest vein. There has been nothing written about Swift so clever, and if we except Lord Orrery's silly letters, we suspect we might add nothing so unjust.

Though suitable credit was given to Swift's talents, all of which were admirably characterized, yet when he came to speak of the moral side of the dean's nature he saw nothing but darkness.

PHILADELPHIA
21 to 23 January 1853

My dear lady's kind sad letter gave me pleasure, melancholy as it was. . . .

At present, I incline to come to England in June or July and get ready a new set of lectures, and bring them back with me. That second course will enable me to provide for the children and their mother finally and satisfactorily, and my mind will be easier after that, and I can sing *Nunc Dimittis* without faltering. There is money-making to try at, to be sure, and ambition,—I mean in public life; perhaps that might interest a man, but not novels, nor lectures, nor fun, any more. I don't seem to care about these any more, or for praise, or for abuse, or for reputation of that kind. That literary play is played out, and the puppets going to be locked up for good and all.

Does this melancholy come from the circumstance that I have been out to dinner and supper every night this week? O! I am tired of shaking hands with people, and acting the lion business night after night. Everybody is introduced and shakes hands. I know thousands of Colonels, professors, editors, and what not, and walk the streets guiltily, knowing that I don't know 'em, and trembling lest the man opposite to me is one of my friends of the day before. I believe I am popular, except at Boston among the newspaper men who fired into me, but a great favorite with the *monde* there and elsewhere. Here in Philadelphia it is all praise and kindness. Do you know there are 500,000 people in Philadelphia? I daresay you had no idea thereof, and smile at the idea of there being a *monde* here and at Boston and New York. Early next month I begin at Washington and Baltimore, then D. V. to New Orleans, back to New York by Mississippi and Ohio, if the steamers don't blow up, and if they do, you know I am easy. What a weary, weary letter I am writing to you. . . . Have you heard that I have found Beatrix[3] at New York? I have basked in her bright eyes, but Ah, me! I don't care for her, and shall hear of her marrying a New York buck with a feeling of perfect pleasure. She is really as like Beatrix, as that fellow William and I met was like Costigan.[4] She has a dear woman of a mother upwards of fifty-five, whom I like the best, I think, and think the handsomest,—a sweet lady. What a comfort those dear Elliots are to me; I have had but one little letter from J. E. full of troubles too. She says you have been a comfort to them too. I can't live without the tenderness of some woman; and expect when I am sixty I shall be marrying a girl of eleven or twelve, innocent, barley-sugar-loving, in a pinafore.

They came and interrupted me as I was writing this, two days since; and I have been in public almost ever since. The lectures are enormously *suivies* and I read at the rate of a pound a minute nearly. The curious thing is, that I think I improve in the reading; at certain passages a sort of emotion springs up, I begin to understand how actors feel affected over and over again at the same passages of the play;—they are affected off the stage too, I hope I shan't be.

Crowe is my immensest comfort; I could not live without someone to take care of me, and he is the kindest and most affectionate henchman ever man had. I went to see Pierce Butler yesterday, Fanny's[5] husband. I thought

[3]A character in Thackeray's novel *Henry Esmond.*

[4]A character in *Pendennis.*

[5]Fanny Kemble, the well-known actress, divorced in 1849.

she would like me to see the children if I could, and I asked about them particularly, but they were not shown. I thought of good Adelaide coming to sing to you when you were ill. I may like everyone who is kind to you, mayn't I? . . . What for has Lady Ashburton never written to me? I am writing this with a new gold pen in such a fine gold case. An old gentleman gave it to me yesterday, a white-headed old philosopher and political economist. There's something simple in the way these kind folks regard a man; they read our books as if we were Fielding, and so forth. The other night some men were talking of Dickens and Bulwer as if they were equal to Shakespeare, and I was pleased to find myself pleased at hearing them praised. The prettiest girl in Philadelphia, poor soul, has read *Vanity Fair* twelve times. I paid her a great big compliment yesterday, about her good looks of course, and she turned round delighted to her friend and said, "*Ai most tallut,*" that is something like the pronunciation. Beatrix has an adorable pronunciation, and uses little words, which are much better than wit. And what do you think? One of the prettiest girls in Boston is to be put under my charge to go to a marriage at Washington next week. We are to travel together all the way alone—only, only, I'm not going. Young people when they are engaged here, make tours alone; fancy what the British Mrs. Grundy would say at such an idea!

There was a young quakeress at the lecture last night, listening about Fielding. Lord! Lord, how pretty she was! There are hundreds of such everywhere, airy looking little beings, with magnolia—no not magnolia, what is that white flower you make bouquets of, camilla or camelia—complexions, and lasting not much longer. . . . God bless you and your children, write to me sometimes and farewell.

To Miss Perry

BALTIMORE,—WASHINGTON
Feby. 7th. to 14th. '53

Although I have written a many letters to Chesham Place, not one has gone to the special address of my dear K. E. P., and if you please I will begin one now for half an hour before going to lecture 1. In another hour that dreary business of "In speaking of the English Humourous writers of the last, etc." will begin,—and the wonder to me is that the speaker once in the desk (to-day it is to be a right down pulpit in a Universalist Church and no mistake), gets interested in the work, makes the points, thrills with emotion and indignation at the right place, and has a little sensation whilst the work is going on; but I can't go on much longer, my conscience revolts at the quackery. Now I have seen three great cities, Boston, New York, Philadelphia, I think I like them all mighty well they seem to me not so civilized as our London, but more so than Manchester and Liverpool. At Boston is very good literate company indeed; it is like Edinburgh for that,—

a vast amount of toryism and donnishness everywhere. That of New York the simplest and least pretentious; it suffices that a man should keep a fine house, give parties, and have a daughter, to get all the world to him. And what struck me, that whereas on my first arrival, I was annoyed at the uncommon splendatiousness

—here the letter was interrupted on Monday at Baltimore, and is now taken up again on Thursday at Washington—never mind what struck me, it was only that after a while you get accustomed to the splendor of the dresses and think them right and proper. Use makes everything so; who knows? you will be coming out in Empire ruffs and high waists by the time I come home. I have not been able to write a word since I came here on Tuesday; my time has been spent in seeing and calling upon lions. Our minister Mr. Crampton is very jolly and good-natured. Yesterday he had a dinner at five for all the legation, and they all came very much bored to my lecture. To-day I dined with Mr. Everett;[6] with the President[7] it may be next week. The place has a Wiesbaden air—there are politics and gaieties straggling all over it. More interruption and this one has lasted three days. Book indeed! How is one to write a book when it is next to impossible to get a quiet half hour? Since I wrote has come a short kind letter from dear old Kinglake,[8] who continues to give bad accounts from Chesham Place. God bless all there, say I. I wish I was by to be with my dear friends in grief, I know they know how to sympathize (although we are spoiled by the world, we have no hearts you know &c. &c.; but then it may happen that the high flown romantic people are wrong, and that we love our friends as well as they do). I don't pity anybody who leaves the world, not even a fair young girl in her prime; I pity those remaining. On her journey, if it pleases God to send her, depend on it there's no cause for grief, that's but an earthly condition. Out of our stormy life, and brought nearer the Divine light and warmth, there must be a serene climate. Can't you fancy sailing into the calm? Would you care about going on the voyage, only for the dear souls left on the other shore? but we shan't be parted from them no doubt though they are from us. Add a little more intelligence to that which we possess even as we are, and why shouldn't we be with our friends though ever so far off? . . .

Why presently, the body removed, shouldn't we personally be anywhere at will—properties of Creation, like the electric something (spark is it?) that thrills all round the globe simultaneously? and if round the globe why not *Uberall* [Everywhere]? and the body being removed or else where disposed of and developed, sorrow and its opposite, crime and the reverse, ease and disease, desire and dislike &c. go along with the body—a lucid Intelligence

[6]Edward Everett, then Secretary of State.

[7]President Franklin Pierce.

[8]Probably Alexander W. Kinglake, who later wrote a history of the Crimean War.

remains, a Perception ubiquitous. *Monday*. I was interrupted a dozen times yesterday in the course of these profitless *Schwärmereien* [Reveries].—There's no rest here for pilgrims like me. Have I told you on the other side that I'm doing a good business at Baltimore and a small select one here? the big-wigs all come and are pleased; all the legations and old Scott[9] the unsuccessful candidate for the Presidency &c.? It is well to have come. I shall go hence to Richmond and Charleston and then who knows whither? not to New Orleans, I think the distance is too great. I can't go a thousand miles fishing for half as many pounds. Why not come back and see all the dear faces at home? I try and think of something to say about this country; all I have remarked I could put down in two pages. Where's the eager observation and ready pencil of five years ago? I have not made a single sketch. The world passes before me and I don't care—Is it a weary heart or is it a great cold I have got in my nose which stupefies me utterly? I won't inflict any more megrims upon you,

from your affectionate friend and brother

W. M. T.

To Mrs. Elliot and Her Sister Miss Perry

Richmond, Virginia
March 3rd. 1853

Fragment

I am getting so sick and ashamed of the confounded old lectures that I wonder I have the courage to go on delivering them. I shan't read a single review of them when they are published; anything savage said about them will serve them right. They are popular enough here. The two presidents at Washington came to the last, and in this pretty little town the little Atheneum Hall was crowded so much that it's a pity I had not hired a room twice as big; but £2500 is all I shall make out of them. Well that is £200 a year in this country and an immense comfort for the chicks.—Crowe has just come out from what might have been and may be yet a dreadful scrape. He went into a slave market and began sketching; and the people rushed on him savagely and obliged him to quit. Fancy such a piece of imprudence. It may fall upon his chief, who knows, and cut short his popularity.

The negroes don't shock me, or excite my compassionate feelings at all; they are so grotesque and happy that I can't cry over them. The little black imps are trotting and grinning about the streets, women, workmen, waiters, all well fed and happy. The place the merriest little place and the most picturesque I have seen in America, and on Saturday I go to Charleston—

[9]General Winfield Scott.

shall I go thence to Havannah? who knows. I should like to give myself a week's holiday, without my demd lecture box. Shake every one by the hand that asks about me.

I am yours always—O! you kind friends——

W. M. T.

To Miss Perry

Savannah, Georgia,—[1855]
Feast of St. Valentine

This welcome day brought me a nice long letter from K. E. P., and she must know that I write from the most comfortable quarters I have ever had in the United States. In a tranquil old city, wide-streeted, tree-planted, with a few cows and carriages toiling through the sandy road, a few happy negroes sauntering here and there, a red river with a tranquil little fleet of merchant-men taking in cargo, and tranquil ware-houses barricaded with packs of cotton,—no row, no tearing northern bustle, no ceaseless hotel racket, no crowds drinking at the bar,—a snug little languid audience of three or four hundred people, far too lazy to laugh or applaud; a famous good dinner, breakfast etc, and leisure all the morning to think and do and sleep and read as I like. The only place I say in the States where I can get these comforts—all free gratis—is in the house of my friend Andrew Low of the great house of A. Low and Co., Cotton Dealers, brokers, Merchants—what's the word? Last time I was here he was a widower with two daughters in England, about whom—and other two daughters—there was endless talk between us. Now there is a pretty wife added to the establishment, and a little daughter number three crowing in the adjoining nursery. They are tremendous men these cotton merchants.

When I had finished at Charleston I went off to a queer little rustic city called Augusta—a great broad street 2 miles long—old quaint looking shops—houses with galleries—ware-houses—trees—cows and negroes strolling about the side walks—plank roads—a happy dirty tranquility generally prevalent. It lies 130 miles from Charleston. You take 8½ hours to get there by the railway, about same time and distance to come here, over endless plains of swampy pine-lands—a village or two here and there in a clearing. I brought away a snug little purse from snug little Augusta, though I had a rival—A Wild man, lecturing in the very same hall: I tell you it is not a dignified *métier*, that which I pursue.

What is this about the *Saturday Review?* After giving Vernon Harcourt 2/6 to send me the first 5 numbers, and only getting No. 1, it is too bad they should assault me—and for what? My lecture is rather extra loyal whenever the Queen is mentioned,—and the most applauded passage in them I shall have the honour of delivering to-night in the Lecture on George II, where the speaker says "In laughing at these old-world follies and ceremonies shall we not acknowledge the change of to-day? As the mistress of St. James passes me now I salute the sovereign, wise, moderate, exemplary of life, the good mother, the good wife, the accomplished Lady, the enlightened friend of Art, the tender sympathizer in her people's glories and sorrows."

I can't say more, can I? and as for George III, I leave off just with the people on the crying point. And I never for one minute should think that my brave old Venables would hit me; or if he did that he hadn't good cause for it.

Forster's[10] classification delights me. It's right that men of such ability and merit should get government recognition and honourable public employ. It is a compliment to all of us when one receives such promotion. As for me I have pestered you with my account of dollars and cents, and it is quite clear that Kings or Laws cannot do anything so well for me as these jaws and this pen—please God they are allowed to wag a little longer. I wish I did not read about your illness and weakness in that letter. Ah, me! many and many a time every day do I think of you all.

Enter a servant (black) with the card of Bishop Elliott. . . . .

If you are taking a drive some day, do go and pay a visit of charity to my good cook and housekeeper Gray, and say you have heard of me, and that I am very well and making plenty of money and that Charles is well and is the greatest comfort to me. It will comfort the poor woman all alone in poor 36 yonder. What charming letters Annie[11] writes me with exquisite pretty turns now and then. St. Valentine brought me a delightful letter from her too, and from the dear old mother; and whether it's the comfort of this house, or the pleasure of having an hour's chat with you, or the sweet clean bed I had last night and undisturbed rest and good breakfast,—altogether I think I have no right to grumble at my lot and am very decently happy, don't you?

16th Feb. My course is for Macon, Montgomery and New Orleans; no Havannah, the dollars forbid. From N. O. I shall go up the Mississippi, D. V., to St. Loüis and Cincinnati, and ye who write will address care of J. G. King's Sons, New York, won't you?

Yours afft.
W. M. T.

An Imaginary Letter from New York

September 5, 1848

Dear Madam:—

It seems to me a long time since I had the honour of seeing you. I shall be glad to have some account of your health. We made a beautiful voyage

[10]John Forster, English writer and intimate friend of Dickens.

[11]His daughter.

of 13½ days, and reached this fine city yesterday. The entrance of the bay is beautiful; magnificent woods of the Susquehannah stretch down to the shore, and from Hoboken lighthouse to Vancouver's Island, the bay presents one brilliant blaze of natural and commercial loveliness. Hearing that Titmarsh[12] was on board the steamer, the Lord Mayor and Aldermen of New York came down to receive us, and the batteries on Long Island fired a salute. General Jackson called at my hotel, (the Astor house) I found him a kind old man, though he has a wooden leg and takes a great deal of snuff. Broadway has certainly disappointed me—it is nothing to be compared to our own dear Holborn Hill. But the beautiful range of the Allegheney mountains, which I see from my windows, and the roar of the Niagara Cataract, which empties itself out of the Mississippi into the Oregon territory, have an effect, which your fine eye for the picturesque, and keen sense of the beautiful and the natural would I am sure lead you to appreciate.

The oysters here are much larger than ours, and the canvass backed ducks are reckoned, and indeed are, a delicacy. The house where Washington was born is still shown, but the General I am informed, is dead, much regretted. The clergy here is both numerous and respected, and the Archbishop of New York is a most venerable and delightful prelate; whose sermons are however a little long. The ladies are without exception the—But here the first gong sounds for dinner, and the black slave who waits on me, comes up and says, "Massa, hab only five minutes for dinnah." "Make haste, git no pumpkin pie else," so unwillingly I am obliged to break off my note and to subscribe myself,

My dear Madame
Your very faithful servt.,
W. M. Thackeray.

From A MISSISSIPPI BUBBLE

. . . How they sang; how they laughed and grinned; how they scraped, bowed, and complimented you and each other, those negroes of the cities of the Southern parts of the then United States! My business kept me in the towns; I was but in one negro-plantation village, and there were only women and little children, the men being out a-field. But there was plenty of cheerfulness in the huts, under the great trees—I speak of what I saw—and amidst the dusky bondsmen of the cities. I witnessed a curious gayety; heard amongst the black folk endless singing, shouting, and laughter; and saw on holidays black gentlemen and ladies arrayed in such splendor and comfort as freeborn workmen in our towns seldom exhibit. What a grin and bow that dark gentleman performed, who was the porter at the colonel's, when he said, "You write your name, mas'r, else I will forgot." I am not going into the slavery question, I am not an advocate for "the institution,"

[12] Michael Angelo Titmarsh was a pen-name of Thackeray.

as I know, madam, by that angry toss of your head, you are about to declare me to be. For domestic purposes, my dear lady, it seemed to me about the dearest institution that can be devised. In a house in a Southern city you will find fifteen negroes doing the work which John, the cook, the housemaid, and the help, do perfectly in your own comfortable London house. And these fifteen negroes are the pick of a family of some eighty or ninety. Twenty are too sick, or too old for work, let us say: twenty too clumsy: twenty are too young, and have to be nursed and watched by ten more. And master has to maintain the immense crew to do the work of half a dozen willing hands. No, no; let Mitchell, the exile from poor dear enslaved Ireland, wish for a gang of "fat niggers;" I would as soon you should make me a present of a score of Bengal elephants, when I need but a single stout horse to pull my brougham.

How hospitable they were, those Southern men! In the North itself the welcome was not kinder, as I, who have eaten Northern and Southern salt, can testify. As for New Orleans, in spring-time,—just when the orchards were flushing over with peach-blossoms, and the sweet herbs came to flavor the juleps—it seemed to me the city of the world where you can eat and drink the most and suffer the least. At Bordeaux itself, claret is not better to drink than at New Orleans. It was all good—believe an expert Robert—from the half-dollar Médoc of the public hotel table, to the private gentleman's choicest wine. Claret is, somehow, good in that gifted place at dinner, at supper, and at breakfast in the morning. It is good: it is superabundant—and there is nothing to pay. Find me speaking ill of such a country! When I do, . . . smother me in a desert, or let Mississippi or Garonne drown me! At that comfortable tavern on Pontchartrain we had a *bouillabaisse* than which a better was never eaten at Marseilles: and not the least headache in the morning, I give you my word; on the contrary, you only wake with a sweet refreshing thirst for claret and water. They say there is fever there in the autumn: but not in the spring-time, when the peach-blossoms blush over the orchards, and the sweet herbs come to flavor the juleps.

I was bound from New Orleans to Saint Louis; and our walk was constantly on the Levee, whence we could see a hundred of those huge white Mississippi steamers at their moorings in the river: "Look," said my friend Lochlomond to me, as we stood one day on the quay—"look at that post! Look at that coffee-house behind it! Sir, last year a steamer blew up in the river yonder, just where you see those men pulling off in the boat. By that post where you are standing a mule was cut in two by a fragment of the burst machinery, and a bit of the chimney-stove in that first-floor window of the coffee-house, killed a negro who was cleaning knives in the top-room!" I looked at the post, at the coffee-house window, at the steamer in which I was going to embark, at my friend, with a pleasing interest not divested of melancholy. Yesterday, it was the mule, thinks I, who was cut in two: it may be *cras mihi* [tomorrow to me]. Why, in the same little sketch-book, there is a drawing of an Alabama river steamer which blew up on the very next voyage after that in which your humble servant was on board! Had I but waited another week, I might have. . . . These incidents give a queer zest to the voyage down the life-stream in America. When our huge, tall, white, paste-board castle of a steamer began to work up stream, every limb in her creaked, and groaned, and quivered, so that you might fancy she would burst right off. Would she hold together, or would she split into ten million of shivers? O my home and children! Would your humble servant's body be cut in two across yonder chain on the Levee, or be precipitated into yonder first-floor, so as to damage the chest of a black man cleaning boots at the window? The black man is safe for me, thank goodness. But you see the little accident *might* have happened. It has happened; and if to a mule, why not to a more docile animal? On our journey up the Mississippi, I give you my honor we were on fire three times, and burned our cook-room down. The deck at night was a great firework—the chimney spouted myriads of stars, which fell blackening on our garments, sparkling on to the deck, or gleaming into the mighty stream through which we labored—the mighty yellow stream with all its snags.

How I kept up my courage through these dangers shall now be narrated. The excellent landlord of the "Saint Charles Hotel," when I was going away, begged me to accept two bottles of the very finest Cognac, with his compliments; and I found them in my state-room with my luggage. Lochlomond came to see me off, and as he squeezed my hand at parting, "Roundabout," says he, "the wine mayn't be very good on board, so I have brought a dozen-case of the Médoc which you liked;" and we grasped together the hands of friendship and farewell. Whose boat is this pulling up to the ship? It is our friend Glenlivat, who gave us the dinner on Lake Pontchartrain. "Roundabout," says he, "we have tried to do what we could for you, my boy; and it has been done *de bon cœur* [heartily]" (I detect a kind tremulousness in the good fellow's voice as he speaks). "I say—hem!—the a—the wine isn't too good on board, so I've brought you a dozen of Médoc for your voyage, you know. And God bless you; and when I come to London in May I shall come and see you. Hallo! here's Johnson come to see you off, too!"

As I am a miserable sinner, when Johnson grasped my hand, he said, "Mr. Roundabout, you can't be sure of the wine on board these steamers, so I thought I would bring you a little case of that light claret which you liked at my house." . . . No wonder I could face the Mississippi with so much courage supplied to me! Where are you, honest friends, who gave me of your kindness and your cheer? May I be considerably boiled, blown up, and snagged, if I speak hard words of you. May claret turn sour ere I do!

Mounting the stream it chanced that we had very few passengers. How far is the famous city of Memphis from New Orleans? I do not mean the Egyptian Memphis, but the American Memphis, from which to the American Cairo we slowly toiled up the river—to the American Cairo at the confluence of the Ohio and Mississippi rivers. And at Cairo we parted company from the boat, and from some famous and gifted fellow-passengers who joined us at Memphis, and whose pictures we had seen in many cities of the South. I do not give the names of these remarkable people, unless, by some wondrous chance, in inventing a name I should light upon that real one which some of them bore; but if you please I will say that our fellow-passengers whom we took in at Memphis were no less personages than the Vermont Giant and the famous Bearded Lady of Kentucky and her son. Their pictures I had seen in many cities through which I travelled with my own little performance. I think the Vermont Giant was a trifle taller in his pictures than he was in life (being represented in the former as, at least, some two stories high): but the lady's prodigious beard received no more than justice at the hands of the painter; that portion of it which I saw being really most black, rich, and curly—I say the portion of beard, for this modest or prudent woman kept I don't know how much of the beard covered up with a red handkerchief, from which I suppose it only emerged when she went to bed, or when she exhibited it professionally.

The Giant, I must think, was an overrated giant. I have known gentlemen, not in the profession, better made, and I should say taller, than the Vermont gentleman. A strange feeling I used to have at meals; when, on looking round our little society, I saw the Giant, the Bearded Lady of Kentucky, the little Bearded Boy of three years old, the Captain, (this I *think;* but at this distance of time I would not like to make the statement on affidavit,) and the three other passengers, all with their knives in their mouths making play at the dinner—a strange feeling I say it was, and as though I was in a castle of ogres. But, after all, why so squeamish? A few scores of years back, the finest gentlemen and ladies of Europe did the like. . . . Have you ever looked at Gilray's print of the Prince of Wales, a languid voluptuary, retiring after his meal, and noted the toothpick which he uses? . . . You are right, madam; I own that the subject is revolting and terrible. I will not pursue it. Only—allow that a gentleman, in a shaky steamboat, on a dangerous river, in a far-off country, which caught fire three times during the voyage—(of course I mean the steamboat, not the country,)—seeing a giant, a voracious supercargo, a bearded lady, and a little boy, not three years of age, with a chin already quite black and curly, all plying their victuals down their throats with their knives—allow, madam, that in such a company a man had a right to feel a little nervous. I don't know whether you have ever remarked the Indian jugglers swallowing their knives, or seen, as I have, a whole table of people performing the same trick, but if you look at their eyes when they do it, I assure you there is a roll in them which is dreadful.

Apart from this usage, which they practise in common with many thousand most estimable citizens, the Vermont gentleman, and the Kentucky whiskered lady—or did I say the reverse?—whichever you like, my dear sir—were quite quiet, modest, unassuming people. She sat working with her needle, if I remember right. He, I suppose, slept in the great cabin, which was seventy feet long at the least, nor, I am bound to say, did I hear in the night any snores or roars, such as you would fancy ought to accompany the sleep of ogres. Nay, this giant had quite a small appetite, (unless, to be sure, he went forward and ate a sheep or two in private with his horrid knife—oh, the dreadful thought!—but *in public*, I say, he had quite a delicate appetite,) and was also a tea-totaler. I don't remember to have heard the lady's voice, though I might, not unnaturally, have been curious to hear it. Was her voice a deep, rich, magnificent bass; or was it soft, fluty, and mild? I shall never know now. Even if she comes to this country, I shall never go and see her. I *have* seen her, and for nothing.

You would have fancied that, as after all we were only some half-dozen on board, she might have dispensed with her red handkerchief, and talked, and eaten her dinner in comfort: but in covering her chin there was a kind of modesty. That beard was her profession: that beard brought the public to see her: out of her business she wished to put that beard aside as it were: as a barrister would wish to put off his wig. I know some who carry theirs into private life, and who mistake you and me for jury-boxes when they address us: but these are not your modest barristers, not your true gentlemen.

Well, I own I respected the lady for the modesty with which, her public business over, she retired into private life. She respected her life, and her beard. That beard having done its day's work, she puts it away in her handkerchief; and becomes, as far as in her lies, a private ordinary person. All public men and women of good sense, I should think, have this modesty. When, for instance, in my small way, poor Mrs. Brown comes simpering up to me, with her album in one hand, a pen in the other, and says, "Ho, ho, dear Mr. Roundabout, write us one of your amusing," &c. &c., my beard drops behind my handkerchief instantly. Why am I to wag my chin and grin for Mrs. Brown's good pleasure? My dear madam, I have been making faces all day. It is my profession. I do my comic business with the greatest pains, seriousness, and trouble: and with it make, I hope, a not dishonest livelihood. If you ask Mons. Blondin[13] to tea, you don't have a rope stretched from your garret window to the opposite side of the square, and request Monsieur to take his tea out on the centre of the rope? I lay my hand on this waistcoat, and declare that not once in the course of our voyage together did I allow the Kentucky Giant to suppose I was speculating on his stature, or the Bearded Lady to surmise that I wished to peep under the handkerchief which muffled the lower part of her face.

"And the more fool you," says some cynic. (Faugh, those cynics, I hate 'em!) Don't you know, sir, that a man of genius is pleased to have his genius recognized; that a beauty likes to be admired; that an actor likes to be applauded; that stout old Wellington himself was pleased, and smiled when the people cheered him as he passed? Suppose you had paid some respectful compliment to that lady? Suppose you had asked that giant, if, for once, he

[13]Tight-rope performer.

would take anything at the liquor-bar? you might have learned a great deal of curious knowledge regarding giants and bearded ladies, about whom you evidently now know very little. There was that little boy of three years old, with a fine beard already, and his little legs and arms, as seen out of his little frock, covered with a dark down. What a queer little capering satyr! He was quite good-natured, childish, rather solemn. . . .

I have said the B. L. had another child. Now this was a little girl of some six years old, as fair and as smooth of skin, dear madam, as your own darling cherubs. She wandered about the great cabin quite melancholy. No one seemed to care for her. All the family affections were centred on Master Esau yonder. His little beard was beginning to be a little fortune already, whereas Miss Rosalba was of no good to the family. No one would pay a cent to see *her* little fair face. No wonder the poor little maid was melancholy. As I looked at her, I seemed to walk more and more in a fairy tale, and more and more in a cavern of ogres. Was this a little fondling whom they had picked up in some forest, where lie the picked bones of the queen, her tender mother, and the tough old defunct monarch, her father? No. Doubtless they were quite good-natured people, these. I don't believe they were unkind to the little girl without the moustaches. It may have been only my fancy that she repined because she had a cheek no more bearded than a rose's.

Would you wish your own daughter, madam, to have a smooth cheek, a modest air, and a gentle feminine behavior, or to be—I won't say a whiskered prodigy, like this Bearded Lady of Kentucky—but a masculine wonder, a virago, a female personage of more than female strength, courage, wisdom? Some authors, who shall be nameless, are, I know, accused of depicting the most feeble, brainless, namby-pamby heroines, for ever whimpering tears and prattling commonplaces. *You* would have the heroine of your novel so beautiful that she should charm the captain (or hero, whoever he may be) with her appearance; surprise and confound the bishop with her learning; outride the squire and get the brush, and, when he fell from his horse, whip out a lancet and bleed him; rescue from fever and death the poor cottager's family whom the doctor had given up; make 21 at the butts with the rifle, when the poor captain only scored 18; give him twenty in fifty at billiards and beat him; and draw tears from the professional Italian people by her exquisite performance (of voice and violoncello) in the evening;—I say, if a novelist would be popular with ladies—the great novel-readers of the world—this is the sort of heroine who would carry him through half a dozen editions. Suppose I had asked that Bearded Lady to sing? Confess, now, miss, you would not have been displeased if I had told you that she had a voice like Lablache,[14] only ever so much lower.

My dear, you would like to be a heroine? You would like to travel in triumphal caravans; to see your effigy placarded on city walls; to have your levées attended by admiring crowds, all crying out, "Was there ever such a

[14]Luigi Lablache, noted opera singer whose voice was a powerful bass.

wonder of a woman?" You would like admiration? Consider the tax you pay for it. You would be alone were you eminent. Were you so distinguished from your neighbors—I will not say by a beard and whiskers, that were odious—but by a great and remarkable intellectual superiority—would you, do you think, be any the happier? Consider envy. Consider solitude. Consider the jealousy and torture of mind which this Kentucky lady must feel, suppose she should hear that there is, let us say, a Missouri prodigy, with a beard larger than hers? Consider how she is separated from her kind by the possession of that wonder of a beard? When that beard grows gray, how lonely she will be, the poor old thing! If it falls off, the public admiration falls off too; and how she will miss it—the compliments of the trumpeters, the admiration of the crowd, the gilded progress of the car. I see an old woman alone in a decrepit old caravan, with cobwebs on the knocker, with a blistered ensign flapping idly over the door. Would you like to be that deserted person? Ah, Chloe! To be good, to be simple, to be modest, to be loved, be thy lot. Be thankful thou art not taller, nor stronger, nor richer, nor wiser than the rest of the world!

Offenbach Observed

Jacques Offenbach, who was born in Germany, at Cologne, in 1819, went to Paris when he was fourteen and eventually became a French citizen. At twenty-nine he was orchestra leader of the famous Theatre Français. Six years later he was made manager of the Bouffes Parisiennes, where he produced many of his own comic operas. Of these the most popular was ORPHEUS IN HADES, *which has continued to be revived for nearly nine decades since its first production.*

From OFFENBACH IN AMERICA

Hotels and Restaurants

On arriving at New York [1876], I put up at the Fifth Avenue Hotel, which deserves a description, as in Europe one can form no idea of this kind of establishment. There is every convenience at hand; a dressing-room, bath, and closet are provided for each room. The ground floor of the hotel is an immense bazar—a little commercial city, in which every trade is represented. There is the hair-dresser of the hotel, the hatter, the tailor, the druggist, the bookseller, even the boot-black of the hotel. One might arrive at a hotel as lightly dressed as Adam before the fall, as long-haired as Absalom before he caught in the tree, and depart as respectable as the famous Comte d'Orsay[1] of fashionable memory. Everything is to be found in the Fifth Avenue Hotel —everything, with the exception, however, of a polyglot; this alone is entirely wanting. Among the two hundred waiters of this gigantic establishment you would seek in vain for one who spoke French. This is not very pleasant for those who cannot speak English; but, in compensation for this, what numberless comforts! . . .

You have . . . the right of eating all day long. From eight to eleven o'clock, there is breakfast; from twelve to three in the afternoon, lunch; from five to seven, dinner; from eight to eleven, tea. The dining-room is on the first floor; as soon as you appear at the door of this immense hall, where fifty tables are methodically arranged, the steward meets you, and shows you to a seat. Resistance, fancy or preference for one corner rather than for another, are vain. The *maître d'hôtel* (steward) is also master of

[1]Alfred Comte d'Orsay (1801–52), French leader of fashion.

the hotel, and will place next to you whoever he chooses, without as much as asking your leave. When you are seated, the waiter, without asking what you will take, brings you a large glass of ice-water; for there is one thing worthy of note in America: it is, that, of all the fifty tables in the room, there is not one upon which anything but ice-water is drunk; if by chance you see wine or beer before a guest, you may be certain that he is a European.

After the glass of water, the waiter hands you the list of the eighty dishes of the day—I do not exaggerate; you make your choice, selecting three or four; and the most comical part of the business is, that all you have ordered is brought you at once. If you have unfortunately forgotten to mention the vegetables you desire, then the fifteen vegetables down on the bill-of-fare will all be brought you at the same time. So that you find yourself suddenly surrounded by thirty dishes—soup, fish, meat, vegetables, and sweets, without counting the rear-guard of desserts, which is always composed of at least a dozen varieties. All is arranged before you, bidding defiance to your stomach; the first time it makes you dizzy and takes away all appetite. . . .

. . . There are . . . no restaurants which can properly be called American.

The Americans keep the hotels, but the kitchen seems entirely surrendered to foreigners. Nothing is easier than to eat a meal in the French, Italian, Spanish, or German style. Nothing is more difficult for a stranger than to eat an American dinner in America.

I had almost forgotten to mention the most interesting of all restaurants—the restaurant that *serves meals gratis!*

It would certainly never occur to one of our French hotel-keepers to open a free *table d'hôte*. In spite of the Irishman's assertion, that it is possible to get rich while losing on each article by making it up on the quantity, neither Bignon, nor Brébant, nor the Café Riche have yet made such an attempt; and one must really go to a progressive country in order to see such things.

At all events, several well-known New York restaurants serve meals for nothing—provided you take a drink, even if it only cost ten cents. On Sundays, when, thanks to the police, the restaurants dare not sell drinks, it is all the better for the consumer. Lunch is served as usual, and I can state this as a fact, having seen it at the Brunswick myself; and they say that living is expensive in America.

And it must not be supposed that this gratuitous meal is composed of mere trifles. Here is a bill of fare, copied on the spot:

Ham
An enormous piece of roast-beef
Pork and beans
Potato salad
Olives, pickles, etc.
Cheese
Crackers

Wholesome and abundant fare as may be seen. The most substantial part is the roast-beef, from which the guests are privileged to cut, themselves, such slices as they like.

A large pile of plates stands on a sideboard, convenient free lunch, together with forks and knives, in abundance; but the guests, as a rule, prefer using their own fingers; some going so far as to help themselves by the handful out of the salad-bowl. I shudder still, just to think of it!

The head-waiter, to whom I expressed my horror and astonishment, tried his best to soothe my feelings.

"This offends us less than it does you. *Time is money*, you see; and these gentlemen are in such a hurry!"

Waiters in hotels and restaurants are often very peculiar types!

For instance, as I have already mentioned elsewhere, when you sit down at the table, a waiter brings you a glass of ice-water; you might sit there for two hours in company with your ice-water without anybody interfering with you.

You must call another waiter, who hands you the bill-of-fare. Meantime you are dying of thirst, and you want something else to drink besides water. The waiter who took your order goes leisurely for a third one, who brings you at last the desired drink; but you are mistaken if you think yourself safe now: it is another waiter who alone has the privilege of using the corkscrew. At least such is the case at the Brunswick. This annoying proceeding having occurred several times, I declared at last that I would leave the house if this farce was not dropped. When I came to breakfast the following morning, every one of the twenty or thirty waiters of the restaurant were drawn up in line on my passage, and every one gravely held a corkscrew in his hand. Since then the service at the Brunswick is considerably more prompt.

On the evening of my arrival in New York, I dined with some friends in my room at the Fifth Avenue Hotel. The soup had just been served, when I fancied I heard a sound like whistling. I looked around in astonishment to discover the bold individual. Of course, it was not one of the guests; it was the waiter. My first impulse was to get up and kick him out; but my friends, who had noticed the same extraordinary phenomenon, beckoned me to keep still. We continued our dinner. As to the musician, though timid at first, he became gradually bolder, and soon ventured upon little trills, finally essaying the most difficult pieces. At one time, as if overcome by sudden melancholy, he would indulge in the gloomiest of tunes; then suddenly, and without any apparent reason, the liveliest and merriest melodies burst forth from his lips.

The dinner over, I called the waiter's attention to the impropriety of which he had been guilty, in giving us music at the table without having been requested to do so.

"You see, sir, I love music, and I use it to express my thoughts. If a dish is not to my taste, I whistle melancholy airs; when a dish suits me, I whistle lively tunes. But when I fairly worship a dish . . ."

"Like the frozen charlotte we had just now?" I interrupted.

"Monsieur noticed it? Oh! then I whistle my merriest tunes."

"And do you think that tune from the *Grande Duchesse* you were whistling just now particularly gay?"

"Your music, sir, is always so funny!"

I don't very much fancy hearing my music whistled; so I requested the steward in future not to send me a whistling waiter.

Second Sketch of a Waiter

This is rather curious too.

It was in Philadelphia I had the pleasure of meeting the fellow. It was half-past nine in the evening when we arrived in that city, and we were, my friends and myself, literally starved. Having inquired for a good restaurant, we were directed to Pétry's; so to Pétry's we went, and here we are at the table.

"Waiter!"

"Well, sir?"

"Give us first a good Julienne soup."

The waiter makes a wry face.

"I should not recommend it to you, sir; the vegetables here are so very tough."

"Well, never mind the soup; have you any salmon?"

"Oh! yes, sir, we have salmon, of course, and we have had it a good long time too; possibly it may not be as fresh as you might wish."

"How then about a Chateaubriand, nice and rare?"

"The cook don't know how to get them up, sir."

"Strawberries?"

"They are not fit to eat, sir."

"And the cheese?"

"I'll ask it to come up, sir; it is quite able to walk by itself."

"I say, waiter, you will never make your master's fortune."

"My first duty, sir, is to please my customers."

"If I was Mr. Pétry I would soon discharge you."

"Mr. Pétry did not wait for your advice, sir. You see me here to-night for the last time."

Whereupon he bowed to us in his best style; after which we had an excellent supper.

Waiter Number Three

Delmonico's waiters' style deserves a special mention.

We were invited one evening, by a theatrical manager, to a supper, in company with the leading actors of his theatre. The supper was excellent.

Like all other good things, it came to an end. The time for a smoke and a chat having come, we remained in our parlor, smoking and sipping iced drinks. There was then no further necessity for the presence of a servant; nevertheless I noticed, not without astonishment, our waiter returning very often, and listening to our conversation. As I was not the host, I thought it best to say nothing. As to the other guests, none seemed to have noticed this strange proceeding.

When about to part, I took occasion to invite the manager and his artists to a supper in the same restaurant.

Supper over, the same occurrence took place. This time I observed the waiter more attentively, and I noticed that he went all around the table, examining closely every one of the guests. He went away after that, but returned within a few minutes and renewed his examination and his perambulations.

"Waiter, you have come several times without being called; let this be the last, please."

"Sorry, sir," he answered; "but we have orders from Mr. Delmonico to walk every five minutes into every parlor and private room."

"Is Mr. Delmonico connected with the police, then, that he sends you to listen to what his guests say?"

"Don't know, sir. Sure Mr. Delmonico would dismiss me if his instructions were not strictly obeyed."

"Is Mr. Delmonico afraid we are going to carry off his napkins and spoons; does he think we are likely to forget for a moment that a decent behavior is *de rigueur* in his famous restaurant? I am sorry to tell you, my friend; it is now half-past one, and we intend remaining here till seven; you will, therefore, have to repeat your visit sixty-six times more if you follow your instructions."

"I'll do it, sir."

I need not say that, after thus giving vent to our indignation, we did not carry out our threat. We left a little late (it was nearly two o'clock), vowing never to be caught again in this way.

New Yorkers, who don't care to have the whole town know in the morning how they spent the previous evening, will do well to keep an eye on those waiters who obey Mr. Delmonico's orders so punctually.

Gilmore's Garden

I breakfast hurriedly, for my one wish, my one desire since arriving, is to see the famous covered Garden where . . . I am about to display my talents; I hastened then to Gilmore's Garden.

Imagine a vast covered garden. In the centre of a great mass of tropical plants stands the stage, large enough to accommodate an orchestra of a hundred to a hundred and twenty musicians. All around are grass-plots, shrubbery, and flower-beds, among which the public circulate. Facing the entry is a large cascade, which imitates Niagara Falls during the interludes. The corners of the Garden are occupied by little Swiss cottages, which can hold seven or eight persons, and which advantageously supply the place of boxes in a theatre. A large gallery, with ordinary boxes and tiers of seats, afford facilities for those who like seeing and hearing from an elevation, to satisfy their taste.

The *ensemble* reminds one somewhat of the old *Jardin d'Hiver*, once so popular in the Champs-Elysées. The hall has a capacity of eight to nine thousand persons. It is brilliantly lit up; colored glasses are hung in festoons of the most picturesque effect.

Delighted with the hall, I asked Mr. Grau, the manager, a few particulars upon the orchestra I was to lead.

"We have engaged," he answered me, "the hundred and ten musicians you asked for; and I can assure you they are the best in New York."

I soon discovered that he had not deceived me.

I had the rare good fortune of gaining the sympathy of my orchestra from the start; and here is how it happened: The musicians have here a vast and powerful organization, and have constituted a society, outside of which there is no salvation. Any one who wishes to join an orchestra must first become a member of the society. There is no exception to this rule; from the leader to the drummer inclusively, all must belong to it.

I had been advised of this state of things by Boulard,[2] who had already led one or two rehearsals, and who had been obliged to join the association in order to be allowed to lead.

On my entering the hall, the musicians received me with a regular ovation, for which I returned thanks in a few words.

We begin the rehearsal with the overture of "*Vert-Vert.*" I had scarcely led sixteen bars when I stopped the orchestra, and, addressing the musicians:

"Excuse me, gentlemen," I said. "We have scarcely begun, and you have already failed in your duty."

General astonishment.

"What! I am not a member of your association, and you allow me to lead!"

Whereupon there was a general laugh. I waited until this had subsided, and then added, quite seriously:

"Since you have not thought proper to mention it to me, I must myself request to be admitted into your society."

They protested; but I insisted, saying that I entirely approved of their institution, and should consider it an honor to belong to it.

My request was received with long and loud applause. I had conquered my orchestra, and from this moment we were all members of the same

[2]M. Boulard accompanied Offenbach as orchestra leader.

family, and the most perfect *harmony* never ceased to prevail among us. It is fair to add that the orchestra was composed in a superior manner; for each of my pieces two rehearsals were always sufficient to insure a most brilliant rendering.

American Women—Introductions—Central Park

Ladies, and even young girls, enjoy here the greatest freedom. I have an idea that when Lafayette went to America to fight for Liberty, he only had the ladies in view, for they alone are really free in free America.

My friends Meilhac and Halévy,[3] in the *Vie Parisienne*, assert that Parisian ladies alone possess the art of walking on the street; but they had not seen American women going, coming, getting out of the way of carriages, picking up their skirts with an elegant gesture, and revealing the most exquisite ankles with the most consummate skill.

It must be confessed that there are perhaps no women so fascinating as American women. In the first place, they are handsome in a proportion wholly unknown in Paris. Out of every hundred you meet, there are ninety who are lovely. Moreover, they know how to dress; their toilets are of the most exquisite and perfect taste. They look as if they had all just come from Worth's.

One thing alone I shall venture to criticise on their dress; that is, the little pocket, located just above the knee, where, in olden times, the ladies hung their purse. This pocket is exclusively devoted to the handkerchief. When, from a distance, a bit of white linen is seen issuing from this aperture, one is apt to wonder whether an accident has befallen the lady, and whether it is not a certain nameless garment which is thus revealed through a rent in the skirt.

All the American ladies you meet hold their purses tightly in their hands, lest some pick-pocket—of which there are perhaps as many in New York as in Paris—should be tempted to thrust a profane hand in their pocket. *Shocking!* In the afternoon young girls may be seen alone visiting the first-class restaurants and taking their lunch as quietly as an old European bachelor. Others are seen on some corner of Fifth Avenue, or elsewhere, waiting for their carriages, to which they have given orders to meet them, and drive to Central Park.

A strange fact for the depraved Parisian who is fond of following pretty women on the street, is that no one in New York or in any other city of the United States would venture to take up his line of march behind a youthful Yankee maiden, and still less to speak to her, even to offer her an umbrella.

In order to be able to offer her this object, with or without your heart, you must be presented, or *introduced*, as they say. But do not imagine that

[3]Librettists of several of Offenbach's operettas as well as his *Vie Parisienne.*

the formalities of an introduction are either very formidable or very difficult to accomplish. In the absence of a common friend, a simple "Personal" in the *Herald* will answer.

I spoke of the Central Park just now. It is the favorite drive of the most elegant society; but it does not in any way resemble our Bois de Bologne. Imagine a great rocky plain, skillfully concealed beneath well-kept lawns, a few groves of fine trees, one or two little lakes, and magnificent drives; such is the New York *Bois*. Every day a procession of carriages may be seen there. . . . American carriage manufacturers seem particularly bent upon inventing the most fantastic vehicles, all of which belong in a degree, more or less remote, to two leading styles: the first, which is enormously heavy, is a kind of landau of the Middle Ages, a massive coach, a monster berline, which, it is true, is capable of accommodating many people quite comfortably. But the aspect of these houses on wheels remains always horrible. A large window behind, with an ever-dangling curtain, makes it higher still. The other style, on the contrary, is of extreme lightness. It consists of a diminutive box, with or without top, seating one or two persons at most, and mounted on four great wheels, so thin and so slender that they impart to the carriage the appearance of a huge spider. These buggies, as they are called, have sometimes their tops raised; but as this is open on all sides, they always look as if they were in rags. It is not rare to see young ladies of the highest classes driving alone one of these light vehicles drawn by two powerful horses.

The first time I visited Central Park it was in company with a gentleman well known in New York, and at almost every step he met some friend. I noticed that he bowed very low to some, while to others he scarcely touched the brim of his hat. I asked him what it meant. He replied, quite seriously: "The gentleman to whom I have just bowed so respectfully belongs to the best New York society, and is worth a million of dollars. The one coming now is only worth a hundred thousand, and so he does not stand as well as the former one; I treat him, therefore, with less ceremony."

These are shades which are observed in America, where there is no aristocracy save that of labor and of the dollar.

Liberty in America

France, growing more and more generous, said to herself one fine morning: "What could I do to be agreeable to America on the occasion of her Centennial? Suppose I present her with a statue?"

All right for a statue, then. A subscription was opened; Frenchmen and Americans both contributed, and it was unanimously resolved that the statue should represent *Liberty enlightening the World*. M. Bartholdi . . . was commissioned to carry out the work. This new statue was . . . finished without trouble, and the sculptor then went over to select a proper site for his *Liberty enlightening the World*.

A parenthesis: I don't exactly understand the choice of this subject. The New World is said to possess all the liberties, and consequently needs no further enlightening.

I close the parenthesis.

After long examination, M. Bartholdi found at last the desired spot: a magnificent position; a natural pedestal rising from the waters—in short, Bedloe's Island.

"Here it shall stand!" he exclaimed.

He loses no time, hires workmen, and takes them to the island to dig the foundations. While his men were working, the artist was contemplating with emotion the rapidly deepening excavation, beholding in his imagination, and already standing there, the magnificent monument with which his name was to be eternally connected. Suddenly he felt a hand touching him on the shoulder.

The sculptor looks around, and finds himself in presence of a policeman.

"What are you doing there?" the policeman graciously asks.

"I am digging the foundations for *Liberty enlightening the World*."

"And who has given you permission to dig this hole?"

"Why, it is——"

"You don't know who?"

"Excuse me, sir, it is America herself!—America who has given me an order for a statue, and I was looking for a suitable spot for the erection of the monument; this one is excellent."

"This is all very interesting; but notwithstanding all the liberty that prevails in America, you must learn, sir, that you have no right to dig such a formidable hole without permission; you will please, therefore, follow me to the Mayor."

The laborers, who had stopped work at the sight of the policeman, had already put on their coats, and were about leaving the ground.

"Don't go," shouted the sculptor, in despair; "I shall be back with the authorization in five minutes."

Five minutes!

The artist had not foreseen one thing, nay, several things.

To build on public property without permission is as much an impossibility in the United States as anywhere else.

The Mayor could not take the responsibility upon himself; so he convoked the municipal council. The latter thought the subject too important to be decided without consulting the Governor. The Governor could do nothing without consulting the President of the Republic; the latter could only carry out the decisions of the House of Representatives, which must themselves be approved by the Senate.

Why not do for *Liberty enlightening the World* what was done for the quarantine? Build an island on piles! Here is an idea worthy of the monument. But let the construction be secure, for in case a heavy storm should arise, Bartholdi's island might be set adrift. Who knows where chance might lead it? To the French coast, perhaps, or to Paris, which, in the meantime, might have become a seaport?

America is indeed the land of liberty!

If you cannot dig a hole without disturbing the whole government hierarchy, you may, however, go where you like, marry whom you please, and eat what you fancy.

There is, however, one melancholy restriction to all this superabundant liberty; you cannot drink what you please every day in the week.

One Sunday, after leading my orchestra with considerable spirit, under a tropical heat, I rushed into a bar for a glass of beer.

The proprietor of the establishment answered with a woful look:

"Impossible, sir; I have no waiters."

"What! no waiters? And what have you done with them all?"

"Every one of them has been arrested for having insisted upon serving drinks to our customers against the legal prohibition."

"Is it forbidden to drink on Sunday?"

"Strictly forbidden, sir."

"I am going to see about that."

I run to the Brunswick and order boldly:

"A sherry cobbler!"

"I am sorry, sir, to be obliged to disappoint you; the bar is closed, and all my waiters have been arrested."

"But I am dying with thirst."

"The only thing we can give you, sir, is a glass of soda."

Such was, indeed, the state of things in New York. Three hundred waiters had been arrested on that Sunday for carrying refreshments to customers. The customers who called for the drinks may consider themselves lucky enough that they were not arrested themselves.

What a singular liberty!

Nor has anybody the right to hang himself in America.

A drunkard tries to hang himself, but fails, and is brought back to life after a few hours. When he has recovered his senses he is taken before the judge, who sentences him to six months' imprisonment. Usually it is only three months, but in this case it was an old offender, who had tried it once before. The third time he will be condemned to death. In order to take one's own life the previous authorization of the Governor is required.

Negro emancipation is another grand reform! The dear negroes are free, perfectly free; let me tell you how.

They cannot enter either the cars or any other public conveyances; on no account do the theatres admit them; and if they are received in the restaurants, it is only to wait on the white guests. This is an illustration of Liberty, Equality, and Fraternity.

You think, perhaps, that only negroes are deprived of certain liberties; you are mistaken.

The proprietor of the *Cataract Hotel,* at Niagara Falls, had the following advertisement inserted in the principal daily papers:

"Being a citizen of a perfectly free country, and having the right to do as I please in my own house, I have decided:

"First and only Article—'From and after this day, Jews will be excluded from this hotel.'"

It may be interesting to add that after a lapse of two years this liberal hotel-keeper was compelled to give up his establishment for want of business.

The first Sunday I was at leisure after my arrival in Philadelphia, I proposed making a visit to the Exhibition. I found it closed. The exhibitors were restrained from showing their products on Sunday.

I thought of going to the theatre in the evening. Closed too. And the concerts also, just the same as in New York.

Sunday is the only day the working man can call his own. He might avail himself of his few hours of rest for his instruction and recreation, or to improve himself in his calling by the contemplation of the admirable industrial productions which the foremost manufacturers of both hemispheres exhibit here! The Exhibition is closed for him. Again, he might seek to refresh his mind by witnessing some play in a good theatre. Yet on this day everything is closed: exhibition, theatres, concerts. If there is any one worthy of respect, it is a working man. After his week's toil he needs one day of mental recreation. He may take his family out, but he cannot enjoy with them the refreshment even of a glass of beer. And what is the consequence? While his wife and children go to church or take a walk, he stops at home and takes to whiskey.

While almost unrestricted liberty is given to industry, invention, and manufactures, the results prove often somewhat inconvenient. If an American conceives an idea, he proceeds at once to carry it out. See, for instance, the rapid development of the cars which have in such a short time driven out the omnibuses. Just now the cars are all the fashion; they are everywhere, and as the streets can only afford space for a limited number, one inventor has imagined to construct elevated railways, and has already commenced the execution of his project. Here is an incident connected with this:

A lady who had just purchased a charming little residence on Broadway, left for the country immediately after, and returned after five or six months to take up her quarters in the new house. Having arrived late at night, she slept soundly. The next morning, a sound like that of thunder, and shrill whistles, suddenly awake her. She runs to the window:

She beholds a passing train, with passengers gazing curiously out of every window. She faints.

When she recovered her senses, her first thought, even before closing the window, was to send for a lawyer, and commence a suit for damages against the new company. The house, which had cost her two hundred thousand dollars, was now only worth one quarter of that sum; but she had the privilege of selling it again.

There is one day in the year when the Americans are allowed absolutely unrestricted liberty, the Fourth of July, the anniversary of the national independence. Everything is permitted on this day, and Heaven knows what use and abuse are made of this license! I have preserved a number of the *Courrier des Etats-Unis,* which gives some curious incidents of that memorable day.

Leaving aside many accidents of minor interest, I will confine myself to the more serious casualties. The article is headed: *The Reverse of the Medal.*

"Our first accounts of the casualties and accidents occurring in New York were very incomplete.

"A young girl of nineteen, Mary Henley, residing at No. 261 Sixteenth street, was walking with two of her friends on the Eighth Avenue. Near twenty-second street, fire-crackers were thrown at the girls, in celebration of the glorious day. They paid no attention to it, however, and it was only when they had reached the next block that Mary Henley felt herself burning, and her dress on fire. Terror-stricken, she started running, her clothes ablaze from her head to her feet. The efforts of several men were required to hold her, so agonizing were her pains. The flames were extinguished, but it was too late. Mary Henley was injured beyond possibility of recovery. During the pyrotechnical exhibition in the City Hall Park, a bomb exploded in the midst of a group of spectators: there were five wounded, three of whom are in a dangerous condition.

"Finally, we have before us a list of forty-nine persons, mostly children, wounded during the day or night on the Fourth of July. Some have lost an eye, others a hand; some have had a leg or a rib broken; others the face or other parts of their body badly burned. A few have injured themselves in handling fire-arms, throwing crackers, and falling from roofs and windows. But nine-tenths at least ascribe their wounds to pistol-balls fired by 'unknown persons.' It would only be charitable to believe that these 'unknown persons' were simply awkward fellows.

"These disastrous occurrences are not confined to the city of New York; every large city in the United States suffers from them.

"The celebration of the Centennial in Washington 'was very quiet.' What would have happened had it been more brilliant?

"The rowdy element was very noisy, and four assassinations were committed by drunkards before nightfall.

"Many people visited Washington's tomb at Mount Vernon; unfortunately, even this sacred spot was not free from riot and bloodshed. Several drunken men had a fight with knives. No arrests were made."

In Philadelphia now:

"The Fourth of July was most disastrous for Philadelphia. Besides the conflagration mentioned in another column, which resulted in the death of four persons, this city suffered a ruinous fire, caused by the foolish recklessness with which fire-arms are handled. Boys were firing a cannon near the lumber-yard of Collins & Co., at the foot of Laurel street. A burning piece of wad fell on some shingles, and set fire to them.

"Thus began a fire that destroyed property to the amount of $250,000, and reduced to ashes the whole square situated between the river bank and the east side of Delaware Avenue and Laurel and Shackamaxon streets.

"Every cannon shot may be estimated, on an average, to have caused a similar loss, the most of which falls upon the insurance companies."

These few extracts will give an idea of the number of accidents, fires, and deaths occurring on the Fourth of July in the United States.

As to myself, I am free to confess that these excesses increase greatly my respect for our effete governments, which forbid squarely all liberties that endanger the lives of citizens, and which afford us the protection of our brave gens d'armes. I have seen unlimited liberty. Thank you! I prefer our sergents-de-ville [police].

Philadelphia

Here I am in Philadelphia. It is eleven o'clock at night. I put up at the Continental Hotel, a reproduction, as regards size, of the Fifth Avenue Hotel at New York. There are, however, even more people than usual; for the Americans give a dinner to-day to the Emperor of Brazil,[4] who is staying at the hotel. From my apartment I hear a band of music, not entirely harmonious, which is playing *Orphée aux Enfers* [Orpheus in Hades]. Are they saluting the departure of Dom Pedro, or my own arrival? —it is, perhaps, for both, unless the music has been ordered, which is most probable, to play during dinner.

The next day, at ten o'clock, I went down to the dining-room for breakfast. It was a repetition of the New York meal. There is, however, one thing which gives a peculiar and curious appearance to the room; it is that all the waiters are negroes or mulattoes. To be received as waiter in this hotel, it is necessary to have a coating of liquid blacking on your face. The dining-room is immense, and it is a curious sight to see about thirty tables of different sizes, chiefly occupied by pretty women in elegant dresses, around which some forty or fifty negroes are skipping about. The negroes are not bad-looking, but the mulattoes have magnificent heads. I have an idea that Alexandre Dumas must have passed some time in this country; for the portrait of our great novelist is reproduced here to perfection.

As soon as I had breakfasted I started for the Exhibition, for I had forgotten that it was Sunday. On Sunday the Exhibition is closed; the houses

[4] Dom Pedro II (1825–91), second emperor of Brazil.

and taverns are closed; everything is closed in this joyous city; it is exceedingly gay. The few people that one meets are coming from church, with their Bibles and funeral faces. Should you be guilty of smiling, they look at you with horror; should you laugh, they would have you arrested.

The streets are very fine, and wide enough to rival the Boulevard Haussman. On both sides are houses of red brick, with window-frames in white marble; here and there pretty little mansions; but the churches are very numerous. The pretty women of Philadelphia probably require much praying for, and I see no great harm in the fact.

A new City Hall is being built, in white marble, and will cost two hundred million of francs.

My two friends and I did not know how on earth to spend our Sunday. We were advised to go to Indian Rock, in Fairmount Park. It takes two hours to go there, but the park is endless.

The people of Philadelphia are proud of this immense garden, and with reason, for it is impossible to imagine anything finer or more picturesque. Here and there are little cottages nestling in the shrubbery; small streams winding under the trees, green valleys, shady ravines, splendid woods; it is magnificent.

From time to time one sees a tavern, a public-house full of people. The men, according to the American fashion, stretched in rocking-chairs, or on ordinary chairs, resting their feet upon some object higher than their heads. They all had large glasses of red, green, or yellow lemonade before them. Strong drinks are forbidden—on Sunday one must confine himself to mild drinks. The law cannot be the same for all, for a carriage, driven by two residents of the place, quite drunk (and I hardly suppose the lemonade could have produced this effect), nearly ran into ours several times. These questionable observers of the Sunday law passed us several times, and seemed bent upon upsetting us. On reaching Indian Rock, our coachman gravely dismounted from his box, and took hold of the reins of the horse driven by the two drunken men. He begged these gentlemen to get out of their carriage. On their refusal, a policeman gravely got into their carriage, lifted out one of them, handing him over into the arms of another policeman, who received him with the greatest politeness; he then gravely took the reins and drove off with the other. A dozen words were not exchanged between them; all was done silently, gravely, methodically.

The Miseries of a Musician

Besides the concerts which I had engaged to direct, I had promised Mdlle. Aimée[5] to lead at some of the representations which she intended giving in America. According to my promise, I had held the baton or leader of the

[5]Perhaps Mlle. Aimée Desclée, who had sung in some of Offenbach's operettas in Paris.

orchestra in New York, at the theatre where Mdlle. Aimée sang. I thought I had thus discharged my obligation towards her; but when my series of concerts were over in Philadelphia, she came to inform me that she was about starting for Chicago, and begged me to lead a last representation at X——. I have special reasons for not giving the name of the town. I intended myself going to Chicago, and X—— being on the way, I consented. I reached X—— early in the morning. The piece for the evening was *La Belle Parfumeuse*. I went to the theatre, so as to have at least one rehearsal with my orchestra.

I went to my desk, gave the signal, and the musicians began.

I knew my score by heart. What, then, was my surprise at hearing, instead of what I expected, some strange sounds which bore no likeness to my opéretta. I could make out the tunes, but the scoring was entirely different from mine. Some inventive local musician had thought proper to compose a new score according to his own ideas!

My first impulse was to leave the rehearsal at once, and to give up all thought of leading the orchestra in the evening. Mdlle. Aimée, however, begged me so hard to stay, representing that I was on the bills, that the public would be angry if I did not appear, that the performance would even be impossible, that I finally allowed myself to be coaxed. I resumed my bow, and gave the signal of attack to my orchestra. What an orchestra! It was small, but wretched. Out of twenty-five musicians eight were pretty good, six were indifferent, and the others decidedly bad. To guard against all eventualities, I first of all requested a second violin to take a kettle-drum, and I gave him my instructions privately. This was a lucky thought, as will be seen hereafter.

The rehearsal was so deplorable, that when it was over I made new efforts to be excused from leading. It was time lost; I found it impossible to escape from the execution of my music.

"Come what may," I thought, "I have promised to lead two acts. I will lead them, with the help of Providence."

What a performance! You should have heard it. The two clarionets emitted false notes every instant—except, however, when they were needed. In the comic march of the first act I have noted a few bars purposely out of tune, and this always produces an amusing effect. When they had reached this particular passage, the clarionets stopped, and went on merely counting time; the fool who had scored my music had written this piece for the quartette only. At the rehearsal I had begged these gentlemen (the clarionet players) to play, no matter what, in this place, feeling certain that the false notes would come naturally. But I had reckoned without my host; relying upon their text, the rascals absolutely refused to go on.

"We have pauses to mark; we must mark them; there is nothing written for us."

"But, gentlemen, the false notes you utter when there are no pauses are not written either, and nevertheless you do not spare them."

It was impossible to convince them. As for the hautboy, he played from time to time as he felt inclined; the flute blew when he could; the bassoon slept half the time; the violoncello and double-bass, placed just behind me, skipped note after note, and smuggled in a base of their own fancy. While leading with the right hand, I had at every moment to stop either the bow of the double-bass or that of the violoncello. That was to parry the false notes. The first violinist, an excellent one, was always too hot; the thermometer stood above 100 degrees in the room, and the poor fellow was continually trying to wipe his forehead. I appealed to him in a beseeching tone: "If you forsake me, my friend, we are lost!" He put away his handkerchief mournfully, and took up his instrument; but the flood of false notes kept constantly raising. Happily the first act was drawing to a close.

An enthusiastic success!

I fancied I must be dreaming.

All this was nothing to the second act. Still following my own score, as originally written, I turned to the flute, who should, according to the text, have struck in at this point; but it was the trombone on the right who responded instead.

The two clarionet players had, according to my score, a song in tierce. The local musician had given it to the cornet-à-piston, who played false, and to the bassoon, who was still asleep. At last, and not without much difficulty, we reached the finale. I doubted very much whether we should get through it. The duet between Rose and Bavolet went on after a fashion, but it went on. The finale follows the duet, and as the latter ends in C, I have of course made for the entry of Clorinde, which begins in B major, the modulation in C sharp, E sharp, E. The bass plays the sharp. My little march had been scored by the musician of X—, for the famous clarionets, the hautboy player, who did not play, and the bassoon, who was sleeping more soundly than ever. I made desperate signs to his neighbor, who woke him suddenly. If I had only known, I would have let him alone; for instead of striking the A sharp, he struck up E sharp with all the strength of his lungs. Five notes too high! The unfortunate artist who played Clorinde naturally followed the natural ascension, and also started the melody five notes too high. The orchestra, paying no attention to all these particulars, went on playing five notes too low, and one may imagine the cacophony. I made desperate signs to Clorinde and to the musicians, while the perspiration was streaming from my face. An inspiration from heaven at last came to my aid. I made an energetic and desperate sign to the drummer. He understood me, and a vigorous roll that made the windows rattle—a roll of thirty bars, that lasted until the end of the duet, and which completely drowned, heaven knows, how many false notes. The public certainly never understood why, during a mysterious scene in the middle of the night, that drum was heard so loud and so long; perhaps they took it for a flash of genius on the part of the composer. Such was it.

indeed, for it saved the situation. I never think without a cold shudder of the horrors which the rolling of that drum covered up.

After this piece of eccentricity I expected a torrent of abuse from the newspapers, when giving an account of the performance; on the contrary, it was praise, and only praise, which they bestowed upon me for the masterly manner in which I had led.

Oscar Wilde Lectured

Oscar Fingal O'Flahertie Wills Wilde (1856–1900) was twenty-six when he came to America. It was ten years later that his first great success came with the play LADY WINDERMERE'S FAN. *Nevertheless he was already famous as the leader of a movement—art for art's sake—and the affectations of his cult had been satirized in Gilbert and Sullivan's operetta* PATIENCE *(1881).*

On the afternoon of May 11, 1882, Oscar Wilde walked onto the stage of Wallack's Theatre in New York, wearing a dark velvet coat trimmed with much lace, knee breeches, dark stockings and patent leather pumps. Standing before a stage library set and surrounded by an indiscriminate collection of bric-à-brac, he gave this lecture:

ART DECORATION

In my first lecture, I gave you something of the history of Art in England. I sought to trace the influence of the French Revolution upon its development. I said something of the song of Keats and the school of the pre-Raphaelites. But I do not want to shelter the movement which I have called "The English Renaissance" under any palladium, however noble, or any name, however revered. The roots of it have indeed to be sought for in things that have long passed away, and not, as some suppose, in the fancy of a few young men, although I am not altogether sure that there is anything much better than the fancy of a few young men. When I appeared before you on a previous occasion, I had seen nothing of American art save the Doric columns and Corinthian chimney-pots visible on your Broadway and Fifth-avenue. Since then I have been through your country to some fifty or sixty cities, I think. I find that what your people need is not so much high imaginative art, but that which hallows the vessels of every-day use. I suppose that the poet will sing and the artist will paint regardless whether the world praises or blames. He has his own world and is independent of his fellow-men. But the handicraftsman is dependent on your pleasure and opinion. He needs your encouragement and he must have beautiful surroundings. Your people love art, but you do not sufficiently honor the handicraftsmen. Of course, those millionaires who can pillage Europe for their pleasure need have no care to encourage such; but I speak for those whose desire for beautiful things is larger than their means. I find that one great trouble all over is that your workmen are not given to noble designs. You cannot be indifferent to this, because art is not something which you can take or leave. It is a necessity of human life.

And what is the meaning of this beautiful decoration which we call art? In the first place, it means value to the workman, and it means the pleasure which he must necessarily take in making a beautiful thing. The mark of all good art is not that the thing done is done exactly or finely, for machinery may do as much, but that it is worked out with the head and the workman's heart. I cannot impress the point too frequently that beautiful and rational designs are necessary in all work. I did not imagine until I went into some of your simpler cities that there was so much bad work done. I found where I went bad wall-papers, horribly designed and colored carpets, and that old offender, the horse-hair sofa, whose stolid look of indifference is always so depressing. I found meaningless chandeliers and machine-made furniture, generally of rosewood, which creaked dismally under the weight of the ubiquitous interviewer. I came across the small iron stove which they always persist in decorating with machine-made ornaments, and which is as great a bore as a wet day or any other particularly dreadful institution. When unusual extravagance was indulged in it was garnished with two funeral urns.

It must always be remembered that what is well and carefully made by an honest workman after a rational design increases in beauty and value as the years go on. The old furniture brought over by the Pilgrims two hundred years ago, which I saw in New England, is just as good and as beautiful today as it was when it first came here. Now what you must do is to bring artists and handicraftsmen together. Handicraftsmen cannot live, certainly cannot thrive, without such companionship. Separate these two, and you rob art of all spiritual motive. Having done this, you must place your workman in the midst of beautiful surroundings. The artist is not dependent on the visible and the tangible. He has his visions and his dreams to feed on. But the workman must see lovely forms and beautiful forms as he goes to his work in the morning and returns at eventide. And, in connection with this, I want to assure you that noble and beautiful designs are never the result of idle fancy or purposeless day dreaming. They only come as the accumulation of habits of long and delightful observation. And yet such things may not be taught. Right ideas concerning them can certainly only be obtained by those who have been accustomed to rooms that are beautiful and colors that are satisfying.

Perhaps one of the most difficult things for us to do is to choose a notable and joyous dress for men. There would be more joy in life if we should accustom ourselves to use all the beautiful colors we can in fashioning our own clothes. The dress of the future, I think, will use drapery to a great extent and will abound with joyous color. At present we have lost all nobility of dress, and in doing so have almost annihilated the modern sculptor. And in looking around at the figures which adorn our parks one could almost wish that we had completely killed the noble art. To see the frock coat of the drawing-room done into bronze or the double waistcoat perpetuated in marble, adds a new horror to death. But indeed, in looking through the history of costume, seeking an answer to the questions we have propounded, there is little that is either beautiful or appropriate. One of the earliest forms is the Greek drapery, which is so exquisite for young girls. And then, I think we may be pardoned a little enthusiasm over the dress of the time of Charles I, so beautiful, indeed, that in spite of its invention being with the cavaliers, it was copied by the Puritans. And the dress for the children at that time must not be passed over. It was a very golden age of the little ones. I do not think that they have ever looked so lovely as they do in the pictures of that time. The dress of the last century in England is also peculiarly gracious and graceful. There is nothing bizarre or strange about it, but it is full of harmony and beauty. In these days, when we have suffered so dreadfully from the incursions of the modern milliner, we hear ladies boast that they do not wear a dress more than once. In the old days, when the dresses were decorated with beautiful designs and worked with exquisite embroidery, ladies rather took a pride in bringing out the garment and wearing it many times and handing it down to their daughters—a process which I think would be quite appreciated by modern husbands when called upon to settle their wives' bills.

And how shall men dress? Men say they don't particularly care how they dress, and that it is little matter. I am bound to reply that I do not believe them and do not think that you do. In all my journeys through the country, the only well-dressed men that I saw—and in saying this I earnestly deprecate the polished indignation of your Fifth-avenue dandies—were the western miners. Their wide-brimmed hats, which shaded their faces from the sun and protected them from the rain, and the cloak which is by far the most beautiful piece of drapery ever invented, may well be dwelt on with admiration. Their high boots, too, were sensible and practical. They only wore what was comfortable and therefore beautiful. As I looked at them, I could not help thinking with regret of the time when these picturesque miners should have made their fortunes and would go East to assume again all the abominations of modern fashionable attire. Indeed, so concerned was I that I made some of them promise that when they again appeared in the more crowded scenes of Eastern civilization they would still continue to wear their lovely costume. But I don't believe they will.

Now, what America wants today is a school of rational design. Bad art is a great deal worse than no art at all. You must show your workmen specimens of good work, so that they may come to know what is simple and true and beautiful. To that end I would you have a museum attached to these schools—not one of those dreadful modern institutions where there are a stuffed and very dusty giraffe and a case or two of fossils, but a place where there are gathered examples of art decoration from various periods and countries. Such a place is the South Kensington Museum in London, whereon we build greater hopes for the future than on any other one thing. There I go every Saturday night, when the Museum is opened later than usual, to see the handicraftsman, the wood-worker, the glass-blower and the worker in metals. And it is here that the man of refinement and culture comes face to face with the workman who ministers to his joy. He comes to know more of the nobility of the workman, and the workman, feeling the appreciation, comes to know more of the nobility of his work.

You have too many white walls. More color is wanted. You should have such men as Whistler among you to teach you the beauty and joy of color. Take Mr. Whistler's symphony in white, which you no doubt have imagined to be something quite bizarre. It is nothing of the sort. Think of a cool, gray sky, flecked here and there with white clouds, a gray ocean and three wonderfully beautiful figures robed in white leaning over the water and dropping white flowers from their fingers. Here are no extensive intellectual scheme to trouble you and no metaphysics, of which we have had quite enough in art. But if the simple and unaided color strikes the right keynote, the whole conception is made clear. I regard Mr. Whistler's famous peacock room as the finest thing in color and art decoration which the world has known since Correggio painted that wonderful room[1] in Italy where the little children are dancing on the walls. Mr. Whistler finished another room just before I came away—a breakfast-room in blue and yellow. The ceiling was a light blue, the cabinet furniture was of yellow wood, the curtains at the windows were white and worked in yellow, and when the table was set for breakfast with dainty blue china, nothing can be conceived at once so simple and joyous.

The fault which I have observed in most of your rooms is that there is apparent no definite scheme of color. Everything is not attuned to a keynote as it should be. The apartments are crowded with pretty things which have no relation to each other. Again, your artists must decorate what is more simply useful. In your art schools I found no attempt to decorate such things as the vessels for water. I know of nothing uglier than the ordinary jug or pitcher. A museum could be filled with the different kinds of water vessels which are used in hot countries. Yet we continue to submit to the depressing jug with the handle all on one side. I do not see the wisdom of decorating dinner-plates with sunsets and soup-plates with moonlight scenes. I do not think it adds anything to the pleasure of canvas-back duck to take it out of such glories. Besides, we do not want a soup-plate whose bottom seems to vanish in the distance. One neither feels safe nor comfortable under such conditions. In fact, I did not find in the art schools of the country that the difference was explained between decorative and imaginative art.

The conditions of art should be simple. A great deal more depends upon

[1]Probably the mural in the Camera de Correggio at Parma.

the heart than the head. Appreciation of art is not secured by any elaborate scheme of learning. Art requires a good healthy atmosphere. The motives for art are still around about us as they were around about the ancients. And the subjects are also easily found by the earnest sculptor and the painter. Nothing is more picturesque and graceful than a man at work. Only idle people are ungraceful. The artist who goes to the children's playground, watches them at their sport, sees the boy stoop to tie his shoe, will find the same themes that engaged the attention of the ancient Greeks. And such observation and the illustrations which follow will do much to correct that foolish impression that mental and physical beauty are always divorced.

To you more than perhaps to any other country has nature been generous in furnishing materials for art workers to work in. You have marble quarries where the stone is more beautiful in color than the Greeks ever had for their beautiful work, and yet day after day I am confronted with the great building of some stupid man who has used the beautiful material as if it were not precious almost beyond speech. Marble should not be used save by noble workmen. There is nothing which gave me a greater sense of barrenness in travelling through the country than the entire absence of wood-carving on your houses. Wood-carving is the simplest of the decorative arts. In Switzerland the little barefooted boy beautifies the porch of his father's house with examples of skill in this direction. Why should not American boys do a great deal more and better than Swiss boys?

There is nothing to my mind more coarse in conception and more vulgar in execution than modern jewelry. This is something that can be easily corrected. Something better should be made out of the beautiful gold which is stored up in your mountain hollows and strewn along your river beds. When I was at Leadville and reflected that all the shining silver I saw coming from the mines would be made into ugly dollars, it made me sad. It should be made into something more permanent. The golden gates at Florence are as beautiful today as when Michael Angelo saw them.

We should see more of the workman than we do. We should not be content to have the salesman stand between us, who knows nothing of what he is selling save that he is charging a great deal too much for it. And watching workmen will teach that most important lesson, the nobility of all rational workmanship.

I said in my last lecture that art would create a new brotherhood among men by furnishing a universal language. I said that under its beneficent influences war might pass away. Thinking this, what place can I ascribe to art in our education? If children grow up among all fair and lovely things, they will grow to love beauty and detest ugliness before they know the reason why. If you go into a house where everything is coarse you find things chipped and broken and unsightly. Nobody exercises any care. If everything is dainty and delicate, gentleness and refinement of manner are unconsciously acquired. When I was in San Francisco I used to visit the

Chinese quarters frequently. There I used to watch a great hulking Chinese workman at his task of digging, and used to see him every day drink his tea from a little cup as delicate in texture as the petal of a flower. Whereas in all the grand hotels of the land, where thousands of dollars have been lavished on great gilt mirrors and gaudy columns, I have been given my coffee or my chocolate in cups an inch and a quarter thick. I think I have deserved something nicer.

The art systems of the past have been devised by philosophers who looked upon human beings as obstructions. They have tried to educate boys' minds before they had any. How much better would it be in these early years to teach children to use their hands in the rational service of mankind! I would have a workshop attached to every school, and one hour a day given up to the teaching of simple decorative arts. It would be a golden hour to the children. And you would soon raise up a race of handicraftsmen who would transform the face of your country. I have seen only one such school in the United States, and this was in Philadelphia, and was founded by my friend Mr. Leland.[2] I stopped there yesterday and have brought some of their work here this afternoon to show you. [Mr. Wilde here turned from the stand to an adjoining table and held up the different articles he spoke of.] Here are two discs of beaten brass; the designs on them are beautiful, the workmanship is simple and the entire result is satisfactory. The work was done by a little boy twelve years old. This is a wooden bowl, decorated by a little girl of thirteen. The design is lovely, and the coloring delicate and pretty. [The bowl was painted black and yellow, and looked like a sunflower with the colors run into each other.] Here you see a piece of beautiful wood-carving, accomplished by a little boy of nine. [This was a small rectangular piece of wood, and the carving was not visible to the audience.] In such work as this children learn sincerity in art. They learn to abhor the liar in art—the man who paints wood to look like iron, or iron to look like stone. It is a practical school of morals. No better way is there to learn to love Nature than to understand Art. It dignifies every flower of the field. And a boy who sees the thing of beauty which a bird on the wing becomes when transferred to wood or canvas will probably not throw the customary stone. What we want is something spiritual added to life. Nothing is so ignoble that art cannot sanctify it.

[2]Charles Godfrey Leland (1824–1903) who attempted to introduce handwork into Philadelphia schools, and edited a series of "Art-Work Manuals."

Arnold on Civilization

Matthew Arnold won a notable rank in English literature by two achievements: the poetry that he wrote during the earlier part of his career and the critical essays of his later years. He was born in 1822, attended Rugby—of which his father was the famous headmaster—and graduated from Balliol College, Oxford, in 1845.

Beginning in 1851 he was inspector of schools in England for thirty-five years and contributed a great deal to their improvement. He had published EMPEDOCLES ON ETNA, SOHRAB AND RUSTUM, *and* THE SCHOLAR GIPSY *when he was appointed professor of poetry at Oxford, where he lectured from 1857 to 1867. In 1865 he wrote the first series of his* ESSAYS IN CRITICISM. *His analyses ranged from literature to society and religion. After lecturing in America and Canada in 1883–84 he published this essay in* THE NINETEENTH CENTURY, *London.*

CIVILIZATION IN THE UNITED STATES

Two or three years ago I spoke in this Review on the subject of America; and after considering the institutions and the social condition of the people of the United States, I said that what, in the jargon of the present day, is called "the political and social problem," does seem to be solved there with remarkable success. I pointed out the contrast which in this respect the United States offer to our own country—a contrast, in several ways, much to their advantage. But I added that the solution of the political and social problem, as it is called, ought not so to absorb us as to make us forget the human problem; and that it remained to ask how the human problem is solved in the United States. It happened that Sir Lepel Griffin, a very acute and distinguished Indian official, had just then been travelling in the United States, and had published his opinion, from what he saw of the life there, that there is no country calling itself civilized where one would not rather live than in America, except Russia. Certainly then, I said, one cannot rest satisfied, when one finds such a judgment passed on the United States as this, with admiring their institutions and their solid social condition, their freedom and equality, their power, energy, and wealth. One must, further

go on to examine what is done there towards solving the human problem, and must see what Sir Lepel Griffin's objection comes to.

And this examination I promised that I would one day make. However, it is so delicate a matter to discuss how a sensitive nation solves the human problem, that I found myself inclined to follow the example of the Greek moralist Theophrastus, who waited, before composing his famous *characters*, until he was ninety-nine years old. I thought I had perhaps better wait until I was about that age, before I discussed the success of the Americans in solving the human problem. But ninety-nine is a great age; it is probable that I may never reach it, or even come near it. So I have determined, finally, to face the question without any such long delay, and thus I come to offer to the readers of this Review the remarks following. With the same frankness with which I discussed here the solution of the political and social problem by the people of the United States, I shall discuss their success in solving the human problem.

Perhaps it is not likely that any one will now remember what I said three years ago here about the success of the Americans in solving the political and social problem. I will sum it up in the briefest possible manner. I said that the United States had constituted themselves in a modern age; that their institutions complied well with the form and pressure of those circumstances and conditions which a modern age presents. Quite apart from all question how much of the merit for this may be due to the wisdom and virtue of the American people, and how much to their good fortune, it is undeniable that their institutions do work well and happily. The play of their institutions suggests, I said, the image of a man in a suit of clothes which fits him to perfection, leaving all his movements unimpeded and easy; a suit of clothes loose where it ought to be loose, and sitting close where its sitting close is an advantage; a suit of clothes able, moreover, to adapt itself naturally to the wearer's growth, and to admit of all enlargements as they successively arise.

So much as to the solution, by the United States, of the political problem. As to the social problem, I observed that the people of the United States were a community singularly free from the distinction of classes, singularly homogeneous; that the division between rich and poor was consequently less profound there than in countries where the distinction of classes accentuates that division. I added that I believed there was exaggeration in the reports of their administrative and judicial corruption; and altogether, I concluded, the United States, politically and socially, are a country living prosperously in a natural modern condition, and conscious of living prosperously in such a condition. And being in this healthy case, and having this healthy consciousness, the community there uses its understanding with the soundness of health; it in general, as to its own political and social concerns, sees clear and thinks straight. Comparing the United States with ourselves, I said that while they are in this natural and healthy condition, we, on the contrary, are so little homogeneous, we are

living with a system of classes so intense, with institutions and a society so little modern, so unnaturally complicated, that the whole action of our minds is hampered and falsened by it; we are in consequence wanting in lucidity, we do not see clear or think straight, and the Americans have here much the advantage of us.

Yet we find an acute and experienced Englishman saying that there is no country, calling itself civilized, where one would not rather live than in the United States, except Russia! The civilization of the United States must somehow, if an able man can think thus, have shortcomings, in spite of the country's success and prosperity. What is civilization? It is the humanization of man in society, the satisfaction for him, in society, of the true law of human nature. Man's study, says Plato, is to discover the right answer to the question *how to live?* Our aim, he says, is very and true life. We are more or less civilized as we come more or less near to this aim, in that social state which the pursuit of our aim essentially demands. But several elements or powers, as I have often insisted, go to build up a complete human life. There is the power of conduct, the power of intellect and knowledge, the power of beauty, the power of social life and manners; we have instincts responding to them all, requiring them all. And we are perfectly civilized only when all these instincts in our nature, all these elements in our civilization, have been adequately recognized and satisfied. But of course this adequate recognition and satisfaction of all the elements in question is impossible; some of them are recognized more than others, some of them more in one community, some in another; and the satisfactions found are more or less worthy.

And, meanwhile, people use the term *civilization* in the loosest possible way, for the most part attaching to it, however, in their own mind some meaning connected with their own preferences and experiences. The most common meaning thus attached to it is perhaps that of a satisfaction, not of all the main demands of human nature, but of the demand for the comforts and conveniences of life, and of this demand as made by the sort of person who uses the term.

Now we should always attend to the common and prevalent use of an important term. Probably Sir Lepel Griffin had this notion of the comforts and conveniences of life much in his thoughts when he reproached American civilization with its shortcomings. For men of his kind, and for all that large number of men, so prominent in this country and who make their voice so much heard, men who have been at the public schools and universities, men of the professional and official class, men who do the most part of our literature and our journalism, America is not a comfortable place of abode. A man of this sort has in England everything in his favor; society appears organized expressly for his advantage. A Rothschild or a Vanderbilt can buy his way anywhere, and can have what comforts and luxuries he likes, whether in America or in England. But it is in England that an income of from three or four to fourteen or fifteen hundred a year does so much for its possessor, enables him to live with so many of the conveniences of far richer people. For his benefit, his benefit above all, clubs are organized and hansom cabs ply; service is abundant, porters stand waiting at the railway stations. In America all luxuries are dear except oysters and ice; service is in general scarce and bad; a club is a most expensive luxury; the cab-rates are prohibitive—more than half of the people who in England would use cabs must in America use the horse-cars, the tram. The charges of tailors and mercers are about a third higher than they are with us. I mention only a few striking points as to which there can be no dispute, and in which a man of Sir Lepel Griffin's class would feel the great difference between America and England in the conveniences at his command. There are a hundred other points one might mention, where he would feel the same thing. When a man is passing judgment on a country's civilization, points of this kind crowd to his memory, and determine his sentence.

On the other hand, for that immense class of people, the great bulk of the community, the class of people whose income is less than three or four hundred a year, things in America are favorable. It is easier for them there than in the Old World to rise and to make their fortune; but I am not now speaking of that. Even without making their fortune, even with their income below three or four hundred a year, things are favorable to them in America, society seems organized there for their benefit. To begin with, the humbler kind of work is better paid in America than with us, the higher kind, worse. The official, for instance, gets less, his office-keeper gets more. The public ways are abominably cut up by rails and blocked with horse-cars; but the inconvenience is for those who use private carriages and cabs, the convenience is for the bulk of the community who but for the horse-cars would have to walk. The ordinary railway cars are not delightful, but they are cheap, and they are better furnished and in winter are warmer than third-class carriages in England. Luxuries are, as I have said, very dear—above all, European luxuries; but a working-man's clothing is nearly as cheap as in England, and plain food is on the whole cheaper. Even luxuries of a certain kind are within a laboring man's easy reach. I have mentioned ice; I will mention fruit also. The abundance and cheapness of fruit is a great boon to people of small incomes in America. Do not believe the Americans when they extol their peaches as equal to any in the world, or better than any in the world; they are not to be compared to peaches grown under glass. Do not believe that the American Newtown pippins appear in the New York and Boston fruit-shops as they appear in those of London and Liverpool; or that the Americans have any pear to give you like the Marie Louise. But what laborer, or artisan, or small clerk, ever gets hot-house peaches, or Newtown pippins, or Marie Louise pears? Not such good pears, apples, and peaches as those, but pears, apples, and peaches by no means to be despised, such people and their families do in America get in plenty.

Well, now, what would a philosopher or a philanthropist say in this case? which would he say was the more civilized condition—that of the country where the balance of advantage, as to the comforts and conveniences of life, is greatly in favor of the people with incomes below three hundred a year, or that of the country where it is greatly in favor of those with incomes above that sum?

Many people will be ready to give an answer to that question without the smallest hesitation. They will say that they are, and that all of us ought to be, for the greatest happiness of the greatest number. However, the question is not one which I feel bound now to discuss and answer. Of course, if happiness and civilization consists in being plentifully supplied with the comforts and conveniences of life, the question presents little difficulty. But I believe neither that happiness consists, merely or mainly, in being plentifully supplied with the comforts and conveniences of life, nor that civilization consists in being so supplied; therefore, I leave the question unanswered.

I prefer to seek for some other and better tests by which to try the civilization of the United States. I have often insisted on the need of more equality in our own country, and on the mischiefs caused by inequality over here. In the United States there is not our intense division of classes, our inequality; there is great equality. Let me mention two points in the system of social life and manners over there in which this equality seems to me to have done good. The first is a mere point of form, but it has its significance. Everyone knows it is the established habit with us in England, if we write to people supposed to belong to the class of gentlemen, of addressing them by the title of *Esquire*, while we keep *Mr.* for people not supposed to belong to that class. If we think of it, could one easily find a habit more ridiculous, more offensive? The title of *Esquire*, like most of our titles, comes out of the great frippery shop of the Middle Age; it is alien to the sound taste and manner of antiquity, when men said *Pericles* and *Camillus*. But unlike other titles, it is applied or withheld quite arbitrarily. Surely, where a man has no specific title proper to him, the one plain title of *Master* or *Mr.* is enough, and we need not be encumbered with a second title of *Esquire*, now quite unmeaning, to draw an invidious and impossible line of distinction between those who are gentlemen and those who are not; as if we actually wished to provide a source of embarrassment for the sender of a letter, and of mortification for the receiver of it.

The French, those great authorities in social life and manners, find *Mr.* enough, and the Americans are more and more, I am glad to say, following the French example. I only hope they will persevere, and not be seduced by *Esquire* being "so English, you know." And I do hope, moreover, that we shall one day take the same course and drop our absurd *Esquire*.

The other point goes deeper. Much may be said against the voices and intonation of American women. But almost every one acknowledges that there is a charm in American women—a charm which you find in almost all of them, wherever you go. It is the charm of a natural manner, a manner not self-conscious, artificial, and constrained. It may not be a beautiful manner always, but it is almost always a natural manner, a free and happy manner; and this gives pleasure. Here we have, undoubtedly, a note of civilization, and an evidence, at the same time, of the good effect of equality upon social life and manners. I have often heard it observed that a perfectly natural manner is as rare among Englishwomen of the middle classes as it is general among American women of like condition with them. And so far as the observation is true, the reason of its truth no doubt is, that the Englishwoman is living in presence of an upper class, as it is called—in presence, that is, of a class of women recognized as being the right thing in style and manner, and whom she imagines criticizing *her* style and manner, finding this or that to be amiss with it, this or that to be vulgar. Hence self-consciousness and constraint in her. The American woman lives in presence of no such class; there may be circles trying to pass themselves off as such a class, giving themselves airs as such, but they command no recognition, no authority. The American woman in general is perfectly unconcerned about their opinion, is herself, enjoys her existence, and has, consequently, a manner happy and natural. It is her great charm; and it is moreover, as I have said, a real note of civilization, and one which has to be reckoned to the credit of American life, and of its equality.

But we must get nearer still to the heart of the question raised as to the character and worth of American civilization. I have said how much the word civilization really means—the humanization of man in society; his making progress there towards his true and full humanity. Partial and material achievement is always being put forward as civilization. We hear a nation called highly civilized by reason of its industry, commerce, and wealth, or by reason of its liberty or equality, or by reason of its numerous churches, schools, libraries, and newspapers. But there is something in human nature, some instinct of growth, some law of perfection, which rebels against this narrow account of the matter. And perhaps what human nature demands in civilization, over and above all those obvious things which first occur to our thoughts,—what human nature, I say, demands in civilization, if it is to stand as a high and satisfying civilization, is best described by the word *interesting*. Here is the extraordinary charm of the old Greek civilization: that it is so *interesting*. Do not tell me only, says human nature, of the magnitude of your industry and commerce; of the beneficence of your institutions, your freedom, your equality; of the great and growing number of your churches and schools, libraries and newspapers; tell me also if your civilization—which is the grand name you give to all this development—tell me if your civilization is *interesting*.

An American friend of mine, Professor Norton,[2] has lately published the early letters of Carlyle. If any one wants a good antidote to the unpleasant effect left by Mr. Froude's *Life of Carlyle*, let him read those

[2]Charles Eliot Norton (1827–1908).

letters. Not only of Carlyle will those letters make him think kindly, but they will also fill him with admiring esteem for the qualities, character, and family life, as there delineated, of the Scottish peasant. Well, the Carlyle family were numerous, poor, and struggling. Thomas Carlyle, the eldest son, a young man in wretched health and worse spirits, was fighting his way in Edinburgh. One of his younger brothers talked of emigrating. "The very best thing he could do!" we should all say. Carlyle dissuades him. "You shall never," he writes, "you shall never seriously meditate crossing the great Salt Pool to plant yourself in the Yankee-land. That is a miserable fate for any one, at best; never dream of it. Could you banish yourself from all that is interesting to your mind, forget the history, the glorious institutions, the noble principles of old Scotland—that you might eat a better dinner, perhaps?"

There is our word launched—the word *interesting*. I am not saying that Carlyle's advice was good, or that young men should not emigrate. I do but take note, in the word *interesting*, of a requirement, a cry of aspiration, a cry not sounding in the imaginative Carlyle's own breast only, but sure of a response in his brother's breast also, and in human nature.

Amiel,[3] that contemplative Swiss whose journals the world has been reading lately, tells us that "the human heart is, as it were, haunted by confused reminiscences of an age of gold; or, rather, by aspirations towards a harmony of things which every day reality denies to us." He says that the splendor and refinement of high life is an attempt by the rich and cultivated classes to realize this ideal, and is "a form of poetry." And the interest which this attempt awakens in the classes which are not rich or cultivated, their indestructible interest in the pageant and fairy tale, as to them it appears, of the life in castles and palaces, the life of the great, bears witness to a like imaginative strain in them also, a strain tending after the elevated and the beautiful. In short, what Goethe describes as "was uns alle bändigt, *das Gemeine*—that which holds us all in bondage, the common and ignoble," is, notwithstanding its admitted prevalence, contrary to a deep-seated instinct of human nature and repelled by it. Of civilization, which is to humanize us in society, we demand, before we will consent to be satisfied with it—we demand, however much else it may give us, that it shall give us, too, the *interesting*.

Now, the great sources of the *interesting* are distinction and beauty: that which is elevated, and that which is beautiful. Let us take the beautiful first, and consider how far it is present in American civilization. Evidently this is that civilization's weak side. There is little to nourish and delight the sense of beauty there. In the long-settled states east of the Alleghanies the landscape in general is not interesting, the climate harsh and in extremes. The Americans are restless, eager to better themselves and to make fortunes; the inhabitant does not strike his roots lovingly down into the soil, as in rural England. In the valley of the Connecticut you will find farm after

[3]Henri Frederic Amiel (1821–81).

farm which the Yankee settler has abandoned in order to go West, leaving the farm to some new Irish immigrant. The charm of beauty which comes from ancientness and permanence of rural life the country could not yet have in a high degree, but it has it in an even less degree than might be expected. Then the Americans come originally, for the most part, from that great class in English society amongst whom the sense for conduct and business is much more strongly developed than the sense for beauty. If we in England were without the cathedrals, parish churches, and castles of the catholic and feudal age, and without the houses of the Elizabethan age, but had only the towns and buildings which the rise of our middle class has created in the modern age, we should be in much the same case as the Americans. We should be living with much the same absence of training for the sense of beauty through the eye, from the aspect of outward things. The American cities have hardly anything to please a trained or a natural sense for beauty. They have buildings which cost a great deal of money and produce a certain effect—buildings, shall I say, such as our Midland Station at St. Pancras; but nothing such as Somerset House or Whitehall. One architect of genius they had—Richardson.[4] I had the pleasure to know him: he is dead, alas! Much of his work was injured by the conditions under which he was obliged to execute it; I can recall but one building, and that of no great importance, where he seems to have had his own way, to be fully himself; but that is indeed excellent. In general, where the Americans succeed best in their architecture—in that art so indicative and educative of a people's sense for beauty—is in the fashion of their villa-cottages in wood. These are often original and at the same time very pleasing, but they are pretty and coquettish, not beautiful. Of the really beautiful in the other arts, and in literature, very little has been produced there as yet. I asked a German portrait-painter, whom I found painting and prospering in America, how he liked the country? "How *can* an artist like it?" was his answer. The American artists live chiefly in Europe; all Americans of cultivation and wealth visit Europe more and more constantly. The mere nomenclature of the country acts upon a cultivated person like the incessant pricking of pins. What people in whom the sense for beauty and fitness was quick could have invented, or could tolerate, the hideous names ending in *ville*, the Briggsvilles, Higginsvilles, Jacksonvilles, rife from Maine to Florida; the jumble of unnatural and inappropriate names everywhere? On the line from Albany to Buffalo you have, in one part, half the names in the classical dictionary to designate the stations; it is said that the folly is due to a surveyor who, when the country was laid out, happened to possess a classical dictionary; but a people with any artist-sense would have put down that surveyor. The Americans meekly retain his names; and, indeed, his strange Marcellus or Syracuse is perhaps not much worse than their congenital Briggsville.

So much as to beauty, and as to the provision, in the United States, for

[4]Henry Hobson Richardson (1838–86), designer of Trinity Church, Boston.

the sense of beauty. As to distinction, and the interest which human nature seeks from enjoying the effect made upon it by what is elevated, the case is much the same. There is very little to create such an effect, very much to thwart it. Goethe says somewhere that "the thrill of awe is the best thing humanity has." . . .

But, if there be a discipline in which the Americans are wanting, it is the discipline of awe and respect. An austere and intense religion imposed on their Puritan founders the discipline of respect, and so provided for them the thrill of awe; but this religion is dying out. The Americans have produced plenty of men strong, shrewd, upright, able, effective; very few who are highly distinguished. Alexander Hamilton is indeed a man of rare distinction; Washington, though he has not the high mental distinction of Pericles or Caesar, has true distinction of style and character. But these men belong to the pre-American age. Lincoln's recent American biographers declare that Washington is but an Englishman, an English officer; the typical American, they say, is Abraham Lincoln. Now Lincoln is shrewd, sagacious, humorous, honest, courageous, firm; he is a man with qualities deserving the most sincere esteem and praise, but he has not distinction.

In truth everything is against distinction in America, and against the sense of elevation to be gained through admiring and respecting it. The glorification of "the average man," who is quite a religion with statesmen and publicists there, is against it. The addiction to "the funny man," who is a national misfortune there, is against it. Above all, the newspapers are against it.

It is often said that every nation has the government it deserves. What is much more certain is that every nation has the newspapers it deserves. The newspaper is the direct product of the want felt; the supply answers closely and inevitably to the demand. I suppose no one knows what the American newspapers are, who has not been obliged, for some length of time, to read either those newspapers or none at all. Powerful and valuable contributions occur scattered about in them. But on the whole, and taking the total impression and effect made by them, I should say that if one were searching for the best means to efface and kill in a whole nation the discipline of respect, the feeling for what is elevated, one could not do better than take the American newspapers. The absence of truth and soberness in them, the poverty in serious interest, the personality and sensation-mongering, are beyond belief. There are a few newspapers which are in whole, or in part, exceptions. The *New York Nation*, a weekly paper, may be paralleled with the *Saturday Review* as it was in its old and good days; but the *New York Nation* is conducted by a foreigner,[5] and has an extremely small sale. In general, the daily papers are such that when one returns home one is moved to admiration and thankfulness not only at the great London papers, like the *Times* or the *Standard*, but quite as much at

[5]Edwin Lawrence Godkin, born in Ireland in 1831. He attacked Tammany Hall fearlessly.

the great provincial newspapers too—papers like the *Leeds Mercury* and the *Yorkshire Post* in the north of England, like the *Scotsman* and the *Glasgow Herald* in Scotland.

The Americans used to say to me that what they valued was news, and that this their newspapers gave them. I at last made the reply: "Yes, news for the servants' hall!" I remember that a New York newspaper, one of the first I saw after landing in the country, had a long account, with the prominence we should give to the illness of the German Emperor or the arrest of the Lord Mayor of Dublin, of a young woman who had married a man who was a bag of bones, as we say, and who used to exhibit himself as a skeleton; of her growing horror in living with this man, and finally of her death. All this in the most minute detail, and described with all the writer's powers of rhetoric. This has always remained by me as a specimen of what the Americans call news.

You must have lived amongst their newspapers to know what they are. If I relate some of my own experiences, it is because these will give a clear enough notion of what the newspapers over there are, and one remembers more definitely what has happened to oneself. Soon after arriving in Boston, I opened a Boston newspaper and came upon a column headed: "Tickings." By *tickings* we are to understand news conveyed through the tickings of the telegraph. The first "ticking" was: "Matthew Arnold is sixty-two years old"—an age, I must just say in passing, which I had not then reached. The second "ticking" was: "Wales says, Mary is a darling"; the meaning being that the Prince of Wales expressed great admiration for Miss Mary Anderson. This was at Boston, the American Athens. I proceeded to Chicago. An evening paper was given me soon after I arrived; I opened it, and found under a large-type heading, "*We have seen him arrive*," the following picture of myself: "He has harsh features, supercilious manners, parts his hair down the middle, wears a single eyeglass and ill-fitting clothes." Notwithstanding this rather unfavorable introduction I was most kindly and hospitably received at Chicago. It happened that I had a letter for Mr. Medill, an elderly gentleman of Scotch descent, the editor of the chief newspaper in those parts, the *Chicago Tribune*. I called on him, and we conversed amicably together. Some time afterwards, when I had gone back to England, a New York paper published a criticism of Chicago and its people, purporting to have been contributed by me to the *Pall Mall Gazette* over here. It was a poor hoax, but many people were taken in and were excusably angry, Mr. Medill of the *Chicago Tribune* amongst the number. A friend telegraphed to me to know if I had written the criticism. I, of course, instantly telegraphed back that I had not written a syllable of it. Then a Chicago paper is sent to me; and what I have the pleasure of reading, as the result of my contradiction, is this: "Arnold denies; Mr. Medill [my old friend] refuses to accept Arnold's disclaimer; says Arnold is a cur."

I once declared that in England the born lover of ideas and of light could not but feel that the sky over his head is of brass and iron. And so I say that, in America, he who craves for the *interesting* in civilization, he who requires from what surrounds him satisfaction for his sense of beauty, his sense for elevation, will feel the sky over his head to be of brass and iron. The human problem, then, is as yet solved in the United States most imperfectly; a great void exists in the civilization over there; a want of what is elevated and beautiful, of what is interesting.

The want is grave; it was probably, though he does not exactly bring it out, influencing Sir Lepel Griffin's feelings when he said that America is one of the last countries in which one would like to live. The want is such as to make any educated man feel that many countries, much less free and prosperous than the United States, are yet more truly civilized; have more which is interesting, have more to say to the soul; are countries, therefore, in which one would rather live.

The want is graver because it is so little recognized by the mass of Americans; nay, so loudly denied by them. If the community over there perceived the want and regretted it, sought for the right ways of remedying it, and resolved that remedied it should be; if they said, or even if a number of leading spirits amongst them said: "Yes, we see what is wanting to our civilization, we see that the average man is a danger, we see that our newspapers are a scandal, that bondage to the common and ignoble is our snare; but under the circumstances our civilization could not well have been expected to begin differently. What you see are *beginnings*, they are crude, they are too predominantly material, they omit much, leave much to be desired—but they could not have been otherwise, they have been inevitable, and we will rise above them"; if the Americans frankly said this, one would have not a word to bring against it. One would *then* insist on no shortcoming, one would accept their admission that the human problem is at present quite insufficiently solved by them, and would press the matter no further. One would congratulate them on having solved the political problem and the social problem so successfully, and only remark, as I have said already, that in seeing clear and thinking straight on *our* political and social questions, we have great need to follow the example they set us on theirs.

But now the Americans seem, in certain matters, to have agreed, as a people, to deceive themselves, to persuade themselves that they have what they have not, to cover the defects in their civilization by boasting, to fancy that they well and truly solve, not only the political and social problem, but the human problem too. One would say that they do really hope to find in tall talk and inflated sentiment a substitute for that real sense of elevation which human nature, as I have said, instinctively craves—and a substitute which may do as well as the genuine article. The thrill of awe, which Goethe pronounces to be the best thing humanity has, they would fain create by proclaiming themselves at the top of their voices to be "the greatest nation upon earth," by assuring one another, in the language of their national historian, that "American democracy proceeds in its ascent as uniformly and majestically as the laws of being, and is as certain as the decrees of eternity."

Or, again, far from admitting that their newspapers are a scandal, they assure one another that their newspaper press is one of their most signal distinctions. Far from admitting that in literature they have as yet produced little that is important, they play at treating American literature as if it were a great independent power; they reform the spelling of the English language by the insight of their average man. For every English writer they have an American writer to match. And him good Americans read. The Western States are at this moment being nourished and formed, we hear, on the novels of a native author called Roe,[6] instead of those of Scott and Dickens. Far from admitting that their average man is a danger, and that his predominance has brought about a plentiful lack of refinement, distinction, and beauty, they declare in the words of my friend Colonel Higginson,[7] a prominent critic at Boston, that "Nature said, some years since: 'Thus far the English is my best race, but we have had Englishmen enough; put in one drop more of nervous fluid and make the American.'" And with that drop a new range of promise opened on the human race, and a lighter, finer, more highly organized type of mankind was born. Far from admitting that the American accent, as the pressure of their climate and of their average man has made it, is a thing to be striven against, they assure one another that it is the right accent, the standard English speech of the future. It reminds me of a thing in Smollett's dinner-party of authors. Seated by "the philosopher who is writing a most orthodox refutation of Bolingbroke, but in the meantime has just been presented to the Grand Jury as a public nuisance for having blasphemed in an alehouse on the Lord's day"—seated by this philosopher is "the Scotchman who is giving lectures on the pronunciation of the English language."

The worst of it is, that all this tall talk and self-glorification meets with hardly any rebuke from sane criticism over there. I will mention, in regard to this, a thing which struck me a good deal. A Scotchman who has made a great fortune at Pittsburg, a kind friend of mine, one of the most hospitable and generous of men, Mr. Andrew Carnegie, published a year or two ago a book called *Triumphant Democracy*, a most splendid picture of American progress. The book is full of valuable information, but religious people thought that it insisted too much on mere material progress, and did not enough set forth America's deficiencies and dangers. And a friendly clergyman in Massachusetts, telling me how he regretted this, and how apt the Americans are to shut their eyes to their own dangers, put into my hands a volume written by a leading minister among the Congregationalists, a very prominent man, which he said supplied a good antidote to my friend

[6]Edward Payson Roe (1838–88) author of *Barriers Burned Away*.

[7]Thomas Wentworth Higginson (1823–1911).

Mr. Carnegie's book. The volume is entitled *Our Country*. I read it through. The author finds in evangelical Protestantism, as the orthodox Protestant sects present it, the grand remedy for the deficiencies and dangers of America. On this I offer no criticism; what struck me, and that on which I wish to lay stress, is, the writer's entire failure to perceive that such self-glorification and self-deception as I have been mentioning is one of America's dangers, or even that it *is* self-deception at all. He himself shares in all the self-deception of the average man among his countrymen, he flatters it. In the very points where a serious critic would find the Americans most wanting he finds them superior; only they require to have a good dose of evangelical Protestantism still added. "Ours is the elect nation," preaches this reformer of American faults—"ours is the elect nation for the age to come. We are the chosen people." Already, says he, we are taller and heavier than other men, longer lived than other men, richer and more energetic than other men, above all, "of finer nervous organization" than other men. Yes, this people, who endure to have the American newspaper for their daily reading, and to have their habitation in Briggsville, Jacksonville, and Marcellus—this people is of finer, more delicate nervous organization than other nations! It is Colonel Higginson's "drop more of nervous fluid," over again. This "drop" plays a stupendous part in the American rhapsody of self-praise. Undoubtedly the Americans are highly nervous, both the men and the women. A great Paris physician says that he notes a distinct new form of nervous disease, produced in American women by worry about servants. But this nervousness, developed in the race out there by worry, overwork, want of exercise, injudicious diet, and a most trying climate—this morbid nervousness our friends ticket as the fine susceptibility of genius, and cite it as a proof of their distinction, of their superior capacity for civilization! "The roots of civilization are the nerves," says our Congregationalist instructor, again; "and, other things being equal, the finest nervous organization will produce the highest civilization. Now, the finest nervous organization is ours."

The new West promises to beat in the game of brag even the stout champions I have been quoting. Those belong to the old Eastern States; and the other day there was sent to me a Californian newspaper which calls all the Easterners "the unhappy denizens of a forbidding clime," and adds: "The time will surely come when all roads will lead to California. Here will be the home of art, science, literature, and profound knowledge."

Common-sense criticism, I repeat, of all this hollow stuff there is in America next to none. There are plenty of cultivated, judicious, delightful individuals there. They are our hope and America's hope; it is through their means that improvement must come. They know perfectly well how false and hollow the boastful stuff talked is; but they let the storm of self-laudation rage, and say nothing. For political opponents and their doings there are in America hard words to be heard in abundance; for the real faults in American civilization, and for the foolish boasting which prolongs them, there is hardly a word of regret or blame, at least in public. Even in private, many of the most cultivated Americans shrink from the subject, are irritable and thin-skinned when it is canvassed. Public treatment of it, in a cool and sane spirit of criticism, there is none. In vain I might plead that I had set a good example of frankness, in confessing over here, that, so far from solving our problems successfully, we in England find ourselves with an upper class materialized, a middle class vulgarized, and a lower class brutalized. But it seems that nothing will embolden an American critic to say firmly and aloud to his countrymen and to his newspapers, that in America they do not solve the human problem successfully, and that with their present methods they never can. Consequently, the masses of the American people do really come to believe all they hear about their finer nervous organization, and the rightness of the American accent, and the importance of American literature; that is to say, they see things not as they are, but as they would like them to be; they deceive themselves totally. And by such self-deception they shut against themselves the door to improvement, and do their best to make the reign of *das Gemeine* eternal. In what concerns the solving of the political and social problem they see clear and think straight; in what concerns the higher civilization they live in a fool's paradise. This it is which makes a famous French critic speak of "the hard unintelligence of the people of the United States"—*la dure inintelligence des Américains du Nord*—of the very people who in general pass for being specially intelligent—and so, within certain limits, they are. But they have been so plied with nonsense and boasting that outside those limits, and where it is a question of things in which their civilization is weak, they seem, very many of them, as if in such things they had no power of perception whatever, no idea of a proper scale, no sense of the difference between good and bad. And at this rate they can never, after solving the political and social problem with success, go on to solve happily the human problem too, and thus at last to make their civilization full and interesting.

To sum up, then. What really dissatisfies in American civilization is the want of the *interesting*, a want due chiefly to the want of those two great elements of the interesting, which are elevation and beauty. And the want of these elements is increased and prolonged by the Americans being assured that they have them when they have them not. And it seems to me that what the Americans now most urgently require, is not so much a vast additional development of orthodox Protestantism, but rather a steady exhibition of cool and sane criticism by their men of light and leading over there. And perhaps the very first step of such men should be to insist on having for America, and to create if need be, better newspapers.

To us, too, the future of the United States is of incalculable importance. Already we feel their influence much, and we shall feel it more. We have a good deal to learn from them; we shall find in them, also, many things to beware of, many points in which it is to be hoped our democracy may not be like theirs. As our country becomes more democratic, the malady here may no longer be that we have an upper class materialized, a middle class vulgarized, and a lower class brutalized. But the predominance of the common and ignoble, born of the predominance of the average man, is a malady too. That the common and ignoble is human nature's enemy, that, of true human nature, distinction and beauty are needs, that a civilization is insufficient where these needs are not satisfied, faulty where they are thwarted, is an instruction of which we, as well as the Americans, may greatly require to take fast hold, and not to let go. We may greatly require to keep, as if it were our life, the doctrine that we are failures after all, if we cannot eschew vain boasting and vain imaginations—eschew what flatters in us the common and ignoble, and approve things that are truly excellent.

I have mentioned evangelical Protestantism. There is a text which evangelical Protestanism—and for that matter Catholicism too—translates wrong and takes in a sense too narrow. The text is that well-known one: "Except a man be born again he cannot see the kingdom of God." Instead of *again*, we ought to translate *from above;* and instead of taking the kingdom of God in the sense of a life in Heaven above, we ought to take it, as its speaker meant it, in the sense of the reign of saints, a renovated and perfected human society on earth—the ideal society of the future. In the life of such a society, in the life *from above*, the life born of inspiration or *the spirit*—in that life elevation and beauty are not everything; but they are much, and they are indispensable. Humanity cannot reach its ideal while it lacks them, "Except a man be born *from above*, he cannot have part in the society of the future."